ENGLISH PLACE-NAME SOCIETY. VOLUME LIII
FOR 1975–1976

GENERAL EDITOR
K. CAMERON

THE PLACE-NAMES OF
DORSET

PART II

ENGLISH PLACE-NAME SOCIETY. VOLUME LIII

THE PLACE-NAMES OF DORSET

By

A. D. MILLS

PART II

THE HUNDREDS OF COGDEAN, LOOSEBARROW,
RUSHMORE, COMBS DITCH, PIMPERNE, BADBURY,
CRANBORNE, WIMBORNE ST GILES,
KNOWLTON, MONKTON UP WIMBORNE

ENGLISH PLACE-NAME SOCIETY

1980

Published by the English Place-Name Society

© English Place-Name Society 1980

ISBN: 0 904889 04 1

Printed in Great Britain at the
University Press, Cambridge

The collection from unpublished documents of material for all the
Dorset volumes has been greatly assisted by generous grants
received from the British Academy.

CONTENTS

MAPS

Sixpenny Handley parish,
to be included in Part III

Key to hundreds and parishes

IX Cogdean
1 Branksome
2 Canford Magna
3 Charlton Marshall
4 Corfe Mullen
5 Hamworthy
6 Kinson
7 Longfleet
8 Lytchett Matravers
9 Lytchett Minster
10 Parkstone
11 Poole
12 Sturminster Marshall

X Loosebarrow
1 Almer
2 Morden
3 Spettisbury

XI Rushmore
Winterborne Zelstone

XII Combs Ditch
1 Anderson
2 Blandford St Mary
3 Bloxworth
4 Winterborne Clenston
5 Winterborne Tomson
6 Winterborne Whitchurch

XIII Pimperne
1 Blandford Forum
2 Bryanston
3 Durweston
4 Fifehead Neville
5 Hammoon
6 Haselbury Bryan
7 Langton Long Blandford
8 Pimperne
9 Steepleton Iwerne
10 Stourpaine
11 Tarrant Hinton
12 Tarrant Keynston
13 Tarrant Launceston
14 Tarrant Rawston
15 Winterborne Houghton
16 Winterborne Stickland

XIV Badbury
1 Chalbury
2 Colehill
3 More Crichel
4 Gussage St Michael
5 Hinton Martell
6 Hinton Parva
7 Holt
8 Horton
9 Pamphill
10 Shapwick
11 Tarrant Crawford
12 Wimborne Minster

XV Cranborne
1 Alderholt
2 Ashmore
3 Cranborne
4 Edmondsham
5 Farnham
6 Hampreston
7 West Parley
8 Pentridge
9 Shillingstone
10 Tarrant Gunville
11 Tarrant Rushton
12 Turnworth
13 Verwood
14 Witchampton
15 East Woodyates

XVI Wimborne St Giles
1 Wimborne St Giles
2 West Woodyates

XVII Knowlton
1 Long Crichel
2 Gussage All Saints
3 Woodlands

XVIII Monkton Up Wimborne
1 Chettle
2 Tarrant Monkton

East Dorset: Hundreds and Parishes

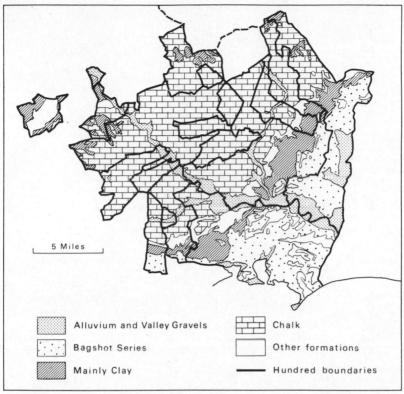

East Dorset: Geology, also showing Hundreds

IX. COGDEAN HUNDRED

In c. 1086 GeldR the hundred had roughly the same extent as it now has (Anderson 128, VCHDo 3 135). Charlton Marshall is a detached par. to the NW. Kinson par. is now in Ha.

Cocdene hundret c. 1086 GeldR, *Chogden'hundredum* 1182 P, *hundr' de Cocdene* 1212 Fees, 1244, 1268 *Ass*, 1275 RH, *Co(c)keden(e)* 1244, 1288 *Ass et freq* to 1554 *AddCh*, *-denne* 1280 *Ass*, *Cogden(e)* 1244 *ib*, 1247 FF, *-deane* 1664 HTax, *Kocdene* 1249 FF, *Gogden'* 1268, 1288 *Ass*, *Cokden(e)* 1288 *ib*, 1327 *SR*, 1332 SR, 1346 FA, *Cokkeden* 1303 ib, *Co(o)kkedene* 1512, 1514 *Pars*, *Cockden* 1539 *Ct*, named from Cogdean Elms in Corfe M. par. *infra*, the meeting-place of the hundred.

Branksome

This par. was formed in 1894 out of Kinson par.; in 1905 it was added to the borough and par. of Poole.

BRANKSOME (SZ 050926) seems to have taken its name from a house called *Branksome Tower* 1863 Hutch[3]. In view of the absence of early forms, this is probably a late transferred name from *Branksome Tower*, the setting of Scott's *Lay of the Last Minstrel*, published in 1805; this Branksome is near Hawick in Roxburghshire, Scotland.

ALDERNEY HEATH, GRAVEL PIT & PLANTS, cf. *Alderney Ctg* 1826 Gre, *-Manor* 1886 *DROMap*; the first el. may be OE **alren** 'growing with alders', cf. foll. ALDER FM. BLACK ROCK (lost), 1822 *EnclA* (Canford M.), where the old bdy of Canford meets the sea. BOURNE BOTTOM (1811 OS), BOURNE MOOR RECREATION GROUND, BOURNE VALLEY (1886 *DROMap*), from R. Bourne which rises in this par., cf. Bourne in Kinson par. *infra*. BRANKSOME MANOR. COY POND (GDNS), *v.* **coy** 'a decoy', cf. The Decoy in Wareham 1 162. FERN BARROW, 1811 OS. FOX HOLES, 1886 *DROMap*, *v.* **fox-hol**. HEATHERLANDS (Kelly), 1886 *DROMap*. THE HERMITAGE. HILLMORTON (a house). HILLTOP

1

BUNGALOWS. KINSON POTTERY, near to the spot marked *Kenson* 1811 OS, from Kinson par. *infra*. MOORLAND LODGE. NAZDAR HALL. NEWTON FM. NEWTOWN, 1863 Hutch[3], *Newton* 1886 *DROMap*. OAK HO. ROSSMORE, *v*. **ros, mōr**. ST CLEMENT'S HALL. TALBOT VILLAGE FM, cf. Kinson par. *infra*. TRINIDAD GDNS ESTATE. UPPLEBY HO.

Canford Magna

The pars. of Kinson, Longfleet and Parkstone all *infra* were formed out of this par. in 1833; it was added to the borough and par. of Poole *infra* in 1933.

CANFORD MAGNA (SZ 030985)
 Cheneford 1086 DB, *Keneford* 1181 P (p), 1196 ChancR (p)
 Kaneford 1195 P, 1210 Cur *et freq* to 1337 Pat, *Caneford(e)* 1200 (1335) Ch, 1210 Cur (p) *et freq* to 1440 Pat (-*als. Canford als. Caunford*)
 Kanesford 1219 FF (p), *Cansford* 1487 Pat
 Canford(e) 1307 Pat, 1341 Cl (p) *et passim*, '-otherwise *Caneforde*' 1455 Cl, *Mochel Canford* 1472 Smith, *Canfford* 1529 Ct, *Cannford* 1588 *AD*, *greate Canford* 1612 *DCM-Deed*, *Canford Magna* 1774 Hutch[1]
 Canneford 1408 (1410) Pat, *Candeforde* 1550 *Midd*

Probably 'Cana's ford', as suggested by Ekwall DEPN, *v*. **ford** (here across R. Stour); an OE pers.n. *Cana* is first recorded in DB (cf. Feilitzen 213), but is evidenced in several other p.ns., among them the lost hundred-name of *Canendone* 'Cana's hill' which lay just N of Canford Magna and which was no doubt named from the same man, *v*. Badbury hundred *infra*; cf. also John-, Roger *Canewei*, -*wey* 1332 SR (taxed under Lytchett Minster par. *infra*) whose surname may be from a local p.n. meaning 'Cana's way', *v*. **weg**. The absence of any early forms with -*nn*- makes derivation from OE **canne** 'a can' in the topographical sense of 'a hollow' (thus Zachrisson DTR 147, Smith EPN I 80) unlikely. *Mochel*-, *Great*-, -*Magna* to distinguish it from Little Canford on the other bank of R. Stour in Hampreston par. *infra*, *v*. **micel, mycel**. The bounds of Canford Magna are given in 1822 *EnclA*.

ASHINGTON (SZ 002984), 1822 *EnclA*, *Esseton* 1242-3 Fees, *Ashamton* 1327 *SR* (p), *Asshton* 1463 *MinAcct* (p), cf. *Ashenton*

Bridge 1791 Boswell, probably 'farm of the *Æschæme*' ('dwellers by the ash-tree'), *v.* **æsc, hǣme** (gen.pl. *hǣma*), **tūn**, cf. Bockhampton in Stinsford 1 367. The two forms dated 1396 and 1415 given in Fägersten 110 probably belong under Ashton in Winterborne St M. par. 1 375.

CANFORD PARK (SZ 035985), '(new) park of *Caneford*' 1291 Cl, 1309 Pat, *Caneford park* 1347 Ipm, *parcum de Caneford(e)wode* 1374 *MinAcct*, 'the park and lawn of *Canford*' 1429 Pat, *Canforde Parke* 1583 *SPDom, the two parkes of Canford* 1586 *DCMDeed, the Great Parke* 1587 *ib*, cf. *Hr & Lr Park, The Parks, Park Md* 1841 *TA, v.* **park**, cf. The Lawns *infra*, 'chace and warren of *Canford*' 1307 Pat, *warenn*' 1463 *MinAcct*. 'Great' distinguishes this park from Leigh Park in Wimborne M. par. *infra*; there were three parks in the manor of Canford in the reign of Ed I (Hutch[3] 3 289), the third being that at Knighton foll., cf. Parkstone par. *infra, v.* Wilson, DoNHAS 98 6–9.

KNIGHTON (SZ 049977), 1612 *DCMDeed, Kny(g)hteton* 1288 *Ass, Cnihtetona, Knygheton iuxta Caneford* n.d. (1372) *ChrP, Knyghton* 1348 Ipm, 1463 *MinAcct et freq* to 1544 *Ct, Knyghetun* 1544 *ib*, 'the farm of the youths or retainers', or 'farm of the knights, farm held by knight service' if the name is of post-Conquest origin, *v.* **cniht** (gen.pl. *cnihta*), **tūn**. There was a park here in 1348 Ipm, cf. *parcum de Knyghton, Knyghton Parke* 1463 *MinAcct, Knighton Parke* 1612 *DCMDeed, v.* **park**, cf. prec.

LAKE FM (SZ 999989), *La(c)ke* 1565 *Comm, Lake* 1575 Saxton, e17 *BRA et passim*, no doubt the home of John *atte Lake* 1332 SR, cf. John *Lake* 1374 *MinAcct, Gillingham's Mill now Lake Mill, Lake Mill Stream, Over Lake* 1822 *EnclA, v.* **lacu** 'a stream, a water-course', **atte, uferra**; the farm stands on a small tributary of R. Stour called *Chelwell Water* 1822 *EnclA*.

MERLEY HALL FM, MERLEY HO (SZ 010983), MERLEY POND, HR MERLEY, *farme called Merle* 1565 *Comm,* (*Meryfeilde als.*) *Myrle(y)* 1575 *DCMDeed, Merley* 1612 *ib, Merly Fm & Ho* 1811 OS, probably 'glade or clearing by a pool' (i.e. Merley Pond), *v.* **mere**[1], **lēah**.

MOORTOWN FM (SZ 039978), COPPICE & CTGS, *Mourton* 1374 *MinAcct, Morton* 1463 *ib, Mo(u)reton(e)* 1465 *Ct,* 1520 *Rent,* 1543 *Ct, Mo(o)retowne* 1542 *ib,* e17 *BRA, -toune* 1544 *Ct,* 'marshland farm', *v.* **mōr, tūn.**

OAKLEY (FM) (SZ 021986), 1774 Hutch[1], *Ocle* 1327 *SR,* 1332 *SR* both (p), 1475 FF, *-ley* 1463 *MinAcct, Okleye* 1360 Ipm, *Okel(e)y* 1497 ib, 1519, 1529 *Ct, Ock(e)ley* 1520 *Rent, Oakely* e17 *BRA,* 'oak-tree glade or clearing', *v.* **āc, lēah**; a common p.n.

STRATFORD (lost), *vill' de Startford, Stratteford* 1280 *Ass, Stratford* ('water-mill at-') 1347 Ipm, *molend' de Stratforde* 1374, *-Strafford* 1463 *MinAcct,* 'ford on a Roman road', *v.* **strǣt, ford.** The ford was possibly where the Roman road from Badbury to Poole Harbour (Margary 4d) crossed R. Stour or its tributary (*v.* Lake Fm *supra*) near the NW corner of Canford Magna par. at SY 993998 or 996991.

ARDMOY, a house-name, like many of the other names in this section. ARROWSMITH COPPICE & RD, cf. *Altmt near Arrowsmiths* 1841 *TA,* Edward *Arrowsmith* 1799 Hutch[3]. ASHINGTON LANE, 1822 *EnclA, -Close* 1822 *ib,* from Ashington *supra.* AUDLEM LODGE. BARROW HILL, 1811 OS, cf. *Barrow How* 1822 *EnclA, v.* **beorg, howe** 'enclosure' (cf. the f.n. How Croft *infra*); tumuli marked 6". BEAR WOOD, 1840 *TA* (Kinson), cf. *Bear Barn* 1839 *ib, Bear Mdw, Moor & 2 Acres* 1840 *ib,* from **bearu** 'wood' or **bær**[2] 'woodland pasture'. BEAUFORT HO. BEECHLEY CTGS. BIG COVERT. BISHOP's CTG, cf. William *Bysshopp* 1543 *Ct.* BLEAK HO., cf. *Bleak Hills* 1841 *TA, v.* **bleak.** BOAT HO (CLUMP). BONSHAW. BRAKE HILL, altered from *Blake Hill* 1811 OS, cf. *Blake Hill Moor Fm* 1811 ib, *Blake Hill or Furzy Fd, Gt & Lt Blake Hill* 1822 *EnclA,* 'dark hill' from **blæc** (wk.obl. *blacan*), **hyll**; a stream called *Black Water* 1811 OS flows nearby into R. Stour, cf. *Blackwater Bottom & Hill* 1822 *EnclA.* BROADSTONE, an ecclesiastical par. formed in 1906. BROADSTONE HO. BROOKDALE. THE BUNGALOW. BURNT HILL, cf. *Burnt Cl* 1841 *TA.* BURWOOD. CANFORD BRIDGE, (*-Md*) 1822 *EnclA, -Fd* 1844 *TA,* cf. Nicholas *atte Brigge* 1327 *SR,* William *atte Brygge* 1340 NI, *v.* **atte, brycg.** CANFORD HEATH (PLANTS.), *the hethe* 1542 *Ct, lez Hethe* 1554 *AddCh, the Lawndes and Heath of*

Canford Eliz ChancP, *Canford Heath* 1811 OS, cf. *the greate waste of...Canford* 1612 *DCMDeed*, v. **hǣð**, *The Lawns infra*. CANFORD PRIOR (lost), 1604, 1774 Hutch[1], 'the manor of Canford-priory' 1578 ib, *the Pryory manor of Canford* 1675 *WRO*, cf. *Priors Lande als. Talbotes* 1575 *DCMDeed*, *Prior Md* 1841 *TA*, from its possession by the priory of Bradenstoke W, *v.* **priory, prior**. CANFORD SCHOOL, *the howse of Canforde* 1583 *SPDom*, *Canford House* 1587 *DCMDeed*, 1826 Gre, *Nunnery* 1811 OS; the house was let to Teresan nuns in 1804 (Hutch[3] 3 295) and became a school in 1923. CHURCH (dedication unknown according to Kelly), cf. *ecclesiam de Caneford* 1280 *Ass*, *-de Kaneford* Ed 3 *Brad*, *the Churche of All Hallowes in Canford* 1519 *Ct*, cf. *Church Hill* 1822 *EnclA*, *Canford Chapel and Burying Grd* 1844 *TA*. COBBLES. CORFEDALE NURSERIES, CORFE HILLS, from Corfe Mullen par. *infra*. COSY CORNER. COURT HO. COVALS. CREEKMOOR BRIDGE (1811 OS), CLAY PIT, FM HO, HO (*Creekmoor* 1811 OS), LAKE (a channel in Poole Harbour), LANE, & MILL (*Iron Mill* 1826 Gre, *Mill Ho etc*, *Foundry* 1844 *TA*, cf. *Mill Grd* 1844 *ib*), *Creek-*, *Crickmoor* 1822 *EnclA*, *Creekmoor* (*Heath*) 1844 *TA*, 'marshland by a creek or inlet' (with reference to Holes Bay *infra*), *v.* **crike, mōr, lacu**. DARBY'S CORNER, 1841 *TA*, cf. *Darby's Lane* (*End*) 1822 *EnclA*. DAWSON'S HOLE, on R. Stour, *v.* **hol**[1]. DELPH HO, THE DELPH (1822 *EnclA*), cf. *Delf Wd* 1811 OS, *v.* **(ge)delf** 'a pit, a quarry'; near Gravel Hill *infra* and a disused pit marked 6″. DIRTY LANE COPPICE, 1844 *TA*, cf. *Dirty Lane Bridge* 1791 Boswell, *Dirty Lane* (*Acre*) 1822 *EnclA*. DUNYEATS (a house), DUNYEAT'S HILL, *Gt Dunyards Hill* 1822 *ib*, possibly to be associated with *firm' de Du'wedd* 1520 *Rent*. FAIRLIE HO. FAIR MDW. FENNERS. FERN HILL (lost), 1811 OS. FIGBURY [BARROW] (Kelly), *-Hill* 1811 OS. FIVE OAKS. FROGMOOR CTG. THE GABLES. GARDEN COPPICE, cf. *-Plot* 1844 *TA*. GISBOROUGH HALL. THE GRANGE, cf. *hospital' infra grang' manerii* 1463 *MinAcct*. GRAVEL HILL (PLANT.), *Gravel Hill* 1822 *EnclA*, near Gravel Pits (6″), cf. *Gravel Pit adjoining Park* 1844 *TA*. THE GROVE, 1822 *EnclA*, cf. *East Grove or Croft* 1822 *ib*. HALF MOON CLUMP, from its shape. HARRABY GREEN. HARVEY RD, cf. *Close by Harveys* 1844 *TA*. HATCH HOLE, on R. Stour, *v.* **hæc(c)** 'a hatch, a sluice', **hol**[1], cf. foll. HATCH POND RD, cf. *Altmt at Hatch Pond* 1841 *TA*, cf. prec. HAWKESBURY [BARROW] (Kelly), *Hakesbury Hill*

1811 OS. Haymoor Bottom, 1822 *EnclA*, *Canford Bottom* 1811 OS, cf. *le Haymoures* 1544 *Ct*, *v.* hēg, mōr. Heather Dell. Hillbourne. Hillbrow. Hillcroft. Holes Bay, 1661 Hutch[1], 1811 OS, from bay[1], with a surname (cf. John *Howles* 1544 *Ct*) or hol[1] 'a hollow', cf. Creekmoor *supra*; the S part was called *Longford Bay* 1661 Hutch[1], *v.* lang[1], ford. Holland's Hill Coppice, *Hollands or Ansteys Coppice* 1844 *TA*, cf. *Hollond* 1542 *Ct*, *Gt Hollings* 1822 *EnclA*, *Hollands Fd* 1844 *TA*, 'hollow land', *v.* hol[2], land; *Anstey* is probably a surname, perhaps from Ansty in Hilton par. *infra*. John O' Gaunt's Kitchen, *-of-* 1774 Hutch[1], part of the old manorial bldgs, cf. Canford School *supra*, Gaunt's Ho in Hinton M. par. *infra*. Knighton Fm (1822 *EnclA*), Heath, Ho, Lane & Lodge, cf. *Knyghton Meade* 1544 *Ct*, *Knighton* (*Cross*) *Bridge* 1791 Boswell, *Knighton Cross*, *-Bottom* 1811 OS, *-Plant.* 1841 *TA*, all from Knighton *supra*. The Lawns (lost), 1863 Hutch[3] ('a large tract of barren heathy ground'), 'launds of *Caneford*' 1275 Cl, *the lawnes-*, *the lawndez of Canford* 1542 *Ct*, *Canforde Laundes* c. 1586 Tres, *v.* launde 'an open space in woodland', cf. Canford Park, Canford Heath *supra*. Livett's Hill Coppice, *Levits Hill* (*Coppice*) 1844 *TA*, a surname. Lodge Hill, 1811 OS, on Canford Heath, cf. *the lodge* 1542 *Ct*, *v.* loge. Long Coppice (2 ×). Luters Hill (lost), 1811 OS, cf. *cotag' voc' Lytters* 1544 *Ct*, *Luters Grd* 1841 *TA*, a surname. Malaya. Manning's Brick Works & Heath. The Maples. May Vale. Merley Lane (*Merly-* 1822 *EnclA*, cf. *Merley Lane Bridge* 1791 Boswell) & Park (*Merly-* 1822 *EnclA*), Hr & Lr Merley Rd, cf. *Merley Barrows Plant.* 1822 *ib*, all named from Merley *supra*. Merton Grange, cf. The Grange *supra*. Miegunyah. Mill Pond, cf. *Mill grd* 1844 *TA*, near to Creekmoor Mill *supra*. The Moors, cf. Walter *in themore* 1332 SR, *Moor(s)*, *Far & Near Moor*, *Lr & Upr Moor*, *Middle Moor* 1822 *EnclA*, *v.* mōr. Mount Pleasant (Clump). New Covert. Newtown Fm, *Newtown* 1811 OS, *-Cl* 1822 *EnclA*. Northbrook Fm & Ho. Northmead Copse. Oakley Lane (*Oclelane* 1466 *Ct*) & Straight, cf. *Oakley Mdw* 1822 *EnclA*, named from Oakley *supra*, *v.* lane, strait 'a narrow lane'. Old Orchard, 1822 *EnclA*, (*le*) *Oldeorchard* 1374 *MinAcct* (*gardin' voc'-*), 1463 *ib* (*firm' de-*), cf. *le Orchard* 1347 Ipm, *Orchard Plot* 1822 *EnclA*, *v.* ald, orceard. Park Ctgs, near Canford Park *supra*. Pen-

NINGTON COVERT, *Pennington's Plot* 1841 *TA*. PERGIN'S ISLAND, 1811 OS, *Perguain als. Pelham, Periams Island* 1774 Hutch[1], *Perham's Island* 1822 *EnclA*, in Holes Bay *supra*, cf. John *Perham* 1463 *MinAcct*. THE PINES. PLAINFIELD FM, near Plane-field Ho in Longfleet par. *infra*. POND COPPICE, near Merley Pond *supra*. POUND (CLOSE), cf. *murus circa ponfald'* 1374 *MinAcct*, v. **pund**. ROSE LAWN COPPICE, *Rose Lawn* 1844 *TA*, cf. The Lawns *supra*. ROSEMERYON. RUSHCOMBE BOTTOM, -*Moor or Bottom, Rushcomb* 1822 *EnclA*, v. **risc, cumb**. RYDAL MOUNT POULTRY FM. THE SHRUBBERY. SOPER'S LANE. SOUTH LODGE. SPRINGS, 1822 *EnclA*, a plantation. STOAT'S HILL, cf. (*Lr*) *Stote Fd* 1841 *TA*, perhaps ME **stote** 'a stoat', or a surname. SWISS CTG. TRUNK HOLE, on R. Stour, perhaps ModE **trunk** 'a perforated floating box in which live fish are kept', v. **hol**[1]. TULGEY WD, no doubt from Lewis Carroll's poem *Jabberwocky* (l.15). TYCOED CTGS. UPTON HO (1826 Gre) & LAKE (a channel in Poole Harbour, v. **lacu**), from Upton in Corfe Mullen par. *infra*. VICARAGE, *the parsonage* 1542 *Ct*. VINEYARD COPSE. WATERLOO (RESERVOIR), named from *Waterloo Iron Foun-dry* c. 1850 (ex. inf. E. J. French). WHEELER'S LANE, cf. *Wheelers* 1822 *EnclA*. WHITE BARN. WHITEHOUSE RD, -*Hill* 1844 *TA*. WIDWORTHY, perhaps to be associated with *Wude-wurth, Wydeworth* 1244 *Ass* both (p), v. **wudu, widu** 'a wood', **worð, worðig** 'an enclosure'. WIMBORNE LODGE, from Wim-borne Minster par. *infra*. WITHY BED, cf. *Withy Bed Bottom, the Willow Bed* 1822 *EnclA*. YAFFLE HILL.

FIELD-NAMES

The undated forms are 1841 *TA* 37 (Middle division) or 1844 *TA* 38 (Western division). Spellings dated 1242 are Ch, 1275 Cl, 1280, 1288 *Ass*, 1327 *SR*, 1332 SR, 1374, 1463 *MinAcct*, 1412 FA, 1520 *Rent*, 1554 *AddCh*, 1575, 1587, 1612 *DCMDeed*, e17 *BRA*, 1648 *DCMCt*, 1664 HTax, 1675 *WRO*, 1774 Hutch[1], 1791 Boswell, 1811 OS, 1822 *EnclA*, 1826 Gre, and the rest *Ct*.

(a) Alloes (*Allows or Allice's Moor* 1822, cf. John *Alwy* 1327); Bailey Croft (*v.* **baillie**); Barley Croft; Barn Cl; the Bean Gdn 1822; Gt Bedford; the Bee Gdn 1822; Berry Fd (*Bory-* 1463, *Buryfeld* 1463, 1542, cf. Henry *atte Burgh* 1374 (Poole), v. **burh** (dat.sg. **byrig**) 'fortified place', **atte**); Betes 1822; Bethays; Birds' Plot 1822; Bodenhill (perhaps to be associated with Budden(s) Fd *infra*); Border 1822; Borums; Bottom Cl; Brakers; Bratch Coppice & Md 1822, Breach (*prat' voc' le Brec(c)he* 1463, 1520, *Brache Mead* 1587, v. **brēc, brǣc**); Long Brewers 1822; Brick Kiln Cl & Fd, Brick Yd (cf. *tenement called*

Bricks 1675, *Brick Kiln* 1811); Broad Cl; Long Broad Lds 1822; Broom 1822 (cf. *Bromecrofte* 1575, *v.* **brōm**); Bucklands; Budden(s) Fd (cf. John *Budden* 1529); Bugsby Fd (cf. Katherine *Bugbee*, William *Bugbye* 1664); Burts (Cl); Bushes (*-Md* 1822); the Butts 1822 (*v.* **butte**); Byberry Cl 1822; Callas Mdw als. Amy's Ham 1822 (*v.* **hamm**, as freq in this par.); Canford Pdk & St. 1822 (cf. *Canford Street Bridge* 1791); Captains Md; Carter's Park & Rope Walk 1822; Cathays 1822; Catherine's Ash 1822; Cheese Cl (*-Copse* 1822); Chill green; Chimney Cl; Clot Cl 1822; Clover Cl (*-Copse* 1822); Cockstile (*Cock's Tail* 1822, cf. *Kokeshowe* 1463, from **howe** 'enclosure' (cf. How Croft *infra*) and the surname *Cock*); Cogdale Cmn 1822; Collier's Plot 1822; Collins Fd; Common Cl & Plot (cf. *Common Close Green Bridge* 1791); Coppice (Cl); Cow Leaze; Cromwell's Hole 1822 (in R. Stour, *v.* **hol**[1]); Crossway 1822; Davids Fd; Dawbennys 4 & 6 acres (*Estate called Daubeneys* 1822); Deer Mdw 1822; Denshires Ctg; Dowagers; Dowlands (cf. *Dawcrofte* 1544, John *Dawys* 1543); (The) Drove; Dryford 1822; Duck(s) Cl (cf. *terr' apud Doukes*, John *Duk* 1463); Dyches Cl 1822; Eastern Cl; East Grove or Croft 1822; East Heath 1822; East Md; East Side Fd 1822; Edgars; 18 & 11 Acres; Engine Stream or Back Brook 1822; Gt Ewelands; Fent Md 1822 (cf. f.ns. in Hampreston par. *infra*); Fir Plant.; 15 Acres 1822; Fish Pond and Bank (cf. *Fysshewer* 1463, *Fishwear Pdk* 1822, *v.* **fisc, wer**); Fisher's Bridge 1791; 5 Acres; Nthr Foreland; 14 Acres; Fox Holes (*v.* **fox-hol**); Furze Bridge 1791; Furze Plot; Furz(e)y Cl & Plot; Giddy Md Green Bridge 1791, Giddy Md 1822 (*v.* **gydig**); Gillinghams 1822 (cf. Richard *Gyllyngham* 1529, Lake Fm *supra*); Great Cl, Fd & Plot; Lt & Gt Green Hill(s); Greening How 1822; Gutch's Mdw 1822; Ham (cf. *Hammes* 1520, *v.* **hamm**); Hanton 1822; Harpit Cl; Gt Hayes (*v.* **(ge)hæg**); Head Acre 1822; Henson Hill 1822; Heath Plot (cf. *Heathehayes*, *Hethehyll* 1544, *v.* **hǣð, (ge)hæg, hyll**); Heath(e)y Cl or Kidgells (*Kidgill* 1822); Heathy Cl, How, Pce & Plot; Hendys (cf. *Handey* 1822); Herring How; High Plot; Higher Cl, Grd & Plot; Hill Cl & Fd (cf. *Hill Cl Lake, Hill St.* 1822, John-, Peter *atte Hulle* 1332, *v.* **atte, hyll**); Hollys Hill (cf. William *Hoghlys* 1327, Robert *Holles* 1664); Home Cl (Copse & Plant.); Home Cl or Hop Grd; Homers acre and moors; Homestall; Honey Md Coppice (*Honey Md* (*Leg*) 1822); Out Hooks (cf. Walter *atte Hok* 1332, *v.* **atte, hōc, ūt(e)**); How Croft & Moor, Gt How (an el. *how(e)* is common in the minor names and field-names of this part of the county, as e.g. in this par. and in the pars. of Corfe M., Kinson, Hampreston, etc., all *infra*. On the evidence of these names, and of instances of the word in independent use (e.g. *unius ho(u)we* (freq), *clausis...vocat' Howys* 1427 *HarlRoll* (relating to Leigh in Colehill par. *infra*), *a close or howe...called Littell Lowlandes* 1591 *DLMB* (in Pamphill par. *infra*)), it is clear that the el. *how(e)* signifies 'enclosure'. As a term in independent use it has been noted as early as 1350 *HarlRoll* (N/29 m.2r), and it is frequent in f.ns. from the mid-15th cent. (e.g. *Kokeshowe* 1463 *MinAcct*, *v.* Cockstile *supra*). OE **hōh** 'heel, spur of land'(ME *how(e)* from dat.sg.) can hardly have developed the sense 'enclosure', and it is more likely that *how(e)* in these names represents a dial. form of *haw(e)* from OE **haga**[1] 'enclosure'); Hungar Hill (*Phillips's-* 1822, *v.* **hungor**, cf. Phillips *infra*); Inner Cl; Inner Fd 1822; Island (or Willow Bed) (cf. *Island Plot* 1822); James('s) Plot & Well (cf. *James's Hill* 1822, John *Jamys* 1539); Jefferie's Acre & Cl 1822; Jeremiah

Lane; Kennel Md 1822 (cf. *Kennel* 1826); Kings Cl (cf. *King's Bridge Md, King's Ham* 1822, Richard *Kyng* 1332); Knowles (*Knowle* 1822, v. **cnoll**); Lamb Leys 1822 (v. **lǣs**); Lane Cl; Large Cl 1822; Leg Lane 1822 (v. **leg**); Lime Kiln Plot 1822; Lion (P.H.) 1826; Little Cl & Ham; Lockyers Grd (cf. *Lockyer's Coombes* 1822, Richard *Lokyar* 1543, v. **cumb**); Long Acre & Croft 1822; Long Cl, Ditch, Fd & Ham; Longlands; Loose Hill (probably **hlōse** 'pig-sty'); Marble Ld; Marks Plot; Marle Cl 1822 (cf. *quadam marlera* 1288); Marsh Cl & Md (cf. *prat' in la Mers(s)h(e)* 1374, 1465, *Lt Marsh* 1822, v. **mersc**; the form *Marcheffurlonche* 1544 probably also contains **mersc**, with **furlang**); Mead's 5 Acres 1822; Middle Cl, Fd, Grd & Plot; Middle Heath & Mdw 1822; Mile Stone; Mill Ham ((*la*) *Mulham* 1374, *Milleham* 1463, *Mylhame* 1520, *Millhams* 1587, v. **myln, hamm**, from foll.); Mill Ho (cf. Thomas *atte Mulle* 1332, *molend'* 1374, *Steyresmyll* 1463, *Sterys Myll* 1546 *Surv*, v. prec.; there were two mills in Canford in 1086 DB (VCHDo 3 90), cf. *Stratford supra; Steyres-, Sterys-* probably represent the surname *Steer*); Minchin Hill 1822; Moody; Morris' Ham 1822; Mount Ivy; Nags Head Inn; Netherwood Mdw 1822 (*Nitherwode* 1374, *Nathre-, Nather-, Nether-, Notherwod(de)* 1463, *Nether-, Nitherwud* 1529, 'lower wood', from **niðerra, neoðerra** and **wudu**, cf. Overwood *infra*); New Acres 1822; New Cl, Plant. & Plot; New Fm (or Sandpits); Newman's Oak 1822; New Inn P.H. 1822; Nits Cl (-*How* 1822, v. **howe**); North Cl; North Moor 1822; the Nursery 1822; Oakfords Grd; Oak House or Oak Ham(s) (*le Okehowe* 1543, v. **āc, howe, hamm**; the possible confusion of the pl. form *howes* with the word *house* is to be noted); Old Cl; Old Croft or Gt Green Hill; Outer Cl; Outer Fd 1822; Over Fd (cf. foll.); Overwood (*claus' voc' Overwo(o)de* 1465, 1542, v. **uferra** 'higher'); Padmoor (v. **padde** 'toad'); Pancake; Paris Ld 1822; Peaks' Lane 1822; Peat Moor; Perry Islands 1822 (v. **pirige**); Phillips (cf. *Philipclose* 1463, William *Phelipp* 1332); Picks Cl; Pightle (v. **pightel**); Pill('s) Croft, Pill Hows (Border) (v. **pyll** 'pool', **howe**); Pissmoor (*Posemour* 1374, -*more* 1520, *Puse-* 1463, *Pysemore* 1465, *Peasemoor* 1822, v. **pise, peosu** 'pease', **mōr**, cf. *Pesel-* 1542, *Pesyllmo(u)re* 1543 which may be an alternative name for the same place, probably '(moor at) pease hill', v. **hyll**); Pit Copse (cf. *Pitt Hows* 1822, v. **howe**); Pitmans Hill; Pleasure Grd; Ploughed Cl; Plowmans (cf. John *Plowman* 1664); Point Cl 1822; Pond Cl, Moor & Pce; Potters (cf. Robert *Potter* 1664); Purlieu (v. **purlewe**); (Gt) Quity; Redcross Bridge 1791; Red Lion Home Cl, Red Lion P.H.; Reeks Cl (cf. John *Ryke* 1529); Road Plot; Rolles Hedge; Rooks Park (cf. John *Rouke* 1543); Rosy Plot; Rough Cl; Rush 1822 (v. **rysce** 'rush bed'); Rushy Plot & Withy bed; Ryeberry (v. **ryge, beorg**); Rye Cl (cf. *Rye How* 1822); Saddle Back (v. **saddleback**); Salt Croft (-*Cl* 1822); Samways('s) Plot; Lt Sand Pce 1822; Sandy Lane 1822; School Ho; Sedgeford; Servers; 7 Acres; Shape croft (v. **scēap**); Shells; Shepherd Cl (cf. *Shepherd's Wd* 1822); Skinners; Smackhams (cl); Smithy Fd; South Moor & Plot 1822; Sparrows Heathy Cl; Spears Plot; Spinney; Square Cl; Stage 1822; Stanley Green 1822; Stone Plots; Stoney grd; Stony Park 1822; Swan Inn; Swans nest (cf. *the Kinges grac' game of Swannes* 1542, *Swan* (island) 1774, *Swan Cl* 1822, v. **swan**[1]); Swimming Mdw 1822; Swing Fd or Swin Hill 1822; (Long) Tadmoor 1822 (*claus' voc' Taddemere* 1463, v. **tadde** 'a toad', **mere**[1] 'a pool'); 10 Acres; Thornhill Cl; 3 Acres; Three Peal

Bottom 1822; Triangle Cl & Fd; Trinds Lawn; Trining Bridge 1791; the
Turn Stiles 1822; Tutwell Plot 1822; 12 Acres; Twitchams (*la Twychen, -yn*
1465, *cotag' voc' Tuchyn* 1544, *v.* twicen(e) 'cross-roads'); Upper Grd;
Wares Plot (cf. *John Weares house* 1664 (Kinson)); Washing Pond 1822; Water
Plot (cf. Stephen *atte Watere* 1327, *v.* atte, wæter); Webb Arms Inn Plot,
Webbs Moor (cf. Sir John *Webb* 1664); Well Hole 1822 (cf. Walter *atte Wolle*
1332, John *atte Woll* 1465, *v.* atte, well(a), wyll(a)); West(ern) Cl; Western
Fort 1822; West Heath & Plot 1822; West Hows (*v.* howe); West Side Fd;
Wheat Cl 1822; Whetstone's Bridge 1791; Whitclose (cf. foll.); Whitcombe
(*claus' voc' Whit-, Whytcombe* 1465, 1466, *v.* hwīt, cumb); Whitmoor (*Whyte-*
1519, *Whyttmo(u)re* 1544, *Whitmore Bridge* 1791, *White Moor* 1822, *v.* hwīt,
mōr); Behind Williams's (cf. Richard *Williams* 1648); Willow How or
Cummings (cf. *Cunnings* 1822); Winds Lawn (*-Moor* 1822); Woodlakes Cl
1822 (*Wodelake* 1374, *Wodde-* 1463 (*pastur' voc'-*), *Wodlake* 1520, *Woodlakes*
1587, *v.* wudu, lacu 'a stream'; it was near (*la*) *Wodehey* 1374, *Woddeheys*
1463, *Wodhays* 1520, *Woodhayes* 1587, *v.* (ge)hæg); Yeatmans Cl (cf. John *atte*
Yate 1463, 1466, *v.* atte, geat); Yonder Cl.

(b) *the bekon, a vale...called Bycam* 1542 (*v.* (ge)bēacon); *the Bell Acre*
1538 WimCW, 1663 Hutch³, *the Bill acre* 1540 ib (in Netherwood Mdw *supra*,
so called because it 'hath byn alwayes apperteyning to the maintenance of the
said bells', i.e. those of the minster church at Wimborne, *v.* belle, Hutch³
3 224); *Brodenesham* 1463 (*v.* hamm, probably with a surname); *Canfordmede*
1463, *prat' de Canforde* 1543 (*v.* mǣd); *Chadenwich* 1374 (the OE pers.n.
Ceadda and wīc); *Crabelane* 1520 (*v.* crabbe); *Crisc(c)h'* 1374 (reading
uncertain); *Culuerham* 1374, 1463, *Couluerhouss(e)(ham)* 1520, *Culverhay*
1587 (*v.* culfre 'dove', hamm, hūs, (ge)hæg, cf. the dove-cot (*columbura*)
mentioned Ed I Hutch³ 3 289); *terre in Curtell* 1544, *Curtall* 1554 (Professor
Löfvenberg compares OFr cortil(le) 'garden, enclosure'); *Daschlake* 1374
(*v.* lacu, *Dasch-* may represent *de Asch-, v.* æsc, cf. Reaney s.n. *Dash*); *aque*
voc' Dedwill 1520 (*v.* dēad, well(a)); *croft'voc' Durnelee* 1374 (*v.* derne, dyrne,
lēah); *Durnelynch(e)clif* 1374, *-clyffe* 1463 (*v.* derne, dyrne, hlinc, clif);
Dyxsons land 1519; *Froudemere* 1465 (perhaps the OE pers.n. *Frōda* and mere¹
'pool'); *in le Grene* 1327, *in the Greyne* 1332 both (p) (*v.* grēne²); *Greneclose*
1519, *Gryneclosse* 1544 (*v.* grēne¹, clos(e)); *Guymede* 1374, *Geremede* 1463 (*v.*
mǣd; Professor Löfvenberg suggests that *Guy-* may be a scribal error for
Gur- and that, if so, the first el. may be an OE *gyre 'dirt, mud', on which
v. Löfvenberg 85); *Hyghfeld* 1463 (*v.* hēah, feld); *Idenle* 1412 (*v.* lēah);
Keepers ham 1587 (*v.* hamm); *Kyrton* 1520 (second el. probably tūn;
Professor Löfvenberg suggests that the first el. may possibly be an OE pers.n.
*Cyra, cognate with OE *Cora in Corringham Li (DEPN)); *vill' de...Langele*
1280 (*v.* lang¹, lēah); *Langemour* 1374 (*v.* lang¹, mōr); *Makedoune* 1463
('Mac(c)a's hill', from the OE pers.n. *Mac(c)a* found in Makeney Db 589,
etc, and dūn); *Math(e)uesham, -hay* 1463 (the ME pers.n. or surname *Matthew*
with hamm and (ge)hæg); *croft' voc' Merveile* 1463 (probably the ME
surname *Merveyle* from OFr *merveille* 'marvel', or the same word used as
a complimentary name for productive land); *atte Niwelond* 1332 (p) (*v.* atte,
nīwe, land); *cottage called Norris Hay* 1675 (cf. John *Noreys* 1332, *v.* (ge)hæg);
Ordes- 1463, *Ordysham* 1520 (*v.* hamm; first el. an OE pers.n. *Ord* found

in Ordsall Nt 90, etc); *Oselake* 1463 (probably 'Osa's stream', from the OE pers.n. *Ōsa* and **lacu**); *ten' voc' Panett* 1542 (probably the surname *Pannett*); *Porslande* 1543 (probably 'land set aside for the benefit of the poor', *v.* **po(u)re, land**, or from the surname *Poor*); *Westmostrawland* 1544 (*v.* **westmest, land**; Professor Löfvenberg suggests that *-raw-* may represent the adj. *raw* (OE *hrēaw*, ME *raw*), cf. ModE dial. *raw-lay* 'grass land which has been ploughed to grow a crop' (recorded from Devon, EDD)); *Redeford* 1465 (*v.* **rēad** 'red' or **hrēod** 'reed', **ford**); *le Rewes* 1374, *Rewen* 1520 ('the rows (of trees, etc)', *v.* **rǣw**; *-en* is a ME wk.pl., *v.* *-en*[5]); *pastur' in la Roky* 1374 (possibly from **hrōc** 'rook' with **ēa** 'stream' or **ēg** 'island'); *Rotherford* 1520 ('ford used by cattle', *v.* **hrīðer, hryðer, ford**); *Ryve acre* 1612; 'the vale of *Sirewater*' 1242 ('clear stream', *v.* **scīr**[2], **wæter**); *lez Southebarowe* 1554 (*v.* **sūð, beorg**); *South(e)mede* 1463, 1520, *-Meade* 1587 (*v.* **mǣd**); *Strodebrigge-* 1463, *Stroderidgeford(e)* (sic) 1554 (*v.* **strōd, brycg, ford**); *Townemede* 1465 (*v.* **toun**); *cotag' voc' Tonipp* 1542 (reading uncertain); *cotag' voc' Tynkers* 1542; *Westhey* 1463 (*v.* **(ge)hæg**); *Westend* 1520 (*v.* **ende**[1]; this is probably the western division of the manor, called 'the west end' in Hutch[3] 3 312, cf. note under Kinson par. *infra*); *Wymarecruch* 1242 (the OE pers.n. *Wīgmǣr* and **crūc**[3] 'a cross'); *Wyreberge* 1275 (said to be in the 'launds of *Caneford*', *v.* *The Lawns supra*; Smith 2 46 cites *Werybarowe* 1544 which perhaps belongs here, and he may be correct in supposing that the form '*Wyrebarowe* by *Pole*' 1462 Pat also belongs here and not under Worbarrow 1 103; in any case the names may be identical in origin, cf. also Wor Barrow in Wimborne St G. par. *infra*).

Charlton Marshall

Formerly a tithing and chapelry in Spettisbury par. *infra* (Hutch[3] 3 284, 516).

CHARLTON MARSHALL (ST 902038)

 Cerletone 1086 DB, *-tona* Exon

 Cerlentone, -tonia 1087–1100, c. 1165 France

 Cherlentona, -tune 1166–87 France, *-ton* 1188 *AD, Cherlinton(e)*? John *AddCh*, 1219 Sarum

 Cheorleton 1187 France

 Cherleton(e) 1201 P, 1242 Ch, 1244 *Ass*, 1256 FF (p) *et freq* to 1428 FA, *-juxta Wymburn* 1266 FF, *-iuxta Canford* 1270 (1372) *ChrP, -Marescal* 1288 *Ass, -infra Spectebury* 1460 *DCMDeed, Cherlton* 1347 Pat, 1429 *EgCh* (*-iuxta Blaneford*)

 Cherelton 1244 *Ass*, 1589 Eton

 Charleton 1337 Fine, 1340 Pat *et freq* to 1571 *Eton* (*-Marshall*), *-Prioris* 1340 NI, *-juxta Speghtebury* 1390 FF

 Charilton 1383 Cl, *Chareletoun* 1453 *MinAcct*

 Carleton 1575 Saxton

'Farm of the peasants', *v.* **ceorl** (gen.pl. *ceorla*), **tūn**, cf. Canford M. par. *supra*, Wimborne M. par., Spettisbury par., and Blandford F. par. *infra*; the early forms in *C(h)erlen-, -in-* probably represent an analogical ME wk.gen.pl. *-ene, v.* **-ena**, cf. Wo 105. The affix *Marshall* is from the family which gave name to Sturminster Marshall par. *infra*, cf. Henry *Marescot* (for *-scal*) 1258 Ch (grantor of lands in Charlton Marshall to Tarrant abbey), Ralph *le Mareschal* 1280 ib (witness to a charter confirming the same grant), *v.* Hutch³ 3 522, 524, and cf. foll.; *-Prioris* alludes to the possession of the chapel and tithes of Charlton Marshall by the priory of Spettisbury from l11, *v.* VCHDo 2 119–120.

CHARLTON PARVA (lost), 1575, *Charleton Rectoris de Stourmynstre Marchall* 1447, *Charleton Sturmynstr'* 1448, *Firm' de parva Charleton* 1459, *Charleton Parva* 1462–1571 (*-in Charleton Marshall*) all *Eton*, 1716 Eton, *Charlton Makerell Parva* 1508, *Charelton Parva* 1589 both *Eton, v.* **parva**. This manor, along with the rectory of Sturminster Marshall, belonged to Eton College from m15, *v.* Hutch³ 3 365, 524; according to Hutch³ 3 524, it was 'situate near the river on the eastern side of the parish', cf. Charlton Manor and Manor Fm *infra*. *Makerell* may show confusion of this name with Charlton Mackrell So, although the surname does occur in the area, cf. the f.n. Mackrells Leaze in Sturminster Marshall par. *infra*.

ABBESS OF TARENTS (lost), 1795 Boswell, *The Manor of the Abbess of Tarent* 1774 Hutch¹, lands granted to Tarrant abbey in 1258 Ch, *v.* Hutch³ 3 524. BIRCH CLOSE, called *Brunes Cl* 1811 OS, cf. *Brune's* 1795 Boswell (a manor), from the family of William *le Brune* 1301 Hutch³ 3 522, cf. Manor Fm and the f.n. *Neweschepey* both *infra*. CHARISWORTH, a farm, perhaps an old name in **worð**, but there are no early forms; a form *Kaerswurth*, tentatively identified with this name by Fägersten 111, belongs under Keysworth in Wareham par. 1 159. CHARLTON DOWN, 1863 Hutch³, *le Downes* 1508 Eton, *le doun* 1559 *ib*, cf. *culturam...versus montem, le Foredoun* 1447 *ib, v.* **dūn, fore**. CHARLTON HO & MANOR (perhaps to be associated with the manor of Charlton Parva *supra*, cf. Manor Fm *infra*). CHARLTON ON THE HILL, a hamlet only 50′ above the village itself. CHURCH, cf. *ecclesiam...de Cherlenton* 1188 *AD, capella de Cherleton*

1428 FA, *Church Acre* 1451 Hutch³, 1800 *EnclA*. GLEBE FM.
GORCOMBE CTGS & WD, (*le Hedlond de*) *Gorcombe* 1447 *Eton, v.*
cumb; first el. **gāra** 'point of land' or **gor** 'dirt'. GRAVEL LANE,
cf. *Gravelly md* 1800 *EnclA, Graund acres infra.* GROSVENOR
BUSHES. HILL CREST, a house on the crest of a 250′ ridge. HOLLY
BRAKE, *v.* **bræc¹**. KITEHILL PLANT., *v.* **cȳta**. LYCH GATE.
MANOR FM (2 ×); one is near to Birch Cl *supra*, the other to
Charlton Manor *supra*. NEW TOWN. NEWLANDS. RED BARN FM,
cf. *Barne close* 1630 Eton. RIVER'S EDGE, near R. Stour.
SPARROWBUSH FM. THORNCOMBE, a hamlet partly in Blandford
St M. par. *q.v.*

FIELD-NAMES

The undated forms are 1800 *EnclA* (DRO Record Book IV p. 490). Spellings
dated 1327 are *SR*, 1448², 1449, 1450, 1452 *MinAcct*, 1540, 1570, 1ı8 Hutch³,
1559², 1613, 1630, 1667, 1716, 1727 Eton, and the rest *Eton.*

(*a*) (Bank) Bincklinch (*litel-, Longbyklynche* 1447, possibly 'bees' nest
ridge' from **bīc** and **hlinc**, with **lȳtel, lang¹**, cf. *le Byorchard* 1447 which is
probably from **bēo** 'a bee' and **orceard**); Blandford Cl, -Lane (Cl) ('close lying
by Blandford Lane' 1613, cf. Blandford St Mary par. *infra*); Brofland
(*Broferland close* 1630, probably 'broad furlong', *v.* **brād, furlang**); Brottland
(perhaps to be associated with *le Bere* [? *hefed* erased] *londes* 1447, 'the barley
(head)lands', cf. *Berfurl'* 1447, *v.* **bere, hēafod-land, furlang**); Cirlings;
College (from its possession by Eton College); Coombe Cl (cf. *Combe* 1613,
v. **cumb**); Corner Md; Crickets Plot; Cross (Cl, Fd, Gdn & Orchd); Lr,
Middle & Upr Drove (Lane) (*le droveWeyeshull* 1447, *drove hedge* 1613, *v.*
drāf, weg, hyll); Elm Cl; Etalls; Forster; Freke's 1ı8 (from John *Freke* 1570);
French Grass; Front Fd; Great Cl; Hell Fd; Home Cl & Grd (cf. *the Home
Fd* 1727, *Homegraunge infra*); Hope good; Long Grd; Lunny; Main Crate
(*v.* **croft**); Marsh Lane, Up Marsh (*the Marshe* 1571, (*via . . . ducent' versus
prata et pastur' voc'*) *Upmers*(*c*)*h*(*e*) 1447, 1559¹, *v.* **mersc, upp**); 9 Acres; Oak
Cl; Pancras Cl; Rickyard; Spinny Cl; Tan yd; 3 Acres; Well Cl; Were (*v.*
wer, cf. 'the fishery within the manor of *Charleton Parva*' 1716).

(*b*) *Acrehey* 1559² (*v.* **æcer, (ge)hæg**, as freq in this par.); *Bareleggethorn*
1447 (*v.* **þorn**; the first part of the name is probably a ME surname *Barelegge*
'bare leg', cf. Reaney *s.n.* Barefoot); *Blanchardisley* 1540 (the ME surname
Blanchard (< OFr), with **lēah**); *Burell londes* 1447 (cf. Henry *Burall* 1447,
v. **land**); *Buryclose* 1447, *-berne* 1448¹, *-hall*(*e*) 1448¹, 1591 (dom' voc'-) (ME
bury 'manor' (from dat.sg. *byrig* of OE **burh**), with **clos**(**e**), **bere-ærn, hall,**
cf. *le Hyde londes infra*); *Catsbrayne* 1613 (*v.* **cattes-brazen**); *Charleton Mede*
1447, 1571 (*v.* **mǣd**); *Chykyns Thorne* 1447 (the surname *Chicken, v.* **þorn**);
Childbergh 1447 (*v.* **cild** 'young person', **beorg**); *Cotens heye* 1447 (the
surname *Cot*(*t*)*en*); *toft' voc' Crishey* 1559¹ (possibly **cærse** 'cress'); *Culuyrhey*
1450 (*v.* **culfre**); *Ded*(*e*)*folkefurlong*(*e*) 1447 (no doubt an old burial site, *v.*

dēad, folc, furlang); *1 acra...iac' ex opposito le Dowe* 1447 (if the form is reliable, ME *dogh, dow(e)* 'dough', used of soft ground, cf. G.Kristensson, *Studies on Middle English Topographical Terms*, 1970, p. 24); *le dychewey* 1447 (*v.* **dīc, weg**); *Grenehey* 1447 (*v.* **grēne**[1]); *ten' voc' the Ferme* 1569 (*v.* **ferme**); *cultura voc' le Fryingpanne* 1447 (an early instance of this field-name, *v.* **fryingpanne**); *Graund acres cope* 1447 (first el. possibly **grand** 'gravel', cf. Gravel Lane *supra* and foll., with **æcer**; *cope* may represent **cop(p)** 'hill-top'); *le Grundewatereputt, le Watergrandelputtes,* (*furl' voc'*) *Suthwater(e)grundelhull* (*busshes*) all 1447 (*v.* **wæter, pytt, sūð, hyll, busc**; the el. represented by -*grandel*-, -*grunde(l)*- (if all these forms belong together) is obscure, but -*grandel*- may be an **-el**[3] derivative of **grand** 'gravel' (cf. prec. and the mutated **grendel** 'gravelly place'), and -*grundel*- a similar derivative of **grund** 'ground, bottom' with a meaning 'deep place' or the like (cf. ModE *grundel*, ME *grundyl* 'a groundling, a small fish' and *Grundelacr'* Brk 341). Some of these names are no doubt represented by the *TA* f.n. Water Gunnell Fd in Spettisbury par. *infra*); *via voc' HarnesWey* 1447 (possibly from **(ge)hērness** 'a jurisdiction', *v.* **weg**); *le Hyde londes, le Overebury-, le Nether bury Hide-, Hydelondes* 1447 (*v.* **hīd, land, uferra, neoðerra**; for -*bury*-, *v.* **Buryclose**, etc *supra*); Homegraunge 1449 (*v.* **home, grange**, cf. Home Cl *supra*; there was a grange of the hospital of St Giles of Pont Adomar in Charlton M. in 1325 Hutch[3] 3 524); (*le*) *Inslade* 1447 (*v.* **in, slæd**); *Juddas* 1613 (the pers.n. or surname *Judah, Judas, v.* Reaney s.n. *Jude*); *Kingsmells close* 1575 (cf. Richard *Kyngysmyll* 1508; the surname may refer to a 'king's mill' in this par., cf. *le Mullepounde infra*); *langacre* 1447 (*v.* **lang**[1], **æcer**); *le Mullepounde* 1448[2], *le Pownde* 1452 (*v.* **myln, pund**, cf. *aqua molendini domini* 1447, *molend' aquatic'* 1597; the royal manor of Charlton Marshall and Pimperne had two mills in 1086 DB (VCHDo 3 65), cf. the surname in *Kingsmells close supra*); *Netherfurl'* 1447 (*v.* **neoðerra, furlang**); *the North fyld* 1571 (*v.* **feld**); *downe called the North Sleight* 1571 (*v.* **slæget**); *Parke* 1613 (*v.* **park**); *Rowefurlong* 1447 (*v.* **rūh** (wk.obl. *rūgan*) 'rough'); *cultura voc'-, via voc' Ryp(p)ewey(e)* 1447 (*v.* **weg**, perhaps with OE **rip(p)** 'a strip, an edge'); (*le*) *Neweschepey* (*als. dict' Brunschepey*) 1447, *old shapee* 1613 (*v.* **scēap, (ge)hæg, nīwe, ald**; *Brun*- is probably a surname, *v.* Birch Close *supra*); (*via voc'*) (*le*) *Smal(e)wey* 1447 (*v.* **smæl, weg**); *S(o)uthfeld* 1447, *the South fyld* 1571 (*v.* **feld**); 'the south west field' 1613; *le Stort* 1447 (*v.* **steort**); *cultura voc' Sunder-, Sundorton* 1447 ('detached, or private, farm'), *v.* **sundor, tūn**); *le Taddeacr'* 1447 (*v.* **tadde** 'a toad', **æcer**); *Waddon* 1447, 1450 (*v.* **wād, dūn**); *atte Watere* 1327 (p) (*v.* **atte, wæter**); *Nether Wernehull, Wernehull Thorne* 1447 (*v.* **neoðerra, hyll, þorn**; *Werne-* could be from OE **wrǣna, wærna** 'a stallion', or OE **wrenna, wærna** 'a wren', or an OE pers.n. *Werna*, cf. Ekwall Studies[2] 67–8 and *wærnan hyll* Brk 706); *Westfeld* 1447 (*v.* **feld**); *Whites* 1667 (a surname); *le Whiteweyhill* 1447 (*v.* **hwīt, weg, hyll**).

Corfe Mullen

Part of this par. (Upton, etc) was transferred to Lytchett Minster par. in 1930.

CORFE MULLEN (SY 976984)
> Corf 1086 DB, 1212 Fees, 1244 Ass (p), 1327 SR
> Corf le Mulin 1176, 1177 P, Corfmulin Hy 3 Ipm, -molyn(e),
> -Molyn 1268 Ass et freq to 1428 FA, -Mulyn, -mulyn 1283
> Misc, 1288 Ass, 1353 Cl, Ipm, Corf(f)(e) Malyn 1375 Cl,
> -Mallen 1661 DCMCt, -Molen 1395 Cl, 1487 Ipm, 1672
> DCMCt (-als. Corfe Hubert), -Moleyn, -moleyn 1412 FA et
> freq to 1536 Wim, -Mullen 1545 (16) Bartelot, 1605
> DCMCt (-als. Corffe Hubard), 1742 DCMDeed (-otherwise
> Corfe Hubert), -Mullin 1545 (16) Bartelot, -Molyn als.
> Corffe Hubert 1671 DCMCt, -Mullein als. Corff Mullein St
> Nicholas vel Corff Hubbard 1610 NichHosp
> Croft molendina John LN
> Corf(f)(e) Huberd, -huberd 1303, 1428 FA, 1484 Eton,
> -Hubert 1346, 1431 FA, 1478 FF, 1487 Ipm, -Hiberd 1484
> Eton, -Hubarde, -hubart 1539 Ct
> Corf(f)(e) Giles 1484 Eton, 1539, 1543 Ct
> Corf(e) St Nicholas 1774 Hutch[1], 1863 Hutch[3]

'A cutting, a pass', with reference to its situation between two hills, v. corf, cf. Corfe Castle 1 5. The affix Mullen is from OFr molin 'a mill', referring to the valuable mill here, which rendered 20 shillings (a high value) in 1086 DB (VCHDo 3 90), v. Mill infra; the isolated form Croft molendina contains Lat molendinum 'mill', the spelling Croft showing metathesis and a development of final -t also found in the ME spellings for Corfe Castle 1 6. The affix Huberd, Hubert is either from Hubert de Burgo who held Corf in 1212 Fees (90), or from Hubert la Veylle who held ⅛ of a knight's fee in Corf Huberd in 1303 FA; Giles is probably from Giles de Hardyngton who held ¼ of a knight's fee in Corfmolyn in 1346 FA, cf. Egidius de Erdyngton 1327 SR. Corfe St Nicholas is so called because it 'anciently and now belongs to St Nicholas's hospital near Sarum' (Hutch[3] 3 359), cf. St Nicholas Lands 1610 NichHosp and St Hubert's Church infra.

COGDEAN ELMS (SY 993980), -*Elm(e)s* 1774 Hutch[1], named from *Kocdene* 1249 FF, 1280 *Ass* (*vill' de-*), *Cokkeden(e)* 1280 *ib*, 1374 *MinAcct, Cog-* 1288 *Ass, Coke-* 1455 Cl, *Cokden* 1463 *MinAcct, Cogdean* 1774 Hutch[1], cf. *Cogdean* (*Lane*) *Cl* 1839 *TA*, probably 'cocks' valley', from **cocc**[2] (gen.pl. *cocca*) and **denu**; it gives name to Cogdean hundred *supra*, the court of which was formerly held here (as in 1249 FF and 1463 *MinAcct*). The valley (part of it now called Happy Bottom *infra*) extends NE and is crossed by a N–S Roman road (Margary 4d). Anderson 129 suggests that the 'cocks' may have been waterfowl, since these frequent the marshy valley bottom. There were 'some large elms' here in 1774 (Hutch[1] 2 129), *v.* **elm**.

THE KNOLL (SY 976973), KNOLL CLUMP, COPSE & FM, *La Cnolle* 1228 FF, *atte Knolle* 1327 *SR*, 1332 SR both (p), *Knoll* 1697 *DCMCt, The Knoll* 1863 Hutch[3] (a house), cf. *Knowle Cl* 1742 *DCMDeed, -Hill* 1839 *TA*, from OE **cnoll** 'a hillock', *v.* **atte**.

SLEIGHT (SY 986978), 1811 OS, *atte Sleyte* 1327 *SR*, 1332 SR both (p), from **slæget** 'a sheep pasture', *v.* **atte**.

UPTON (SY 984932), UPTON FM & HEATH, *Vp-, Upton* 1463 *MinAcct*, 1485 Pat *et passim, Uppon* 1522 *Russ, Upton Farme* 1612 *DCMDeed*, cf. *Upton-wood* 1661 Hutch[1], 'higher farm', *v.* **upp, tūn**, cf. Upton Ho & Lake (named from this place) in Canford Magna par. *supra*, and the analogous Upton in Osmington par. 1 213; it lies at only c. 50', but must have been named in relation to an even lower settlement such as at Hamworthy par. or Lytchett Minster par. both *infra*. There is mention of a 'cony-warren or pasture' here in 1485 Pat, and of [the church of] *Saynt Peter in Upton* in 1519 *Ct*.

ALLEN HILL, *Allen's-* 1839 *TA*. ATWELL'S COPSE. THE BARRACKS. BEECH GROVE. BELDAM HOWE (lost), 1811 OS, *Beldams How* 1637 (1704) *DCMCt, close called Beldam* 1740 DCMDeed, *Belham Howe* 1826 Gre, (*Gt & Lt*) *Beldam's How, Beldams How Coppice* 1839 *TA*, the surname *Beldam, v.* **howe** 'enclosure'. BROG STREET (a hamlet), 1811 OS, possibly from **brocc** 'badger' or **brōc** 'brook' (it is near a stream), with **strete** in the sense 'hamlet, straggling village'; for the sound develop-

ment, cf. Brogdale K 290. BROOK LANE, near a stream, cf. prec.
BROOM CLOSE, (*East*-), (-*Copse*) 1839 *TA*, cf. *Broomfield* 1839
ib. BUTLER'S COPSE, cf. *Butlers Acre & 3 Acres* 1839 *TA*.
CANDYS FM, *Condys* 1811 OS, (*South*) *Candies, Candie's 4 acres
& cl* 1839 *TA*. CARTER'S SIDING (railway). CHALK PIT COPSE.
CHERETT'S CLUMP, cf. Thomas *Cherrett* 1664 HTax. CLAY
HILL (lost), 1811 OS, near Beacon Hill Clay Works (6″) named
from Beacon Hill in Lytchett Minster par. *infra*, cf. *Clay Pit*(*s*)
1839 *TA*. CORFE EDGE (a house near par. bdy) & LODGE. THE
COTTAGE. COURT FM & HO, *Court* 1811 OS. THE CROFT. CROSS
(Remains of), 'the great stone called the cross in the
churchyard' 1662 Hutch[3], 'a square cross base' 1863 ib, cf. St
Hubert's Church *infra*. DECOY POND, *v.* **decoy**. DOMINYS (lost),
1759 *DCMDeed*, 1811 OS, *Dominey's cl* 1839 *TA*, cf. Robert
Domeny 1664 HTax. DORSET NURSERY. DRAGLENS HEDGEROW,
Drags Lds 1839 *TA*. DRINMERE, a house. EAST END, 1811 OS,
cf. *East End Cl* 1839 *TA*, a hamlet in the E of the par., *v.* **ende**[1].
FLORENCE CTG. GLENDON, a house. GRANT'S COPSE. GRAVEL
PIT (freq), 1839 *TA*. HAPPY BOTTOM, *v.* Cogdean Elms *supra*.
HAYWARDS LANE, cf. *Haywards Ham* 1637 (1704) *DCMCt*,
Haywards (*Coppice, 5 Acres & 3 Acres*) 1839 *TA*, Annis
Hayward 1664 HTax, *v.* **hamm**. THE HERMITAGE. HIGH DITCH
COPSE, *High Ditch* 1839 *TA*, cf. *Ditch Acre* 1839 *ib*, *v.* **dīc**. HILL
FM, *Hill Fm Lane* 1839 *TA*. HILL VIEW. HIMMON COPSE,
Himmon 1839 *TA*. HOME FM. JOINER'S COPSE, *Joyner's Coppice*
1839 *TA*, cf. *Joiner's Grd* 1839 *ib*. KENNEL COPSE, cf. *Keepers
Ho...and Kennel* 1839 *TA*. LAMBS' GREEN, 1811 OS, *Lambs
Green Cl* 1839 *TA*. LOCKYER'S SCHOOL, endowed by Richard
Lockyer 1730 Hutch[3] 3 481, cf. *Lockyers Ho* 1839 *TA*. MILL,
cf. *Millstreete* 1663 (1707) *DCMCt*, *Water Corn Mill* 1839 *TA*,
v. **myln, strǣt**; on the important early mill here, *v.* par. name
supra. MILTON, not near prec., but possibly 'mill farm', from
myln and **tūn**; there is a stream ¼ mile E. MOUNTAIN CLUMP,
Mountain's Coppice 1839 *TA*, cf. *Mounteynes* 1695 *DCMCt*,
Hr & Lr Mountains 1839 *TA*, perhaps a whimsical use of
monteyne 'a mountain' to describe the hillock here (marked
Mound 6″), but possibly a surname. MOUNT PLEASANT. MUL-
LOCK. NAKED CROSS, 1839 *TA*, a cross-roads, cf. Bare Cross in
Church Knowle par. *supra*, *v.* **nacod**. THE NEST. NEWTOWN,
1811 OS, cf. *New Town Cl* 1839 *TA*. OLD COURT COPSE, -*Coppice*

1839 *TA*, cf. Court Fm & Ho *supra*. ORCHARD COPPICE, cf. *Orchard Cl* 1778 DCMDeed, *-Plot* 1839 *TA*, *(Lt) Orchard* 1839 *ib*. OTTERBURN, a house. PALMERSTON RD, cf. *ten' called Palmer's*, widow *Palmer* 1740 *DCMDeed, Palmers Moor Coppice* 1839 *TA*. PARDY'S COPSE. PARK COPSE, *-Coppice, The Park* 1839 *TA*, v. **park**. BIG & LITTLE PAYNE. PEALS MARSH (lost), 1811 OS. PENTRE CTGS. THE PINE CLUMP. PONY DRIVE. POOR CMN. RED LANE (COPSE), cf. *Redland* 1697 *DCMCt, E & Gt Red Lawn* 1839 *TA, v.* **rēad, land**. ROMAN TOWER, a house. HR & LR RUSSELL'S COPSE, cf. *Russell's (Moor)* 1839 *TA*. ST HUBERT'S CHURCH, earlier 'The Chapel of Corf-Mullen... dedicated to St Nicholas' 1774 Hutch¹ 2 129, both dedications perhaps having been suggested by the manorial affixes of Corfe Mullen *supra*, cf. 'the chapel of *Cormolin*' 1285 FF, *prists-* 1653 (1704), *Preists house* 1688, *the churchouse* 1661 all *DCMCt, Church cl* 1839 *TA*, and Cross *supra*. SAND PIT. SOUTH VIEW NURSERY. SPUR COPSE, cf. *Spurcock's Coppice* 1839 *TA*. STONY DOWN (PLANT.), cf. *Stony Hill* 1657 *DCMCt, (Lt-)* 1839 *TA, Stonehill* 1697 *DCMCt*. TAYLORS (lost), 1811 OS. TILEKILN COPSE, *v.* **tilekiln**. THE TOWERS. VIOLET FM. WATERLOO CTGS. WESTWAYS. WHITEHALL FM, cf. *Corf' Hall'* 1512 *Pars, atte Hal(l)e infra, v.* **hall**. WHITE HO. WINDYRIDGE. WITHY BED, 1839 *TA*.

FIELD-NAMES

The undated forms are 1839 *TA* 71. Spellings dated 1327 are *SR*, 1332 SR, n.d. (1372) *ChrP*, 1406, 1740, 1742 *DCMDeed*, 1600 *Hen*¹, 1635, 1656, 1778 DCMDeed, 1664 HTax, 1811 OS, 1822 *EnclA* (Canford Magna), and the rest *DCMCt*.

(a) Addle Md (*v.* **adela** 'a filthy place'); Allswood Coppice; Arnold's Plot; Backrells; Bankers Hill; Barn Cl; Barnes's cl (cf. John *Barnes* 1664); Bartlett's Plot (cf. Lawrence *Bartlett* 1664); Bear Md (*v.* **bearu** 'wood' or **bǣr²** 'woodland pasture'); Bedwell Cl (probably 'well provided with a vessel', *v.* **byden, well(a)**, cf. Bedwell Hrt 138); Black Down (Hill); Black Lane Plot; Blackmoor (*-more* 1742); Blind Slade (*v.* **slæd**); Bon(i)fore Hill (perhaps ModE **bonfire**); Botherd; Boundary Rd (a Roman road (Margary 4d) here forming the par. bdy, cf. *Bound Rd* 1822); Brambles cl; Brass Fd; Breach Cl; (old) Brickkiln(s) (cf. *Brick Kiln* 1811); Broad Moor (Ld & Lane); Brook's cl; Bushy Cl Coppice; Butcher's Hill & Lane; (N) Butts (*v.* **butte**); Clarke's 4 & 2 Acres, Clarke's Lane (Plot) (cf. Thomas *Clarke* 1664); Coombe Cl (cf. *Combefield* 1697, *v.* **cumb**); Corfe Hill Cl; Corfe Md (*Corff mead* 1657, *le Com'on mead* 1677, *Corfe (Common) Md(w)* 1742, *v.* **mǣd**); Cowleaze, Lt Cowleys; Crumpets (Bottom), Crumpit's Bottom (near Crumpet's Fm in

Sturminster Marshall par. *infra*); N & S Cummings (cf. *Kemming* 1742); Dean's 5 acres (1822); Denny 6 acres; Diett's Acre, Gt Dyett's, Middle Dites (cf. John *Diett* 1664 (Lytchett Matravers)); Drax's Cl; Duck Plot; East Cl, Fd & Md; 8 and 3 Acres; Eweleaze (Park); Far Hays (*v.* (ge)hæg); Inner 5 acres; Foots cl; 4 Acres; Furmages (cf. John *Formage* 1600); Garden Plot; Gib's Cl (*Gibbs* 1653, cf. William *Gibbes* 1332); Great Cl; Great Wd (1742 (*Corfe-*)); Green Cl, Ground (Cl) & Stile; Green's (Grd) (*Green's* 1740); Grove Cl (cf. *the Grove* 1778); Half Acre Pce & Plot; Hanging Grd; Harrington's; Hayley's Cl (cf. *Haylyes tenement* 1653 (1704), Richard *Hayle* 1664); Heath (& Plant.); Hercules Plot; Hill Md; Hobby's (Altmt); Home Cl & Plot; the Homestead; Hop Gdn; House cl coppice (probably pl. of howe 'enclosure', cf. foll.); (Further, Gt & Lt) How, (Lt) How Cl (*the Hows* 1652 (1704), *le how* 1677, *v.* howe); (N) Hurgate; Hr & Lr Hurst, Hurst Coppice (*v.* hyrst); Hussey's Coppice & Plant. (cf. Robert *Hussey* 1664); (Far & Near) In(n) Md (*In meade* 1697, *v.* in, mæd); Kennion cl (cf. *Cemmen greene* 1662); Kiln Plot (cf. Brickkiln(s) *supra*); Kite Whistle (perhaps to be associated with *Wastle meade* 1697, which may be from weard-setl 'a watch house', *v.* cȳta)'; Lake How (-*Howes* 1740, *v.* howe); Lane, (E & S) Lane Cl; Lea Croft (*v.* lēah); Lick Hays (perhaps from lēac 'leek' and (ge)hæg); Liswell (probably from lisc 'reeds' and well(a)); Little Coppice & Wd ((*Corfe*) *Little Wood* 1742); Long Cl; Longdown Hill; Long Grd & Md (-*meade* 1681); Lords Coppice & Copse Cl; Lousebarrow (*v.* lūs, beorg, cf. Loosebarrow hundred *infra*); Lower Cl; Mackrell's md; Mead; Middle Fd; Minen's cl; (Far, Near, Lt & Middle) Moor, The Moor, Moors; Morn's Cl; Mundys; 9 Acres; Nether House (probably pl. of howe); Netherway (Cl); New Barn and Sheep Yd; New Grd; Odd Barns, Odd Burns (Coppice & Upr Ground), Odd Burns Corfe Fd (cf. foll.); Odd Crates (*Odcroft* 1697, *v.* croft; *Od(d)-* is probably the surname *Odd* from the OE pers.n. *Odda*); Oxenleys (-*Lease* 1742, *v.* oxa, lǣs); Paradise (*v.* paradis); Peaked-, Picked Cl (*v.* peked, pīcede); Pigeon cl; Pill Hill, South Pill Hows (probably from pyll 'pool, stream', with howe, but cf. William *atte Pile* 1327, 'at the stake', *v.* pīl, atte); Piplin Cl; Playstile; Porters Cl; Puddies (cf. Isabel *Poude* 1327); Reck's Hill; Red Hill; Rick yd; Rickett's (Down) Hill; Rush How (*v.* howe); Rushy Cl & Plot; School cl, the Schoolhouse; 7 Acres; Shittletons; Middle Plot or Silas's, Silas's North Plot; (Green) 6 Acres; Small Plot; South Plot; (Paddock) Spinney (cf. *East Paddock* 1742); Stotfield (cl) (*v.* stott); Sturminster mdw (from Sturminster Marshall par. *infra*); Sweet Moor (*v.* swēte); 10 Acres; Thousand Acres (a small field); 3 Acres; Three Halves (*v.* half); Toms How (*v.* howe); The Turbary Altmt; Underwood; Upper Cl; Vineyard; Wakes Cl; Want Hill Cl (*v.* wante 'mole', cf. Gl 1 81); Warlands Grd; Wash Md (*v.* wæsce); Way Cl; West Cl & Fd (-*Feild* 1677); Western Bows (perhaps boga 'a bow' in the sense 'river bend', cf. Bowes YN 304); West Md; Westmoor's Plot and Drove; White fess; White Lion (P.H.); Wind Mill Fd; Woodyard.

(b) *Baglands* 1677 (*v.* bagga or bagge); *Borsehay dech* 1661 (*v.* bors, (ge)hæg, dīc); *Broadcraft* 1677 (*v.* croft); *Broodhowes* 1742 (probably for *Broad-*, *v.* howe); *Buth Close* 1742; *Gilmers Ham* 1697 (*v.* hamm); *terra de la Girde, la Gerde, Yerde* n.d. (1372), *Zurd, atte ʒurd* (p) 1372 ChrP (*v.* gerd, gierd 'measure of land'); *Great Mead* 1740; *atte Hale* 1327, *atte Halle* 1332 both (p) (the same person, *v.* **hall**); *the Ham* 1740 (*v.* **hamm**); *Hattfield* 1742 (probably **hǣð** 'heather'); *Helvin* 1740; *Longcraft* 1677 (*v.* **croft**); *North Crofts* 1740; *Pamphew* 1742; *Peartree* 1677; *Pikes* 1656; *Press Hays* 1742; *Raynham* 1637 (1704); *le running acre* 1697 (*v.* **running**); *Sellhay* 1681 (*v.* **(ge)hæg**); *South Keys* 1742; *Stroode* 1677 (*v.* **strōd**); *Welch How* 1652 (1704) (*v.* **howe**); *Wellclose* 1677; *Westwood* 1635; *Wheathowes* 1742 (*v.* **howe**); *Wilkins* 1697.

Hamworthy

This par. was added to the borough and par. of Poole *infra* in 1905.

HAMWORTHY (1″) (SY 994912), HAMWORTHY JUNCTION, LR HAMWORTHY

Hamme 1236 Fees, 1268 *Ass*, 1280 *ib*, 1285 FF (*-juxta la Pole*) *et freq* to 1476 Cl, *Hammes* 1247 FF, *Hanme* 1288 *Ass*, *Hame* 1463 *MinAcct* (*-iuxta Pole*), 1554 *AddCh*, e17 *Cecil*, *Hampne* 1484 *Eton*, *Hamd* (sic) 1504 Ipm, *Ham als. Ham Worthy* 1612 *DCMDeed*, *Ham, Hamworthy, Upper or South-Ham, Hr & Lr Ham* 1774 Hutch[1]

Southam juxta Poule 1407 IpmR, *Southaunnes* (for *-hammes*) *juxta Poule* 1412 FA, *Southamme* 1465 *Ct*, *South Ham or Hamworthy* 1565 Hutch[3]

Hamworthy 1463 *MinAcct*, 1520 *Rent et passim*, *-or South-Ham* 1661 Hutch[1], *Hamwurthy* 1535 VE, *-worthie* 1539 *Ct*, 1613 *AddCh*

Hampne Worth 1484 *Eton, Hamworthe* 1540 *Ct*

'The enclosure', *v.* **hamm**, with the later addition of **worðig** 'enclosure' (from 1463), alternating with the synonymous **worð** (from 1484) of which **worðig** is a derivative. The name is discussed by M. Gelling, NoB **48** 145ff, who suggests that this is one of several names in the S of England where **hamm** appears to have the sense 'promontory' (with reference to the situation of Hamworthy on a marked peninsula between Lytchett Bay and Holes Bay, i.e. on a site 'enclosed' by water), cf. however, K. I. Sandred, NoB **64** 82ff. 'South' probably in relation to Hampreston par. *infra* (6 miles NE), *v.* **sūð**. Hutch[1] 2 129 describes Hamworthy as 'divided into 2 parts, Higher and Lower', cf. *duar' partium manerii de Hamworthie* 1613 *AddCh*, and the use of the pl. form *Hammes* in 1247 and 1412; *Higher* (or *Upper*) *Ham* and *Lower Ham* are now Hamworthy Junction (from the railway) and Lower Hamworthy respectively (the land rises to over 50′ at the former), cf. also *Hither Ham* 1612 Hutch[1], apparently used of the extreme E tip of the promontory which was anciently part of Poole par. There is mention of *hundred' de Hamworthy* in 1463 *MinAcct.* Smith 1 98 notes that Hamworthy is always called *Ham* by 'the natives of the place'.

STREET-NAMES. FERRY RD, named from Ferry (*v.* Poole par. *infra*); a ferry here is mentioned by Leland 1 254 and shown on 1774 Map, cf. *over the passadge* (from Poole) *nere to a place callyd Broome hille* 16 Hutch[3] 1 38, *v.* **passage**; *Broome hille* is *Bromehill* 1612 Hutch[1], *Broom Hill Stone* 1751 Map, 'broom hill', *v.* **brōm, hyll**; it lay in *Hither Ham* for which *v.* par. name *supra*. HARBOUR RD, *Ham-street* 1774 Map, cf. *Ham-quays, Carter's Quay* 1774 ib, *Ship yds & sheds* 1838 *TA*. Inns include *The Red Lion Inn* 1838 *TA, Royal Oak, Shipwrights Arms & Sloop* all 1824 Pigot.

ROCK LEA BRIDGE, HILL & POINT (SY 973911), ROCK LEA RIVER, (*loc' voc'*) *Rodeclyve atte Welle* 1341 (1792) *DCMDeed*, 1341 Hutch[3], *Redecliue atte Welle* 1364 ib, 'a little hill called *Radcliff Atte Well*', 'a spring called *Attewell*' 1626 Hutch[1], *Attwell lake,* 'the ancient bounds called *Redcliff* and *Attewell*' 1667 ib, *Rookley-, Rockly Point* 1774 ib, *Rock Point, Rock Lea River* 1811 OS, *Rockley Hill* 1822 *EnclA, -Point* 1838 *TAMap*. The early forms are all from perambulations of the port of Poole, the liberties of which extended W to this place, and mean 'the reedy bank at the spring', *v.* **hrēod, clif** (dat.sg. *clife*), **atte, well(a)**; on the 14th cent. forms with analogical medial *-e-* (*Rode-, Rede-*), cf. Radipole par. 1 239. The use of the form *Attewell* for the spring is an interesting case of metanalysis. *Attwell lake* ('the stream near (the spring called) *Attwell*') probably refers to Rock Lea River (a channel in Lytchett Bay), *v.* **lacu**. On the late development of *-(c)liff* to *-(k)ley*, cf. Catsley in Corscombe par. *infra*.

ADDLE PATH (lost), 1811 OS, *v.* **adela** 'a filthy place'. ALMSHOUSES. BENNETT'S PLACE. THE BULWARKS, *Key called Bulwarks* 1751 *DROMap*, at the tip of the Hamworthy promontory anciently part of Poole par., *v.* **bulwerk**. CLAY PIT(S), *The Clay Pits* 1838 *TA*, cf. *Clay Houses* 1811 OS. HAM COMMON, *-Heath* 1811 OS, *Inclosed Cmn, (The) Inner & Outer Cmn* 1838 *TA*. HAM HILL, *v.* par. name *supra*. HAMWORTHY PARK. HARKWOOD FM, probably named from *Harcuits Point* 1838

TAMap (a promontory in Holes Bay), cf. John *Harcourt* 1664 HTax. THE HOMESTEAD. LAKE (HO), *Lake* 1811 OS, *Lake Ho*, *Moor & Pdk* 1838 *TA*, cf. *Lake Bridge* 1791 Boswell, *v.* lacu. RECTORY formerly MANOR HO. ROPE WALK(S) (lost), 1774 Map, 1811 OS. TOLL GATE (lost), 1811 OS. TURLIN FM (*Talland*-1811 OS, *Tirland*- *1838 TA*), HO & MOOR (*Turlings*- 1811 OS, *Tirling*- 1838 *TA*), cf. *Tirland Coppice & Point* 1838 *ib*, perhaps analogous with Turleigh W 125 (*Turlinge* 1341, *Torlyng* 1362, *Turlin* 1699), which the editors of PN W take to be from þyrelung 'piercing' (with reference to a deep curving valley), cf. also EPN **2** 222, but which Ekwall PN -ing 231 thinks is a compound of turf 'turf' or trun 'round' and hlinc 'ridge'.

FIELD-NAMES

The undated forms are 1838 *TA* 99. Spellings dated 1791 are Boswell.

(a) Ayle's Ho & Gdn; Barfoots (Gdn) (cf. Walter *Barfot* 1332 SR); Beach; Beale's Md & Plot; Bengers; Bingham's Dock (cf. Richard *Bingham* 1639 Hutch³); Black Down (cf. *Blackdown Bridge* 1791); The Bogs; Cansiers; Church Cl (cf. 'chapel of *Hamme juxta la Pole*' 1285 FF); Clump Grd; Cockroads (*v.* cocc-rodu); Common Plot; Long Dunfords (cf. Dunford Cl in Longfleet par. *infra*); (Home & Middle) 8 Acres; 11 Acres; Encroachment; Farm Md; 5 Acres; Lr & Upr Folly, Brook's Folly (*v.* folie); Foot path Fd; Furzy Grd & Plot; Garden Cl; Green Cl; The Green; Greens; Ham Coppice; Ham Corner 1751 DROMap; Hazzards; Home Cl & Plant.; Horse Lane & Moor; One Hundred Acres (a small field); Island 4 & 6 Acres; Island Moor; Kitcats 2 houses (probably a double pl. of howe 'enclosure'); Lambs Leaze (*v.* læs); Leaward Hays (probably from leeward 'sheltered', with (ge)hæg); Little Coppice; Long Grd; Mead Grd; Mitchells Moor; The Moor, Upr Moor; Nap Cl (*v.* cnæpp); Lr 9 Acres; Oakleys; Orchard; Oxen Leaze (*v.* oxa, læs); Paddock; Pinneys Plot; Ponges Plot; Red Lion Plot (from *The Red Lion Inn supra*); Rough Grd & Pasture; 7 Acres; Severdhays Bridge 1791; Home 6 Acres; South Shore Md; Star's Plot; Stony Down; 10 Acres; Timber Yd; Titus's Bridge 1791; Trokepond Bridge 1791; 12 Acres; The 2 Acres; Well Cl; Woodbine Ctg.

Kinson

This par. was transferred to Ha in 1930. It was originally the E division of Canford Magna par. *supra* (this was divided into three parts from at least the 16th cent., *v.* Hutch³ **3** 295), but was formed into a separate par. in 1833. Branksome par. *supra* was formed out of it in 1894.

KINSON (SZ 068961)

Chinestanestone 1086 DB, *Kyn(e)stan*- 1231 FF, 1259 ib, 1288

Ass, 1409 Cl, *Kinestanes-* 1238 Pat, *Kynstants-* 1288 *Ass*, *Kyn(n)(e)sten(e)s-*1303 FA, 1327 Cl, 1412, 1431 FA, *Kynstaneston* 1393 FF, 1399 Cl, *Kinstanton* 1774 Hutch[1] *Kingeston* 1225 Cur, *Kyng(e)ston* 1268 *Ass*, 1303 FA *et freq* to 1554 *AddCh*, *Kingston or Kinson* 1795 Boswell *Kunestonston* 1244 *Ass* (p), *Knustanstone* (for *Kun-*) 1314 Ipm *Ken(e)stan(es)ton* 1280 *Ass*, 1326 FF *Cunston* 1374 *MinAcct*, *Konston* 1463 *ib* *Kyn(e)ston(e)* 1431 FA, 1465, 1519 *Ct*, 1575 Saxton *Kyndeston* 1489 Ipm *Kenston* e17 *BRA*

'Cynestān's farm', from the OE pers.n. *Cynestān* and **tūn**; the pers.n. has been confused with **cyning** 'king'.

CUDNELL (FM) (SZ 060966), *Codnell* 1520 *Rent*, *Cuddnell-(howe)* 1544 *Ct*, *Cuddinghill* 1546 *Surv*, *Cudnell* e17 *BRA*, *Cudnal* 1811 OS, possibly 'Cuda's hill or nook', from the OE pers.n. *Cuda* and **hyll** or **halh**, with **howe** 'enclosure', cf. Cudnall Gl 2 97 and the surname of John *Cud* 1340 NI (Lytchett Matravers); the same pers.n. may be found in the lost name *Cotenham* 1463 *MinAcct*, *Cudnam* 1519 *Ct*, *v*. **hamm**.

ENSBURY (FM & PARK) (SZ 081965), *Eynesburgh* 1463 *MinAcct*, *-berow* n.d. Hutch[3], *-bruth* 1520 *Rent*, *Emys(s)borowe* (*Meade*) 1544 *Ct*, *Ensbury* e17 *BRA*, 1822 *EnclA* (*-Green*, *-Md*), (*-Fd*) 1840 *TA*, *En(de)sbury* 1774 Hutch[1], *Emsbury Green* 1811 OS, probably 'Ægen's fortified place', from an OE pers.n. *Ægen* (a short form of names in *Ægen-*, suggested by DEPN for Eynsford K, etc) and **burh**, cf. Eynesbury Hu 255 which is 'Ēanwulf's **burh**' (*Eynes-* from 1234). Ensbury is near R. Stour.

ASHLEY CTG, cf. Edward *Assheley* 1520 *Rent*, *v*. **æsc**, **lēah**. ASHRIDGE. BANKES' HEATH, from the *Bankes* family, lords of the manor of Canford from m17, *v*. Hutch[3] 3 301, cf. William *le Bonk* 1327 *SR*. BOURNE, from R. Bourne, cf. Bourne Bottom in Branksome par. *supra*. BUTCHER'S COPPICE. BUTLER'S FM. DUCK LANE, 1822 *EnclA*. DUKE'S COPPICE & CTG, *Gt & Lt Dukes*, *Dukes Wd* 1840 *TA*, cf. John-, Walter *le D(o)uk* 1327 *SR*. EGLINGTON. FAYREMEAD. HEADLESS CROSS, cf. Heedless William's Pond in Stinsford par. 1 370. HEAD'S FM. HIGHMOOR,

-*Moors* 1886 *DROMap*. HILLSIDE, cf. *Hill Side* 1840 *TA*. HIROPI, a house. EAST HOWE (FM), HIGH HOWE LANE, WEST HOWE (FM), HOWE LODGE, *East, West & High Howe* 1811 OS, *Howe Cl or Long Howe, Howe Lane* 1822 *EnclA*, cf. *How croft* (*wd*) *& grd* 1840 *TA*, possibly from **hōh** 'heel of land, ridge end'; West Howe and *High Howe* are at the end of a 200' ridge, East Howe is at 100', all overlooking the Stour valley. However, it is more likely that these names are from ME **howe** 'enclosure', an el. common in the f.ns. of this par., *v*. discussion under the f.n. How Croft in Canford M. par. *supra*. KINGSBROOK, cf. *William Kings house* 1664 HTax and par. name *supra*. KINSON FM or MANOR FM, *Kingston Fm* 1811 OS, *Kinson Fm, the Manor Fm* 1863 Hutch³, cf. *Kinson Fm Lane* 1822 *EnclA*. LOLLIPOP FM. LUSH BARROWS, -*Barrow* 1811 OS, probably 'small barrows', from **lūs** and **beorg**, cf. Loosebarrow hundred *infra*. THE MOUNT. NUTLEY WAY, *v*. **hnutu, lēah**. PELHAMS, 1863 Hutch³ ('house called-'). PITT'S FM. POOLE LANE, (-*3 Acres*) 1822 *EnclA*, 1840 *TA* (-*Fd & Plot*), from Poole par. *infra*. RESTMORE. RINGWOOD RD, to Ringwood Ha. RUDDLES-FORD (lost), 1811 OS, *Redeylesford* 1463 *MinAcct, Ryddelysforde* 1546 *Surv, Riddles Ford* 1822 *EnclA*, cf. *Riddles Croft Copse* 1840 *TA*, possibly from an OE pers.n. *Rēðel or *Hrēðel* suggested for Riddlesden YW 4 172 (or from a surname derived from such a pers.n., cf. John *Retyle* 1465 *Ct* who held lands in Longfleet par. *infra*), with **ford**; the crossing over R. Stour was where a small lane runs NE to meet the river near the old Do–Ha county bdy. However, if the first part of the name has a different origin, *Rhydleford* Gl 2 235 and Ruddles Pool Brk 20, of uncertain meaning, may need to be compared. ST ANDREW'S CHURCH, cf. (the church of) *Sainct(e) Michell (tharchangell) in Kynston* 1519 *Ct*, 1546 *Surv, Church Mdw & Plot* 1840 *TA*. SLADE'S FM & LANE. TALBOT VILLAGE, 1863 Hutch³, built by Georgina *Talbot op. cit.* 3 302. THATCHED HO. VERNOLD'S COPPICE. WALLIS DOWN, 1811 OS, cf. *Wallis Ford* 1811 ib (where a N–S road crosses R. Bourne); the first el. may be a surname, cf. Richard *Waleys* 1332 SR. WATER LANE FM, *Waterlayne* 1543 *Ct*, 'arable strip, or lane, by the river', from **wæter** and **leyne** or **lane**, on bank of R. Stour; on 1811 OS it is called *Boat Fm*, cf. Boat Ho (6"). WATERSIDE, near R. Stour. WHEELERS LANE. WHITE FM. WOODLANDS. WOODSIDE.

FIELD-NAMES

The undated forms are 1840 *TA* 119. Spellings dated 1332 are SR, 1340 NI, 1463 *MinAcct*, 1554 *AddCh*, 1664 HTax, 1822 *EnclA* (Canford Magna), 1839 *TA* schedule in local form, 1873 *TA* alt.app., and the rest *Ct.*

(*a*) Acre (Plot); Allotment Pasture; Amen Style (near to Headless Cross *supra*, but not on the par. bdy, cf. Amen Corner Brk 76); Am(e)y's Cl & Plot; Austins Brambles & Moor; Barn Cl & Plot; Beaminsters Wd; Bells Cl 1839; Bengyfield (*Bingy-* 1839); Berhams; Berry Hill (*v.* **beorg**); Black Hole; Bottom Cl & Plot; (Lt) Brake, Brake Wd (*v.* **bræc**[1]); Brambles; Break Heart (a derogatory name for poor ground); Broad Cl; Broomy Cl & Wd; Burts (Plot & Wd) (cf. John *Burt* 1664); Butts Hr 3 acres 1839; Captain Kings; Carrion Cl; Cartshead How (*v.* **howe**); Cast How (*v.* **howe**); Claypit; Cliggs; Cobborns 4 Acres & Plot (cf. Henry *Collborne* 1664); Cockram Mdw (*Cockerham-* 1822); Gt Cook Hill, Cooks (cf. John *Coke* 1466); Coopers Hides, Orchd & Plot (cf. Hydes *infra*); Copse (Acres); Corbins 5 Acres 1839 (cf. John *Corbyn* 1543); Corner Plot; Hatchett & Lt Cotty (probably from **cot** and **(ge)hæg**, with **hæcc-geat** 'a hatch-gate'); Court Cl; Cowleys (*v.* **læs**); Cow Yd and Lane; (Chalk) Craft (*v.* **croft**); Cudnell Gt & Lt Md(w) (*v.* Cudnell *supra*); Curtiss' Fd and House (possibly a pl. form of **howe**); Davis's (cf. John *Davy* 1340); Dolphin P.H.; Dominys Hill Grd; Doves Hill (cf. John *Dove* 1529); Durdalls Intake (*v.* **intake**); Earlys Fd 1839; East Cl; Eggthorne (*-Thorn Cl* 1822); 8 & 18 Acres; Elliotts Plot (cf. John *Elyot* 1332); Emland 1839; Eweland; Fern(e) House 1839, -How (*v.* **howe**); Field Acre & 4 Acres; 5, 4 & 14 Acres; Framptons Hill; Furze Cl; Furzy Cl, Grd & Plot; Galley Pool 1822 (in R. Stour); Gibs's (cf. Henry *Gibbe* 1332); Great Cl; Green Fd & Plot; Gubbins pond cl 1839, Gubbens; Ham (*v.* **hamm**); Hansty- 1839, Ansteys Moor (*v.* **ānstiga** 'narrow path', or a surname); Harts Brambles & Wd (cf. Duke *Hart* 1664); Heathy Acre & Plot, Far & First Heathy Grd; Hedge Row(s); Gt & Lt Hencocks (Wd), Hancocks- 1839 (*claus' pastur' voc' Hancock'* 1544, cf. William *Hancocke* 1543); Henslade; Hermy; Higher Cl & Fd; Hill Cl (Lake) & Mdw; Hill(e)y Fd & Grd; Hobbery; Hobbys (cf. Ralph *Hoby* 1465); Home Bush Cl (cf. *Holm Bush* 1822, *v.* **holegn**); Home cl, fd, Pasture & Plot; the Homestead; Horse Cl 1839; Houselands (cf. Kinson Heath *infra*); Hugh Moor; Hundred Acres (a small field); Huntsmans; Hydes (*-Close* 1822, probably to be identified with *ij pec' terre voc' Hyd'* 1519, *ij pec' terre voc' Hyws* 1544 (denoting the same land), *v.* **hīd, hīwisc**); In Ox, Ox 10 Acres (*v.* **inhoke** 'land temporarily enclosed'; omission of *In* in the second form is due to confusion with the prep. **in**); Island; Jerratts Plot; Jolliffs Cl; Josephs (Lane); Kinson (Lane) Cl & Mdw; Kinson Heath 1822, Heath (Cl & Plot) (*Lez heth' de Kyngston* 1554 (*ii lez hethe howses iacen' in-*), *v.* **hǣð**; *howses* is probably a double pl. of **howe** 'enclosure', rather than from *house* (**hūs**)); Kitchells; Kitchers Fd & Md; Kits Croft; Lt Lag or 11 acres (*v.* **lagge**); Lake Mdws, -Mead 10 Acres; Lane end grd; Large Mdw; Larks Lays (*v.* **lāwerce, læs**); Latch Acre (*v.* **læc(c)**); Lay cl 1839; Lime Kiln; Little Mdw; Little Moor(e) (Copse); Little Plot; Lockyers Coombs (cf. John *Lockyer* 1664, *v.* **cumb**); Long Cl, Fd & Moor; Lower Cl & Grd; Low Plot; First & Inner Marsh, Marsh 10 Acres; Lt Michaels 1839; Middle Cl & Fd;

Mignes Fd; Mill Hams (*v.* **hamm**; there was a mill at Kinson in 1086 DB, *v.* VCHDo 3 90); Moor Hays (*v.* **(ge)hæg**); Inner, Lr & Upr Moor (cf. *Brodemoure* 1544, *v.* **brād, mōr**); Mountain; New Plot; 9 Acres; 9 Corners; Nippers Cl; Nither-, Netherway (Wd) (*v.* **neoðerra**); Norrises, Norris Hays & Wd; North's Plot; Oat Cl 1839; Orchard (Plot); Oxford 1839, -Plot; Park (cf. '*Kinstanton* Park' 1347 Hutch³ 3 290); Parry (*v.* **pirige**); Peak (*v.* **pēac**); Pellands; Picked Jaws (with reference to its shape, *v.* **pīcede** 'pointed'); Pick Purse (a derogatory name for poor ground); Jack Pierce 1839; Pitchard (-*Cl* 1822); Plot Gdn & Wd; Pond Cl; Poole Plot (from Poole par. *infra*); Potatoe Plot; Pubwell Plot; Pye Corner (*v.* **pēo, pīe** 'insect' or **pie²** 'magpie'); Hr & Lr Quarry 1839; Gt, Harveys & Roses Quomp, Quomp Corner (*Comp* (*als.* Coomb) *Corner* 1822, possible **camp¹** 'enclosed piece of land', cf. Walter *Rose* 1664); Rabbitts 1839; Redgate Hill & Moor; Red Hill; Reekes Cl (cf. John *Reekes* 1664); River side; Roberts's; Robbit plot; Rod (possibly **rod¹**, **rodu** 'clearing'); Rough Pce; Rushy Plot; Scaffold Barn Cl 1839; Scotts Island & Mdw; Scull Pit (Wd); Second Cl; 7 Acres; Shoulder of Mutton P.H.; Side Fd; 6 Acres; Small Plot; Soldier; Sourer Hays (*v.* **(ge)hæg**); Sow Ditch Cl, Saw- 1839; Stoney Cl 1873; Stony Plot; Taylors Fd (cf. John *le Taillur* 1332); (Long) 10 Acres; Thorne Crofts, -Craft 1839; 3 Acres; Tillers Plot (cf. Thomas *Tylly* 1529); Toms cl, Toombs; Townsend; Triangle Fd; Trims Plot; Trum How (probably to be identified with *Trenhowe* (perhaps for *Tron-*) 1463, possibly from **trun** 'round', *v.* **howe** 'enclosure'); Turf House Yd; 12 & 2 Acres; Upper Grd; Water Fd & Plot; Warrens; Way Cl; Waymans Cl (cf. Katherine *Weyman* 1664); Weedy Plot; Whitefield (-*Felde* 1519, *v.* **hwīt, feld**); Willows 1839; Wills 6 & 12 Acres, Upr Wills (cf. Walter *Willes, -ys* 1465); Withy Copse.

(*b*) *Dunborghe* 1546 *Surv*; *Ma(rs)sons Clos(s)e* 1519, 1544 (*v.* **clos(e)**); *Mistenetrust* 15 Hutch³ (a close; form probably corrupt); *clausor' voc' Voydehowen'* 1466 (from **voyde** 'vacant, useless' and **howe** 'enclosure', *-en* representing a ME wk.pl.).

Longfleet

This par. was formed out of Canford Magna par. *supra* in 1833; it was added to the borough and par. of Poole *infra* in 1905.

LONGFLEET (SZ 020918), *Langeflete* 1230 P, 1288 *Ass*, 1374 *MinAcct*, 1520 *Rent*, 1543 *Ct*, *-fleatte* 1543 *ib*, *-flethe* 1544 *ib*, *Langflete* (*iuxta Mare*) 1463 *MinAcct*, 1465, 1529 *Ct*, *-f(f)let(t)* 1529 *ib*, 1554 *AddCh*, *Longfle(e)t(e)* 1575 Saxton, c. 1586 Tres *et passim*, 'long inlet or creek', from **lang¹** (wk.obl. *langan*) and **flēot**, with Lat **mare** 'the sea', referring to Holes Bay in Canford Magna par. *supra*. The bounds of Longfleet are given in 1836 Hutch³ 3 303.

HICKFORD or THICKFURZE (lost), 1795 Boswell, surviving in HECKFORD RD (6″), is *Thic-*, *Thikfurs* 1374 *MinAcct*, *-fyrres*, *-furrez*, *Thykfurres* 1463 *ib*, *Hikfurs* 1472 Smith, *Thickefurs* 1520 *Rent*, *Thycffursys* 1529 *Ct*, *Thickfurses als. Hickford* 1661 Hutch[1], *Hycle-* (probably for *Hyck-*) 1543 *Ct*, *Hyck-* c. 1586 Tres, *Hickford(e)* 1597 *DROMap*, *Hicksfordes* e17 *BRA*, *Heckford or Thickfurse* 1751 *DROMap*, *Heckford Fm* 1822 *EnclA*, *-Fd* 1843 *TA*. 'Thick furze', from þicce[2] and fyrs; the forms in *Hick-* arise from initial *Th-* being mistaken for the def. art. and then dropped as in Elbridge K (OE þel), Ede Way Bd (OE þēod), etc, whilst the final cl. has been confused with (the pl. of) the word *ford*.

STERTE (SZ 011918), 1863 Hutch[3], *Strette iuxta Pole* 1520 *Rent*, *Sterts* 1811 OS, cf. *Stert Fm* 1822 *EnclA*, *Street Fd* 1843 *TA*. Probably from steort 'tail of land', with reference to a low-lying promontory in Holes Bay; for the metathesis of *r* in two of the forms, cf. Woodstreet 1 190. Formally the name could perhaps be from strǣt 'paved way, Roman road', but this is not very likely. The Roman road from Badbury to Poole Harbour (Margary 4d) led to Hamworthy 1½ miles W and could not in itself be the road referred to, and there is no evidence that this road originally forked, one branch passing near Sterte to Poole on the opposite bank of Holes Bay; however, for the discovery of Roman occupation debris and a coin-hoard at Sterte, in fact in *Street Fd* itself, *v.* RCHM 2 604.

TATNAM FM (SZ 013920), *Totnesham* 1520 *Rent*, *Tot(t)nam* 1529 *Ct et freq* to 1543 *ib*, *Tottenham* 1661 Hutch[1], *Tatnam* 1826 Gre, cf. *Tatnam Cl & Fd* 1843 *TA*. The second el. is probably hamm 'enclosure, etc' rather than hām 'homestead'; the first el. is probably the OE pers.n. *Tot(t)a* found in Tottenham Mx 78, etc. The form *Totnes-* is probably analogical, a str.gen.sg. ending *-es* having been added to ME *Tot(e)n-* from OE *Tot(t)an-* (wk.obl.), *v.* -an.

BUSHELL MILL FM, *Bushell's Mill Bridge* 1791 Boswell, *Bushels Mill* 1811 OS, cf. *Longe fleete mill* 1649 *DCMCt*, *Inner and Outer Mill Pond* 1843 *TA*, Michael *Bustall* (sic) 1664 HTax. CHURCH (St Mary's), *Longfleet Church* 1811 OS. COUNTRY HO. DARBY'S LANE, cf. *Darby's corner* 1836 Hutch[3], *-grd* 1843 *TA*,

Richard *Durbey* 1664 HTax. DENBY LODGE. FLEET'S CORNER, cf. *Fleet grd* 1843 *TA*, *v.* **flēot** 'creek', cf. par. name *supra*. HENNING'S FM, cf. Michael *Hening* 1664 HTax. HOLES BAY JUNCTION (railway), from Holes Bay in Canford Magna par. *supra*. LADIES' WALKING FD, just outside the old bdy of Poole par. *infra*. THE LAURELS. LONGFLEET LODGE. OAKDALE. PARR'S PLANT., cf. John *Pers* 1519 *Ct*. PLANEFIELD HO, -*Lodge* 1826 Gre, *Plainfield* 1822 *EnclA*, *v.* **plain**. POPLARTREE FM. POUND LANE, *v.* **pund**. SANDPIT LANE, cf. *Sandy Lane* 1836 Hutch[3], *Sand pit cl* 1843 *TA*. SELDOWN LANE & RD, cf. *The Common of Cell Down* 1751 *DROMap*, *Seldown* (*Ho & Point*) 1836 Hutch[3], first el. possibly **sele**[1] 'a hall', cf. Seldon D 144, or **celle** 'a cell'. STANLEY COURT, -*green* 1843 *TA*, *Stanleys Green* 1811 OS, *v.* **stān, lēah**, or a surname. TURBARY ALTMT, *v.* **turbary**. WHITE HO LAUNDRY.

FIELD-NAMES

The undated forms are 1843 *TA* 131. Spellings dated 1327 are *SR*, 1520 *Rent*, 1664 HTax, 1751 *DROMap*, 1811 OS, and the rest *Ct*.

(*a*) Bank Cl; Barn Cl; Beacons Green; Belt; Bore Cl; Coppice Md & Ctg; Cowleaze; Dolery's Md; Dunford Cl, Dunford's Plot (cf. Thomas *Durneford* 1664); East Fd; The 8 Acres; Fenny Cl and 6 Acres; the 4 Acres; Furzy Cl; Garden Plot; George Inn (Fd); Graces Grd, South Graces (probably to be associated with *firm' voc' Graserth* 1520, *v.* **gærs-yrð** 'the customary ploughing of grassland'; Grants; Great Cl, Grd & Mdw; Heath; Lr Heathy Cl; Hill Grd; Holly Fox; Home Cl, Fd, Grd & Plot; Hosiers Plot; The Island, Island Plot; Ley Cl (*v.* **lǣge**); Little Mdw & Plot; Long Cl & Grd; Longfield; Lower Cl; Mackrells Plot (cf. William *Mackerill* 1664); Marsh; Mead Hayes (*v.* **(ge)hæg**); Middle Cl; (the) Moor (*the more* 1542, *v.* **mōr**); Moor Coppice & Grd; New Cl; New England; Outer New Grd; The New Inn; Paddock; Pains How (cf. John *Payn* 1327, *v.* **howe**); The Park; Middle & S Path Fd; Point Cl; Portmahon Castle Inn (*Port Mahon* 1751); Potters Cl; Putnams 1811; Rope Walk; Rushy Grd; Sandy Hayes (*v.* **(ge)hæg**); Sea Cl & Grd; 7 Acres; Spinning Sheds; Spring Cl; Streets Plot; Tan yd Fd; Three Corner Grd; Gt & Lt Titus; Lt Tucks; Twiners (cf. George *Twines* 1539); 2 Acres; Union Ho 1811; Upper Cl; Waste; Well Cl & Hole; Late Willow's leasehold; Witteridges.

(*b*) *the comen of Langeflete* 1542; *venella qui ducit versus Plerescroce* 1466 (*v.* **cros**, possibly with a ME form of the surname *Player*); *Sesershaye* 1542 (probábly the pers.n. *Caesar*, *v.* **(ge)hæg**); *le Stonye Lake* 1544 (*v.* **stānig, lacu**); *viam a Streynbrydge* 1543 (*v.* **brycg**).

Lytchett Matravers

LYTCHETT MATRAVERS (SY 947955) ['litʃət mə'trævəz]
Lichet 1086 DB, 1297 Ipm, 1357 Pat, Litsed 1236 Fees,
Lischet 1243 ib, Liscete 1244 Ass, Licet l13 AddCh (p),
Lychet 1288 Ass, 1357, 1399 Cl, Lycchet 1314 Ipm, Li-,
Lychette 1339 Pat
Li-, Lyc(c)het(t) Mautrauers, -vers(e) 1280, 1288 Ass, 1293
Ilch et freq to 1484 Eton, -Mautrevers(e) 1340 NI, 1416 Pat,
-Mawtravers 1461 DCMDeed, -Matravers 1508 Eton,
1588 AddCh, Lisset- 1296 (16) Bodl, Lische(t) Ma(u)travers,
uers 1327 SR, 1332 SR, Lychit Mauterveys 1451 Pat,
Litchett Matreevers 1673 Drax
Luchet Mautravers 1291 Tax, 1325 Pat, 1349 Fine,
-Matrauvers 1428 FA
Lechet Mautravers 1351 Fine, Lechiot Matreuers 1575 Saxton

Probably a Brit name meaning 'grey wood' from PrWelsh
*lẹd and PrWelsh *cẹd, as suggested by Ekwall DEPN, Jackson
327, 332–4, 563, cf. Litchett Ha and also Lichfield St with the
first part of which it is identical; the same name probably occurs
in Co as Ludcott, Lidcutt, etc (at least five instances) and in
Wales as Llwytgoed (at least twice) (ex. inf. O. Padel). There
was 'woodland ½ league in length and width' here in 1086 DB
(VCHDo 3 91), cf. Forest Bourne Fm in Lytchett Minster par.
infra. The manorial affix distinguishes it from Lytchett Minster,
where some of the early unaffixed forms may strictly belong;
it was held by Hugh Maltrauers in 1086 DB (VCHDo loc. cit.,
Hutch³ 3 314; his surname is given in Exon p. 410 (So)), and
by John Mautravers in 1306 Ch, 1327 SR, etc, cf. Langton
Matravers 1 33. It was also called Upper-, Higher Lichet 1774
Hutch¹, Higher Lytchet 1811 OS, cf. Lytchett Minster par.
infra.

DULLAR FM (SY 942981) & WD, Dulre 1268 Ass (p), e14 Wim
(p), 1310 FF (p), 1332 SR (p), 1353 AddCh (p), 1469, 1484
IpmR, Dolere 1288 Ass (p), Doullere 1295 Wim (p), Dullere
1296 ib (p), 1468 HarlCh, Dolre 1302 Wim (p), Doulre e14 ib
(p), 1421 IpmR, Durle 1327 SR (p), Duller 1468 HarlCh, 1774
Hutch¹, 1837 TA (-Coppice), Dollar F. 1811 OS. This is a
difficult name. Professor Löfvenberg notes that if the name is

of native origin, it may possibly be a compound whose second
el. is OE **ærn, renn** 'house' with loss of -*n* as in Dinder So
(DEPN), Quither D 216, cf. Ekwall, Studies[1] 64. He further
suggests that the first el. may be related to dial. *dulkin* 'a dell
or dingle, with water at the bottom; a ravine' (EDD, recorded
from Gl) which is apparently a diminutive of a word **dul* or the
like, and points out that there may have been an OE **dolu,
dulu 'valley' (from PrGerm **dulōn-*), corresponding to MHG
tole 'ditch', G dial. *Dole* 'covered drain' and related by
gradation to OE **dæl** 'valley'. The farm lies at about 200′ in
a small dry valley sloping away from a 230′ ridge.

ARNOLD'S CTG, -*Mdw* 1837 *TA*. BARTOM'S HILL, *Bartrim's*
1837 *TA*, cf. Richard *Bartram* 1664 HTax. BROCK HILL, *v.* **brocc**
'badger', cf. *Badgers Earth* 1837 *TA*. CASTLE FM (1811 OS)
& HILL (1837 *TA*), -*Cl* 1837 *ib*, *v.* **castel(l)**; the significance is
not clear. CHALK PIT CTG, -*Fd* 1837 *TA*, pit marked 6″. LT
CHARBOROUGH PLANT., near Charborough in Morden par.
infra. CHEQUERS INN, 1837 *TA*, *Chequer-* 1756 Hutch[1], cf.
Chequer Cl, Grd & Md 1837 *TA*. CUZENAGE COPPICE, *Cozinage
Coppice, Hr & Lr Cozenage* 1837 *TA*, *v.* **cozenage** 'deception,
fraud'; near par. bdy. DOLMAN'S HILL, *Dolman Hill* 1837 *TA*,
Dolemans Hill (Gate) 1838 *TAMap*. DROVE COPPICE, 1837 *TA*,
-*Plot* 1837 *ib*. DUNGEON PIT, *Dungeon* 1837 *TA*, *v.* **dungeon**.
DYETT'S COPPICE, *Dyke's-* 1837 *TA*. EDDYGREEN FM, *Neddy
Gr.* 1811 OS, *Eddy Green* 1837 *TA*. ELDER MOOR, *Alder-* 1837
TA, *v.* **alor, mōr**. ELLEN CLUMP, *v.* **elle(r)n**. FOX HILL,
FOXHILLS (DAIRY & LANE), *Fox Hills* 1837 *TA*. GARDEN WD,
1837 *TA*, -*Cl* 1837 *ib*. GATE'S HILL. GREENFIELD COPPICE,
Green Fd, -Veal 1837 *TA*, *v.* **feld**; on the voiced form *Veal* for
Field, *v.* Phonol.; the first el. is probably **grēne**[1] 'green', but
cf. Robert *in le Greyne* 1332 SR, *v.* **grēne**[2] 'a grassy spot'.
HALL'S HILL. HENBURY BARROW, from Henbury in Sturminster
Marshall par. *infra*. HIGH WD, 1811 OS, cf. *Higwood* (sic)
Coppice 1837 *TA*; at 200–300′. HILL FM, 1811 OS, near foll.
HILL WD, *Helwoode* 1590 Hen[2], *Hell Wd* 1837 *TA*, cf. Ralph-,
Roger *de Helle* 1327 *SR* (Lytchett Minster), *Hell Fm Wd* 1822
EnclA, *Hell Gate Lane* 1837 *TA*, *v.* **hell** 'hell', a derogatory
name. HOLLY CTG. HOWEN'S COPPICE, 1837 *TA*, -*Bottom Cl,
-Hither & Yonder Cl* 1837 *ib*. HUNTICK FM, cf. *Huntwitch Hill*

1822 *EnclA* (Canford Magna), perhaps analogous with Huntwick YW 2 90, 'the hunter's dwelling', from **hunta** (gen.sg. *huntan*) and **wīc**. THE KENNELS, cf. *N & S Kennel Cl 1837 TA*. LOOP CTG, HR LOOP FM (*Grays F.* 1811 OS), LR LOOP FM (*Loop F.* 1811 ib), cf. 'the fields of *Lowpe'* 1376 Hutch³, *Loop Green* 1837 *TA*, John *Lhoupe* 1340 NI; more early forms are needed for an etymology. LUSCOMBE CTGS & WD, *Loscomb* 1774 Hutch¹, *Loscombe Coppice* 1837 *TA*, 'valley with a pig-sty', from **hlōse** and **cumb**, cf. Loscombe in Netherbury par. *infra*. LYTCHETT HEATH FM, HO & WD, cf. *Heath Grd* 1837 *TA*. MANOR HO, *Lytchet Ho* 1811 OS, cf. *Mansion* 1837 *TA*. MEMORY CLUMP. NEW GROUND (lost), 1811 OS. OLD PARK (FM), PARK PLANT., WEST PARK FM, *Litchet Parke* 1583 *SPDom*, *Wool Park* 1811 OS, *Old, E, S & W Park, Coney Park, Park Cl* 1837 *TA*, *v.* **park, coni,** Cantor & Wilson 2 149–150; on the form *Wool* for *Old, v.* Phonol. PEATON'S FM. PERHAM'S Row, 1837 *TA*, *-Cl* 1837 *ib*, *v.* **rāw**, here 'a row of trees' as elsewhere in this par. PHILLIPS'S COPPICE, *Phillip's-* 1837 *TA*. PIT BOTTOM (CTGS), cf. *Pit Bridge Md & Plot, Pit Cl* 1837 *TA*, *v.* **pytt.** POND CLOSE, 1837 *TA*. POST ROW. QUARR FM, *-Hill* 1837 *TA*, *v.* **quarre.** QUARRY COPPICE, 1837 *TA*. RECTORY, cf. *ye Parsonage house* 1664 HTax. ST JOHN'S CLUMP. ST MARY'S CHURCH, *ecclesie de Lisset Matravers* 1296 (16) *Bodl, -de Lichett Mautrauers* 1370 *Ilch*, cf. Rectory *supra*; *ecclesiam de Liscete* 1244 *Ass* probably belongs here rather than to the church at Lytchett Minster *infra*. SANDPIT FM, cf. *Sandpit* 1837 *TA*, near foll. LR SANDY COPPICE, SANDY LANE, near prec. SIMMONS'S BOTTOM, cf. William *Symond* 1332 SR. STAFFORD ROW, *-Md* 1837 *TA*, *Stoford side* 1600 *Hen¹*, cf. *Stafford's Plot* 1837 *TA*, 'stony ford', *v.* **stān, ford,** with **sīde**; a lane crosses two small streams here. TEN ACRE ROW, cf. *10 Acres* 1837 *TA*. TRAVELLERS' REST. WARMWELL FM, *v.* **wearm, well(a),** cf. Warmwell par. 1 169; a stream rises here at a spring marked 6″. WIMBORNE RD, to Wimborne Minster par. *infra*. WINDMILL BARROW (FM); tumulus marked 6″ on the crest of a ridge. WINTER'S COPPICE, 1837 *TA*.

FIELD-NAMES

The undated forms are 1837 *TA* 135. Spellings dated 1637 are *DCMSurv*, 1664 HTax, and 1822 *EnclA* (Canford Magna).

(*a*) Ashly Cl (*v.* **æsc, lēah**); Banky Cl; Barley Md; Barn Cl & Plot; Beach; Beales Grd (cf. John *Beale* 1664); Birch Coppice; Hr Blacknep (*v.* **blæc, cnæpp**); Bleak Hill (*v.* **bleak**); Bottom Cl & Coppice; Bramble Ld; Breach (Coppice & Row) (*v.* **brǣc**); Brick Kiln Cl, Green, Grd & Yd; Bridge Cl; Brinson('s) Cl & Grd; Broom Cl & Coppice; Brow (*v.* **brū**); Bushy Cl & Coppice; Butter's Fd (cf. Thomas *Butler* 1664); Butts (*v.* **butte**); Chalky Knap (*v.* **cnæpp**); Chantry Coppice & Md (*v.* **chantry**, cf. Hutch³ 3 333); Lr Chevire Cl; Clap Gate Grd (*v.* **clap-gate**); Coneygar Plant. (*v.* **coninger**); Coppice Grd; Copse Cl; Cotman's (Md) (cf. Thomas *Cotman* 1664); Cowleaze; Cow Pound; Crooked Coppice; Crucked Cl; Crumpets Pond (near Crumpet's Fm in Sturminster Marshall par. *infra*); Crumpley Md (cf. William *Crumpleaze* 1637 (Lytchett Minster), *v.* **crumb, crump** 'crooked', **lǣs**); Deep Wd; Dry Cl; East Hay (*v.* **(ge)hæg**); 8 & 11 Acres; Elms Grd; Fern Cl; 15 Acres; Fir Plot; 5 Acres (Row); Fortune Cl; 4 & 14 Acres; French grass; Furzy Cl; Gages Moor (cf. John *Gaich* 1664 (Lytchett Minster)); Gate-, Gazemoor Pond (perhaps to be associated with prec.); Gilbert's Grd; Glebe Coppice; Gomeridge; Gould's Cl; Gravel Pit; Great Cl, Md & Orchd;Green Cl; Grosvenors Orchd; Middle Grd Row; Grove Cl (Coppice); Gunimer Hill; Half Acre; Hanging Cl & Grd; Hellier's Plots; Hellow Grd; Hr Herne Cl (*v.* **hyrne**); Higher Cl, Grd & Md; Hill Cl & Grd; Hill foot; Hills Coppice; Hilly Grd & Plot; Hither Cl, Grd & Md; Hole Fd; Hollis (Croft); Home Cl, Coppice, Fd, Grd, Md(w) & Plot; Homestead; Hutchins's Coppice, Hill, Row & Well; Jennings; Jenny's Md; King Lane; Kite Hill (*v.* **cȳta**); Leigh Cl (*v.* **lēah**); Little Cl, Coppice, Fd & Wd; Long Cl, Coppice, Cross, Md, Orchd & Plot; Longfield; Longhayes (*v.* **(ge)hæg**); Lower Cl, Down, Grd & Md(w); Mabers Cl; Manover Coppice & Grd; Mead (Plot); Middle Cl; Mill Ham (*v.* **hamm**); Moor (Cl); New Cl & Inclosure; 9 Acres; North Cl; Oat Cl; (Old) Orchard; Palmer's Cl; Pare Toy; Path Fd; Peak; Peaked Cl (*v.* **peked**); Pear Tree Cl; Pi(d)geon Cl; Pond Cl; Puss'(s) Md (cf. Mary *Purse* 1664); Quilton Hill; (Lt) Red Fd; Rickett's Drove; Robert's Coppice & Grd; Row Fd & Park (*v.* **rāw** 'a row' or **rūh** (wk.obl.. *rūgan*) 'rough', cf. Old Park *supra*); Rowness (-*nest* 1822); Rust Bridge (*v.* **rust**, cf. foll.); Rusty Pce; Salters Plot; Scuds (cf. Theophilus *Skutt* 1664); 7 Acres (Row); Shetler's Cl; Short Cross; 6 & 16 Acres; South Cl; Sparks Coppice; Spittle Fd (*v.* **spitel**; the allusion is not clear); 3 Acres; 3 Corner Grd; 12 & 2 Acres; Vines Cl; Vineyard; Watering Place & Pond (*v.* **watering**); Well Cl & Coppice (*v.* **well(a)**); West Cl; (Eastward or Yonder) Whetcombe, Hthr & Peaked Whitcombe (*v.* **hwǣte** 'wheat', **cumb, eastward, peked**); Whistlers Grove; Wormhill Pond (*v.* **wyrm**); Yonder Cl, Coppice, Grd & Md.

Lytchett Minster

Part of Corfe Mullen par. *supra* (Upton, etc) was transferred to this par. in 1930.

LYTCHETT MINSTER (SY 961931) ['litʃət]
  Licheminster, Lyccemynistr' 1244 *Ass, Lyce-* 1253, 1262 FF, *Lycheministr(e)* 1288 *Ass, Lychet(t)-, Lichet(t) Minystre, -Min(i)stre, -Mynstr(e), -Mynster* 1280 *ib,* 1285 FF *et freq* to 1539 *Ct, -Menstr'* 1348 *DCMDeed, Lyschet Monaster'* 1281 FF (p), *Liscett* 1311 Ipm, *Lischet Munstre* 1327 *SR,* 1332 OR, *Lytchet or Lichet Mynstre* 1329 Ipm
  Lechet Ministre 1269 FF, *Lechard Mynstre* 1435 Cl
  Luchet Mynstre 1314 FF
  Sowthlichett(e) 1550 *Midd, South(e) Li-, Lytchett(e)* 1583 *SPDom,* 1597 *Feth, South Lochiot* c. 1586 Tres
  Be(e)re Lychet 1564 *Hen²,* 1565 *Hen¹, Lychett Minstre als. Beire Lychett* 1567 *ib, Beire Lichet als. Lichet Mynstre* 1575 *ib, Lytchett Minster cum Beere* 1590 *Hen²*

v. Lytchett Matravers par. *supra.* 'Minster' is OE **mynster** '(large) church', probably with reference to the church at Sturminster Marshall par. *infra,* of which Lytchett Minster was a chapelry (Hutch³ 3 365, DoNHAS 38 67, Taylor 79), but cf. Church *infra.* 'South' in relation to Lytchett Matravers (*v.* **sūð**), in contrast to which it was also called *Lower-, Nether Lichet* 1774 Hutch¹. For the affix *Be(e)re, v.* foll.

BERE FM (SY 942935), 1838 *TA, (firm' de) Bear(e)court(e)* 1374 (16), 1483 (16), 1532 (16) all *Hen¹, Bere court* 1520 *Rent, Bere* 1420, 1601 *Hen¹, Beere* 1534 *Ct,* 1590 *Hen²,* cf. *Be(e)relane* 1420 *Hen¹,* 1590 *Hen², Be(e)re Wood(e)* 1564 *ib,* 1601 *Hen¹, Bere Cl & Corner* 1838 *TA,* from **bær²** '(woodland) pasture' or **bearu** 'wood', cf. Bere Regis 1 273, with **court** 'manor house'; its importance is suggested by its use as an affix to the par. name *supra.*

BULBURY CAMP (SY 928942) & COPPICE, LR BULBURY FM, ROUGH BULBURY, *Burle-, Bulrebury* 1306 Ipm, *bosco voc' Bulberye* 1567 *Hen¹, Burliborowe Woode, east Burrelbarow* 1590 *Hen², Bullbury* 1774 Hutch¹, *Hr & Lr Bulberry* 1838 *TA.* The final el. is **burh** (dat.sg. *byrig*) 'earthwork', with reference to

Bulbury Camp, a hill-fort; the first part of the name may mean 'wood or clearing by the earthwork' from **burh** (gen. sg. *burge*) and **lēah**, as is suggested for the f.n. Burlington (*Burle-* 1333) in Dorchester par. 1 361.

NEWTON FM (SY 937932), *atte Niweton* 1332 SR (p), *Newton...via reg'* 1420 *Hen*[1], *Newtown* 1811 OS, cf. *Streets or Newtown Coppice* 1838 *TA*, 'new farm', *v.* **nīwe, tūn, atte** 'at the'; *Streets* is probably a surname but may refer to the Dorchester-Lytchett Minster road, cf. the 1420 form, *v.* **strǣt**.

ORGAN FORD (BRIDGE & FM) (SY 939924), ORGAN HO (-MANOR 1"), (*firma de*) *Argent(e)* 1194, 1195, 1197 P, 1196 ChancR, *molend' de Erghente* 1244 *Ass*, *Irgente* 1332 SR (p), *terra de Argenta* n.d. (1372) *ChrP*, *ergentemede* 1420 *Hen*[1], *Argaunte* 1534 *Ct*, *Orgons, Urgons* 1590 *Hen*[2], *Organfo(u)rde* 1593 *DCMDeed*, 1597 *Feth*, *Orgayne als. Organt* 1600 *Hen*[1], *Organ Green, Ho & Md* 1838 *TA*, *v.* **mǣd, ford**. This is a difficult name, but it may be of Fr origin. It is possible that it is to be connected with OFr, AN *argent* (< Lat *argentum*) 'silver', also 'silver money'; this word is apparently found in 12th cent. surnames in England (cf. Geoffrey *Argent* 1180 (Nth) cited by Reaney), but there is no evidence for its occurrence in English p.ns.[1] It is perhaps more likely that *Argent(e)* is a transferred p.n. from Argent (Cher) (*v.* A. Dauzat & Ch. Rostaing, *Dictionnaire étymologique des noms de lieux en France*, Paris 1963, p. 26) or some other place in France rather than an original coinage (Tengvik 69 connects the surname of Reginald *de Argente* 1273 (Essex) with Argent (Cher)), cf. Richmond YN 287 which was named from one of the Richemonts in France. The estate of *Argent(e)* was held by a certain Lecia *de Brouilla*, *-de Broil* in 1194–5.[2] In Northern Fr usage, the spelling *gh* before a front

---

[1] On 'silver' as a theme in p.ns., Professor Löfvenberg draws my attention to his discussion of English r.ns. containing OE *seolfor, sylfor* 'silver' or a derivative OE **seolfre, *sylfre* 'silvery stream', i.e. 'clear or sparkling stream', in Löfvenberg 181–2, cf. also DEPN s.n. Monksilver, EPN s.v. **seolfor**. In this semantic connection it may be worth noting that Organ Ford is where Sherford River was once crossed by a ford, and that the name Sherford, originally denoting another crossing 1¼ miles W at what is now Sherford Bridge in Morden par. *infra*, may mean 'bright ford' or 'ford over the *Sher*' ('the bright one').
[2] Professor Löfvenberg points out that the likelihood of *Argent(e)* being a transferred name from Argent (Cher) may be strengthened by the existence in Cher of a place called

vowel (as in the 1244 form) may indicate the pronunciation [g]
(Feilitzen § 126),[3] but if the original pronunciation of the medial
-g- was [dʒ] rather than [g], it is possible that [g] is a spelling
pronunciation, perhaps originating as late as the 16th cent. and
perhaps reinforced by popular association of the name with the
word *organ* 'wild marjoram, pennyroyal'. Professor Jackson
thinks that any connection with PrW *argant* 'silver' is very
doubtful, pointing out that the -g- in this word was the palatal
or velar voiced fricative [j] or [ɣ], cf. the r.ns. Arrow He and
Erring Burn Nb in Ekwall RN 17–18, 150.

SLEPE (SY 927933), *Slape juxta Lychetmenistre* 1315 Drew,
Slepe 1327 *SR*, 1332 SR both (p), 1504 Ipm, 1590 *Hen*², 1774
Hutch¹ (*-and Cockamore*), 1795 Boswell (*-cum Cockmore*),
Sleeping Green 1811 OS, *Slepe Cmn & Green*, *Slepe Peak* Cl
1838 *TA*, *v.* slǣp 'a slippery muddy place', cf. Slepe in Arne
1 73; *Cock(a)more* may be 'cocks' moor' from cocc² (gen.pl.
cocca) and mōr.

BAKER'S ARMS P.H., cf. *Bakers Plot* 1838 *TA*. BEACON CTGS,
HEATH, HILL (1838 *TAMap*, cf. *Bacon Hill Plant.* 1838 *TA*)
& HILL FM, *v.* Lytchett Beacon *infra*. BLACK HILL. CHURCH,
cf. 'chapel of *Lychet ministre*' 1285 FF, *atte Church(e)* 1327 *SR*,
1332 SR both (p), *the Churche house* 1590 *Hen*², St Mary's
Church in Lytchett Matravers par. *supra*, *v.* cirice, atte. CLAY
PIT, 1838 *TA*. CLIFTON HO. THE COMMON, *Lytchet Cmn* 1811
OS. COTTAGE FM & WALK. ELMWOOD. FISH POND. FOREST
BOURNE FM, near foll., cf. *bosc' de Lychet* 1450 *MinAcct*, *Lytchett
Forest* 1811 OS, Bailie Gate in Sturminster Marshall par. *infra*;
a spring is marked 6″, *v.* burna. FOREST HILL (CTG), near prec.
FRENCH'S COPPICE & FM. GREEN WORLD FM. HIGHGATE CTGS,
probably an access to the forest, *v.* geat, cf. Forest Bourne Fm
supra. NORTH HOLTON FM, *v.* Holton in Wareham par. 1 159.
HOME COPPICE, near Pike's Fm *infra*, *v.* home. KICHERMAN'S

Breuilly, this being a derivative (with the common Fr suffix -*y*) of Br(e)uil which would
be a regular development of the *Brouill/Broil* in the surname of the 12th cent. owner
of the estate; however, there is still the problem of the etymology and pronunciation
of the name Argent in OFr (it is first recorded in 1012 in the Lat form *Argentum*
according to Dauzat & Rostaing op.cit.).
³ Dr D. H. Evans, on this and other grounds, is inclined to interpret the evidence of
the spellings for Organ Ford as favouring a pronunciation [g] and as suggesting
derivation from an original form *argant-.

CTG. LYCH GATE. LYTCHETT BAY, *S. Lichet-* 1661, *Lichet Bay* 1774 Hutch[1], *v.* **bay**[1]. LYTCHETT BEACON, *Lechiot becon* 1575 Saxton, *Litchet Beacon* 1774 Hutch[1], a hill commanding 'a very extensive prospect of Pool-Bay. Here was formerly a beacon' (Hutch[1] 2 130), *v.* **(ge)bēacon.** LYTCHETT BRICK WORKS, *Brick Kiln* 1811 OS, cf. *Brick Kiln Grd & Yd, Bricks Md* 1838 *TA.* SOUTH LYTCHETT MANOR, *Sans Souci* 1811 OS ('free from care'), cf. *South Lytchett Ho* 1838 *TA.* THE MANSE. MANSION HILL, near Lytchett Heath Ho in Lytchett Matravers par. *supra.* THE MARSH, cf. *Marsh Green* 1811 OS, *-Cmn* 1838 *TA, v.* **mersc.** ONE ELM. OTTER ISLAND, *Utter-heath* 1774 Hutch[1], *Otter Heath Island* 1838 *TA, v.* **oter.** PETER'S FINGER P.H., 1838 *TA,* cf. *Peters Cl & Grd* 1838 *ib,* thought locally to be a corruption of *St Peter ad Vincula* (M.H.). PIKE'S COPPICE & FM, *Pikes Coppice, 15 Acres & Middle Grd, 7 Acres (Pykes)* 1838 *TA.* PIT BOTTOM SPINNEY, cf. *Pit Bridge (Md), Pit Fm* 1838 *TA,* near Pit Bottom in Lytchett Matravers par. *supra.* THE PLANTATION. POST GREEN, 1826 Gre, *(-Ho)* 1838 *TA, v.* **post.** RACE FM. RANDALL'S CTG & FM. ROUND HILL. ST ALDHELM'S CHURCH. ST LEONARD'S FM. SANDY LANE, cf. *Sandhill* 1601 Hen[1], *v.* **sand, hyll.** SHOT LAKE WD, cf. *Shuthill 4 Acres* 1838 *TA,* perhaps from **scēot**[3] 'steep slope' or **scyte** '(steep) slope or hill'; a stream flows through the wood, *v.* **lacu.** SIX ACRE WD, cf. *(The) 6 Acres* 1838 *TA.* THREE OAKS (CTG). TROKES COPPICE, 1838 *TA, -Grd* 1838 *ib,* cf. *terr' Petri Troke voc' the Grove* 1601 Hen[1], *v.* **grāf(a).** UPTON RD, to Upton in Corfe Mullen par. *supra.* YARRELL'S FM, THE YARRELLS.

FIELD-NAMES

The undated forms are 1838 *TA* 136. Spellings dated 1244 are *Ass,* 1327 *SR,* 1332 SR, n.d. (1372) *ChrP,* 1534, 1543 *Ct,* 1564, 1590 *Hen*[2], 1637 *DCMSurv,* 1664 HTax, 1774 Hutch[1], and the rest *Hen*[1].

(a) Acre Plot; Agness Md; Anvils Drove; Arnolds Coppice & Md; Bank; Barn Cl & Plot (cf. *Barnhulle* 1420, *v.* **bere-ærn, hyll**); Barn(e)s Cl & Home Plot (cf. Thomas *Barnes* 1600); Barton Yd; Bennetts Moor; Bennily Cl; Bixes Orchd; Boat Grd; (Furzy) Breaches, Heath Breach Grd, Breach Wd (cf. *Breachehyll* 1564, *claus' voc' le Breache* 1601, *v.* **brǣc, brēc, hyll**); Brewers Coppice, Md & Moor (cf. Thomas *Brewer* 1664); Broad Cl, Lane & Leaze (*v.* **lǣs**); Brook Cl; Bucks Cove (cf. John *Bucke* 1483 (16), *v.* **cove**); Bull Cl & Hays (*v.* **(ge)hæg**); Cart Ho Cl, Gdn & Plot; Clark's Cl; Cole Hill (or 7 Acres) (possibly **col**[1] 'charcoal'); Coombers Md & Plot; Coppice (Cl & Plot);

Cowards Md; Cozenage Md (cf. Cuzenage Coppice in Lytchett Mat. par.
supra); Crockers (Grd); (The) Drove, Drove Plot; Dry Md; Durrells Grd;
(The) 8 Acres; Fern Grd; 5 Acres (Home Grd); Foes Plot; Forrell Cl; (The)
4 Acres; Fox Hills (Row) (cf. Foxhill(s) in Lytchett Mat. par. *supra*); Franks
Plot; Furmages (Grd) (cf. John *Formage* 1601); Further Grd & Plot; Furzy
Grd & Pasture; Garden Plot (near Bowling Green); Gilberts (Md & Moor)
(cf. Thomas *Gilbert* 1664); Gravel Pit; Great Grd & Wd; Green; (Pear Tree
or) Green Cl; Green Coppice & Md; Greens Moor & Wd (cf. Nicholas *Greene*
1664); Ground; Groves (cf. Trokes Coppice *supra*); Hampers Grd; Hardings
5 Acres (cf. Christopher *Harding* 1664, Hooks *infra*); Gt Hazel Gare (cf. *le*
Gore 1420, *Gorehethe* 1601, *v.* **gāra, hǣð**); Hither Grd; Holton Bridge 1838
TAMap (from Holton in Wareham par. 1 159); Home Cl, Grd, Md & Plot;
Hardings Inner Hooks, Outer Hooks (*v.* **hōc**, cf. Hardings 5 Acres *supra*);
Horse Leaze (*v.* **lǣs**); Hough Fd, Grd & Md (*v.* **hōh** 'heel of land'); House
Moor; 100 Acres (a medium-sized field); Hungry Hill (a name for poor land,
v. **hungrig**); Inner Grd; Islander Clarks folly (*v.* **folie**); Jones' Plot; James
Land Grd & Md; Kings Lane Grd (cf. King's Bridge in Wareham par. 1 163);
Knapps at Organ Green (*v.* **cnæpp**, Organ Ford *supra*); Lr Land Grd, Large
Lands (cf. Nicholas *de la lond* n.d. (1372), *v.* **land**); Lane; Lanes Grd;
Further & Hthr Lawn (*v.* **launde**); (The) Leg (*v.* **leg**); Gt & Lt Lennet(t)s,
Lennetts Moor & Plot; Lenningtons Md; Lilly Cl; Little Cl & Plot; Long
Cl (or Crawford Pdk), Long Cl Coppice (*v.* **crāwe,** ford); Long Grd & Md;
Lower Plot; (The) Mead, Mead Ham (*v.* **hamm**); Meads Plot; Middle Grd
& Plot; Millers Wd Corner Coppice (cf. *molendinarius ibidem* 1543); Gt Mill
Md (cf. *the Mill* 1664); Lt, Middle & Upr Moor, (The) Moor (cf. Thomas
Attemore 1244, Robert *de la more* 1327, *Moreheye* 1420, *le Common More* 1601,
v. **mōr, atte, (ge)hæg**); New Grd & Inclosure; 9 Acre Row, 9 Acres; North
Cl & Fds; Nuthays (Md) (*v.* **hnutu, (ge)hæg**); Oaks Cl & Moor; Old Rd; (Old)
Orchard; Osmonds Grd(s) (cf. William *Osmund* 1327 (Corfe Mullen)); Peaky
Cl; Philips's Coppice (cf. Alice *Phelipes* 1327); Picked Cl (*v.* **pīcede**);
Plowmans Grd; Pollards Plot; Pond Cl (Md); Popes Grd; Pound Cl, Pound
Hill Cmn (cf. *punfoldum domini* 1420, *v.* **pund**); Punch Bates; Quan (sic,
probably for Quarr) Hill (cf. *Quarryes of stone very apte for buildynge* 1565,
Old quarre 1600, *v.* **quarre**); Radmoor Cl, Coppice & Md (*Roddesmore* 1590,
v. **hrēod** 'reed, reed-bed', **mōr**); Reeks Barn Cl & Gdn (cf. Henry *Reeks*
1637); Rohers Fd; Rolls Grd; Round Grd; Row (of Wood); Rowness Grd
(cf. Rowness in Lytchett Mat. par. *supra*); Rush Cl; Rush Heath Cmn; Rushy
Grd; Russells; Salterns (*v.* **salt-ærn**); Saw Pit Grd (*v.* **saw-pit**); Scatts 7 Acres
(cf. *lande called Scuttes horne* 1590, *v.* **horn**, cf. Scuds in Lytchett Mat. par.
supra); Seagulls; (The) 7 Acres; Sherwoods Plot; Shitlers Cl (cf. Thomas
Shetler 1664); Small Gdn; Spear Grd (*v.* **spear**); The Squares; Stanleys
Orchd; (Outer) Stiching(s) (*v.* **sticcen**); Stony Down (Plant.); Stronds Moor
& Plot; Strongs Grd & Ho (cf. William *Strong* 1664 (Corfe Mullen)); Tarbots
Home Grd; (The) 10 Acres; Terrard lot on the Cmn, Terrards Plot; (Higher
Cl or) 3 Acres; 3 Ashes; 3 Corner'd Grd; Trendalls; 2 Acres; Vernigore 1774
(an island at low water in Lytchett Bay, *v.* **fearnig, gāra**); Watery Lane Grd;
Way Cl; Welch Nut Plot (*v.* **welsh-nut**); Well Grd; West Pce; White horn(s)
(furzy) grd, White horn Md (*v.* **hwīt, horn**); The Wood; Wood Md

(*Woodemeade* 1601); Wood Rows (*v.* **rāw**). A f.n. of recent origin is Pylons (B.K. 255).

(*b*) *Amitels ferme* 1590; *Bo*(*u*)*leslonde* 1420 (cf. William *Bole* 1332, *v.* **land**); *Bromeclose* 1601 (*v.* **brōm**); *cursum aque voc' Freshwater lake* 1601 (*v.* **fersc, wæter, lacu**, cf. *Freshwater* Wt 122); *Gaynes Woode* 1590; *marisc' voc' le Hechyn* 1420 (*v.* **hēcing**); *Huntynge thornes* 1601 (*v.* **hunting, þorn**); *lokyars Court yeate* 1601 (*v.* **court, geat**, cf. *domum*...*Nich' Lokyar* 1601); *le Re* 1420 (probably '(place) at the stream', *v.* **atter, ēa**); *Southafellgor* 1534 (*v.* **gāra**); *atte Stighele* 1327 (p) (*v.* **atte, stigel**); *Uppehulle* 1327 (p) ('upon the hill', *v.* **uppan, hyll**); *Wethermore* 1601 (*v.* **weðer, mōr**); *Wyngeates* 1600, *-yeate* 1601 (*v.* **wind-geat**).

Parkstone

This par. was formed out of Canford Magna par. *supra* in 1833; it was added to the borough and par. of Poole *infra* in 1905.

PARKSTONE (SZ 038913), *Parkeston*(*e*) 1326 FF, 1463 *MinAcct et freq* to 1543 *Ct*, *manor of* (*Kyneston or*) *Parkestone* 1494 Ipm, (*camp' de*) *Parkyston* 1529 *Ct*, *Parkston*(*e*) c. 1586 Tres *et passim*, *Parkson* 1774 Hutch[1], probably simply 'the park (boundary) stone', from **park** and **stān**, perhaps with reference to an early park in the manor of Canford, cf. Canford Park in Canford Magna par. *supra*, *v.* Kinson par. *supra*.

STREET-NAME. BRITANNIA RD, named from *Britania Inn* 1826 Gre.

NORTH HAVEN LAKE & POINT (SZ 035874), *Northavensford* 1341 Hutch[1], *Northhavenefford* 1341 (1792) *DCMDeed*, *le Northauen forde* 1364 Hutch[3], *Northe Havyn Poynt* 1539 LP, *Northaven Pointe* 1581 Hutch[3], *North Haven Point* c. 1586 Tres, *-or Celes* 1774 Hutch[1], *-or Coles* 1795 Boswell, *North Haven* 1811 OS, at the entrance to Poole Harbour opposite South Haven Point in Studland par. 1 50, *v.* **norð, hæfen**[1], **ford, point**; there is now a ferry here, cf. *The Foord and Passage where the wains pass* c. 1800 *DROMap*. For *Celes*, *Coles*, *v.* Sandbanks *infra*.

SALTERNS BEACON, ESTATE, HO & PIER (SZ 036896), *Part of Little Sea now the Saltern* c. 1800 *DROMap*, (*The*) *Salterns* 1811 OS, 1843 *TA*, cf. *a Salterneslane vsque Cokdenswych, de Saltmershelane vsque Cokdeneswiche, Saltmersshe* 1463 *MinAcct*, *Salt Marsh* 1843 *TA*, *v.* **salt-ærn** 'a building where salt is made or sold', **salt**[2] 'salty, brackish', **mersc, lane**; for *Little Sea*, *v.*

Parkstone Bay *infra*. *Cokden(e)swych*, *-wiche* probably means 'salt-works in, or belonging to, Cogdean hundred', *v*. wīc, Cogdean hundred *supra*; the meaning 'salt-works' for wīc (contested by Smith EPN s.v. wīc (3, iii), affirmed by Ekwall OE wīc 22–8) seems likely here in view of the context in which the name appears and of the following other references to salt-works in the manor of Canford, all possibly to be associated with the area of Salterns on the N shore of Poole Harbour: *quatre Wichwerkes de Seel* 1368 *AD* ('four wichworks of salt', i.e. 'four salt-works', *v*. geweorc), *iiij Wichwrekkes* (sic) 1374, *iiij Whichwerkes* 1463 both *MinAcct* (held by priory of Breamore Ha), cf. also 'salt-pit (*salina*) at *Waldflete* in *Caneford*' 12 Hutch³ 3 312 (granted to priory of Bradenstoke W, *v*. flēot 'estuary', possibly with w(e)ald 'high woodland, hill'), and the f.n. *Wrykesham* 1463 *MinAcct* (from hamm, possibly with (ge)weorc '(salt-)works').

ALEXANDRA PARK. ARDMORE, a house-name, like many of the other names in this section. BALHOLM GRANGE. BELMONT COURT. BERKELEY TOWERS. BLAKE DENE, near to foll. BLAKE HILL (Ho), *Black Hill* 1811 OS, (*Gt & Lt*) *Blakehill* 1843 *TA*, *v*. blæc, hyll. BLUE LAGOON, near Salterns *supra*. BOWLING GREENS, *-Green* 1826 Gre, 1843 *TA* (P.H.). BRANKSOME CHASE, CHINE (GDNS) & PARK, from Branksome par. *supra*, *v*. cinu, as elsewhere in this par. BRIDLE PATH. BULLPITT BEACON, a buoy in Poole Harbour, but probably named from an on-shore feature, *v*. bula, pytt. CANFORD CLIFFS (CHINE), from Canford Magna par. *supra*. CASA NARA. CASTLE EVE ESTATE (Kelly), *Castle Eve* 1826 Gre, no doubt a P.H. CASTLE HILL, THE CASTLE, *Castle* 1826 Gre. CERNE ABBAS, from the par. of that name *infra*. CHURCH (St Peter's), *Parkstone Church* 1843 TA, cf. the chapel in Parkstone marked c. 1586 Tres. CLIFF GDNS, cf. *Cliffe Ho* 1822 *EnclA*, *Cliff Ho Gdn* 1843 *TA*. COLLISTON HO. COMPTON ACRE(S), *-Acre* c. 1800 *DROMap*. CONSTITUTION HILL (RD), 1822 *EnclA*, near where the old par. bdys of Longfleet, Kinson and Parkstone met. COPSE CLOSE, cf. *Coppice Plot* 1843 *TA*. COURTENAY LODGE. THE DELL. EDENHURST. THE ELMS. FIRGROVE. FISH POND. FLAG FM, *Lilliput Fm* 1811 OS, near foll., cf. Lilliput *infra*. FLAGHEAD, FLAG HEAD CHINE, *v*. hēafod, cinu; first el. perhaps flagge 'rush, iris', unless this is

an allusion to the hoisting of a flag here. FOREST LODGE.
FORSYTE SHADES. FROGMOOR (lost), 1811 OS, v. frogga, mōr.
GABLEHURST. THE GLEN. GLEN DOONE. GLENMORAG. GRATA
QUIES. GRAY RIGG. GREYSTOKE. GREYSTONES. HAVEN FERRY
CAFÉ, HAVEN HOTEL, cf. *Haven Ho & Plaine* c. 1800 *DROMap*,
cf. North Haven *supra*. HEATHSIDE. HIGHMOOR. HOLMWOOD.
HUNGER HILL, cf. *Hunger Fd* 1843 TA, derogatory names for
poor land, v. hungor. INGLEWOOD. INVERCLYDE. LANGDON, cf.
a place called Langton Barowe 1546 *Surv*, v. lang[1], tūn, beorg.
LEDGARD HO. LILLIPUT (HO & PIER), *Lillypute* 1783 *Marten*,
Lilliput 1811 OS, the name of the imaginary country peopled
by pygmies in Swift's *Gulliver's Travels* (1726), cf. Flag Fm
supra. The name is probably to be associated with Isaac *Gulliver*
(of West Moors) (1745–1822) who may have been the house's
first occupant, the addiction to Swift's story being further
suggested by the baptismal name of *Lemuel* Gulliver of East
Orchard (1823 *Marten*) who was probably of the same family
(*Lemuel* is the name of Swift's hero) (M.H.), v. Gulliver's Fm
in W Parley par. *infra*. LUSCOMBE (VALLEY), *Loscomb* 1822
EnclA, v. hlōse 'pig-sty', cumb, cf. Luscombe in Lytchett
Mat. par. *supra*. THE MANSE. MARTELLO TOWERS. MILL HILL
CLOSE, MILL LANE, cf. *Iron Mills* 1811 OS. MOUNT GRACE.
MOUNT HO. NIRVANA. NORTH LODGE. OAK CTGS (lost), 1826
Gre. THE OLD RIDE (v. ride). OVERCOOMBE. PARKBURY. PARKS-
TONE BAY, *Little Sea* 1661 Hutch[1] (*Gosts Bay als*.-), c. 1800
DROMap. PARKSTONE CTG (lost, 1826 Gre), HO, LAKE (a
channel in Poole Harbour, v. lacu) & PARK (cf. *The Park* 1843
TA). PARKSTON GREEN (lost), 1811 OS. THE PATCH. PENNYS
HILL (lost), 1811 OS, cf. Robert *Penny* 1664 HTax. PENWOOD.
PERRAN LODGE. PIGEON BOTTOM. THE PINES. THE PLATEAU.
POOLE BAY, HEAD (*The Head* 1811 OS, v. hēafod 'promon-
tory'), HEATH (lost, 1811 OS) & PARK, named from Poole par.
infra; part of Poole Heath is called *Mines heath* 1707 Hutch[3],
named from *The Mynes* 1575 Saxton, c. 1586 Tres (worked for
copperas and alum). PONSONBY PLACE (lost), 1826 Gre. POTTERY
FM, near SOUTH WESTERN POTTERY, cf. *Potters Ho* 1843 *TA*,
Peter *Potter* 1332 SR. REDLANDS. RUDHEATH. ST ALDHELMS.
SANDBANKS, *the Sand Banks* c. 1800 *DROMap* (-*vulgarly called
Cales*), 1843 *TA*, cf. Walter *atte Sonde* 1327 *SR, ground called
Cales* 1579 *DCMDeed, Cales Pound* c. 1800 *DROMap*, from

sand, banke, atte, pund, and the surname *Cale, v.* North Haven
supra. SANDECOTES. SMUGGLER'S CHINE. OLD SMUGGLER'S
WELL. STRETTON COURT. SWAIN'S HALL, cf. Edward *Swayn*
1332 SR. THE TEAK HO. THERAPIA. TWELVETREES PLACE.
UPWOOD. WESTERN COURT. WESTLANDS. WESTMINSTER RD.
WESTON'S ISLAND & POINT, cf. Anna *Weston* 1543 *Ct.* WHIN-
THORPE. WHITLEY LAKE, a channel in Poole Harbour, but
probably named from an on-shore feature, *v.* hwīt, lēah. THE
WICK. WILDERTON. WOODLANDS. WOODSIDE (2 ×).

FIELD-NAMES

The undated forms are 1843 *TA* 163. Spellings dated c. 1800 are *DROMap*.
(*a*) Barn Cl & Fd; Beacon Chine c. 1800 (*v.* (ge)bēacon, cinu); Bittman
Chine c. 1800; Bog; (Late Jupes) Brick Kiln; Broad Cl; Broad Shard c. 1800
(*v.* sceard); Carrot Cl; Cload's Hill c. 1800; Common; Cowleaze; Farm Cl;
Forked Cl (*v.* forked); 4 Acres; Furze; Furzy Grd; Great Grd; The Grove;
Hawkleys Plot; Heath; Further Furzey Holes, Outer Holes (*v.* hol[1]); Home
Cl; Jews Fd, Md & Plot; The Land Mark Bank c. 1800; Lime Kiln (Cl); Long
Plot; Meadow; Middle Fd, Mdw & Plot; The Moor; New Cl; North Fd,
Mdw & Plot; Nursery; The inclosed part of Oakman c. 1800; Pasture Pce;
Pill Cl, East Pill (*v.* pyll 'tidal creek, pool'); Plantation; Plott; Pond Cl; Rose
& Crown Inn; Ryalls; Sistern's Hedge now Perry Bakers c. 1800; South
Mdw; Spring Cl; 10 Acres; Upper Plot; West Fd & Plot; Withey Bed Cl;
Wood.

Poole

A borough, incorporated in 1248, constituted a county in 1559, extended in
1905 to include the pars. of Branksome, Hamworthy, Longfleet and Parkstone,
and again in 1933 to include the par. of Canford Magna.

POOLE (SZ 008904), *Poles* 1180–1186 P (p), *Pole* 1183, 1195
ib both (p), 1199 Cur (p), 1231 Cl, 1280 *Ass et freq* to 1484
Cl, *Pola* Hy 3 (1371) Pat, 1227 FF, 1230 Pat *et freq* to 1268 *Ass*
(*aquam portus de-*), 1288 Ch, *la Pole* 1220 Cur, 1224 Pat *et freq*
to 1428 Cl, *le Pole* 1386 Pat, (*la*) *Poule* 1300 Cl *et freq* to 1412
FA, *Pool(e)* 1392 Fine *et passim*, 'the pool or creek', with
reference to Poole Harbour *infra, v.* pōl[1]; *-s* in the earliest forms
is a pl. ending, possibly AN (cf. Zachrisson IPN 94).

POOLE STREETS & BUILDINGS

Spellings dated 1697 are *Eg*, 1751 *DROMap*, 1774 Map, 1822 *EnclA* (Canford Magna), 1824 Pigot and 1863 Hutch[3].
BAITER ST., from Baiter *infra*, cf. East St *infra*; it was earlier *Hileys Lane* 1751, cf. Peter *Hielys*, (*Mr*) *Hielys Close*, *-tennement* 1697. BARBERS PILES, 1822, near *Barbers Lane* 1751, cf. *Pile Close* 1563 Poole, *v.* **pīl** 'a pile'. BAY HOG LANE, 1751, perhaps from a surname *Bayhog* 'one who bays hogs, a hog hunter'. CASTLE ST.; the N end was earlier *Fish St.* 1697, 1751 (near to *The Fish Shambles ib*, *The fish-market* 1863); the S end was earlier *Phuddie* (sic) *Lane* 1751, *Pluddie-lane* 1774, *v.* **pluddy** 'pool, puddle'. CHAPEL LANE, 1863, from *St Paul's Church ib*; it was earlier *Pound Lane* 1751, cf. *lez pownde* 1540 *Ct*, *Pound Close*, *-Garden* 1697, *v.* **pund**, cf. Pound St. *infra* which must take its name from a different pound. CHURCH ST., 1574 Poole, 1751, *Chruch* (sic) *St.* 1697, from St James's Church *infra*. DEAR HAY LANE, 1826, *deerehayes lanne* 16 Hutch[3], *Dair-* 1751, *Deerhay Lane* 1774, from 'a close called *Dyer Hayes*' 1484 Hutch[3], 'deer enclosures' from **dēor** and **(ge)hæg**. DRAKE ST. (TPlan), *Drakes Alley* 1751, cf. Frances *Drake* 1697. EAST QUAY RD, cf. The Quay, West Quay *infra*. EAST ST., 1824, earlier *Baietor-*, *Baytor Lane* 1607 Poole, *Baiter Lane* 1751, from Baiter *infra*, cf. Baiter St. *supra*. GLOBE LANE, cf. *the Globe* (inn) 1697; it was earlier *Levets-*1751, *Levites lane* 1774, cf. William *Levytt* (mayor) 1596 Hutch[3], and Levet's Lane *infra*. GREEN LANE, near foll. GREEN RD, earlier *-Lane* 1751, from *Baiter Green ib*, *v.* Baiter *infra*, cf. prec. and *Corporation Green* 1666 Poole. HIGH ST., 1549 Hutch[3] *et passim*. HILL ST., 1751, *Hell St.* 1649 Poole, 1697, *v.* **hell** 'hell', a derogatory name. HUNGER HILL, 1751, *Hungerhulle* 1437 Poole, *-hill* 1549 Hutch[1], a name for poor land, *v.* **hungor, hyll**. KING ST., 1863, earlier *Market Lane* 1751, off Market Place *infra*. LAGLAND ST., 1774, *close in Lage Lane, Lagelane St.* 1697, *Leg Lane* 1721 Poole, 1774 Hutch[1] (*-or Lackland-street*), *Lag Land* 1751, probably from **lagge** 'marsh', with **lane** (later confused with **land**). LEVET'S LANE, *Levels-lane* 1774, altered to *Lovel's-* 1863 Hutch[3] in key to same map; the modern name seems to show confusion with the old name for Globe Lane *supra*. LOVE LANE, earlier *West Butts Lane* 1751, *v.* West Butts St. *infra*; there was another *Love Lane* 1751, off Green Rd *supra*. MARKET PLACE, 1826, cf. 'A market house in *the Pyllorye St.*' 16 Hutch[3], *the Markett* 1697, *The Market House and Shambles, The Corn Market* 1751, *the Butter Market* 1822, *v.* King St. *supra* and foll.; Hutch[3] 1 32 says the Market House was known as *Guildhall*. MARKET ST., 1751 (*-als. Pillory St.*), *Markett St.* 1697, off prec.; the N end was earlier *the Pyllorye St.* 16 Hutch[3], *Pillory St.* 1697, 1774, *v.* **pillory**. MOUNT ST., *Gt Mount Lane* 1751, cf. *Lt Mount Lane ib* now part of High St. *supra*, *v.* **mont**. NEW ORCHARD, 1751, near Old Orchard *infra*. NEW ST., 1697, 1751 (*Wine or-*), no doubt where wine was sold, *v.* **wine**. NIGHTINGALE LANE, 1623 Poole, 1774, *Nightingal-* 1751. NILE ROW. NORTH ST., 1824, earlier *Water Lane* 1751, *v.* **wæter**. OLD ORCHARD, 1751, near New Orchard *supra*. POUND ST., cf. Chapel Lane *supra*. PROSPEROUS ST. THE QUAY, *le Key* 1472 *Ct*, *the (greate) key(e)* 16 Hutch[3] *et freq*, *the little new key* 1679 Hutch[1], *the Ballast Key, the Key yard* 1697, *The little key* 1751, *New-quay* 1774, *Quay-head* 1824, *v.* **key**, cf. *Key Lane* 1751, Thames St. and West Quay

both *infra*. SKINNER ST., 1863, near to *Skinners Alley* 1751, probably where skinners lived, but cf. John *Skynner* 16 Hutch³, Grace *Skiner* 1697. STRAND ST., 1658 *Poole, Strond Streate* 1607 *ib*, *the Strand Streete* 1676 *ib*, v. **strand** 'shore'. TAYLOR'S BLDGS, 1824. THAMES ST., 1822, *The(a)mes St.* 1697, also called *Key St.* 1751, v. The Quay *supra*. TOWNGATE ST., *Town(e) Gates Lane* 1697, 1751, cf. *towne gate close* 1697, named from *The Town Gate* 1751, *Pool Gate* 1756 Hutch¹, *Turnpike gate* 1774, cf. Richard *de la Gate* 1288 *Ass*, v. **geat**. WEST BUTTS ST., *West-butt-street* 1774, *West Butt's Rd* 1822, named from *(the) West Butts* 16 Hutch³, 1751 *et freq*, cf. *West Butts Green* 1751, *West Butts shore* 1792 Hutch³, *Love Lane supra*, v. **butt²** 'archery butt', cf. Smith 2 35. WESTON LANE, *Westons-* 1751, cf. *Westons shopp, Margaret Westons tennement* 1697. WEST QUAY, 1822, v. The Quay *supra*. WEST ST., 1697, '(the) West Street' 16, 1549 Hutch³.

Lost st.ns. include *Bell Lane* 1751 (from *Bell Inn* 1697); *Bennets-alley* 1774 (cf. Henry *Benet* 1472 *Ct*); *Blackwell Street* 1563 Poole; *Broad Way* 1751; *Buttons Lane* 1751; *Carters-lane* 1774 (cf. John *Carter* (mayor) 1670 Hutch³); *Cinnamon Lane* 1751 (no doubt where this spice was sold); *Comptons-alley* 1774; *Crabb Lane* 1751; *Crocked-* 1751, *Crooked lane* 1774; *Ditch Lane* 1751; *Fowlers Lane* 1751; *Frickers Alley* 1751; *Hancock Alley* 1751 (cf. Thomas *Hancock* 1546); *Hosiers-lane* 1824; *the Jetty* 1697 (v. **jetty**); *Lights Lane* 1751; *Lit(t)le Lane* 1607 Poole, 1751; *Mud Lane* 1751; *the Parade* 1822; *Paradise St.* 1751 (cf. *Pardice Celler* 1697, v. **paradis**); *Pelleys Lane* 1751 (cf. *house formerly Pellys*, Robert *Pelly* 1697); *Perry Gdn* 1563 Poole, 1751 (v. **pirige** 'pear-tree'); *Petty Lane* 1751; *Rickurd' Lane* 1607 Poole; *Rogers Lane* 1751 (cf. Robert *Rogers* 1540 *Ct*, a descendant of whom endowed *Mr Rogers's Almes Houses* 1751, cf. *the allmes howse infra*); *Rope Walks* 1751; *Rozers Lane* 1751; *St Clement's Alley* 1863 (cf. *St Clement* (inn) 1824); *Salisbury court* 1824, -*St.* 1751, 1824 (cf. *Salisbury Prison infra*); *Short Way* 1751; *Smock Alley* 1751 (perhaps where smocks were sold); *Stoney Lane* 1751; *Suttons Piles* 1751 (cf. *Barbers Piles supra*); *Thomas's Alley* 1751 (cf. 'the lond of John *Thomas*' 16 Hutch³); *Toops Lane* 1751 (cf. Christopher *Toupe* 1609 Hutch³).

Buildings include *the allmes how(e)se* 16, 1561 Hutch³, *The Old Almes Houses* 1751 (mentioned from 1429 according to Hutch³ 1 64, cf. *Rogers Lane supra*); *the new brewhouse* 1697; *The Bridewell* 1812 Hutch³ (a prison); *The Custom House on the Key* 1751, *Old Custom Ho* 1822; *The Free School* 1751; *the gaiole* 1601 Hutch³, *The Town Gaol* 1812 *ib* (cf. *The Town Hall over the Prison* 1751); *Havilands Celler* 1697; *Lordis-*1485 Pat, *Lordes halle* 1486 *ib* (v. **hlāford, hall**); *the parsonage howse* 1584 Hutch³; *the Powder House* 1822; *Mr Rookes Iron Celler* 1697; 'A little prison by the key called *Salisbury*' 16 Hutch³, *Salisbury Prison* 1751 ('so named from the earls of Salisbury' according to Hutch¹ 1 8, cf. *Salisbury court, -St. supra*); *the Schele* 1697 (probably for *Schole*, 'school'); *Sir Peter Thompson's Ho* 1751; *The Town Hall over the Prison* 1751; *The Town Ho* 1751 (replaced 1822 by another building of same name, v. Hutch³ I 33); *Waterloo-buildings* 1824; *Western Fort* 1751; *le Wolle-* 1463 MinAcct, *le Wolhouse* 1522 Russ, *lez Wolehowse* 1554 AddCh (tolnet' dom' voc'-), *Great Celler* 1697, *The Great Cellar of Kings Hall* 1751, *The Great Cellar or King's-hall or Wool-house* 1774 Hutch¹ (v. **wull, hūs**); *The Work Ho* 1751 (replaced 1838 by *the Union Ho*, v. Hutch³ 1 32).

Inns include *Air Balloon* 1824; *Angel* 1794 Poole; *Antelope Inn* 1697, *Old Antelope* 1824, cf. *New Antelope* ib; *Bakers Arms* 1824; *Bell Inn* 1697 (cf. *Bell Lane supra*); *Blew Anchor* 1697; *the Bull Head* 1697; *the Crowne Inn* 1697; *Dolphin* 1824; *Eight Bells* 1824; *Fethers Inn* 1697; *Fountain* 1824; *Georg Inn* 1697; *the Globe* 1697 (cf. Globe Lane *supra*); *the Grayhound Inn* 1697; *Jolly Sailor* 1824; *King and Queen* 1824; *Kings Arms* 1697; *the Kings head* 1697; *Lamb Inn* 1697; *Lion and Lamb* 1824; *Lord Nelson* 1824; *New Inn* 1824; *New London Tavern* 1824; *Old Inn* 1824; *Poole Arms* 1824; *Portsmouth Hoy* 1824; *the Reed Lyon* 1697; *Rising Sun* 1824; *the Royal Oake* 1697; *St Clement* 1824 (cf. *St Clement's Alley supra*); *the Shipp Inn* 1697; *the Sun* 1697; *Swan Inn* 1697; *the 3 Crowns* 1697; *The Three Mariners* 1764 Poole; *Two Brothers* 1824; *Wellington* 1824; *The Whitt Beare* 1697.

BACK WATER CHANNEL, in Holes Bay, *v.* **back**. BAITER (TPlan), 1543 Hutch[1] ('common at-'), 1751 *DROMap* (-*Green*), 1863 Hutch[3] (*the*-), *Bayter* 16 Hutch[3], 1697 *Eg*, giving name to Baiter St. *supra* and *Baietor*-, *Baytor Lane* 1607 *Poole* (now East St. *supra*); it was originally used of 'the projecting slip of land' (Hutch[3]) forming the W side of Parkstone Bay, possibly 'rock or rocky outcrop in the bay', from **bay**[1] and **torr**, cf. the f.n. Wind Mill fd *infra*. CHURCH (St James's), 'church of *la Pole*' 1339 Pat, *Saincte James in Pole* 1519 *Ct*, cf. Church St. *supra*. FERRY (to Hamworthy), cf. *passage & pasage ho* 1697 *Eg*, *the Passage Ho* 1740 Hutch[1], *v.* **passage**; it gives name to Ferry Rd in Hamworthy par. *supra q.v.* HOSPITAL ISLAND, from Isolation Hospital. POOLE BRIDGE, 1863 Hutch[3]. POOLE HARBOUR, 1811 OS, *la hauene de la Pole* 1364 Hutch[3], *the haven of Pole*, *Poole Haven* 1535–43 Leland (*the mouth of*-, *the water of*-), cf. *aquam portus de Pola* 1268 *Ass*, *the bay of Pool* 1774 Hutch[1], *v.* **hæfen**[1], cf. North Haven Point in Parkstone par. *supra*, South Haven Point in Studland par. 1 50; the areas of mud in the Harbour are called *the Mudlands* 1822 *EnclA* (Canford Magna). QUAY CHANNEL, *le Streme...iuxta le Key* 1472 *Ct*, *v.* **strēam**, The Quay *supra*. STAKES (lost), 1811 OS, *Pool stakes* 1774 Hutch[1], in Poole Harbour.

FIELD-NAMES

The undated forms are 1697 *Eg* (Poor Rate Book, MS 2437). Spellings dated 1350 are Pat, 1374 *MinAcct*, 1472, 1519, 1529, 1540 *Ct*, 1520 *Rent*, 1542, 1563, 1649, 1666, 1777 Poole, 1661, 1740 Hutch[1], 1751 *DROMap*, 1774 Map, and the rest Hutch[3].

(a) Ashes Stables; back syd (*v.* **backside**); Barrets tennement; Bowling

Green 1774; Cloads Cl (cf. *Cloades tenement, widdow Cloade* 1649); Cocks Tennement; Deal Yd 1751; Dennets tenement; Dewys-, Dueys cl (cf. Robert *Dewey* 1529); Goderds-, Godards Cl (cf. Richard *Goddarde* 1559); Gre(e)n(e) Cl (*Green Close* 1666); Grundys tennement; Halls tennement; Old Harts Grave 1740; Hennings tennement (cf. Stephen *Henning*); Horse Island & Lake 1751; Jollifs tennement; Leeks meade (cf. John *Leeke* 1609); Lyme Keel cl (*v.* līm, cyln); Lowsy Bank 1751 (*v.* lousi); Mill Cl (1777, cf. 'garden called the *Mill Post*' 1549, named from an early windmill at Hunger Hill *supra*); Mount Rails 1751; Nichelas tennement (cf. Robert *Nyclys* 1580); Oyster Bank 1751 (a bed of discarded oyster shells, *v.* Hutch[1] 1 10); Phillips tennement; Picketts tennement; Pidwines (*Great & Little Pydwins* 16, *Pitwines* 1542, *Pynt Wynes* 1751); Reeds Ho & Cl (cf. Morgan *Rede* 1540); De Samways Gdn & tennement (cf. John *Samways*); Thc Sand Pitts 1751; Sear tenement; Skailes Craft Point 1751, Sealescraft otherwise Scalescroft 1822 (a surname with **croft, point**); Skutts tenement (cf. William *Skutt*); Stic(k)lands (perhaps a surname, but cf. Winterborne Stickland par. *infra*); Swampey Grd & Ld; Towne Cl; Towne Ld tennement; Verins gdn; Vines tennement; Way(e)s Tennement; the West Shore 1863; Wills tennement (cf. George *Wills*); Wind Mill fd 1751 (cf. 'close called *Windmill Hill*' 16, *Windmill Point* 1661, probably with reference to the windmill to be erected at Baiter *supra* in 1543 (Hutch[1] 1 3) and shown in 'A Prospect of the Towne of Poole' 1774 (ib), *v.* **windmill**).

(*b*) Brygeheys 1519 (*v.* **brycg, (ge)hæg**); *Cole Corner* 1563; *de la Court* 1472 (p) (*v.* **court**); *the Hill Close* 1563; 'Horwood's land' 16; *Knigesheys* 1519 (*v.* **(ge)hæg**); *Mesurer's Gap* 1609 (cf. William *Mesurer* 1609, *v.* **gappe**); *the Misone* 1563 (*v.* **mixen**); *atte Nasshe* 1350 (p) (*v.* **attc(n), æsc**); *No Man's Land* 16; *plac' voc' Shullourd* 1374, *Sholard* 1520 (possibly from **scell** (WSax **sciell**) 'shell, shell-fish, mussel' and **ord** 'a point', cf. Oyster Bank *supra*); *Town's End* 1563.

Sturminster Marshall

Almer par. *infra* was transferred to this par. in 1933. On the 'liberty' of Sturminster Marshall, *v.* Hutch[3] 3 336.

STURMINSTER MARSHALL (ST 949002) ['stəːRmistəR]
(*æt*) *Sture minster* 873–888 (e11) BCS 553
Sturministris c. 1080 France, *-minstre* 1086 DB, *-ministra* 1154–8 (1390) Ch, *-minstr(i)a* 1162–4 France, *-min(i)str(e)*, *-minister*, *-myn(i)stre*, *-mynystre*, *-mynster* 1204 ClR, 1212 Fees *et passim*, *-men(i)str(e)* 1206 P (p) *et freq* to 1391 DCMDeed with variant spellings *-menystre* (1304 *Wim*) and *-menustre* (1348 Pat), *-munstr(e)* l13 AddCh, 1332 SR, 1353 *AddCh*, 1374 Cl, *-mistre*, *-mystre*, *-myster* 1340 Pat *et freq* to 1508 *AddCh* with variant spelling *-mistir* (1379 Cl), *-mester* 1512 *Pars*, *Sturemynstre* 1286 *Wim*, 1337 Fine,

1340 Pat, -*menstre* 1335 *Wim*; with affix -*Marescal* 1268
Ass, 1280 Cl, -*Mare(s)chal(l)* 1284 Cl *et freq* to 1465 Pat,
-*Marischal* 113 *AddCh*, -*Mar(s)chal(l)* 1288 *Ass et freq*,
-*Marescalli* e14 *Wim*, 1306 Cl, -*Mars(s)hall* 1318 Pat *et
freq*, -*marechel*, -*al* 1330 *Wim*, -*Marchel* 1423 Pat, -*Marshell*
1493 *Ilch*

Esturmin(i)stre, -*minstr(i)a* 1152–1204 France, -*milistria* 1162
  ib, -*munstr'* 1268 *Ass*, -*minstre Mareschal* 1327 *HarlCh*,
  1330 Pat, *Estur(e)menistre* 1266, 1366 ib, *Est'ministr'* 1268
  Ass

Stormen(i)str(e) 1210–12 RBE *et freq* to 1348 *DCMDeed*,
  -*ministr(e)*, -*mynstre*, -*mynster* 1268 *Ass et freq* to 1412 Cl,
  -*myster* 1548 *DLCt*, *Storemen(i)stre* 1273 Ipm, 1335
  Wim; with affixes as above

Stourmistre 1244 FF, 1344 Pat, Fine, -*myn(y)str(e)*, -*mynster*,
  -*mynstyr* 1280 *Ass et freq* to 1461 *DCMDeed*, -*munstre* 1345
  Wim, -*menstre* 1348 Pat, 1366 Cl, -*myster* 1475 Pat, 1508
  DCMDeed, *Stouremynstre* 1344 Fine *et freq* to 1396 ib,
  Stowremynster 1514 *Pars*, *Stower Mister* 1677 *DCMCt*;
  with affixes as above

Turmin(i)str', *Thurmynistr'* 1244 *Ass*, *Thurmunstr'* 1269 Cl
Stirmystermarchall 1469 Pat
Stromynstre Marchall 1504 *DLCt*
Sturmister Marshall als. Moorecourt 1678 *DCMCt*, 1690
  Drax

'The church on R. Stour', *v.* **mynster**, RNs. *infra*, cf.
Lytchett Minster par. *supra*, Sturminster Newton par. *infra*.
The manorial affix is from the *Marshals*, earls of Pembroke, of
whom William *Marescallus* or *Mareschal* was here in 1204
Hutch[3], 1212 Fees, 1218 Pat, etc, cf. Charlton Marshall par.
supra. It was also called *East Sturminster* 1774 Hutch[1], from its
situation relative to Sturminster Newton. On the AN spellings
Estur- with prosthetic *e* before *st*, -*milistria* with interchange of
n and *l*, and *T(h)ur-* with loss of *s*, *v.* ANInfl 55, 141, 67. For
Moorecourt, *v.* Moorcourt Fm *infra*. There is mention of
Sturministre Marescall hundred in 1307 Ipm.

STREET-NAMES. BALL'S LANE, cf. William *Ball* 1627 *DCMSurv*; CHURCH ST.,
cf. *la Churche Weye* 1246 *Wim*, *v.* St Mary's Church *infra*; MARKET PLACE,
1774 Hutch[1], cf. *la Chupyng Stret* 1345 *Wim*, *v.* **cēping** 'a market'. A lost

st.n. is *Charborow-* 1508 *DCMDeed, Charburrow Way* 1677 *DCMCt,* cf. *viam que ducit de Sturminstr' versus Cherbergh* 1325 *Wim, v.* Charborough in Morden par. *infra.* For a lost *Green St., v.* Green Lane *infra.*

EAST ALMER FM & LODGE (SY 920993), (*vill' de*) *Estalmere, Est Almere* m13–1335 *Wim,* 1268 *Ass,* 1290 Ipm, 1391 FF, *manerio*...*de Almere que dicitur Est Almere* 1294 *Wim, dec' de Almer* 1484 *Eton, East Aylemer als. Combe Aylmer* 1673 *Drax,* 'east' in relation to Almer par. (olim *West Almere*) q.v. *infra, v.* ēast, cf. Combe Almer *infra.* There is mention of *parcum de Estalmere* e14 *Wim,* cf. Henbury Park *infra.*

BAILIE GATE & HO (SY 947990), BAILEY GATE STATION, *baylye yeate* 1516 *Pars,* named from *Le Bailly* 1412 FA, *the Baylye* 1515 *Pars,* cf. (*terr' super*) *Baily-, Bayly(e) Hyll, -Hill* 1508 *DCMDeed et freq* to 1693 *DCMCt, the Bayle-* 1513 *Pars, the Bayly Lane* 1514 *ib, Bayly Ash Furlong* 1694 *ib, Baily-House* 1774 Hutch[1], *Bailey Corner* 1811 OS, *Bailey Leaze* 1839 *TA, v.* **baillie** 'a bailliff's jurisdiction or district', perhaps with reference to a division of the wood of Lytchett (cf. Forest Bourne Fm in Lytchett Minster par. *supra*) or to 'the bailiwick of keeping the banks of the *Frome* and *Stoure*' mentioned in 1338 FF, with **gcat, hyll, lanc, æsc, lǣs,** cf. Bailey Ridge in Lillington par. *infra.*

COMBE ALMER (SY 948975), *Cumb(e)* 1228 FF, 1244 *Ass,* 1249 FF *et freq* to 1288 *Ass, La Cumbe* e14 *Wim, Combe* 1268 *Ass et freq* to 1539 *Ct, Coumbe* 1280 *Ass,* 1362 Cl (*-by Stormynstre Marchall*), *Combe Almere* 1327 *SR,* 1332 SR, *-Maresshall* 1426 Cl, *Combe otherwise Coombesett* 1558–1579 ChancP, *Combe Bessett, Combe Sturmister als. Sturmister Marshall* 1588 *AddCh, Combe Almer als. Combe Marshal* 1604 Hutch[3], from **cumb** 'a valley'; for the affixes -*Almer* and -(*Sturmister*) *Marshal(l), v.* East Almer and par. name *supra; Bes(s)ett* (probably for -*Bas(s)ett*) is manorial, cf. *Rog' Basset*...*domus aule* 1329 *Wim.*

HENBURY FM, HO & MANOR (SY 963982), *Henne-* 1244 FF, *Henn-* 1244 *Ass, Hembyr* 1249 FF, *Hymbur* 1249 ib, 1280 *Ass,* -*bir* 1280 ib, *Him-, Hymburi* l13 *AddCh, Hymbury* 1327 *SR,* 1334 *Wim,* 1352 *AddCh et freq* to 1476 Cl, -*bere* 1504 Ipm, *Hyn-* 1545 Hutch[3], *Henbury* 1546 *Surv,* 1664 HTax, *Henbury Higher or Upper Hymbury, Henbury Lower* 1774 Hutch[1], probably '(at)

the high or chief fortified place', from **hēah** (wk.obl. *hēan*) and
burh (dat. sg. *byrig*), cf. Broadhembury D 557, Henbury Gl 3
130; the ground here rises to 275' at *Henbury Hill* 1811 OS. In
spite of the two earliest forms cited, the first el. is less likely to
be *henna*, gen.pl. of **henn** 'a hen', cf. Encombe in Corfe Castle
par. 1 12. The *i*-forms for the first el. (if OE *hēan*) are probably
due to the change *ēa* > *īe* > *ī*, and the spellings also show ME
assimilation of *nb* to *mb*. Henbury Ho & Manor are respectively
Lower-, *Higher Henbury* 1811 OS, Henbury Fm is *Henbury
Dairy* 1826 Gre.

MOORCOURT FM (ST 930007), *Moreis* ? 1204 BM I, *Moors Court*
1346 Hutch[3], *Morescourte* (*maner'*) 1469 IpmR, *-courts* 1484 ib,
Moorecourt(e) 1626 *Bartelot*, 1678 *DCMCt* (*Sturmister Marshall
als.-*), *Mores-Court* 1774 Hutch[1], *More's or Moor Court* 1863
Hutch[3], an early manorial name, perhaps to be associated with
the ancestors of Robert *Moure* 1340 NI, *v.* **court** 'manor-house',
manere, cf. par. name *supra*.

NEWTON PEVERIL (FM) (SY 939998), *Neuton* 1260 FF, *Niweton*,
Neweton Peverel 1306 Ipm, *Neweton* 1329 ib, *Niwton* 1332 SR
(p), *Nyweton* n.d. (1372) *ChrP* (*-iuxta Almere*), 1412 FA,
Neuton by Stouremynstre Marchall 1375 Fine, *New(e)ton by
St(o)urmynstre Marshall, -Marchall* 1377 Cl, 1431 Fine, *Newton*
1431 FA *et freq*, (*the fearme of*) *Newton Peverell* 1583 *Comm*,
'the new farm', *v.* **nīwe, tūn**, cf. East Almer *supra*; Andrew
Peverel held lands in *Stourmistre* in 1244 FF, cf. Bradford
Peverell par. 1 334.

WESTLEY FM & WD (ST 926003), *Westleye* (*by Neweton Peverel*)
1306 Ipm, *boscum de Westlee* 1325 *Wim*, *Westlee closes* 1571
Drax, *Westley Close, copic' voc' Wenstley* (sic) *Coppes* 1593
Lane, *Westly farme* 1690 *Weld*[1], *Westley Grd & Wd, Westleys
8 Acres* 1839 *TA*, 'west wood or woodland glade', *v.* **west, lēah**,
with **copis**, cf. prec.

GT ALMER WD, *Boscum de Estalmere* e14 *Wim*, *v.* East Almer
supra, cf. Lt Almer Wd in Almer par. *infra*. AUSTEN'S PLANT.,
-Cl 1839 *TA*, cf. Thomas *Asten* 1664 HTax. BARROW HILL.
BLACK HORSE P.H. BLUETT'S (lost), 1795 Boswell (a 'manor'),
from the family of Simon *Bluet* l13 *AddCh*, Richard *Bluet* 1586
Hutch[3] 3 344. BONVILLE'S (lost), 1795 Boswell (a 'manor'),

from the family of John *Bonvil* 1397 Hutch[3] 3 344, cf. *clausum heredis d'ni Bonnevyle* 1508 *Eton*, Mapperton in Almer par. *infra*. CAVE'S CORNER, at a corner of the par. CHALK PIT, *the chalke pytt* 1571 *Drax*, cf. *Chalke Pytt Felde* 1593 *Lane, Chalk Pit Fd* 1839 *TA*. LT CHARBOROUGH PIT, from Charborough in Morden par. *infra*. CHURCH DAIRY, near St Mary's Church *infra*. CHURCH HO (remains of); according to Hutch[3] 3 367 'it is called the "tiled house" and also the "minster buildings", and a tradition in the village says that monks were formerly resident here'; perhaps to be associated with the 'vicarage of St Peter's' 1358 Pat, or with the grange of the hospital of St Giles of Pont Audemer (to which the church, then St Peter's, was appropriated) mentioned in 1324 Hutch[3] 3 361 note a, cf. St Mary's Church *infra*. CHURCH HO. (HR) COMBE FM, COMBE ROW, cf. *Coombe cmn* 1839 *TA*, near Combe Almer *supra, v.* rāw 'row of trees'. COXDITCH, *Cock ditch* 1693 *DCMCt, v.* dīc. CRUMPET'S FM, LR CRUMPETS, *Crumpets* (*Pit Close*) 1839 *TA*, no doubt 'crooked pit' from **crumb** and **pytt**, with later explanatory addition of **pytt**, cf. Crumpets Pond in Lytchett Matravers par. *supra*; gravel pits of irregular shape are marked here 6". FIELD DAIRY, *Sturminster F.* 1811 OS. FOX COVERT, cf. foll. FOX HOLES CTGS & WD, *Foxholes* 1839 *TA, v.* **fox-hol**. GORGE'S (lost), 1795 Boswell (a 'manor'), from the family of Ralph *de Gorges* l13 *AddCh*, 1305 Hutch[3] 3 344. GREEN LANE, cf. (*la*) *Grenestrete* 1339 *Wim*, 1593 *Lane* (*v acr' in-*), *Green-street* 1663 *DCMSurv* (*Summer feild called-*), *Greenestreete Fd* 1678 *DCMCt*, (*vie voc'*) *Greene Way* 1677, 1693 *ib, v.* **grēne**[1], **strǣt, weg**. HENBURY PARK (*The Park* 1839 *TA*, cf. *parcum de Sturmenistr'* 1244 Cl, Cantor & Wilson 1 112, and foll.) & PLANT. (*Hynbury Wood* 1545 Hutch[3]), from Henbury *supra*. HERON GROVE, situated at the edge of Henbury Park *supra*, so first el. is perhaps to be associated with *la Parkes hurne* 1339 *Wim*, 'the corner of the park', if this form in fact refers to Henbury Park, *v.* **park, hyrne**; however *Heron* may be a surname, cf. John *Harang* l13 *Wim*. HOVEL'S CTGS. JUBILEE BRICK WORKS & CTGS. LIMEKILN COPPICE, cf. *le lime pitt* 1687 *DCMCt, Lymepitts* 1693 *ib*. LION LODGE (PLANT.). LOOP'S (lost), 1795 Boswell (a 'manor'), from the family of Thomas *Loop* 1581 Hutch[3] 3 350. MAGG'S BRIDGE, cf. *the bridge going into the greate meade, the bridge at William Cotmans* 1690 *Weld*[1]. MILLMORE, *Myll'moore*

1593 *Lane*, cf. Adam *atte Mulle* 1329 *Wim, molendinum* ...*apud Stourmynstre Marchall* 1449 *DLCt, Lake mill* 1773 Bayly, Mill Ho Grd 1839 *TA*, *v.* **myln, mōr, atte**; there were two mills at Sturminster Marshall in 1086 DB, *v.* VCHDo 3 89. MOOR LANE, cf. *le comen moore* 1513 *Pars, ye Moore close* 1514 *ib, ditch along by Moor* 1691 *Weld*[1], *v.* **mōr.** NEW BLDGS. NEWTON CTG & RD, cf. *Newton Marsh* 1811 OS, from Newton Peveril *supra.* NOTTING HILL, part of *Henbury Hill* (cf. Henbury *supra*) with a gazebo on it, perhaps transferred from Notting Hill Mx 129. PHILPOTT'S ROW, cf. The Row *infra.* RED LION INN, 1839 *TA.* THE ROW, cf. *Row* 1839 *TA*, *v.* **rāw.** ST MARY'S CHURCH, 'the church (of St Peter) of *(E)sturminstr(i)a, -min(i)stre*' 1152–1204 France, *ecclesie de Esturmunstr*' 1268 *Ass et freq,* 'church of *Stormenistre Marchal*' 1285 FF, cf. *cemiterium* 1508 *Eton, Church Acre* 1677 *DCMCt,* Church St., Church Dairy & Ho all *supra.* HR SANDY COPPICE, *Sandy Coppice* 1839 *TA,* cf. Lr Sandy Coppice in Lytchett Matravers par. *supra.* SPRING COPPICE, 1839 *TA (Lt-),* cf. foll. SPRINGFIELD FM. SQUARE PIT. STAG GATE (PLANT.), a gate (surmounted by a stag) of Charborough Park in Morden par. *infra.* STURMINSTER FDS (lost), 1811 OS, cf. *in campo ville de Stourminstre* 1325 *Wim, in comunibus campis de Sturmyst' Marshall* 1593 *Lane.* THREE CORNERED CLUMP. TIREL'S (lost), 1795 Boswell (a 'manor'), from the family of Hugh *Tirel* 1343 Hutch[3] 3 350. TOWNSEND, 1839 *TA, Townesend Cl* 1593 *Lane, v.* **toun, ende**[1]. VINES CLOSE. WADHAM'S (lost), 1795 Boswell (a 'manor'), from the family of William *Wadham* 1508 *AddCh,* Nicholas *Wadham* n.d. Hutch[3] 3 350. WEST WD (2 ×). WHITE MILL BRIDGE, [*pons de*] *Wytemull* 1341 *Wim, Whytt(e)myll(e) Brygge* 1514, 1515 *Pars, Whitemyll bridge* 1593 *Lane, the bridge at Whitmill Casway* 1690 *Weld*[1], named from White Mill in Shapwick par. *infra,* probably also the bridge referred to as *pontem de Stourminstre Marshal* 1337 DorR, *pons voc' Sturmynsterbrigge* 1468 *MinAcct,* but cf. Maggs' Bridge *supra, v.* **brycg, cauce.**

FIELD-NAMES

The undated forms are 1839 *TA* 211. Spellings dated 113[2], 1352, 1588 are *AddCh,* 1298 Ipm, 1327 *SR,* 1331, 1557, 1832 Hutch[3], 1332 SR, 1332[2], 1465 Pat, 1348, 1350, 1448, 1462, 1508 *DCMDeed,* 1366 Misc, 1382 FF, 1404 Cl, 1426 *Midd,* 1504 *DLCt,* 1508[2] *Eton,* 1512–1525 *Pars,* 1571, 1682, 1683, 1692[2]

Drax, 1593 *Lane*, 1627, 1653, 1663 *DCMSurv*, 1664 HTax, 1677, 1678, 1686, 1687, 1689, 1692, 1693, 1694 *DCMCt*, 1690, 1691 *Weld*[1], and the rest *Wim*.
(*a*) Bakers Cl, Grd & 10 Acres (cf. William *le Baker* 1332); Bangers Barn; Bartons grd; Bests cl (cf. Thomas *Beste* 1504); Bottom Fd; Breach Cl (*le Brache* e14, *brache* 1571, *le Breache* 1593, *Breech* 1689, *v*. **brēc, brǣc**); Bullans Cl (*Bullens*- 1593); Burland (perhaps (**ge**)**būr-land** 'land occupied by peasants'); Bushey Cl & Leaze (*Bus*(*s*)*che Clo*(*o*)*se*, -*Closee* 1512–1516, *Busschy close* 1525, *Bushie lease* 1653, *v*. **busc, lǣs**, cf. *Bush*(*h*)*edge* 1677, 1687); Chinns plot (cf. Nicholas *Chynne* l13); Clipper cl (perhaps identical with *Clepit*- 1653, *Claypit Cl* 1663, cf. *Clay Pitts* 1677, *v*. **clǣg, pytt**); Conygar (*v*. **coninger**); Cotmans Grd (cf. Thomas *Cottman* 1664, Maggs' Bridge *supra*); Cottage Leaze (*v*. **lǣs**); Court and pasture; Cowleaze; Crabtree Cl; Crumplers Cl, Crumplico Plot, David Hay & Lane (cf. Christopher Davys 1664, v. (ge)hæg); Dean Cl (cf. *le-*, *the dene* 1508, *Deanes Bottome* 1677, *v*. **denu, botm**); Dung-, Duns Hay(e)s (*v*. (**ge**)**hæg**); Durhams plot and Barn; Dykes Cl (cf. Elizabeth *Dycke* 1593); 8 Acres (*culturam que vocatur eyȝtacres* e14, *v*. **eahta, æcer**); Firs; (The) 5, 4 & 14 Acres; Frog Lane; Furze(y) Cl & Grd; Gallops 1832 (cf. John *Gallopp* 1627); Late Galpins Ctg; Golds Plot (cf. Robert *Golde* l13); Greens (7 Acres); Hr Hams (*v*. **hamm**); Hardens (Ho) (cf. John *Hardinge* 1627); Hay Barn Leaze (*v*. **lǣs**); Higher Grd; Hilly Grd; Home Cl (Orchd); Home Fd, Grd, Mdw & Plot; Hoopers Cl; House Plot; In Md (*v*. **in**); King Orchd Ctg; Lights Grd (cf. Andrew *Light* 1664); Long Cl (1653), Fd & Grd; Long Johns; Lower Grd; Mackrells Leaze (cf. *Relict' Thom' Makerel* 1327, *v*. **lǣs**); Manor Ho; the Marsh (cf. *Wynterbourne Mersch* 1339, *v*. **mersc**; R. Winterborne flows through the par.); Mead Plot; Middle Cl & Fd (*the myddle fyld*(*e*) 1571); Milking Cl (*v*. **milking**); Mow Plot (*v*. **mow**); New Fd; Newfoundland (possibly a transferred name, but cf. 1 314; it is not a remote field); The 9 Acres ((*camp' voc*') *nyneacres* 1593, 1693, *Novem* (sic) 1693, cf. *Nyne Acres Quary* 1677); Oak Fd (cf. *Oclond* e14, *v*. **āc, land**); Old Hayes (*hill of Oldehey* 1298, *Old*(*e*)*hayes* 1571, 1593, *v*. **ald,** (**ge**)**hæg**); Ox Leaze; Parkers Cl (cf. Abraham *Parker* 1664); Parsonage Plot (cf. 'vicarage of St Peter's' 1358, *clausum vicarii vel Rectoris* 1508[2]); Pit (Fd); The Plot; Pond(s) Cl; Pounders; Pudding Fd (*v*. **pudding**, perhaps denoting soft ground, or for *pudding-grass* 'pennyroyal'); Robins Ho & Orchd; Roundabout 8 & 7 acres; Round Cl & Mdw; Ryelands (*Rilands* 1653); Saverns Grd; 7 Acres (*Septem acre* l13, *Sevenacre* e14); Short Cl; Small Cl & Ho; South Fd (Pdk) (*in campo australi* e14 *et freq*, the *Southfylde called Penworthe* 1571, cf. *Pendeworthe infra*); Starve Lds; Staysons; (The) 10 Acres (*10 Acres* 1653); 3 Grounds; 12 Acres; Long 2 Acres; Watts Cl; Well Cl; West Fd (*in campo occidentali* 1246 *et freq*); West Leaze (-*lease* 1653, *v*. **lǣs**); Whitemans Plot; Willis's (grd and barn); Wood Fd (cf. *Wodacre* e14, *Little Woodsheard* 1677, *v*. **wudu, æcer, sceard**).

(*b*) *in campo de Estalmere* m13 (cf. East Almer *supra*); *Apeshull* 1246 (*v*. **æspe** 'aspen-tree', **hyll**); (*H*)*aschemede* 1512, 1513, *Ashmead Copice* 1653, *Ash Mead* 1691 (*v*. **æsc**, cf. *Hachemede infra*); *Aunlett Croft* 1516; *Barly Cl* 1653; *Barries* 1593 (probably a surname); *Beauchampesmaner* 1404, 1465 (from the *Beauchamp* family which was here from 1299 (Hutch[3] 3 338–9), *v*. **manere**); *Beere Way* 1693 ('road to Barford' (in Pamphill par. *infra*), or 'to Bere Regis' (1 273)); (*West*)*ber*(*e*)-, (*Estere-*, *Vest*)*berforlang*, -*furlong* l13, e14, *la Berlynche* e14 (v. **bere** 'barley', **furlang**, **ēasterra**, **hlinc**, cf. Barlinch So (DEPN)); *vna acra iacet Byestoune* 1295, *bi-* e14, *Byesteton(e)* 1322 ('east of the village' (probably East Almer *supra*), v. **bī, ēastan, toun**); *la-, le blakethurne* l13, e14 (v. **blæc, þyrne**); *cultur' q' voc' (le) Bottes* e14, *lez buttes* 1593 (v. **butte**); (*acr'*) *super Bovie* 1677, -*Boorne* 1693 (probably the same place); *claus' voc' Bradpollis* 1512 (a surname from Bradpole par. *infra*); *Broad Lds* 1677; *Bromehill* 1593 (v. **brōm**); *Bro(o)de Croft* 1512, 1513, *Bradcraftes* 1571 (v. **brād, croft**); *claus' voc' Brownys* 1512 (cf. the *New Inne infra*); *claus' voc' Brytons* 1512 (the surname *Briton, Breton*); *le Cauxey, le Cawxey* 1515 (v. **cauce**); *Chypylthorn* 1525 *AOMB*, *Chipple-* 1571, *Chipell-* 1591, *Cheple Thorne* 1677, *camp' voc' Chipthorn* 1593 (perhaps **cipp** 'log' or an OE pers.n. ***Cippa** (cf. DEPN s.n. Chipley), with **hyll, þorn**); *le Chur Aker* e14 (v. **cerr** (WSax **cierr**) 'a (river) bend'; *Clift* 1693 (v. **clif**); *Cockrode* 1653, -*road* 1663 (v. **cocc-rodu**); *hill of Colflad* 1298 (form doubtful); *Cornes Cl* 1653 (cf. William *Corne* 1593); *Cors(s)ersham* 1512, 1513 (v. **hamm**); *Cot(t)haies* 1653, 1663, -*hayes* 1686 (v. **cot, (ge)hæg**; (*cultura voc'*) *La Croft(e)* e14, 1335 (v. **croft**); *Crowthorne* 1513 (v. **crāwe, þorn**); *Culuerham* 1448, *Culverhayes* 1593 (v. **culfre, hamm, (ge)hæg**); *Deadland* 1693 (cf. foll.); *Dedde Lake* 1514, *Dead(e) Lacke* 1593, 1690 (*the bridge at-*), -*lake* 1677 (v. **dēad, lacu**, cf. Dead Lake D 5); *Dedde poole* 1513 (v. **pōl**[1], cf. prec.); *Dedman' feld* 1593 (probably an old burial site, v. **dēad**); *Dokham* 1298, *prat' voc' Dockum* 1508[2], *Dokking, Doccing* 1515, *Dokkeham* 1519, *Dockeham* 1593, *Dock(h)am(e) (Meade)* 1653, 1663, 1678 (v. **docce, hamm**); *Dowcraftes* 1571 (ME *Dow-*, a pet-form of *David*, v. **croft**); (*le*) *drof-* 1348, *drafaker* 1350, 1462 (v. **drāf, æcer**); *Alde-* l13, *Ealde-* e14, *Eldecroft(e)* e14, 1335, 1426 (v. **ald** (WSax **eald**), **croft**); *Efurlang* 1298, *Eyforlong* 1516, *Everlongs* 1593, *Everland* 1693 (v. **ēg, furlang**; *Elmon' Stubbe* 1508 (v. **elmen, stubb**); *El(le)forlang, -vorlang* e14 (v. **elle(r)n**); *in campo orientali (de Estalmere)* l13, *Estfelde* e14 (v. **ēast, feld**, East Almer *supra*); *Estgardin* 1369 (v. **gardin**); *Ettelonde* l13 (v. **ete, land**); *Faber Crosse* 1512, 1515 (*Seynt Sonday crosse vell-*), *Seynt Sondays crosse* 1516 (the ME pers.n. or surname *Faber*, v. **cros**; *Seynt Sonday* is St Dominic, v. NED s.v. *Sunday*); *the farmers fields* 1653; *Flookes hedge* 1593 (cf. Richard *Flouk* 1332); *Fookes Heade Flg* 1677 (cf. Robert *Fuke* l13, v. **hēafod**); *de la forlane* l13 (p) (**fōr** 'pig' or **fore** 'front'); *Foremeade* 1593 (v. **fore**); *de la ȝerde* 1302, *de la Yurd, de Virga* e14, *atte ȝurd* 1334 all (p) (v. **atte, gerd** (WSax **gierd**)); *the great(e) meade, -meadow* 1690; *la guldenelonde* e14 (v. **gylden, land**); *Hachemede* 1512 (v. **hæc(c)**, but perhaps identical with (*H)aschemede supra*); *Hamstede* e14 (v. **hām-stede**); *Hefdacre* e14 (v. **hēafod, æcer**); *Heg Acre* l13 (...*iuxta Hayam*), *le hegeakres* e14 (v. **hecg** 'hedge'); *de la Hele* e14, *Atte Hyle* 1321, *in le hyle* 1327, *in the Hyle* 1332, *atte Hale* 1352 all (p), *Hylemede* 1366 (v. **healh** (dat.sg. **hēale**), **mǣd**); *Henforlang* e14 (v. **henn**); *le Hethe Fylde* 1525 *AOMB* (v. **hǣð**); *la hulle* 1246, *super montem* 1322, *Hyll Cl* 1593 (v. **hyll**, cf. John *Uppehulle* 1327, 'up on the hill', v. **uppan**); *la Holeden* 1339 (v. **hol**[2], **denu**); *Holme mede* 1525 (v. **holegn**); *Hooke land* 1694 (v. **hōc**); *Hoverþeweye que ducit versus Craford* e14 ('(land) across the road to Crawford (in Spettisbury par. *infra*)', v. **ofer**[3], **weg**); *haya...que voc' Hoyrawe* e14 (probably for *Hey-*, v. **hege, rāw**); *Pykyd Hurst* 1512, *Picked-, Pycked & Rounde Hurste* 1627, *Hurst (lease)* 1653 (v. **pīcede** 'pointed', **round, hyrst**, læs); (H)ywenemede 1300, 1335 (v. hīwan (gen.pl. hīw(e)na) 'household', mæd); Inseland 1512, Ingelond (sic) 1513, Endsland 1691; Jacob(be)s drove 1593, 1693 (v. drāf); Kateby Put e14 (v. pytt); Ken(e)ley(e) e14 (the OE pers.n. Cēna and lēah, cf. Kenley Sa, Sr); Kyllyngwort(t)hys (cloose) 1512, -Closys 1513 (perhaps a surname from Killingworth Nb); Knave acr' 1693 (v. cnafa); the lampe halfe acre 1508, Lampeland 1537 (v. lampe); Langgehegge e14 (v. lang¹, hecg); Laxted forlong e14 (the first el. may be the OE pers.n. *Leaxa found in to leaxan oc in Winterborne T. par. infra, perhaps with stede 'site'); Lytellonde 1295, Litlelonde, Litelemede e14 (v. lȳtel, land, mæd); Lockeforlange 1325 (v. loc(a)); Long Acres e14; Long Combe 1677 (cf. Combe Almer supra); Long(ge) Croft 1512, Longe craftes 1571 (v. croft); Loudsor Acre m13; newe Marvyll 1571 (cf. Merveile in Canford Magna par. supra); Michelesbodok 1468 (the ME pers.n. Michel); Mideforlong 1295, Medfurlong l13, Mid-, Medforlang e14, le Middle Furlong 1693 (v. midd 'middle'); Mochyl-, -el-, Muc(c)hel(l)-med(e) 1514, 1515 (v. mycel); New Croft 1512; the New Inne 1519 (claus' quond' Brownys super quod quond' stetit-) (v. inn, cf. Brownys supra); de la Nordene l13² (p) (cf. in borialiori cumba l13, v. norð, denu); in campo boreali l13, in campo boriali de Sturmenstre Mar' e14, the northe fylde 1571; Norvilus Hegge 1329 (cf. John Norvile 1329, v. hecg); loc' voc' Old Strete 1516 (v. strǣt, no doubt with reference to the Dorchester–Badbury Roman road which crosses the par. near Moorcourt Fm, cf. the f.n. Kingway in Almer par. infra); campo de Pendeworthe e14, Peynde- 1335, Penworth(e) 1571 (the Southfylde called-), 1677, Pennorthe 1593, Penneth 1663 (Summer feild called-), 1689 ('Penda's enclosure', from the rare OE pers.n. Penda and worð, cf. Pinbury Gl 1 73); Pitts Acre 1677; Plowmans 1571 (cf. Benjamin Plowman 1664); Poyschis- 1348, Possche- 1350, Po(o)ssheslond(e) 1416, 1462, Poysche hurst 1512, Poysche-, (le) Poische hegge 1513–1516, Poysche Mede 1513 (the ME surname Poissh (1332 SR 5), with land, hecg, mæd, cf. Hurst supra); le Possokes, Possokesdone e14 (v. dūn; Possokes is obscure); Post hedge 1593 (v. post); Pykyd Acre 1515 (v. pīcede); Quenegore 1298 (v. cwēn, gāra); Ridon Hill 1677 (probably 'rye hill' from ryge and dūn); Rodways 1593, -way 1677 (v. rād-weg); Roubergh' 1334 (v. rūh, beorg, cf. foll.); Roweley(e), Roweleys-forlong, -hegge e14 ('(furlong and hedge at) the rough clearing', v. rūh (wk.obl. rūgan), lēah, hecg); the Runynge Acre 1593 (v. running); Sangers Md 1653; la Schylond (sic) 1339, Shippelond 1508, Sheepeland 1694 (v. scēap, scī(e)p); le Schyphurdes Gore e14 (v. scēap-hirde, gāra); Scottes-, -is goose leese, -leez 1514, 1515 (v. læs, cf. Richard Scutt 1512, Stotteslond infra); Shoddeslane 1331, Shotesdene 1332² (cf. Stephen Shudde 1329, v. lane, denu); Six Acres 1653; claus' voc' Skytys 1512; Slootree- 1653, Slootry Close 1663 (v. slāh-trēow); Smeþedone e14 (v. smēðe¹, dūn); Stabelborghe e14 (v. beorg, first el. ME stable 'a stable'); Stanylond e14, Stone-, Stony(e) Croft 1512, 1513, Ston(y)e Lane 1513, 1515 (v. stān, stānig, land, croft, lane); dom' voc' Staples 1512, pontem de Le Staples 1513, le Staples brigge 1514, Stapull Byrge 1525 (v. stapol 'post', brycg); Stotteslond e14 (v. stott, or the surname Stott, but perhaps for Scott-, cf. Scottes goose leese supra); Sturmynster leez 1515 (v. læs); Sturmester Mede(e) 1513, 1515, Sturmister Meade 1588 (cf. pastur' de Sturminstre e14, ye medew of Sturmyster 1512, le Mede scherde 1515, the common meadoes of Sturmynster Marshall 1571, v. mæd, sceard); Symoneslond ll3, *Symondeslond*, *-put* e14 (the ME pers.n. *Simon(d)*, *v.* **land, pytt**); *the tenents fields* 1653; *Thornford* 1693 (*v.* **þorn, ford**); *Thorne Goale* 1677 (perhaps **go(u)le** 'ditch'); *Totyesthorn* e14 (probably a pers.n. (cf. ODan *Toti*), *v.* **þorn**); *Ye Vycary Leez* 1512 (*v.* **vicarie, læs**); *Wereweye* 1339, *Werland* 1677 (first el. perhaps **wer** 'a weir', with **weg, land**); *Biwestewode* 1322 ('(land) to the west of the wood', *v.* **bī, westan, wudu**); *la Westrelinche* ll3 (*v.* **westerra, hlinc**); *la Wetelond(e)* 1339, 1345 (*v.* **wēt, land**); *the Wheat feilds* 1690, *Wheate Land* 1693 (*v.* **hwǣte**); *Whitys* 1508 (cf. Walter *le White* 1327); *Whitting Ash* 1677, 1693, *Whiting gates* 1693 (*v.* **whitten** 'water elder, mountain-ash'); *Wychegrave* 1298, *Whychegraue* 1448, *Wiche Grove* 1593 (*v.* **wice** 'wych-elm', **grāf(a)**)); *Wirfurlong* ll3, *Wyrforlong* e14 (probably from **wīr** 'bog myrtle', cf. foll.); *le Wirthorne* e14 (*v.* **þorn**. Professor Löfvenberg notes that this would seem to be an early instance of dial. *wire-thorn* 'the yew' (Taxus baccata), recorded by EDD only from NCy; he adds, however, that the term may be used here to denote some kind of wild myrtle, comparing OE *wīr-trēow* 'myrtle' and NED s.vv. *myrtle* (sense 2c) and *myrtle-tree*); *terram Willelmi in La Yle* 1325 (*v.* **ile**).

X. LOOSEBARROW HUNDRED

In c. 1086 GeldR this small hundred (then called *Celeberge*) had its present extent except that it then included West Morden (now a tithing in Rushmore hundred, though in Morden par. *infra*) (Anderson 125, VCHDo 3 136, Eyton 117-8).

Celeberge hundret c. 1086 GeldR
Lusebergehdr' 1130 PR, *-berga(hundredum)* 1170–1185 P, *-berg(h)(e)* 1219, 1226–8 Fees, 1244 *Ass*, 1251–2 Fees, 1268 *Ass et freq* to 1332 Pat, *-berehe* 1265 Misc, *-borgh* 1303 FA, *-burgh* 1315 Fine, 1352, 1369 Pat, *Lusburgh* 1268 *Ass*, 1344 Fine, 1414 Cl, *-bergh* 1303, 1428 FA, *-bargh* 1470, 1475 *Weld*[1], *Dimidium Hundredum de Lusseberwe* 1280 *Ass*
Loseberg(h)(e) 1212 Fees, 1280 *Ass*, 1315 Ipm, 1316 FA, 1326 *Wim* (*quartem partem hundredi et bedelrie de-*), 1340 NI, 1361 IpmR, *-berwe* 1280 *Ass*, *-burgh* 1323 Inq aqd, *-bargh* 1431 FA, *Losberg* 1268 *Ass*
Lesseberewe (sic) 1275 RH
Louseberouwe 1306 Ipm, *-burgh* 1318 Pat, 1388 FF, *-bergh* 1330 Pat, 1332 SR, 1343 Orig, Pat, *Lousbergh(e)* 1376 FF, 1389 *Wim*, *Lowsbarrow* 1692 *Weld*[1]

The 11th cent. name is from Charborough in Morden par. *infra*. Loosebarrow means 'louse-infested, or small and insignificant, barrow or hill', from **lūs** (gen.pl. *lūsa*) and **beorg**; according to Hutch³ 3 494 it was the name of a barrow (then almost levelled) 'near the west end of Charborough Down', where the hundred courts were formerly held, so that the change of name does not indicate a change of meeting place (cf. Rowbarrow hundred 1 4). The name Loosebarrow is identical with *on lusa beorg* 934 BCS 699, cf. *on lusebeorg* 940 ib 748 (both W), and probably with the f.ns. Laus-, Laws-, Lowsborough in Dorchester 1 362, Lousebarrow in Corfe M. par., and Lush Barrows in Kinson par. (all *supra*); for a discussion of the meaning and form of the name, *v.* Forsberg 182–6. In 1332 SR the tithing of Spettisbury in this hundred is itself called *Lousebergh*, *v.* Spettisbury par. *infra*.

Almer

This par. was transferred to Sturminster Marshall par. *supra* in 1933.

ALMER (SY 914989)
    (*of-*, *on*) *elmere* 943 (15) ShaftR (S 490), *Elmerham* 1166 RBE
    (cf. Hutch³ 1 711), *Elmer* 1211 Cur, *Elmere*, *-mera* 1211 ib
    (p)
    Almer(e) 1212 Fees, 1227 FF, 1228 Cl, 1231 FF, 1235–6 Fees,
      1246 Ipm *et passim*, *Au(e)mer(e)* 1244 Ass, *Alle-* l13 Wim,
      Ail- 1270 (1372) ChrP, *Aylmer(e)* 1288 Ass, *Alme* 1434
      Midd
    Almor(e) 1244 Ass, 1664 HTax, 1692 Weld[1]
    Westalmere e14 Wim, *-Almere* 1408 FF

'Eel pool', *v.* **ǣl, mere**[1], with reference to a pool on R. Winterborne just SE of the village, cf. Elmer Sx 142; the pool is no doubt that called *Almer Pond* 1844 *TA* and that referred to in *mesuagium desuper Le Mere, Merfurlong* l13, William *de la Mere* 1295, e14 all *Wim*, Reginald- 1327 *SR*, John *atte Mere* 1332 SR, *v.* **furlang, atte**. The 943 forms occur (with reference to the pool) as the starting and finishing points in the bounds of Mapperton *infra*, which in OE times and in DB was the name of the estate later comprising the modern par. of Almer. *Elmerham* 1166 may mean 'homestead, or enclosure, at *Elmer*', *v.* **hām, hamm**. *Au(e)mere* shows AN vocalization of *l*, *v.* ANInfl 146f. *Almor(e)* shows confusion of the second el. with

mōr 'moor'. *West-* distinguishes this place from the adjacent East Almer in Sturminster M. par. *supra, v.* **west**.

MAPPERTON (FM) (SY 906987)

> (*at-, to*) *Mapeldertune* 943 (15) *ShaftR* (S 490)
>
> *Mapledretone* 1086 DB, *Mapeldureton, Mapeldorthon* 1244 *Ass, Mapeldor-* 1268 *ib, Mapelder-* 1280 *ib, Mapilderton(e)* 1288 *ib*
>
> ?*Mapertune* 1086 DB, *-tona* Exon, *Maperton* 1212 Fees, 1385 FF, 1545 *Whil* (*-otherwyse called Maplerton*), 1692 *Weld*[1]
>
> *Mapellerton* 1316 FA, *Mapelerton* 1326 Ipm, 1327 Cl *et freq* to 1441 *Midd* (*-Filoll*), 1453 *ib* (*-Bonevyle et Filoll*), *Maplerton* 1434 *ib*, 1863 Hutch[3]

'Maple-tree farm', *v.* **mapuldor, tūn**, cf. Mapperton par. *infra*. On the doubtful identification of DB *Mapertune* (Exon *-tona*) (½ hide here was an outlying member of the manor of Puddletown), *v.* Eyton 118 fn., VCHDo 3 66. The 15th cent. affixes *-Filoll* and *-Bonevyle* are from the families of Hugh *Fyllol* e14 *Wim*, William *Filloil* 1335 *ib*, John *Filiol* 1406 Hutch[3] 3 495, and John *Bonvil* 1397 ib 3 344, cf. Bonville's in Sturminster M. par. *supra* and *furlong voc' Bonesyfylye, Bonevyle* 1426 *Midd*. The bounds of Mapperton are given in 943 (15) *ShaftR* (S 490) *v.* par. name *supra*, Forsberg 205, cf. Grundy 1 244ff.

LT ALMER WD, 1844 *TA*, cf. Gt Almer Wd in Sturminster M. par. *supra*. WEST ALMER FM & LODGE. THE BORDER, a narrow wood bordering a road. COLL WOOD CTG, GREAT COLL WD, *Colwod(e)* 1284 Cl, 1460 *DCMDeed, copse calledde Colewoode* 1549 *Midd, Coll Wood* 1587 *ib*, 1844 *TA, Great Colwood* 1863 Hutch[3], possibly 'wood where charcoal was burnt', from **col**[1] 'coal, charcoal' and **wudu**, cf. Little Coll Wd in Spettisbury par. *infra*, Cole Wd in Wool 1 191. However the first el. may be **coll** 'hill' with reference to the hill spur here. The wood is on the par. bdy, and is that referred to in the OE bounds of the adjacent par. of Winterborne T. in the forms *to widesgete* 'to the gate of the wood' and *anlang wides* 'along the wood', *v. infra*. CROSS (remains of). HIGHER BARN. LEGG'S CLUMP. PARLIAMENT HO, at a point where the bounds of three pars.

meet. OLD RECTORY WD, cf. *terr' Rectoris de Alme(re)* 1434
Midd. ST MARY'S CHURCH, cf. *ecclesie de Almere* 1323 *AddCh.*
WORLD'S END (P.H.), 1811 OS, *Worlds End (Marsh)* 1844 *TA.*

FIELD-NAMES

The undated forms are 1844 *TA* 5. Spellings dated 943 (15) are *ShaftR* (S 490);
1327 are *SR*, 1332 SR, 1426, 1434 *Midd*, 1664 HTax, 1682, 1683, 1692 *Drax*,
1791 Boswell, and the rest *Wim.*

(*a*) Hr & Lr Almer Bridges 1791, Almer Pond (*v.* par. name *supra*);
Bravelands Md; Bushes Cl; Cowleaze; Crawford Bushes Fd (from Gt
Crawford in Spettisbury par.); Crumplers Leaze; David Lane Fd; (Lt)
Down; 11 Acres; Glebe Ld; Great Fd & Md; (Hr) Ground(s); Hayleaze;
Hedgerow (cf. *of* (for *on*) *þa hege reawe, onlang heie reawe* 943 (15), *v.* **hege-ræw**);
Hill Croft (cf. *le hulle* 1426, *v.* **hyll**); Hills Md; Home Cl ((*le-*) 1682, 1683)
& Fd; Inside Fd; (Lt) Kingway, Kingway Fd (*Kyngwey* 1426, *v.* **cyning, weg**,
with reference to the Dorchester–Badbury Roman road which crosses this
par.; the road is also referred to in *on þe elþen* (for *elden*) *stret, of þare streate*
943 (15), 'the old street', *v.* **ald**, WSax **eald** (wk.obl. *ealdan*), **strǣt**, cf. *Old*
Strete in Sturminster M. par. *supra*; for the form *elþen*, cf. the similar scribal
confusion of OE *þ*, *ð* and *d* in two other late copies of charters from *ShaftR*
noted under *Hollish* in Corfe C. 1 14); Lime Kiln; Little Md; Long Fd; Long
Marsh (cf. (*le*) *marsh close* 1682, 1683, *v.* **mersc**); Mapperton Drove & Hill;
Meadow; New Breach (*v.* **brǣc**) & Md; 9 Acres; Oakley's Cl (cf. John *de Ocle*
1335, probably from Oakley in Canford M. par. *supra*); Orchard; Park or Cold
Arbor (cf. *le Lese park* 1426, *v.* **lǣs, park, cald, here-beorg**); Pasture Plot;
Gt & Lt Peak (*v.* **pēac**); Plantation; Pond (Fd); Rickyard; Sellers Ld (cf.
Elizabeth *Seller* 1664); South Md; Water Swallow Fd (*v.* **swealg** 'a pit'); Tag
Hill (*v.* **tagga** 'a young sheep'); Warlands (cf. *Werland* in Sturminster M.
par. *supra*); Well Fd; West Fd; Wood Fd (cf. *to wþe* (for *wde*), *Innen wde* 943
(15), *v.* **wudu**; for the scribal confusion, cf. Kingway *supra*).

(*b*) *to þere alde dich, þanne andlang diche* 943 (15) (*v.* **ald** (wk.obl. *aldan*),
dīc); *Almer Greene* 1692 (*v.* **grēne²**); *Brodemede* 1426 (*v.* **brād, mǣd**); *Cacke*
ulle e14, *Cattehull* 1426 (cf. *Catelesforlang* e14, probably from **catt** (gen.pl.
catta) and **hyll**, with **furlang**; *Cacke-* is probably for *Catte-*, with *ck* due to
misreading of *tt* as *cc*); *to-, of cellor* 943 (15) (perhaps a poor spelling for OE
ceolor 'throat, channel, gorge'); *le Combe* 1426 (*v.* **cumb**); *on anne crundel,*
of þane crundele 943 (15) (*v.* **crundel**); *on þa dich* 943 (15) (*v.* **dīc**); *Elfurlongespitt*
1426 (cf. *Elforlang* in Sturminster M. f.ns. *supra*, *v.* **pytt**); *Furnedon* 1426 (*v.*
dūn; first el. possibly **fergen** (WSax **fi(e)rgen** 'hill', or an OE **(ge)fierne*
'fern brake', cf. Fern Down in Hampreston par. *infra*); *Geldynges-* 1426,
Goldyngescote 1434 (the surname *Gelding* or *Golding*, with **cot**); *on grenenhille*
943 (15) (*v.* **grēne¹** (wk.obl. *grēnan*), **hyll**); *to-, of horgate* 943 (15) (at the point
where the bounds of Almer and Winterborne T. meet at the S tip of Gt Coll
Wd, and identical with *on hornget, of horngetes hirne* 942 (15) *ShaftR* (S 485(1))
in the bounds of Winterborne T. par. *infra*, *v.* **geat** 'gate', **hyrne** 'corner,
angle'; the first el. is **horn** (of which **hyrne** is a derivative) 'horn, something

shaped like a horn', with reference either to an animal's horn used to decorate the gate (cf. EPN 1 261, Hornchurch Ess 112) or to the hill spur here (for the loss of *n* in *hor-*, *v*. Forsberg 204), cf. Gt Coll Wd *supra* and also the f.n. Woodhorn ¼ mile S of Gt Coll Wd in Winterborne Z. par. *infra*); *on hþete* (for *hwete*) *cumb, anlang cumbes* 943 (15), *Whatcombe* 1434 (*v*. hwǣte 'wheat', cumb; this OE bdy point is wrongly identified with Whatcombe in Winterborne W. par. by Fägersten 68, *v*. Forsberg 205); *Hydelond* 1434 (*v*. hīd, land); *in le Hyle* 1327, *in thehyle* 1332 both (p) (cf. Sturminster M. f.ns. *supra*); *Langelond* 1434 (*v*. lang[1], land); *Langemede* 1426 (*v*. mǣd); *Langethorn* 1426 (*v*. þorn); *Leunespitt* 1426 (the surname *Leon* or a reduced form of the OE pers.n. *Lēofwine, v*. pytt); *on-, of limbenlee* 943 (15) (*v*. lēah; first el. perhaps corrupt for linden 'growing with lime-trees'); *to-, of molenhame* 943 (15) (*v*. hamm; first el. perhaps corrupt for *melen-, v*. myl(e)n 'mill'); *atte More* 1332 (p) (*v*. atte, mōr; *le piledlond* 1426 ('strip marked by stakes', *v*. pīl, -ede, land); *on Ruþanþorn* (for *Ruwan-*), *of þane þorne* 943 (15) (*v*. rūh (wk.obl. *rūgan, rūwan*), þorn); *on sex þorne, of sex þorne* 943 (15) (*v*. þorn 'thorn-tree'; first el. probably sex 'six'); *anlang standene* 943 (15) (*v*. stān, denu; this bdy point is wrongly associated with Den Wood in Winterborne T. par. *infra* by Fägersten 67, *v*. Forsberg 205); *on-, of stanhecheres ande* 943 (15) (*v*. ende[1]; *stanhecheres* is probably for *stanæceres* (Tengstrand 181), *v*. stān, æcer); *on anne þorn þiuel* 943 (15) (*v*. þorn, þȳfel); *on anne weie* and *an lang weies* both 943 (15) (*v*. weg); *on weritun, of wertune* 943 (15) (*v*. tūn; first el. possibly wering 'weir, dam' alternating with wer); *le Westfeld* 1426 (*v*. west, feld); *Wikele* 113, *Weeckley Wood* 1692 (*v*. wīc, lēah); *on windee bergh, of þane berghe* 943 (15) (*v*. beorg; the first el. is perhaps corrupt for *windie* from OE windig 'windy', cf. Woodbury Hill in Bere R. 1 277 with which this form was wrongly identified by Fägersten 70).

Morden

In 1894 parts of the out-parishes of Wareham St Martin and Lady St Mary were added to Morden, but a large area in Morden in 1844 (*TA*) is now included in Wareham St Martin. Charborough was formerly a separate parish. West Morden is a tithing in Rushmore hundred *infra*.

MORDEN (SY 916956), EAST & WEST MORDEN
    Mordune 1086 DB (2 ×), n.d. AD I, *-dun(a)* 112 Hutch[3], 1219
    Fees, 1250 ib (*Est-*), 1288 *Ass, -don(e), -dona* 1086 DB (3 ×),
    Exon (2 ×), 1173–5 (1329 Ch, 1194 P, 1196 FF, 1212 Fees
    et freq to 1568 *Drax* (*Easte-, Weast-*), with additions *-Roberti*
    1242–3 Fees, *Est-* from 1250 Fees, *West-* from 1275 RH,
    Mordoun 1399–1422 Cl, *Morton* 1268 *Ass*
    Morden 1196 Cur(P), 1250 Fees (*Est-*) *et freq* to 1596 *AD*
    (*Easte-, Weste-*), *Est Morden als. Morden Matravers* 1562
    Hutch[3], *Morden East or Matraverse* 1795 Boswell, *Moredenn* 1280 QW, *Mooreden* 1664 HTax

Moredon 1226–8 fees, 1547 *Drax (Est-, West-), Eastmoredon als. Moredon Mawtrevers* 1564 *ib, Moridon* 1412 FA *Estmerdun* 1250 Fees, *Merdone* 1316 FA *Mourdon(e)* 1340 NI, 1346 FA, 1357 *Cecil (West-)* 1381 DCMDeed, 1408 *Midd (West-), Westmourden* 1343 Ipm, *Estmoordon* 1436 Fine

'Hill in marshy ground', *v.* mōr, dūn, cf. Morden C 61, Sr 53, with ēast, west; the spellings for the second el. show influence from denu, denn and tūn. The affix -*Matravers* is from the *Matravers* family of Lytchett Matravers par. *supra* who held the manor of East Morden from the 14th cent. (Hutch[3] 3 511); the affix -*Roberti* is no doubt from *Robertus* de Porton 1226–8 Fees (p. 378).

CHARBOROUGH HO (SY 924978)
Cereberie 1086 DB, -*beria* Exon, -*berg* 1253 FF, 1268 *Ass*, -*brug* 1268 *ib*, *Chereberge* 1212 Fees, -*bergh* 1274 Ipm, -*berwe* 1275 Cl, 1280 Pat, -*burch* 1288 *Ass*, *Cerberge* 1274 Cl, 1280 *Ass*, -*bergh* 1280 *ib*, *Cherberwe* 1274 Cl, Fine, -*bergh* 1316 FA *et freq* to 1489 Ipm, -*borgh* 1389 Fine, -*burgh* 1389 Pat *et freq* to 1428 FA
Chiresbire c. 1185 Templar, *Serisberewe* 1275 RH
Cheleberge 1204 PatR, 1215 ClR, 1251 Ch, -*bir* 1227 Fees
Chauberg(e) 1206 Cur, 1428 FA
Chernebrug 1219 Fees
Cherlegh (sic) 1252 Fees
Scerebrg 1288 *Ass*
Charbergh 1340 NI, -*burgh* 1431 FA, -*bor(r)ow* 1508 DCM-Deed, 1693 DCMCt, -*borughe* 1535 VE, -*bar(r)ow* 1575 Saxton, 1692 *Weld*[1], -*burrough*, -*burrow* 1696 DCMCt, *Charebury* 1450 *MinAcct*

The second el. is beorg 'hill, barrow', later influenced by burh 'fortified place'. The first el. may be an old name for R. Winterborne (on which Charborough is situated) identical with R. Cerne (a derivative of PrWelsh or PrCorn *carn 'cairn, rock', *v.* RNs. *infra*), as suggested by Fägersten 75, Ekwall DEPN on the basis of the isolated form in *Cherne-* (1219) and on a comparison of the spellings with those of Charminster 1 338 (which also show early loss of -*n*-). Cf. also Charney Basset, Cherbury Camp Brk 389–390, 704–705. OE *cearr(e) 'a turn, a bend' (with reference to the gentle curve in the course of R. Winterborne here) might also be thought of for the first el., but as Professor Löfvenberg points out, the persistent early spellings with single *r* make this unlikely. Initial *C-* for *Ch-* and *-l-* for *-r-* (dissimilation of *r—r* to *l—r*) are AN features, both of them evidenced in the form *Celeberge* cited under Loosebarrow hundred *supra, v.* ANInfl 18f, 120.

SHERFORD (BRIDGE & FM) (SY 915934), *Sireford* 1244 *Ass* (p), *S(c)hyre-* 1311 Banco, 1408 *Midd, Shir-* 1420 *Hen*[1], 1470 *Weld*[1], *Sher-* 1473 *ib et passim, Shereford(e)* 1590 *Hen*[2], *Easte-, West Sharforde, Sharfordes meades* 1602 *DCMDeed, Sherford Bridge* 1811 OS, 'bright or clear ford', *v.* scīr[2], ford; the bridge, no doubt the site of the ford, is where the Blandford–Wareham road crosses Sherford River. It is in fact possible that the name of the river was originally *Sher* (< scīr[2]) 'the bright one', and that the name Sherford means 'ford over the *Sher*', cf. Shere Sr 248, Ekwall RN 362.

WHITEFIELD (FM & WD) (SY 902946), *claus' voc' Whytewell* 1422 *Midd, Whitewell* 1671 *Drax (cottage called-),* 1846 *TA* (-*Close,* -*Cross,* -*Wood*), *Whitefield* 1811 OS, -*Mill* 1826 Gre, 'white spring or stream', *v.* hwīt, well(a), with reference to the springs or the stream marked 6″, cf. Whitfield in Bradford P. 1 335 which has a similar late development -*well* > -*field.* The form *Wytefeld* 1244 *Ass,* tentatively identified with this place by Fägersten 76 (it occurs in fact only as a surname under Cogdean hundred), clearly does not belong here. The former mill here (also marked 1811 OS) was called *Rudgewaye Mylle* 1550 *Midd, v.* the f.n. Ridgeway *infra.*

BEACON HILL, 1811 OS, -(*Hill*) *Close* 1846 *TA, v.* (ge)bēacon. BLOXWORTH BOG, from Bloxworth par. *infra.* BOAR HILL LODGE. BRIMLAND WD, 1846 *TA.* BROOKS FM, cf. John *Brookes* 1664 HTax. HR BULBURY FM, BULBURY PLANT., from Bulbury in Lytchett Min. par. *supra.* CANNON CLUMP. CHALK PITS, cf. *Chalk pit Fd, Chalk Croft, Lr Chalk Cross* 1846 *TA.* CHAPEL WD, near Methodist Chapel (6″). CHARBOROUGH PARK (1846 *TA,* cf. *The Old Park* 1848 *ib*) & TOWER (*Obelisk* 1811 OS). CHITTEN HILL. CHURCH (St Mary, in Morden), cf. *ecclesiæ sanctæ Mariæ de Morduna* l12 Hutch[3], 'the church of *Mordon*'

1306 FF, *Le Chauntrey house* 1597 Hutch[3], *Churchway* 1671 *Drax, ye viccaridge house* 1664 HTax, *Church Ld* 1846 *TA*. CHURCH (St Mary, in Charborough), cf. *ecclesiam de Cereberg* 1268 *Ass*, v. Charborough *supra*. COCKETT HILL (GATE), *Cock Hill Gate* 1838 *TAMap* (Lytchett Mat.); first el. possibly cocc[1] 'hillock'. COLD BARROW, a small hillock, v. beorg. COLLINS'S LANE, cf. William *Collins* 1664 HTax. DUKE'S HILL. EAGLE PLANT. EAST COPPICE. EVERETT'S WD. FORTY ACRE BOTTOM, cf. *Forty Acres* 1848 *TA*. FROGMOOR (COPPICE). FRY'S WD, 1846 *TA*, cf. William *le Frye* 1332 SR (Almer). FURZE HILL. GALLOP'S LANE. GILES'S LANE. GOODWIN'S LANE, cf. Stephen *Godwyn* 1332 SR (Spettisbury). GREEN LANE, cf. *Green Rd* 1846 *TA*. THE HANG (a copse), probably ModE hang 'slope, bend'. HAWK WD. HAZEL COPPICE. HERON COPPICE, *Herns Wood* 1846 *TA*, cf. Henry *in thehurn* 1332 SR, *v.* hyrne. HIGHER POND, *Pond* 1846 *TA*. HIGH WOOD CTG, *Highwood* 1848 *ib.* HILL FM, near Cockett Hill *supra*. HUNTING BRIDGE, near Morden Park *infra*. THE KENNELS. KIDNEY CLUMP, so called from its shape. LOBBETT'S BARROW, *Loppetts Barrow Wd* 1846 *TA*. LONGCUTTER'S COPPICE. LOUSLEY WD, 1846 *TA*, probably from hlōse 'pig-sty' and lēah, cf. Loseley Sr 185. LOWER ST. MARSH BRIDGE & WD, cf. *Brodermerse* (for *Brodemerse*) 1274 Ipm, William *atte Merssh* 1332 SR, *The Marsh* 1848 *TA*, *v.* mersc, brād, atte. MILL BOG, near Morden Mill *infra*. MILLER'S FM (1846 *TA*), MILLER'S CORNER PLANT. MILL POND, 1848 *TA*, near Saw Mill *infra*. MORDEN BRICKYARD, *Brickyard and Common* 1846 *TA*. MORDEN MILL, 1811 OS, cf. *Nich' Colyere...molend' aquatic'* 1408 *Midd, Colyeresmulle* 1422 *ib*, mill in Mordon 1647 SC, Adam *atte Mulle* 1327 *SR*, *v.* myln, atte, and cf. the former mill at Whitefield *supra*; there were mills at three of the manors of *Mordune, -done* in 1086 DB (VCHDo 3 85, 97, 110). MORDEN PARK (CTGS), *Morden Park* 1811 OS (partly in Wareham St M. par.). E MORDEN DROVE (cf. *Drove Lane Pce* 1846 *TA*) & WITHY BED. W MORDEN BOG (cf. *Pond Md and Bog* 1846 *TA*) & FM (cf. *Easter East Morden Farme* 1671 *Drax*, *v.* ēasterra 'more easterly'). NEW BARN. NEW LANE. NEW PLANT. (2 ×). OLD NURSERY. PARADISE LANE, *v.* paradis. PARK CORNER, at the corner of Morden Park *supra*. PEACOCK LODGE. THE PEAK, a triangular copse, cf. *Peak Cl, Peaks* 1846 TA, *v.* pēac. POUND WD, cf. *Pounds Hill, Pound* 1846 *ib*, *v.* **pund**. PUMP HO. QUARR HILL, *v.* **quarre**. ROUND HO (*Lodge* 1811 OS), -PLANT. SANDHILL CLUMP. SANDY KNAP (lost, just S of E Morden), 1811 OS, *v.* **cnæpp**. SAW MILL, 1848 *TA*. SCUTT'S GATE, on par. bdy near *Scutts 7 Acres* in Lytchett Min. par. *supra*. SHRUBBETTS, perhaps 'place characterized by brushwood', from **scrubb** and the suffix **-et**. SNAILSBREACH FM, SNAIL'S BRIDGE, *claus' voc' Snaylesbreche* 1422 *Midd*, -*Snallys Breche* 1550 *ib*, *Snails Bridge Cl* 1846 *TA*, *v.* **bræc** 'land broken up for cultivation'; the first el. is OE **snægl** 'snail', here possibly used as a pers.n., cf. Snailslinch Sr 173. The form Snail's Bridge may be partly due to popular etymology, although there is in fact a bridge here. SQUARE CLUMP (2 ×). STONE PIT, -*Fd* 1846 *TA*. WELL HO. WHITMORE BOTTOM, *Whitmoor Pond* 1811 OS, *v.* **hwīt, mōr**. WIRE DROVE, perhaps to be associated with the lost f.ns. *Wirfurlong, Wirthorne* in the adjacent par. of Sturminster M. *supra*. WEST WITHY BED.

FIELD-NAMES

The undated forms are 1846 *TA* 152 (Morden) and 1848 *TA* 47 (Charborough), marked †). For some fields in Morden *TA* but now in Wareham St M., *v.* Wareham par. 1 166. Spellings dated 1213, 1768, 1863 are Hutch[3], 1319, 1323 *Ct*, 1327 *SR*, 1332 SR, 1408, 1415, 1419, 1422, 1550 *Midd*, 1620 *Lane*, 1664 HTax, and 1671 *Drax*.

(a) Balletts Wd (cf. *Rich' Balletts house* 1664); Balthays (perhaps the same surname *Ballett* with **(ge)hæg**); Bema's Hill; Biltham; Blackthorn Fd & Shard (*v.* **blæc-þorn, sceard**); Little Bodle(s); Boggy Pasture; Brake (*v.* **bræc**[1]); Breach (Wd) (*v.* **bræc**); Bush Moor; Bushy Pce and Pond; †Carpenters Ho and Gdn (cf. Margery *Carpenter* 1664); Carrot Cl; Charborough Down 1863; Chelley (a common) 1768; Clay Pits; Close(s); Inner Common heath; Corner Cl; Cut hedge (*v.* **cut**); Dirty Flg; Dyetts Fd (cf. *Tho' Dyetts house* 1664); Elder Stubs (*v.* **ellern, stubb**); (Hr, Middle & Lr) Field; Flat Fd; The Folly; Galtons Cl (cf. John *Galton* 1664); †Gardeners Ho and Gdn; Go lane and hop yd; Golds Cl & 7 Acres; Grants Grd; Green Barrow; Hanging Fd (*v.* **hangende, hanging**); Hollybush Fd; Home Cl; Honey Blood (perhaps alluding to soil colour or texture); Hornbys Cl; Horse Moor; †The Hound Walk; Hoziers or Oziers 1863 (*v.* **osier**); Hutts Cl; Joyces Wd; †Keeper's Ho and Gdn; Kings Fd; Knowle Hill (*Knoll* 1671, *v.* **cnoll**); Long Cl & Fd; Mallards Cl; Masons Grd; Mead (cf. *Morden Meade* 1671); Moor (cf. *Thomas in le more* 1319, *Mooreclose, little Moore* 1671, *v.* **mōr**); W Morden Common; E Morden Heath (cf. *Broiheriæ de Mordona* 1213); Moses Grd; Mount Pleasant; Neal Down; New Cl (1671) & Enclosure; North Close(s); Northover (*v.* **ōfer**[1] or **ofer**[2]); Orchard (Md) (-*Close* 1671); Boggy Orles and Pasture (cf. John-, Thomas *Urell* 1415, *mes' q' Thomas Hurell nuper tenuit* 1419); Paddock (freq); Parsonage Enclosure; Pill Cl & Pasture (*v.* **pyll**); Pit; †Plantation; Plummers Ld; Ridgeway (Closes, Fd & Wd) (cf. *Rudgewaye Mylle* 1550, *v.* **hrycg-weg**; the fields are located just S of Whitefield *q.v. supra*, near the Poole–Dorchester road); Rough Pce; Rowden Fd (perhaps **rūh, denu**); Rudd Cl; Ryles and Closes; †Shepherds Fd; Shoulder of Mutton Cl (so called from its shape); 6 (and 7) Acres; †16 Acres; †Slaughter Ho; Sloes (near Blackthorn Shard *supra, v.* **slāh**);: Sussex Cl and Pdk; Suttons Cl; 10 Acres; Tithing Barn and Yd; †Old Toll Ho; Touless Cl; 20 Acres; Upper Lodge; (Lt) West Fd; †West Md; White Barrow; Wood (cf. Nicholas *atte Wode* 1327, *v.* **atte, wudu**); Worlds Fd & Pdk.

(*b*) *attenassche* (p) 1327 (*v.* **atte(n), æsc**); *Bablings pitt* 1671; *Blackmore meere* 1671 (*v.* **mere**); *Cleyardesplase* 1422 (*v.* **place**); *the Common Feild* 1671 (cf. *camp' de Mourdon* 1408, *Morden feilde* 1620); *Middle Close* 1671; *cottage called Smedge* 1671; *atte To(u)neshende* 1323, 1332, *-Toneseynde* 1327 all (p) (*v.* **atte, tūn, ende**[1]); *Wareham Meade* 1671 (from Wareham par. 1 152).

Spettisbury

Charlton Marshall par. *supra* was formerly a tithing and chapelry in this par. (Hutch[3] 3 284, 516).

SPETTISBURY (ST 909029) ['spetsbəri]

> *Spehtesberie* 1086 DB, *Spestesberia* Exon, *-byry* 1301 Ipm, *Spectesb'i* 1162 P, *-bury* 1294 Pat, 1385 IpmR, 1386 Cl, Ilch, *Spettes-* 1349–1372 Pat, 1598 *Drax*, *Speghtesbury* 1399, 1401 FF, *Speytesburi*, *-bury* 1435 FF, 1469 *Ilch*, *Speytis-* 1472 *MinAcct*, 1540 Hutch[3], *Spytes-* 1497 *Ilch*, *Spetis-* 1535 VE, 1692 *Weld*[1], *Spetsbury* 1664 HTax, *Speytysbery* 1558 79 ChancP, *Spettesborough als. Spettesbury* 1599 *Drax*, *Spittesburye, -ie* 1571 *HarlCh*, 1608 *Lansd*, *Spetesbury* 1700 *Fort*

> *Spesteberie* 1086 DB, *Spetteberi* 1242 Ch, *-bury* 1291 Tax, 1294 Pat *et freq* to 1460 Hutch[3], *Spectebur'* 1268 *Ass* (p), 1288 *ib*, *-byr'* 1288 *ib*, *-bury* 1291 Tax, 1297 Pat *et freq* to 1461 ib, *Spittebir* 1280 Ch (p), *Speyhtebir'* 1280 *Ass*, *Spetebir'*, *-bur'* 1288 *ib*, *Espeghte-* 1312 Inq aqd, *Spe(y)ghtebury* 1312 Pat, 1313 Inq aqd, Orig *et freq* to 1390 FF, *-byry* 1378 Pat, *Speghti-* 1313 ib, *Speght-* 1341 ib, *Spehte-* 1341 Cl, *Spect-* 1346 FF, *Specce-* 1388 Cl, *Speightebury* 1391 Pat

> *Poststeberia* 1087–1100 France, *Posteberies* 1099 ib, *-bere* 1166–87 ib, *-beri* 1187 ib, *-byr'* 1188 *AD*, *Poste(r)biri* 1219 Sarum

Spactebir' 1205 Hutch³ *Speburg* 1221 Cur
Spesbury 1575 Saxton *Septisbury* 1692 *Weld*¹

The second el. is **burh** (dat.sg. *byrig*), here in the sense
'pre-English earthwork' with reference to the Iron Age hill-fort
of Crawford Castle or Spettisbury Rings *infra*. The first el. is
an unrecorded OE **speoht, speht** 'the green woodpecker', as
first proposed by Fägersten 76; the word corresponds to OHG
speht, MLG *specht*, it occurs as ME *specht* from c. 1450 (NED
s.v. *speight*), and it is also the first el. of Spexhall Sf (DEPN).
It is probably used as a pers.n. here, although the name could
be taken to suggest that the abandoned fortification was frequented by this bird, cf. EPN 1 61 for other instances of **burh**
with words denoting birds. For the AN spellings with prosthetic
E- (*Espeghte-*) and with loss of *S-* (*Poste-*, etc), *v.* ANInfl 55,
67. In 1327 *SR* this tithing in Loosebarrow hundred is called
[*C*]*rauford* (*v.* Gt Crawford *infra*) and in 1332 SR it is called
Lousebergh, *v.* the hundred name *supra*.

Gᴛ Cʀᴀᴡꜰᴏʀᴅ (lost, about ST 915015), 1863 Hutch³, *Craveford*
1086 DB, *Crawe-*, *Craueford* 1242–3 Fees, 1272 Ipm, 1280
Ass, (*Magna-*) 1288 *ib*, 1291 Tax *et freq* to 1367 Fine, *-forth* 1280
Ass, *Crau-*, *Crawford(e)* 1242 Ch, 1244 *Ass* (p), 1253 FF, 1258
Ch, 1268 *Ass* (p) *et freq* to 1497 *Ilch* with affix *Magna-* from 1308
FF, *Great-* from 1315 Pat, -*Magna* 1795 Boswell, *Craford(e)* e14
Wim, 1512 *Pars* (-*Magna*), 1571 *Drax*, 1692 *Weld*¹, (*Great*)
Croweford 1331 Pat, 1462 *Weld*¹, *Magna Crafard* 1427 *ib*, 'crow
ford', *v.* **crāwe** (obl.sg. -*an*), **ford**. The ford was no doubt at
Crawford Bridge *infra* where the Almer–Tarrant Crawford
road crosses R. Stour; the manor lay 'contiguous to Middle-
street on the south' (Hutch³ 3 521). The affixes *Magna* and·
Great distinguish it from Tarrant Crawford par. *infra* (earlier
Parva or *Little Crawford*), where some of the early unaffixed
forms cited above may strictly belong. For the DB identification,
v. DBGazetteer 119, cf. VCHDo 3 110.

Mɪᴅᴅʟᴇsᴛʀᴇᴇᴛ (lost, about ST 913023), 1863 Hutch³, *Middel-
stret(e)* 1278 FF *et freq* to 1497 *Ilch*, *Myddelstrete* 1493 *ib*,
Middlestre(e)te 1598, 1599 *Drax*, 'middle street or hamlet', *v.*
middel, strǣt; the manor lay 'in the middle between Spettisbury and Great Crawford' (Hutch³ 3 519), and along the middle

one of three minor roads running SW–NE through the par., cf.
South Fm *infra*. On the location of this place, *v*. further Taylor,
DoNHAS **88** 207.

BOTTOM PLANT., -*Fd* 1838 *TA*, *v*. **botm**. CHARLTON BARROW
(1863 Hutch³), CHARLTON HILL COPPICE (-*Hill* 1838 *TA*), from
Charlton Marshall par. *supra*. CHURCH (St John the Baptist),
cf. 'the church of *Spettebury*' 1338 Pat, *ecclesiam de Speytisbury*
1540 Hutch³, *Churchacr* 1460 *DCMDeed*, *v*. **cirice, æcer**.
CLAPCOTT'S FM, cf. John *Clapcott* e19 Hutch³. LITTLE COLL
WD, 1811 OS, *Little Colwood* 1544 Hutch³, cf. Great Coll Wd
in Almer par. *supra*. CRAWFORD BRIDGE, 1811 OS, 'the bridge
of *Crauford*' 1242 Ch, *ponte de Crauford* 1280 *Ass, Craufordes-*
1337 DorR, *Craffordbrigge* 1468 *MinAcct, Crayford(e) Bridge*
1535–43 Leland, 1618 *Map*, *v*. **brycg**, Gt Crawford *supra*.
CRAWFORD CASTLE (1811 OS) or SPETTISBURY RINGS, *Spetisbury*
Rings 1838 *TA*, cf. *Castle Coombe & Plant*. 1838 *ib*, *v*. **castel(l),**
hring, cumb, Gt Crawford and Spettisbury *supra*. CROSS (site
of). THE GABLES. HICKSON'S COPPICE, *Hixons Plant*. 1838 *TA*.
HIGHER BLDGS. HILL BARN, cf. *the Hill Pasture* 1809 *EnclA*.
HOME PLANT., cf. *Home Fd* 1838 *TA*. LOUSE LANE, *v*. **lūs**.
MIDDLE BLDGS. NEW BARN (PLANT.). NEWFOUNDLAND, a plan-
tation, perhaps so called from its remoteness. NORTH FM,
Spettisbury Fm 1811 OS. OAK BED, *v*. **bedd**. RECTORY, cf.
Parsonage Ho 1838 *TA*. RENDEZVOUS LODGE (*Lodge* 1811 OS)
& PLANT. ST MONICA'S PRIORY, *The Nunnery* 1838 *TA*, occupied
by various communities of nuns c. 1800–1927, *v*. Hutch³ **3**
519–20, cf. The Summer Ho *infra*; it was called *Sion Ho* 1863
Hutch³ after the London house of that name. SOUTH FM,
Middlestreet Fm 1811 OS, *v*. Middlestreet *supra*. SPETTISBURY
Ho, 1863 Hutch³. THE SUMMER HO (on site of Benedictine
Priory), *Summerhouse* 1838 *TA*, cf. *situs in quo prioratus fuit olim*
edificatus 1447 *Eton*; for the former priory here, a cell of the
abbey of Préaux, *v*. VCHDo **2** 119–121. TARRANT, a plantation,
no doubt an allusion to the abbey of Tarrant which had lands
in Spettisbury in 1293 Hutch³ **3** 516, 521. WEST END, at the NW
end of the village, *v*. **ende**¹.

FIELD-NAMES

The undated forms are 1838 *TA* 191. Spellings dated 1324 are Hutch[3], 1327 *SR*, 1332 SR, 1460 *DCMDeed*, 1598 *Drax*, 1664 HTax, c. 1700 *DCMSurv*, 1809 *EnclA*, 1811 OS, 1840 *TA* alt. app.

(a) Aldersmead; Almar Way Fd (*v.* Almer par. *supra*); Angles Pitt Fd; Ash Corner (Plant.); Ballett's Grd (cf. Morden f.ns. *supra*); Bannell Mdw (*Bavnwell als.* Bavnell 1460, possibly analogous with Banwell So (DEPN), Bannall's Fm Wo 56, Bannel Nth 280, Bannawell D 218 all of which may mean 'slayer's spring or stream' or 'poisonous spring or stream', from **bana** and **well(a)**); Barrow Fd (*v.* **beorg**); Berry Hill Town (*Bury Hill* 1809); Biggs Fd; Gt & Lt Breach (*v.* **brǣc**); Buth Mdw; The Cleft (*-Clift* 1809, *v.* **clif** or **cleft**); Close; Coindy Whistle (spelling uncertain); The Common Mead (*-meadow* c. 1700); Coombe Cl and Parsons Coombe (*v.* **cumb**); the Cowleaze 1809; Crawford Down & Fd (cf. *Crawford Fm* 1809, *-Cmn* 1811, from Gt Crawford *supra*); Crook (*v.* **crōc** 'a bend', with reference to a sharp double bend in the lane at New Barn *supra*); the Dairyhouse 1809; Doctors Cl; Down Barn, Cl & Fd (*v.* **dūn** or **dūne**); Little Down (*v.* **dūn**); The Drove; Dyches; 18 Acres; Field Cl 1809; Foley Fd & Plant.; Furlong (*Gt-* 1809); Galton(')s (Little Fd, Orchd & Mdw); Garden Grd 1840; Garlands-, Carlands Cl (cf. William *Garland* 1324); The Gt Meadow; The Green; Green Plot; The Hanging (*v.* **hanging**); Hilliards Cl; Hills; Holly Grd; Hookland (*v.* **hōc**); Horse Lawn; Housefield; The Island; Kelleway's Fd; Knights Fd & Gdn 1809; Little Fd; Longmans; Louder; Lovells Marsh & Orchd 1809; Many Mds; Meaders Orchd; Meadow (Ld); Meadow Marsh 1809 (cf. Thomas *de Marisco, -in la Marssch* 1324, *-in the Merssh* 1332, *v.* **mersc**); Middle Fd (Plant. & Ridge) (*v.* **hrycg**); Middle Md & Plant.; Mitchel's (cf. Katherine *Michell* 1664); New Breach (*v.* **brǣc**); New Cl (Barn and Yd); Out Md 1809 (*v.* **ūt(e)**); Paddock; Paper Ld; Parlour Cl (*v.* **parlour**); Parsons Hill, Marsh, Nap (*Parsonage Knap(p)* 1809, *v.* **cnæpp**) & Orchd (cf. Rectory, Coombe Cl *supra*); Pitt Fd (cf. Reginald *atte Putte* 1327, *-in theputte* 1332, *v.* **atte, pytt**); Plantation; the Schoolhouse 1809; Sheepland; Shop Fd (*v.* **sc(e)oppa** 'shed'); Southfield 1809; Sparrowline (*v.* **spearwa, leyne**); Spetisbury Down (cf. (pasture) *super montem* 1324, Down Barn *supra*) & Mdw; Spetisbury Mills (cf. *cottage called Milclyfe* 1598, *v.* **myln, clif**; there was a mill at the larger of the two DB manors of Spettisbury in 1086 (VCHDo 3 92), and there is mention of a mill in 1312 Pat); Three Corners (cf. *Morgans three Corner'd Plot* 1809); Town Md 1809; Travellers Rest Fd (no doubt from a P.H.); Walices Plot (cf. Richard *le Wal(l)eys* 1324, 1327); Water Gunnell Fd (on par. bdy near North Fm *supra*, no doubt to be associated with the 15th cent. f.ns. *le Grundewatereputt, le Watergrandelputtes*, etc in Charlton M. par. *supra*); Water Swallow (*v.* **swealg** 'a pit'); West Pce.

(b) *le Conynger als. le Orchard* 1460 (*v.* **coninger, orceard**); *atte Stone* (p) 1332 (*v.* **atte, stān**); *Vernolde* 1460 (perhaps a compound of **fearn** 'fern' and **ōlde** 'steep slope' (*v.* Ekwall Studies[2] 144)).

XI. RUSHMORE HUNDRED

This small hundred, consisting of Winterborne Zelstone par. *infra* and West Morden in Morden par. *supra*, was originally only a tithing, probably of Combs Ditch hundred *infra*; it was annexed to Hasler hundred 1 70 in the 13th cent. and later became a separate hundred (Anderson 122).

theginga de Rysemore 1275 RH, *hundr' de Haselore et Rys(sh)e-mor(e)* 1278 QW, 1288 *Ass, (hund' de) Ryss(h)e-* 1285 FA, 1425 Cl, *Ris(s)e-* 1288 *Ass*, 1316 FA, 1319 *MinAcct, Riss(t)hemor(e)* 1314 Ipm, 1319 *Ct*
tethyng de Russhemore, hundr' de Haselore et Russhemor' 1278 QW, *villata de-, hund' de Russemor(e)* 1280 *Ass, (hund' de) Runs-* (sic) 1296 Ipm, *Rus(s)(c)h(e)-* 1307 ib, 1323 *Ct et passim, Russe-, Rossemor(e)* 1342 Pat, *hund' de Haselore et Russhemour* 1327 SR, *hundred of Russheme and Hasellore* 1509 *BrEll, Ruys(he)mo(r)* 1546 *Ct*

'Marshy ground where rushes grow', from **risc, rysc** and **mōr**. According to Hutch[3] 1 336 (and earlier Hutch[1] 1 122), Rushmore is 'a small spot of ground, near a gate of the same name, planted with ash-trees, near Winterborne; a meadow or two there is called by the same name. It is in the parish of Morden, between Bloxworth and Winterborne, on the confines of the three parishes'; it is *Ruysmore* 1408 *Midd, Russhemore* 1546 *Lane, Rus(h)mo(o)re (Lane)* 1671 *Drax*, 1686, 1698 *Pick, Rush Moor* 1845 *TA* (Bloxworth). Fägersten 72 identifies the name Rushmore with *an lang riscemeres* 943 (15) *ShaftR* (S 490) 'along the rushy pool' (or 'stream', *v.* **mere**[1], Tengstrand 262), apparently used to describe that part of the OE bdy of Mapperton (in Almer par. *supra*) formed by a small tributary of R. Winterborne rising at Botany Bay Barn in Bloxworth par. near to the area called Rushmore; Fägersten *loc. cit.* takes **Riscmere* to be the original name and simply assumes later confusion of **mere**[1] with **mōr**. Anderson 122 follows this identification, but instead considers the charter form *-meres* to be corrupt for *-mores*. On the other hand, it is perhaps unnecessary to assume identification of the two forms; **Riscmere* and **Riscmōr* may well be independent names, each referring to a different feature of this marshy area (cf. the nearby Marsh Fm & Lane in Bloxworth par., and Marsh Bridge in Morden par.).

Winterborne Zelstone

WINTERBORNE ZELSTONE (SY 899978)

?*Wintreborne* 1086 DB (f. 75), *-borna* Exon, *Winterburn'* 1214 Cur, *-born'* 1226 ib, *Wynterburn* 1227 FF, *-born(e)* 1285 FA *et freq* to 1546 *Ct*
Wynterburn(e) Malreward' 1230 P, 1268 *Ass*, *Winter-*, *Wynterborn(e)-*, *-burn(e) Maureward(e)* 1242–3 Fees, 1268 *Ass et freq* to 1620 *CH* with variant spellings *-bourne* 1280 *Ass*, *Marleward* 1280 *ib*, 1285 FA, *-Maylward* 1291 Tax, *-Maurward* 1340 NI, *-Maryward* 1383 IpmR, *-Maurewod* 1416 ib, *-Mawreward* 1422, 1428 *Midd*, 1437 ib (*-als. Wynterborne Seleston*), *-Marwood(e)* 1601 *Hen*[1], 1626 DoIpm, *-Malward* 1619 *CH*, *Wynterbourne Marewarde by Bere* 1409 Cl, *-Maleward* 1428 FA
Marlewardeston 1275 RH
Wynter-, *Winterbo(u)rn(e) Selyston* 1350 FF, 1431 FA, 1432 *Midd*, 1514 Hutch[3], *-Seleston(')* 1398 *Cecil*, 1403 IpmR, 1419–1433 *Midd*, 1422 FF, 1468 IpmR (*-als. Wynterborn Maureward*), *-Sheleston* 1415 *Midd*, *-Syllis-*, *-Syllyston* 1518 Hutch[3], *-Celston* 1528 ib, *-Selston* 1535 VE, 1550 *Midd*, *-Zelston* 1626 DoIpm, *Seleston* 1428 ib, *Selston Wynterborne* 1484 IpmR, *Zelston Winterborne* 1795 Boswell

One of several places named from R. Winterborne, a tributary of R. Stour, *v.* RNs. *infra*. The identification of the DB form is that of Eyton 97, 100 (also Fägersten 73), cf. VCHDo 3 65, DBGazetteer 129, Winterborne Came par. 1 261. The affixes are manorial. The family of *Mal-*, *Maureward* was here from 12th–16th centuries, cf. William *Maureward* 1227 FF, Geoffrey *Maldreward* (sic) 1230 P, etc, and for the same affix, cf. Kingston (Maurward) in Stinsford par. 1 369, and Shipton Gorge par. *infra*; the surname occurs with **tūn** 'estate' in 1275. The affix *Selys-*, *Seleston*, etc is no doubt from the family called *de Seles* (probably from Zeals W 182) and **tūn**, as supposed by Fägersten 73; a Henry *de Seles* was a witness to a charter concerning the adjacent par. of Almer in c. 1276 (15) *ShaftR* (f. 28) (also cited in Hutch[3] 3 494), cf. also Robert *de Seles* 1268 *Ass* (Hasler hundred).

HUISH (SY 905979), 1795 Boswell, *atte Hiwy*[*sh*] 1327 *SR* (p), *atte Ywyssch'* 1332 SR (p), *Hywyss(c)h* 1340 NI (p), 1462 FF, *Wynterbourn Hywyssh* 1350 ib, *Haiwyssh* 1419 *Midd, Huwyssh* 1423, 1426 *Midd, Huse* 1656 Hutch[3], *Hewish* 1811 OS, 'a household, a measure of land that would support a family', *v.* **hīwisc, atte**; on R. Winterborne, cf. par. name *supra.*

BUSHES BARN & PIT, (*Hr, Lr & Lt*) *Bushes, Bushes Pit* 1839 *TA, v.* **busc**, but possibly a surname. CHANTELL'S CORNER. GRAVEL PIT. HUISH PIT, possibly to be identified with *on anne water pet, of þane pitte* 943 (15) *ShaftR* (S 490) in the OE bounds of Mapperton in Almer par. *supra, v.* **wæter, pytt**, Huish *supra.* RECTORY. ST MARY'S CHURCH, cf. 'the church of St Peter at *Winterborne Maureward'* 1385 Hutch[3], *eccles' de Wynterborne Mawreward* 1422 *Midd, Church Cl, Churchyard* 1839 *TA.* SPEAKS, from the *Speke* family which possessed a farm here in the 18th cent. (Hutch[3] 1 708). VERMIN LANE, *Vermin Lane* (*Plot*) 1839 *TA*, perhaps from ModE **vermin** 'animals of a noxious or offensive kind'. WINTERBORNE DAIRY, FM & LANE. WINTER-BORNE WITHY BED, *Withy bed* 1839 *TA*, cf. (*ongen*) *Wiþig þeuel* 943 (15) *ShaftR* (S 490), *v.* **wīðig, þȳfel** 'a thicket'.

FIELD-NAMES

The undated forms are 1839 *TA* 259. Spellings dated 1319, 1546 are *Ct,* 1664 HTax, and the rest *Midd.*

(*a*) Anthills; Barn Cl & Fd; Bear Cl (perhaps **bere** 'barley'); Bere Lane (Plot) (near the road to Bere Regis 1 273); Billows's; Bloxworth gate (*v.* Bloxworth par. *infra*); Breach (*v.* **bræc**); Broad Md; Brownings (18 acres & 2 acres), Brownings Peak (*v.* **pēac**); (Above) Chalk Pit; Common; Coppice Cl; (By) Copyhold; Court Cl; Cowards (Ho); Cowleaze; Dry Md; Dyots orchd (cf. John *Dyot* 1437); Long 8 acres; Eweleaze; 5, 4 & 14 Acres; Furmages Grd, Furnages Ho; Gallops Tenement; Gascon (perhaps from **gærs-tūn** 'paddock', cf. Goschen in Anderson par. *infra*); Gilberts Ho; Ham (*v.* **hamm**); Haywards Orchds; Hewish Md (from Huish *supra*); Hobbys Bars (cf. *terr' iuxta Hobbysthon* (probably for -*thorn*) 1437, Richard *Hoby* 1495, *v.* **barre, þorn**); Home Fd; Honeyburns Orchd (cf. Robert *Honiborne* 1664); 100 Acres; Inside Fd; Jeans's (Grd); Jeffery's; Joyces Ho; Kiddles Homestead; Kingway (with reference to the Dorchester–Badbury Roman road, cf. the same f.n. in Almer par.); Leg (*v.* **leg**); Little Md; Long Fd; Mead; Meadens (5 Acres); Middle Fd; Gt & Lt Moor; Morden Gate, By Morden Lane (from Morden par. *supra*); Nicholas's; 9 Acres; North Cl; Orchard (*le*- 1426, *v.* **orceard**); Outside Fd; Paddock including Plant.; Peak (*v.* **pēac**); Pit Grds; Plot; Redmans Orchd; Redpits; Ropers Tenement; Ruftord Fd; 7 & 6 Acres;

Stephens Plot; Stickland Fd & Md, Sticklands Cowleaze (cf. *William Stickland* 1664 (W Morden)); Stonehayes Mead(s) (*v.* **stān, (ge)hæg**, but perhaps a surname); Strangeman's Plot; 10 Acres; Thorny Moor; Townmead; 2 Acres; West Md (*le Westmede* 1432, *v.* **mǣd**); Woodhorn (*Wodeherne* 1495, *v.* **wudu, hyrne, horn**); Woolfrys (Plot) (cf. Thomas *Wulfrice* 1546, *Roger Woolfreys house* 1664).

(*b*) *le Blyndelane* 1423 (*v.* **blind**); *atte brigge* 1319 (p) (*v.* **atte, brycg**); *semita pedestre et equestre...in mora ex parte boriali de Chalfecroft ducens de Wynterborne versus Warham* 1426 (*v.* **calf** (WSax gen.pl. *cealfa*), **croft**); *le Colehey* 1433 (*v.* **(ge)hæg**; first el. perhaps **cāl** 'cole, cabbage'); *tenement voc' Colehopkins* 1550 (*mes' q' Nicholas Hopkyns nuper tenuit* 1419; *Cole-* represents ME *Col(l)*, a pet form of *Nicholas*); *le Downe* 1433 (*v.* **dūn**); *les Elmys* 1437 (*v.* **elm**); *la Estmede* 1423 (*v.* **ēast, mǣd**); *lez Fursys* 1428 (*v.* **fyrs**); *le Gore* 1428 (*v.* **gāra**); *Lenkethorne* 1428 (*v.* **þorn**; first el. possibly an OE pers.n. **Len(d)ca*, on which *v.* DEPN s.n. Linkfield Sr); *Magattehayes* 1495 (*v.* **(ge)hæg**; first el. either the pers.n. *Magot*, a hypocoristic form of *Margaret* found as a surname in Do in 1332 SR, or an early example of dial. **maggot** 'magpie' (of identical origin), or ME **magotte** 'worm or grub'); *Maysterioneslond* 1426 ('master John's land', *v.* **land**); *Roberdyscote* 1426 (cf. *ten'...quondam Margare Roberddys* 1439, *v.* **cot**); *le Stubbes* 1423 (*v.* **stubb**).

XII. COMBS DITCH HUNDRED

This hundred is now in two portions originally connected by the tithing of Winterborne Muston in Winterborne Kingston 1 284 which was earlier in it (Hutch³ 1 160, VCHDo 3 135). Rushmore hundred *supra* was probably originally a tithing of this hundred, and the hundreds of Pimperne and Bere Regis possibly include other parts of the original area (Eyton 121–2, Anderson 127, VCHDo 3 135).

> (*Con*)*cresdic hundret* c. 1086 GeldR
> *Kilkesdich* 1205, 1206 P, *Culke-*, *Colke(s)dich* 1268 *Ass*
> *Cunekesdich* 1207 P, *-dych* 1300 Ipm, *Cunkes-* 1244, 1288 *Ass*, 1303 FA, *Cunke-* 1244 *Ass*, *Kunekes-* 1265 Misc, *Chunekes-* 1296 Ipm, *Cunkis-* 1428 FA, *Kunkesdich(e)*, *-dych(e)* 1459–1466 Lane, *Cunkesdik* 1300 Ipm
> *Conkesdich(e)*, *-dyche* 1244 *Ass*, 1307 Ipm *et freq* to 1469 Lane, *Conewes-* (for *Conekes-*) 1251–2 Fees, *Con(n)ekes-* 1268, 1280, 1288 *Ass et freq* to 1423 Midd, *Koneke-* 1268 *Ass*, *Coneghes-* 1280 *ib*, *Konekes-* 1317 *MiltC*, *Coukesdich(e)*, *-dyche* (for *Conkes-*) 1338 Ipm *et freq* to 1414 Cl, *Conckysdyche* 1542 LP
> *Cuningedych* 1244 *Ass*, *Cominges-* 1269 FF, *Conyng-* 1273 Banco, *Coningesdich(e)*, *-dych* 1275 *ib*

Cokesdich 1275 Cl, 1288 *Ass*, *Kokesdich* 1288 *ib*
Cumebusdich 1275 RH   *Cokenesdych* 1280 *Ass*
Coombes Ditch 1664 HTax

Named from the Iron Age-RB boundary bank and ditch known as COMBS DITCH (6"); this runs NW–SE (facing NE) and for most of its length forms the hundred bdy. It is referred to as (*anlang*) *cunucces dich* 942 (15) *ShaftR* (S 485(1)) in the bounds of Winterborne T. par. *infra*, (*on*) *cinninces* (for *cunnuces*) *dic* 943 (15) *ib* (S 490) in the bounds of Mapperton in Almer par. *supra*, *Coombe Ditch* 1800 *EnclA* (Charlton M.), *v.* dīc. The first el. is PrWelsh *cönǭg or PrCorn *conǭg (Brit *cunāco-) of doubtful meaning (*v.* Jackson in JEPN 1 46, cf. Ekwall RN 92 and DEPN s.n. Cannock St for the older supposition that the el. meant 'hill', cf. also NTCB s.n. Cannock); the same word is found in Conock W, Consett Du, and probably also in Conkwell So 38 ((*on*) *cunuca leage* 957 (e12) BCS 1001) and in the early forms of Chester le Street Du (*Cunca-*, *Cunceceastre* c. 1050 DEPN). The name *cunnuces dīc* no doubt means 'the ditch called *Cunnuc*', *v.* -es².

Anderson

The par. of Winterborne Tomson *infra* was added to this par. in 1933 (Kelly); the two pars. originally formed one tithing (Hutch³ 1 160).

ANDERSON (SY 881975)
  ?*Wintreburne* 1086 DB, *Winterburn* 1235–6 Fees
  Wynterburne-, *-born'* Fif(*f*)(*h*)as(*s*)e 1268 *Ass*, 1293 Ipm,
    Wynterb(o)urn(e) Five(*e*)sse(*s*) 1284, 1285 Cl, *-Fifaysches*,
    -Fisaisshe (for *Fif-*) 1285 Pat *et freq* with variant spellings
    Winter-, Wyntir-, Wyntur-, *-born(e)-*, *-Fif-*, *-Fyf-*, *-Vif-*,
    -Vyf-, *-Viv-*, *-Vyv-*, *-has(se)*, *-(h)as(s)h*, *-(h)as(s)ch(e)*,
    -heysse, *-hache*, *-ayssh(e)* to 1431 FA, *Fyfhasche* 1327 *SR*,
    Fifassch 1332 SR
  Andreweston 1331 FF, 1340 NI, 1451 *MinAcct*, *Andr(e)us-*
    1342 Pat, 1377 Cl, *Andres-* 1428 Pat, 1460 *Lane*, 1469
    IpmR (*Wynterborne-*), *Anderston* 1428 FA, 1536 *Pars*
    (*-Fyveasshes*), 1549 *Lane*, 1597 *PlR* (*Winterborne-*), 1795
    Boswell, *Andryweston* 1447 *MinAcct*, *Wynturbourne*
    Andreston alias dict' *Wynturbourne Vyueasshe* 1477
    DCMDeed, *Anderson* 1617 *Add*

Named from R. Winterborne, *v.* RNs. *infra.* For the possible identification of this place with one of the DB manors called *Wintreburne, v.* Eyton 121–2, DBGazetteer 129, cf.VCHDo 3 135. The affix *Fifash*, etc means 'five ash-trees', *v.* fīf, æsc, cf. Five Ash Down, Five Ashes Sx 392, 396. *Andreweston,* etc is probably from the dedication of the disused St Andrew's Church in Winterborne T. par. *infra, v.* tūn; this church lies only ¼ mile from the manor house of Anderson.

DOWN BARN, cf. *The Down* 1837 *TA, v.* dūn. GOSCHEN, *Garston* 1284 Cl, *Gascoigne* 1837 *TA, v.* gærs-tūn 'paddock'. MANOR HO. RECTORY, cf. *Parsonage Md* 1837 *ib.* ST MICHAEL'S CHURCH, cf. 'the chapel of *Andreuston'* 1342 Pat, although this may refer to St Andrew's Church in Winterborne T. par. *infra.* WELL HO, cf. *Well Fd* 1837 *TA.*

FIELD-NAMES

The undated forms in (*a*) are 1837 *TA* 7, in (*b*) 1284 Cl. Spellings dated 1327 are *SR*, 1332 SR, 1340 NI, 1460, 1617 *Lane* and 1902 SCat.

(*a*) Barn Md; Bartletts Ho and Cl; Btm & Old Cowleaze; Dogkennel Leaze; (Goods) 8 Acres; 18 Acres; Gallops Ctg; The Green; Highway Fd (beside the Badbury–Dorchester Roman road (Margary 4e)); Home Cl; Knights Ctg; Little Fd; Long Fd; Mallards Tail (*v.* tægl); Pains Grd; Picked Fd (*v.* pīcede 'pointed'); Plunb (sic) Pits (*Plum-* 1902, perhaps ModE plumb adj. 'sheer' (of the sides) rather than plūme 'plum-tree'); Smalls Ctg; Stock Md (*v.* stocc); 10 & 12 Acres; 20 Acres (and 9 Acres in one) (*Twenti-, Nyenacres* 1284, *v.* twēntig, nigon, æcer); (Gt) Wood Fd.

(*b*) *Betacres* (*v.* æcer, as freq in this par.; first el. probably bēte[1] 'beet'); *La Breche* (*v.* brǣc); *Enleveacres* (*v.* en(d)leofan); *Estmed* (*v.* ēast, mǣd); *Fifteneacre* (*v.* fīftēne); *Hegeforlange* (*v.* hecg, hege, furlang (as freq in this par.)); *in la-, in le Hyle* 1327, 1340, *in le Hile* 1332 all (p) (probably from the WSax dat.sg. form *hēale* of healh 'nook, corner of land'); *Lortemerforlange* (cf. Henry *de Lortemere* 1319 FF (Winterborne W.), *v.* lort(e) 'dirt, mud', mere[1] 'pool'); (*La) Marle* 1284, 1460, 1617 (*v.* marle); *Rochelon* (*v.* roche[1] 'rock', lane); *Scortstiche* (*v.* sc(e)ort, sticce[1]); *Stanes* (*v.* stān); *Staniforlange* (*v.* stānig); *Stretforlange* (*v.* strǣt, probably with reference to the Roman road (Margary 4e) which crosses this par.); *Westmed* (*v.* west, mǣd); *La Worth* (*v.* worð).

Blandford St Mary

A detached part of the par. of Turnworth (Thorncombe) was added to this par. in 1887, and part of the par. of Langton Long Blandford (Littleton, etc) was added in 1933 (Kelly).

BLANDFORD ST MARY (ST 892053) ['bɑ:nvəRd]
  Bleneford(e) (2 × or 3 ×) 1086 DB, *Blaneford(e)* (2 ×) 1086 ib,
    1244 *Ass*, 1327 *SR*, 1332 SR
  Parva Blaneford 1205, 1225 ClR, 1236 Fees, 1288 *Ass*, *Parva
    Blaneforde Martel* 1210–12 RBE, *Blaneford Martel* 1302,
    1339 FF, 1391 Pat, *Blandford Martell* 1506 ib
  Blaneford(e) St Mary, *-Sancte Marie* 1254 FF *et freq* to 1426
    Cl, *Blaneford Mar(ie)*, *-Mary* 1291 Tax, 1340 NI, 1397 Cl,
    Blan(e)ford Beate Marie 1421 IpmR *et freq* to 1466 *Weld*[1],
    Seyntmaryblan(d)ford 1450 *MinAcct*, 1488 Ipm, *Blandford
    maries* 1575 Saxton, *St Mary Blandford* 1703 *Fort*
  Blaneford Mon(i)alium 1316 FA

Parva (Lat **parva** 'small') and *St Mary* to distinguish this par. from Blandford Forum and Langton Long Blandford pars. *q.v. infra*. *St Mary* is 'either from the dedication of its church, or because it belonged to the nunnery of St Mary in Clerkenwell' (Hutch[3] 1 163); the latter association also explains the affix *-Mon(i)alium* (Lat *monialis* 'a nun'). The family of *Martel* possessed the manor, or part of it, from the time of Hy 2 (Hutch[3] 1 163), cf. William *Martel* 1210–12 RBE. The form *Blaneford Philippi de Tylly* 1242–3 Fees may also belong here, *v.* discussion under Langton Long Blandford par. *infra*. For the identification of the DB forms, *v.* Eyton 121–2, VCHDo 3 86, 91, 100, 110, DBGazetteer 117.

THORNCOMBE (FM) (ST 870032), *Tornecome* 1086 DB, *-cumba* 1160–62 (1336) Ch, *-combe* 1292 Cecil, *-coumbe* 1325 *MinAcct*, *Thornacumba-*, *Thornecumbe iuxta-*, *-prope Blaneford*, *Thorcumba* ?John *AddCh*, *Turnecumb(a)* 1203 RC, 1234 Cl, *Thor(e)-cumbe* 1234 Pat, 1244 FF, *Thorncumbe* 1236 FF, 1280 *Ass*, 1285 Cecil, *Thornecombe* 1398 IpmR *et passim*, cf. *Thorncomb Down* 1634 Hutch[3], 'valley where thorn-trees grow', *v.* þorn (gen.pl. þorna), cumb. The forms in *Turne-* show influence from the cognate þyrne 'thorn-bush', cf. Turnworth par. *infra* of which Thorncombe was formerly a detached part (1840 *TA*).

THE BELT, *v.* **belt**. B PLANT., like V Plant. and Y Plant. *infra*, named from its shape. THE DOWN HO, 1863 Hutch[3], *Chettledown Ho* 1811 OS, cf. Little Down *infra*; Henry *Chettle* and his heirs held the manor of Blandford St M. from 1546 (Hutch[3] 1 163), cf. Chettle par. *infra* from which the family no doubt took its name. FOX GROUND DOWN, cf. *Foxelond* 1535 Hutch[3], *v.* **fox, land**. HIGHER FM. HILL CTG. IVY CTG. KNIGHT'S, late HUSSEY'S (a farm, lost), 1795 Boswell, cf. Walter *le cnith* John *AddCh*, *Knights Md* 1837 *TA*. LADY CAROLINE'S DRIVE, probably a reference to Lady Caroline Damer, died 1775 (M.H.). LITTLE DOWN, cf. *Lr & Upr Down* 1837 *ib*, *v.* **dūn**. LITTLE WD, 1837 *ib*. LONG COPSE, *-Coppice* 1837 *ib*. LOWER FM. MANOR FM & HO. MAGGOT CLUMP, probably dial. **maggot** 'magpie', cf. Winterborne Z. f.ns. *supra*. MIDDLE FM. MOORE'S FM. NEW LODGE. NEW PLANT. NORTH LODGE. OLD CLUMP. OLD LODGE. THE PLANT. RABBIT WARREN. ST MARY'S CHURCH, *Ecclesia Sancte Marie de Blaneford* 1268 *Ass*, 1291 *Tax*, 1428 FA. ST MARY'S DROVE, from prec. V PLANT. and Y PLANT., cf. B PLANT. *supra*.

FIELD-NAMES

The undated forms are 1837 *TA* 21, but those marked † are 1840 *ib* 233 (Turnworth). Spellings dated ?John are *AddCh*, 1337 *Ass*, 1702[1], 1703 *Fort*, 1702[2], 1707, 1765, 1768, 1789 Almack, 1877 *TA* alt.app.

(*a*) †Barn Fd; Biles (Orchd or Pdk); (King Croft or) Brick Kiln Fd; Butts Cl; †Chalky Fd; Chantry Md 1702[2]; (Marsh & Woar) Cow Leaze (*Woar* is probably to be associated with *Worth* 1768, *v.* **worð**, but cf. the f.n. Woar in Steeple par. 1 100); †Down Cl; Drove (Md(w)); Duck Moor; Hr Earth Fd, Lr Earth Pit(s) (perhaps from **erð** 'ploughing', or with reference to a fox earth, *v.* **eorðe**); †Elbury; Farm Cl (1703); 15 Ash Fd; Foundering Bank Mdw (from ModE *founder* 'to collapse'); Gipsey Corner; Gould Fd; Gravelly Napp 1765 (*v.* **cnæpp**); (N & S) Great Fd; Great Mdw; Green Cl; Harveys Md; Gt & Lt Horse Leaze (cf. *Horse Cl* 1702[1]); Kite Hills (*v.* **cȳta**); †Little Fd; †Long Fd; Long Pond Fds; Lr End Grds; Lower Mdw; (†)Middle Fd; †New Pce; (Lr) Nursery; Old Orchd; Peak (Fd), †Peaked Fd (*v.* **pēac, peked**); Pigeon Cl (*Culver Cl or-* 1789, *Pigeon House Cl* 1707, *v.* **culfre**); Pit Fds; Plump (sic, *Pump-* 1877) and Well Cl; †Rough Grd; Field 'Thornes' (a surname); Three Gates Fd; 20 Acres; Two Bush Fds; Wallnut Tree Cl; Wheat Rick Fd; Withey Bed.

(*b*) *de La Lea* ?John (p) (*v.* **lēah**); *Suthcoum*[*b*] 1337 (*v.* **sūð, cumb**).

Bloxworth

BLOXWORTH (SY 881948), EAST BLOXWORTH
  (*in*) *Blacewyrðe* 987 (13) KCD 656 (S 1217, Finberg 613)
  Blocheshorde 1086 DB, -*borda* Exon
  Blokesw(u)rth(e) 1200 Cur (p), 1201 FF, 1213 ClR *et freq* to
    1366 Pat, -*wrd*' 1212 Fees, -*worth(e)* 1268 Ass *et freq* to 1465
    Pat, *Blokysworthe* 1370 DCMDeed
  Blockeswurth 1223 Pat (p), -*worh* 1244 FF (p), -*worth(e)* 1258
    For, 1268 *Ass*, 1280 *ib* (*Est*-, *West*-) *et freq* to 1431 FA,
    -*wort* 1288 *Ass*, *Blokkesworth(e)* 1244 *ib*, 1327 *SR et freq* to
    1459 *Lane* (*Est*-), 1466 *ib* (*West*-), 1500 *ib* (*Est*-, *West*-),
    Blockus-, *Blocckesw(o)rth*' 1268 *Ass*, *Blockeseworth* 1291
    Tax, *Blockysworth* 1303 FA
  Blockeswerdi (probably for -*wordi*) 1250 Pap
  Blekeswrthe 1251 FF, *Ble(c)kesworth*' 1280 *Ass* (p)
  Blakesworth(') 1280 Ch (p), 1288 *Ass*
  Bloxkesworth 1417 Fine, *Bloxworth(e)* 1440 ib *et passim*,
    -*wourth* 1550 *Midd*, *Bloxcewurth*', -*worth*' 1545, 1546
    Lane, *East(e) Blox(e)worth(e)* 1557 *ib*
  Bloxforde 1575 Saxton

'Blocc's enclosure', from an OE pers.n. *Blocc* and **worð**, cf.
Bloxham O 394, Bloxholm Li and Bloxwich St (DEPN) all of
which are held to contain this pers.n., and cf. Blockley Wo 98
which contains a wk. form *Blocca*. The OE spelling points
rather to the OE pers.n. *Blaca* with the variant **wyrð**, but it is
probably corrupt; the charter itself from which it is taken may
be spurious (S 1217). The isolated form *Blokeswerdi* (probably
for -*wordi*) shows interchange of the second el. with **w(e)orðig**
and *Bloxforde* shows confusion with **ford**. The present village
is the former West Bloxworth, *v.* **ēast**, **west**.

THE KNOLL (SY 892939), *Knowle* 1811 OS, the home of
Robert *atte Knolle* 1327 *SR*, 1332 SR, cf. *Knolhay* 1463 *Weld*[1],
Knolehayes 1686 *Pick*, *v.* **cnoll** 'hillock', **atte**, **(ge)hæg**.

MARSH FM (SY 874973), 1845 *TA*, *Marsh* 1661 Hutch[3], the
home of Henry *atte Mers(c)h(e)* 1327 *SR*, 1332 SR, William *atte*
Merssh' 1461 *Lane*, cf. *Mersshfeld* 1460 *ib*, (*North*) *Marsh Fd*,
The Marsh 1845 *TA*, *v.* **mersc**, **atte**, **feld**.

STROUD BRIDGE (SY 889916), 1811 OS, -*Bar* 1826 Gre, named from *Stroda* 1303 FA, *Strode* 1332 SR, 1500 *Lane*, *Stroude* 1340 NI, 1346 FA, 1544 *Lane*, *Stroode* 1544 *ib* all (p), cf. *Stro(w)des landes*, -*londes* 1574 *ib*, *v.* **strōd** 'marshy land overgrown with brushwood', **barre, land**.

GT & LT ADBURY, 1845 *TA*, perhaps to be associated with Joan *atte Bergh'* 1327 *SR*, 1332 SR, *v.* **beorg** 'hill, tumulus', **atte**. THE BELT, HR BELT, *v.* **belt**. BLOXWORTH DOWN (1811 OS), HEATH (1811 ib) & HO (1811 ib, cf. *Ferme of Blox(e)worthe* 1557 *Lane*). BOTANY BAY BARN, 1845 *TA*, a transferred p.n.; it is in the extreme NE corner of the par. BOUNDARY OAK, on the par. bdy. BROAD BREACH, -*Wd* (*Bewleys Breach and-*) 1845 *TA*, cf. *Brechelond(e)* 1459, 1546 *Lane*, *Breachland* 1620 *ib*, *Little-*, *Smale breach(e)* 1618 *ib*, *the breache Copice* 1621 *ib*, (*le-*, *the*) *Breach(es)* 1674–1690 *Pick*, (*East*) *Breach* 1845 *TA*, *v.* **bræc** 'land broken up', **land**. THE CLUMP. COMMON CHALK PIT WD, *the Common Chalke pitt* 1674 *Pick*, *Common Chalk Pit* (*Coppice*), *Chalk Pit Fd* 1845 *TA*. DERHAM'S COPPICE, *Derrhams Coppice & Grd* 1845 *ib*, cf. John *Derrome*, Matthew *Dearam* 1664 HTax. DRYCLOSE CHALK PIT. FOX POUND. HALF MOON (2 ×), coppices so called from their shape. HORSE CLOSE, 1845 *TA* (*Row in-*), *v.* **row**. HUMBER'S COPPICE & LEG, cf. Richard *Carpentar' de Humbir'*, -*byr'* 1288 *Ass*, Alexander *Humber* 1664 HTax (Winterborne W.), *v.* **leg**; the surname is derived from a p.n. (r.n.) *Humber*. JAMES'S COPPICE, *Samuel James Coppice* 1845 *TA*, cf. *Mathew James' Fd* 1845 *ib*. JUBILEE OAK. KEEPER'S LODGE. LARCH PLANT. THE LODGE. LONG CROSS PIT, cf. *Long Cross(e) feilde* 1621 *Lane*, -*Fd* 1845 *TA*, at a junction of roads, *v.* **cros** or **cross**. LONG WALK. MARSH LANE, to Marsh Fm *supra*. MORDEN LANE, to Morden par. *supra*. NEW BARN. NEWPORT (LANE), *Newport* (*Barn & Farmhouse*) 1845 *TA*, just N of the village, perhaps a transferred name from Newport elsewhere. OAK HILL, OAKHILL MIRE POND, *v.* **mire**. RECTORY, cf. *grang' Rectorie* 1463 *Weld*[1], *The Parsonage Ho*, *Old Parsonage Grd*, *Parsonage Md & 3 Acres* 1845 *TA*. ST ANDREW'S CHURCH, cf. 'the chapel of *Blokeswerdi*' 1250 Pap, 'the church of *Blokesworth*' 1465 Pat. SCOTCH PLANT. STEPHEN'S FM. STICKLEHILL BARN, *Stickhill* 1618 *Lane*, *Stickle Hill* (*Barn*) 1845 *TA*, perhaps 'hill where sticks are got', from **sticca** and **hyll**, with later addition of ModE *hill*. SUGAR HILL, a stretch of the Bere R.–Wareham road where it crosses Bloxworth Heath, perhaps identical in origin with Sugar Hill W 292 the first el. of which is **scēacere** 'a robber'. WATERLEY WD, *Waterlegh'* 1458, 1461 *Lane, Watersley* 1460 *ib, Waterley* (*wood*) 1845 *TA*, perhaps 'wet glade', from **wæter** and **lēah**, but the first el. may be the pers.n. *Wa(l)ter*. THE WILDERNESS, *-Wider-* (sic) 1845 *TA* (a wood). WITHY BED, 1845 *TA*. WOODLAKE, 1617–1621 *Lane, -diche* 1620 *ib, Wood Lake Farmhouse & Lane* 1845 *TA*, *v.* **wudu, lacu** 'stream', **dīc**; perhaps with reference to the stream ⅒ mile S, a feeder of Sherford River. WOOLSBARROW, 1774 Hutch[1] (*-or Oldbury*), *Wool Barrow* 1845 *TA*, an earthwork near which are several tumuli, *v.* **beorg** or **burh**; the first el. may be **ūle** 'owl', hence 'haunted by owls', cf. Oldberrow Wo 267, *Oldborough* K 142.

FIELD-NAMES

The undated forms are 1845 *TA* 22. Spellings dated 1327 are *SR*, 1332 SR, 1408, 1550 *Midd*, 1458, 1459, 1460, 1461, 1462, 1464[2], 1546, 1617, 1618, 1620, 1621 *Lane*, 1463, 1464 *Weld*[1], 1664 HTax, 1673 *DCMDeed*, and the rest *Pick*.

(*a*) Back Grds; Bacon Hill; Balhams Md; Barn Cl (*Barne-* 1690); Bencroft Fd & Trees, New Bencroft (*v.* **bēan, croft**); Under Bere Wd (*v.* Bere Wd in Bere R. par. 1 273); Bloxworth Green (cf. Adam *in le Gre(y)ne* 1327, 1332, *v.* **grēne**[2]); Brick Kilns & Pits; Broad Cl; Butland (first el. probably **butte**); Calves Grd; Chapmans Fd (*Chapmanes-* 1458–1460, *Chepmanesfeld* 1460, cf. Thomas *Chapman* 1458, *v.* **feld**); Chicks Grd; (Hr, Middle & Lr) Churchill (*two Churchill Closes* 1686; a group of fields on Bloxworth Down (200′) and quite separate from foll., so perhaps from PrWelsh or PrCorn **crūg* 'hill' with explanatory OE **hyll** as in Long & More Crichel pars. *infra*); Church Hill (named from St Andrew's Church *supra*, cf. prec.); The Clover Grd; Coppice Ld (cf. *le Coppice* 1674); Copythorne (*Cappidthorn* 1460, *v.* **(ge)-coppod** 'polled', **þorn**, cf. Copthorne Sr 287); (The) Cow Leaze; Croles (probably the surname *Crole*); Green, Hr & Lt Cut Furze (*v.* **fyrs**; first el. **cut** 'a water-channel' or the pa.part. of the vb. *cut*); Davis' Md; Day Cl (*v.* **dey** 'a dairy'); Dodds Cl; Dyotts (cf. William *Dyette* 1550); The Eweleaze; First Flg; 4 & 14 Acres; Frys Mdw (cf. Nathaniel *Frye* 1686); Furmages Fd; Further Grd; Gilletts Grd; Goods Coppice; Great Md; Gulleys (a surname); Heatherleys (cf. Simon *Hatherly* 1698); Home Grd (cf. *Home Closes* 1618); Kite Hill (*v.* **cȳta**); Little Grd; Long Cl or Lt Ryalls (*Long Close* 1686, *v.* Ryalls *infra*); Long Fd; Long Lds (Coppice); Long Orchd; Manuels Firs (cf. Robert *Manuell* 1686, *v.* **fyrs** or **firr**); Martinote Grd (sic, probably to be connected with *Marke Nole way* 1686, *Martins hole Lane* 1696); The Mead; Middle Grd; Millers Grd, Md & 7 Acres; The Moor (cf. *Morelond'* 1460, *v.* **mōr, land**); New Down; Newfoundland (near the par. bdy); New inclosure; The 9 Acres;

Notleys (probably a surname from some p.n. such as Nutley in Winterborne K. 1285); Old Bank; Old Pound; The Park; (Lt) Peak (le Peake 1674, v. pēac); Petty Cl (v. pety); Plantation; Plot; Pond Fd; Pound Md; Puckers Md; Red Hill & Lds; Rick yard (cf. le Reeke Barton 1700, v. rickebarton); Rook Ditch (v. hrōc); Row (freq, v. row); Rushy Md; (Lt) Ryalls (Ryehill 1686, v. ryge); Sand Hills (Santhill 1621, Loveridges Sandhills 1686, v. sand, with the surname Loveridge); Sawpit Fd; School Ho; Shortwood (1686, v. sc(e)ort); Shrubbery; The 6 Acres; Smallways (Coppice) (v. smæl); The Springs; Strangemans E & W Breach, Strangemans Md (cf. William Strangeman 1664, v. Broad Breach supra); Strip; Old Sues (probably from the pers.n. Sue, a pet-form of Susan); 10 & Lt 3 Acres; 12 Acres (Twelve- 1674); 20 & 25 Acres; 22 Acres (Wd); Westfield and Long Courte (v. court); Wey Cl (v. weg); Woodside Barn & Plot (cf. Woodclose 1690); Woolley Down (perhaps identical in origin with Woolley Brk 291, etc, 'wolves' glade' from wulf and lēah); Yonder Grds.

(b) Aisshlegh' 1459, Ashly Wood 1620 (v. æsc, lēah); Beverlands 1684 (v. beofor); Bradmer(e) 1546 (v. brād, mere[1]); closes called Ye Breackes, Tharrable & Bushey Breackes 1673 (v. arable, bræc[1]); Brenylham 1550 (perhaps from brēmel 'bramble' and hamm); Brodecroft 1463 (v. brād, croft); Bromhull 1461, Bramlandes 1617 (v. brōm, hyll, land); Charelton 1462 (v. ceorl, tūn); Clive 1690 (v. clif (dat.sg. clife, nom.pl. clifu)); (Greate) Cokers 1686, 1697 (a surname); the Common 1674; Kokesdiche 1620, (le) Cookes Close 1673, 1674, Cookes 1674 (the surname Cook, v. dīc); Courte Koll 1673 (v. court, perhaps with coll 'hill'); la Crundell 1458–1461 (v. crundel); Field Gates 1690; the Fower Acres 1673 (v. fēower); Fryarnebridge 1550 ('friars' bridge', v. frere (ME wk.pl. -ene)); Parrock called Fyldeshay 1686 (probably the surname Field (< feld), v. pearroc, (ge)hæg); Giffords 1699 (a surname); Girehull' 1408 (v. hyll; first el. possibly *gyre 'dirt, mud', on which v. Löfvenberg 85); le grove 1690 (v. grāf(a)); Hasel(l)headge 1618 (v. hæsel, hecg); la Holt 1459–1461 (v. holt); Jolliffs lane 1674; Knyghteshey 1460 (v. cniht, (ge)hæg); Lancherhedge 1686 (v. landsc(e)aru); le lanes 1696 (v. lane); Litle Paddock 1686; Long(e) Lane 1618, 1684; Lose- 1618, Loosehangers 1696 (v. hlōse 'pig-sty', hangra); Merlin Pitt 1686 (probably from marling and pytt); Middel- 1460, Midlegrove 1618 (v. middel, grāf(a)); New meade 1618; Nyweton' 1461 (v. nīwe, tūn); Ouerlonde 1546 (v. uferra 'higher', land); Papilhill 1460, 1461, -hull 1462 (v. hyll; first el. possibly papol 'a pebble'); Pykes 1686 (probably a surname); via regia vocat' Portwey 1458–1460 (v. port-weg; probably the road to Wareham); Smokland 1459 (v. smoke, land); atte Stapele 1332 (p) (v. atte, stapol); prat' voc' Stokbrigg' 1464 (v. stocc, brycg, cf. Stockbridge in Lillington par. infra); Thersshefoldes 1464[2] ('enclosures where threshing was done', v. þersc, fald, cf. Threshfield YW 6 105); the Turffe Howse 1618 (v. turf, hūs); Wenesherd' 1458–1461 ('gap fit for a wagon', v. wægn, sceard); Whitbarrowe 1621 (v. hwīt, beorg); Whitmyll 1550 (v. hwīt, myln); White-, Whit(t)well (Closes) 1673 (v. hwīt, well(a)).

Winterborne Clenston

WINTERBORNE CLENSTON (ST 840028)

?*Wintreburne* 1086 DB (ff. 79b, 82), -*burn* 1232 Pat
Winterborn' Clench 1242–3 Fees
Clenchton' 1268 *Ass, Clenges-* 1316 FA, *Clenches-* 1327 *SR,*
1332 SR, 1340 NI, 1510 *MP, Cleyncheston(e)* 1349 Pat,
Clenston 1574 *Add* (-*als.*
Clencheston), (-*alias Winterborne
Clenston*) 1625 *AddCh,* 1774 Hutch[1] (*Higher & Lower-*)
Wynterborn Cleyngestone 1273 Ipm, *Wynterborne-, -burn'
Chencheston'* (sic) 1288 *Ass, Wynter-, Winterburn-,
-bo(u)rn(e) Clencheston(e)* 1303 FA *et freq* to 1510 *PlR,*
-*Clencheton* 1318 FF, 1397 Pat, -*Cl(e)yncheston* 1370 FF,
1378 Fine, -*Cleynston* 1514 *PlR,* -*Clenston* 1535 VE *et
passim,* -*Cleynston* 1544 *PlR*
Wynturburne Clenchston 1428 FA, *Clenston Winterborne* 1795
Boswell

Named from R. Winterborne, cf. Winterborne Z. par. *supra.*
The identification of the DB form(s) is that of Eyton 121–2
(also Fägersten 66), cf. VCHDo 3 135, DBGazetteer 129,
Winterborne Came 1 260. The manorial affix is from Robert
Clench 1232 Pat, *v.* tūn. For *Higher & Lower Clenston,* appar-
ently to be identified with the two former manors of *Winter-
borne Phelpston* and *Winterborne Nicholston* in this par., *v. infra,*
Taylor 56.

WINTERBORNE NICHOLSTON (lost), 1574 *Add, Wynter-, Winter-
burn'-, -bo(u)rn(e) Nicholeston(e)* 1283 AD VI, 1324 *Wim,* 1329
Hutch[3], -*Ni-, -Nycholaston* 1286 ib, 1544 *PlR,* -*Nicoles-,
-Necholeston* 1343–5 Ipm, -*Nicholson* 1625 *AddCh, Wynter-
born-, -burn Nicole* 1285 Ipm, 1286 Cl, *Nicholeston* 1340 NI,
Niclaston 1412 FA, *Wynterbourne Nicholai* 1428 ib, *Lower
Clenston or St Nicholas* 1795 Boswell, *v.* par. name *supra.* The
affix may be from the dedication of the church as suggested by
Hutch[3] 1 195 (*v.* St Nicholas's Church *infra*), but it is perhaps
more likely that it is manorial in origin and that the dedication
of the church to St Nicholas came later (cf. Osmington 1 212),
v. tūn. The pers.n. and surname *Nicholas* (from Lat *Nicolaus,*
gen. *Nicolai*) and its vernacular form *Nicol* were extremely
common, and a *Nicholas de Benham* is mentioned as holding

land in *Wynterburn Nicole* in 1286 Cl. According to Hutch[3] 1 195, *Winterborne Nicholston* 'seems to have lain near the present church and churchyard', in the S of the par., cf. *op. cit.* 1 193 for a former chapel near here, and *v.* Clenston Fm *infra*.

WINTERBORNE PHELPSTON (lost), 1544 *PlR*, 1574 *Add*, 1625 *AddCh*, *Wynterburn Philip's* 1244 FF, *Winterburn Philippeston*, *Wynterburn Phelipston* 1299 Banco, *Winterburne Felipeston* 1307 ib, *Wynterbourn Phelpeston* 1544 *PlR*, *Higher Clenston or Phillipson* 1795 Boswell, *v.* par. name *supra*. As with prec., the affix may be from a church dedication as suggested by Hutch[3] 1 195 (although there are no remains of a church, *op. cit.* 1 191), but it is more probably manorial in origin even though the *Philip* in question has not been noted, *v.* tūn. *Phelp* is a ME contracted (and vernacular) form of this common pers.n. and surname, *v.* Reaney s.n. *Philip*. *Winterborne Phelpston* lay in the N of the par. (Hutch[3] 1 191), *v.* Clenstone Fm *infra*.

CHARITY WD, part of Clenston Wd *infra*, so called because it belonged to 'Williams's Charity', *v.* foll. CLENSTONE FM, *Little*-1690 Hutch[3], *Upper Clenston farm* 1770 ib, *Charity Fm* 1811 OS, perhaps to be identified with *Higher Clenston*, *v.* foll., par. name and *Winterborne Phelpston supra*; this farm, together with nearby woodland, belonged to 'Williams's Charity' on which *v.* Hutch[3] 1 236–7, cf. prec. CLENSTON FM, *the fearme of Clenston* 1646 SC, *the farme of Clinsson* 1647 ib, perhaps to be identified with *Lower Clenston*, cf. prec., *v.* par. name and *Winterborne Nicholston supra*. CLENSTON LODGE & WD (*-Woods* 1770 Hutch[3], *Clenstone Wd* 1839 *TA*). HEATHY FD COPPICE, (*-Copse*) 1839 *TA*. MANOR HO. NEW BARN. OATCLOSE WD. OLD RECTORY, cf. *Parsonage Md* 1839 *TA*. ST NICHOLAS'S CHURCH, perhaps originally the church of *Winterborne Nicholston supra*, cf. *Ecclesia Sancti Andr' de Wynterborne Chencheston'* (sic) 1288 *Ass*, *ecclesia de Clencheston* 1510 *MP*.

FIELD-NAMES

The undated forms in (*a*) are 1839 *TA* 249, in (*b*) 1324 *Wim*. The fields marked † (a small detached portion) are now in Winterborne Stickland par. *infra*. Spellings dated 1324 are *Wim*, 1327 *SR*, 1332 SR, 1349 Pat, and 1647 *Bartelot*.

   (*a*) Bate Leaze (identical with the f.n. Beat Leaze in Puddletown par. 1

323); Broadland; Calves Cl; Clenstone Coppice & Down; †Copse; Copse Cl; Cowleaze; Dry Md; Egnes Fd; 11 Acres; Eweleaze; †Fair Mill (Down); Further & Nthr Ganson (sic) (*le Garston* 1324, *v.* **gærs-tūn**); Great Md; Higher Fd; Homestead; Hop Gdn; Long Fd & Md; Middle Fd; Mill Md (cf. *Clenston Mille* 1647); North Fd; Park; The Range (*v.* **range** 'row (of trees, buildings, etc)'); Rowe Plot (from **rūh** 'rough' or **rāw** 'a row'); Shepherds Ho; 6 Acres; South Fd; Square Fd; Strip; Stubbey Down (Copse) (*v.* **stubbig**); 12 Acres; Warren Fd; West Fd (*occident' camp'* 1324); Withey Bed.

(b) *Addreputte* (*v.* **næddre, pytt**); *camp' oriental'*; *le Gorþorne* (*v.* **gāra** or **gor, þorn**); *Lancer Acre* (*v.* **land-sc(e)aru, æcer**); *atte Lane* (p) 1327, 1332, 1349 (*v.* **atte, lane**); *Langeþorne* (*v.* **lang¹, þorn**); *þe Schortmarle* (*v.* **sc(e)ort, marle**); *Terrys croft* (the pers.n. or surname *Terry* (< OFr *T(h)ierri*), and **croft**); *Watforlange* (*v.* **wēt**, WSax **wǣt** 'wet', **furlang**).

Winterborne Tomson

Since 1933 in Anderson par. *supra.*

WINTERBORNE TOMSON (SY 885974)
   (at) *Winterburne* 942 (15) *ShaftR* (S 485(1)), *?Wintreburne* 1086 DB
   Winterborn' Thom' 1242–3 Fees
   Wynterborn' Thā(m)ston' 1268 *Ass*, *Wynter-, Wyntreburn-, -bo(u)rn(e) Thomaston* 1280 FF, 1297 Pat *et freq* to 1428 *Midd*, -*Tomaston* 1412 FA, *Winterbourne Thomastone* 1330 Pat, *Wynturburne Thomston* 1428 FA, *Thompson Winterborne* 1795 Boswell
   Thomaston 1316 FA, 1367 Pat, 1426 *Midd*, 1484 Hutch³ (-*Pegges*), *Thomaseston* 1340 NI, *Thomston* 1428 FA, *Tomaston* 1433, *Tompston* 1495 *Midd*, *Tomson* 1575 Saxton, 1617 *Add*

Named from R. Winterborne, cf. Winterborne Z. par. *supra.* For the possible DB identification, *v.* Eyton 121–2, DBGazetteer 129, cf. VCHDo 3 135. The affix *Thom', Thomaston*, etc is probably manorial in origin, although the *Thomas* in question has not been noted, *v.* **tūn**; however, the form *Winterburn' Tome Malfillastre* 1204 P may belong here. The later affix -*Pegges* is no doubt from the family of *P(u)eg* which gave its name to Pegg's Fm (formerly a manor) in Iwerne M. par. *infra*; like Winterborne Tomson, this manor was later held by the *Hussey* family, *v.* Hutch³ 1 195, 3 540.

DEN WD, *Denwodforlange* 1284 Cl, *v.* **denu** 'valley', **wudu, furlang**; Fägersten 67 cites the bdy point (*anlang*) *standene* 943 (15) *ShaftR* (S 490) under this name, but cf. Forsberg 205, *v.* under Almer par. *supra.* ST ANDREW'S CHURCH (disused), *ecclesia Sancti Andree de Wynterborn' Thāston'* 1268 *Ass,* 'chapel of *Wyntreburn Thomaston'* 1297 Pat, *Church & Church Yd* 1838 *TA,* cf. *Parsonage Ho & Gdn* 1838 *ib,* Anderson par. *supra.* TOMSON FD BARN, cf. *Barn Mdw, (Coppice in) Higher & Middle Fd* 1838 *TA.* TOMSON FM, *-Manor Fm* 1838 *ib.*

FIELD-NAMES

The undated forms in (*a*) are 1838 *TA* 231, in (*b*) 942 (15) *ShaftR* (S 485(1)).

(*a*) Crawford Way Fd ('the road to (Gt) Crawford' (in Spettisbury par. *supra*), here with reference to the Dorchester–Badbury Roman road which is *Crawford Way* 1838 *TAMap*); Gt, Hr, Lt & Upr Down (*v.* **dūn**); Gore Fd (cf. *þurh þane garen infra, v.* **gāra**); Hr Coppice; Lr & Upr Hundred Acres (two quite large fields); Long Fd; Middle Croft; Paradice Md (*v.* **paradis**); Pidgeon Ho Mdw; Rooke Hayes (*v.* **hrōc, (ge)hæg**); The 10 Acres.

(*b*) *to nearn þan-, of þan anstigan* ('narrow path', *v.* **nearu, ānstiga**; Professor Löfvenberg points out that *nearn þan* is probably corrupt for dat.sg. *nearuwan*); *one þo berges astward* (*v.* **beorg** 'hill, tumulus'); *anlang broke* (*v.* **brōc**); *to-, of chelfgraue* (*v.* **calf** (WSax **cealf**), **grāf(a)**); *on þene depe crundel* (*v.* **dēop, crundel**); *to þane ealde seale* (*v.* **ald** (WSax **eald**), **salh** (WSax **sealh**)); *þurh þane garen* (*v.* **gāra**; Gore Fd *supra* lies c. ¼ mile S of this point); *anlang herepaþes, on lang þane herepaþe* (*v.* **here-pæð**); *on hornget, of horngetes hirne* (cf. *horgate* in Almer par. *supra*); *lang land share, of dune an lang land share* (*v.* **land-sc(e)aru**); *to leaxan oc* (the OE pers.n. **Leaxa* (*v.* Forsberg 71), **āc,** cf. the f.n. *Laxted forlong* in Sturminster M. par. *supra*); *one meairweie, anlang weies* (*v.* **(ge)mǣre, weg**); *to midelgete, of midelgate* (*v.* **middel, geat**); *on þe sherd, of þene sherde, of þane shearde* (*v.* **sceard**); *tou þares túnes hirne* (*v.* **tūn, hyrne**); *one wicweie neþerward* (*v.* **wīc, weg**); *to widesgete, anlang þides* (for *-wides*) (*v.* **wudu, widu, geat,** *v.* Coll Wood in Almer par. *supra*); *an lang wdes* (*v.* **wudu**).

Winterborne Whitchurch

Part of Milton Abbas par. (that known as 'Whitchurch End') was added to this par. in 1933 (Kelly).

WINTERBORNE WHITCHURCH (-WHITECHURCH 1″) (ST 836001)
     ?*Wintreburne* 1086 DB, *Winterburn'* 1200 Cur
     Winterburn Albi Monasterii 1201 FF *et freq* to 1299 (e15)
          MiltRoll with variant spellings *Wynter-, -born-*
     Winterburn' Blancmustier 1212 P, *Winterburn and Blaunc-*

muster 1249 FF, *Wynter-*, *Winterburn-*, *-born Bla(u)ncmuster* 1253, 1256 FF, *-Blaun(c)mynstre*, *-minstre* 1275, 1276 Banco, *-Blauncmusters* 1280 Ch, *-Blaumuster*, *-Blauncmoster* 1303 FA, *vill' de Blanckmuster* 1288 *Ass*
Winterborn' Rocheford' 1242–3 Fees
Wynterborn' (et) Wytecherch(e) 1268 *Ass*, *Wynterburne-*, *-bo(u)rn(e) Whyt(e)chirch(e)* 1288 *ib*, 1294 Cl, *-W(h)yt-*, *-Whitchurch(e)* 1288 *Ass et passim* with variant spellings *-Withcherche* 1331 Ipm, *Wynt(o)ur-* 1399 Cl, 1428 FA, *-chirche*, *-chyrche* 1428 ib, 1497 Ipm, *Winterburn and Witchirch* 1294 Misc
Wycchirch (for Wyt-) 1291 Tax, *Whitchirche* 1294 Cl, *W(h)yt-*, *Whit(e)church(e)* 1316 FA *et freq* to 1575 *PlR*, *Whitechurch Winterborne* 1795 Boswell

Named from R. Winterborne, cf. Winterborne Z. par. *supra*. For the possible DB identification, *v.* Eyton 121–2, DBGazetteer 129, cf. VCHDo 3 135. The affix means 'white church', from OE **hwīt** and **cirice**, alternating with Lat *albus* and *monasterium*, OFr *blanc* and *moustier*; the name is a common one (cf. Bk 86, O 63, etc) and possibly denotes a church built of stone (as distinct from a wooden one), cf. Whitchurch C. par. *infra*, EPN 1 273. The affix *-Rocheford'* is from the family of this name which held a manor here from the 13th–15th centuries (Hutch[3] 1 196–7), cf. John *de Rocheford* 1294 Cl, 1319 FF, 1340 NI, *-de Rogeford* 1316 FA, etc. Other forms which possibly belong to (manors in) this par. are *Winterburne Gurewambe* a1165, c. 1165 (both p1305) MontC (for the identification, *v.* T. Bond, DoNHAS 11 146) and *Wynterburne Leton'* 1288 *Ass*; the affix *-Gurewambe* is no doubt manorial, although no family of this name has been noted here; *-Leton'* is probably OE **lēac-tūn** 'leek enclosure', or, if manorial, a surname from a p.n. of this origin.

LA LEE FM (ST 833011) [lə'li:], *la Le* 1244 *Ass* (p), 1553 *PlR*, *La Lee* 1280 Winch, 1288 *Ass*, 1321 *Winch et passim*, *La Leye* 1291 Tax, *La Lea* 1310 Inq aqd, 1311 Pat, *Lee* 1317 MiltC, *Laley* 1560 Hutch[3], *Law Lee* 1664 HTax, 1688 *PlR*, *Lalee* 1774 Hutch[1], 'the clearing in a wood' or, since the name is probably of post-Conquest origin, 'the meadow', *v.* **la**, **lēah**, cf. Lee Wood *infra* which lies adjacent to the farm. The survival of the

Fr def.art. la as an independent word, and the absence of alternation with Engl *the*, are noteworthy, and suggest strong Fr influence (the manor was held by Milton abbey).

WHATCOMBE FM & HO (ST 837013), HR & LR WHATCOMBE, *Watecumbe* 1288 *Ass*, 1316 FA, *-combe* 1332 SR, *Whatecumbe* 1288 *Ass*, *-combe* 1412 FA, *Wadecombe* 1327 *SR*, *Wynterborn Wateco(u)mbe* 1343–5 Ipm, 1370 FF, *-Whatecombe* 1402 IpmR, *Watco(u)mbe* 1363 Cl, 1647 *Bartelot*, *Whatcombe* 1510 *MP et passim*, *Wynterbourn-* 1544 *PlR*, *Winterborn Whatcomb(e)* 1774 Hutch[1], *Hr & Lr Whatcomb* 1811 OS, probably 'wet valley', *v*. wēt (WSax wǣt), cumb, rather than 'valley where wheat is grown', *v*. hwǣte, cf. Whatcombe Brk 299; like the village itself, this place is on R. Winterborne. Fägersten 68 identifies *on hwete cumb* 943 (15) *ShaftR* (S 490) with this name, but this is not possible as pointed out by Forsberg 205, *v*. under Almer par. *supra*. The form *Winterburn' Guah(e)bon* 1235, 1236 Cl is identified with Whatcombe in the indexes of those calendars; the affix is no doubt manorial, but no family of this name has been noted here.

CLIFF WD, *-Lane* 1839 *TA*, cf. *Bushey & Corn Cliff* 1839 *ib*, *v*. clif. THE CLUMP. DAIRY HO. DOLWAY CTGS, *Dolwey*, *Daleweyforlang* 1317 *MiltC*, *Dolway* 1839 *TA*, perhaps 'way by shared land', from dāl and weg; the place is near the par. bdy. DOWN BLDGS, EAST DOWN CTGS & PLANT., cf. *la Indoune*, *la Southdoune* 1317 *MiltC*, *le West downe* 1553 *PlR*, *West Down* 1839 *TA*, *Down(e) Close* 1688 *PlR*, 1839 *TA*, *Whitchurch Down* 1811 OS, *East Down (Plant.)* 1839 *TA*, *v*. dūn, in 'inner', cf. Whatcombe Down *infra*. EAST FM. FIELD BARN, cf. *Whitechurch fd* 1839 *TA*. HOLLOWAY'S WD, 1839 *ib*, cf. *Luc(a) de Holeweye* 1303 FA, *v*. hol[2], weg. HORSE CLOSE PLANT., *(Plant. in) Horse Cl* 1839 *TA*. LEE WD, 1546 Hutch[3], 1839 *TA*, cf. *Lee Fd* 1839 *ib*, *v*. La Lee Fm *supra*. LOWER STREET, *Lr Whitchurch* 1811 OS, *v*. strǣt, here denoting the lower end of the straggling village. PEAT HILL, *v*. pete. THE PLANTATION, cf. *Plantation (freq)* 1839 *TA*. ST MARY'S CHURCH, cf. *Philipus le chapeleyn de Wynterborn' de Albo Monastr'* 1268 *Ass*, *Ecclesia Albi Monasterii* 1428 FA, *v*. par. name *supra*. SCENT CLOSE PLANT., first el. probably senget 'place cleared by burning', possibly with lēah as in St Chloe Gl 1 98, Saintlow *ib* 3 219, with later adaptation to *close*. STONE PITS. VICARAGE. WARREN CLOSE PLANT., *Warrens Close (Plant.*), *Gt Warren Fd* 1839 *TA*, *v.* **wareine**. WELL HO, cf. *Well Grd* 1839 *ib*. WEST FM. WESTON'S WD, 1839 *ib*, probably a surname, from the common p.n. *Weston*. WHATCOMBE COMMON (cf. *The Common* 1839 *ib*), DOWN (1839 *ib*) & PARK (*Park* 1317 *MiltC*, *The Park* 1839 *TA*, *v.* **park**), cf. Whatcombe *supra*. WHITCHURCH HILL BARN, cf. *Hilacres* 1317 *MiltC*, *Hillclose Gate* 1627 *Bartelot*, *v.* **hyll**.

FIELD-NAMES

The undated forms in (*a*) are 1839 *TA* 254, in (*b*) 1317 *MiltC*. Spellings dated 1249 (14) are Cerne, 1317 *MiltC*, 1321 *Winch*, 1554, 1597, 1688 *PlR*, and 1664 HTax.

(*a*) Barn Fd (cf. *Barne mead* 1688); Blandford Bottom (from Blandford St M. par. *supra*, *v.* **botm**); Burnbake (*v.* **burnbake**); Burrow Fd (*v.* **burg**); Bushy Cl; Calves Mdw; Chalky Fd & Grd; Corn Grd; Cow Down (Plant.), Cowleaze (freq) (cf. *Cow close* 1688); (Hr & Lr) Croft (cf. *Overcroft, Croftesthorne* 1317, *v.* **uferra, croft, þorn**); Cucumber Gdn; 8 Acres; Elm Nursery; (Btm) Eweleaze; 15 Acres; Flockshard (perhaps 'gap through which a flock (of sheep) could be driven', *v.* **flocc, sceard**, cf. Shepherds' Shore W 251); French Grass Fd (*v.* **french grass**); Great Close Plant.; Great Fd (Plant.) & Mdw; The Grove; Hanging Plant. (*v.* **hangende, hanging**); Harbins Md; Higher Fd; Highway Fd (by Blandford–Dorchester road); Hogsdown; Home Fd, Mdw, Orchd & Pce; The Home Paddock; Hunts Down (cf. Robert *Hunt* 1664); Hum Furland (perhaps for *Hurn*, *v.* **hyrne, furlang**); Kitchen Gdn; Kite Hill (*v.* **cȳta**); Little & Lower Fd; Mastermans Grd; Middle Fd (*medius camp* 1317); Morris' Sleight (cf. *Sleithefurlang* 1317, *v.* **slæget, sleget, furlang**); North Fd (*camp' borial'* 1317); Orchard (Cl); Over Fd (*v.* **uferra**); Parrick (cf. *le wood parrock* 1688, *v.* **pearroc**); Peaked Fd (*v.* **peked**); (Lime Pit and) Peaky Fd (*v.* **peaky**); Plott; The Pound; Round Mdw; Serree Cl; 7 Acres; Shrubbery; Smoky Hole; South Fd; 10 Acres; Thistle Croft; Thorney Grd; Three Furlong Grd; 28 Acres; Two Ctgs; Gt & Lt Water Mdw; West Hill; Windmill Fd.

(*b*) Boltons 1664 (a surname); *la Broche* (probably for -*Breche*, *v.* **brǣc**); la Cumbe (*v.* **cumb**); *Foxle(e)* (*v.* **fox, lēah**); *Garston'* 1249 (14) (*v.* **gærs-tūn**); *Nether-, Overgerdelond* (*v.* **neoðerra, uferra, gerd, land**); *Atgodewynesthorne* ('(land) at Godwine's thorn-tree', from the OE pers.n. *Godwine* and **þorn**, *v.* **æt**); *La Grotene* (apparently OE ***groten** 'sandy' used as a noun to denote 'sandy soil' or 'a sandy place', cf. the analogous *le Groten* Sr 36, W 66); *Hevedlond* (*v.* **hēafod-land**); *Hywissch-* 1317, *Hiwisshecroft(e)* 1321 (*v.* **hīwisc**, croft); *the Joyners Howse* 1597; *Knapforlang* (*v.* **cnæpp, furlang**); (*West*)-*langwode* (*v.* **west, lang¹, wudu**); *Layndone* (*v.* **leyne, lain, dūn**); *Levidiforhurde* (*v.* **hlǣfdige, forierð, -yrð**; perhaps land dedicated to the Virgin Mary); *Middelforlang* (*v.* **middel, furlang**); *Mustardes wodde* 1554, *Musterds wood* 1688 (the surname *Mustard*, *v.* **wudu**); *Bynorthebury* ('(land) to the north of the fortified place', *v.* **bī, norðan, burh** (dat.sg. *byrig*)); *Osmonds Close* 1688; *Roudone, Roweleye, -lee* ('rough hill and clearing', *v.* **rūh** (wk.obl. *rūwan*), **dūn, lēah**); *cot' voc' Scamas* 1554 (probably a surname); *Bytwunewode* ('(land) between the woods', *v.* **betwēonan, wudu** (dat.pl. *wudum*), cf. *in bosco exteriori* 1321); *Virniforlang* (*v.* **fearnig, furlang**); *camp' occidental'*.

XIII. PIMPERNE HUNDRED

The present hundred is an amalgamation of the small GeldR hundred of Pimperne and the greater parts of the GeldR hundreds of *Hunesberge* and *Langeberge* (Eyton 131–2, 137–8, Anderson 133–4, VCHDo 3 138–40). The two last disappeared at the beginning of the 13th cent. Of the area now in this hundred, the GeldR hundred of Pimperne contained only Pimperne itself, Steepleton Iwerne and Stourpaine. The old hundred of *Hunesberge* contained the present pars. of Bryanston, Durweston, Fifehead N., Hammoon, Haselbury B. and Winterborne Stic., Okeford F. (now in Sturminster N. hundred), Shillingstone and Turnworth (both now in Cranborne hundred), and Plumber in Lydlinch (now in Sherborne hundred). The old hundred of *Langeberge* contained the present pars. of Langton Long B., Tarrant H., Tarrant K., Tarrant L. and Tarrant Raw., Chettle and Tarrant M. (both now in Monkton Up Wimborne hundred), Ashmore, Farnham, Tarrant G. and Tarrant Rush. (all now in Cranborne hundred). Winterborne Hou. par. was probably in Combs Ditch hundred in c. 1086 GeldR (Eyton 121–2). Turnworth par. was in Pimperne hundred in 1316 FA, 1332 SR. Lower Fifehead or Fifehead St Quintin in Fifehead N. par. was a tithing in Cranborne hundred in 1327 *SR*, 1332 SR, 1664 HTax. Pimperne hundred was appurtenant to the manor of Pimperne and belonged to the Honour of Gloucester. The pars. of Haselbury B. and Fifehead N. form a detached unit, and Hammoon par. is also detached. Blandford F., a borough in 1332 SR, 1664 HTax, etc has been included in this hundred for topographical convenience as by Hutch[1] 1 75.

PIMPERNE HUNDRED, *Pinpre hundret* c. 1086 GeldR, *Pinpre* 1212 Fees, *Pimper, Pympere* 1244 *Ass, Pimpre* 1255 *AD, Pympre* 1269 Cl, *Pimpr'* 1280 *Ass; Pinpern* 1265 Misc, *Pynperne* 1288 *Ass,* 1290 Pat (*-Forinsecus*), *Pympern(e), Pimpern(e)* l13 *AD,* 1268, 1280 *Ass et passim,* '*Pymperne* foreign' 1290 Fine, *Pemperne* 1664 HTax. Named from Pimperne par. *infra* which was the *caput* of the hundred and to which it was annexed. Lat *forinsecus* ('foreign') denotes the 'out-hundred'.

HUNESBERGE HUNDRED (lost), *Hunesberge hundret* c. 1086 GeldR, *Hunebergahdr'* 1175 P, *Hundesburg'* 1212 Fees. Probably 'Hūn(a)'s hill or barrow' from the OE pers.n. *Hūn* or *Hūna* and **beorg**, cf. (*be*) *Hunesbiorge* KPN 228, *Honesberie* hundred Wa 267, Anderson 133. The site of the barrow (or hill) is not known.

LANGEBERGE HUNDRED (lost), *Langeberge hundret* c. 1086 GeldR, *Langebergahdr'* 1160 P, *Langeber'*, -*berg'*, -*burgh* 1212 Fees, 'long (hill or) barrow', *v.* **lang¹, beorg**, possibly with reference to Pimperne Long Barrow in Tarrant H. par. *infra* (as suggested by Hutch³ 1 214), to Chettle Long Barrow in Chettle par. *infra* (as alternatively suggested by Anderson 134), to the Long Barrow (marked 6″) in Tarrant Raw. par. *infra*, or to some other long barrow within the area of this old hundred.

LOST OR UNIDENTIFIED NAMES IN PIMPERNE HUNDRED: *Brounescroft* 1366 Pat (the surname *Brown*, **croft**); *Childeford* 1280 *Ass* (*v.* **cild** (gen.pl. *cilda*) 'young person', **ford**, cf. Chilford C 99); *Fayleswode* 1366 Pat (*v.* **wudu**, perhaps with an unvoiced form of the surname *Vaile*); (*manor and farm of*) *Furmage* 1566 Hutch³, 1661 *AddCh* (apparently the surname *Furmage* (from OFr *fourmage* 'cheese') which occurs locally, e.g. Edmund *Fyrmadge* c. 1580 *Hen¹* (Durweston), *clausum Johannis Formage* 1601 *ib* (Lytchett Min.)); *Pykemull'* 1280 *Ass*, -*mill'* 1288 *ib* (*v.* **myln**, first el. perhaps **pīc¹** 'point'); (*Le*) *Wodehous* 1366 Pat, 1412 FA (*v.* **wudu, hūs**).

Blandford Forum

Parts of this par. were transferred to Pimperne par. and Bryanston par. in 1886 and 1894.

BLANDFORD FORUM (ST 886065) ['blɑːnvərd]
  ?*Blaneford* 1086 DB, -*ford(e)* 1182–1186 P, 1199 FF, 1205, 1214 P, 1216 ClR, PatR, 1219 Fees, 1226 Cur *et freq* to 1458 *AddCh*, *Burgus de Blaneford(e)* 1244, 1280, 1288 all *Ass*, *Blanford(e)* 1348 Pat *et freq* to 1547 *Ct*, *Blandeford* 1377 Pat
  Beneford (sic) 1189 France, 1200 (1280) *HarlCh*, *Bleneford(e)* 1191–1195 P, 1222 ClR, 1278 QW, *Bleinefort* 1201 (1231) *AddCh*
  Blaneford super Stur 1279 Pat, '-upon *Stures*' 1279 Fine
  Blaneford(e) Forum 1297 Pat *et freq* to 1470 *Rawl*, *Blanford-* 1340 NI *et freq* to 1501 *DLCt*, *Blanforth-* 1441 EL, *Blandford-* 1506 Pat *et passim*, *Blanneford Forum* 1512 *Pars*

Cheping Blaneford 1288 FF, *Chuping-, -yng Blaneford* 1310, 1344 FF, *Blanford Chepyng* 1311 Pat, *Cheping-, -yngblan(e)ford* 1319, 1330 FF *et freq* to 1429 *EgCh*, 1466 FF (*-al. Blanford Forum*), *Chapynblanford' alias dict' Blanford' Forum* 1466 Weld[1] *Blaneford forinc'* (possibly for *-forum*) 1327 *SR*

Possibly 'ford where gudgeon are found', from **blǣge** (gen.pl. *blǣgna*) 'the blay, the gudgeon' (a small fresh-water fish) and **ford**, as suggested by Ekwall Studies[1] 62. For other early forms of the name, *v.* Blandford St M. par. *supra*, Bryanston par. and Langton Long B. par. both *infra*. The DB form *Blaneford* (f. 79b, second entry) is tentatively placed here by VCHDo 3 87, but identified with Bryanston par. *infra* by Eyton 131–2, DBGazetteer 117. According to Drew, the probably corrupt form 'the church of *Blendfort*' 1101–1118 (e17 copy) France (identified with Blandford in the index to France, and cited under Blandford F. by Fägersten 50) belongs under Blynfield in Cann. The affixes allude to the situation of Blandford F. on R. Stour (*v.* RNs. *infra*) and to its early importance as a market town (*v.* Lat **forum**, OE **cēping** (WSax **cī(e)ping**), cf. Fair Fd, Market Place *infra*). If the affix *-forinc'* in 1327 is not a scribal error but denotes Lat *forinsecus*, it must refer to the part of the town outside the hundred of Pimperne, i.e. the old borough (*burgus* from 1244) which lay to the E of Salisbury St.; the bounds of *The Borough of Blandforde* are given in 1591 *DLMB* (Vol. 116, f. 48). The area of the town to the W, within the hundred, was referred to as the *Warnership(p) of. Pim-, Pymperne* 1636 NED, 1664 HTax, 1774 Hutch[1], from *warrenership* 'the office of warrener or gamekeeper', *v.* **warener**, cf. *chace of Pymperne* 1316 Fine, 1317 Cl, *Warennarius* 'the warrener (of the hundred)' 1547 *Ct, v.* **chace**. There is mention of *Hund' de* ('the hundred of') *Blaneford'* in 1244 *Ass*.

BLANDFORD FORUM STREETS AND BUILDINGS

BRYANSTON ST., *-stone-* 1824 Pigot, to Bryanston par. *infra*. DAMORY ST., *Dammerie Lane* 1591 *DLMB*, named from Damory Court *infra*. EAST ST., 1774 Hutch[1], *the Kinges High Waye* 1591 *DLMB*. FAIRFIELD RD, cf. Fair Fd *infra*. MARKET PLACE, 1774 ib; a market at Blandford is mentioned in 1218

Cl (Hutch³ 1 216), 1409 EL and in 1468 *MinAcct* (*shamell' in foro*), cf. also *Market-st, Sheep Market-hill* 1824 Pigot and the former market cross (Hutch³ 1 220) mentioned in 1425 EL. PARK RD, to Bryanston Park now in Bryanston par. *infra*. PLOCKS, 1824 Pigot, from dial. **plock** 'small plot of ground'. ST LEONARD'S AVE, cf. St Leonard's Chapel *infra*. SALISBURY RD & ST. (1774 Hutch¹), to Salisbury W; the former is *Sarum High Waie* 1591 *DLMB*, *the Great road* 1784 *SalisT*, the latter is perhaps 'the High Street' 1403 EL, 1694 DCMDeed. SHORT'S LANE. THE CLOSE. WEST ST., cf. *iter quod se ducit de Blaneford Forum versus Dorchestre* 1458 *AddCh*. WHITE CLIFF MILL ST., 1824 Pigot, leading to Whitecliff Mill in Pimperne par. *infra*.

Lost street-names include *the Almes House Lane* 1591 *DLMB* (cf. 'the alms-houses' *infra*); *le Churchestrete* 1501 *DLCt* (cf. Church of Saints Peter & Paul *infra*), *the Comen Lane* 1391 *DLMB*, *Townslane* 1303 *DLCt*.

Buildings include 'the alms-houses' 1568 Hutch³ (cf. 'the new alms-house called Ryves's alms-house' 1774 Hutch¹, from George *Ryves* who endowed it 1685); *Corn-Exchange* 1861 Hutch³; *Dashwood's bakehouse* 1690 ib (cf. John *Dashewood* 1547 *Ct*); *The Guilde Hawll* 1591 *DLMB*; 'The Hurdle House' 1623 BlandF; 'the (Free-)school house' 1568, 1861 both ib.

Inns (forms from 1824 Pigot unless otherwise stated) include *Black Bear, Black Dog, Blue Boar, Cock & George, Cricketter's,* 'tenement or hospice called *le Crowne*' 1465 EL, *the Crown Inn* 1774 Hutch¹, *Fleur d'Lis, George, Greyhound* 1753 BlandF, *Half Moon, King's Arms, New Inn, Portman's Arms, Red Lion, Three Choves, White Bear* 1837 *TA, White Hart.*

DAMORY COURT (lost, about ST 888064), 1774 Hutch¹, 'the manor called *Damemarieplace* of *Chepyngblaneford*' 1363 Pat, *Dame Mary-, -Marie Place de Chepyngblaneford* 1363 Inq aqd, Orig, *the Daumarye Courte* 1591 *DLMB, Damerie-, Damery Court next Blandford* 1616 DoIpm, *Damory-house* 1774 Hutch¹, formerly considered (by Coker cited in Hutch³ 1 222 and by Hutch¹ 1 80) to have been named from a family called *Damory*, but as pointed out by Fägersten 51 probably an allusion to the possession of this manor by the abbey of St Mary, Fontevrault (*v.* Hutch³ 1 222, 1189 France p. 384, 1363 Inq aqd p. 334), *v.* **place, court.** Hutch¹ 1 80 adds: 'A little N of this house was a remarkable oak, called *Damory Oak*'. Cf. Damory Court Ctgs & Fm in Pimperne par. *infra*.

BLANDFORD BRIDGE, cf. *pons de Blaneford* 1268 *Ass et freq* to 1341 *Wim, atte Brigg*' 1332 SR (p) (Bryanston), *Blandfordes-brigge* 1337 DorR, *Blanford Bridg(e)* 1535–43 Leland, *Blandford Bridg* 17 *CecilMap, v.* **brycg, atte**; in 1774, Hutch¹ 1 79 notes that 'At the west end of the town is a great bridge of five arches, and east of that two lesser ones'. CHURCH OF SAINTS PETER &

PAUL (Kelly), cf. *ecclesia Sancti Petri de Blaneford* 1288 *Ass*, le *Churchestrete supra.* FAIR FD, cf. '*cultura* called *La Fayre*' 1284 Cl, *Fairlond* 1423 Hutch[3], v. **feire, land**; Hutch[3] 1 216 notes that 'A fair was granted here 35 Ed I [1307]' and that 'Here are now three fairs'; in fact there is mention of a fair at Blandford in 1279 Pat. THE HAM, on R. Stour, v. **hamm**. THE MARSH, 1617 BlandF, *the Comen Marshe* 1591 *DLMB*, v. **mersc**, also on R. Stour. ST EALDHELMS. ST LEONARD'S CHAPEL, 'a ruined ecclesiastical building, now used as a barn' (1861 Hutch[3] 1 241), cf. 'the hospital of St Leonard juxta Blandford' 1420 ib 1 283 which must be the 'house of lepers' stated by Hutch[1] 1 98 to be mentioned in a deed of 1282, v. St Leonards Fm in Langton Long B. par. *infra*, cf. VCHDo 2 100.

FIELD-NAMES

For some fields in Blandford F. *TA* but now in Bryanston or Pimperne, v. under those pars. The undated forms are 1837 *TA* 20. Spellings dated 1284 are Cl, 1288[1] FF, 1288[2] *Ass*, 1458 *AddCh*, 1591 *DLMB*, 1592 Hutch[3], 1623 BlandF, and 1861 Hutch[3].

(a) Lt Bowling Green 1861 (cf. *The Bowling Green* 1623); Cow Leaze; The Island; Meadow; Oak Mdw; Picket Cl (perhaps from **pīcede** 'pointed'); Pleasure Grd; Rope Cl; 10 Acres.

(b) *the backwater* 1591 (v. **lagge**); *the Bridge Lagg* 1591 (v. **lagge**); *barne called Bridmere* 1591; *Duntch Meade* 1591; *Atte Halle* (p) 1288[1] (v. **atte, hall**); '*cultura* called *le Marler*' 1284 (OFr **marliere** 'marl-pit'); *the Outhaies* 1591, *The Out hays* 1623 (v. **ūt, (ge)hæg**); '*cultura* called *Pilewen*' 1284 (perhaps 'wen-shaped barrow or mound marked by a stake', v. **pīl, wenn**); *The Play Close* 1592 ('for the use of shooting at the butts', Hutch[3] 1 221); *de la Sale* (p) 1288[2] (either from **sealh** 'willow', dat.sg. *seale* (with a short diphthong from the nom. form), or from **sæl** 'hall'); *Shortegge* 1284 (v. **sc(e)ort, ecg**); *campus australis* 1458; *Stoke Mede* 1397 EL, *Stok(e)mede* 1403 ib, *Stoke Meadowe* 1591 (probably to be associated with Hyde (earlier *Stokehyde*) in Tarrant H. par. *infra*, v. **mæd**); *de la Stone, -Stane* (p) 1288[2] (v. **stān**).

Bryanston

Parts of Blandford F. par. were added to this par. in 1894, and parts of Pimperne and Winterborne Stic. pars. in 1897.

BRYANSTON (ST 875069)
?*Blaneford* 1086 DB, -*ford*' 1212 Fees, 1232 Cl, *Blaneford Brion* n.d. (Hy 3) Osm, -*Brian* 1268 *Ass*, 1270 Ipm

Brianeston(e) 1268, 1288 *Ass*, 1291 Tax *et freq* to 1451 Pat
with variant spelling *Bryanes-; Brianis-, Bryaniston'* 1268,
1288 *Ass, Briames-* 1285 FA, *Bramps-, Bryam(p)s-* 1288
Ass, Branes- 1291 Tax, *Brien(e)s-, Bryens-* 1295 Ch *et
freq* to 1445 Pat, *Bryans-, Brianston(e)* 1314 Ch *et passim,
Brauneston* 1410 Pat

'Brian's estate', *v.* **tūn**, named from *Brian de Insula* who held
this manor early in the reign of Hy 3 (*B. de Insula* 1232 Cl,
Brianus de Insula de Blaneford 1232 Pat, *v.* Hutch³ 1 248) and
who also gave his name to *Bradford Brian*, now Bradford Fm
in Pamphill par. *infra*. For the possible identification of one
of the DB manors called *Blaneford* with Bryanston, *v.* Blandford F. par. *supra*.

BROADLEY CTG, PLANT. & WD (ST 850060), (*silvam de-, terre
arabilis de*) *Bradele, Bradele(ye)combe* 1334 (15) *MiltC, Brade-
legh* 1344 Pat, *-ley* (*in Stykelane*) 1431 FA, *Little Bradley* 1586
Hutch³, *Broadly Grounds* 1650 ib, *Bradley* (*Wd*) 1811 OS,
'broad wood or clearing', *v.* **brād, lēah**, with **cumb** 'valley';
part of this wood was formerly in Winterborne Stic. par. *infra*.

BEECH CLUMP. BRYANSTON (LOWER) FM, *-Farms* 1837 *TA*.
BRYANSTON PARK, *Deer Park, Fatting Park, the Park* 1837 *ib*
(Blandford F.), *v.* **fatting**, cf. Old Park *infra*. BRYANSTON
SCHOOL, on the site of *Brians-* 1664 HTax, *Bryanston House*
1861 Hutch³. THE BUSHES (LINHAY),), *v.* **busc**, Do dial. **linhay**
'lean-to shed' (Barnes 79, EDD). CLIFF CTGS, THE CLIFF
(LINHAY), *v.* **clif**, cf. prec. FAIR MILE PLANT. & RD, a straight
1½ mile stretch of road. THE HANGING, *v.* **hanging**. HIGHER
BARN CTGS, *Bradley* 1811 OS, *v.* Broadley *supra*. HR & LR
INCLOSURE. MIDDLE HILL (lost), 1811 OS. MIDDLE LODGE.
MORGAN'S WD, cf. Jo' *Morgan* 1664 HTax (Blandford F.). NEW
RD. NORTON (LIMEKILN) COPPICE, near *North Down* 1811 OS,
so perhaps 'north hill' from **norð** and **dūn**, cf. Norton in
Durweston par. *infra*. OLD PARK (CTG, LINHAY & WD), *v.*
linhay, cf. Bryanston Park *supra*. PARK PLANT., in Bryanston
Park *supra*. QUARLESTON (DOWN), formerly in Winterborne
Stic. par. *infra* and no doubt to be associated with Quarleston
Fm in that par. 2 miles SW. THE ROOKERY. ST MARTIN'S
CHURCH (old and new). SHEEP LINHAY, near SHEEPWASH, *v.*

linhay. SHOTHOLE, near Old Park *supra* and Old Warren Plant. *infra*, cf. ModE **shot-hole** 'a small hole in a fortified wall through which to shoot' (NED s.v. sense 2), perhaps used of a hunting station from which game could be shot. OLD WARREN CTGS & PLANT.

FIELD-NAMES

There are no names in (*a*).
(*b*) *atte More* (p) 1332 SR (*v.* **atte**, **mōr**).

Durweston

DURWESTON (ST 858086) ['dʌrestən]
Derwines-, Dervinestone 1086 DB, *-tona* Exon, *Deruunestuna* 1100-22 (1270) Ch, *Derewineston*(') 1204 FF, Cur, 1221, 1223 ib, *-tun* 1227 FF, *Derwenes-* 1242 Ch, *Derwyneston* 1244, 1280 *Ass*
Dirwines- 1091-1106, *Dyrwines-* 1135-7, *Direwinestun* 1135-66 all MontC, *Dirrewynes-* 1283 FF, *Dyrweneston* 1338 ib
Darwinestone 1166 RBE (p)
Durwinestona 1166 LN (p), *Durewnes-* 1212 Fees, *Dur(e)-wines-, Dur(e)wyneston* 1242-3 ib, 1277 FF, 1280 Ch (p), Ipm, 1288 *Ass et freq* to 1399 Pat, *Durwynis-* 1268 *Ass*, *Durnewynes-* 1288 ib, *Durwyns-* 1316 FA, *Dur(e)wen(e)s-* 1359, 1379 Cl, *Durrewyneston* 1402 *DCMDeed, Durweston* 1412 FA *et passim, -Fitz Payn* 1533 *Weld*[1], 1534 *Hen*[1], *Durwyston* 1431 FA, *Dureweston* 1455 Cl, *Duryston* 1464 *Hen*[2]
Dorwyn(e)ston 1398 IpmR, 1399 Cl, *Dorwinestan* (sic) 1425 IpmR, *Dorweston* 1428 FA, 1483 *Hen*[1], 1583 *AddCh*, *Dowreston* 1547, 1548 *Ct*

'Dēorwine's farm', from the OE pers.n. *Dēorwine* and **tūn**. The affix is from the family of *Fitz Payn* which held this manor in the 15th or early 16th cent. (Hutch[3] I 265), cf. Okeford Fitzpaine and Wootton Fitzpaine pars. *infra*. Hutch[1] I 89, followed by Hutch[3] I 265, suggests that *-wines-* in the early forms of the name may contain some allusion to the two acres of vineyards (*vinee*) recorded at one of the two manors of

Durweston in 1086 DB, an amusing instance of antiquarian etymologizing (in Do, vineyards in DB occur only here and at Wootton Fitzpaine, both manors belonging to Aiulf the chamberlain, *v.* VCHDo 3 100).

KNIGHTON (FM) HO (ST 857082), *Dervinestone* 1086 DB (f. 79b), *Knicteton'* 1212 Fees, *Kny(g)hteton(e)* 1242–3 ib, 1288 *Ass et freq* to 1402 *DCMDeed* with variant spellings *Knyt(t)e-*, *Knygte-*, *Knythe-*, *Kynghee-*, *Knyghthe-*, *Knyghtte-*, *Kynghte-*, *Knyghe-*; *Knythton'* 1288 *Ass* (p), *Kyngtedon* 1316 FA, *Knyghton* 1346 ib *et freq* to 1548 *Ct*, '-*by Bryanston'* 1399 Pat, -*Fm* 1837 *TA*, *Kyngthton* 1412 FA, *Knygh(t)ston* 1534, 1537 *Hen*[1], 'the farm of the thanes or retainers of a high personage', *v.* cniht (gen.pl. *cnihta*), tūn, cf. Bryanston par. *supra*. The DB manor of *Dervinestone* (cf. par. name *supra*), assessed at 2½ hides, was held TRE by five *taini* or thanes (cf. W Knighton 1 207) and in 1086 by William (*de Estre*) (VCHDo 3 87); the identification of this manor with Knighton is suggested by the fact that 2½ hides in *Knicteton'* were held by Richard *de Estre* in 1212 Fees (87) (Eyton 131–2, VCHDo 3 60).

DAIRY HO. DURWESTON BRIDGE, FM (1837 *TAMap*) & LODGE. DURWESTON MILL, *Mill* 1811 OS, cf. *molendinorum domini* 1538 *Hen*[1], *firma molendini aquatici, prat' voc' Mylham* 1564 *Hen*[2], *Myll' hammes* c. 1580 *Hen*[1], *the Mill Ham* 1590 *Hen*[2], *v.* myln, hamm. ENFORD BOTTOM (1811 OS) & FM (1837 *TA*), *Enford* 1838 *ib* (Shillingstone), on R. Stour, perhaps analogous with Enford W 328, 'duck ford', *v.* ened, ford. FIELD GROVE (CTGS), *bosci domini vocat' Fylgrove* 1564 *Hen*[2], *Great Feyldegrove Woodd* 1567 *Hen*[1], *copice of wood cawled Filgroes* 1583 *AddCh*, *Filgraves* 1590 *Hen*[2], *Filgroves* 1811 OS, 'grove in open country', *v.* feld, grāf(a). FOLLY BARN (1811 OS) & CLUMP, THE FOLLY, cf. *Folly Fm & Wds* 1837 *TA*, *v.* folie. FOUR ACRE COPPICE. FREE DOWN BORDER, *Freedowne* 1609 *Weld*[1], cf. *ye downe* c. 1580 *Hen*[1], *v.* frēo, dūn, border 'edge, boundary' (here a narrow plantation). MILL POND, near Durweston Mill *supra*. NORTON CTGS, LANE & WD, *Norden* c. 1580 *Hen*[1], -*don* 1784 *SalisT*, probably 'north hill', from norð and dūn, the second el. showing confusion with denu 'valley' and tūn 'farm'; it is in the N of the par., and lies to the N of Sutcombe Wd *infra*. THE PLANTATION. HR & LR PRESSHAM WD, *Presham*

Coppes Woode 1590 *Hen*[2], on R. Stour, perhaps 'priest's river-meadow', from **prēost** and **hamm**, with **copis**. RECTORY, *Rectoria de Durweston* c. 1580 *Hen*[1], cf. *terr' Rector'* 16 *Hen*[2], the *Parsonage Pexy'shole* 1784 *SalisT*, the last form apparently meaning 'hollow haunted by a pixie or pixies', from **pixie** (common in SW dial.) and **hol**[1]. ROUNDBUSH WD. ST NICHO-LAS'S CHURCH, cf. 'the church of *Knyghtheton'* 1297 Pat, *Church Cl & Ld* 1784 *SalisT*; the churches of Knighton and Durweston were united in 1381 (Hutch[3] 1 266). SHEPHERD'S CORNER FM, cf. *Edythe Shepherd...cottage* c. 1580 *Hen*[1]. SUTCOMBE WD, *copice of wood cawled Suttcombe* 1586 *AddCh*, *Sutcombe Coppes Woode* 1590 *Hen*[2], *Sudcomb coppice* 1784 *SalisT*, 'south valley', *v.* **sūð, cumb**, with **copis**. TRAVELLERS' REST. TWO GATES, a coppice. WEBSLEY COPPICE & FM.

FIELD-NAMES

The undated forms are 1784 *SalisT*. Spellings dated 1283 are FF, 1332 SR, 1381 *DCMDeed*, 1399 Cl, 16, 1564, 1590 *Hen*[2], 1534, 1535, c. 1580 *Hen*[1], 1547 *Ct*, 1622 *Weld*[1], and 1664 HTax.

(*a*) Arnold's Gdn; Bartlett's Orchd; Bray's Mdw (*Brayes Meede* 16, a surname with **mǣd**); ye bridlepath Gate; Corn Island; Croft; Farm Island; Fernylands (*ye fearne land* c. 1580, *v.* **fearn**); Garden Bush (fd); Gateway fd (*terr' voc' Gatewaye* 1564, *v.* **geat**); Goosehaum (*Goosham* 1564, *goose Hammes* c. 1580, *v.* **gōs, hamm**); (Clarks & Cox's) Haycomb (*Haycome* c. 1580, *v.* **cumb**, cf. Walter *Clarke* 1664; first el. probably **hēg** 'hay'); Heathern Drove (perhaps **hǣðen** 'heathy', with -*r*- possibly due to the influence of the noun *heather*); Heath Knoll (*v.* **cnoll**); Island Drove (cf. *Ilandes* 16, Corn & Farm Island *supra, v.* **ēg-land** (WSax **īeg-land**)); Joyce's Fd; Kendals Ho; Keynes's two Acres; Knighton fore-down (*v.* **fore**); Knighton bottom Common Fd, Knighton little & upper Common Fd; Knighton Mead(ow) (cf. *Knyghton Close* c. 1580); (Clark's little) Knoll (*v.* **cnoll**, cf. Haycomb *supra*); Mair Drove (perhaps **mere**[2] 'a mare'); Milton Lane (to Milton A. par. *infra*); Morren's Cl; (the) North (Common) Fd; Pidgeons Wall; the Pound (-*e* 1590, *poundfald domini* 1535, *v.* **pund, pund-fald**); Privetts (cf. Robert *Pryvett* c. 1580); Ridge Hill (*v.* **hrycg**); Sommers's Down Platt, Sommers's Lane (*v.* **plat**[2], cf. John *Somer* 1332); South Cl; Udals Cl; Watts's Cl (*Wattes-* 16, the surname *Watts*); Withiby (*Wethebere* 16, cf. *ye Wethebed* c. 1580, *v.* **wīðig, bearu, bedd**).

(*b*) *Buckes Close* 16 (cf. John *Bookes* 1664); *Courte Close* c. 1580 (*v.* **court**); *Cowardes Drove* c. 1580 (*v.* **drāf**; first el. **cū-hyrde**, or a surname); *Epyngrove* c. 1580 (*v.* **grāf(a)**; the first el. may be the OE pers.n. *Eoppa*, cf. Epney Gl 2 187); *ye field* c. 1580; *Hafe hewez* c. 1580 (reading doubtful, possibly -*howez*, from *howe*; the first el. may be **hæfer**[1] 'a he-goat' or **hæfera** 'oats');

Howcombe 1622 (*v.* **cumb**; first el. uncertain); *Keyles* 1547 (no doubt a surname; this was perhaps the name of an inn (in Knighton), since gaming is said to have taken place here); *le landcher' de Bryanston* 1381 (*v.* **landsc(e)aru**, Bryanston par. *supra*); *lyme kyll'* 1534 (*v.* **līm-cyln**); *ye mead* c. 1580 (*v.* **mǣd**); *atte More* (p) 1332 (*v.* **atte, mōr**); *Northe Meede* 16 (*v.* **mǣd**); *Sheepeground* c. 1580; *Southe Clyffe* c. 1580 (*v.* **clif**); *Southe Meede* 16 (*v.* **mǣd**); *Stokham* 1381, *Stockume* 16 (perhaps 'stumpy enclosure', or 'enclosure made of stocks', from **stocc** and **hamm**); *Tacton* 1283, *Tatton* 1399 (perhaps analogous with Acton 1 34); *Twytchynge* c. 1580 (*v.* **twicen(e)** 'cross-roads'); *the tythinge mans acre* c. 1580 (*v.* **tēoðung-mann**).

Fifehead Neville

Lower Fifehead or Fifehead St Quintin was transferred to this par. in 1920 from Belchalwell, formerly a distinct par. in Cranborne hundred, now in Okeford Fitzpaine par. *infra*.

FIFEHEAD NEVILLE (ST 768110)

> *Fifhide* 1086 DB (f. 82), 1235–6 Fees, -*hyde* 13 Salkeld (p), 1268 *Ass* (p), -*hude* 1332 SR, *Fifid(e)* 13 Salkeld (p), 1244 *Ass* (p), *Fyfhid(e)*, -*hyde* 13 Salkeld, *Fyv-* 1316 FA (p), *Vifhide* 1316 ib, *Fyffehed* 1548 Ct
> *Fif-, Fyf(h)id' Nouile* 13 Salkeld, *Fyf-, Fif(h)ide-, -(h)yd(e) Neuile* 13 ib, 1288 *Ass et freq* with variant spellings *Fyff-, Vyf-* (1303 FA), *Fyfe-, Fife-, -Neuill(e), -Neuyle, -Nevile, -Nevyle, -Neovill* (1346 FA), -*Nevill, -Nevyll(e)* to 1487 *Weld*², *Wyfhideneuil'* 1280 *Ass, Fyfhud' Neuyle* 1287 Salkeld, *Fifede nevill'* 1288 *Ass, Fyfed(e)-* 1428 FA, 1491 Ipm, *Fyffehed(e)-* 1496 Salkeld, *Fiffed-, Fyffed-* 1603 *Weld*², *Fifehead-* 1650 *ParlSurv et passim* with variant affixes as above, *Fifehuyde Nevyle or Fyfete Nevile* 1486 Ipm, *Fyvett-* 1549 Salkeld, *Fif(f)et(t) Nevell* 1583 SPDom, 1654 Salkeld, *Fiffed alias Fifehead alias Fiffed Nevell* 1655 ib, *Fyfehead alias Fyffett Neavell* 1675 ib

'(Estate of) five hides', from **fīf** and **hīd**, a common p.n., cf. foll. and Fifehead Magdalen par. *infra*. This manor was assessed at five hides in DB (VCHDo 3 96), and was held by William *de Nevill'* in 1235–6 Fees (the surname is from Néville or Neuville in France, *v.* Tengvik 102, IPN 127).

LOWER FIFEHEAD or FIFEHEAD ST QUINTIN (ST 773103)

> *Fifhide* 1086 DB (f. 78b), 1217, 1222 ClR, 1303, 1346 FA,

1332 SR, *-hid(a)* 1205, 1223 Cur, *Fyffhude* 14 *Cecil, Vyfhyde* 1303 FA, *Fyfhyde* 1327 *SR,* 1431 FA, *Fifyde* 1428 ib, *Fyfehuyd(e)* 1494 *Cecil, Lower Fifett* 1647 SC *Fifhyde Johannis de Sancto Quintino* 1242–3 Fees, *-Johannis* 1268 *Ass, Fifhide-* 1268 *ib, Fifeld Quintyn* 1472 Pat, *Fifhide Seint-* 1323 FF, *Fyffyde Seynt Quyntyn* 1412 FA, *Fyffed Quiteine* 1480 IpmR, *Fiffehede Quynteyn* 1495 Ipm, *Fiffhide quintine* 1619 *CH, Fifehead Quinton* 1641 *Salkeld Bell Challwell Fifehead* 1664 HTax

Cf. prec.; this manor was also assessed at five hides in DB (VCHDo 3 82). Richard and Herbert *de Sancto Quintino* (from one of the places called St Quentin in France, *v.* Tengvik 113) are mentioned in connection with this manor in 1205 Cur, cf. *William de Sancto Quintino* 1288 *Ass,* Maud *de Sancto Quintyno* 1332 SR, John *Seyntquyntyn* of *Fifhyde* 1374 Pat, John *Quynteyn* 1416 *HarlCh*; the same family gave its name to Frome St Quintin par. *infra, v.* Hutch³ 2 643. For the development *Fifeld-* in 1472, cf. Fifield O 351, W 207. For the 1664 form, *v.* Hutch³ 3 373 and note under par. heading *supra.*

ALL SAINTS' CHURCH. BADBURY COPSE, *-Coppice* 1842 *TA, coppice called Badbury* 1736 *Salkeld,* cf. Badbury hundred *infra.* BADGERS LANE, *Barges-* 1842 *TA.* BRAKETHORNE COPSE, *Brokehorn Coppice* 1842 *ib,* cf. *Brokehorn Md or Calves Cl* 1842 *ib,* perhaps from **brōc** and **horn** if the *TA* forms are reliable. COCKCROW COPSE, *Cockrow* 1840 *TA,* possibly from **cocc-rodu** 'clearing where woodcock were netted', with loss of final *-d* and modern rationalization of *-row* to *-crow.* DARK LANE. DEADMOOR COMMON, DREADMOOR COPSE, *coppice called Deadmore* 1736 *Salkeld, Deadmoor Cmn & Md, Gt Deadmoor Wd, Lt Deadmoor Coppice* 1842 *TA, v.* **dēad** 'dead', perhaps in the sense 'disused', **mōr,** cf. Gl 4 118 for an analogous 12th cent. name; the common is marked *Fifehead Common* on 1811 OS, cf. foll.; the modern variant *Dread-* is no doubt due to popular etymology. FIFEHEAD CMN, cf. *(the) West Com(m)on* 1666, 1697, *Fifehead Nevill Little Common or Gobson Common* 1697, *ye Lower Comon* 1709, *the Higher Common* 1787 all *Salkeld, (Hr & Lr) Fifehead Common* 1842 *TA;* the form *Gobson* is no doubt to be taken with *common called Goleson* 1603 *Weld²,* but it remains obscure. (LR) FIFEHEAD FM. FIFEHEAD MILL, *Mill* 1811 OS, cf.

Robert- 1332 SR, William *atte Mulle* 1376 *Ass*, *Nicholas atte Mulle de Vyfhyde Neuuylle* 1427 *DCMDeed*, 'two Water Mills' 1603 *Weld*[2], *Frost Mill* 1762 *Salkeld* ('before with Richard *Frost*'), *v.* **atte, myln**; there were mills at both manors of *Fifhide* in 1086 DB (VCHDo 3 82, 96). GREEN CLOSE LANE, *Green Cl including lane* 1840 *TA*. HARELY FM, *Harley (Meade)* 1607 *DROMap*, *Harl(e)y (Living)* 1736 *Salkeld*, *Harely* 1811 OS, *Hareley Farm Ho, Harely Gt or Long Md* 1842 *TA*, *Hartley* 1826 Gre, *v.* **lēah**; the first el. is probably **hara** 'hare', but if the last form is reliable, the name should perhaps be associated with Adam *de Hert(e)legh*', *-leye* 1288 *Ass*, a juror in Pimperne hundred, in which case the first el. is **heorot** 'a hart, a stag' (for loss of *-t*, cf. Harford Gl 1 200). HOME COPSE & FM, cf. *the Homeclose* 1603 *Weld*[2], *Home Cl, Coppice & Orchd, Home Md (or four Acres)* 1842 *TA*, *v.* **home**. KITFORD COPSE, *-Coppice* 1840 *ib*, from Kitford in Ibberton par. *infra*. MANOR HO. OLD QUARRY, cf. *Quar-* 1782 *Salkeld*, *Quarr(y) Close* 1842 *TA*, *v.* **quarre**. PLUMBER COPPICE, from Plumber in Lydlinch par. *infra*. RECTORY. SEDGE COPSE, *v.* **secg**[1]. SMETHERD FM, *Smitheard* 1744 *Salkeld*, *Smetherd* 1811 OS, *Smithard Drove, Ho & Plain* 1842 *TA*, perhaps 'smithy yard', from **smiðð̄e, smeð̄e** and **geard**. WOODROW, *Woderove* 14 GlastF (p), *Woodrow Brake, Orchd & Pit, Woodrow Md or six Acres* 1842 *TA*, *v.* **wudu, rāw**, with **bræc**[1], cf. an identical name 1 mile SW in Haselbury B. par. *infra*; the 14th cent. form may show influence from OE *wudurofe* 'woodruff', cf. Reaney s.n. *Woodroff*; it is called *Rawles* 1811 OS, cf. John *Rawelles* 1564 *Salkeld*, *v.* Hutch[3] 1 269. ZOAR FM (*Zoar* 1811 OS) & LANE, perhaps a jocular name from ModE *soar* 'altitude attained in soaring, act of soaring or rising high' (from 1596 NED) with reference to the situation of farm and lane on a small 300′ hill spur, and with Do dial. voicing of *S-* to *Z-*.

FIELD-NAMES

The undated forms are 1842 *TA* 84, but those marked † are 1840 *ib* (Belchalwell). Spellings dated 1288 are *Ass*, 1332 SR, 1547 *Ct*, 1603 *Weld*[2], 1607 *DROMap*, 1650[1], 1689 Hutch[3], 1664 HTax, 1791 Boswell, and the rest *Salkeld*.

(a) Anns Orchd; †Ash Flg; Bear Croft (*Bare-* 1736, cf. ½ *acram (que iacet) sub la ber(a)* 13, *v.* **bær**[2] '(woodland) pasture' or **bearu** 'wood'); †Bole Ham (*v.* **hamm**, cf. William *Bole* 1332); Bottom Grd or Cowleaze; Brake (*freq, v.* **bræc**[1]); Breach (Coppice) 1787 (*Breche* 1603, *v.* **brǣc**); Gt & Lt Broad Cl 1734; †Hr & Lt Broad Fd; Broadleaze 1744 (*brode Lease* 1603, *v.* **lǣs**); Broad Md (*Little-* 1734); †Brook Flg; Gt & Lt Bucks; Butts Gdn; †Capperage (Ham, Md & Wd); Chaff hay Cl (*v.* (ge)**hæg**; first el. possibly **ceaf** 'chaff' or **cealf** 'calf'); Clift Md (*Clift* 1782, *v.* **clif**); Cockers Pit (Drove & Orchd) (cf. John *Coker* 1689); †Hr Cockrams; †Common Cl; Corn Flg; †Corn Grd; †(Gt & Lt) Cowleaze; †The Crate (*v.* **croft**); Davis's Ho; †Drong Way (*v.* **drong**); †Dry Cl; †8 Acres; Everley Coppice, Everley on the Hill (*Everleigh* 1603, 'wild boar wood', *v.* **eofor, lēah**, cf. Everleigh W 329); (Lt) Fernhill (*v.* **fearn**); Fifehead Bridge 1791 (cf. *the parish bridge* 1666); Fifehead Fds (1640); †Fifehead Grd; †5 Acres; 40 Acres 1736; 4 Acres 1736; Frith or Gt Mead (*Little Frethers* (sic) 1603, *Fryth* 1675, *Little Frith* 1688, *v.* **fyrhð**); (Gt) Furland 1787 (½ *acram in les Forland'* 13, *v.* **fore, land**); †Furnip (probably for *Turnip-*) Grd; Furze Brake (*v.* **fyrs, bræc**[1]); Furzy Cl; Gannetts Cl (cf. Joseph *Gannet* 1650[1]); Garden Grd; Goblets (cf. John *Gopet* 1332); Half Grd; †Ham(s) (*v.* **hamm**); Henville Orchd; Hr or Middle Piece; †Hill(s), Hill Wd; Hilly or Hanging Grd, Hilly Grd Garden; †Hilly Piles (near Pile Md *infra*); Holbrooke Green Bridge 1791 (*v.* **hol**[2], **brōc**); Homers or Gt Furlong (cf. *meadow called Furlong* 1749); Hop-yard; Hose Md (*Hose* 1782, cf. the discussion under Hose Hill Brk 205); Huddlestons Gt & Lt Ham, Huddlestons Middle Flg & Broad Croft (*v.* **hamm**); Ker-, Kirleys Coppice & Orchd (cf. *terr' nuper Kyrleys lond* 1547, Edward *Kerlie* 1664, *v.* **land**); †King Cl Ham; Lake Md; Little Fd & Flg (cf. *Schortforlange* 13, *v.* **sc(e)ort, furlang**); †Little Ham; Little Wood 1709 (*Little Wood Close* 1666); †Long Cl; Long Fd & Ham (Plant.); †Long Lands (*Lang(e)land'*, *-londe* 13, *v.* **lang**[1], **land**); (End of) Long Md (or Lt Browns) (cf. *closes called-* 1603, *roveles tenement called Brownes* 1666, John *Broun* 1327, *-Brun* 1332); †Long Md; Long Pce; †Lower Fd; Lower Pce; †Gt, Hr & Lt Manfield (first el. probably (ge)**mǣne** 'common'); (Hr or) Middle Pce; Milking Plot; Milk Wells (4 *closes called Milkwell* 1650[2], *v.* **meoluc, well(a)**, cf. Milkwell Du (EPN)); New Orchd; †9 Acres; North Cl (for the use of the Poor) (on this charitable benefaction, *v.* Hutch[3] 1 272); North or Ham Coppice; North Green; †Home & Lr Orchard, Orchard Cl; Over Cl (1603, *v.* **uferra**); Paddock (1749); Park (*Parke* 1782); Parsons Coppice; †Pile Md (*v.* **pīl**); Perryhay 1743 (1650, *v.* **pirige**, (ge)**hæg**); †Plantation; Plympthorn Coppice (first el. perhaps ModE dial. *plim* adj. 'filled out', cf. NED s.v. *plim* vb.); Priest Md, Priest Thorn Coppice & Md; (Green, Hthr & Lr) Punwell (the first el. could be **pund** 'a pound'); Lt Reach (*v.* **rǣc**); Ridouts Cl, Grd, Orchd & Willow Bed, Ridouts Md late Atchinsons (cf. John *Ridout* 1664); Ridgey Grd or Summer Leaze (*v.* **lǣs**); Gt & Lt Sandhill (cf. *lang-, Sc(h)ort(e)sandun(e), -don'* 13, *Sandon(e)* 1288, *v.* **lang**[1], **sc(e)ort, sand, dūn**); School Ho; †7 Acres; †Shorts Mdw & Orchd (cf. William *Short* 1641); 6 Acres; South Coppice; Stephens Pleck (*v.* **plek**); †8 & 3 Acres Stilings, Gt & Lt Stillings (perhaps reflecting an OE (WSax) ***sti(e)lling**, corresponding to Angl ***stelling** 'a cattle shelter'); †Stone Md; 10 Acres; Hr, Lr & Middle Villars; †(Hr & Lr Green) Wadden, †Pit Waddon, Navel Waddon, Parsons & Rolls Waddon (*Wadden* 1736, *v.* **wād**, with **dūn** or **denu**, cf. Richard *Rolls* 1666); Well Cl 1744 (1688); Whites Cl & Orchd (cf. John *Whyte* 1549); Woodclose (1603); Woodleaze 1744 (-*Lease* 1603, *v.* lǣs); Woodman's door Cl.

(*b*) (*the*) *Barton Farm*(*e*) 1624, 1679 (*v.* bere-tūn); *la Butweye* 13 (*v.* weg, with butt[1] or butte); *some tymes Crockhorns Land* 1603 (cf. John *Crokehorne* 1547); *Fifylde Woode* 1607 (from par. name *supra*); *Foots House* 1666 (cf. John *Fote* 1516); *de la Lee* (p) 13 (*v.* lēah); *Matrauars Woode* 1607 (a surname); (*cot*(*t*)*age called*) *Mayne Place* 1603, -*Meane Place* 1624, 1691, -*Maine* 1679 (probably a surname, cf. Nicholas *Mayne* 1332 (Pimperne), from Broadmayne 1337, *v.* place); *terre in campo aquilonari* 13 ('north field'); *Pellies Plaine* 1666 (a surname and plain); *in campo australi* 13 ('south field'); *Staffordes House* 1666 (cf. John *Stafford* 1664); *in duodecim acris* 13 ('twelve acres', *v.* æcer); *Wa*(*y*)*thay* 1640, 1691 (*v.* (ge)hæg; first el. perhaps ME waite 'a watch', or the surname *Wayt*); *atte Yate* (p) 1332 (*v.* atte, geat).

Hammoon

HAMMOON (ST 817146) [hə'muːn]
> *Hame* 1086 DB, *Ham* Exon, *Hamme* 1202 P, 1228 FF, 1252 Pat *et freq* to 1331 Fine, *Leham* 1204 Cur, *Ham* 1205, 1208 ib, *Hama* 1235–6 Fees
> *Ham Galfridi de Moiun* 1194 P, *firma de Hamma-* 1195 ib, *firma de la Ham Galfridi de Moun* 1197 ib
> *Hamme* Mayun 1268 *Ass*, -*Moun* 1280 *ib*, -*Mohun* 1303 FA *et freq* to 1431 ib, -*Mooun* 1346 ib, -*Mowen* 1392 Pat, -*mown*(*e*) 1408 FF, 1428 FA, *Amme Moyun* 1297 Pat, *Hampme Mohun* 1331 Ipm, *Ham*(*e*) *Moh*(*o*)*un* 1340 NI, 1495 Ipm, *Hampne Moune* 1412 FA, *Hammo*(*u*)*ne* 1428 IpmR, 1444 Fine, 1548 Ct, *Hampmohun* 1611 *DuCo*, *Ham*(*m*)*oone* 1611 *ib et passim*

'The enclosure or river meadow', *v.* hamm, cf. Hampreston par. *infra*; Hammoon is surrounded on three sides by R. Stour. The manor was held by William *de Moion* in 1086 DB (VCHDo 3 93), cf. John-, Geoffrey *de Moiun* 1202 P, William *de Mohun* 1228 FF, '-*de Moun* of *Hamme*' 1252 Pat, etc; the family derives its name from Moyon in Normandy, cf. Winterborne Houghton par. *infra*, Tormoham D 523, Mohun's Ottery ib 642. The shift of stress in the modern form of the name is noteworthy. There is mention of a mill here in 1086 DB (VCHDo 3 93), cf. *molendinum de Hamme* 1288 *Ass*. The form *Archethamm* 939 adduced by Ekwall DEPN for this name does not belong here, *v.* under E Orchard par. *infra*.

EAST FM. HAM DOWN COPSE, *Ham Down* 1839 *TA, v.* **dūn,** par. name *supra.* MANOR FM & HO. RECTORY, cf. *Parsonage Fd, Ho & Md* 1839 *TA.* ST PAUL'S CHURCH. TAN-HILL COPSE, -*Wd* 1811 OS, *Tanhill Coppice & Grove, Gt & Lt Tanhill(s)* 1839 *TA,* first el. possibly OE **tān** 'twig, shoot'.

FIELD-NAMES

The undated forms are 1839 *TA* 97. Spellings dated 1547 are *Ct,* 1611 *DuCo,* 1650 *ParlSurv,* 1791 Boswell.

(a) Hr & Lr Brackey Md; Broad Cl; Courts Gdn; Crab Cl (*v.* **crabbe**); Cranes Md; Cribb Houses & Yd (*v.* **cribhouse**); Downs Grd; Everlands; Gawsons Md; Glebe Corn Grd; Goosehams (*v.* **hamm**); Green Cl; Hammohun Bridge 1791 (*v.* par. name *supra*); Inland Mdw (*v.* **inland**); Inn Mdw (*v.* **in** or **inn**); Jackleasehays (*v.* **jack** 'insignificant', **lǣs, (ge)hæg**); Little Fd adjoining Cribhouse; Legs (*v.* **leg**); Mays (cf. Richard *Maye* 1547); Gt & Lt Nordens; Gt Orchard; Oxenleaze (*v.* **oxa, lǣs**); Gt Park, Park Md; Parkers Leaze ((-*Meadowe*) 1650); Ridout Plot and Island (cf. Ridouts Cl in Fifehead N. par. *supra*); Rushy Md; Sturtle Pits (Mdw) (perhaps analogous with Sturthill in Shipton G. par. *infra*); Three Plots; Town Md; Late Upwards Ho & Mdw; Dry & Wet Wedber (*v.* **wīðig, bearu**); Gt & Lt West Fd; Wet Furlong Mdw; Yew Tree Cl & Orchd.

(b) *Bakers Leaze* 1611 (*v.* **lǣs**).

Haselbury Bryan

HASELBURY BRYAN (ST 754083) ['hɑːzəlbəʀ], *Hasebere* 1201 Cur, 1280 *Ass,* 1311 Ipm, -*berg(e)* 1201 Cur, *Haselber(e)* 1237 FF, 1268 *Ass,* 1275 Banco, 1281 Cl *et freq* to 1489 *AD,* -*in Blakemor(e)* 1268 *Ass,* 1346 *AddCh,* 1435 Cl, -*juxta Stokewak* 1305 FF, *Hesil-* 1261 Cl, *Heselber(e)* 1380 Pat, *Haselberg*' 1268 *Ass,* -*beare* 1412 FA, -*beyre* 1556 *Prideaux, Asal-* 1291 Tax, 1428 FA, *Hasal-* 1400 *MinAcct, Hasilber(e)* 1458 *AD et freq* to 1547 *Prideaux* (-*Bryan*'), -*beare* 1462 Pat, *Hasselbere* 1547 *Ct, Haselbury Bryant* 1811 OS, 'hazel wood', from **hæsel** and **bearu,** identical in origin with Haselbury Plucknett So (DEPN). Guy *de Bryene* was here in 1361 FF, 1388 Cl, cf. Alice *de Briene* 1393 *MinAcct* (the surname is from Brienne in France). It is on the edges of Blackmoor Vale *infra,* cf. also Stoke Wake par. *infra.* Eyton 131–2 (tentatively followed by VCHDo 3 93) identifies the DB manor of *Poleham* (f. 81b) held by William *de Moyon* with Haselbury Bryan, but for the identification of this form with East Pulham, *v.* DBGazetteer 120, Pulham par. *infra.*

DROOP (FM) (ST 754083), *Thorpe* 1580 *SPDom*, *Throope*, *Thrup(p) Hills* 1607 *DROMap*, *Thrope* 1774 Hutch[1], *Droop* 1799 Hutch[3], 1838 *TA* (-*Hills & Orchd*), *Throop* 1811 OS, *v.* **þrop** 'outlying farm, secondary settlement'; it is ½ mile E of the village.

KINGSTON (ST 751098), 1811 OS, *Kingeston* 1580 *SPDom*, *Kinston* 1605 *DROMap*, *Kinson* 1774 Hutch[1], 'king's farm', *v.* **cyning, tūn**; according to Hutch[3] 1 275, 'Richard de Hasilbere held the manor of Hasilbury of King John in chief'.

CROCKERN STOKE (lost), *Crokkernestoke*, *Sto(c)k(e) et Crock-*, -*Crokkern*' 14 GlastF, *Crockernestock by Haselbere* 1333 Pat, *Crockerne Stocke et Turberville* 1346 *AddCh*, *Cro(c)kern(e)stoke* 1349 Hutch[3], 1385 FF, 1435 IpmR, *Crokkernstokke* 1386 FF; *Crokkere Stokke, -stok(k)e* 1308 Ipm, 1340, 1370 FF, 1441 Pat, *Stock Crokeres* 1315 Drew, *Cro(c)ker(e)sto(c)k* 1318, 1361 FF, *Stokkecrokkere* 1340 NI, *v.* **stoc** 'secondary settlement', cf. foll. and the adjacent par. of Stoke Wake *infra.* The first part of the name is probably 'house where crocks or pots are made', from **crocc** and **ærn**, cf. Crockern Tor D 193, Crockernwell ib 428 and the synonymous Potterne in Verwood par. *infra.* An alternative though less likely explanation, as noted by Fägersten 55 note 1, is that it is from **croccere** 'a potter' in a ME wk.gen.pl. form with *-ene*, *v.* **-ena**, cf. Buckhorn Weston par. *infra.* The -*s* in the form *Stock Crokeres* may be a pl. or be due to metanalysis. The -*Sto(c)ke* of this name and foll. may be preserved in Stockfield Fm *infra* (at ST 755090) as suggested by Fägersten 55; Crockern Stoke is included under Lydlinch par., though for no apparent good reason, by Hutch[3] 4 191. The form *Stokke iuxta Fyffhude* 14 *Cecil* may belong here or under foll., cf. Fifehead Neville par. *supra.*

TURBERVILLE STOKE (lost), *Sto(c)keturbervil(l)e* 1318, 1370 FF, *Turberevilistokke* 1340 ib, *Crockerne Stocke et Turberville* 1346 *AddCh*, *Turbervilstok* 1361 FF, *Turbervylestoke* 1385 ib, 1435 Cl, *Stoke Turlevile* 1619 *CH*, cf. prec. Andrew *Turberville* was a witness to a charter concerning the manor of Haselbury B. in 1339 Hutch[3] 1 275; for other branches of this family, cf. Bryants

Puddle 1 289, Winterborne Muston 1 284, and Melbury S. par. *infra*.

WONSTON (ST 743081), 1774 Hutch[1], *Wolmerston'* 1280 *Ass*, *Wom(e)ston* 1580 *SPDom*, 1607 *DROMap*, 'Wulfmær's farm', from the OE pers.n. *Wulfmǣr* and **tūn**.

WOODROW (FM) (ST 741098), 1774 Hutch[1], 1838 *TA* (*Gt-*, *-ground*), *-rowe* 1580 *SPDom*, 1607 *DROMap*, 'row of trees', *v.* **wudu, rāw**, cf. Woodrow in Fifehead N. par. *supra*.

ALMSHOUSES. BACK LANE FM, earlier *Thorrington* 1811 OS, perhaps 'thorn farm', from **þorn** and **tūn**, cf. Thorrington Ess (DEPN) and Thickthorn Lane, Thorncroft both *infra*. THE CAUSEWAY, cf. *Causey-* 1607 *DROMap*, (*Gt*) *Cassey Close* 1838 *TA*, *v.* **cauce** 'raised way'. CHURCHFOOT LANE, leading to St James's Church *infra*. CONEY LANE, *v.* **coni** 'a rabbit'. FIVE ELMS, 1811 OS, 1838 *TA* (*-lynch*), *v.* **hlinc**. FRIZZEL'S HILL, perhaps from **fyrs** and **hyll**, with later explanatory **hyll**, cf. *Furzy hill* 1838 *TA*; for the metathesis in **fyrs**, cf. Friezland Gl 1 194. HADDON COPSE, *Ha(y)den* 1607 *DROMap*, *Haddon* (*brow*), *Gt & Lt Haddon* (*copse*) 1838 *TA*, probably 'hay hill', from **hēg** and **dūn**, with **brū**, the second el. showing confusion with **denu** 'valley' in the earliest form, cf. Haydon par. *infra*; the copse lies above the 300′ contour. HARELY COPSE, *Harley-* 1838 *TA*, cf. *Browns, Gilberts & Hobses Harley*, (*Gt, Lt, Long & Yonder*) *Harley* 1838 *ib*, from Harely Fm in Fifehead N. par. *supra*, cf. George *Browne* 1664 HTax, Alice *Gilberd* 1327 *SR*, Barnaby *Gilbert* 1664 HTax, and with the surname *Hobbs*. HASELBURY COMMON (lost), 1811 OS. HASELBURY MILL, 1811 OS, cf. *Longheres Mylle, the Mylle Pounde* 1567 *Glyn* (cf. William *Longhere* 1567 *ib*), *Millhams* 1838 *TA*, *v.* **myln, pund, hamm**. HIGH HOUSE FM, cf. *High House Grd* 1838 *ib*. LOCKETTS COPSE & FM, *Lockets* 1697 *Salkeld*, *-Fm* 1774 Hutch[1], from the family of John *Lo(c)ket* 1386 FF, 1404 Hutch[3] 1 276. MANOR FM & HO. MARSH COPSE, *Hr, Lr & Middle Marsh* (*Coppice*) 1838 *TA*, cf. *Marsh Close* 1607 *DROMap*, *v.* **mersc**. MOUNT PLEASANT FM, *Mount Pleasant* 1811 OS, a complimentary name. PARK GATE, 1811 ib, *-ground* 1838 *TA*, cf. Walter *atte ghate* 1327 *SR*, *-atte Yate* 1332 SR, *v.* **park, geat**; it is not clear to what park the name refers. PARTWAY LANE, *Porte Waie* 1607

DROMap, Partway 1838 *TA*, cf. *Port(e)way-, -Waie Close, -Mead* 1607 *DROMap, v.* **port-weg** 'road leading to a market town' (probably Sturminster Newton 4 miles NE). PIDNEY, 1838 *TA, Pidnell (Mead(e))* 1607 *DROMap, Pitney Mead* 1838 *TA*; the second el. is possibly **hyll** 'hill' (the place lies on the 300' contour), the first el. may be an OE pers.n. *Pyd(d)a* postulated for Piddington Nth 150, O 184, etc. PLECK (HILL), cf. *West Placke, Placke-, Plecke Close* 1607 *DROMap, v.* **plek** 'small plot of ground'. POVERT BRIDGE, *Poford Bridge* 1698 *Bundy, Povard* [bridge] 1791 Boswell, cf. *Poford Lane, -Mead* 1607 *DROMap, Povert* 1838 *TA, v.* **ford**; Professor Löfvenberg suggests that the first el. may be ME *po* 'pea-fowl' and compares Pow Fd Hrt 281. PYLE WELL, cf. Thomas *de La Pile* 1268 *Ass, Pile-* 1607 *DROMap, Pill Mead* 1838 *TA, v.* **pīl** 'stake, shaft'. RECTORY, 1838 *TA*, cf. *The Personadg Land* 1607 *DROMap, Parsons Mdw* 1838 *TA*. RIDGE (DROVE), cf. *Ridge Comon* 1580 *SPDom, Rudge Common* 1607 *DROMap, -Mdw* 1838 *TA, v.* **hrycg**, cf. Ridge Fm in Lydlinch par. *infra*. ST JAMES'S CHURCH, cf. *ecclesia de Haselberg'* 1268 *Ass*, 'the church of *Haselbere* 1318 FF, *the Church House* 1580 *SPDom, Church Close, -Thorns* 1607 *DROMap, Church Cross, (Lt) Church Thorn(s), Church(wood) Lane Grd* 1838 *TA*. SAW MILL. SHORTS BARN (lost), 1811 OS, 1838 *TA (-Cowleaze)*, cf. *Shorts Home Mdw* 1838 *ib*, Henry *Short* 1664 HTax. SILLY HILL, *Little Silly* 1838 *TA*, probably to be associated with *Selwaie Brook, Selway Mead* 1607 *DROMap*, perhaps from **sele²** 'willow copse' and **weg** 'way'. STIVVICKS BRIDGE, *Stib(b)erd Bridge, -Lane, Stebbard* 1607 *DROMap, Stipick' Bridge* 1698 *Bundy, Stiffeck* [bridge] 1791 Boswell, *Stibbicks (Mdw)* 1838 *TA*; the earliest forms suggest that this name may be analogous with Stibbard Nf for which Ekwall Studies² 163–4 proposed derivation from **stīg** 'path' and ***byrde** 'border, bank'; a track from the village runs S along the bank of a tributary of R. Lydden and here joins another track to cross the stream, so that 'bank with a path on it' would be an appropriate description. STOCKFIELD FM, *-Barn* 1811 OS, *Stocke Feild* 1607 *DROMap*, perhaps named from the lost *Crockern Stoke* or *Turberville Stoke supra*, but possibly from **stocc** 'tree stump'. STUT LANE, cf. *(Corn) Stut, Gt & Lt Stut* 1838 *TA*, probably to be associated with *Stirts* 1607 *DROMap, v.* **steort** 'projecting piece of land'; this corner of the par. projects into Fifehead N. par. *supra*. THICKTHORN LANE, *Thicke Thorne Lane* 1607 *DROMap*, *v.* **þicce**[2] 'thick, dense'. THORNCROFT, *Dowes Thorne Crofte* 1607 *ib*, *Gt*, *Lt & Middle Thorn Croft*, *Thorn Croft Coppice & Drove* 1838 *TA*, *v.* **þorn**, **croft**, with the surname *Dowe*. WEST LANE.

FIELD-NAMES

The undated forms in (*a*) are 1838 *TA* 101, in (*b*) 1607 *DROMap*. Spellings dated 1298 are FF, 1327 *SR*, 1332 SR, 1339, 1546, 1861 Hutch[3], e16, 1550, 1556, 1563, 1567, 1570 *Prideaux*, 1607 *DROMap*, 1664 HTax, and 1791 Boswell.

(*a*) Acre (cf. *Acre Close* 1607, *v.* **æcer**); Allers (*Nallars* 1607, *v.* **alor** 'alder'; *N*- from metanalysis of ME **atten** 'at the'); Antelope Inn; Appletree hay (*Apled(or)e Haye* 1607, *v.* **apuldor** 'apple-tree', (**ge**)**hæg**); Barley Cl; Beatham(s) (*v.* **beat, hamm**); Beltons cowleaze (*terr' voc' Beltons* 1550, *-Belston(e)s* 1556, 1570, *-stone* 1563, 1567, perhaps analogous with Belstone D 131 from **belle** 'a bell' and **stān**, or a surname from that place); Beny's; Betty Hays Mdw; Binghams (Lt Mead); Birds Cl (cf. Sarah *Burt* 1664, Brites *infra*); Birds nest; Black Grd; Black Hill, W Blackhill Gdn (*Blackhills* 1607, *v.* **blæc**); Black lane plot; Bottom Ground(s) (5 Acres); Bottom Mdw; (Lt) Brandish (*Brand(e)s* 1607, the surname *Brand*); Breastlands (*Brestlands*, *Bresland* (*Marsh Lande*) 1607, perhaps from **brēosa** 'gadfly'); (Middle) Breeches, Breaches, Hr Breech cowleaze (*Bre(a)ches* 1607, *v.* **bræc**); Brites (cf. Maud *Bret* 1327, *-Brut* 1332, Ralph *Bryt* 1339); Broad Croft (*-Crofte* 1607); (Lt) Broadlands (*-Lands* 1607); Gt & Lt Brookes (*Brooke* 1607, *v.* **brōc**); Brooklands (*-land* 1607); Bull Brooks & Mdw; Butts (*v.* **butte**); Caines('s) Hill & Plot; Caperage (adjacent to Capperage in Fifehead N. par. *supra*); (Gt) Castlemans (a surname); Clavel(l)s (a surname); Close; Clover Grd; Cobs Grd (Orchd) (cf. William *Cobb* 1664); Cockhill (perhaps **cocc**[1] 'hillock'); Common(s) Cl (freq, *Common Close(s)*, *-Close Lane* 1607); Condix (possibly from **conduit** 'drain', or a surname, *v.* Reaney s.n. *Conduit*); Coombs leg (*Co(o)mes* 1607, from **cumb**, or a surname, and **leg**); Cop Crouch (*Copt Cruch(e)* (*Mead*) 1607, 'headless cross', from (**ge**)**coppod** and **crūc**[3], with **mǣd**); Coppice (Cl), Copse Grd; Corner Grd; (Lt) Corn Grd, Corn Grd Hill; Cowleaze, -lease (freq); Crib house (plot) (*v.* **cribhouse**); Croft (*-e* 1607, *v.* **croft**); Culverhays (*Culuer Haye* 1607, *v.* **culfre**, (**ge**)**hæg**); Cummidge Mdw; Dole Mdw (*-Meade* 1607, *v.* **dāl**); Drove plot (cf. *The Droue*, *Common* (*Droue*) *Lane* 1607, *v.* **drāf**); (Long) Dry Cl (*Drye-* 1607); Dry Grd; Lt Dunford; 8 Acres; Fat ox (*Fatt ox Close* 1607, a complimentary name for good pasture for cattle); Fern Plot; Five Maples; Floodlands (*Flud-* 1607, *v.* **flōd**); (Hthr & Yonder) 4 Acres; Foxhill (1607); Freathe, Gt & Lt Frith (Mdw) (*Frethes*, *Frithes*, *Frethe Mead* 1607, *v.* **fyrhð** 'wood'); Frogwells (*Frogwell* (*Meade*) 1607, *v.* **frogga**, **well(a)**); Furlong (*Furland*, *Furlong Close* 1607, *v.* **furlang**); (Gt & Lt) Furzy Grd; Garstang (*Gassons* 1607, *v.* **gærs-tūn** 'paddock'); Gartles Cl (cf.

Honor *Gatrell* 1664); Gaulers Mdw (*-Heye* 1607, cf. John *Gawler* 1664, *v.* (ge)hæg); Great Wood (cf. *Hasilbera wood* 1546); Green Cl; Grove (*The Groue(s)* 1607, *v.* grāf(a)); Hagmans (Orchd) (*Hangmans* 1607, a surname, or the occupational term); Ham Orchd (*Hame, Hammes* 1607, *v.* hamm); Hanging Grd (*v.* hangende); Haselbury Grd; Helly Cl (perhaps 'hilly', but cf. *Helliars* 1607, from the surname *Helliar*); Hides (Mdw) (*Hides* 1607, probably a surname); High Gate Mdw; (Lt & Lr) Hill (cf. *Hill Close* 1607); (Lt) Hoar (probably from ōra¹ 'bank', cf. *Nore Meade* 1607 which may show metanalysis of ME *atten ore* 'at the bank', *v.* atten); Holly well (perhaps to be associated with *Hallwell* (*Mead*) 1607, *v.* well(a); first el. possibly hālig 'holy'); Home Grd (freq) & Md (*Home Ground, -Mead(e)* 1607, cf. *Home Close ib, v.* home); Honey Md; Horse Cl; Hose (adjacent to Hose Md in Fifehead N. par. *supra*); Hundred Acres (a small field); (Gt & Lt) Inox (*Innox* 1607, *v.* inhoke); Gt Irish; Jarvis (*Iaruis* 1607, the surname *Jarvis*); Jensons Mdw; Keet Bridge 1791 (*Keat-* 1607, perhaps from cȳta 'kite' or cyte 'hut', cf. Reaney s.n. *Keat(s)*); Lane Common Cl; Leap gates (*v.* hlīep-geat); (Athwart) Leg(g) (*v.* athwart, leg); Little Heath & Md; Loders Common Cl (cf. Joan *Loder* 1664); Long Cl (*Long(e) Close* (*Meade*) 1607); Long hedge (1607); Longlands (*Longe Lands* 1607); Long Mdw (*Long Mead(e)* 1607); Lucehills (Coppice) (*v.* lūs); (Hthr, Lt, Middle & Yonder) Lynch, -Linch (*v.* hlinc); Marl pits; Marsh maidens (cf. Marsh Copse *supra*; *maidens* may be a surname or from *maiden* 'tree grown from seed, unlopped tree' (*v.* Barnes 80)); Mayes (a surname); Meadow; Meads; Mitfield lands (mead) (perhaps to be associated with *Metforlands, Methams* (*Mead*) 1607, *v.* furlang, hamm, mǣd; for a possible first el., cf. *Met(e)lond* 1 184); Moose (perhaps mēos 'marsh, bog'); Moses's Mdw (*Moyses Meade* 1607, the pers.n. *Moses*); Muddles (Orchd) (probably a surname); New Cl; Nil Grd; 9 Acres; North Mead(ow); Northover plot (*v.* ōfer¹ or ofer²); Okeford charity grd (from Okeford F. par. *infra*); (Long, Old & Young) Orchard; Paddock; Parch Cl; Pease Cl, Peaselands (*v.* pise); Phillis thorn (*Phillis* 1607, the pers.n. *Phillis* or *Phill*); Piltons Plot; Pit Plot; Piveland (cf. *Piluerland infra*); Plantation; (Lt) Play cross (*Plea Crofte* 1607, first el. perhaps plega 'play, sport'); Plot; Polly Acres; Pond Mdw; Poors land (cf. *the Poor Lands* 1799 Hutch³ 1 281, a charitable endowment); Prankets; Rabbits; Redlands (*Red(e)land(e)s* 1607, *v.* rēad, land); Lt Rough Grd; (Lt) Runhams (*Rownams* 1607, probably from rūh (wk.obl. rūwan) 'rough' and hamm); Rushy Cl & Grd (cf. *Rush(e) Moore* 1607, *v.* risc, rysc, mōr); Saunders Mdw (cf. William *Sanders* 1664); 7 Acres; (Lt & Long) Shags (*Shadgs, Shagges* 1607, *Shagg's Fm* 1861, cf. Richard *Sheg* 1327, 1332); Shoulder of Mutton (so named from its shape); 6 Acres; Sleck (cf. N dial. *sleck* 'soft mud, ooze'); Small Hams (*v.* hamm); Smitherd Leg & Md (from Smetherd in Fifehead N. par. *supra*, *v.* leg); Smiths shop; Spirtly Md (*v.* spyrt, lēah); Spring Cl; Square Grd; (Gt) Stavelands (*Stafordland(e)* (*Lane*) 1607, perhaps from stān and ford, with land, or the surname *Stafford*); Stone Lds (*Stonye-* 1607, *v.* stānig); 10 Acres; Thorney Grd; 3 Acre Orchd, 3 Acres; Three Cornered Grd; Tiley Bridge 1791; Timley (this and foll. perhaps contain an OE pers.n. *Tima* suggested by Ekwall DEPN for Timworth Sf); Timmer; Lt Trogwells; 20 Acres; 2 Acres; Wattinghams (*Wortingham* 1607, first el. perhaps wyrt-tūn 'vegetable garden', medial *-ing* being analogical, *v.* **hamm**; however Professor Löfvenberg points out that the first el. may be an OE pers.n. *Wyrta*, supposed by Ekwall, PN -*ing* 44, to lie behind Worting Ha); Weep hills (*Whiphills* 1607, *v.* **hwip(pe)** 'brush-wood'); Well Grd; Wheat Grd (cf. -*Close* 1607); Whitemarsh (*Whit(t) Marshe* 1607, *v.* **hwīt, mersc**); Whites Cl (cf. John *le Wyte* 1298, Ralph *White* 1664); Williams Wd; Woodsend (*v.* **ende**[1]); Woollands (*Wolland(s) (Copies)* 1607, first el. perhaps **well(a)**, WSax **wyll(a)** 'spring, stream', *v.* **land, copis**); Wry acres (*Rye Acre* 1607, *v.* **ryge**); Youngs Grd (cf. Richard *Young* 1664).

(*b*) *Beer Bridg* (*Mead*) (first el. **bearu** 'wood', cf. par. name *supra*, or **bǽr**[2] 'woodland pasture'); *Bellipot Grene* (*v.* **grēne**[2]; the first part may be a humorous surname, cf. eModE *belly-cup* '? cup with a swelling body' (NED)); *Berry(e) Close, -Haye, -Meade* (first el. perhaps **beorg** 'hill' or **berige** 'berry', *v.* **(ge)hæg, mǽd**); *Bittom* 1607 (*v.* **bytme**); *Bro(w)defyld(es)* 1550–1567 (*v.* **brād, feld**); *Chaffes* (*Mead*) (the surname *Chaff*); *Chalke Hills* (*v.* **cealc**); *Dunghilles* (*v.* **dunghill**); *East Haye* (*v.* **(ge)hæg**); *The Farme Woode*; *Gylls Close* (the surname *Gyll*); *Gore Mead* (*v.* **gāra**); *Haucksam* (perhaps from **hafoc** and **hamm**); (*The*) *Hawes* (*v.* **haga**[1]); *Haysham* e16 (perhaps from **hǽs** and **hamm**); *Hilliatts* (perhaps 'hill gates', from **hyll** and **geat**, or a surname); *Kichin Mead* (*v.* **cycene**); *The Lagge* (*v.* **lagge**); *Linch* (*v.* **hlinc**); *Middle Close*; *Munke Meade* (*v.* **munuc**, perhaps with reference to the possession of lands here by Glastonbury abbey, *v.* Hutch[3] 1 276); *Niston; North Greene* (*v.* **grēne**[2]); *Ouerhaye, Out Hayes* (*v.* **uferra, ūt(e), (ge)hæg**); *Oxye Mead* (perhaps from **oxa** and **(ge)hæg**); *Parte Acres*; *Piluerland* (perhaps from **pīl** and **furlang**, cf. Pyle Well *supra*); *Pitnes; Pitt Close, -Meade* (*v.* **pytt**); *Portland* (cf. Partway Lane *supra*); *Quarye Close* (*v.* **quarre**); *Reuells* (a surname); *Rudges* (*v.* **hrycg**, cf. Ridge *supra*); *The Shelfe* (*v.* **scelf**); *Shery Crose* (*v.* **cros**); *Slad(e) Mead* (*v.* **slæd**); *Smalland* (*v.* **smæl, land**); *Twinborne* (*Mead*) (by R. Lydden, 'between the streams', *v.* **betwēonan, burna**); *Upper Mead; Woodforland, -Mead* (*v.* **wudu, furlang**); *Worres; Worth* (*v.* **worð**); *Yellands* (probably 'arable land left unused', from **eald** and **land**, cf. Yelland D 115, 311, etc).

Langton Long Blandford

Part of this par. (Littleton, etc) was transferred to Blandford St Mary par. *supra* in 1933.

LANGTON LONG BLANDFORD (ST 898059)

> *Bleneford* 1086 DB (2 × or 3 ×), *Blæneford* Exon, *Blaneford* 1280 Pat, 1310 Cl
>
> *Longa Bladeneford* (sic) 1179–80 P, *Longa(m) Blaneford(')* 1212 Fees, 1228 Cl, 1291 Tax, 1329 Pat, 1428 FA, *Lang(e)blan(e)ford(e)* Hy 3 Ipm, 1244 *Ass et freq* to 1548 *Ct*, -*alias*/*otherwise Lang(e)ton Boteler, -Botyler, -Botil(l)er* 1420 Fine *et freq* to 1466 *Weld*[1], -*otherwise Langeton Latyle by Blaneforde Forum* 1421, 1426 Cl, -*alias dict' Langton'*

Latyle 1466 *Weld*[1], *Long(e)blan(e)ford(e)* 1242 Ch, 1279 Cl
et freq to 1661 *AddCh*
Blaneford' Michael' Belet 1217 ClR, *Blaneford' Belet* 1242–3
Fees
Blaneford Philippi de Tylly, Langeblaneford' Tilly 1242–3
Fees
Langeton 1273 Banco, 1288 *Ass*, 1316 FA, 1394 *Russ (-iuxta
Blaneford forum) et freq* to 1443 *Weld*[1], *Langton* 1412 FA,
1548 *Ct*, 1598 AD, *Langhton* 1506 Pat
Blaneford' Langeton' 1280, 1288 *Ass, Langeton Blaneford*
1309 Ipm, 1316 Cl, *Langton Long Blandford* 1598 AD
Langeton(e) Botiller, -Botelir 1303 FA, 1327 *SR et freq* with
variant spellings *-Botelyr, -Botyler, -Botelir* to 1370 *Ass,
Langton Boteler* 1428 FA, *-Botyler alias dicta Langblaneford*
1431 ib, *-Butler* 1598 AD, 1664 HTax, *-Botiler* 1795
Boswell
Langeton(e) Latyle 1327 *SR*, 1370 *Ass et freq* with variant
spellings *-Latil(l)e, -Latylle* to 1431 FA, *Langton Latell*
1598 AD, *-Latile* 1795 Boswell
Langgeton(') Gulden(') 1332 SR, 1340 NI, *Gylden Langton*
1546 Hutch[3], *Langton Gundon* (sic) 1664 HTax

Long- distinguishes this par. from Blandford F. and Blandford
St M. pars. *q.v. supra, v.* **lang**[1] 'long'; *Langton-* means 'long
farm or estate', *v.* **tūn**, cf. Langton Fm & Ho, Littleton (Fm
& Ho) *infra.* For the identification of the DB forms, *v.* Eyton
131–2, VCHDo 3 98, 111, DBGazetteer 122. Michael *Belet* is
mentioned in 1216 ClR, cf. Emma *Belet* 1254 FF. The family
of *-de (la) Tylly, -(de) Latylle* had lands both here and in
Blandford St M. par. *supra* (Hutch[3] 1 163, 282f), and the form
Blaneford Philippi de Tylly may in fact belong under the latter,
cf. Robert *de Tilli* 1205 ClR, Oliva *de Tylly* 1225 ib, Richard
de la Tille 1236 Fees, John *de la Tyl(l)e, -de la Tille, -de la Tyele*
1288 *Ass*, 1290 FF, 1309 ib, *-de Latille* 1316 FA (he held
Langeton jointly with Joan *le Botiller*). *Langeton Botiller* was a
distinct manor; the family of *le Botiller* was here from 1280, cf.
John *le Botiller* 1280 Pat, *-le Botyl(l)er* 1280 Misc, 1303 FA, *-le
Boteler* 1288 *Ass*, etc. *Langgeton Gulden* seems to have been
another name for *Langeton Latyle*; the tithing called *Langetone
Latyle* in 1327 *SR* is *Langgeton' Gulden'* in 1332 SR, and in

1334 Cl, Ipm Henry *le Guldene* held at his death the manors of *Lang(e)blaneford* and *Langeton Latile*, cf. also Roger- 1309 FF, Henry *le Gildene* 1327 *SR*, *-de Gulden* 1329 Pat, *-le Gulden*' 1332 SR, Elizabeth *de Gulden* 1346 FA. There were two mills at Langton Long B. in 1309 FF.

LITTLETON (FM & HO) (ST 894047), *Liteltone* 1086 DB, *Litletun*', *-ton* (p) 1220 Cur, *Littleton*' 1242–3 Fees *et passim* with variant spellings *Lytle-*, *Lit(t)el-*, *Litil-*, *Lyt(t)yl-*, *Lyt(t)el-*; *Littleton juxta Blaneford Martel* 1310 FF, *Lytelton by Blaneforde St Mary* 1421, 1426 Cl, 'little farm or estate', from lȳtel and tūn, so named to distinguish it from Langton (Long Blandford) which is situated on the opposite bank of R. Stour. There was a mill here in 1086 DB (VCHDo 3 86).

LOPHILL FM (ST 906047), *Lob Hill Clump, Drove & Ho* 1839 *TA, a place called Lobhill* 1861 Hutch[3], probably to be associated with *Lepen* 1225 Hutch[3], '*Lobepenn* in the field of *Longeblaneford*' 1242 Ch, *v.* lobb 'something heavy', hyll; *-pen(n)* is probably from penn[2] 'a fold', *Le-* in the spelling from 1225 may be a reduced form of *Lobe-* or represent the Fr def.art. le. As is noted for all of the p.ns. containing the el. lobb in D (where it occurs five times, twice as simplex, once each with pyll, tūn and well(a), *v.* PND 33), this place is situated by a fairly steep slope; the farm lies at 100′ near R. Stour below a projecting hill which rises to 300′ at Buzbury Rings in Tarrant K. par. *infra*; a track down the hill, also forming the par. bdy, passes through the farm towards a ford on R. Stour.

ALL SAINTS CHURCH, cf. 'the church of All Saints, *Langeblaneford*' 1333 Pat, 'a chantry in the chapel of St Thomas in the parish church of *Langeblaneford*' 1391 ib, *Church Fd* 1839 *TA*; there is mention of 'the church of *Lytelton*' in 1421 Hutch[3], cf. *Chapel Cl* 1839 *TA, v.* Littleton *supra*. B. Plant., *East & West B. Coppice* 1839 *TA*, shaped like the letter *B*. BINGLEDON WD, first el. perhaps bing 'hollow', with lēah and dūn; the wood is on a 300′ ridge, with a marked hollow to the W. BUZBURY PLANT., from Buzbury Rings in Tarrant K. par. *infra*. DAIRY CTGS. THE DOWN WD, near Little Down *infra*. HALF MOON COPPICE, *Half Moon* (*Plant.*) 1839 *TA*, from its shape. HIGHER BLDGS. HOLLY CLUMP. HUNGRY CTGS & DOWN, *v.*

hungrig. LANGBOURNE, by the *Pimperne* stream (*v.* Pimperne par. *infra*), cf. *on þa burnestowe* in the OE bounds of Tarrant H. only ½ mile upstream from this place, *v.* **lang**[1], **burna**. LANGTON COPPICE (1839 *TA*), FM (1784 *SalisT*), HO (1811 OS), LODGE FM & NORTH LODGE. LITTLE DOWN, cf. *Down* 1839 *TA*. LITTLE WD. LITTLETON DROVE, cf. *Drove* 1839 *ib*. LODGE, *Langton Lodge* 1861 Hutch[3]. LONDONDERRY, *-Coppice* 1839 *TA*, no doubt a transferred name from N Ireland. LONG COPPICE, cf. *Long Plant.* 1839 *ib*. LONG FRIDAY, 1839 *TA*, alternatively called *Good Friday* 1839 *ib*, now the name of a long narrow plantation, *v.* **frīgedæg**. NUT COPPICE. OLD ROAD WD. THE PARK, cf. *Park Gate Plant. North & South* 1839 *ib*. PLEASURE GRD. POUND CL (lost), 1811 OS, *v.* **pund**. ST LEONARD'S FM, 1784 *SalistT*, cf. *Saint Leonards Lands* 1814 *EnclA*, named from St Leonard's Chapel in Blandford F. par. *supra*. SCOT-LAND, either a transferred name or from **scot** 'tax' and **land**. THE SHRUBBERY. SNOW'S DOWN, from the family of George *Snow* who held the manor of Langton Long B. a1800 Hutch[3]. SOUTH LODGE. THORNCOMBE NORTH BELT & SOUTH BOLT (sic), cf. *Thorncombe Bottom* 1811 OS, from Thorncombe in Blandford St M. par. *supra*, *v.* **belt, botm**. WIMBORNE BELT, cf. *By Winborne Turnpike* 1839 *TA*, by the road to Wimborne M. *infra*.

FIELD-NAMES

The undated forms are 1839 *TA* 122. Spellings dated 1327 are *SR*, 1332 SR, 1340 NI, 1421 Hutch[3], and 1441 EL.

(*a*) Adam and Eve; Backlawn; Hr Barn Fd; (Clump) Barrack Fd, 7 Acres including Barracks; Below Plant.; Black Lane (NE Piece) (cf. William *atte Lane* 1327, Richard *in thelane* 1332, *-in la Lane* 1340, *v.* **atte, lane**); Bottom Fd; Burn bake (fd) (*v.* **burnbake**); Bush Fd; Butlers Mead(ow) (Plant.) (the surname *Butler* < ME *Botiller*, cf. par. name *supra*); (Hr) Charmouth (perhaps a transferred name from Charmouth par. *infra*); Clover Fd; Clump Fd & 10 Acres; Conygar Fd (*v.* **coninger**); Coppice (by River), Coppice Fd, Copse; Corner Fd; Cow Down; Cowleaze; Donkey Plot; Drying Plot; Duntish Md (perhaps a transferred name from Duntish in Buckland N. par. *infra*); Fir Plant.; Folly Plant.; 14 Acres; Fry's Land (Plant.) (cf. Richard *le Frie* 1327, William *Ffrye* 1421); Furze Fd, Furzy Grd; Glebe 8 Acres North & South, Glebe 17 Acres North; Good's Md; Great Md; Grotten (Do dial. *grotten* 'a run or pasture for sheep' (Barnes 67, EDD s.v. *gratton*), *v.* **græd-tūn**); Guinea Fd (perhaps with reference to cost or rent, or a transferred p.n.); (Wood by) Ham (*v.* **hamm**); N & S Hill; Home Mdw; Green Horseleaze,

Horse Leaze Row; Kennel Coppice & Hill; Lambing Barton; Langton Cliff; Limekiln Down; Littleton Down; Lynch (*v.* **hlinc**); Martins Mdw; Middle Fd; Milestone Fd (Coppice); The Moor; New Fd(s); North Fd & Plant.; Orchard (Plant.); Paddock (Plant.); Pit Fd; Plot; Pond Down (Plant.); Plot S of Rickbarton; 7 & 17 Acres; Shepherd's Fd (cf. Roger *Shepheard* 1664); 60 Acres; South Cl & Plant.; Square Fd; (North) 10 Acres; Three Cornered Fd; Three Corners; (Lr) Tichford (probably 'kid ford', from **ticce(n)** and **ford**, cf. Tickford Bk 23); 12, 28 & 26 Acres; Water Mdw; Well Cl.

(*b*) (manor of) *Cokerscourt(e)* 1466 *Weld*[1] (*v.* **court**, cf. Robert *Coker* 1426 Hutch[3] 1 283); *Gretelansher* 1441 (*v.* **grēat, land-sc(e)aru**); *Hedaker* 1441 (*v.* **hēafod, æcer**); 'the field of *Langetone*' 1441 (*v.* par. name *supra*).

Pimperne

Parts of Blandford F. par. (including Nutford) were transferred to this par. in 1886 and 1894, and parts of the pars. of Tarrant H., Tarrant L. and Tarrant M. were added in 1933.

PIMPERNE (ST 903094)

(*to*) *pimpern*, (*of-*, *to*) *pimpernwelle* 935 (15) *ShaftR* (S 429)
Pinpre 1086 DB, 1177–1194 P, 1197 *AddCh*, 1212 Fees, 1220 Cur, 1230 P (p), *Pinpra* 1086 Exon, *Pinpr'* 1220, 1226 Cur
Pimpr(e) 1178–9 P, 1189 France, 1219, 1220 Cur, ClR, 1221 ib, 1223, 1224 Pat, Cur, 1225, 1227 FF, 1228 *AddCh*, 1233 Lib, 1238 Pat, 1255 *AD*, *Pympr(e)* 1200 (1280) *HarlCh*, 1220 Cur, 1262 Ipm, 1263 Cl, 1288 *Ass*, *Pinipre* (probably for *Pimpre*) 1204 ClR, *Pimper(e)* 1219, 1221 Cur
Pympern(e) 13 AD II, *Salkeld*, 1285 *Cecil*, 1288 *Ass*, 1290 Fine, 1291 Tax, 1296 Ipm, 1303 FA *et freq* to 1548 Ct, *Pimpern(e)* 1210–12 RBE, 1224 Cur, 1234 Pat, Cl, 1242 Ch, 1290 Pat, Ch, c. 1300 *AD et passim*
Pumpr' 1221 Cur
Pynperne 1234 *Cecil*, 1290 Pat, 1382 Fine, 1406 Pat, *Pinperne* 1234 *Cecil*, 1268 *Ass*
Pempre 1290 Cl
Pympernet 1307 Pat
Pemphorne c. 1586 Hutch[3]

This is a difficult name. The form *pimpern* cited from the OE bounds of Tarrant H. refers to the small stream which flows from Pimperne village SW to R. Stour (cf. Langbourne in Langton Long B. par. *supra*), and *pimpernwelle* in the same charter probably refers to the spring where the stream rises, *v.*

well(a). Ekwall (RN 326, DEPN) thinks that the name may be
of British origin, and suggests derivation from PrWelsh *pïmp
or PrCorn *pimp 'five' and PrWelsh or PrCorn **prenn**
'tree', the r.n. being a back formation from the p.n. Professor
Jackson agrees that this derivation is perfectly feasible, but
points out that the early forms with -*np*- and those without final
-*n* would need to be explained on English grounds (as the latter
at least can be, *v. infra*).

However Tengstrand (MN 96) suggests that a Gmc origin for
the name is possible. Like Ekwall he supposes that the early
spellings in -*re*, -*ra*, -*er* are due to loss of -n (on this cf. also
Ekwall Studies[1] 66), but adduces various Gmc words in *pimp*-
indicating small, rounded shape (e.g. ModE *pimple* 'small
rounded tumour or swelling' (from c. 1400 NED), ModE dial.
pimp 'a pimple', 'a small bundle of firewood') and suggests
that Pimperne may originally have been a collective hill-name,
secondarily applied to the stream, from the stem *pimp*- and an
OE combinative suffix *-*ern* with a collective sense (cf. also
Iwerne C. and Iwerne M. pars. *infra*). The name would have
reference to the group of hills projecting W, N & E towards the
village, or to Pimperne Down *infra*, a large irregularly shaped
ridge. For the first part of the name Tengstrand *loc.cit.*
compares Pimp's Court K (KPN 317, *Pinpa, -e* 1086, *Pinpe,
Pympe* 1242–3 *et freq*) which is situated on a ridge with a
rounded end, projecting from a larger tract of high ground, and
not far from R. Loose. Two names possibly more closely
analogous to Pimperne may now also be adduced: Pimperleaze
Rd W 180 (*Pimper-, Pinper-* 1196, 1198, *Pymper-* 1321), a
country road crossing a hill spur towards a small stream, and
Pimperne (1811 OS) in Melbury O. par. *infra*, again situated
in undulating country, on a hill near a stream. Professor
Löfvenberg comments: 'This is a very difficult name, and I can
offer no solution or even suggestion. But if we start from a word
*pimp of Germanic origin, it seems to me impossible to account
for the numerous forms with -*n*- in front of the following -*p*-.
A change of an original -*n*- to -*m*- would be natural. From a
formal point of view the second el. may well be OE **ærn**
'house'.' However, -*np*- for -*mp*- is perhaps only orthographical
(cf. *Panptune* DB for Ponton L (DEPN) and the common AN
n for *m* before (original) *b* in DB and 12th-cent. spellings like

Cuntone, Contone for Compton (various counties, DEPN), *Crunwelle, Cronwell(a)* for Cromwell Nt 185, *Lanbecote* for Lamcote ib 240, etc, *v.* Feilitzen 85).

In the form from 1307, *-et* may represent the Fr diminutive suffix *-ette, v. -et(t)(e).* For the former *chace* and *warnership* of Pimperne, *v.* under Blandford F. par. *supra,* cf. Pimperne Fox Warren & Wd *infra.*

NUTFORD CTGS & FM (ST 879080), LT NUTFORD
    Nortforde 1086 DB, *Notforda* Exon
    Nu[t]ford 1189 France, *Nutford(e)* c. 1191–7 ClR (p), 1222
      ib, 1225, 1227, 1234 all FF, 1238 Ch, 1242–3 Fees *et passim,*
      Nutfort 1197 AddCh, *Nufed* 1200 (1280) *HarlCh, Neudfort*
      1201 (1231) *AddCh, Nutteford* 1228 *ib, Netford*' 1265 Cl,
      Notford(e) 1338 Ipm, 1339 Cl *et freq* to 1486 Ipm
    Blakemitford (for *-nutford*) 1252 FF, *Blakenotford* 1280 *Ass,*
      1317 Pat, 1319 FF, 1339 Ipm, 1344 FF (*-juxta Blaneford*),
      1352 Pat ('*-by Blaneford*), *Blake Nortfford* 1288 *Ass*
    Nutford Barnage iuxta Chyping' *Blaneford* 1288 *Ass, Nutford*
      Barnard (sic) 1311 Hutch[3]
    Lytil-Notford 1423 Hutch[3]

'The ford (on R. Stour) where nuts grow', from **hnutu** and **ford**, with **blæc** 'black, dark' and **lȳtel** 'little', cf. Blandford F. par. *supra.* The affix *-Barnage* is manorial, cf. *terram Hamelini filii Radulfi Barnage* 1197 *AddCh,* Reginald *Barnage* 1311 Hutch[3], Richard-, Joan *Bernage* 1332 SR. Some of the early unaffixed forms may strictly belong under France Fm in Stourpaine par. *infra.*

WHITECLIFF MILL (lost, at ST 882076), 1846 *TA, molend*' *de La Whyteclyve, -de la Whiteclyue* 1288 *Ass, -de Whiteclyve* 1318 *Ct, -de Wyhutecliue* 1369 *MinAcct, -de Whitclyuemylle* 1392 *Rawl, -mull*' 1393 *ib, those two mills called Whitcliffe Mills* 1661 *AddCh, Whitley Myll* 1591 *DLMB, -Mill* 1664 HTax, 1811 OS, 'the white cliff', from **hwīt** and **clif**, cf. Whitecliff in Swanage I 56. The place was on the bank of R. Stour just S of Nutford Fm *supra,* cf. *Nutford Mill* Hy 2 Hutch[3], *molendinum de Nutfort* 1197 *AddCh,* Robert *atte Mulle* 1382 EL, *Millway bottom* 1784 *SalisT,* Mill Down *infra, v.* **atte, myln.** The royal manor of Pimperne and Charlton Marshall had two mills in 1086 DB (VCHDo 3 65).

BARNES HOMES (near Blandford F., erected by the *Barnes* family). BERKELEY HO. CAMP DOWN (CTGS & PLANT.), *Camp Down* 1811 OS, named from the earthwork marked Camp 6″, but cf. the statement in Hutch[1] 1 79 that in 1756 there was a 'a camp...in Pimpern, consisting of two regiments of dragoons and six of foot'. CEMETERY FM, near Cemetery 6″. COTTAGE FM, cf. *Cottage Fd* 1829 *EnclA*. COWARD'S FM, cf. Nicholas *Coward* 1664 HTax. DAMORY COURT CTGS & FM, cf. *Damery Fd* 1784 *SalisT*, named from *Damory Court* in Blandford F. par. *supra*. FERNS PLANT., cf. *Fern Fd* 1829 *EnclA*. FRANCE DOWN CTGS, from France Down in Stourpaine par. *infra*. LETTON, *Litten Hill bottom* 1784 *SalisT*, possibly to be associated with William *de Latton*' 1327 *SR*, *-Lacton*' 1332 SR (Tarrant K.), perhaps from lēac-tūn 'herb garden'. MANOR FM. MAZE (Site of), *Miz Maze* 1814 *EnclA*, *Maze Fd* 1861 Hutch[3], *v.* mizmaze, Hutch[3] 1 292. MILL DOWN, *Mulledoune* 1382 Fine, *v.* myln, dūn, near *Whitecliff Mill supra*. NEW BARN. NEWFIELD FM, cf. *the New Field* 1784 *SalisT*. NORDON, N of Blandford F., perhaps from norð and dūn. PIMPERNE DOWN, 1811 OS, cf. *The Down* 1837 *TA*. PIMPERNE FOX WARREN & WD, cf. Roger *atte Wode* 1332 SR, 1340 NI, *v.* atte, wudu; for the *chace* and *warnership* ('office of warrener') of Pimperne, *v.* Blandford F. par. *supra*. POOR DELF, *v.* (ge)delf 'a pit'. PRIOR'S LANE, 1861 Hutch[3], *Pryors Lane End* 1814 *EnclA*, in allusion to the priory of Breamore Ha which held land here from the time of Hy 3 (Hutch[3] 1 292); the nearby pond (site marked 6″) is thought by Hutch[3] *loc. cit.* to have been an ancient fish-pond. RECTORY, cf. *Parsons Pitt, Parsons Stubbs* 1784 *SalisT*, *v.* pytt, stubb. ST PETER'S CHURCH, cf. *ecclesie de Pymperne* 1288 *Ass*. STUD HO, STUDHOUSE FM, *v.* stōd. WELL HO.

FIELD-NAMES

The undated forms are 1814 *EnclA* (DRO 70), but those marked † are 1837 *TA* 20 (*v.* Blandford F. par. *supra*). Spellings dated 1296, 1544, c. 1586 are Hutch[3], 1332 SR, 1547, 1548 *Ct*, 1657 DCMDeed, 1784 *SalisT*, and 1846 *TA* 157 (Nutford).

(a) Ansty's Altmt (cf. Stephen *Anestayse* 1332 (Durweston)); Ballis's (cf. Richard *Bal* 1332 (Blandford F.)); Birch Coppice; One Acre Blandford lane end 1784 (cf. Blandford F. par. *supra*); Bluffits; the Bough Flg 1784; Boyes Lane (cf. John *de Boys* 1332); †Brick Kiln Fd; Broad Mdw; Buddens Cl;

Burnbake(s), The Burnt Bake (*v.* **burnbake**); †Colts Corner; the Common Fd 1784; Court Cl (cf. *clausum curiæ* 1296); (Old) Cow Down; Crab Tree Coppice & Row; Crawford Mdw (perhaps from **crāwe** 'crow' and **ford**); Crosses Corner 1829 *EnclA*; By the Cross Way 1784 (*v.* **cross**); Down Pond; †Dry Mdw; (Gt & Lt) East Fd; East Wood Coppice (*Estwood* 1544, *v.* **ēast**); †The 8 Acres; Fatting Grd (*v.* **fatting**); †Hr & Lr Field; 5 Acres 1846; †(The) 4 Acres; Godwins Pond; Gore (Grd) (cf. *Mayngore* 1548, *v.* **gāra**, perhaps with **main**[1] 'demesne land'; †Green Fd; Green Knapp Half an Acre (*v.* **cnæpp**); †Gunners Grd; †Ham Mdw (*v.* **hamm**); Hanging Cl 1829 *EnclA*; Harvest Pitt 1784; †Hatches (*v.* **hæc(c)**); Heath Fd 1829 *EnclA*; Home Cl; Iron Grd; †Kite's Corner; †Lambourn Down (perhaps **lamb, burna**); Landshare 1846 (*v.* **land-sc(e)aru**); Landway bottom 1784; Lilly Bank; Long Elm(s); †Major's Mdw; †Middle Fd; the Middle Flg 1784; Middle Hill 1784; †9 (and 11) Acres; †Nutford Fd (*v.* Nutford *supra*); †(Old) Orchard; the old way 1784; Paddock; Pimperne Fm 1784; †Pimperne Fd; Pimperne Mead(ow); By the Pitt 1784; Pitts tenement 1784; Plantation and Lime Kiln; Hr & Yonder Pleck, The Plecks (*v.* **plek**); Poins; Red Land 1784; the Rick Yard (Gate) 1784; Ridout's Arable Altmt (cf. Nicholas *Ridhoud'* 1332 (Tarrant H.)); Salisbury Lane (to Salisbury W.); Sergiants Grd; Shaston Lane (*Shaftesbury*-1784, to Shaftesbury par. *infra*); Shawl(s) Coppice & Row; †16 Acres; Sleight (*v.* **slæget**); †Smoke Acre (*v.* **smoke**); 3 Acres head lands on Lincks 1784 (*v.* **hēafod-land, hlinc**); †3 Acre Mdw; 3 Stitches 1784 (*v.* **sticce**[1]); Turnpike Plot (cf. *the Turnpike to Blandford* 1784); †(The) 12 Acres; †Lr 20 Acres; †Hr 21 Acres; 2 Acres Head lands 1784; Tythingman's Ld (*v.* **tēoðung-mann**); The Upper Fd; Vanstons Ash 1784; West Fd 1829 *EnclA*; White Lane; Wills Round Grove; Woodhouse Grd; Wool Ld 1784 (perhaps from **well(a)**, WSax **wyll(a)** 'spring, stream').

(b) (*terr' nup'*) *Bar(r)ettes* 1547, 1548; *Hedley* c. 1586 (possibly 'heath clearing' from **hǣð** and **lēah**); *Pympernethornes* 1364 *Cecil* (*v.* **þorn**); *Shawewood* 1544 (*v.* **sc(e)aga**); *Sparrowes* 1657 (a surname); *atte wych* (p) 1327 (*v.* **atte, wīc** 'farm' or **wice** 'wych-elm').

Steepleton Iwerne

STEEPLETON IWERNE (IWERNE STEPLETON 1″) (ST 863113)
Werne 1086 DB, *Iwerna* Exon
Stepelton(e) 1210–12 RBE, 1235–6 Fees, 1288 *Ass* (p), 1316 FA, 1327 Cl, 1331 Ipm, 1341 Cl, *Steple-* 1234 Pat, 1547 *Ct*, 1550–3 BM I, *Stepilton* 1412, 1428 FA
Stupelton(e) 1244 *Ass* (p), 1279 Ipm, 1280 QW, *Ass*, 1285 Ipm, 1288 *Ass*, 1291 Tax, c. 1300 *AD* (p), 1303 FA, 1327 SR, 1332 SR, 1340 NI, 1346, 1428, 1431 all FA, *Stupleton* 1278 QW, 1280 *Ass*, 1428 FA
Stipelton 1291 Tax, 1412 FA, 1428, 1431 IpmR, *Stypyl-* 1385 Pat, *Stypleton* 1547 *Ct*

Stapelton(e) 1316 FA (p), 1331 Ipm
Iwernestapleton 1346 FF, -*Stupelton* 1359 ib, -*Stupleton* 1431
  IpmR, *Iverne Stupulton* 1435 FF, *Ewerne Stipleton* 1594
  DCMDeed
Steepleton Preston 1795 Boswell, 1839 *TA*, 1939 Kelly
  (*Steepleton Iwerne or-*)

One of three pars. named from R. Iwerne, *v.* Iwerne Minster
par. and RNs. *infra*; for the DB identification, *v.* Eyton 131–2,
VCHDo 3 94, DBGazetteer 126. It is probable that the meaning
of *Steepleton* is 'village (*v.* tūn) with a church steeple or tower'
rather than 'village at a steep place' (although this could refer
to its situation in the Iwerne valley under Ranston Hill), *v.*
stēpel (WSax stīepel), cf. Steeple par. 1 95, Winterborne
Steepleton par. *infra*, Hutch[3] 1 298. *Preston* is probably from
Preston, in Iwerne Minster par. *infra*, part of which may once
have been in this par. (*Preston* was a tithing in Pimperne
hundred in 1327 *SR*, 1332 SR, 1548 *Ct*, and Hutch[3] 3 540
describes it as 'part in Blandford and part in Shaftesbury
division'). For the forms *Stapel-*, *-staple-* cf. NED s.v. *staple*
sb[1], sense 1b.

ASHY COPPICE, *Ashton cops* 1618 *Map*, *v.* æsc, tūn, copis.
BECKFORD LODGES, *Lodges* 1826 Gre, from the *Beckford* family
here in the 18th cent. BOYNE'S COPPICE & LANE, cf. Boyne's
Lane Pleck in Iwerne Courtney par. *infra*.
CRABTREE COPPICE. EVERLEY COPPICE, DOWN & FM (*Steepleton
Fm* 1811 OS), EVERLEY HILL FM, probably 'wild boar wood'
from eofor and lēah, cf. an identical name in Fifehead N. par.
supra). GRAMMARS HILL, the surname *Grammar*. PIMPERNE
STUBS, cf. Pimperne par. *supra*, *v.* stubb. ST MARY'S CHURCH.
SHALE'S COPPICE. SMUGGLERS' LANE. STEEPLETON HO (1826
Gre) & SHRUBBERY.

FIELD-NAMES

(*b*) *Atteforde* (p) 1327 *SR* (*v.* atte, ford); *Breaches* 1618 *Map* (*v.* bræc).

Stourpaine

STOURPAINE (ST 861094) ['stauəpein]
  Sture 1086 DB (2 ×), 1245 Sarum, 1280 Ass, Stures 1208
  Cur, 1212 Fees, 1245 Sarum, 1270 (1372) ChrP, 1288 Ass,
  Estur' 1208 Cur, Sturis 1210 P, 1245 Sarum, Stoure 1372
  ChrP
  Sture(s) Paen 1242–3 Fees, 1268 Ass, -Payn 1280 QW, Ass,
  1288 ib, Store Payn 1303 FA, Stour(e) Payn, -payn(e) 1303
  ib et passim, Stowre- 1394 Pat, Stowerpayn 1548 Ct
  Stoure Ereschus 1313 FF

Named from R. Stour, v. RNs. infra; for the DB identifi-
cations, v. Eyton 137–8, VCHDo 3 101, 114, DBGazetteer 126.
The affix -paine is from the Payn family which held the manor
during the 13th and 14th centuries ('Pagan son of William'
1226 FF, Bartholomew Payn 1303, 1316 FA, 1327 SR, Richard
Payn 1332 SR, etc). The affix -Ereschus is also manorial, from
Richard Orescuilz 1210 P, -(de) (H)orescuel, de Oriscoill n.d.
(1372) ChrP, whose family gave name to Sandford Orcas par.
infra, cf. Hutch³ 1 312, Reaney OES 291; the form Sture Oscut
(for -Oscul?) 1280 Ass (203 m.4d, 204 m.4d) may also belong
here. There was a mill at the larger of the two manors of Sture
in 1086 DB (VCHDo 3 101), cf. molendinum de Stures n.d.
(1372) ChrP.

ASH (FM) (ST 864103), Aisse 1086 DB, Esse 1244 Ass (p), c.1270
Seymer, 1288 Ass, Aysse 1270 (1372) ChrP, As(s)h(e) 1280 QW,
Ass, 1316 FA (p), 1327 SR et passim, As(s)ch(e) 1280 QW, Ass,
1332 SR, Esshe, Heshe 1288 Ass, Ayssh(e) 1372 ChrP, 1412,
1431 FA, 1548 Ct, Ayshebozon 1547 ib, 'the ash-tree', v. æsc
(dat.sg. æsce), cf. Ash in Netherbury par. infra; the affix -bozon
is from the family of Joan Buzun who held Lazerton infra in
1256 FF, cf. Hutch³ 1 311, John Boson 1332 SR (Tarrant
Rush.).

FRANCE FM (ST 867082), Nodford 1086 DB, Not(t)ford(e)locky
1265 Cl, 1431 FA, -Lok(') 1280 QW, Ass, -Locki 1288 FF,
-Lok(k)y 1303, 1346 FA, Natford Lok(') 1280 QW, Ass, Nutford
Locky 1288 ib, -Lokky 1316 FA, -Lokke 1428 ib, Franc' 1368
Cl, Nutford Lockey als. France 1587 Hutch³, France or Fraunce

1774 Hutch[1], v. Nutford Fm in Pimperne par. *supra*; for the DB identification, v. Eyton 137–8, VCHDo 3 113. The affix *-locky* is from the family of Richard *Loky* 1244 *Ass* (mentioned in connection with Blandford), Jordan- 1275 RH, Henry *Locky* 1288 *Ass* (both mentioned in connection with Badbury hundred). Hutch[1] 1 81 supposed that the later name France was 'from some Frenchman that possessed it in the Norman times'; more plausibly, Fägersten 58 considers that it may be an allusion to land held in Nutford by the abbey of Fontevrault (cf. *Lib' Abbatisse de Fonte Eboraldi...Nutford' et Blaneford'* 1280 *Ass*), cf. PN Brk 542 for an even earlier instance of *Fraunce* as a transferred name. On the other hand, France is possibly manorial in origin, perhaps from the family of William *Fraunc'* 1327 *SR* (Pimperne), cf. French's Fm in Wimborne St G. par. *infra*, France Wd Sx 401

HOD HILL (ST 855108) & WD, 1840 *TA*, *Hod-hill* 1774 Hutch[1], cf. *due acre...iacent in campo Australi quod vocatur sub Hod*, (*viam que vocatur*) *Hodweye* c. 1270 *AddCh* (entries concerning the neighbouring par of Shillingstone, v. Hodway Lane in that par. *infra*), '*Hod* meadow' 1302 AD I (2 ×), possibly from OE hōd[1] 'a hood', in allusion to the shape of the 470' hill, but more probably from an OE hōd[2] 'a shelter', with reference to the Iron Age hill-fort (incorporating a Roman fort) which crowns the hill, marked Camp 6", v. hyll, cf. Hood D 297, YN 195, EPN s.v. hōd, DEPN s.n. Hood. Dr Gelling notes that if either explanation is correct, the apparently early shortening of the vowel is surprising, especially as *Hod* was a simplex name in c. 1270.

LAZERTON FM (ST 863103) ['læzətən]
>   *Werne* 1086 DB (f. 84), *Iwernelazerton* 1346 FF
>   *Lacerton* Hy 3 Ipm, 1795 Boswell (*-or Lazerton*), *Laterton*(')
>   1280 QW, *Ass*
>   *Lathirton'* 1235–6 Fees, *Latherton'* 1242–3 ib
>   *Lasceton'* 1244 *Ass* (p), *Lasteton* 1256 FF
>   *Lazereton* c. 1270 *Seymer*, *Lazerton*(e) 1280 *Ass*, 1288 Orig,
>   *Ass*, 1316, 1428 FA, *Lasar-* 1326 Ipm, 1327 Cl, *Laserton*
>   1341 ib
>   *Lacheston'* 1280 *Ass*, *Lacherston'* 1288 *ib*
>   *Laston'* 1327 *SR*, 1332 SR, *Las'ton* 1340 NI

This farm stands on R. Iwerne, *v.* Iwerne Minster par. and RNs. *infra*; for the DB identification, *v.* Eyton 137–8, VCHDo 3 111, DBGazetteer 122. The final el. of Lazerton is clearly **tūn** 'farm, estate', but the first part of the name is difficult. If the spellings in *-t-*, *-th-*, *-st-* may be taken to be errors of transcription for *-c-*, *-ch-*, *-sc-*, and if those in *-c-*, *-sc-*, *-z-*, *-s-* may be seen to be due to Fr influence (cf. Zachrisson ANInfl 21ff, IPN 102), then the first el. could be, as Professor Löfvenberg suggests, an OE (WSax) ***lǣcere** 'a leech gatherer or leech dealer', with early shortening of the vowel in the compound. There was a mill at Lazerton in 1086 DB (VCHDo 3 111), and there was formerly also a church here, *v.* Chapel Md *infra*.

Ash Down (*Ash Furze Down* 1840 *TA*), Ash Oaks Coppice (*Ash okes* 1618 *Map*, *Ash Oak(s) Coppice* 1840 *TA*, *v.* āc), from Ash *supra*. Church (All Saints), cf. *ecclesie sancte trinitatis de Sturis* n.d. (1372) *ChrP*. Church Ho, from prec. Conygar Clump, *Conegre-* 1840 *TA*, cf. *Conygore Hill* 1811 OS, *Conegre Coppice & Pce*, *Above Conegre* 1840 *TA*, *v.* **coninger**. Down End Fm Bldgs, cf. *Down End* 1840 *ib*, near France Down *infra*. The Down, 1840 *ib*. Elder Dean Coppice, 1840 *ib*, possibly to be identified with *Elendene* 1227 FF, *v.* **elle(r)n** 'elder-tree', **denu** 'valley', Hinton Bushes in Tarrant H. par. *infra*. France Ctgs, Down (1840 *ib*, *Furze Down* 1811 OS) & Firs, France Oaks Coppice, cf. *France Mdw* 1837 *TA*, from France Fm *supra*. Free Down, *Ash Free Down* 1840 *TA*, *v.* frēo, Ash *supra*. Furzeland Barn & Coppice, *Furzeland Fd (Barn) & Coppice* 1840 *TA*, *v.* **fyrs, land**. Higher Barn. Little Coppice. Manor Fm & Ho (site of), cf. *Manor Pound* 1840 *TA*, Hutch[3] 1 305. Paradise Pond (1811 OS) & Wd ((-*Wd*) 1840 *TA*, *v.* **paradis**. Parsonage Fm, near Vicarage (6″). Shady Bushes, 1840 *ib*, a wood. Stourpaine Bushes, Down (*Stowerpaine-* 1811 OS) & Ho (cf. *Stourpain Farmhouse* 1840 *TA*). Upper Barn, 1840 *ib*.

FIELD-NAMES

The undated forms are 1840 *TA* 204. Spellings dated 1244 are *Ass*, 1327 *SR*, 1332 SR, 1340 NI, 1480 *DCMDeed*, 1664 HTax, 1817 Hutch[3].

(*a*) Above the house, -the Road; Allens Orchd; Under & Yonder Ash hedge, Ash Md (cf. *campis de Esse* 1244, *v.* Ash *supra*); Biggs Cl; (Grass & Middle) Bottom (*v.* **botm**); Bottom Fd; Under & Upon Box Linch, Box Linch

Plant. (v. **box, hlinc**); Breeches (v. **bræc**); Bridge Oaks; Brimley Lawn; Broad Leys (v. **læs**); Butcher's Fd; Butlers Orchd & 3 Acres; Cats Grd; Chapel Md (*Chappel-Close* 1774 Hutch[1] 1 106, the site of the former church of Lazerton *supra*, in 1331 dedicated to St Andrew); Chopping Knife (so named from its shape); Clerk's Acre (cf. Richard *le Clerk* 1340); Close; Clump Acre; Coffin Acre; Cole Hill (Snuffhalf) (cf. Colehill par. *infra ; Snuffhalf* perhaps means 'the half of little value', v. NED s.vv. *snuff* sb.[1] sense 1d, *snuff* sb.[2] sense 2b); Comb Pit acre (v. **cumb**); Common E & W of Turnpike Rd; Common Pleck (v. **plek**); Cow Leaze; Croft (Orchd); Crooked Joan; Cross Cl; Cuckoo Plot; Custon Corner; Down Fd; Drove Fd; Dry Mdw; Everetts 4 Acres; (E of) Farm 10 Acres; (Above) Fiford (Acre); 14 Acres; Foyals Orchd (cf. *Foyle's* (*living*), Edward *Foyle* 1861 Hutch[3] 1 239); Friars Stitch (v. **sticce**[1]); Gascons Pond (possibly from **gærs-tūn** 'paddock'); (Below) Great Linch (v. **hlinc**); Great Mdw; (W) Green Flg; Hr & Lr Greenhill; The Ham Mdw (v. **hamm**); Harveys Barn (cf. Nicholas *Hervy* 1327); Garden (Havlin's); Hill Md (Handkerchief half & Tuffin's half) (v. **half**; Handkerchief half is a small triangular field); Hod Drove Acre, Under Hod Linch, Hod Pce & Pit Lds (from Hod Hill *supra*, v. **hlinc**); Home Md; Horse Leys, Lambs Leys (v. **læs**); Lazerton Fd (v. Lazerton *supra*); Limepit Fd with Stable Yd; Loders Cl; Above Long Linch (v. **hlinc**); Lower Fd 1829 *EnclA*; Lower Flg; Maredon; The Marsh, Marsh Cl & Clump; Middle Bottom, Fd, Flg & Md; New Cl; New's Tenement 1817; North Hill (Shortlons) (v. **sc(e)ort, land**); Oakey Coppice (perhaps **āc, (ge)hæg**); Oak Coppice and Plant.; Oak Fd; Old Clover; Paddock (cf. *le West Parrok'* 1480, v. **pearroc**); (Hr & Lr) Park; Peaked Grove (v. **peked, grāf(a)**); Pickaxe (so named from its shape); Piece; Pigeon house Cl; Pilley's Grave; Plantation; Plums; Ragged hedge; Reads Ho & Orchd (cf. Thomas *Reed* 1664); Rivers' Arms Inn; Sheeps Drove; 6 Acres; Slades (v. **slæd**, or a surname); South Md; Ste(a)rt (v. **steort** 'tail of land'); Stone Cl; Sutton (possibly 'south farm', v. **sūð, tūn**); 10 Acre Mdw; 10 Acres; Thirt Over Comb (v. **thwart-over, cumb**); Thirt the Path (v. **thwart**); Tuffins Acre; Two Twelves; Under the hedge; Walls Flg (Linch), Walls Linch (v. **hlinc**); Walnut Acre; Well Fd; Westons Water; Wheat Lds; Wire Shard (v. **sceard** 'gap'; first el. perhaps **wīr** 'bog myrtle'); Withy Bed, Withy Nash (*Withy Hays* 1829 *EnclA*, v. **wīðig, (ge)hæg**; *Nash* is from ME *atten ashe* 'at the ash-tree', v. **atten, æsc**, Ash *supra*).

(*b*) Knolleys 1618 *Map*; atte Lane 1327, in thelane 1332 both (p) (v. **atte, lane**); atte Wode 1332 (p) (v. **wudu**).

Tarrant Hinton

Part of this par. was transferred to Pimperne par. *supra* in 1933.

TARRANT HINTON (ST 936112)
(*at*) *Terente* 871–877 (15) *ShaftR* (S 357(1)), (*in*) *Tarente ib* (S 357(2)), (*ad*) *Tarentam* (rubric), (*ad*) *Terentam* 935 (15) *ib* (S 429)

Tarente 1086 DB (f. 78b), 1227, 1245 FF, *Tarent'* 1212 Fees
Tarent(e) Hyneton(') 1280 *Ass*, 1285 FA, 1288 *Ass et freq* to
1428 FA, *-Hynton* 1340 NI, 1435 FF, *-Henton* 1428 FA,
Tarant Hynton juxta Pymperne 1358 Hutch[3], *Hinton Tar-
rant* 1795 Boswell
Hineton' 1280 *Ass, Hynton* 1548 *Ct*
Hyneton' et (sic) *Goundevile* 1327 *SR, Hyneton' Goundeuyle*
1332 SR

One of eight Do pars. named from R. Tarrant, *v.* RNs. *infra.*
Hinton means 'farm or estate belonging to the religious
community', from **hīwan** (gen.pl. *hī(g)na*) and **tūn**, cf.
Piddlehinton par. 1 309, Hinton St M. par. and Hinton Martell
par. both *infra*; Tarrant Hinton belonged in 1086 DB (VCHDo
3 82) to Shaftesbury abbey, to which it had been granted by
Alfred and Athelstan (S 357, 429). The bounds of the manor
are given in S 429. The affix *-Goundevile* must be from the
family which gave name to the adjacent par. of Tarrant Gunville
infra.

HYDE FM (ST 906093)
*Hugoni de La Hyda de pimpern ius . . . in una hyda terre in villa
de pimperne* e13 *Wim, Hyda(m)* 1227 FF, 1314 *AD* (p),
Hida 1242 Ch (p), *la Hyde, -Hide* 1288 *Ass,* c. 1300 *AD*
(*p*) *et freq* to 1358 Hutch[3] (*-in Tarente Hynton juxta
Pimperne), Le Hyda juxta Blaneford* 1316 FA, *atte Hude*
1327 *SR* (p), (*Stoke and*) *Hide* 1366 FF, *De la Hide maner'
in Tarent Hynton* 1402 IpmR, *Hyde or Stoke Hyde* 1795
Boswell
Stokehyde, -Hyde 1437, 1480 Hutch[3], 1483 IpmR *et freq* to
1518 Hutch[1], *Stokehide* 1495 Ipm, 1774 Hutch[1] (*-near
Blanford), Stocke hide* 1591 *DLMB*

'The hide of land', *v.* **hīd, atte,** cf. Pimperne par. and
Blandford F. par *supra*, Hutch[3] 1 315. *Stokehyde* may be '(the
part of) the manor of Hyde attached to (East) Stoke', *v.* E Stoke
par. 1 145; lands in Hyde were held during the 15th and 16th
centuries by the same families (*Chauntmarle, Cheverel,* etc)
which held the manor of E Stoke (Hutch[3] 1 315, 411–13).
Probably to be associated with this place is the f.n. *Stoke Mede*
in Blandford F. par. *supra.*

BARTON HILL, *Barton's hill* 1839 *TA, Barton field or Barton hill* 1861 Hutch[3], *v.* **bere-tūn**. BRIXEY'S FM. CHURCH (St Mary's), cf. Andrew- 1327 *SR*, Adam *atte Church(e)* 1332 SR, *Church Mdw* 1839 *TA*. CROWN INN, 1839 *ib.* HIGH LEA HILL, *Hayley (Fd)* 1839 *ib*, probably 'clearing used for hay', *v.* **hēg** (WSax **hī(e)g**), **lēah**. HINTON BUSHES, 1784 *SalisT*, (*-Fd*) 1839 *TA*; this wood, and Pimperne Wd in Pimperne par. *supra*, are on the site of the wood referred to in the OE bounds of Tarrant H. as *þane wde* ('the wood') 935 (15) *ShaftR* (S 429), cf. 'a certain angle of wood called *Northwude juxta Elendene* 1227 FF, *bosco de Tarrent* 1369 *MinAcct*, *v.* **norð, wudu**, Elder Dean Coppice in Stourpaine par. *supra*. HORSE SHOE CLUMP, a round clump of trees, perhaps formerly the shape of a horseshoe. LITTLE DOWN PLANT. MANOR FM. NEW BARN, -(*Lower*) *Fd* 1839 *TA*. NINETY EIGHT & NINETY NINE PLANTS., perhaps so called because planted in 1898 and 1899. NORTH FM. OLD TURNPIKE, a junction on *Turnpike Rd* 1839 *TA*, cf. 'the Salisbury and Blandford turnpike traverses the whole length of the parish' (Hutch[3] I 314). PIMPERNE LONG BARROW, *Long Barrow* 1811 OS, lying just inside the bdy of Tarrant H. with Pimperne; it possibly gave name to the DB hundred of *Langeberge, v.* Pimperne hundred *supra*. RECTORY, cf. *Parsonage Hr & Lr Field* 1839 *TA*. SPRAKE'S BLDGS. (N & S) TARRANT HINTON DOWN, cf. the bdy point *to dungete* 935 (15) *ShaftR* (S 429) which was at the NW corner of the par. near to the present N Tarrant Hinton Down, *v.* **dūn** 'hill', **geat** 'gate, pass', and cf. *Down* 1839 *TA*. THICKTHORN BAR & COPPICE, *Thickthorn Coppice, Corner, Fd & Mdw* 1839 *ib*, from Thickthorn Fm in Long Crichel par. *infra*; *Bar* here is used of a narrow belt of trees, *v.* **barre**.

FIELD-NAMES

The undated forms in (*a*) are 1839 *TA* 221, in (*b*) 935 (15) *ShaftR* (S 429). Spellings dated 1227 are FF, 1327 *SR*, 1332 SR, 1664 HTax , 1791 Boswell.

(*a*) Blackgrove Fd (*v.* **grāf(a)**); Bloodhurst (*v.* **hyrst**); Bown's Bottom Fd, Bown's Greenway, Bown's Hr & Lr Fd (cf. Richard *Bounde* 1332, *v.* **grēne**[1]); Broad Cl; Crabbs Burnbake, Hr & Lr Burnbake (*v.* **burnbake**); Lr Bye Fd (*v.* **byge**[1] 'a bend'; near R. Tarrant); Coombs Down; (The) Croft; Drove Down & Fd; Dryground; 8 Acres; Hr End Mdw; Farquharson Arms' Inn (from the *Farquharson* family, lords of the manor since e19, *v.* Hutch[3] I 315); Farm Down & Mdw; Fords Cl; Furze Brake & Fd (*v.* **bræc**[1]); Great Bridge

1791; Hide Fd, Peaked Hide (from Hyde Fm *supra*, *v.* **peked**); Home Fd; Little Fd; Long Cl; Malthouse Orchd; Meadland's Fd (cf. *med ham infra*); Middle Fd; Morey's Md (cf. Thomas *Morey* 1664); The Park; Peaked Fd (*v.* **peked**); Rookery; 6 Acres; The Sleight (*v.* **slæget**); Town Fd Down; Westlane Bridge 1791; Whitewood's Down, Fd, Mdw & Orchd; Wood Md; Yard Fd (*v.* **geard** or **gerd**); Yew Tree Fd.

(b) *to bacging berghe, þanen on þane oþerne beoit* (sic) (probably 'barrow called after Bacga', from the OE pers.n. *Bacga*, **-ing-**[4], **beorg**; *beoit* is corrupt, but possibly represents *beorc* for *beorg*); *on þat beorhlem* (probably corrupt, perhaps from **beorg** 'hill' and *lēam*, dat.pl. of **lēah** 'wood, clearing'); *on þa burnestowe middewardde* (*v.* **burn-stōw** 'bathing place', or 'watering place for cattle', cf. Langbourne in Langton Long B. par. *supra*); *þiyres ouer chelesbergh'* ('Cēol's barrow', from the OE pers.n. *Cēol* and **beorg**, with **þwēores** 'across', **ofer**[3] 'over'); *be westen cockes þorne* (perhaps '(to the west of) Cocc's thorn-tree', from an OE pers.n. **Cocc* (cf. the wk. form **Cocca* postulated to enter into several p.ns, *v.* DEPN s.n. Cockbury) and **þorn**, but **cocc**[1] 'a heap, a hillock' or **cocc**[2] 'a cock' are also possible, *v.* **bī, westan**); *one dat* (for *ðat*) *dich* (*v.* **dīc**); *to fildene lane uppende* ('the upper end of the lane of the dwellers in open country', *v.* **filde**[2] (gen.pl. *fildena*), **lane, upp, ende**[1], Tengstrand 99ff); *oð þanne ford* (*v.* **ford**); *an lang þere fures* (from **furh** 'furrow', with analogical gen.sg.); *wið norþen þanen graetem beorge* ('towards the north of the great barrow', *v.* **wið, norþan, grēat** (wk.obl. *-an*), **beorg**; the barrow (marked 6″) is situated in the field now called Twissell Barrows in Tarrant L. par. *infra*); *Hauodacre* 1227 (*v.* **hēafod, æcer**); *anlang herepaþes* (*v.* **here-pæð**); *to horsedich* (*v.* **hors** (gen.pl. *horsa*), **dīc**); *to þare hwitendich, and þanen and lang dich* (*v.* **hwīt** (wk.obl. *-an*) 'white', **dīc**); *on þone med ham suðe wardne* (*v.* **mǣd, hamm**); *to þare rede hane* (*v.* **rēad** 'red', **hān** 'stone'); *Smalelande* 1227 (*v.* **smæl, land**); *to þan stanegan crundel* (*v.* **stānig, crundel**); *atte Sturte* (p) 1327 (*v.* **atte, steort** 'tail of land'); *to tatanbeorge, and of þane berge* ('Tāta's barrow', from the OE pers.n. *Tāta* and **beorg**); *on worres berg, of þane beorge* ('Worr's barrow', from the OE pers.n. *Worr* and **beorg**).

Tarrant Keynston

TARRANT KEYNSTON (ST 925041) ['keinstən]

Tarente 1086 DB (f. 77b), 1199 P (*-Willelmi de Cahaignes*), 1201 FF *et freq* to 1292 Cl, *Tarrent* 1242 Ch

Tarent(*e*) *Kaaign*(*es*) 1225 Sarum, m13 *Salis*, *-Kahaines* 1225 Osm, *-Kay*(*g*)*nes*, *-Kaynegnes* 1242 Ch *et freq* with variant spellings *-Kahaynes*, *-Kay*(*n*)*gnes*, *-Cay*(*g*)*nes*, *-kaymes*, *-kenes*, *-Keynes* to 1432 Cl, *Tarrent*(*e*) *Kahaynes* 1237 Pat, Ch, *-Kaynes* 1316 FA, 1344 Ipm, *Tharent*(*e*) *Kaynes*, *-Kaenes* 1242–3 FF, *Terente Kaynes* 1252 ib, *Tarente de Kaynes* 1285 FA

Kenysteton' 1268 *Ass*, *Kayneston*(*e*) 1278 Pat, 1280 *Ass et freq*

to 1431 FA, *Caynes-* 1332 SR, *Keynes-* 1386 Fine, *Keyns-*
1547 Ct, *Kaynston* 1548 *ib*, *Caynston* 1575 Saxton, *Keinson*
als. *Keinston* 1624 *Fort*, *Keynson* 1700 *ib*
Keynes 1280 *Ass* (*man' de-*), 1364 Pat
Tarent(e) Kyneton' (sic) 1288 *Ass*, -*Keyneston* 1303 FA *et freq*
with variant spellings -*Cayneston*, -*Kayneston* to 1469 Cl,
Tarrant' Kaynston' 1512 *Pars*, *Tarrannte Keynston'* 1597
PlR, *Tarrant Kayns-*, -*Kainston* 1617 *Maslen et passim*,
Keynson 1700 *Fort*, *Ke(i)nston Tarrant*, -*Terrant*
1624–1626 *ib*

Named from R. Tarrant, *v.* Tarrant H. par. *supra*, RNs.
infra; for the identification of the DB form, *v.* Eyton 131–2,
VCHDo 3 60, 73. The manor was held by William *de Cahaignes*
in 1199 (P), and was in the possession of this family until the
end of the 14th cent. (1201 FF, 1212 Fees, 1237 Pat, etc), cf.
Coombe Keynes par. 1 114, *v.* **tūn** 'estate'.

ALL SAINTS' CHURCH, cf. 'church of All Saints, *Tarente*' 1235
Ch, 'St Michael's Church in *Tarent Kaines*' 1383 Hutch[3] 3
122. ASHLEY WD, 1645 Hutch[3], *Ash(e)lie Wood* 1624 *Fort*, cf.
vie que vocatur asseweye n.d. (1372) *ChrP*, *v.* **æsc**, **lēah**, **weg**.
BROOKFIELD. BUZBURY RINGS, *Buzbury* 1811 OS, an Iron
Age-RB multivallate hill-slope enclosure, the second el. being
no doubt **burh** (dat.sg. *byrig*) 'fortified place'; the form '(down
called...) *Barseden*' (for *Burse-*, -*don* ?) 1242 Ch may belong
here, and the first el. of both names may be the OE pers.n.
Beorhtsige, cf. Buzzacott D 36. DOWN BARN, *West Down Barn*
1838 *TA*, cf. Keynston Down *infra*. FORD, cf. *Tarenteforde*
1145–66 Templar (p. 190), *Cleffordehal infra*, *v.* **ford**. KEYNSTON
DAIRY HO, cf. *Bottom Fd Dairy Ho* 1838 *TA*. KEYNSTON DOWN,
cf. *Keynes Down* 1542 Hutch[3], *Schipenedone* 1270 *Ass*, *Hogen
Downe Corner* 1624 *Fort*, *Downe Feild* c. 1700 *DCMSurv*, *East
& Lt Down*, *Down Cl* 1838 *TA*, *v.* **dūn**; *Schipene-* and *Hogen-*
are gen. pl. forms in -*en* (*v.* -*ena*) of **scēap** (WSax **scī(e)p**)
'sheep' and **hogg** 'young sheep', cf. 'pasture for 500 sheep
called hoggs' 1535 VE (Hutch[3] 1 322). KEYNSTON LODGE.
KEYNSTON MILL, -*stone-* 1811 OS, *the Mill house with the two
watermills thereunto belonginge* 1624 *Fort*, *Keynson Mills* 1700
ib, *two grist Mills and a Mault Mill* c. 1700 *DCMSurv*, cf. (*the*)
Mil(l) croftes 1624 *ib*, *Mill Croft* 1838 *TA*, *the Mill ham(s)* 1624,

1700 *Fort, Millway feild* 1624 *ib, the Mill barne* 1676 *ib, v.* **myln, croft, hamm**; there were two mills at Tarrant K. in 1086 DB (VCHDo 3 73), cf. also *molendinum . . . quod est subtus curiam meam in eadem villa et molendinum super Stures cum prato et mesuagio quod Brutel tenuit* n.d. (1372) *ChrP, molendinum quod vocatur Prutelesmille, -mulle super ripam de Stures* 1288 *Ass, v.* R. Stour in RNs. *infra*; the pers.n. *Brut-, Prutel* is probably from ME *brotel, brutel* 'fickle, untrustworthy'. MANOR FM, cf. *the Farme house Keyneton* 1664 HTax, *Tarrant Keynston Farme* 1677 *Fort, The Mannor house* c. 1700 *DCMSurv.* RECTORY, *the Rectory with the Gleab Land* c. 1700 *ib.* TRUE LOVERS' KNOT (P.H.).

FIELD-NAMES

The undated forms are 1838 *TA* 222. Some fields in Tarrant K. *TA* are now in Tarrant Rush. par. *infra*. Spellings dated 1242 are Ch, 1243 FF, 1288 *Ass,* 1327 *SR,* 1332 SR, 1346, 1428 FA, n.d. (1372) ChrP, 1542 Hutch[3], 1617 *Maslen,* 1624, 1627, 1676, 1677, 1700 *Fort,* 1664 HTax, c. 1700 *DCMSurv.*

(a) Baines Flg; Batts or Butts Fd ('culture called *Buttes'* 1243, *Butts Close* c. 1700, *v.* **butte**); Benjafields Mdw; Blandford Lane Pce (cf. *magne vie que tendit apud Blaneford'* n.d. (1372), *v.* Blandford F. par. *supra*); Bookes hay c. 1700 (*v.* (ge)hæg); Broadlands (*Brod-* c. 1700, *v.* brād); Collis lane c. 1700 (cf. Jane *Collis ib*); The Common Pasture Down; Coneygear (Flg) (*the Connigar Close* 1624, *Conniger Furlong* 1677, *the Cunnygares* c. 1700, *v.* **coninger** 'rabbit-warren'); The Coppice Woods c. 1700; Corn Crate (*v.* **croft**); Cowards or Falls Plot; The Croft c. 1700; Dry Cl c. 1700; Dunbury Cl c. 1700 (cf. Dunbury in Winterborne Hou. par. *infra*); Field; a peice of greensward ground called Forehead Cloth c. 1700; Hthr & Yonder Furlong; Furzy Bit (*-pitt* 1677, *v.* **pytt**); Glaziers Md; Great Mdw (*the great mead(owe of Tarrant Keynston)* 1676, 1700); Green; Green Crate (*v.* **croft**); Green Hayes (*-Hay* c. 1700, *v.* (ge)hæg); Green Way; ye Hams c. 1700 (*v.* **hamm**); Hard Md; Harris Ham Mead (*v.* **hamm**); Hayters (Home) Fd (cf. William *Hayter* c. 1700); Heath Close(s) (*-Close* c. 1700, cf. *the Heath, Heath Lane ib*); Heath Wood (c. 1700, perhaps to be connected with *bosco qui vocatur Ethenwode* 1288, *v.* hǣð, hǣðen, wudu); Higher Cl c. 1700; Hind water (*-Close* c. 1700, *v.* **hind** 'a hind' or **hindan** 'behind'); (the) Home Feild c. 1700; Horwoods Ham c. 1700 (*Harwoodes-* 1624); Keynston Feilds c. 1700 (*Keynson-* 1700, cf. *in campo de Kaynyston'* 1387 (e15) *MiltRoll*); Keynston Lane c. 1700; Keynston Mead(ow), Keyns Mdw or Keyns Marshe (*Kainston Meade* 1617, *Kaynes mead, Kainston Marshe* 1624, *v.* mǣd, mersc, cf. par. name and Great Mdw *supra*); Kerleys Plot; Lady Hole, -Holt c. 1700 (*-Hole* 1676, perhaps with reference to lands belonging to Tarrant abbey, *v.* hlǣfdige, hol[1] or holt, Hutch[3] 1 321–2); Langton Barrow Md (*Clarkes Mdw als.-* c. 1700, *v.* Langton Long B. par. *supra*); Leg Cl, The Leg (*v.* **leg**); Little Cl c. 1700;

Long Cl (1676); Malthouse Cl (cf. *a Mault Mill* c. 1700); Mead(ow) (cf.
Medgare 1242, *v.* **mǣd, gāra**); Middle Fd; Newbury (c. 1700); New Cl (*(the)
new(e) close* 1624); 19 and 20 Acres; Old Road planted; Orange; Orchard;
Orchard Cl (1677); Paddock; Pauls c. 1700 (cf. Henry *Paul ib*); Peak Fd (*v.*
pēac); Pikes Cl c. 1700; Pitts c. 1700; Plantation; Poors Gdns; Pouncy's
living; Preston Bridge Cl c. 1700 (*v.* Preston in Tarrant Rush. par. *infra*);
Richards Cl (c. 1700); Ridout's Fd; Rolesbury (perhaps to be identified with
Rasbury c. 1700); Rook Hay (*Rookehaies* 1676, *v.* **hrōc, (ge)hæg**); Rudland
Feild c. 1700; Rushton Lane & Md (*v.* Tarrant Rush. par. *infra*); The Sheep
Sleight (called Hintons Hill) c. 1700 (*Hintons Hill* 1676, *v.* **slæget**); Shorleys
Cl c. 1700; The 6 Acres; Great Slade, Upr or Btm Slade (*v.* **slæd**); Strip;
Townsend(s) Cl & Fd; Trottles Cl (*Trottle als. Vinalls Hay* c. 1700, cf. Brune
Trottle 1664 (Haselbury B.), *v.* **(ge)hæg**); *the Wheate barne* 1700; Whiteshard
c. 1700 (*v.* **hwīt, sceard**); Woodhills (*Lower-, Upper-* 1677); Yeatmans Mdw
& Upr Dean Mds (*v.* **denu**); Yew tree Fd; Yonder Fd.

(b) 'the hamlet of *Bernoldesclif*' 1242 (from the OE pers.n. *Beornweald* and
clif 'steep bank'); *in rode de Bro(c)hole* (*vie que vocatur asseweye usq'-*) n.d.
(1372) (cf. Ashley Wd *supra, v.* **rād** 'riding way' or **rod**¹ 'clearing', **brocc-hol**
'badger hole'); *Clefforde-, Cliffordeshal* 1242, *Cliffordeshal(l)e* n.d. (1372)
(near *Bernoldesclif supra*, '(hall or nook at) the ford near the steep bank', *v.*
clif, ford, hall or **halh** (dat.sg. *hale*), cf. Clifford Gl I 239); *the earth pitt* 1624;
Edwardes Crosse 1627 (*v.* **cros**); *Goldecrofte* 1242 (*v.* **croft**; the first el. may
be **gold** 'gold', **golde** 'marigold', or a surname); *atte Hale* (p) 1346, 1428
(*v.* **atte, halh** (dat.sg. *hale*)); *Highwood* 1542; *Holdeley* 1242 (possibly 'sloping
clearing' from **hald**² and **lēah**, cf. Hanlye Sx 262); *(le) New breach(e) feylde*
1627 (*v.* **brǣc**); *the north Feild* 1624; 'the old garden called *Olbergecroft*' 1242
(perhaps from the OE (fem.) pers.n. *Wulfburh*, and **croft**); *Old Crofte* 1624
(cf. prec.); 'land called *Quarentaine*' 1242 (cf. NED s.v. *quarenten(e)* 'a lineal
or square measure containing forty poles; a furlong or rood' (from 1809), said
to be from MedLat *quarentēna* (AFr *quarenteyne*); this term, spelt *quarentina*,
is common in DB, *v.* VCHDo 3 21)); *Rogeresbreche* 1242 (given by *Roger* de
Bosco *ib* to Tarrant abbey, *v.* **brǣc**); *Serleford* 1243 (*v.* **ford**, cf. Roger *Cerle*
1332 (Tarrant L.)); *Thorendon* 1242 (*v.* **þorn, dūn**); *atte Wych(e)* (p) 1327,
1332 (*v.* **atte, wīc** or **wice**).

Tarrant Launceston

Part of this par. was transferred to Pimperne par. *supra* in 1933. It is a chapelry
of Tarrant Monkton par. *infra*.

TARRANT LAUNCESTON (ST 943096)
   Tarente 1086 DB (f. 79), *Tarent(')* 1082 France, 1189 Cart-
      Ant, 1246 Ch, *Tarenth* Hy I France, *Darent* 1180–87 ib,
      Tarenta 112 *AD*
   Tarente Loueweni(e)ston', -Louinton' 1280 Ass, *Tarente de
      Lowyneston* 1285 FA, *Tar(r)ent(e) Lo(u)wyn(e)ston* 1288

FF, 1316 FA, 1417 FF, -*Loweston* 1390 Cl, IpmR, 1402 Pat, -*Lounston* 1397 Fine *et freq* to 1439 Pat, -*Launston* 1397 IpmR, -*Lon(e)ston* 1412 FA, 1443, 1455 Pat, -*Louston* Hy 5 *HarlRoll et freq* to 1467 IpmR, -*Lanston* 1455 Cl, *Tirant-*, *Tyrant Launceston* 1468 Pat, 1472 IpmR, *Terraunt Lawynston alias Tarraunt Launceton* 1486 Pat, *Tarrent Launceston* 17 Cecil, *Tarrant Lawston* 1664 HTax, *Launceston Tarrant* 1795 Boswell

Louineston', *Lowyneston'*, *Louynton'* 1280 *Ass*, *Lowynston'* 1327 *SR*, *Launston* 1431 FA, 1575 Saxton, *Launceton* 1547 *Ct*

Named from R. Tarrant, *v.* Tarrant H. par. *supra*, RNs. *infra*; for the DB identification, *v.* Eyton 131–2, VCHDo 3 83. Launceston probably means 'Lēofwine's farm or estate', from the OE pers.n. *Lēofwine* and tūn, although since it may be of post-Conquest origin, the first part may rather be the ME surname *Lowin* derived from this pers.n. There is mention of a mill here in 1280 *Ass*.

CHAPEL (Site of), 'the chapel of *Tarent(e) Low(yn)eston'* 1288 FF, 1402 Pat, cf. *Launceston Chapel Yard, Chapel Cl* 1839 *TA*. THE DAIRY. HYDE HILL PLANT., *v.* hīd 'hide of land'. LAUNCESTON DOWN (1811 OS), FM & WD (1839 *TA*, cf. Roger *de bosco* l12 *AD*). OLD BUTTS, *v.* butt[2] 'archery butt' (mound marked 6″). PENFOLD BELT, *Hr & Lr Penfold* 1839 *TA*, *v.* pynd-fald 'a pinfold', belt. RACE DOWN, from *Blandford Race Ground* 1811 OS; Blandford races were 'commonly held on a down in the parish of Tarent Monkton or Launston in July or August, since the year 1729, and revived 1744' (Hutch[1] 1 75), but were 'discontinued since 1843' (Hutch[3] 1 215). TELEGRAPH CLUMP, *Telegraph* 1811 OS. VANITY HILL WD. WELL BOTTOM PLANT., *Well Bottom* 1839 *TA*, *v.* well(a), botm.

FIELD-NAMES

The undated forms are 1839 *TA* 223. Spellings dated l12 are *AD*, 1548 *Ct*, 1664 HTax.

(a) Cellers Md; Charn hill; Culver Cl (*v.* culfre); 8 Acres; Farm Middle Fd; 4 Acres; Heathy Bottom; Higher Cl & Md; Horse Leaze (*v.* lǣs); Hunger hill (*v.* hungor); Knight's Ctg; Long Grd; Lower Cl; Mount Fd; New Fd & Orchd; Parsonage Fd; Round-about (skirted on two sides by a lane, *v.*

PNBrk 281); Scrag's Fd; Smart's Fd; 10 Acres; Till(e)y's Cl & Fd; 20 Acre Pce; Twissell Barrows (two fields, in one of which is situated a tumulus (marked 6"), near a junction of lanes, *v.* **twisla** 'fork', **beorg**; the barrow is that referred to as *graetem beorge* in the Tarrant H. charter, *v.* under that par. *supra*; the f.n. is *Liversell Barrows* according to Grundy 6 86); West Fd; Woor Md (by the *Pimperne* stream, possibly from ōra[1] 'bank', with prosthetic *w*-before *o*, or, as Professor Löfvenberg suggests, **wōr** 'wood-grouse'); Young's Grd (cf. Henry *Young* 1664).

(*b*) *unam acram iuxta acram Gunilde vidue que tendit super stretam* l12 (the ON fem. pers.n. *Gunnhildr; stretam* probably refers to the Roman road (Margary 46) which crosses the par., *v.* **strǣt**); *curs' aque apud Launceton Ford* 1548 (*v.* **ford**; the ford may be that on R. Tarrant marked 6" just S of par. bdy in Tarrant M.); *in campo aquilonali* l12; *in campo australi* l12.

Tarrant Rawston

TARRANT RAWSTON (ST 938066)

> *Tarente* 1086 DB (f. 83b, second entry), *Tærenta* Exon, *Tarent* 1242 Ch
>
> *Tarente Willelmi de Antioche* 1242–3 Fees, *Tarente Antyoche*, *-Hantych*' 1288 *Ass*, *-A(u)ntioch(e)* 1291 Tax *et freq* to 1346 Cl, *Tarraunt Aunteoch*' 1299 (e15) *MiltRoll*, *Tarrente Antioch* 1316 FA
>
> *A(u)ntyocheston(*') 1268 *Ass*, 1399, 1404 FF, 1412, 1431 FA, *Annchiatheston* (for *Aunthiaches*-) 1340 NI, *Antiocheston* 1428 FA, 1542 Hutch[3] (*-als. Rawson*), *Anteocheston* 1547 Ct
>
> *Auntioch(e)* 1327 *SR*, 1332 SR
>
> *Tarent(e) Auntyocheston* 1399 FF, *-Antiocheston* 1459 Pat, 1524 Hutch[3]
>
> *Tarrant Rawston* 1535 VE (*-als. Antyocke*), 1664 HTax, *Rauston* 1575 Saxton, *Rawson Tarrant* 1795 Boswell

Named from R. Tarrant, *v.* Tarrant H. par. *supra*, RNs. *infra*; for the DB identification, *v.* Eyton 131–2, VCHDo 3 107. William *de Antioch(e)*, *-de Antiochia* occurs in connection with this place in l12 *AD*, 1242 Ch (Sarah, his sister, gave *Tarent* to Tarrant abbey) and 1242–3 Fees, cf. also Nicholas *Antioch(e)* (*als. de Antyoch*) 1299 Ipm, 1314 *AD*, etc, *v.* **tūn**; the same family gave name to Antioch Fm in Stalbridge par. *infra*. The later affix *Rawston*, as suggested by Fägersten 61, probably contains the pers.n. *Ralph* as in Rawston D 384; it may be more

than a coincidence that the DB manor was held in 1086 by one
Radulfus (*Ralph*), but earlier forms are needed. There was a mill
here in 1086 DB (VCHDo 3 107).

THE CLIFF, *Cliff* 1811 OS, *Rawston Cliff* 1838 *TA*, *v.* **clif.**
DOWN BARN, near Rawston Down *infra*. LONG BARROW. PAR-
SONAGE HO, *the-* 1664 HTax, cf. *Parsonage Fd, Hill & Md* 1838
TA. RAWSTON DOWN, 1838 *ib*, *Rushton* (sic) *Down* 1811 OS, cf.
Down Wd 1811 ib, showing confusion with the adjacent par. of
Tarrant Rushton, cf. foll. RAWSTON FM, *Rushton* (sic) *Fm* 1811
OS, cf. prec. ST MARY'S CHURCH, 'the parish church of our
Lady of *Tarent Antiocheston*' 1524 Hutch[3]. STUBB'S COPPICE,
cf. *Rawston Stubbs* 1838 *TA*, *v.* **stubb** 'tree-stump'.

FIELD-NAMES

Forms are from 1838 *TA* 224.
   (a) Hr Blandford Way (from Blandford F. par. *supra*); Burnbake (*v.*
burnbake); Cowleaze Fd, The Cowleaze; Gt & Lt Croft; The Drove;
Dryfield; Drymead; East Fd; Little Mdw; Hr & Lr Lynch (*v.* **hlinc**); Marsh
Md, The Marsh; Gt Middle Fd; Gt & Lt Warren; Gt Water Md; White's
living.

Winterborne Houghton

WINTERBORNE HOUGHTON (ST 820044) ['hautən]
   Wintreburne 1086 DB (ff. 82, 83b), *-borna* Exon, *Winterburn*
      1229 Ch, 1234 Fees
   Winterburn(') *Fercles* 1208–1211 P, 1236 FF, *-Feroles* (sic) l13
      Hutch[3], *Wynterborn' Fercles* 1280 *Ass*, e15 *PlR*, *-burn'*
      Ferles 1280 *Ass*, *Winterborne Ferkles* 1290 Hutch[3], *Wyn-*
      terbourne Serles (probably for *-Ferles*) 1409 Cl
   Winterborn' Moyun 1242–3 Fees
   Winter-, *Wynterbo*(u)*rn*(e) *Hueton*(e) 1246 Ipm, 1302 AD I,
      -Hout(*t*)*on*(e) 1273 Banco, 1302 AD I *et freq*, *-Hugheton*
      1279 Ipm *et freq* with variant spellings *-burn*(e)-, *-Huweton*
      als. Howeton, *-Hugeton*, *-Hut*(*t*)*on*, *-Heuton*, *-Ho*(u)*gh*(e)-
      ton, *-Howeton; Houghton Winterborne* 1795 Boswell
   How(e)*ton* 1303 FA *et freq* with variant spellings *Hugh*(e)-,
      Ho(u)*gh*(e)-, *Ho*(u)-, *Howghton*

   Named from R. Winterborne, which rises here, *v.* RNs. *infra*;

for the identification of the DB forms, *v.* Eyton 121–2, VCHDo 3 93, 105. The affix -*Fercles* is from the family of Hugh-, Thomas *de Fercles* (misspelt -*Fereles*, -*Feroles* by Hutch¹ 1 114–15, Hutch³ 1 327–8) which held the manor (or a manor) here in the late 12th or early 13th centuries (cf. Geoffrey *de Fercles* 1208 P (Essex)). The affix -*Moyun* is from the family of William *de Moion* to whom the larger of the two DB manors belonged in 1086 (VCHDo 3 93), cf. John *Mohun* 1278, 1286, Reginald-, Roger *de Mayun* 113 all Hutch³, and cf. Hammoon par. *supra.* Houghton is 'Hugh's estate', *v.* tūn, probably with reference to the *Hugh* (de Boscherbert) who held the smaller DB manor in 1086 of the wife of Hugh fitz Grip (VCHDo 3 105), but possibly with reference to *Hugh* fitz Grip himself to whom the manor had presumably earlier belonged and who died a1084, cf. *Wayhoughton* in Broadwey par. 1 201.

COLE COMBE (ST 795064), *Colecumbe, Colcomb* (*boscos de-, parcum de-*) 113 Hutch³, -*combe* e15 *PlR*, 1603 *Weld²*, *Colecombe* 1838 *TA*, *v.* cumb 'valley'; the first el. may be col¹ 'charcoal', cōl² 'cool', cāl 'cabbage', or the OE pers.n. *Cola.*

BOTTOM GRD, *v.* botm. BULLY PLANT. & WD, *Bull(e)y Fd & Wd* 1838 *TA*, probably 'bull enclosure', from bula and (ge)hæg. COMMON WD, 1838 *ib.* DOGSHOLE CTGS, *v.* hol¹ 'a hollow'; the first el. may be dogga 'a dog', or a surname. DUNBURY (LANE & LEG), *pasture called Dunbaro* 1603 *Weld²*, *Dunberry(s)* (*freq*), *Dunberry Copse & Md* 1838 *TA*, 'barrow on the down', from dūn 'hill' and beorg, with reference to a tumulus (marked 6″) on Houghton S Down *infra.* GLEBE FM. GREAT HILL. HEATH BOTTOM, *v.* hæð, botm, cf. *Heath Pond Fd* 1838 *ib.* HOUGHTON DOWN CLUMP (cf. *Houghton Clump* 1838 *ib*), HR HOUGHTON FM, HOUGHTON N DOWN (1811 OS) & S DOWN (1811 ib, cf. *Lt & Lr Down* 1838 *TA*), HOUGHTON WD (1811 OS), *v.* par. name *supra.* LOWER FM. MERIDEN WD, *cops called Morden* 1603 *Weld²*, *Upr Marden, Marden Wd* 1838 *TA*, from denu 'valley', perhaps with mere² 'a mare' although the first form points to mōr 'moor, marshland'; the wood is situated above the valley which gives name to Dogshole and Heath Bottom *supra.* NORTH BARN. OCHILL BARN & WD, *cops called Okhilds* 1603 *Weld²*, *Oxhill Wd* 1838 *TA*, probably 'oak-tree hill' from āc and hyll. PARK BOTTOM & WD, *le Park* 1280 *Ass*, 'the park of Sir Osbert

Gyffard' 1294 Misc, *the park* e15 *PlR, Cops called Gyffordsparke* 1603 *Weld*[2], *The Park, Park Md & Wd* 1838 *TA, v.* **park**, cf. Cole Combe *supra*; the *Gyffard* family held the manor during the 13th cent., cf. Osbert *Gifford* 1229 Ch, *-Giffard, -Gyffard* 1241, l13 Hutch[3] 1 327–9, etc. On this park *v.* further Cantor & Wilson 7 171. RECTORY. RYE CL, (*-Copse & Lane*) 1838 *TA, v.* **ryge**. ST ANDREW'S CHURCH, cf. *ecclesie Sancti Andree de Winterburn Feroles* l13 Hutch[3], *-de Wynterborn' Fercles* e15 *PlR*, 'the church of *Houton*' 1361 Pat. SHITLEY, *Cops called Shitterly* als. *Oxencomb* 1603 *Weld*[2], *v.* **lēah** 'clearing', *Oxencumbe infra*; the first el. is probably **scitere** 'stream used as a sewer', also perhaps simply 'dirty stream', cf. Shitterton 1 276. THE STUBBS, *v.* **stubb** 'tree-stump'.

FIELD-NAMES

The undated forms are 1838 *TA* 250. Spellings dated l13, 1700 are Hutch[3], 1332 SR, e15 *PlR*, 1603 *Weld*[2], 1664 HTax.

(a) Allens Md (cf. William *Allen* 1664); Bealings Dunberry (cf. George *Bealing* 1700, *v.* Dunbury *supra*); Brights Md (cf. John *Breite* 1664); Bulls Md (cf. Ralph *Bule* 1332 (Winterborne Stic.)); Court Cl; Croft (Fd); Davidges Md; 18 Acres; Elfords Cl; 5 & 4 Acres; Furlong; Green Cl; Harveys Md & Pdk; Hicks Md; Home Plot; Inner Copse; Joyces Cl (cf. George *Joyce* 1664); Kit Barrow (perhaps **cyte** 'hut' or **cȳta** 'kite'); Lees Md (*v.* **lǣs**); Lime Kiln Fd; Little Croft & Fd; Long Md; Mildon (Inclosures & Md); Mount Pleasant; New Cl & Grd; North Fd & Hill; Pit Fd; Quarry Fd; Severas Wd; Shappis Md (*cops called Shaphouse* 1603, *v.* **scēap** 'sheep', **hūs**); 6 & 16 Acres; South Closes; Stoney Cliff; Syers Md; Symes Cl & Md; 12 Acres; West Md; Whiteway Fd; Winters Pdk.

(b) (*spina de*) Heywey e15 (*v.* **weg**, probably with **hēg** 'hay', cf. Highway W 269; an earlier spelling is *spina de Hegwene* l13, cf. *Heweneby* ib, but these seem to be corrupt, possibly for *Hegweye, Heweyeb'y*); Holecumb l13 (*v.* **hol**[2], **cumb**); Hudeleforundele l13 (*v.* **fēorðan-dǣl** 'a fourth part'; the first part of the name perhaps represents a wk form *Hūdela* of an OE pers.n. *Hūdel* (*v.* DEPN s.n. Huddleston)); *pasture called Leveridge* 1603 (perhaps the OE pers.n. *Lēofa* and **hrycg**)); *Mereburge* l13, *Merbrigge* e15 (*v.* **brycg**; first el. probably (**ge**)**mǣre** 'boundary' or **mere**[1] 'pool'); *campum de Middlecumbe* l13, *Middelcombe* e15 (*v.* **middel**, **cumb**); *Necway* l13, *-wey* e15 (probably for *Net-, v.* **weg**; first el. probably **nēat** 'cattle'); *Overton Batche* 1603 (*v.* **bæce** 'stream, valley', **batch** 'hillock'; *Overton* is probably 'upper farm' from **uferra** and **tūn**); *Oxencumbe* l13, *Oxyn-* e15, *Oxencombe* 1603 (*v.* **oxa** (gen.pl. *oxna*), **cumb**, cf. Shitley *supra*); *Rodedyck* l13, *Reddyche* e15 (possibly 'reedy ditch', from **hrēod** and **dīc**, though the first el. could be **rēad** 'red' if *Rode-* is an error for *Rede-*).

Winterborne Stickland

Part of this par. was transferred to Bryanston par. *supra* in 1897.

WINTERBORNE STICKLAND (ST 835046)
>Winterborna 1068–84 France, *Winterburne* 1086 DB (3 ×, ff.
79, 83b), *-borna* Exon (2 ×), *Winterburn' canonicorum de
Constantiis* 1210, 1211 P
>*Winterburn Stikellane* 1203 France, *Winter-*, *Wynter-*,
Wyntreburn(e)-, *-bo(u)rn(e) Stike-*, *-Stykelan(e)* 1223 Osm,
1225 ClR, 1244 Cl, 1280 *Ass et freq* to 1385 Pat, *-Stiklane*
1280 *Ass*, *-Stike-*, *-Stykelone* 1338, 1340 Pat, *Wynterborn
Stokelane* 1428 FA
>*Winter-*, *Wynterburne-*, *-born Stikeland* 1205 ClR, 1316 FA,
1379 Pat, *-Sticland* 1310 Inq aqd, *-Stikelland* 1311 Pat,
-Stykelond 1338 ib, *Stickland Winterborne* 1795 Boswell
>*Stike-*, *Stykelane* 1268 *Ass*, 1321 *Winch*, 1327 *SR et freq* to
1548 *Ct*, *Stichelane* 1268 *Ass* (p), *Stickland* 1575 Saxton

Named from R. Winterborne, *v.* RNs. *infra*; for the identification of the DB forms, *v.* Eyton 131–2, VCHDo 3 83, 106,
DBGazetteer 129. The largest of the DB manors was held in
1086 by the canons of Coutances (Manche), *v.* VCHDo 3 36,
83. The affix *-Stickland* means 'steep lane', from **sticol** and
lane, cf. Do dial. *stickle* 'steep' (Barnes 106, EDD) and the OE
bdy point *on þa sticelen lane* 1019 (15) *ShaftR* (S 955(1)) in
Cheselbourne par. *infra* (in fact identified by Ekwall DEPN
with this place, but Cheselbourne is some 6 miles SW of
Winterborne Stickland). Lanes climb the hills to E and W out
of the deep valley of R. Winterborne in which the village lies.
There has been some alternation or confusion of the second el.
with **land** 'land'.

QUARLESTON FM (ST 837039), *Winterburn (Quarel)* 1232 Pat,
Winterborn' Quarel 1242–3 Fees; *Quarellyston'* 1268 *Ass*, *Quar-
(r)(e)l(l)(e)ston* 1280 *ib et passim*; *Wynterburne-*, *-bo(u)rn(e)
Quar(r)el(l)(e)ston* 1288 *Ass et freq* to 1434 Fine, *-Querlestone*
1482 Cl, *Quarleston Winterborne* 1795 Boswell, on R. Winterborne, *v.* par. name *supra*. Named from the family of William
Quarel 1232 Pat, John-, Christine *Quarel* 1332 SR, etc, *v.* **tūn**,
cf. Quarleston (Down) in Bryanston par. *supra*, Hutch[3] 1 332.

BLACKFERN PLANT. CANADA, a transferred name. CROWN INN.
HEDGE END FM, 1861 Hutch[3], formerly *New Fm* 1811 OS,
named from *Hedge End* 1811 ib, *v.* hecg, ende[1]. NEW BARN CTGS.
NEW COPPICE. NEW RD. NORMANDY FM & LODGE, perhaps, as
suggested by Fägersten 63, commemorating the possession of
one of the DB manors here by the Norman abbey of Coutances
(*v.* par. name *supra*), but probably only a name of recent origin.
RECTORY. ROWBARROW, 1811 OS, 'rough barrow', from rūh
(wk.obl. *rūwan*), beorg, cf. Rowbarrow hundred 1 3; a tumulus
is marked 6″. ST MARY'S CHURCH, cf. 'the church of *Winterburn
Stikelane*' 1244 Pat, *Bichurcheweye* 1334 (15) *MiltC*, *v.* bī
'(place) by', cirice, weg. STICKLAND CTG & WD (cf. *Walter atte
Wode* 1327 *SR*, 1332 SR, *v.* atte, wudu), *v.* par. name *supra*.
WATER LANE, by R. Winterborne, *v.* wæter.

FIELD-NAMES

There are no f.ns. in 1919 *TA* 253. The undated forms in (*a*) are 1839 *TA*
249 (Winterborne Cl., of which par. a small area now in Winterborne Stic.
was formerly a detached part). The undated forms in (*b*) are 1334 (15) *MiltC*.
Spellings dated 1321 are *Winch*, 1327 *SR*, 1332 SR, and 1341 (1347) Pat.

(*a*) Copse; Fair Mill (Down) (there were mills at two of the DB manors
of Winterborne Stic. in 1086, *v.* VCHDo 3 83, 106).

(*b*) *Est-*, *Westaisseneslade* (*v.* æscen, slæd); *Aleyneslonde* (the OFr pers.n.
Alein, with land); (land) *Bythe Brodeweye* ('by the broad way', *v.* bī, brād,
weg); (*La Fryth super*) *Chip-*, *Chypmandon*', *Langelonde Bychipmannesweye*
(*v.* fyrhð, dūn, lang[1], land, bī, weg, cf. Philip *Chipman* 1332 (Bryanston));
Cliffurlang (*v.* clif, furlang (as freq in this par.)); *la Combe* (*v.* cumb); (land)
Under Coweslynche (*v.* hlinc, under; first el. probably a surname); *in prima
cultura atte crosse*, *Grosfurlang* (probably for *Cros-*, *v.* atte 'at the', cros, cf.
Ralph *atte Crosse* 1341 (1347); for the former village cross and a tree called
the 'cross tree', *v.* Hutch[3] 1 335); *campus oriental*' ('east field'); (*past*' *voc*')
Eldedon', *-downe*, (land) *under Eldedon*' (*v.* eald (wk.obl. *ealdan*), dūn); *Fyue
acr*' (*v.* fīf, æcer); *Ganeshulle* (*v.* hyll; first el. probably a surname); *la Gore*
(2 ×, *v.* gāra); *crofta viridis* ('green croft'); *Heved-*, *Everdlond(e)* (*v.* hēafod-
land); *la Hyde, Northhide, la Southerhide* (*v.* hīd, norð, sūðerra); *Houndeshulle*
(*v.* hyll; first el. hund 'hound', or an OE pers.n. *Hund*); *atte Lane* 1327 (p),
in thelane 1332 (p) (*v.* atte, lane); *Langefurlang* (*v.* lang[1]); *Langelonde* (*v.* lang[1],
land); *pastura voc*' *Leghes* (*v.* lēah or læs); (land) *atte Lymchende* (probably
for *Lynch-*, *v.* atte, hlinc, ende[1]); *Marlyngputte* (*v.* marling, pytt); *Mechelwode*
(*v.* micel, wudu); *Middelfurlang* (*v.* middel); *Possheslane* 1321 (*v.* lane, cf.
William *Poyssh*' (Pulham)); *atte Rewe* 1321 (p) (*v.* atte, ræw); *Rouwedon*' (*v.*
rūh (wk.obl. *rūwan*), dūn); *Schapcome* (*v.* scēap, cumb); *Sixacres* (*v.* sex,

æcer); *campus austral'* ('south field'); *Spaddon(e)* (v. **dūn**; Professor Löf-venberg suggests that the first el. would seem to be **spadu** 'spade', the meaning of the cpd being perhaps 'hill cultivated by the spade'); *Stanndene, Pertrychestondene* (v. **stān, denu,** cf. William *Pertrich'* 1332 (Tarrant H.)); *Stron(t)ers* (possibly a surname); *(under) Trendele* (v. **trendel**); (land) *Bytwene Tweylynches* (v. **betwēonan, twēgen, hlinc**); *atte Were* 1327 (p) (v. **atte, wer**); *camp' occident'* ('west field'); *(under) Whyteweye* (v. **hwīt, weg**); *(Bithe) Wo(u)welond'* (v. **bī, wōh** (wk.obl. *wōgan*), land).

XIV. BADBURY HUNDRED

The present hundred is an amalgamation of the small GeldR hundred of Badbury and the greater part of the GeldR hundred of *Canendone* which disappeared in the 13th cent. (Eyton 113–4, 117–8, Anderson 129, VCHDo 3 128–130). The GeldR hundred of Badbury contained only Gussage St M., Shapwick, Tarrant C. and part of Wimborne M. (probably corresponding to the modern par. of Pamphill) in the extreme W of the present hundred, as well as Witchampton which is now in Cranborne hundred. The GeldR hundred of *Canendone* comprised the larger E area of the present hundred of Badbury, containing Chalbury, Colehill, Hinton M., Hinton P., Holt and Horton, as well as Hampreston and W Parley both of which are now in Cranborne hundred. Since the 13th cent., Badbury hundred has also contained M. Crichel which was in Knowlton hundred in c. 1086 GeldR. Petersham in Holt was in Cranborne hundred in 1327 *SR*, 1664 HTax, 1795 Boswell.

BADBURY HUNDRED, *Bedeberie hundret* c. 1086 GeldR, *Bade-berihundredum* 1182, 1185 P, *(hundr' de) Badebir(e)* 1212 Fees, 1244 *Ass (-et Canedon'), -bur(')* 1265 Misc, 1280 *Ass, Baddeberi* 1219 Fees, *-bir', -byr(e)* 1230 P, 1244 *Ass et freq* to 1294 *Queens, -bur'* 1275 RH, 1288 *Ass, -bury* 1288 *ib*, 1294 *Queens et freq* to 1552 *DLCt, -byry* 1280 *Ass, -biri* n.d. (1372) *ChrP, -buri* 1310, 1322 Ipm, *Badbir'* 1286 (1313) Ch, 1288 *Ass, -bur'* 1288 *ib*, *-bury(e)* 1379 Pat *et passim*, named from Badbury Rings in Shapwick par. *infra*.

CANENDONE HUNDRED (lost), *Canendone hundret* c. 1086 GeldR, *Canedon'* 1212 Fees, 1244 *Ass (Hundr' de Badebire et-), Kenedun'* 1219 Fees, 'Cana's hill', from an OE pers.n. *Cana* and **dūn**, cf. Canford M. par. *supra* which probably contains the same pers.n. The site of *Canendone* has not been located, but Anderson 129 n. 1 tentatively suggests that the name may be preserved in Canon Hill in Hampreston par. *infra*.

LOST OR UNIDENTIFIED PLACES IN BADBURY HD: *Audelyngton* 1288 *Ass* (*v.* -*ingtūn*, perhaps with the OE pers.n. *Ealdhelm*); *Bendesle* 1288 *ib* (*v.* lēah, first el probably a pers.n.); *Cliueton'* 1244 *ib* (*v.* clif (gen.pl. *clifa*), tūn).

Chalbury

Uddens, formerly a detached part of this par., was transferred to Wimborne M. in 1886, and is now in Holt par.

CHALBURY (SU 018068) ['tʃɔ:lbəri]
   (*on*) *cheoles burge* (*eastgeat*) 946 (14) *Harl* (S 519), (*in an*)
      cheoles byris (*east gete*) 956 (14) *ib* (S 609)
   Chelesbyr' 1244 *Ass*, -*ber'* 1280 *ib*, -*bur'* 1288 *ib*, -*bury* 1297
      Cl, Pat, 1318 FF *et freq* to 1448 *Marten*, *Chelbury* 1428 FA
   Cheselbur' 1288 *Ass*, -*bury* 1291 Tax, *Chesebury* 1428 FA
   Chalesbury 1361 Pat, 1386 IpmR, *Chalbury* 1448 *Marten*,
      1558 *PlR*, -*bery* 1501 Ipm, 1535 VE, 1575 *PlR*, *Challebury*
      1504 *Marten*, *Chawbery* Eliz ChancP, *Chabury* 1575
      Saxton
   Chaldebery 1432 *CampbCh Chelkesbury* 1535 VE

'Cēol's fortified place', from the OE pers.n. *Cēol* and burh (gen.sg. *burge*, *byrig*), with reference to the hill-fort here. For the pers.n., cf. *chelesbergh'* in Tarrant H. par. *supra*, a form tentatively identified with Chalbury by Fägersten 78 but which cannot belong here. The form *byris* in the 956 charter, silently 'corrected' to *byrig* in BCS 958, is probably an analogical gen.sg. in -*s*, cf. Campbell 253 §625. The form *Chese*(*l*)- may be due to metathesis, but there may have been some confusion of the first el. with ceosol 'gravel', as also in later forms with ceald 'cold' and cealc 'chalk'.

DIDLINGTON FM (on site of Chapel) (SU 005077)
   (*æt*) *Didelingtune*, (*into*) *dydelingtune* 946 (14) *Harl* (S 519),
      Dudelingtone, (*æt*) *Dydelingtune ib* (rubrics), (*æt*-, *to*) *Dydyl-
      ingtune* 956 (15) *Harl* (S 609), (*æt*) *Dydylingetune ib*
      (rubric)
   Dedilintone 1086 DB, *Dedlyngton'* 1327 *SR*
   Didelington' 1199–1201 P (p), *Didil*- 1201 ChancR, *Didl*-
      1229 Cl, 1558 *PlR*, *Dydelington* 1288 *Ass*, *Dydlyngton* 1504
      Marten, 1560 *DLCt*
   Dudelinton', *Dudlington'* 1244 *Ass* both (p), *Dudelyngton*(*e*),

-*in(g)ton* 1285 FA, 1288 *Ass et freq* to 1431 FA, *Dudlyngton* 1448 *Marten*, 1501 Ipm, *Duddel-, Duddolyngton* 1552 *DLCt*
Dodelington' 1244, 1268 *Ass*, *Doddelington'* 1280 *ib*, *Dodlyngton* 1559 *DLCt*

'Farm called after Dydel', from an OE pers.n. *Dydel* (a derivative of *Duda, v.* Redin 63) and **-ingtūn**, cf. Ekwall PN -ing 33 s.n. Didling Sx. In the OE charters cited, which describe the bounds of the estate of Didlington (identical with the modern par. of Chalbury), a point on the S bdy is referred to as *on dydelingdune. of dydelingdune* 946 (14) *Harl* (S 519), *on dydeling dune middewearde.* 7 *of dydeling dune* 956 (14) *ib* (S 609), 'on to (the middle of) Dydel's hill, from Dydel's hill', *v.* **-ing**[4], **dūn**, although alternatively *dydelingdune* might be 'hill at *Dydeling*' ('Dydel's place'), *v.* **-ing**[2].

ADDER'S COPSE. BLACK BARN. CHALBURY CMN (*Common* 1840 *TA*), FM & HILL (*Chalbery hill* 1618 *Map, v.* **hyll**). CHURCH, cf. 'the church of *Chalesbury*' 1361 Pat, *ecclesie de Chelesbury* 1448 *Marten*, Henry *de la Churche* 1288 *Ass*, William *atte churche* 1327 *SR, v.* **atte, cirice**. DIDLINGTON LODGE & MILL (*Diddleton Mill* 1811 OS, cf. *Mill Gdn* 1840 *TA*). DUKE'S COPSE, *Dukes Copse & Grd* 1840 *ib*; the manor of Chalbury belonged to the duchy of Lancaster in 1427 Hutch[3] 3 113. OXLEAZE COPSE, 1840 *TA, v.* **oxa, lǣs**. RECTORY. RED CROSS (lost), 1811 OS, *Red(d) Crosse* 1591 *DLMB*, 1595 *DLComm* (in the bounds of Holt forest), at the E corner of Chalbury par.; 'the red way' referred to in the OE bounds of Didlington *supra* (*ofer þone readan weg* 946 (14) *Harl* (S 519), *ofer þane redan weg,* 7 *of þam readan wege* 956 (14) *ib* (S 609)), and again in the OE bounds of Horton par. *infra* (*on þone readan weg, of þam wege* 1033 (12) *SherC* (S 969), *on þane rede wei, of þan weie* n.d. (12) *SherC*), was near here, *v.* **rēad** (wk.obl. *rēadan*), **weg, cros** or **cross**. SIBYL CTGS. STURT'S COPSE, *Sturts Wd* 1840 *TA*, from the *Sturt* family (Hutch[3] 3 114). TELEGRAPH CTG, *Telegraph* 1811 OS. WILTSHIRE WD, 1840 *TA*, cf. Peter *de Wylteshire* 1318 FF, Richard (*de*) *W(h)ilteschir* 1332 SR, 1340 NI.

FIELD-NAMES

The undated forms are 1840 *TA* 45. For f.ns. in Chalbury *TA* now in Holt par. (i.e. Uddens), *v.* under Holt par. *infra*. Spellings dated 946 (14) are *Harl* (S 519), 956 (14) are *Harl* (S 609); 1244 are *Ass*, 1327 *SR*, 1332 SR, 1341 FF, 1448 *Marten*, and 1664 HTax.

(*a*) Ashey Md; Barn Grd & Md; Bottom Grd; Brook Flg (*Brokfurlang* 1341, *-forlong* 1448, *v.* brōc, furlang); Calves Cl, Copse & Moor; (Lt) Clay Lds; Coomb Bottom (*v.* cumb); Copse; Cudnell (*Kodenhilles* 1448, cf. Cudnell in Kinson par. *supra*); Didlington Md; Down Fd, Lt Down (cf. *Chalbury Down* 1840 *TA* (Horton), *v.* dūn); Dry Acre; 18 & 40 Acres; Furz(e)y Croft & Grd; Great Cl; Grove Copse; Upr, Middle & Lr Ground; Hedge Row; Hilly Cl; Home Cl; Homestead; Long Cl; Long Flg (*Longeforlong* 1448, *v.* lang[1]); Marlpit Grd; North Md; Orchard; Paper Mill Md; Pasture; Picked Breach (cf. *le Breche* 1448, *v.* pīcede, brǣc); Picked Cl; Poors Md; Puxey Grd (cf. Puxey in Sturminster N. par. *infra*); Reads Grd; Rooky Md; Sheep down; The 33 Acres; 20 & 25 Acres; Way Fd; Wimbourne Turnpike (the road to Wimborne M., perhaps the road referred to in *regiam viam vocat' Herpath'* 1448, *v.* here-pæð); Withy Bed; Yonder Fd.

(*b*) *Alewourdeslond* 1341 (*v.* land, perhaps with the surname *Alward*); *Blymundestenement* 1341 (*v.* tenement, cf. Laurence *Blymond* 1327); *boddingc weg...from bodding wege* 956 (14) (from an OE pers.n. *Bodd*(*a*), *v.* Feilitzen 204, with -ing[2] or -ing-[4], weg); *Courtecloses* 1448 (*v.* court); (*at*) *crawan forda* 956 (14) (*v.* crāwe (gen.sg. -*an*) 'crow', ford); *to þam ealdan wege, andlang weges* 956 (14) (*v.* (e)ald (wk.obl. -*an*), weg); *on fugelan þæþ. from fugelan paþe* 956 (14) (from an OE pers.n. *Fugola*, a wk. form of *Fugol*, and pæð); *on þa-, of þære haran apuldran* 956 (14) (*v.* hār[2] (wk.obl. -*an*), apuldre); *Heyesende, Heyfurlang* 1341 (*v.* (ge)hæg, ende[1], furlang); *in magno Hethfelde* 1448 (*v.* hǣð, feld); *Hungresbergh* 1341 (probably 'Hūngār's hill or barrow', from an OE pers.n. *Hūngār* (*v.* Reaney s.n. *Hunger*) and beorg); *seo mæd...on ige* 946 (14), *mæd æcras...on ige twegen* 956 (14) ('the meadow-, two acres of meadow on the island', *v.* mǣd, æcer, ēg (WSax ī(e)g)); *Linmede* 1244, *le Inmede* 1448 (*v.* in, mǣd); *on þane langan hlinc. 7 of þan langan hlince* 956 (14) (*v.* lang[1], hlinc); *Lovells* 1664 (a surname); *to-, from mearc broces heafde* 956 (14) ('the source of boundary brook', *v.* mearc, brōc, hēafod); *boscum vocat' Medeheyes* 1448 (*v.* mǣd, (ge)hæg); *Odemere* 1341 (probably 'wood lake', *v.* wudu, mere[1]); *on-, of-, oþ roddan pol(e)* 956 (14) (*v.* pōl[1]; first el. rodde (gen. sg. -*an*) 'rod, shoot' or an OE pers.n. *Rodda*, cf. Rodborough Gl 1 104); *Shortelond* 1341 (*v.* sc(e)ort, land); *campo australi* 1448 ('south field'); *oþ stigla þæþ, of stigela paþe* 946 (14) (*v.* stigel (gen.pl. -*a*), pæð); *on þa twegen ærcas* (probably for *æceras*) 956 (14) (*v.* twēgen, æcer); *Whetfelde* 1448 (*v.* hwǣte, feld); *Yrissheslese* 1448 (*v.* lǣs, cf. John *Yryssh'* 1332 (Gussage St M.)).

Colehill

This par. was formed in 1894 out of the old par. of Wimborne Minster. Part of Hampreston par. *infra* (Pilford, Middle Hill, Canford Bottom, etc) was transferred to this par. in 1913, and in 1933 part of this par. was transferred to Wimborne Minster.

COLEHILL (SU 025013), *Colhulle* 1341 *Wim*, *-hill* 1518 *HarlRoll*, 1795 Boswell; *Collehill*, *-hyll* 1547 *DLMB* (*a hethe called-*), 1552 *DLCt*, 1591 *DLMB*; *Colehill'* 1578 *Fry*, *Cole Hill Lane* 1591 *DLMB*, *Colehill* 1591 *ib* (*the haithe called-*), 1654 *Wim*, 1863 Hutch[3], *Cole Hill* 1811 OS, 1847 *TA* (*-Close & Plot*); *Colleshill* 1593 Hutch[3]. The hill referred to is that NE of Wimborne M., called *Cole Hill* 1847 *TA*, v. **hyll**. The forms are too late for any certainty about the first el., which could be **col**[1] 'charcoal' or **coll** 'hill'.

LEIGH (SZ 025998) [lai], *Lege* 1086 DB, n.d. France, *Leg* 1249 FF, *Legh(e)* 1261 FineR, (*-juxta Wymborn'*) 1291 FF, 1298 ib *et freq* to 1612 *DCMDeed*, *Ley(e)* 1280 *Ass*, 1285 FA, 1387 FF *et freq* to 1554 *AddCh*, *Leya* 1285 FA, *Leygh(e)* 1297 *Wim* (*-iuxta Wymborn' Ministre*) *et freq* to 1465 *Ct*, *Le juxta Caneford* 1337 Hutch[3], *Leigh(e)* 1363 FF *et passim*, *Lye* 1369 *Wim*, 1412 Hutch[3] *et freq* to 1552 *DLCt*, *Le Lye* 15 *Wim*, *Liegh'* 1432 *ib*, *Lyeghe* 1479 IpmR, *Lygh'* 1518 *HarlRoll*, *Leyght* (sic) 1520 *Rent*, *Lyʒghe* 1529 *Ct*, *Lighe* 1539 *ib*, *Leygehe* 1544 *ib*, *Lie or Leigh* 1593 Hutch[3], from **lēah** (dat.sg. *lēage*) 'wood, glade or clearing in a wood', cf. Leigh par. *infra*.

WILKSWORTH FM (SU 007019)
   Wedechesworde 1086 DB (2 ×)
   Wudotheswurde 1107 (1300) Ch
   Wudekesworth' 1244 *Ass*, *-wurth* 1244 *ib* (p)
   Wodekesworth(e) 1244 *Ass* (p), 1280 *ib*, 1281 FF, c. 1290
      DCMDeed (p), 1293 FF, (*-juxta Wymburn*) 1306 *ib et freq*
      to 1439 Cl, *-uuorth'* 1253 ib (p), *-wrth* 1284 FF,
      Woddekesworth' 1462 *Weld*[1]
   Wythekeswurth 1250 Drew, *Wydekesworthe* 1417 *Marten*
   Wodokesuuorth' 1253 Cl, *-worth* 1293, 1449 FF
   Wodekokkes- 1412 FA, *Wodecokes-* 1425 Cl, *Wodcockesworth*
      1535 VE, *Wodecokesworthy* 1433 IpmR
   Wodkysworth 1448 FF, *Lytel Wodekyworthy* 1484 IpmR,
      'Little (*Parva*) *Wodkesworth* or *Wodkeswurth*' 1503 Ipm
   Wilkesworth 1508 *Cecil*, 1593 Hutch[3], (*-als. Honnybrooke*) e18
      Weld[1], *Wilksworth* 1795 Boswell

The second el. is **worð** 'enclosure' (replaced by **worðig** in two 15th cent. forms), with **lȳtel** 'little', cf. Wimborne M. par. *infra*, Honeybrook *infra*. The first el. is probably an OE pers.n. *Wuduc*, a diminutive of the recorded *Wuda* (Redin 58); an OE **wuduc* 'small wood' is formally possible for the first el., but a pers.n. is more likely in combination with **worð**, cf. Fägersten 79–80, Woodcray Brk 141–2. The 15th–16th cent. forms show some confusion of the first el. with *woodcock*. The modern form *Wilks-* may be partly due to influence from Wilkswood 1 36, but Kökeritz 129 accounts for it by supposing a side-form **widuc* (hence the DB form with *e* for *i*, cf. also *Wythekes-* 1250, *Wydekes-* 1417), and by assuming *dk* > *lk* for ease of pronunciation after reduction of the unstressed second syllable.

ASHLEY HO. AVISHAYES. BARLEY MOW (P.H.), 1811 OS. BARROW FIRS. BEAUCROFT (LANE & RD). BEECHWOOD. BIDDLE'S COPSE, cf. (*Lt*) *Bittles* 1847 *TA*, a surname. BROOKSIDE (FM), streams marked 6″. BURT'S HILL, cf. *Burts Mdw*, *Burt Ash* 1847 *TA*, William *Burt* 1664 HTax. CATLEY COPSE, *Catley* (*Copse*) 1847 *TA*, 'wood or glade frequented by (wild) cats', *v.* **cat(t)**, **lēah**, cf. the nearby Dogdean *infra*. CLAPGATE, 1811 OS, *v.* **clap-gate**, on the par. bdy, probably alluding to a gate of the forest of Holt. DEANS GROVE, no doubt with reference to the Dean of Wimborne, cf. Dean's Court in Wimborne M. par. *infra*, but cf. also William *Dene* 1465 *Ct*. DOGDEAN FM & LANE, *Dockedene* 1411 *Wim*, *Dogge Deane*, *Doggdeane* 1591 *DLMB*, *Dogden* 1595 *DLComm*, *Dogdean* (*Lane*) 1847 *TA*, *v.* **denu** 'valley'; the first el. may be **docce** 'dock, water-lily' (as suggested by the earliest form), or **dogga** 'dog', cf. Catley *supra*. ELLIOTT'S GRAVE, cf. Thomas *Elliott* 1664 HTax, *v.* **græf** 'grave, pit'. FURTHER HO. FURZE HILL, 1811 OS, *la furshulle* n.d. (1372) *ChrP*, *v.* **fyrs**, **hyll**. GREENCLOSE, *Green Cl* 1847 *TA*. HIGHLANDS. HIGHWOOD. HONEYBROOK COPSE, HR HONEY- BROOK FM (*-brooke* 1863 Hutch[3]), *v.* Honeybrook Fm in Holt par. *infra*, Wilksworth Fm *supra*. HORNS INN, *Hornes*, (land) *near the Horns* 1847 *TA*. KYRCHIL, apparently named from an archaic form of More Crichel par. *infra*, cf. *Kerchelham* (on R. Stour) c.Ed I Hutch[3] which may be 'river meadow belonging to (More) Crichel', *v.* **hamm**. LEIGH CMN (*Common* 1811 OS), LANE & VINERY, from Leigh *supra*. LONG CLOSE FM, *Long Cl*

1847 *TA*. Lt LONNEN, *close by Little London* 1847 *TA*, doubtless a humorous name for a small hamlet. MERRY FD HILL, *Meriefelde* 1595 *DLComm*, *Merry Fd* 1847 *TA*, 'pleasant field', or 'field where merry-making took place', *v.* **myrge**. NORTHLEIGH (LANE), probably 'north part of Leigh (supra)'. ONSLOW. PARK FM, from Leigh Park in Wimborne M. par. *infra*, cf. *Corders Park, Stoney Park* 1847 *TA*. THE ROW, a narrow wood, *v.* **rāw**. ROWNEY LODGE. ST AUDREY'S. ST MICHAEL & ALL ANGELS' CHURCH. SPRINGFIELD, cf. *Springhill Grd* 1847 *TA, v.* **spring**; a spring is marked (6″)⅓ mile NW. STONE FIRS. SUNDAY'S BARN, *Sundays Barn, Fd & Md* 1847 *ib.* WIMBORNE RD, cf. *viam de Wymbourn apud Colhulle* 1341 *Wim.* WINGREEN. WOODLEAZE (COPSE), *la Wodelese* 1337 Hutch³, *Wood Leaze Coppice* 1847 *TA, v.* **wudu, lǣs**.

FIELD-NAMES

The undated forms are 1847 *TA* 246 (Wimborne Minster). Spellings dated 1312, 1496, 1863 are Hutch³, 1327 *SR*, 1332 SR, 1365 Pat, n.d. (1372) *ChrP*, 1412, 1439 Cl, 1417 *Marten*, 1427¹, 1518 *HarlRoll*, 1468 *MinAcct*, 1472 *Weld*¹, 1479, 1547², 1599, 1617 WimCW, 1523 *AddCh*, 1547¹, 1591 *DLMB*, 1595 *DLComm*, 1621 *CH*, 1664 HTax, and the rest *Wim*.

(*a*) Late Barfoots Mdw (probably a surname from Barford in Holt par. *infra*); Barnes Cl (cf. John *Barne(s)* 1547¹, 1664); Batts Grd; Bounds Md; Broad Fd; Broans Cl; Burdens Plot (cf. John *Burdon* 1312); Chambers (Mdw) (cf. Arthur *Chamber* 1563 *DLCt*, William *Chambers* 1664); Cockpit (*v.* **cockpit**); Coles's, Coles 3 Acres (cf. *Burgagium Thomi Cole* 1390, John *Cole* 1479); Coneygar (*v.* **coninger**); Daws Cl (cf. John *Dawe* 1664); Hthr & Lr 8 Acres; Fox's Mdw; Foyalls Grd & Mdw; Furzy Pce; Late Goffes; (Green) Gooks Hill (*Gokeshull(e)* 1365, 1412, *Gookes Hill Ground, Gokesmoore* 1591, *v.* **hyll, mōr**; first el. ME goke 'cuckoo' or the surname *Goke* from this word); Gravel Pit Grd (cf. *le Gravelputte* 1427¹, (*the*) *Gravel(l) Pitt(e)s* 1518, 1591, *v.* **gravele, pytt**); Gubbers; Habgoods Plot (cf. Holt f.ns. *infra*); Haywards; Hilly Plot; Home Cl; Hookeys (cf. Pamphill f.ns. *infra*); Hop Garden; Hunts Plot (cf. John *le Hunte* 1332); Jacks Corner; Joyles Md; Knotts Grd; Latways; Lawdens Cl (cf. Richard *Lawden* 1617); Leather Cl; Leigh 8 & 9 Acres, Leigh Fd (*campo de Legh*' 1341, *Lighfild*' 1472, *Leyfeld* 1547¹, *v.* **feld**, Leigh *supra*) & Mdw (*prato de Leigh* 15); Loscombe (probably **hlōse** 'pig-sty', with **cumb**); Lovels (cf. John *Lovell* 1547²); Mackrell Plot (cf. Mackrel Cl in Pamphill par. *infra*); (Hr) Mansels; Mill Hams (cf. *Mul(e)ham* n.d. (1372), *the Mill Hammes* 1591, *the lower Mills* 1664, *v.* **myln, hamm**); Millers (cf. Andrew *Miller* 1664); Mitchells Plot (cf. John *Michel* 1332, Mitchells Md(w) in Pamphill par. *infra*); Lr Moor, Moors (*le Mowrys* 1410, *the Mores* 1547, *v.* **mōr**); Muns Plot; Oxhouse; Painters Plot (cf. William *Peynter* 1496); Paradise (*v.* **paradis**); Peak (Coppice) (*v.* **pēac**); Piermans; Pleasure House

Plant. 1863; (Hr) Plot; Pope's Moor (*Popes More* 1621, cf. John *le Pope* 1332); Pot Kiln Cl & Barn; Pottles Mdw (cf. Roger *Potel* 1332); Pound Cl (cf. *pinfald domini...apud Lygh'* 1518, *v.* **pynd-fald, pund**); Ringing Grd; Rooks (cf. Holt f.ns. *infra*); Rough Grd & Pce; Round Hole; Scotts Cl & Fd, Scotts 6 & 7 Acres (cf. John *Scote* 1479, *Scottes Furlonge* 1591, Holt f.ns. *infra*); 7 Acres; Shaves Cl (cf. Nicholas *Schave* 1523); Shippon Cl (*v.* **scypen**); 6 Acres; Slop (from ME **sloppe** 'muddy place'); Stopples; 10 & 3 Acres; Tor(e)y's Cowleaze & Grd (cf. Maud *Torry* 1327); 20 Acres; Walfords 8 Acres (*v.* Walford in Wimborne M. par. *infra*); Webbs Mdw (cf. Thomas *Webb* 1664); Whites (Mdw) (cf. Ciprian *White* 1664); Williams Grd (cf. Davye *Williams* 1599); Wilksworth Lane (*v.* Wilksworth *supra*).

(*b*) *Curlesmylle* 1427[1] (cf. *Corellyscroft(e)* in Wimborne M. par. *infra*, *v.* **myln**); *Dubles Brydge* 1560 *DLCt* (cf. *Duppleshegh* in Pamphill par. *infra*); *Fordiscroft* 1439 ('late of John *atte Forde*' ib, *v.* **atte, ford, croft**); *Hunteheche* 1370, *Hunthegge* 1457 (probably 'huntsman's hedge', from **hunta** and **hecg**); *Newmanfeld* 1457, *Nunam field* 1538 WimCW (perhaps 'field of the newcomers', from **nīwe, mann** (gen.pl. **manna**), **feld**, but cf. John *Newman* 1468, *groundes called Newmans*, *Newnham* (sic) *Lane* 1591, *Newman Lane* 1595); *atte Nywelond'* 1327, 1332 both (p) (*v.* **atte, nīwe, land**); *Olyueresmede* 1417 (the pers.n. *Oliver*, *v.* **mǣd**); *Parkesse Hill* 1591; *la Reccrofte* 1427[2] (*v.* **croft**, first el. uncertain); *claus' voc' Rechoudys* 1464 (cf. Robert *Rechehoud* 1410); *prat' voc' Russch'leygh'* 1427[2], *Russley* 1547[1], *Rushley Park* 1554 Hutch[3] (3 242), *Rushley Meade* 1591, cf. *Russhemo'* 1427[1], *Rushemeade* 1608 WimCW (*v.* **risc, rysc, lēah, park, mǣd, mōr**).

More Crichel

A small part of Gussage St M. par. was transferred to this par. in 1886.

More Crichel (Moor Crichel 1″) (ST 994085)

    Mor Kerchel 1212 Fees, *Morkerchel(l)* 1268, 1280 *Ass*, p1290 *Marten*, *-kercel* 1280 *Ass*, *More Kerchel(l)* 1285 FA *et freq* to 1341 Cl, *-Kerchhulle* 1285 FA, *Morkerchil, -kirchul, -kurchel* 1288 *Ass*, *Mour Curchil* 1328 Pat *et freq* with variant spellings *Mor(e)-, -kurchyl, -kyrchyl, -kyrchel(l), -kurchul(l), -kurchil(l), -kirchil(l), -kurchel(l)* to 1564 *Glyn*, *Mourckyrchull* 1450 Cl; *Moore Crechill* 1541 *Glyn*, *Mo(o)re-, Mourecrychell* 1548 *DCM Deed et freq*, *Maure Crychell* 1554 Hutch[3], *Morecurche* 1575 *Saxton*, *Moore Creechill* 1618 *Map*

    Kerchel Hy 3 Ipm, 1235–6 Fees, *Kirchel'* 1259 Cl, *Kyrchil* 1327 *SR*, *Kyrchel* 1332 *SR*; *Chruchil* 1252 FF, *Crychill* 1376 Pat

    Kerchil Sifrast 1242–3 Fees

Magna Crychell 1518 *HarlRoll, Great Crichel als. More Crichel* 1582 Hutch[3], *Moore or Magna Critchell* 1795 Boswell

OE **mōr** 'marshy ground' to distinguish this place from Long Crichel par. *infra, q.v.* for etymology and earlier forms, cf. Moore in f.ns. *infra*. Richard *de Sifrewast* held the manor in 1212 Fees (92), *v.* Hutch[3] 3 123 and cf. John *Cypherwast'* 1332 SR, Avice *Cyfrewaste* 1564 *Glyn. Magna* to distinguish it from *Little Crichel* in this par.

CHETTERWOOD (ST 973084), *Chetred'* 1215 ClR, 1288 *Ass*, n.d. (1372) ChrP, *Cetred, Cettred(e)* 1242 Ch, *Chetreth* 1243 FF, *Chyttheryd, Chitred* 1331 Cecil, *Chitredd', Chittreade* 1541 *Glyn, Chettered, Chittered* 1547 Hutch[3], 1618 *Map, Chetrede Chace* 1572 Hutch[3], *Chittred Walke* 17 *CecilMap, Chitred Walk or Chitred Chase* 1633 Hutch[3], *Chetter Wood* 1811 OS. Fägersten 80 is almost certainly correct in taking the first el. to be PrWelsh or PrCorn ***cēd** 'a wood'. Professor Jackson suggests that the second el. may be PrWelsh ***rïd** or PrCorn ***rid** 'a ford'; alternatively, if the second el. is of English origin, it could be OE **rīð** 'a stream' (cf. the forms for Hendred Brk 479–480); there is now no ford or stream, but there is a marked valley. All the early forms (except that from 1288 which is *villa de-*) denote a wood, which Chetterwood still is, hence the recent rationalization of *-ed* to *-wood*; it was one of the eight 'walks' in Cranborne Chase *q.v. infra, v.* **walk, chace**.

LITTLE CRICHEL (lost), *Kerchel Freinel* 1212 Fees; *Kerchel, Kertel* 1235–6 ib; *Parua Kerchel(l)* 1244, 1268, 1280 *Ass*, *-Kerchil* 1244 *ib*, *-Cerchel, -Kerchull', -Curchel* 1280 *ib et freq* with variant spellings *Parva-* (until 1431 FA), *Little-* (1270 Ipm *et passim*), *-Cerchehil', -Curchull, -Kerchelle, -Kerchehull, -Kerechel, -Kyrchhylle, -Curchelle, Kirchile* and spellings as for More Crichel *supra* until 1431 FA, *Petite Kirchel* 1280 *Ass*, *Lytylkirchille* 1409 Cl; *parua Crichil* 1268 *Ass*, *Parva Crichull* 1428 FA, *Little Critchell* 1795 Boswell; *parua Chercel* 1280 *Ass*, *Parva Chirchil* 1303 FA. *Little* to distinguish it from the par. name *supra, v.* **lȳtel, parva, petit**, Long Crichel par. *infra. Freinel* is no doubt manorial, though a family of this name has not been noted here, cf. Roger *Fraynel* 1288 Hutch[3] 1 718 mentioned in connection with Studland par.

COCKROW FM, at the edge of woodland, probably from **cocc²** '(wood)cock' and **rāw** 'row (of trees)'. CRICHEL HO & LAKE. CRICHEL MILL, cf. *Mormulle* 1296 (16) *Bodl, Mill Ham* 1843 *TA, v.* **myln, mōr, hamm**, cf. Mill Hill *infra.* CRICHEL PARK, cf. (*Lr*) *Park* 1843 TA. FALCONER'S CTG. FURZY CMN. GUSSAGE CLUMP & ELMS, from Gussage All Sts par. *infra.* HAY BARN CTGS. HOLLY GROVE COPPICE & FM, *Holly Grove* 1843 *TA*, cf. *Holly Down* 1811 OS, -*Mdw* 1843 *TA*. HONEY GROVE. LR & UPR KITEMOOR, *copic' voc' Est-, Westkytemoore* 1541 *Glyn, v.* **cȳta** 'a kite', **mōr**. LONGMAN'S RD. MANSWOOD (FM), *Mangewood* 1774 Hutch¹, *Mange Wood* 1811 OS, perhaps ModE *mange* 'a cutaneous disease of animals caused by a parasite', used of a wood thought diseased, or of a wood thought to harbour the parasite. THE MENAGERIE. MILL HILL (HO, LODGE & WD), *Mill Hill New Leaze, Mill Hill Wd* 1843 *TA*, from Crichel Mill *supra.* NORWOOD COPPICE & PARK, *bynorwode* p1290, *Northewode* 1488, -*Wood* 1564 all *Marten, North Wd* 1843 *TA*, '(place) to the north of the wood', *v.* **bī, norðan, wudu**, with reference to Chetterwood *supra.* OAKHILLS COPPICE, *Okehill cops* 1541 *Glyn, Lr & Upr Oakhills* 1843 *TA, v.* **āc, hyll, copis**, cf. *Ackland* 1829 *EnclA* which may contain the same first el. PARK COPPICE. PETTY'S COPPICE, cf. Edward *Petty* 1664 HTax. THE PLANTATION, cf. *Plantation* 1843 *TA*. QUEEN'S COPPICE, 1842 *TA* (Gussage St M.), -*Copse* 1547 Hutch³, *Quenes Copice* 1611 *Cecil*; this wood was until 1886 a detached part of Gussage St M. par. *infra*, which manor was granted to several Queens of England between 1491 and 1544 (Hutch³ 3 134), cf. Queen's Copse in Holt par. *infra.* THE ROOKERY. ST MARY'S CHURCH, *ecclesiam de Morkerchel'* 1268 *Ass*, 'the church of All Saints, *Mour Curchil'* 1328 Pat, cf. 'the church of *Parva Kirchel'* 1404 Hutch³, *the parsonage* 1564 *Marten*; according to Hutch³ 3 129 'dedicated to All Saints or as some St Mary'. SIX CROSS WAYS, a meeting of six lanes in Chetterwood, *v.* **cross**. STAPLE CROFT, *Stable-* 1843 *TA*. WEST WD, *Westwood* 1541 *Glyn*, (-*gate Cl*) 1843 *TA*, W of More Crichel. WITHY BED, 1843 *TA*.

FIELD-NAMES

The undated forms are 1843 *TA* 151. Spellings dated 1243 are FF, p1290, 1488, 1564 *Marten*, 1327 *SR*, 1332 SR, 1541 *Glyn*, and 1829 *EnclA* (DRO 21).

(*a*) Allotment Fd; Ashes Grd 1829; Barn Plot; Body Cl; Bottom Cl 1829; Bushy Clump; Carters Cl 1829; Common Fd; Cow Leaze; Didlington Moor (from Didlington in Chalbury par. *supra*); Dominys Cl 1829; Dyets Cl 1829; Furzey Grd; Gales 5 Acres & Living; Harding's and Reek's Grd 1829; Home Cl 1829; Horse Moor (cf. Moore *infra*); Hundred Acres; Hunger Hill 1829 (*v.* **hungor**); Lawn (*v.* **launde**); Little Down (*lyttell downe* 1564); Little Fd; Long Cl, Coppice & Md(w); Lower Cl 1829; Moore, Critchell Moors (cf. 'one acre at the moor' 1202 FF, *Vissmor*' p1290, *the Moore lease* 1564, cf. Crichell Mill and par. name *supra*, *v.* **mōr** 'marshy ground', **lǣs**; *Viss-* may represent **wisc** 'marshy meadow'); Hr New Cl 1829; New Fd;North Fds (cf. *in campo orientali ville de Morkerchel* p1290); Orchard (Cl); Palmer's Leg 1829 (*v.* **leg**, cf. *loco qui vocat' Palmecruch*' 1280 *Ass* which may be from ME *palmer* 'pilgrim' and **crūc**[3] 'cross'); Peaked Cl (*v.* **peked**); Pond Cl; Pottles Row (cf. Colehill f.ns. *supra*); Russels Md; Stays Plot; Stony Cl; Stouts Pdk; Walk Fd (cf. Chetterwood *supra*); Walled Gdn; Well Cl 1829; West Coppice.

(*b*) *Bornethornes* 1488 (*v.* **burna** 'spring, stream', **þorn**); *Bradeweye* 1243 (*v.* **brād, weg**); *Chalons cops* 1541 (the surname *Chalon* with **copis**); *Es(se)weye* 1243 (*v.* **æsc, weg**); *Fernegore* 1564 (*v.* **fearn, gāra**); *de la Forde* p1290 (p), *atte Forde* 1327 (p), *Fourd(e)lande, forde brydge* 1564 (cf. *the brydge nexte the Churche, the brydge nexte the parsonage* 1564, *v.* **ford, atte, land, brycg**); *Halsede Weye* 1243 (*v.* **weg**, first el(s). uncertain); *Hammecopice* 1488 (*v.* **hamm, copis**); *cultura que dicitur Polham* p1290, (*common moore callyd*) *Pulham, Pulham Close* 1564 (*v.* **pōl**[1] 'pool, pond', **hamm**); *Prouthaye* p1290 (probably the surname *Prout*, with **(ge)hæg**); *Taddemede* p1290 (*v.* **tadde** 'toad', **mǣd**); *Uincenteshey* p1290 (the pers.n. *Vincent* with **(ge)hæg**); *Wodeforlang*' p1290, *atte Wode* 1332 (p), *the Wood lease* 1564 (cf. *bosco de Curchel* 1280 *Ass*, *v.* **wudu, furlang, atte, lǣs**); *Wydowes Close* 1564 (*v.* **wuduwe**).

Gussage St Michael

Parts of this par. were transferred to Wimborne St Giles par. *infra* and More Crichel par. *supra* in 1886.

GUSSAGE ST MICHAEL (ST 986115)
  Gessic 1086 DB (f. 69 in Wiltshire DB, *v.* VCHDo 3 129)
  Gersich 1167–8 P, *Gersiz* 1212 Fees, *Gissic* 1219 ib, *Gisihc*,
  Gissich' 1280 *Ass*, *Gussich(e)* 1303 FA *et freq* to 1427
  MinAcct, *Guschiste* 1337 Cl, *Gussych* 1338 ib, 1428 FA,
  Gosesich' 1420 *MinAcct*, *Gusesiche* 1421 ib

Gessiz Dinant 1212 Fees, *Gussich(e) Dynaunt* 1275 RH, *-Denaunt* 1291 Tax, 1428 FA, *Gissich' Dymaunt* 1280 *Ass Gyssich(e) St Michael* 1273 Banco, 1292 Ipm, *-Sancti Michaelis* 1280 *Ass, Gissich Sancti Michaelis* 1285 FA, 1288 *Ass,* 1384 *HarlCh* (*-Archangeli*), *Gussich(e)-, Gussych(e) St Michael('s)* 1297 Cl *et freq* to 1440 Pat, *-Michaelis* 1340 NI, *-Myghell'* 1494 Cecil, *Gyssych St Michael's* 1309 FF, *Mighelys Gussech* 1393 Hutch³, *Gussage Mich'is* 1535 VE, *-Michell* 1560 DLCt, *-St Michaell* 1611 Cecil, *Michaels Gussage* 1618 Map, *Gussage St Michael* (*Middle*) 1795 Boswell

Gissiche Bount 1387 IpmR, *-Bowen* 1409 Pat, *Gussych-, Gussich(e) Bohun* 1406 Fine *et freq* to 1429 ib, *-Bohn* 1425 ib, *-Boun* 1431 FA, *Gusshych Benne* 1412 ib, *Gusshich Bhoun* 1425 Fine, *Guysshich Bohun* 1427 *MinAcct, Gussech(e) Bowne* 1461, 1492 Pat, 1509 BrEll, *Gussag(e)bounde* 1547, 1548 Ct, *Gussage Bound als. Gussache Bounde* 1565 Hutch³

For etymology and for other early forms, some of which may strictly belong here, *v.* Gussage All Snts par. *infra.* The affixes *Dina(u)nt* and *Boun(t), Bo(h)un* are manorial. Roland *de Dinan(t)* held this manor in 1167–8 P, 1212 Fees (92); the family of *de Bohun*, earls of Hereford and Essex, held it for at least a century, the first of them to be noted here being Milo *de Bo(h)un* 1275 RH, *v.* Hutch³ 3 133–4. *St Michael* is from the dedication of the church. The late alternative name *Middle Gussage* (first noted 1774 Hutch¹) is from its position between Gussage All Sts par. and Gussage St Andrew (in Six. Handley par.). The form *Great Gissich* 1370 Pat probably belongs here, *Great* perhaps having arisen from a misunderstanding of *Michel* (*Michael*) as from OE **micel** 'great'; the form *Gussich Bethum* 1374 ib may also belong here, if *Bethum* is an error for *Bowum* (representing *Bo(h)un*).

WEEK STREET DOWN (ST 970130), 1842 *TA*, flanking a stretch of the Salisbury–Blandford F. road which would seem to be the 'Week Street', also referred to in the AS bounds of Tarrant H. par. *supra* as *an lang wic herepaþes* 935 (15) *ShaftR* (S 429), 'along the highway to the *wīc*', *v.* **wīc, here-pæð**. The el. **wīc** may simply denote 'a dwelling, a (dairy) farm' (in this or a neighbouring par., cf. Wyke Fm in Gussage All Sts par. *infra*, Geoffrey *atte Wych'* 1332 SR (Tarrant H.)), but it is tempting to suppose that the wīc may have been the RB village (Lat *vicus*) sited 1½ miles NE on Gussage Down in this par. (RCHM 5 24). An old track leaves the present main road just NE of Week Street Down (followed for some way by the W bdy of the par.), passing through the RB village to meet the Roman road (Ackling Dyke) that forms the E bdy of the par. In fact the Wyke Fm in Gussage All Snts par. already referred to is only a further ½ mile E of the same Roman road.

CANADA FM (1″). DOCTOR'S FM, cf. *Doctors Fd & Little Md* 1842 *TA*. DOWN BLDGS, cf. foll. GUSSAGE DOWN (1842 *ib*, *-Downe* 1618 *Map*, cf. *Ancient Down, The Down (Pce), Down End Pce* 1842 *ib*) & HILL. HAWNEFERNE (lost)), 1589, 1863 Hutch[3], *Hawn-* 1795 Boswell; the first el. is probably the OE pers.n. *Hagona* or a ME surname derived from it, cf. DEPN s.n. Haunton St, the second el. may be **fergen** 'wooded hill' or (more likely) **fearn** in the collective sense 'ferny place', cf. Fern Down in Hampreston par. *infra*. HIGHER FM, *Gussage Ho* 1811 OS. LOWER FM. MANOR FM, 1863 Hutch[3]. OGDEN DOWN FM, cf. *Hocken Down* 1842 *TA*, from a pl. form in *-en* of **hogg** 'young sheep', cf. Keynston Down in Tarrant K. par. *supra*. PARSONAGE HILL, 1842 *TA*, near foll. RECTORY. RYALL'S FM, *Ryle's-* 1863 Hutch[3], *Middle-* 1811 OS, cf. *Ryalls Ancient Down* 1842 *TA*. ST MICHAEL'S CHURCH, cf. 'the church of *Gyssych*' 1300 Pap, 'St Michael's Church, *Gussych*' 1338 Cl, 'church of *Great Gissich*' 1370 Pat, *v*. par. name. SOVELL DOWN (1842 *TA*) & PLANT (1842 *ib*), cf. *Gt, Lr & Middle Sovell* 1842 *ib*, perhaps to be associated with *la Southfelde* 1367 *Queens, v*. **sūð, feld**; Sovell Down, etc, lie S of the village.

FIELD-NAMES

The undated forms are 1842 *TA* 95. For some fields in Gussage St M. *TA* but now in Wimborne St G., *v*. under that par. *infra*. Spellings dated 1288 are *Ass*, 1327 *SR*, 1332 SR, Hy 8 *Queens*, 1664 HTax.

(a) Aplins Fd; Biles's Md (cf. Robert *Byle* 1559 *DLCt* (Badbury Hd)); Bottom Fd; Burn Baked (*v*. **burnbake**); Gt Bush Fd; Bussy Md (cf. Bussey Stool in Tarrant G. par. *infra*); Butt Grd (*v*. **butte**); Calves Leys (*v*. **lǣs**); Cashmoor Bratch, Cash Moor Md (from Cashmoor in Six. Handley par. *infra*, *v*. **brǣc**); The Cowleaze, Lr Cow Leaze; Crooked Grd & Hill; Crouch Hill

(*Crouchull* 1332 (p), *v.* **hyll**, first el. possibly **crūc**[3] 'cross', perhaps with reference to the village cross (remains marked 6″) c. 300 yds SW; however, the situation of this field on the lower slopes (200′) of Gussage Hill (384′) makes PrWelsh or PrCorn ***crūg** 'hill' a possible alternative); Davys Hays Plant. (*v.* (ge)**hæg**); The Drove; 8 Acres; Felthams Pce (cf. David *Felltun* 1664); 14 Acres; Frogmore Fd (*v.* **frogga, mōr**); Frys Orchd (cf. George *Fry* 1664); Furzen Grd (*v.* **fyrsen**); Gues Fd & Hill, (Doctor or) Gues Md, Guys Fd (cf. Henry *Guy* 1664, Doctor's Fm *supra*); late Harris's Plot; Hill Fd; Home Fd; Kite Hill (*v.* **cȳta**); Long Md; Lower Md(w) (Altmt); Martins Pond (cf. John *Marten* 1664); Altmt in the Meadow; Middle Fd; Millards Plot; Altmt on the Moor; Nash Md (probably from ME *atten ashe* '(place) at the ash', *v.* **atten, æsc**); 9 Acres; North Fd; Orchard Hill, Lr Orchard; Park (or Travers's) Md (cf. Peter *Travers* 1327); Pound or Home Orchd (cf. John-, Nicholas *atte Ponfold*(*e*) 1327, John *atte Ponfald*' 1332, *v.* **pund, pund-fald**); Prouts Fd & Md(w) (*Prouteslond* Hy 8, the surname *Prout, v.* **land**); Rooky Md; Saw Pit Grd; Square Hill; Stevens Plot; Ston(e)y Plot; Thines Fd; Upper Fd; West Fd Hind Corner; Wilkins Fd; Windmill Fd (a windmill on Gussage Down *supra* is marked on 1618 *Map*); Yew Tree Bratch (*v.* **bræc**).

(*b*) *Attebrigg*', *de la Brigg*' 1288, *atte Brigge* 1327 all (p) (*v.* **atte, brycg**).

Hinton Martell

HINTON MARTELL (SU 014062)

(*to*) *þare hina gemǣre* 946 (14) *Harl* (S 519)

Hinetone 1086 DB, *-ton*(') 1151–57 France, 1212 P (p) *et freq* to 1262 Ipm, *-tun*(') n.d. France, 1212 Cur, *Hyneton*(*e*) Hy 3 Ipm *et freq* to 1342 Cl, *Hynton* 1275 RH (p) *et freq* to 1379 Pat, *Hynetton* 1327, 1341 Cl, *Hyny-* 1388 Pat, *Hynneton* 1399 Cl (p); *Heniton*' 1212 P (p), *Heynetone* 1280 *Ass*, *Henyngton* 1288 *ib* (p), 1431 Cl, *Henton* 1378–1427 Pat, *Henyton* 1468 *MinAcct*; *Hunton* 1272 Ch

Hineton Martel 1226 FF, 1268 Cl, 1328 Ipm, *Hymton*' (sic) *Martel* 1255 Cl, *Hyneton*(*e*) *Martel* 1268 *Ass et passim* with variant spellings *Hynton-* from 1303 FA, *-Martell* from 1387 Cl, *Hemton*' *Martel* 1280 *Ass*, *Henton Martell* 1412, 1431 FA, *-Martill* 1428 ib, 1664 HTax

Hyneton' *Magna*, *Magna Hinton*' 1288 *Ass*, *Hinton-Magna* 1774 Hutch[1], *Hinton Martell* (*Great*) 1795 Boswell

'Farm or estate belonging to the religious community', *v.* **hīwan** (gen.pl. **hīgna**), **tūn**, cf. Piddlehinton par. 1 309, Tarrant Hinton par. *supra*; the 'religious community' is probably the former monastery of Wimborne Minster (VCHDo 2 107ff), since in 1086 DB the church of Wimborne possessed 1½ hides and ½ virgate of land in *Hinetone* held by the Bishop of London (ib 3 70, cf. Hutch³ 3 184). The form *to þare hina gemære* 'to the boundary of the community, i.e. of Hinton', occurs in the AS bounds of the adjacent estate of Didlington (in Chalbury par. *supra*), v. (ge)mǣre. *Martell* is manorial; Eudo *Martel* held the manor in 1212 Cur, 1236 Fees, etc, cf. Broadmayne par. 1 337. *Magna* (or *Great*) distinguishes it from Hinton Parva par. *infra*.

WOODCUTTS FM (SU 013048) & LANE, (*la*) *Wodecote* c. 1290, c. 1300 *DCMDeed*, *Woodcutts* 1811 OS, *Woodcot*(*t*)*s Green & Grd* 1838 *TA*, 'cottage(s) in a wood', v. cot, wudu, cf. Woodcutts in Six. Handley par. *infra*. There is still woodland to the SW at Ashton Wd in Hinton P. par. *infra*, cf. also High Lea and Underwood Fm *infra*, *Hinton Copse* 1811 OS (just N of Woodcutts Fm).

BROOKSIDE, by R. Allen. CLAY HILL. CONEYGAR CLUMP, cf. *Coneygre Md* 1838 *TA*, v. coninger 'rabbit-warren'. EMLEY LANE, *Emley* 1838 *ib*, cf. *Embly* 1841 *ib* (Hinton P.), perhaps 'level wood or clearing', from efn and lēah, cf. Evenley Nth 52 and v. High Lea *infra*. GAUNT'S CMN (*Gaunt-* 1811 OS) & Ho (Gaunts 1774 Hutch¹, *-Ho* 1863 Hutch³), cf. *landes... namyd the great Gawntz* 1535 *Midd*, *Gantts farme* 1646 SC, *Gaunts Hill* 1838 *TA*, probably named from John of *Gaunt*, Duke of Lancaster 1372–99 who was granted a fair at Holt in 1368 (CleggWim 185); the present house was built in 1809, but Hutch¹ 2 91 writes of the earlier house 'tradition says it was a seat of John of Gaunt'; the extensive manor of Kingston Lacy (lying immediately to the SW, v. under Pamphill par. *infra*) belonged to the Duchy of Lancaster (Hutch³ 3 234), cf. John O' Gaunt's Kitchen in Canford M. par. *supra*. GLEBE FM. GORE PIT, v. gāra. HIGH LEA DAIRY & FM, *High Ley, High Leys Flg* 1838 *TA*, cf. *boscum de Langhgeley* c. 1300 *DCMDeed*, v. lēah 'wood, clearing in a wood', lang¹ 'long'; High Lea Fm is on a low hill. MANOR FM. PEAR CLOSE COPSE. PILL WELL, probably pyll 'pool in a river, small stream', with well(a) 'spring, stream'; a small pool and stream are marked 6". PIPER'S HILL, cf. *Pipers Grd* 1838 *TA*, Roger *Pipere* 1332 SR. ROOKS HILL,

-*Cmn, Grd & Rd* 1838 *TA*. ST JOHN'S CHURCH, cf. 'the chapel of *Hineton*' 1151–57 France, 'the church of *Hynton Martel*' 1361 Pat. SWEET APPLE COPSE. UNDERWOOD FM, just N of Ashton Wd in Hinton P. par. *infra*. UPPINGTOWN, cf. *Uppington Grd* 1838 *TA*, probably from OE *upp-in-tūne* '(land) higher up in the village', *v*. **upp, in, tūn**; this is the highest part of the par. WEST END, -Grd 1838 *ib*, 'western quarter of the village', *v*. **ende**[1]. WITCHAMPTON LANE, 1838 *ib*, to Witchampton par. *infra*.

FIELD-NAMES

The undated forms are 1838 *TA* 107. For two fields now in Hinton P. par., *v*. Hinton P. f.ns. *infra*. Spellings dated c. 1290, c. 1300 are *DCMDeed*, 1327 *SR*, 1332 SR, n.d. (1372) *ChrP*, and 1664 HTax .

(a) Batters Grd (cf. Stephen *Batter* 1332); Breach Grd(s), Breach 5, 6 & 3 Acres (*v*. **brǣc**); Carters Hill & Moor; Chalk pit (fd); Hinton Martell Common; Cow Leaze; Dean Bottom, Dean Hill Flg (*la Dene Acre* c. 1300, *v*. **denu** 'valley', **æcer**); Piece of down; Droveway; Duck Moor (*v*. **dūce, mōr**); East Fd (cf. *campo de Hyneton' Martel* c. 1300); East Grd; (Town) Edgarston(e) (perhaps '*Ēadgār's farm*', from the OE pers.n. *Ēadgār* and **tūn**); 8 Acres; Evergan's Ctg & 8 Acres; 5 Acres; Foolish Coppice; The 14 Acres; Lr & Upr Furlong (cf. *in medio furlango* n.d. (1372)); Gatless Coppice; Harpway Flg (*Harp-* may represent OE **here-pæð** 'highway' with reference to the Wimborne-Cranborne road, *v*. Wimbo(u)rne Turnpike *infra* and in Chalbury f.ns. *supra*; the three fields with this name lie alongside this road); Hill Grd; Hilly Cl; Home Cl; Hthr & Further Home (probably elliptical for 'Home Close'); Hone Grd (*v*. **hān** 'a hone, a stone'; situated on par. bdy near bdy stone marked 6″); Horse Cl & Plot, Horse Plat Flg (*v*. **plot, plat**[2]); Inward's Corner; Lambert Grd; Milestone Fd, Millstone Pce (*v*. **mīl-stān**); Millway Flg (*v*. **myln**); The Moor, Moor Flg (cf. Hinton Moor in Hinton P. f.ns. *infra*); Mum-, Munleys Cl & Ctg; North Fd; (The) Park; Picked Acre & Cl (*v*. **pīcede**); Pond Cl; Pound Cl (Flg); Russells Moor (cf. Robert *Russell* 1664); 7 Acres; Snake Land Flg (*v*. **snaca**); South Cmn; Three Cornered Pce; Wimborne Turnpike Rd (cf. Harpway Flg *supra*).

(b) *atte bergh* 1327 (p) (*v*. **atte, beorg**); *Brade-, la Brodelond(e)* c. 1290, c. 1300 (*v*. **brād, land**); *Hauerheye* n.d. (1372) (*v*. **hæfer**[1] 'he-goat', **(ge)hæg**); *le Hoppereslonde* c. 1300 (cf. William *le Hoppere ib*); *Mer(e)heye* c. 1300 (*v*. **(ge)hæg**; first el. perhaps **mere**[2] 'mare' rather than **mere**[1] 'pool' or **(ge)mǣre** 'boundary'); *Suthcrofta* n.d. (1372) (*v*. **sūð, croft**); *Willeheye* n.d. (1372) (*v*. **(ge)hæg** ; first el. probably **well(a)** (WSax *wyll(a)*) 'spring, stream').

Hinton Parva

HINTON PARVA (SU 004038), *Parva Hyneton* 1285, 1303 FA, *Hynton' Parua, Lytle-, Litlehyneton* 1288 *Ass, Parva Hynyngton* 1312 FF, -*Hynton* 1340 NI, *Lytil-* n.d. (1372) *ChrP, Lytell Hynton'* 1459 *Wim, Little Henyngton* 1431 Cl, -*Hynyngton als. Hyneton* 1486 Ipm, *Lytel Henton* 1431 FA, *Little Hinton* 1664 HTax; **lȳtel** 'little' (Lat *parva*) to distinguish this place from Hinton Martell par. *supra*, where earlier spellings without affix, some of which may strictly belong here, are to be found.

ASHTON FM (SU 003041) & WD, *Esseton(')* 1242–3 Fees, 1415 Fine, *Ashton Orchd, Ashton Wd and Grove* 1841 *TA*, 'farm by the ash-tree(s)', *v.* **æsc, tūn**.

STANBRIDGE (CTGS) (SU 004038), *Stanbrig(')* 1230 Cl, 1291 Hutch[3], -*brug(g)(e)* 1254 Drew, n.d. (1372) *ChrP*, 1428 FA, -*brigg(')* 1291 Tax, 1332 SR (p), 1428 FA, *Stambrigge* 1262 Pap, *Stanebrigg* 1297 Cl, Pat, 'stone bridge', *v.* **stān, brycg**, although **brycg** may rather have the sense 'causeway, raised track through marshy ground' since the Wimborne road crosses low-lying land by R. Allen here, cf. Stanbridge in Horton par. *infra*.

HINTON FM. HINTON MILL, *Henton-* 1591 *DLMB, Lt Hinton Mill* 1811 OS; there were three mills in *Hinetone* (which probably included Hinton P.) in 1086 DB (VCHDo 3 70). ST KENELM'S CHURCH, 'the chapel of *Stambrigge*' 1262 Pap, *ecclesia de-* 1291, *capella de Stanbrig* 1295 Hutch[3], *v.* Stanbridge *supra*, cf. *Gt & Lt Chapel Grd* 1841 *TA*.

FIELD-NAMES

The undated forms are 1841 *TA* 108. The two fields marked † were formerly detached parts of Hinton Martell par. *supra* (1838 *TA* 107). Spellings dated 1332 are SR, 1340 NI, n.d. (1372) *ChrP*, 1535 *Midd*, and 1863 Hutch[3].

(a) Bad Md; Gt & Lt Burnetts (from **bærnet** 'land cleared by burning', or a surname); Caplins; Chalk Pit (Fd); Cow Leaze; Down Cl; †Flat Mdw; Green Hill; Hinton Md; Hinton Parva Moor, The Moor, (*atte More* 1332 (p), *atte Mour* 1340 (p), *la ruhemora, la Smethemora* n.d. (1372), *Hynton More* 1535, *Hinton Moor* 1863, *v.* **atte, mōr** 'marshy ground', **rūh** 'rough', **smēðe**[1] 'smooth'); Mead; †Netherlake Mdw (*v.* **lacu**); New Cl; Paddock; Peaked Cl (*v.* **peked**); Slyng or Drove (*v.* **sling**); Square Fd; Water Mdw; Gt & Lt West Fd.

Holt

This par. was formed in 1894 out of the old par. of Wimborne Minster, which from 1886 already included Uddens (formerly a detached part of Chalbury par.) and Mannington (formerly a detached part of Gussage All Saints par.).

HOLT (SU 030039)

Winburneholt 1185 P, 1225–6 FF, *Win-, Wynberncholt(h)* (for *-eholt(h)*) 1199 CartAnt ('chase of-'), 1199 (1233) Ch *(liberam chaciam... de Wsselay et de-), Wynburneholt* 1221 ClR, *Wim-, Wymburn(e)holt(e)* 1230 FF ('forest and chases of-') *et freq* to 1288 *Ass* (*chacia de-*), *Wumburnehold* 1252 Misc, *Wymbo(u)rneholte* 1416 Cl, *-Holte* 1468 *MinAcct Holt(e)* 1286 (1313) Ch, 1307 Pat *et passim, Chacee de Holte* 1468 *MinAcct, le Holte* 1427 *HarlRoll*, 1524 *AddCh, Hollt(t)e* 1523, 1524 *ib*, 1551 *DLCt*

'The wood near Wimborne', *v.* **holt**, Wimborne M. par. *infra, Wysselay infra*. Most of the early references are to the royal chase and forest, first mentioned as *foresta de Winburne* 1086 DB in the entry for Horton (VCHDo 3 81), *v.* Holt Forest *infra*.

BOTHENWOOD (FM) (SU 021025), *Bothenewode* 1323 Ass (Drew), 1349, 1355 *Wim, Bothenwode* 1462 FF, 1472 *Weld*[1], *-wood* 1552 WimCW, *-Woode* 1591 *DLMB, Bethenwode* (probably for *Bothen-*) 1468 *MinAcct, The famose wood of Bathan, now communely caullid of sum Bothom* 1535–43 Leland, *Bothenwood, Bathenwood now corruptly Bonwood* 1774 Hutch[1], cf. *Botherwoods* 1847 *TA, v.* **wudu**. Professor Löfvenberg suggests that the first el. is probably OE **boðen** 'rosemary, darnel; thyme', whence ME *bothen* and dial. *botham, bothen* 'corn marigold' in Do and Ha (EDD, cf. *botherum, botherem* in Barnes 50). The former extent of the wood may be suggested by the context of the 1349 form: *crofta... in villa de Wodekesworthe in Bothenewode, v.* Wilksworth in Colehill par. *supra*. In view of the reduced form *Bonwood* cited by Hutch[1], the spellings *Bornewood Copice* 1547 DLMB, *Bone Woode* 1591 *ib, Bonward Fd* 1847 *TA* may also belong here.

GRANGE (FM) (SU 016027), *atte Graunge* 1327 SR, 1330 FF both (p), *Grange* 1654 *Wim*, cf. *Greadge Lane* (sic) 1595

DLComm, Lt Grange, Grange Fd 1847 *TA, v.* **grange** 'a grange, an outlying farm', atte.

HOLT FOREST (SU 039055), 1847 *TA, foresta de Winburne* 1086 DB, 'forest and chases of *Wimburneholt*' 1230 FF, *chaceam de Wymburne* 1288 *Ass, Chacee de-, Foresta de Holt(e)* 1468 *MinAcct, Common called Holte Foreste* 1583 *SPDom, her Majesties forest and Chase of Holte* 1595 *DLComm,* cf. *Forest Grd & Mdw* 1847 *TA,* Holt Wood *infra.* For other early references to the chase and forest of Holt, *v.* par. name *supra.* The bounds of the forest are given in Ed I Hutch³ 3 245 and in 1595 *DLComm* (44/534), *v.* DoNHAS 88 197–201. Within the forest (S of Holt Lodge Fm *infra*) was *parcus de Holte* 1468 *MinAcct, Holte Parke* 1547 *DLMB,* 1583 *SPDom,* cf. *Parke Corner* 1591 *DLMB,* and also (N of Lodge Hill *infra*) *Olde Parke* (*Coppice*) 1595 DoNHAS, cf. Alderbed Copse *infra, Park Close* 1847 *TA*; on these two parks, *v.* Cantor & Wilson 9 202–205.

HONEYBROOK FM (SU 009029), *Honybrock'* c.1300 *DCMDeed, -bro(u)k'* 1327 *SR,* 1332 SR all (p), *Hr & Lr Honeybrooke* 1863 Hutch³, 'brook by which honey is found', *v.* **hunig, brōc,** cf. Honeybourne Gl 1 245, Hr Honeybrook Fm in Colehill par. *supra*; the place is by a small tributary of R. Allen.

LINEN HILL FM (SU 032066), *Sinen* (sic) *Hill* (*Cl & Grd*) 1847 *TA,* possibly to be associated with *on lindune* (*easteweardre*) 946 (14) *Harl* (S 519), *on lindune estawearde* 956 (14) *ib* (S 609), a point on the AS bdy of Didlington (in Chalbury par. *supra*), in which case the meaning is 'hill where flax is grown', *v.* **līn, dūn.**

(LR) MANNINGTON (SU 063059), *Manitone* 1086 DB, *Manitun'* ?Hy I *Queens, Manton* 1237 Ch, *Mani-, Manyton(')* 1242 Ch, 1244 *Ass et freq* to 1390 Cl, *Mayton* (sic) 1242 Ch, *Maninton(')* 1244 *Ass,* 1278 Drew, *Manington(e)* 1279 Drew, *Manyngton(')* Ed 2 *Queens,* 1376 FF, 1387 IpmR, *Manyntone* 1318 *Queens, Mannyngeton* 1535 Hutch³, *Mannington* 1774 Hutch¹, *Higher & Lower Manaton* 1811 OS, 'farm called after *Mann(a)*', from the OE pers.n. *Mann* or *Manna* and **-ingtūn,** cf. Mannington Nf (DEPN). There is mention of a hermitage here (a gift to Tarrant abbey) in 1237, 1242 Ch, and of a church here in 1244 *Ass.*

PETERSHAM FM (SU 021043)
  Pitrichesham 1086 DB, 1199 CurR, 1236 Cl, 1242–3 Fees,

1280 *Ass*, 1283 *Cecil*, *Pitrechesham* John Abbr, *Pitericesam*
c.1217 Sarum, *Pidrisches-* 1219 Fees, *Pitheriches-* 1244 *Ass*,
Pytriges- 1260 FF, *Piterichesham* 1263 Ipm *et freq* with
variant spellings *Pyt(e)-*, *Pit-*, *-ryches-*, *-reches-*, *-richis-* to
1429 *EgCh*, *Pytrickesham* 1281 Ipm, *Pitresham* 1398 *Cecil*,
Pitreshaump 1412 FA, *Pitersham* 1468 *MinAcct*, 1618 *CH*
Petrishesham 1086 DB, *Petriches-* 1230 Cl *et freq* to 1372
ChrP, *Pettrigges-* 1288 *Ass*, *Petrethesham* (for *-reches-*) 1306
FF, *Petres-* 1382 *Cecil*, 1431 FA, 1468 *MinAcct*, *Petris-*
1398 IpmR, *Peytres-* 1428 FA, *Petrys-* 1472 Cl, *Petersham*
1501 Ipm *et passim*, *-hame* 1591 *DLMB*, *Petrusham* 1508
Cecil, *Petessham*, *Petricham als. Pencham* 1618 *CH*, *Petais-*
ham als. Peducham 1619 *ib*
Putrichesham 1346 FA, *Putresham* 1346 ib, 1494 *Cecil*,
Podychesham 1399 Cl

'Peohtrīc's homestead or enclosure', from an OE pers.n.
Peohtrīc (unrecorded, but cf. *Peohthelm*, *-hūn*, *-rǣd*, etc), and
hām or **hamm**; identical in origin with Petersham Sr 64.

THORN HILL FM (SU 032041), *Tornehelle* 1086 DB, *Thornhill'*
1212 Fees, *þhorhull'* 1219 ib, *Thornhull(e)* 1226 ClR, 1227 Fees,
1244 *Ass et freq* to 1431 FA, *Tornhull'* 1250 Fees, *Thornhell* 1260
FF, *Thorenhull'* 1288 *Ass*, *Thorn(e)hill*, *-hyll* 1468 *MinAcct et*
passim, *Thornnehyll* 1551 *DLCt*, *Thornne* (sic) 1552 *ib*, 'thorn-
tree hill', *v*. **þorn, hyll**, cf. Thornhill in Stalbridge par. *infra*.

UDDENS HO (SU 046028), (*Æt*) *Uddingc* (rubric), (*æt*) *udding*
956 (14) *Harl* (S 609), *Udding* 1297 Banco, 1797 Boswell,
Uddyng 1313 Banco, 1323 Pat, 1331 Cl, Misc, c.1333 *HarlCh*,
1342 Pat, 1501 Ipm, *Uddynge* 1331 Misc, *Oddyng* c.1333
HarlCh, *Vddyng(e)s* 1583 *Glyn*, *Uddinges* 1598 *DLComm*,
Uddings 1648 SC, c.1669 Hutch[3], cf. *Idingewood* 1541 *Glyn*,
Ydyngwod' lease 1583 *ib*, probably 'Udd(a)'s place', from an OE
pers.n. *Udd(a)* and **-ing[2]**, *v*. **wudu, lǣs**; the strong form of the
pers.n. occurs once but is doubtful (Redin 37), the weak form
is found in *Uddanhom* 843 BCS 442 (now Odiam in Smarden
K 407), cf. also *Udding wic* 869 BCS 524 (unlocated), *v*. Ekwall,
PN *-ing* 195. For the possible significance of the late manorial
genitive forms in *-s*, cf. Dodding's Fm 1 274. The bounds of
the AS estate of one hide at *Udding(c)* (*þæs hywisces land gemære*

æt udding, v. **hīwisc**) are given in 956 (14) *Harl* (S 609). Dr Gelling suggests that Uddens may originally have been a stream-name referring to Uddens Water.

WYSSELAY (lost), 1199 CartAnt ('-and *Wynberncholth*, chase of-'), 1199 (1236) Ch, 1267 (1309) ib, *Wsselay* 1199 (1233) ib, *Wisceley* 1267 ib, from **wisc** 'marshy meadow' and **lēah** 'clearing' (a common p.n., *v.* PN Brk 100). The name always occurs as a 'chase' in association with *Wynberncholth*, etc as in the first form, and is therefore likely to have been somewhere in the old forest of Holt, *v.* par. name *supra*.

LT ADAM'S COPSE, (*Lt*) *Adams, Adams Coppice* 1847 *TA*. ALDERBED COPSE, *Alder Bed* 1847 *ib*, cf. *Aldermore Copice* 1595 *DLComm, Olde Parke Coppice* als. *Aldermoore Coppice* 1598 *ib*, *Alder Moor* 1847 *TA, v.* **alor**, cf. Holt Forest *supra*. BAREWOOD COPSE, *Bere Wood Coppice* 1841 *ib*, cf. William *atte Bere* 1327 *SR*, from **bearu** 'wood' or **bǣr²** 'woodland pasture', *v.* **atte**. BARLEY MOW BARN, *-Grd* 1847 *ib*, named from Barley Mow (P.H.) in Colehill par. *supra*. BATCHELOR'S LANE. BEE GDN. BOWERING'S WATER (a ford), 1847 *ib*, cf. William *Bowring* 1664 HTax. BOWER'S FM, *-Cl* 1847 *TA*, cf. Benjamin *Bower* 1763 Hutch³. BRACH COPSE, *-Coppice, Brach Cow Leys, Brachfield* 1847 *TA, Bratch* 1863 Hutch³, *v.* **brǣc** 'land broken up for cultivation', **lǣs**. BROAD BRIDGE (ford marked 6″), cf. *Brudbridge Howe* 1591 *DLMB, Broadbridge Grd & Md* 1847 *TA, v.* **brād**, **brycg, howe**. BROAD LAWN, *v.* **launde**. BROOKSIDE. BROOM HILL, 1811 OS, *Bromehill* 1591 *DLMB, v.* **brōm, hyll**. BULL BARROW (tumulus marked 6″), 1811 OS; *v.* **bula** 'bull', or a corruption of *bowl* barrow, which this is, *v.* RCHMDo 5 34. BURT'S LANE. BUSHY ROW, *v.* **rāw**. CHALKY CLOSE COPSE, *Chalky Close (Coppice)* 1847 *TA*. CHAPEL COPSE. CLAYFORD FM, 1811 OS, *Cleyforde* 1595 *DLComm* (in bounds of Holt forest), cf. *Claipitte* 1468 *MinAcct, v.* **clǣg** 'clay', **ford, pytt**. COCKS' MOOR POND. CROOKED WITHIES, *Croked Wythes* 1598 *DLComm, v.* **croked, wīðig**. CROSS KEYS (P.H.), 1811 OS. CUTLER'S FM, cf. Agnes *Cutler* 1591 *DLMB*. DAFFODIL COPSE, *Daffys Coppice* 1840 *TA*, probably a surname, with later alteration due to popular etymology. DAIRY HO. DRIVER'S PLANT. EARLY'S FM, possibly to be associated with *Erleshey in Foresta de Holt* 1468 *MinAcct*, 'the earl's enclosure', *v.* **eorl**, (ge)hæg, which may be named from the Earl of Leicester to whom the forest was granted in 1267 Ch, cf. *Earl's Mead* 1 72; however the form *Yarlings* 1811 OS (*v.* Holt Lodge Fm *infra*) probably belongs here, in which case the name may be identical with Yarlands 1 205, Yearlings 1 293, etc which possibly mean 'strips used for ploughing' from ere-[3] and **land**. FROG'S HOLE, *Frogs Hole* (*Mdw*) 1847 *TA*, *v.* **frogga, hol**[1]. GARDEN COPSE, cf. *Lodge and Garden* 1840 *TA*. GAUNT'S MAJOR COPSE, near Gaunt's Ho in Hinton M. par. *supra*. GOD'S BLESSING FM, GREEN & LANE, *God-blessing* 1694 Hutch[3], no doubt a name for productive or pleasant land, cf. the surnames of John-, William *Godesblessye* 1332 SR (both taxed in this hundred), and cf. the adjacent f.ns. *Blessing Fd, Blessings Md* 1847 *TA*. GREEN FM, 1847 *ib*, *Grenefarme* 1512 Pars, *v.* **grēne**[1], **ferme**. THE GREEN, *Holt Green* (*Md(w)*) 1847 *TA*, *v.* **grēne**[2]. HART'S LANE (COPSE), *Harts Lane* (*Coppice*) 1847 *ib*, cf. Thomas *Hart* 1664 HTax. HILL FM. HILLY CLOSE COPSE, *Hilly Close* (*Coppice & Md(w)*) 1847 *TA*. HOLT FM. HOLT HEATH, 1847 *ib*, -*Common* 1811 OS, cf. *heathe lying by Holte Moore* 1591 *DLMB*, *Little Heath* (*Grd*) 1847 *TA*, *v.* **hæð, mōr**. HOLT LANE (COPSE), *Holt Lane* (*Coppice*) 1847 *ib*. HOLT LODGE FM, *Holt Lodge* 1645 Hutch[3], 1664 HTax, cf. 'the Keeper's Lodge' 1595 *DLComm*; at the edge of the former park of Holt, *v.* Holt Forest *supra*. Holt Lodge Fm is called *Yarlings* 1811 OS, but this form probably belongs under Early's Fm *supra* which lies ⅓ mile SE. HOLT WD, 1547 *DLMB*, *Holte Wo(o)de* 1468 *MinAcct*, 1591 *DLMB*, *v.* **wudu**, cf. Holt Forest *supra*. HORSE COPSE, *Horses Coppice* 1847 *TA*. HORSE-SHOES, a house name. HUMPHREY'S COPSE, cf. Nicholas *Humfrey* 1591 *DLMB*. LITTLE LODGE, 1645 Hutch[1], cf. foll. LODGE COPSE (-*Coppice* 1847 *TA*) & HILL (1811 OS), cf. *Lodge Mdw & Plot* 1847 *TA*, all named from Little Lodge *supra* which was in the former *Olde Parke*, *v.* Holt Forest *supra*. LONG LANE (FM), *Langlanne* 1524 AddCh, *Longe Lane* 1591 *DLMB*, *the waie at Longelanes end* (in bounds of Holt forest) 1595 *DLComm*, *Long Lane Grd* 1847 *TA*, *v.* **lang**[1], **lane**. LYON'S WD, *terr' voc' Lyons* 1547 *DLMB*, *Lions' Wd* 1847 *TA*, cf. *Lions Cow Leaze & Md, Great Lions Fd* (*Coppice*) 1847 *ib*, the surname *Lyon*. MANNINGTON COPSE (-*Coppice* 1841 *ib*) & FM, *v.* Mannington *supra*. MARGREED COPSE, *Magreeds Coppice, Grd & Mdw* 1847 *ib*. MARTIN'S CLOSE COPSE, *Martins Coppice* 1847 *ib*. MILL (near

Lodge Hill), cf. *molend' de Pitherichesham* 1244 *Ass, domum nigri molendinarii* n.d. (1372) *ChrP*, John *atte Mulle* 1372 *ib, v.* **atte, myln,** Petersham *supra*; there was a mill at Petersham in 1086 DB (VCHDo 3 109). NEWMAN'S FM & LANE, *Newman Lane* 1595 *DLComm, Newmans' Lane* 1841 *TA*, the surname *Newman*. ORGAN LAWN, near Broad Lawn *supra*; perhaps 'where the organ was played', but more probably from ModE dial. *or(i)gan* 'wild marjoram, pennyroyal'. PARADISE CTGS & RD, *Paradise* 1811 OS, *Gt & Lt Paradise, Paradise Md* 1847 *TA, v.* **paradis.** PARK COPSE, *-Coppice* 1840 *ib*, from Uddens Park *infra*. PETERSHAM COPSE, *-Coppice* 1847 *ib*, cf. *Petersame Grene* 1591 *DLMB, Petersham Grove (Fd), Lane & Md(w)* 1847 *TA*, from Petersham *supra, v.* **grēne**[2]. PIG OAK (FM), cf. *Pig Oak Grd* 1847 *ib.* PILFORD COPSE & LANE, *Pylford lane* 1583 *Glyn*, *Pel-, Polforde Lane* 1591 *DLMB, Pillfourde lane* 1595 *DLComm*, cf. *Pelforde Lake* 1591 *DLMB, Pilford Coppice & Gdn* 1847 *TA*, from Pilford in Hampreston par. *infra, v.* **lane, lacu.** PILLMOOR BOTTOM, *Pilemore* 1468 *MinAcct, Pillemores* 1547, 1591 *DLMB, Pilles More* 1547 *ib, Pilsmoore, Pylles More* 1591 *ib, Pilmore Bottom* 1811 OS, *Pills Moor (Plot)* 1847 *TA*, 'marshy ground through which a small stream flows', *v.* **pyll, mōr, botm.** POND HEAD (BRIDGE & COPSE), *Ponds Head Fd, Pond Head Coppice & Md* 1847 *ib*, an 18th cent. dam across a small stream. POPLAR COPSE, *-Coppice* 1847 *ib.* QUEEN'S COPSE, *-Coppice* 1847 *ib*, cf. (lands) *modo in man' regine* 1468 *MinAcct, magna aqua vocat' the quene streme* 1559 *DLCt, the queens cottage* 1591 *DLMB, her Majesties forest and Chase of Holte* 1595 *DLComm, Queen Mdw* 1847 *TA, v.* **cwēn, strēam,** cf. Queen's Coppice in M. Crichel par *supra*. RABBITS' COPSE, *Rabbit Coppice* 1847 *ib.* HR & LR ROW, ROW COPSE (*-Coppice* 1847 *ib*), ROW HILL (FM), cf. *Row Bottom, Grd & Plots* 1847 *ib, v.* **rāw** 'row of houses, hamlet', or 'row of trees'; Row Hill was earlier *Hol(l)te Hyll(e)* 1531 DoNHAS, 1552 *DLCt, Holt Hill* 1811 OS. ST JAMES'S CHURCH, cf. 'the chapel of St James of *Holt*' 1368 Ch, *Capella Sancti Jacobi* 1580 *Comm*, 'messuage called St James's except *the chappell*' 1580 WimCW, *sayncte James howse* 1583 *ib, Holt Chapel* 1679 DoNHAS, 1811 OS. ST JOHN'S MISSION CHURCH. (LT) SCRIVEN'S COPSE, *Scriffers and Five Acres* 1847 *TA, Scrivens* 1863 Hutch[3]. SOUTH COMMON, 1811 OS. SPRING HILL CTGS. STABLE COPSE. STAG'S POND, cf. *Stags*

(*Lane*) 1847 *TA*, Richard *Stagg* 1664 HTax. THE STOCKS
(P.H.). SUMMERLUG HILL (tumulus marked 6″), perhaps from
ModE dial. **lug** 'a square pole or perch', cf. the f.n. Hundred
Lug *infra*. TILE BARN (COPSE), *Tile Barn* (*Grd & Mdw*) 1847
TA. TRENDALL'S COPSE, *Trendalls* (*Coppice & Grd*) 1847 *ib*,
perhaps to be associated with *Trendle slade* 1535 *Midd*, *Trendly
bottome* 1654 *Wim*, which are from **trendel** 'something circular',
with **slæd** 'valley' and **botm** 'valley bottom'. UDDENS PARK,
Udden Parke Corner 1591 *DLMB*, *the Park* 1840 *TA*, cf. *Furze
Park*, *Hr & Lr Horse Park* 1840 *ib*, from Uddens *supra*, *v.*
Cantor & Wilson 1 112. VICARAGE (FM), *ten'tum voc' The Vicar*
(sic) 1547 *DLMB*, *tenement called Vicaridge* 1591 *ib*, *v.* **vicarage**.
WHITE COPSE. WHITE HO HOLDING (local), named from a house
which still existed in 1811 OS. WHITE MOOR (COPSE), -*Coppice*
1847 *TA*, cf. *Whytemore Lake* 1524 *AddCh*, *Whitemoor Grd &
Md* 1847 *TA*, *v.* **hwīt** 'white' (probably in allusion to soil
colour), **mōr** 'marshy ground', **lacu** 'stream'. WHITE SHEET
HILL, LODGE & PLANT., *White Shite Heth* 1547 *DLMB*, *White-
shitte Heath* 1591 *ib*, *White Sheet* 1811 OS, *v.* **hwīt** 'white' (cf.
prec., which is nearby), **hǣð**; the second el. is probably **scyte**
'(steep) slope or hill', cf. PN Brk 903 where possibly analogous
names referring to trackways on chalky ground, which may be
the sense here, are differently explained. Cf. *La Rygway* Ed I
Hutch[3] said to lie between Mannington and Uddens in the
bounds of the forest of Holt, *v.* **hrycg-weg**. THE WILDERNESS.
THE WITHY BED, *Withey Bed* 1847 *TA*, cf. *Whythymere ac le
Howe* 1453 *Midd*, *Withey Moor Mdw* 1847 *TA*, *v.* **wīðig, mere**[1],
mōr, howe. WOOD MIRE COPSE, *Woodmere Coppice & Mdw*
1847 *ib*, *v.* **wudu**, with **mere**[1] 'pool' or **(ge)mǣre** 'boundary'
(it is near par. bdy).

FIELD-NAMES

The undated forms are 1847 *TA* 246 (Wimborne M.), except for those marked
† which are 1840 *TA* 45 (Chalbury, of which par. Uddens was formerly a
detached part), and those marked ‡ which are 1841 *TA* 94 (Gussage All Sts,
of which par. Mannington was formerly a detached part). Spellings dated 956
(14) are *Harl* (S 609); those dated 1286 (1313) are Ch, 1287 FF, 1327 *SR*,
1332 SR, n.d. (1372), 1372 *ChrP*, 1407, 1465 *Wim*, 1422 *Croft-Murray*, 1427
HarlRoll, 1453 *Midd*, 1468 *MinAcct*, 1524 *AddCh*, 1547, 1591 *DLMB*, 1551,
1552 *DLCt*, 1558, 1563, 1568 DoNHAS (**88** 188–202), 1593 Hutch[3], 1595,
1598 *DLComm*, 1618, 1621 *CH*, 1664 HTax, e18 *Weld*[1], and the rest WimCW.

(a) ‡Alder Coppice & Plot (v. **alor**); ‡Amey's Md (cf. Ameysford in Hampreston par. *infra*); ‡Apple Tree Fd; ‡Ash Coppice; Ashley Cl; Bankes Mdw (cf. Nicholas *Bonk* 1327, Thomas *Bank* 1495); ‡Barn Cl; Barn Cl (*Barne-* 1593), (New) Barn Grd & Md; Batts (cf. Thomas *Batt* 1664); Gt & Lt Bells, Bells Md (cf. Henry- 1547, Edith *Bell* 1664); Blinde Lane Grd (cf. *Blinde Lane* 1591, v. **blind**); ‡Bottom Fd; Bottom Grds & Md(w); ‡Brags' Hill; Brick Kiln (Furzy) Grd; Broad Cl; ‡Broad Md (cf. *Brodemede* 1453, v. **brād**); Bushes (Md); Bussons (Mdw) (perhaps to be associated with *Burzen' Forde* 1598, although *Burzen'* is obscure); Butts (Cl) (v. **butte**); ‡Chapel Cl; Gt & Lt Clapper (cf. *Clappse Copse* 1568, v. **clapper** 'a rough bridge or crossing of a stream'); Close; Cobbs; Colt's Grd; Common Cl & Pce; ‡Common Grd; †Coppice; ‡Coppice Cl & Grd; Coppice (Cl), Copse Cl (cf. *the Copice* 1595, v. **copis**); ‡Costlow (probably 'mound where a trial was held', from **cost**[1] and **hlāw**, cf. PN Db 25); ‡Cowleaze (Grd); Cowleys, Cow Leys, Long Cow Leaze (v. **cū, lǣs**); Culver Cl (v. **culfre**); Dames House (Grd) (*claus' voc' Damaske Howus* 1547, apparently ModE *damask* perhaps in the sense 'damask rose', with a pl. form of **howe** 'enclosure', cf. Field 59); ‡Dead Maids' Cl (cf. Deadman's Fd in Pamphill par. *infra*); ‡Drove (Fd, Md & Pce); Drove Grd; ‡Dry Mead Cl; Duch Hole (apparently sic), ‡Duck Md (v. **dūce**); Dungeon Mdw (v. **dungeon**); †8 Acres; 8 Acres; Encroachment; Falls Md (cf. *ten' and a mill called Fallers* 1591); Farm Cl & Grd; 5 Acres; Footpath Mdw; 4 & 14 Acres; Fuller's Hill (cf. William *le Fulur* 1287, *-le fullour* n.d. (1372)); ‡Furze Grd; Furze (Hill) Grd; Furzy Fd & Pce, Rough Furzy Grd (cf. *Fursey Haies* 1591, v. **fyrsig**, **(ge)hæg**); Gastards (cf. Mathew *Gastard* 1664); Giffards, Giffords (cf. Henry *Giffard'* 1332); Gouldens Mdw; Grays Md (cf. John *Gray* 1465); Great Mdw; Green Lane; Grettocks; Gt & Lt Guess Moor; Habgoods Coppice & Md, Habgoods Furzey Grd (cf. Richard *Habgood* 1506, *Richard Habgoods Close* 1591); Hanging Grd (v. **hanging**); (Lt) Hanhams (cf. John *Hannam* 1551); Ham (v. **hamm**); ‡High Harbor (v. **here-beorg** 'shelter (for travellers)'); ‡Hatch Flg (v. **hæc(c)** 'hatch-gate'); †Heath Grd & Ld; (†) Hedge Row; Hills Coppice (cf. John *Hulle* 1407); ‡Hilly Grd & Plot; Hiscocks (cf. John *Hyscoke* 1547, Robert *Hichcock* 1664); Hogmans Cl & Moor, Hogman's Hill Grd (*Hoggmans Hill* 1591, a ME surname); Home Cl, Grd & Md; ‡Home Fd, Grd, Md(w) & Plot; Honeybrook Cl, Coppice, Mdw & Moors (from Honeybrook *supra*); Hospital Fd; ‡House Fd & Grd; Hundred Lug (cf. Summerlug Hill *supra*); Ingrams; Kendalls Coppice (cf. John *Kennell* 1591); Long Cl & Md(w) (*Longmede* 1453, *Longmeade* e18); ‡Long Fd, Flg, Grd & Md; Long Hole; †Long Md; The Long Moor; Luckuses (cf. John *Luckas* 1664); ‡Mannington Cmn & Green Cl (from Mannington *supra*); †Meadow; ‡Meadow Grd; ‡Middle Cl & Plot; Moor; Nap Cl (v. **cnæpp**); New Inclosure & Mdw; 9 Acres; The Old Inn (P.H.); †Old Road (cf. *a lane at . . . Uddinges . . . called Ringwood Waye* 1598, a road to Ringwood Ha, v. Uddens *supra*); Olivers (1618, cf. Edmund *Oliver* 1510); (Old) Orchard, Orchard Md(w) (cf. *le Orcharde* 1427, *Outorchard'* 1468, v. **orceard**, **ūt(e)** 'more distant'); ‡Orchard Cl & Md; Gt & Lt Paradise, Paradise Md (v. **paradis**); ‡Peaked Coppice, Md & Pce (v. **peked**); Pentons Plot; Picked Grd (v. **pīcede**); Pit Cl; Pitneys (cf. William *Pitney* 1664); †Plantation; Pond Cl; ‡Popler Grd; Pound Cl & Mdw (cf. *ponfalld domini*

1552, *v.* **pund-fald, pund**); Ragged Row Grd (*v.* **ragged**, cf. Row *supra*); Red lake (first el. **rēad** 'red' or **hrēod** 'reed', *v.* **lacu**); Rick Cl; Rivals; River Cl; Rooks Hill; Roses Fd (cf. Alice *Roses* 1332, Thomas *Rose* 1664); †Rough Ld; Round Mdw; Rushy Cow Leaze, -Leys; ‡Sandy Fd; Scotts Hill (cf. Robert *Scote* 1286 (1313)); Scriffers; 7, 6 & 16 Acres; Skebridge Md; Small Coppice; Spencers (Moor) (cf. John *le Spencer* 1332, Thomas *Spencer de Hollte* 1524); ‡Square Cl; Steels (Mdw); ‡Stile Grd & Pce; Tanners Orchd (cf. Peter *le Tanner* 1332); 10 & 3 Acres; Three Cornered Grd & Md; The Three Halves (*v.* **half**); Torey's Md (cf. Colehill f.ns. *supra*); ‡Tree Fd; ‡Turnip Fd; 12 Acres; †12 & 2 Acres; ‡Upper Md; Walled Gdn; Warehams 7 Acres (cf. *ten' Johannis Wareham* 1422, Richard *Warham* 1524); ‡Way Fd & Pce; Way Grd; Well Cl & Grd; Wells Grd; Whiteman Plot; Whites; Willis's Grd (cf. John *Willis* 1664); Winters; †Wood; First & Second Wood, Wood Ctg & Plot (cf. John *at Wode* 1453, *v.* **wudu**); Woodford; Woods Drove Md.

(b) *brigmede* n.d. (1372) (*v.* **brycg, mǣd**); *oþ þa brydenan bricgge, 7 of þare brycgge* 956 (14) ('bridge made of planks', *v.* **briden, brycg**); *Burne(d)oke* (*Copice*) 1595 (*v.* **berned, āc**); *on cran mor middeweardne, 7 of cran more* 956 (14) ('marshy ground frequented by cranes', *v.* **cran, mōr**); *on-, of cucan dene, on cucan* (sic) 956 (14) (probably a stream-name **Cuce* from OE adj. **cwicu, cucu** 'live, living', used of water in the sense 'running, flowing', cf. Ekwall DEPN s.nn. Cookridge, Cuckmere, and RN 109, *v.* **denu** 'valley'); *Old Dukes Coppice* 1563, *Dukes Copse* 1568, -*Copice* 1595 (cf. *vnius howe quondam in tenur' Johannis Douke* 1468, Edward *Duke als. Payne* 1547); *Eysmans Hill Copse* 1568 (a surname); *de la forde* n.d. (1372) (p) (*v.* **ford**); *Frizferne* n.d. (1372) (*v.* **fyrs** 'furze', **fearn** 'fern, ferny place'); *on þa fulan lake, 7 of þare fulen lake* 956 (14) ('dirty stream', *v.* **fūl, lacu**); *prat' voc' Gospannes* 1468 (probably 'pens or enclosures for geese', from **gōs** and **penn**[2], **pænn**); *on-, of ham woldes þorn(e)* 956 (14) (from **þorn** 'thorn-tree', apparently with an OE pers.n. **Hāmweald*, though the form may not be reliable); *on þæne heal, 7 of þam heale* 956 (14) (*v.* **h(e)alh** 'nook, corner of land'); *Holtleigh* 1453 (*v.* **lēah**, par. name *supra*); *Horse Fourde* 1595 (in bounds of Holt forest, *v.* **hors, ford**); *claus' voc' le Howe* 1468 (*v.* **howe** 'enclosure'); *Knollecroft* 1372, *Nhollocroft* n.d. (1372) (*v.* **cnoll, croft**); *Lytel(l)mede* 1453 (*v.* **lȳtel**); *Morsels Lane* 1621 (probably a surname); *Nothum (acram prati...versus-)* n.d. (1372) (form perhaps corrupt); *the Ragge Copse* 1568 (*v.* **ragge**); *Reylande* 1468 (from **ryge** 'rye' and **land**, or '(land) at the island', *v.* **atter, ēg-land**); *le Rowelese* 1453 (*v.* **rūh, lǣs**); *le Running Ham* 1621 (*v.* **running, hamm**); *on secg broc...and lang brokes* 956 (14) ('brook where sedge grows', from **secg**[1], **brōc**); *and lang weges* 956 (14) (*v.* **weg** 'way'); *le Welandesshawe* 1468 (from **sc(e)aga** 'a small wood', with the OG pers.n. *Weland*, probably as a surname, cf. *mother Weyland* 1541, John *Weylond* 1551).

Horton

Woodlands par. *infra* was a manor and chapelry in this par.

HORTON (SU 030075)
  oþ hore tuninge gemære, 7*lang hore tuninge gemæres* 946 (14)
    Harl (S 519)
  Hortun, (*to*) *hortune* 1033 (12) *SherC* (S 969), (*æt*) *Hortune*
    1061 (12) *ib* (S 1032), *Hortune* 1086 DB, -*tuna* e12 *SherC*,
    -*tona*(*m*) 1125 (12), 1145 (12) *ib*, -*ton*(*e*) 1212 P, 1221 Cur,
    1231 Cl, 1236 FF *et passim*, *Horton cum Cnolton* 1340 NI

'Dirty or muddy farm', from **horu** and **tūn**, a common p.n.,
cf. Knowlton in Woodlands par. *infra*. The reference to 'the
boundary of the men of Horton' in 946 occurs in the bounds
of the Anglo-Saxon estate of Didlington (in Chalbury par.
supra), *v*. **-ingas** (gen.pl. -*inga*), (**ge**)**mǣre**. The bounds of the
Anglo-Saxon estate of *Hortun* are given in 1033 (12) *SherC* (S
969) and in n.d. (12) *ib* (f. 24v).

BRICKPLACE COPSE, *Brick place Coppice* 1840 *TA*, *v*. **brick**, cf.
Woodlands par. f.ns. *infra*. BRIDGE CTGS, at a place called
Verwood Ford 1811 OS, *v*. *Leftisford* in Verwood par. *infra*.
BURNT FIRS, *Burn firs* 1840 *TA*, *Horton Firs* 1811 OS. CASTLE
CLUMP & COPSE (-*Coppice* 1840 *TA*), *v*. **castel(l)**, perhaps in
allusion to Horton Tower *infra*. CHALK PIT, 1840 *ib*. CLUMP
HILL (FM), cf. *Clump Wd* 1840 *ib*, *v*. **clump**. DAIRY HO. DOE'S
HATCH, on R. Crane, *v*. **hæc(c)** 'hatch, grating, floodgate', cf.
Hatch Flg 1840 *ib*. HART'S BRIDGE, COPSE & FM, *Harts Coppice*
1840 *ib*, cf. John-, Pagan (*le*) *Hert* 1332 SR, Roger *Hart* 1664.
HAYTHORN (CMN, 1840 *TA*), *Heythorne* 1551 *Midd*, *v*. **hæg-þorn**
'hawthorn'. HOMER'S WD. HOPE LODGE, near Temperance
Hall (6"). HORTON CMN, HEATH (FM) (-*Heath* 1840 *TA*),
HOLLOW, HOUSE, INN, PLANT., TOWER (-*Observatory* 1765
Tayl, an 18th cent. folly) & WD (1840 *ib*, cf. John-, William *atte
Wode* 1332 SR, *v*. **atte, wudu**). HORTON NORTH FM, N of the
village. MANOR FM, on the site of the Benedictine abbey (later
priory) of Horton founded in the late 10th cent. and referred
to as (*to*) *þam haligum mynstre æt Hortune*, (*to*) *þære halgan stowe
æt hortune* 1061 (12) *SherC* (S 1032), *Ecclesia Hortunensis*,
Abbatia de Hortune 1086 DB, -*tuna* e12 *SherC*, *priori de Horton*'

1435 *Midd*, cf. *Priors Copse*, St Wolfrida's Church *infra*, *v*. VCHDo 2 71–3. MARLAND PIT, *Marlands pit* 1840 *TA*, perhaps from **marle** and **land**, but more probably a rationalization of **marling** 'marl pit', cf. *in quadam marlera* 1288 *Ass*. MOUNT PLEASANT. PRIORS COPSE, *Priors Hill Coppice* 1840 *ib*, a possession of the former priory, *v*. Manor Fm *supra*. OLD READ'S COPSE, cf. Robert *le Rede* 1332 SR. REDMAN'S HILL, cf. John *Redman* 1664 HTax. ROSE CTG. ST WOLFRIDA'S CHURCH, 'church of *Horton*' 1290 Cl, cf. John *atte Chyrche*, Reginald *atte Chirche* 1281 FF, Henry *de la Chirche* 1288 *Ass*, *v*. **atte, cirice,** Manor Fm *supra*. SLOUGH LANE, *v*. **slōh.** STANBRIDGE MILL, 1811 OS, cf. *Stanbridge Water Mdw*, *Mill Stream* 1840 *TA*, named from a medieval stone bridge across R. Allen, referred to as (*ad/usque/de*) *ponte*(*m*) *petre* 1280 *Ass*, QW (in bounds of Cranborne Chase), *Pons Petreus* e17 Map, *Petersbridge* 17 *CecilMap*, 1620 Hutch[3], *Stone bridge* 1618 *Map*, *pontem petram* 1622 *CH*, *Stanbridge* 1664 RCHM, *Stand Bridge* 1791 Boswell, and probably as *la Stanebrigge* 1311 *Wim*, *v*. **stān, brycg,** cf. DoNHAS 53 215, Stanbridge in Hinton P. par. *supra*. The mill is called *Coleridge Mill* 1826 Gre, *Coleridge* being no doubt a surname. WIGBETH, 1840 *TA* (*-Fd, Mdw & Orchd*).

FIELD-NAMES

The undated forms are 1840 *TA* 113. Spellings dated 1033 (12) are *SherC* (S 969), n.d. (12) are *SherC* (f. 24v), Ed I are Hutch[3], 1324 Cl, 1332 SR, 1448 *Marten*, and 1664 HTax.

(a) Ainsworths Coppice; Alder Bed; Back Settlements; Gt & Lt Bagenham, Bagenham Coppice (*v*. Bagman's Coppice in the adjacent par. of Woodlands *infra*); Bakers Md (cf. Alice *Bakers* 1332); Barn Cl, Coppice, Fd & Pond; Barrow Fd (*v*. **beorg**); Baxards; Bottom Cl; Bowles; Broad Cl; Burn bake (*v*. **burnbake**); Bushy Grd; Butts Md (*v*. **butte**); Calves Plot; Cocks pond (cf. John *Cokkes* 1422 *Midd* (Woodlands)); Common Grd & Pce; Compton's Fd & Md (cf. Thomas *Compton* 1664); Coney gare (*v*. **coninger**); Coppice Grd; Cotts Orchd; Crocker(')s Coppice & Md; Didlington Fd (from Didlington in Chalbury par. *supra*); Drove (pond), Droveway; (The) 18 Acres; 11 Acres; Farm Pce; 5 Acres; Folly Md (*v*. **folie**); 40 Acres; Frog Plot; Furze; Graces Plot; Great Fd & Grd; Green Grd; Hap goods plot (the surname *Habgood*, cf. Holt f.ns. *supra*); Heath; Hedge Row; Higher Grd; Hiscocks; Home Fd & Md (Coppice); the Island 1869 Hutch[3] 3 156 ('a cluster of small farms in the middle of the heath', i.e. Horton Heath *supra*, *v*. **ēg-land**); Kings Hill (possibly a surname, cf. John *le Kyng* 1332, Thomas *King* 1664, but cf. also *Kingescrofte infra*); Lamberts; Lime pit Fd; Little Fd & Grd; Long Cl & Fd,

Longfield; Long Louse Grd, Lousy Grd, Lousy Leazes (v. **lūs, lousi**); Mead
Fd; Meadow; Meal Fd; Middle Fd; The Moor; Morgans (Fd & Md); 19
Acres; The Nursery; Orchard(s); The Park, Furzy & Green Park; Parsons
Md; Pasture; The Peak (v. **pēac**); Peats Hill, Peat Simmons (no doubt 'hill
(and land) belonging to Peter Simmon(s)'); Pinhoins; Plantation (Grd); the
Pond, Pond Cl; Potters; Rough Grd, Mdw & Pce; Row (freq, v. **row**); Saw
Pit Cl (v. **saw-pit**); 7 Acres; Shags Heath 1869 Hutch[3] 3 156 (part of Holton
Heath *supra*; *Shag* is probably a surname); Sheep Leaze; Shergells; Sideland
Cl (v. **sideland**); Smiths Md (cf. Hugh *Smyth* 1332); Sows (Md) (probably
a surname); 10, 30, 3, 20 & 2 Acres; Van Diemans (a transferred name, usually
for a remote field, v. Gl **2** 60); Verwood Heath (from Verwood par. *infra*);
The Walk, Walk Fd (v. **walk**); Water Mdw; Wedge Hill Plant. (from Wedge
Hill in Woodlands par. *infra*); Westbury's Orchd; Wood; Yew Tree (Fd).

(b) *to ballardesham* n.d. (12) (apparently the ME surname *Ballard*, noted
in Reaney from 1196, v. **hamm**); *on þa beorgas* 1033 (12), *on þe buereges* n.d.
(12) ('the barrows', v. **beorg**); *on bisic garan be þære norh ecge, of bisicgaran*
1033 (12), *on Burchesgore bi þare norþhegge, of burchesgore* n.d. (12) (from **birce**
'birch-tree', **gāra, norð, ecg** or **hecg**; *bisic* in the first forms is probably for
biric, the reading given in KCD 1318); *on blacan dune, of þære dune...andlang
blacan dune ecge* 1033 (12), *on blakedune, of þare dune...andlang blakedunegge*
n.d. (12) ('dark hill', v. **blæc** (wk.obl. *blacan*), **dūn, ecg**); *Brokforlong' iuxta
campum de Horton* 1448 (v. **brōc, furlang**); *(on) cealdan broc* 1033 (12),
chealdebrok, on chealdenbrok n.d. (12) ('cold brook', v. **ceald** (wk. obl. *-an*),
brōc); *on-, of ciddesbeara* 1033 (12), *on-, of cheddesbere* n.d. (12) ('Cidd's
wood', from an OE pers.n. *Cidd*, a WSax side-form of *Cedd*, and **bearu**,
cf. Chiddingfold Sr (DEPN)); *in to-, of crockesdich* n.d. (12) (perhaps the lOE
pers.n. *Crōc* from ON *Krókr*, v. **dīc**); 'the two oaks called *deux soers*, i.e. the
two sisters' Ed I (in the bounds of the forest of Holt); *innan-, of east lea* 1033
(12), *on-, of eastlea* n.d. (12) ('east wood or clearing', v. **ēast, lēah**); *atte Forde*
1332 (p) (v. **atte, ford**); *under gorbuerge* n.d. (12) (v. **gāra, beorg**); *on þa hara
apolþore...on þa haran apoldran, of þære apoldran* 1033 (12), *on þe hore
apeldore...on þe hore apeldore, of þare apeldore* n.d. (12) (v. **hār**[2] 'hoar, grey',
apuldor, apuldre 'apple-tree'); *on þa haran stanas, of þam haran stanon* 1033
(12), *on þe horestones...of þan hore stonen* n.d. (12) (v. **hār**[2], **stān**; *-on, -en*
represent OE dat.pl. *-um*); *on þona haran wiðig, of þam wiðige* 1033 (12), *on
þane horewiþeh, of þan hore wiþege* n.d. (12) ('the whitebeam', v. **hār**[2], **wīðig**,
cf. Hoarwithy He (DEPN), ModE dial. *hoar withy*); *on heara wulfrices gemære,
of þam land gemære* 1033 (12), *on hore wlvrichesimere, of þan londimere* n.d.
(12) ('Wulfrīc's boundary', from the OE pers.n. *Wulfrīc* and **(land-)gemære**;
heara in the first charter, interpreted as from **hār**[2] 'hoar' in the second, is
probably corrupt); *on holan broc, of þan broce* 1033 (12), *on holebroc, of þan
broke* n.d. (12) ('brook running in a deep hollow', v. **hol**[2] (wk.obl. *-an*), **brōc**);
þane holewei n.d. (12) ('the hollow way', v. **hol**[2], **weg**); *Horton Crosse* 1591
DLMB, 1595 *DLComm* (v. **cros**); *on þe hwitecroftesdich* n.d. (12) ('the ditch
of the white enclosure', v. **hwīt, croft, dīc**); *on hyrn, up andlang hyrn* 1033
(12), *on hurn up andlang hurne* n.d. (12) (v. **hyrne** 'angle, corner'); *Kingescrofte*
n.d. (12) ('the king's enclosure', v. **cyning, croft**, cf. foll. and the f.n. Kings
Hill *supra*; in 1086 DB 'the King holds the best 2 hides [of the 7 hides of

the manor of Horton] in the forest of Wimborne' (VCHDo 3 81)); *Kingesheigeshurne* n.d. (12) ('corner of the king's enclosure', *v.* **cyning, (ge)hæg, hyrne**); *to þan lange þorne* n.d. (12) ('the tall thorn-tree', *v.* **lang**[1], **þorn**); *lin læge mor*...*on linleaga mor, of linleage mor* 1033 (12), *linlege mor*...*on-, of linlegemore* n.d. (12) ('marshy ground at the clearing where flax was grown', *v.* **līn, lēah, mōr**); *on þone mearc hagan, of þam hagan* 1033 (12), *on þan merhagan, of þan hagan* n.d. (12) ('boundary hedge or enclosure', *v.* **mearc, haga**[1]); *on þa-, of þære gemearcodan lindan* 1033 (12), *on þe-, of þan imerekede linde* n.d. (12) ('the lime-tree with a mark on it', from **gemearcod**, pa.part. of OE *mearcian* 'to mark', and **lind, linde**); *on þone mere* 1033 (12), *on þane mere* n.d. (12) (*v.* **mere**[1] 'pool'); *on þone norh heal, of þam norh heale* 1033 (12) *on þane northheale, of þan norþhele* n.d. (12) ('the northern nook or corner', *v.* **norð, h(e)alh**); *in acs hirste* 1033 (12) (*achirste* KCD 1318), *in okhurste* n.d. (12) ('oak copse', *v.* **āc, hyrst**); *in þane okstub* n.d. (12) ('the oak stump', *v.* **āc, stubb**); *to onesþorne* n.d. (12) ('Ān's thorn-tree', from an OE pers.n. *Ān* (suggested by Ekwall DEPN for Annesley Nt, Onesacre YW), and **þorn**); *Poundeslaunde* 1324 (*v.* **launde** 'a glade'; the first el. may be a surname (*v.* Reaney s.n. *Pound*) or **pund** 'a pound' (cf. the pound marked 6" near Horton Heath)); *to ruwan leges gete, of þan gete* 1033 (12), *to ruanleges gete, of þan gete* n.d. (12) ('gate of the rough wood or clearing', *v.* **rūh** (wk.obl. *rūwan*), **lēah, geat**); *on þæt slæget, of þam slægete* 1033 (12), *on þat sleaget, of þan sleagiet* n.d. (12) (*v.* **slæget** 'a sheep pasture'); *þat slad* n.d. (12) (*v.* **slæd** 'valley'); *in to Sluth an suthe anlang sluth* n.d. (12) (probably the name of a stream; the form may not be reliable, but a spelling for OE **slōh** (dat.sg. *slōge, slō(e)*) is hardly possible; if *Sluth* is correct, cf. ME *sloth(e)* 'miry, muddy place, slough' (thought by NED s.v. to be an alteration of ME *slogh* 'slough') and OE **slytte* 'mud, muddy place' postulated by Löfvenberg 191; on the other hand, if *Sluth* represents *Sluch*, cf. ME *sloche, sliche*, ModE *slutch* 'mud, mire'); *in to þane southevord* n.d. (12) ('the south ford', *v.* **sūð, ford**); *þage* (sic) *strode* n.d. (12) (*v.* **strōd** 'marshy land overgrown with brushwood'); *on suðbeara suþe weardne, of suð beara* 1033 (12), *on-, of Suthbeare* ('south wood', *v.* **sūð, bearu**); *on suþ heal suþeweardne, of þan heale* 1033 (12), *on sutheal suthward of þan heale* n.d. (12) ('south nook or corner', *v.* **sūð, h(e)alh**); *on wænecan wyrþ*...*of wænecan wyrðe* 1033 (12), *on þenecanþwrþe*...*of þenecepwurþe* n.d. (12) ('Wæneca's enclosure', from **worð, wyrð** and a pers.n. *Wæneca, Weneca*, which would be cognate with the OE pers.n. *Wenna* found in Wanborough Sr (DEPN) and *Wennan stan* BCS 476, cf. OG *Wenilo* and *Wenelincg* DB, *v.* Feilitzen 411; *þ-, -þ-* in the later forms are due to scribal confusion of *þ* and *p* (*w*)); *Walerondescrofte* n.d. (12) (from the OG pers.n. *Waleran* and **croft**); *in þat Water anlang Watere* n.d. (12) (*v.* **wæter** 'water'); *to weggeleawe norþ ende* n.d. (12) ('Wegga's mound or tumulus', from the OE pers.n. *Wegga* (on which *v.* Feilitzen 410) and **hlæw**); *in þa wiþgas* 1033 (12), *on þe wiþeges* n.d. (12) ('the willows', *v.* **wīðig**); *on wiþehlakeheafde to wiþehlakevorde* n.d. (12) ('the head and ford of willow stream', *v.* **wīðig, lacu, hēafod, ford**).

Pamphill

This par. was formed in 1894 out of the old par. of Wimborne Minster.

PAMPHILL (ST 988009)

> *Pamphilla* 1168 P (p), *Pamphill* 1524 WimCW, 1774 Hutch[1]
> *Pemphull(e)* 1323 Pat (p), 1407 *Wim* (p), *Pempe Hill* 1598 DLComm, *Pemphill* 1654 *Wim*, 1663 Hutch[3]
> *Peympehull'* 1332 SR (p), *Peymphull(e)* 1340, 1407 *Wim*, 1459 ib (p)
> *Pymphill(')* 1496 Hutch[3], 1579 *Fry*, 1603 WimCW, *Pympe hylle* 1518 ib, *-hill* 1591 DLMB, *-Hill* 1598 DLComm, *Pymphyll* 1524 WimCW, 1525 *Wim*, *-Hill* 1591 DLMB, *Pimphill* 1653 WimCW

This is a difficult name. On the basis of the single 12th cent. form (in the MS *Hug' de Pamphilla*), Ekwall (Studies[2] 145 and DEPN) proposes that the first el. of this name (together with Panton and Ponton L) is an OE word **pamp* 'hill'. However the complete absence of *a*-spellings (and *o*-spellings) among the 14th and 15th cent. forms adduced, as against the constant spellings in *-e-*, *-ey-*, *-y-*, is to be noted. These spellings suggest rather an OE hill-name **Pempe*, a form with *i*-mutation used alongside **Pamp*. It is perhaps less likely that *Pamp-* is only a relatively late development, and that the isolated early form *Pamphilla* is to be explained as due to AN influence, with AN *a* for *e*, cf. Zachrisson IPN 112, Feilitzen 49. Pamphill then is possibly 'hill called **Pamp* or **Pempe*', *v.* **hyll** 'hill'. Pamphill is described by Hutch[3] 3 236 as 'a hamlet situated on an eminence'; the hill itself, in the S of the present par. around Pamphill Green *infra*, is a low hill reaching c.170′ overlooking the valley of R. Stour.

However, there is also the possibility that the first el. of Pamphill is a pers.n. A ME byname *Pe(y)mpe* occurs in this and surrounding pars., e.g. Peter-, Henry *Pempe* c. Ed 1 Hutch[3] 3 269 (witnesses to deeds concerning St Margaret & St Antony's Hospital in this par., *v.* St Margaret's Almshouses *infra*), Alice *Peympe* 1327 *SR* (taxed in Preston in Tarrant Rushton par. 4 miles NW), Henry *Peympe* 1332 SR (taxed in Horton par. 5 miles NE), Peter *Peympe* 1347 *HarlRoll* (Wimborne M.). This may reflect an OE **Pempa*, a form with *i*-mutation of an OE

Pampa (as Professor Löfvenberg points out, this would correspond to the ON byname *Pampi*, which also enters into the Norw farm name Pamperud, *v.* Lind, *Norsk-isländska personbinamn från medeltiden*, col. 275), cf. also a str. form *Pamp* postulated for Pampisford Ca 111, DEPN, Studies[2] 146. Alternatively, therefore, Pamphill may mean '*Pampa's or *Pempa's hill'. Professor Löfvenberg prefers this etymology. The f.n. *Pemphamm' infra* may contain the same first el.

ABBOTT STREET (FM & COPSE) (ST 984007), *Abbodestret(e)* 1340, 1350 *Wim*, 1390 Pat, *Abbot(t)e(s)stret(e)* 1407 *Wim et freq* to 1547 *DLMB*, *Abbostrete* 1523 *AddCh*, 1551 *DLCt*, *Abbott-strete* (*als. Abbottscrofte*) 1591 *DLMB*, *Abstreete* 1664 HTax, *Ab Street* 1811 OS. The first el. is **abbod**, with reference to the possession of this manor by the abbey of Sherborne, cf. *terre nuper Abbat' de Schyrborn* 1551 *DLCt*, Hutch[3] 3 230; 'street' could refer to the Badbury Rings–Poole Harbour Roman road (Margary 4d), the course of which is still traceable here, but the later sense 'straggling village, hamlet' is also possible, *v.* **strǣt**.

OLD BARFORD (SY 964999), BARFORD DAIRY & FM
la Bere 1227 FF (p), c. Ed I Hutch[3] (p), 1294 *Queens*, 1319 *Wim* (p), 1327 *SR* (p), 1329 Ipm, *la Ber'* 1332 SR (p), 1406 *DCMDeed*, *Labere* 1552 *DLCt*; *atte Bere* 1323 Pat (p), *atte Be(e)r'* 1332 SR (p); *Bere* 1269 Cur, *Bere Horsenden* 1269 FF, *-Horsindene* 1280 Banco, *-Horsedene* 1307 ib, *Ber-horsindene* 1281 FF, *Berehorsseden(e)* 1306 Banco, *Bere by Caneford* 1375 Fine, 1377 Cl, *By(e)re* 1387 ib, *Beare* 1412, 1431 FA, 1591 *DLMB*, *Bere-Peverel or Berford or Barford* 1774 Hutch[1], *Beer Peverell or Ford* 1795 Boswell
Ber(e)ford(e) 1244, 1268 *Ass*, c. Ed I Hutch[3], 1286 (1313) Ch all (p) *et freq* to 1598 *DLComm* (all (p) until n.d. (1372) *ChrP*, 1438 *Queens*), *Bireford'* 1244 *Ass* (p), *Berheford'*, *Bereford'* super Sturam n.d (1372) *ChrP*, *Berefford* 1427 *HarlRoll*, *Bereforth* 1518 *ib*; *Barfford super Stoure* 1444 *Queens*, *Barr(e)ford hamme, -mede* 1512, 1513 *Pars*, *Barf(f)ord(e)* 1547 *DLMB*, 1552 *DLCt*, 1648 SC, *Barford ham* 1653 *DCMSurv*, *Barfoot(e)* (*Ham*) 1663 *ib*, WimCW, 1677 *DCMCt*, *Higher & Lower Barford* 1811 OS

'The (woodland) pasture' or 'the wood, the grove', from

bǣr[2] or **bearu**, cf. Bere Regis 1 273, and 'the ford near *Bere*', from **ford**, with **hamm, mǣd**. The manorial affixes are from the families of John *de Horsyndon* 1269 Cur, Joan *de Horsenden* 1269 FF (cf. Horsenden Bk, Horsendon Mx), and Thomas- 1281 FF, Andrew *Peverel* 1329 Ipm (cf. Bradford Peverell 1 334). The earlier *Bere* is probably represented by Barford Dairy (*Lower Barford* 1811 OS), *Bereford* by Old Barford (*Higher Barford* 1811 ib) which is on R. Stour and no doubt the site of the ford.

(Lr) BARNSLEY FM (ST 993031, 997037)

  Bernardeslega 1178 P, -*leg(e)* 1180 ib both (p), 1235 (1372) *ChrP*, -*le* 1212 Fees, 1231 Cl, 1236 (1372) *ChrP et freq* to 1372 *ib*, -*l'* 1235 Cl, -*lee* 1235 (1372) *ChrP*, 1236, 1318 FF, -*leya* 1285 FA, -*leye* 1285 ib, 1288 *Ass*, 1289 FF, -*le(y)gh(e)*, -*leia* n.d. (1372) *ChrP*; *Bernardele* 1280 *Ass*, 1306 FF, 1453 *Midd*, *Bernardleye* n.d. (1372) *ChrP*, *Bernardisley* 1477 *Wim*, -*erdis*- 1552 *HarlCh*

  Burnardesle 1189 (1313) Ch, R 1 (1372) *ChrP*

  Barnardsl' 1270 (1372) *ChrP*, *Barnardeslegh* 1479 *IpmR*, -*ley* 1552 *DLCt*, *Barnesley(e)* 1535 *Midd et passim*, -*lye*, -*lie* 1545 (16) *Bartelot*, *Barnerdisley* 1552 *HarlCh*, *Barnsley* 1591 *DLMB*

'Beornheard's wood or clearing', from the OE pers.n. *Beornheard* and lēah. The surname *Bernard* occurs locally, e.g. John *Bernarde* 1409 *Midd*. There is mention of a mill here in n.d. (1372) *ChrP*.

BRADFORD FM (ST 978054)

  Bradeford(e) 1212 Cur (-*de feodo Briani de Insula*), 1224 ib, ClR, 1235–6 Fees, 1244 *Ass*, 1270 Ipm, 1283 FF (-*juxta Wymburne Menstre*), 1306 (1372) *ChrP*, 1332 SR (p), -*uorde* 1327 *SR* (p), *Bradford(e)* 1535 *Midd et passim*, *Braddeford* 1553 *DLCt*, *Broadford Fm* 1811 OS

  Bradeford(') Brian 1289 FF, 1304 Ipm, 1358 FF, -*Bryan* 1412 FA, 1453 *Midd*, *Burdefford Brian* 1427 *HarlRoll*, *Bradford Briante* 1591 *DLMB*, *Bradford Bryan* 1795 Boswell

'The broad ford', *v.* **brād, ford**, cf. Bradford P. 1 334. The ford was no doubt on the tributary of R. Allen flowing to the N of the farm, perhaps where this was crossed by the Badbury

Rings-Old Sarum Roman road (Margary 4c). The *Brianus de Insula* who was here in 1212 Cur, 1224 ClR (cf. *Reg' de Bryene* 1351 *HarlRoll*) also gave his name to Bryanston par. *supra*.

CHILBRIDGE (FM) (ST 006023)

    Chelebruga c.1140 (1340) Ch, *Chelbruge* c. 1140 *AddCh*, *Chellrug'* (probably for *-brug'*) 1154–8 (1340) Ch, *Chelbrigg* 1326 FF

    Chilbrigg(e) 1307 FF, 1365 Pat, *-brege* 1477 *Wim*, *-brige* 1535 VE, *-bredge* 1591 *DLMB*, *Chylbrygge* 1412 Cl, *-byrge* 1560 *DLCt*

The second el. is **brycg** 'bridge', probably used here in the sense 'causeway through marshy ground' with reference to the road E of the farm which crosses a tributary of R. Allen near Marsh Barn. The first el. may be the OE pers.n. *Cēola*, or **ceole** 'throat, channel, gorge' (perhaps with reference to the course of the road near Daffodil Copse), cf. Chilgrove Sx 49.

COWGROVE (FM) (ST 985001), *C(o)ugraue, -graue* 1288 *Ass*, *Cou-* 1317 *Wim*, *Cowgrave* 1465 *ib*, *Cugrove* 1321 FF, *Cougrove* 1358 ib, c.1500 *Fry*, *Cougerowe* (sic) 1430 *Wim*, *Cowegrove* 1453 *Midd*, *Cowgrove* 1468 *MinAcct et passim*, *Kowe growe* 1535 *Midd*, *Cow Grove* 1664 HTax, 'cow grove or copse', *v.* **cū**, **grāf(a)**, cf. Grove Wd ⅓ mile N, Chaw Mdw ⅓ mile S.

EYE BRIDGE & MD (SY 995995), (6 acres in) *Eye* 1253 Drew, ? *Hya* n.d. (1372) ChrP, *pastur' de-, prat' de Ey*, *Ymede* 1468 *MinAcct*, *Eymede*, *Eylezen* 1547 *DLMB*, *Eye* (*Meade, -Meadow, -Leasinge*), *Ile leises, -Meadowe* 1591 *ib*, *Eye Meade* 1598 *DLComm*, from **ēg**, WSax **ī(e)g** 'an island', replaced in some 16th cent. forms by ME **ile** 'an island', with **mǣd** 'meadow', **lǣs** 'meadowland' (with ME pl. *-en*), cf. Eye He, Mx, etc (DEPN), *v.* Weir Lane *infra*. Eye Md is encircled by R. Stour and its tributaries.

HOGFORD (lost, ST 999015), 1811 OS, (*-Grd* 1847 *TA*), *Hogges-ford'* 1332 SR (p), *Hogeford* 1347 *HarlRoll* (p), 1547 *DLMB*, *Hogfordmyll'* 1468 *MinAcct*, *Hoggeforde Lane* 1598 *DLComm*, probably 'hog('s) ford', from **hogg** and **ford**, with **myln** 'mill', cf. Boresford He (DEPN), Swinford Wo 309; alternatively the first el. could be the pers.n. or surname *Hogg*, cf. PN Bk 68,

Thomas *Hogge* 1523 *AddCh*. It is on R. Allen just E of Hound Hill.

KINGSTON LACY HALL (ST 978013), *Kingestune* c.1170 CartAnt, *Chingeston* 1173 Hutch³, *Kynges-*, *Kingeston(e)* 1176–89 AD VI, 1193 P, 1212 Fees, 1230 FF *et freq* to 1591 *DLMB* with affix *-Lacy(e)* from 1335 Cl, Ipm, *Kynggeston(e)* 1268 *Ass*, 1319 *Wim* (*-Lacy*), 1332 SR, *Kyngesston'* 1280 *Ass*, *Kyngis-* 1387 Cl (*-Lacy*), 1428 FA, *Kyngyston* 1406 *DCMDeed* (*-Lacy*), *Kyngeston Lace* 1401 Pat, *Kynston'* 1468 *MinAcct*, *Kingston-*, *Kyngston Lacy(e)* 1523 *AddCh et passim* with variant spellings *-lacey* 1545 *DCMDeed*, *-Lacie* 1558 *PlR*, *-lasye* 1569 Hutch³, *Kyngynston Lacy* 1523 *AddCh*, *Kingeston-Haul* 1535–43 Leland, *Kynkeston'* 1552 *DLCt*, *Kington Lacie* 1558 *PlR*, *Kingston Hall* 1664 WimCW, 'the king's farm', *v*. **cyning, tūn**, cf. Kingston 1 15. In 1086 DB this manor is not named but is included in the royal group of manors headed by Wimborne M. (Eyton 87, VCHDo 3 65). In 1230 FF the manor was granted to John *de Lasey*, earl of Lincoln, cf. Henry *de Lacy* 1268 *Ass*, 1284 Pat, etc, *v*. Hutch³ 3 233. The present 17th cent. house replaced the earlier one described by Leland as 'a fair maner place', *v*. **hall**. The bounds of the manor of Kingston Lacy are given in 1591 *DLMB* (Vol. 116, ff. 23–24), *v*. also CleggWim 203 ff. The forms *Kingston Crusis* 1537, *-Crucis* 1538 *Midd* probably belong here, the affix representing gen.sg. *crucis* of Lat **crux** 'cross' as in Ampney Crucis Gl, cf. (land at) *Crowche Crosse* 1535 *ib*, from **crūc**³ 'cross' with explanatory **cros**.

STONE (FM) (SU 003007), *tethinga de la Stane* 1268 *Ass*, (*vill' de*) (*la*) *Stone* 1280, 1288 *ib*, *Stone* c.1500 *Fry et passim*, *Stoune* 1523 *AddCh*, 1547 *DLMB*, 1551 *DLCt*, *Wymborne Stone* 1564 *Glyn*, *Stone Ho* 1863 Hutch³, 'the stone', *v*. **stān**. The reference is perhaps to a bdy stone; the place is situated on the road to Blandford F. (Stone Lane 6") ⅓ mile from the present borough bdy of Wimborne M.

TATTEN (ST 987014), *Tadden* (*Fd & Moor*) 1847 *TA*, probably to be identified with *Tadhavene* 1327 *SR*, *Taddehauene* 1332 SR both (p), which is apparently from **tadde, tāde** 'toad' and **hæfen**¹ 'haven, harbour', the name perhaps meaning 'haven for toads' with *haven* in the figurative sense 'place of shelter or retreat' (from a1225 NED) rather than in the sense 'harbour' (from 1031 ib). There is a stream nearby and the ground is marshy; for a similar contemptuous or jocular name, cf. Taddiport D 111.

BARNSLEY CTGS & DROVE, cf. *Barnesley slade, -waye, -waie* 1535 *Midd, Barnsley Mdw & Moor* 1847 *TA*, from Barnsley *supra*, *v.* slæd. THE BELT, *v.* belt. BICKHAM COPSE & FM, *Bickham* (*Coppice, Moor & Plot*) 1847 *TA*, probably to be identified with *Bikcumb'* 1268 *Ass* (p), *Biccombe* c. Ed 1 Hutch[3] (p), which is from cumb 'valley'; the first el. is uncertain, bīc 'bees' nest', bic(a) 'beak-like projection', and the OE pers.n. *Bica* being among the possible alternatives. BRADFORD BARROW, *Broadford-* 1811 OS, *v.* beorg, Bradford Fm *supra*. CHALK PIT COPSE, cf. *Chalk Pit* (*Cl & Fd*) 1847 *TA*. CHAW MDW, *Cheluemede* n.d. (1372) *ChrP, Chalf mede* 1349 *Wim, Chale Meade* 1591 *DLMB*, 'meadow for calves', from WSax cealf (gen.pl. *cealfa*) and mǣd; situated on R. Stour just S of Cowgrove *q.v. supra*. CONEYGAR COPSE, (*le*) *Con(n)ynger(e)* 1409 *Midd*, 1468 *MinAcct*, 1562 *Wim, the Conyng Erth* e16 *Pars, Ye-, the Cunyngry(e)* 1535 *Midd, Conygr'* 1547 *DLMB, Conygarth* 1591 *DLMB, Hr & Lr Coneygar, Coneygar Fd* 1847 *TA*, cf. *the warren of Conneys* 1591 *DLMB*, *v.* coninger, coning-erth 'rabbit-warren', coni 'rabbit'. COWGROVE CMN, *v.* Cowgrove *supra*. CULVERHAYES RD, *Culver Haies* 1591 *DLMB, -hayes* 1847 *TA*, cf. *the Culverhowse* e16 *Pars, v.* culfre 'dove', (ge)hæg, hūs. DAFFODIL COPSE. THE DECOY, *Decoy Copse, Decoy Pond Fd* 1847 *TA, v.* decoy, cf. 1 162. DOG KENNEL COPSE. ELM GROVE. ENTRANCE COPSE, at the E entrance to Kingston Lacy Park. FARRS, *-Grd* 1847 *TA*, cf. Edward *Farre* 1551 *DLCt*, Jeremiah *Farr* 1664 HTax. FITCHE'S BRIDGE, from the family of *Fitch* which possessed High Hall in the 18th cent., *v.* Hutch[3] 3 235-6. GILLINGHAM'S ALMSHOUSES, founded by Roger *Gillingham* in 1695, *v.* Hutch[3] 3 251, cf. *Gillinghams Grd* 1847 *TA*, Walter *de Gillingham* 1284 FF. GROVE WD, *v.* grāf(a), cf. Cowgrove *supra*. HART'S COPSE, *Harts Coppice* 1847 *TA*, cf. John *le Hert'* 1332 SR, Steven *Hartte* 1523 *AddCh*. HIGH HALL (COPSE), *High Hall farm* 1663 WimCW, *High-Hall* 1774 Hutch[1], *High Hale* (sic) *Coppice, High Hall House* 1847 *TA, v.* hēah, hall. HIGH WD, (*-Fd*) 1847 *ib, Hyewoode Copes* 1564, *Hye Wood* 1598 both *DLComm*, *v*. **hēah, wudu, copis**. HILLBUTTS, 1811 OS, *Hilbut(t)s* (*Grd*), *Hill Butts Fd & Grd* 1847 *TA*, possibly so called 'from its having [archery] butts erected here formerly' (Hutch³ 3 230), *v*. **butt²**, but alternatively from **butte** 'short strip at right angles to others, etc'. HOLLOW WAY. HOME COVERT, *v*. **covert**. HOUND HILL, 1811 OS, *Houne Hill* 1591 *DLMB*, cf. *Hound Hill Grd, Moor & Orchd* 1847 *TA*, probably 'hill where hounds were kept', from **hund** and **hyll** (there are still kennels nearby 6"), but the first el. could alternatively be the plant-name **hūne** 'hoarhound'. JUBILEE WD. KEEPER'S LODGE, *-Ho* 1847 *TA*. KIER CTGS. KING DOWN (DROVE & FM), (*the*) *Kinges Downe* 1591 *DLMB*, *Kings Down, Kingsdown Fm* 1811 OS, *King Down* (*Fd*) 1847 *TA*, cf. *Kyngesfeld* n.d. (1372) *ChrP*, *King(')s Cl & Mdw* 1847 *TA*, *v*. **cyning, dūn, feld**; within the former royal manor of Kingston Lacy *supra*, although the f.ns. could contain a surname, cf. *Robert Kynge* 1495 WimCW. KINGSTON LACY PARK, '[the Countess of Lincoln's] park at *Kyngeston Lacy*' 1348 Pat, *The Park* 1847 *TA*, cf. *Park Slade* 1591 *DLMB*, *v*. **park, slæd** 'valley', Cantor & Wilson 1 112. KINGSTON PLANT., cf. *Kyngestone(s)feld*' 1306 (1372), 1372 *ChrP*, *Kyngeston More* 1547 *DLMB*, from Kingston Lacy *supra*, *v*. **feld, mōr**. LAMBING YD, cf. *ponfalld' de Braddeford* 1553 *DLCt*, *v*. Bradford Fm *supra*. LOCUST CLUMP. LODGE DOWN & FM, named from the lodge at the N entrance to Kingston Lacy Park, cf. *The Lodge* 1575 Saxton, *Lodge Fd* 1847 *TA*. MANOR HO. THE MARL PIT, cf. *le marlingpet* 1359 *Wim*, *v*. **marle, marling, pytt**. MARSH BARN & COPSE, cf. *Marsh* (*Fds, Moor & Wd*) 1847 *TA*, *mariscum* 1306 (1372) *ChrP*. NETHERWOOD MD, 1811 OS, 'meadow in *Netherwood*' 1540 Hutch³, cf. *Nethermede* (also by R. Stour) c. Ed 1 Hutch³, *v*. **neoðerra** 'lower', **wudu, mǣd**. THE NURSERY, *Nursery* 1847 *TA*. THE OAKS, cf. *Richard-* 1324 *Wim*, *John atte Ok(')* 1327 *SR*, *William attenoc*' 1332 SR, *v*. **atte(n), āc**. OLD FORD, cf. *John atte Forde* 1372 *ChrP*, *v*. **atte, ford**. OLD LAWN COPPICE & FM, *old land* e16 *Pars*, *Old Land* (*Fd*) 1847 *TA*, *v*. **ald, land**, possibly referring to disused arable land in the NE corner of the par. PAMPHILL GREEN, 1847 *ib*, probably identical with *Feyregren* 1547, *Faire Grene* 1591 *DLMB*, 'green where fairs were held', *v*. **feire, grēne²**, cf. *Site of Old Fair House* 1847 *TA*; two fairs at Pamphill were granted to the churchwardens of Wimborne

M. in 1496 (Hutch[3] 3 224, 274) and are recorded in 1518 WimCW, 1525 *Wim*, etc. LT PAMPHILL, *v.* par. name *supra*. PITT'S DROVE, probably named from Chalk Pits (6″), but cf. *Sidracke Pitt* 1602 WimCW. POUND FM, cf. *Powndes Moore* 1591 *DLMB*, *v.* **pund, mōr**; there is mention of three pounds for cattle in the manor of Kingston Lacy in 1598 *DLComm*. RALPH COPSE. ST MARGARET'S ALMSHOUSES (on site of ST MARGARET & ST ANTONY'S HOSPITAL), *ecclesiæ Sanctæ Margaretæ de Wimborn* John, *domui leprosorum extra Wymborn Mynstre* n.d. (c.13), *capellæ-, domus Sanctæ Margaretæ virginis* c. Ed 1 all Hutch[3], 'the hospital of St Margaret without *Wumburn Ministre*' 1256 Pat, 'the hospital of St Margaret (the Virgin) and St Anthony' 1275, 1286 Pat, (the poor people of) *Seynt Margetts* 1524 WimCW, cf. *Saint Margarets Grd* 1847 *TA*, *v.* VCHDo 2 106-7; in the chapel of this hospital was *Redcote's-, Redcodde's chantry* 1534, 1540 Hutch[3], founded by John *Rototod* (for *Rotecod*), chaplain in 1309 ib (3 189-191), cf. also the f.n. Redcotts *infra* and Redcotts Rd & Lane in Wimborne M. *infra*. ST STEPHEN'S CHURCH, cf. *the chappell of St James in Kyngston* (sic) 1552 WimCW, *the chappell at Kingston* 1663 Hutch[3]; on this chapel, *v.* Hutch[3] 3 226, 228, and cf. St James's Church in Holt par. *supra*. There is mention of a chapel (*gardin' exterior' ex opposito capelle*) in or near Barnsley *supra* in 1306 (1372) *ChrP*, and of a John *atte church'* who held a messuage in the same manor in 1372 *ib*. SANDY LANE, 1535 *Midd*, *v.* **sandig**. STONE LANE & PARK, cf. *Stone Bottom, Fd, Grd & Plot* 1847 *TA*, from Stone (Fm) *supra*. SWEETBRIER DROVE. VINE INN. WEIR LANE, named from *Eywere* 1547 *DLMB*, *Ile Weare Head* 1591 *ib*, 'the weir at Eye', *v.* **wer, hēafod**, Eye Md *supra*. WYNNE COPSE.

FIELD-NAMES

The undated forms are 1847 *TA* 246 (Wimborne M.). Spellings dated 1270 (1372), 1297 (1372), 1306 (1372), n.d. (1372), 1372 are *ChrP*, c. Ed I, 1318, 15, 1442[2], 1465, 1546, 1582, 1637, 1800 Hutch[3], 1318[2] FF, 1327 *SR*, 1332 SR, 1340 NI, 1365 Pat, 1404, 1433 *Marten*, 1409, 1535 *Midd*, 1412 Cl, 1468 *MinAcct*, 1479, 1518, 1604, 1618 WimCW, c. 1500 *Fry*, e16, 1512 *Pars*, 1523, 1524 *AddCh*, 1541, 1564[2] *Glyn*, 1545 (16) *Bartelot*, 1547, 1591 *DLMB*, 1551, 1552, 1559 *DLCt*, 1564, 1598 *DLComm*, 1664 HTax, and the rest *Wim*.

(a) Anthill (Moor); Baker(')s Hams, Mdw & Plot (cf. Richard- 1350 *HarlRoll*, Henry *Baker* 1664; however the forms *Bekere-* (probably for

Bokere-), *Bukeresmede* n.d. (1372) may belong here, with later confusion of the occupational surnames *B(o)ukere* (Fransson 109) or *Bokere* (Thuresson 220) with *Baker*, *v.* **mæd, hamm**); Hr Barford Fd, Bear Coppice, -Copse, Bare-, Bear Grd (cf. *Beare Lande* 1547, all named from Barford (earlier *Bere*) *supra*); Late Batts, Batts Bed & Grd (*cultura voc' Battes* 1306 (1372), cf. Nicholas *le Bat'* 1332); Ben Croft (*Bine Croftes* 1591, *v.* **bēan** 'bean', **croft**); Long Benton; Berry Fd (*la bury* 1297 (1372), *terr' in le Bury(e)* 1409, *Bery-*, *Berifeld(e)* 1535, 1547, 1562, (*camp' voc'-, terr' in*) *le Bery(e)* 1547, 1551, 1552, *Berrye, Berrie* (*Closes*) 1591, *Berrye Fielde* 1598, cf. *Burymore* 1468; from **burh** (gen. and dat.sg. *byrig*) 'fortified place, manor house', with **feld, mōr**, though some of the simplex forms cited may strictly belong under Gt & Lt Burys *infra*, which name is probably identical in origin with Berry Fd); Blandford Way Fd (along the road to Blandford F. *supra*); Bog; Bottom Fd; Bounds; Brimming Mdw (*Brenhamm Meadowe* 1591, *v.* **hamm**, first el. uncertain); (Gt) Broad Moor (Pce) (*Bradmore furlonge* 1535, *Brodemore* 1547, *Broad Moore* 1591, *v.* **brād, mōr**); Brown's Croft (cf. Alice *Brown* 1637); Burley (-*leye* (*coppes*) 1564, 1598, *v.* **lēah, copis**, first el. uncertain); Burnlake (perhaps for -*bake*, *v.* **burnbake**); Gt & Lt Burys (*v.* Berry Fd *supra*); Butlers Coppice (cf. John (*le*) *Boteler* 1332, 1340); Canford Bottom (from Canford M. par. *supra*); Carlton's Grd (cf. Thomas *Garleton* 1664); Cat Ham(s) (*Catthamms* 1591, 'enclosure frequented by (wild) cats', *v.* **cat(t), hamm**); Chard Md (perhaps to be identified with *Swyrde-* c. Ed I, *Schirdemede* 1318, *v.* **mæd**, first el. uncertain); Chilbridge Cowleys (*v.* **cū, lǣs**), Chilbridge Croft (*Chilbredge Croftes* 1591) & Moor (from Chilbridge *supra*); Chosen (Hill) Fd; Common Moor (cf. *the commen of Kyngston Lacye* 1535); The Coppice, Copse Orchd (cf. *the Coppeys* 1535, *v.* **copis**); Corner Acre; Cowgrove Cmn & Grd (from Cowgrove *supra*); Home & Lt Cow Leys (*Coweleise* 1591, *v.* **cū, lǣs**); Cox's Hedge Fd (cf. John *Cokke* 1468, Nicholas *Cockes* 1591, John *Cox* 1664); Crook Hill (*Crokehyll* 1524, *v.* **hyll**, first el. perhaps **crōc** 'bend' (the fields lie at a junction of roads) rather than PrWelsh or PrCorn *crūg 'hill' (which the topography does not strongly support)); Curtis's (Orchd) (cf. Thomas *Curtes* 1552); Daisey Hill Fd; Dampiers; Deadman's Fd: Hr & Lr Ditches (*le Diche* 1468, *terr' voc' Dichis* 1547, *closes called Ditches* 1591, *v.* **dīc**); Doctors Mdw; Down Cl, The Down (Pce) (*v.* **dūn**); Hr 8 Acres (*VIII acres Furlonge* 1591); Hr 11 Acres; Elldridges; 15 Acres; Gt & Lt 40 Acres; Galpins Cow Leaze, Galpin(e)s Grd & Pdk (cf. John *Galpyn* 1457, Thomas *Gawpyne* 1604, -*Galpen* 1618); The Glebe Acre (1800); Great Fd; Green Grd; Hamlake, Hamlet Middle Fd (*Este Hamylock* 1535, *Este-*, *Weste Hamlakes* 1598, possibly 'winding stream' from **hamel** and **lacu**, cf. R. Hamble Ha (RN 189)); Ham Md (*v.* **hamm**); Hanging Cl & Grd (*v.* **hangende**); Hare Grd; Harris's Grd (cf. William *Harris* 1664); Hatch Md (*v.* **hæc(c)**); Higher Fd; High Mdw & Plot; Highmoor; Hilly Grd; Hinton Fd & Moor (*v.* Hinton P. par. *supra*); Hollys Grd & Orchd; Home Farm Grd, Home Fd & Grd; Hooker's Moor, Hookeys Fd (cf. Colehill f.ns. *supra*); Huff Pce; Innock (*Ynhockefeld* 1535, *v.* **inhoke** 'land temporarily enclosed', **feld**); Island; Lane; Middle Large Fd; Leg Plot (*v.* **leg**); Legars; The Lines (*v.* **leyne**); Little Mdw; Lockyers (cf. Ralph *Lockeir* 1664); Long Fd & Grd; Lower Fd; Mackrel Cl (cf. Edward *Makerell* 1523); Mans Croft (*Mannescroft* 1306 (1372), -*croftis* 1372, from the

OE pers.n. *Mann* and **croft** 'small enclosure', cf. *Mannestede* 1524 which would seem to be from the same pers.n. and **stede** 'place'); Meadow (*the Meade* e16, *v.* **mǣd**, cf. *Mennemede* n.d. (1372), the first el. of which may be **(ge)mǣne** 'common' if *Menne-* is for *Mene-*); Middle Fd & Moor; Mitchells Md(w) (*Muchel-* 1318, 1372, 1512, *Michel(l)med(e)* 1468, 1547, *Mitchell Mead(ow)e* 1591, *Mighell Meade, Mychell Meade* (*More*) 1598, 'big meadow', *v.* **micel, mycel, mǣd**, later interpreted as containing the surname *Mitchell*, cf. Mitchells Plot in Colehill par. *supra*); Moor Pasture; Muckles (perhaps the (NCy) surname *Muckle*, but cf. S dial. **muckle** '(a heap of) manure' and Muckleford 1334); New Fd; New Inn (cf. *ten' voc' le Neweinne* 1483, *v.* **inn**); North Fd (*camp' borial' de Kynggestone Lacy* 1319, *the Northfyeld'* e16, *North(e)feld(e)* 1535, 1547, *the meades of the Northe Fieldes* 1598, *v.* **norð, feld**); North Moor ((*the*) *Northe Mo(o)re* 1598, cf. South Moor *infra*); Old Orchd; Paddock; Pamphill (Home) Grd, Pamphill Moor & Plot; Pardys Plot (cf. Ralph *Purdey* 1327); Pattens; Pelleys Coppice (cf. *tenement' Thome Pelley* 1442); Pigeons Cl; Pigs Plot; Pillance; Pills Moor (no doubt analogous with Pillmoor Bottom in Holt par. *supra*, from **pyll** 'pool in a river, small stream', and **mōr**); Plantation; Poor Mdw; Rabbit Grd; Rabs Cowleaze & Grd (*Rabbys* 1442[2], *graungiam sive firmam voc' Rabbis* 1547, *the ferme of Rabbes* 1591, from the surname *Rabb*); (Lt) Redcotts (*Redcottes* (a common) 1591, a surname, cf. St Margaret's Almshouses *supra*, Redcotts Rd & Lane in Wimborne M. *infra*); Rush Fd; Rushy Moor; (Under) Ryalls (*Ryalls* (a common) 1591, 1598); (Gt & Lt) Sand Pit(s); Sedgemoor (*v.* **secg**[1]); Sheep Downs (cf. *the Sheepe Downe called Kinges Downe* 1598, *v.* King Down *supra*); Sims('s) (Grd); 6 Acres, 6 Acre Mdw & Pce; 16 Acres; Hr Small Grd; Small Md(w) (*Smale Medys* 1551, *-medes* 1552, *Small Meade* 1598 (*v.* **smæl** 'narrow', **mǣd**); South Moor; Starley (1598 (a copse), *Serleye* (probably for *Ster-*) 1564, perhaps 'clearing where young bullocks were kept', *v.* **stēor, lēah**); Stones Plot; Sweatherwood; 10 Acres; 35 Acres; Thorne Hill; Three Acre; Three Grounds; Tizzard; Toll House; Trip (*Tripp(e) Furlong(e)* e16, 1591, *Trippbottome* 1591, cf. Do dial. **trip** 'a culvert over a ditch or small watercourse' (Barnes 112), *v.* **furlang, botm**); Two Barrow Fd; Upper Grd; Vartis Lane Pce; Voxley Bottom, Voxleys Md (*Foxleslade* 1306 (1372), *Foxly slade* e16, *Voxleye* 1564, *Foxley(e) coppes* 1598, 'fox wood or glade', from **fox, lēah**, with **slæd** 'valley', **copis** 'coppice'); Wares; Warlands Cl (cf. William *Warlond* 1465 Ct, *Rich' Warlandes house* 1664); Watchhouse Fd (*v.* **watch-house**); White Flgs (*Whyteforlong'* (*al' dict'* Outforlong') 1306 (1372), *Whyte-* e16, *White Furlong(e)* 1591, *v.* **hwīt** 'white', **ūt(e)** 'outer, more distant', **furlang**); White Mice Fd; Wimborne Fd (from Wimborne M. *infra*); Wirey Lane Fd; Withy Pit Fd (cf. *la Wythy-, la Wythibere* 1306 (1372), *v.* **wīðig, pytt, bearu**); Woods (Moor) (cf. Peter *atte Wode* 1327, 1332, *v.* **atte, wudu**); Youngs Gdn, Orchd & Plant. (cf. John *Le Yung* 1318[2], *-le Yonge* 1332).

(b) *Acford'* 1270 (1372) (*v.* **āc, ford**); *Ackettes* 1552 (*v.* **ācet** 'oak wood'); *ten' cum curtillag' voc' Acremanlonde* 1468, *Acreman(s)lande(s)* 1547 (*v.* **æcer-mann** 'farmer', **land**, cf. *custumarii* ('customary tenants') *voc' Acremen* 1468, *tenement called an Acremanlande* 1591); *cottage called Adames* 1591 (cf. Richard *Adam* 1332); *cultura de Addredeston', -Adecedeston'* (sic) n.d. (1372) (perhaps 'Ēadrǣd's farm', from the OE pers.n. *Ēadrǣd* and **tūn**); *toft'*

...*voc' Aforehosse* (sic) *Lande* 1547 (probably 'land in front of the house', *v.* afore, hūs); *parva atteley* 1552, *Atley(e) Coppes* 1564, *-Coppice* 1591, *Litle Atleye* 1598 (from lēah 'wood, clearing', perhaps with the OE pers.n. *Atta*); *Barlane, Barremede* 1372 (*v.* barre 'rod used as a gate fastening', lane, mǣd); *Barrows Haie Parrocks* 1591 (*v.* beorg, (ge)hæg, pearroc); *Bengervyle* 1512, *firma' de Bengerfeldes* 1547, *Benger Fielde* 1591 (perhaps from the surname *Benger* and feld); *Bennell Meade* 1591; *Bolsefurse* 1591 (*v.* fyrs); *Bouchelcrosse* 1468 (*v.* cros, cf. Ralph *Bochel* 1332); *Bradford forlonge, -Waye* 1535, *Bradford Briante Yeatt* 1591 (from Bradford Fm *supra*, *v.* furlang, weg, geat 'gate'); *Bradmere* 1468, *Bredmer* e16, *Brodemer* 1547 ('broad pool', from brād and mere¹); *Brecheburi, cultura voc' la Breche ex parte australi de Buri* 1306 (1372), *the Brach, Bruche* 1547, *Breach* 1591 (*v.* brēc 'land broken up for cultivation', burh (dat.sg. *byrig*) 'fortified place'); *Bremelifurlang'* c.1500, *Bremly Furlong* e16 (*v.* brēmel, -ig³, furlang); *Brianesforlong'* 1306 (1372) (the pers.n. or surname *Brian*, cf. Bradford Fm *supra*); *(les) Brodefurses* 1340², 1461, *-fourses* 1407, *le(z)-, la Brodefurse* 1350, 1407, 1459 (*v.* brād, fyrs); *Brodefurlonge* 1468 (*v.* brād, furlang); *Brodewoke* 1547 (*v.* brād, āc 'oak-tree'); *Brownhill* 1591 (*v.* brūn¹, hyll); *Buckemas* (sic) 1547 (probably for *-mans*, from the surname *Buckman*); *Thomas Buddens Close* 1591; *Burse Hunte Cross* 1547, *cottage at Burse* 1591 (probably from berse 'fenced-in part of a forest', with hunte and cros(s)); *the Buttes, Buttestile* 1591 (*v.* butt² or butte, stigel); *Byndes Croftes* 1591 (probably a surname, *v.* croft); *tenement' voc' Byttemne* 1547, 1552 (possibly bytme 'valley bottom'); *Caffyngyshey* 1306 (1372) (cf. John *Chaffing'* 1270 (1372), Maud *Chaffyng'* 1327, *v.* (ge)hæg); *Capons* 1547, *-als. Dixon's lands* 1563 (from John *Capon* 1349, 1465, cf. *Dixsons infra*); *Caynesmilne* 1244 *Ass* (the surname *Cain*, *v.* myln); *Cheancy Field* 1591; *Chesyll hyll* 1535 (*v.* cisel 'gravel', hyll); *Cokeden* 1547 (probably 'cocks' valley' from cocc² and denu, cf. Cogdean in Corfe M. par. *supra*); *ye conb'* 1552 (probably cumb 'valley'); *(the) Courte Close* e16, 1547 (*v.* court, cf. *curiam de Kingeston'* n.d. (1372)); *Cranhornella* n.d. (1372) (in *South field supra*; from cran 'a crane' and burna 'stream', final el. possibly well(a) 'spring, stream'); *ten' cum curtillag' voc' Dawynlonde* 1468, *tenement voc' Daywens* 1547 (cf. *custumarii* ('customary tenants') *voc' Dawyns* 1468, *ten' voc' Adaywynlond* c.1500, *ten' voc' a Dawyngeland* 1547, *ten' called a Dawen* (sic) 1591; according to CleggWim 176, the *daywyns* were a class of feudal peasant on the manor of Kingston Lacy each of whom owed one day's work in each week throughout the year and occupied a virgate of land; as Professor Löfvenberg points out, this term (cf. *Dawyns* 1468) must be an elliptical use of OE *dæg-wine* 'a day's pay', ME *dai-wine, -wene* 'a day's earnings or pay' (MED s.v. *dai* §13d), cf. N dial. *day-win* 'the day's earnings' (EDD); *Da(y)wynlond* and elliptically *Da(y)wen* (1547, 1591) no doubt denoted 'land cultivated by a customary tenant owing one day's work a week', *v.* land, cf. *Acremanlonde supra*); *Dead Moore* 1591 (*v.* dēad, mōr); *Dixsons* 1547 (from Thomas *Dixon* 1465, cf. *Capons supra*); *Dockham Poole* 1547, *Dacoum-, Daccum Poole* 1591 (in R. Stour, *v.* pōl¹; perhaps 'water-meadow where docks grow', from docce and hamm, but cf. Richard *Dackombe* 1664); *Dovedeslond* 1319, *Donedsclade* (for *Doueds-*) c.Ed I, *dowse slade* 1535 (probably 'David's land and valley', from the ME pers.n. *David*, of which *Dowe* is a pet-form, and

land, slæd); *Dunghill* 1547 (*v.* **dunghill**); *Duppleshegh* 1365, *Dupplishey* 1412, *Dubbles Haies* 1591, *Dobles Hayes* 1598 (*v.* **(ge)hæg**, first el. probably a surname, cf. *Dubles Brydge* in Colehill par. *supra*); *ferny lande* 1535 (*v.* **fearnig**); *Henrie Ferses Coppice* 1591; *Frankemere* 1306 (1372), *Francke Mere hed* 1535 (*v.* **mere**[1] 'pool', **hēafod** 'head'; first el. possibly the OE pers.n. *Franca*, as in Frankley Wo, etc (DEPN), but cf. ME *frank(e)* 'an enclosure for hogs, a sty' (from ? a1400 NED)); (*le*) *Fryth(e)* 1547, *the Frithe Field* 1591 (*v.* **fyrhð** 'wood'); *gander Howsse* 1524 (*v.* **gander**); *Gay(e)s Corner* 1547, *Gaies* 1591 (cf. William *Gay* 1327, 1332); *Gorwey* 1468, *Goreaker* 1524, *Goare* 1591 (*v.* **gāra, weg, æcer**); *Gosspell Bushe* 1591 ('bush where the gospel was read while beating the bounds', *v.* **gospel, busc**; in the bounds of Kingston Lacy); *Gurdynssestyle* e16 (*v.* **stigel**, first el. the surname *Gurden*); *Hamundeshey* n.d. (1372) (the surname *Hamund*, *v.* **(ge)hæg**); *Harpers Haye* 1579 *Fry* (the surname Harper, *v.* **(ge)hæg**); *Harvis* 1547, *Harves Hill* 1591 (cf. John *Harvye* 1664); *Hassell Woodes* 1564 (*v.* **hæsel**); *Hawkyns* 1547 (the surname *Hawkyn*); *atte Ethe* 1407 (p), *le Hethe* 1547 (*v.* **atte, hǣð** 'heath'); *Heuedlond'* 1372 (*v.* **hēafod-land**); *Hickmans* 1547 (cf. Thomas *Hykeman* 1332); *in superiori cultura* n.d. (1372) ('higher furlong'); *Holmersyate* c.1500 (cf. John *Holmer* 1664, *v.* **geat**); *Holminge Stubbes* 1591 ('holly stumps', from **holegn** and **stubb**); *Hong'bargh* 1306 (1372), *Hamborgh'* 1372 (*v.* **beorg** 'barrow, hill', first el. uncertain); *Horse Forde* 1591 (*v.* **hors, ford**); *tenement voc' Howe, iiij claus' voc' Howes, 2 claus' voc' Howes als. Meverell* 1547, *2 closes called Howes* 1591 (*v.* **howe** 'enclosure'; *Meverell* is obscure); *prat' de Hulham* 1270 (1372) (*v.* **hyll, hamm**); *Hunts Field* 1591 (cf. Henry *Hunt* 1479); *Keichesham* n.d. (1372) (the surname *Kei(t)ch, v.* **hamm**); *Kenmynges trowe* 1535, *Kenningbroughe* (sic) 1591 (possibly **trog** 'trough, valley', with a surname); *Kiddes* 1591 (the surname *Kidd*); *Kills* 1591 (cf. *terram Johannes Kill* c.Ed I, Henry *Kyl* 1327); *Kurchelmede* 1404, 1433, *Crichel Mead* 1582 (probably named from L. Crichel par. *infra* or M. Crichel par. *supra, v.* **mǣd**, cf. Kyrchil in Colehill par. *supra*); *the lesing* e16, *Lezyne* 1547 (probably 'the meadows', from **lǣs** with ME pl. *-en*, cf. Eye Md *supra*); *little laye* 1535 (*v.* **lēah**); *Londons* 1547, 1591 (Cf. John *de London de Aultone* 1319); *Longe Downe Furlonge* 1591; *longe lynche* 1535 (*v.* **hlinc**); *Lowelande* 1468, *Littell Lowlandes* 1591 (*v.* **low, land**); *in inferiori cultura* n.d. (1372) ('lower furlong', in *South Fd infra*); *Middell Furlonge* 1591 (*v.* **middel**); *Mistenetrust* 15 (the spelling is probably corrupt); (*molend' de*) *Moremyll'* 1468, *crucem voc Moremyll Crosse* 1523 (*v.* **mōr, myln, cros**); *Morlesham* 1372 (*v.* **hamm**, probably with a surname, cf. Robert *Morly* c.Ed I, Giles *Morel* 1318 *Queens*); *Musterd Crosse* 1591 (*v.* **cros(s)**, cf. Wimborne M. f.ns. *infra*); *le Nethircrofte* 1409 (*v.* **neoðerra, croft**); *Netherlondes Lande Furlonge* 1591 (*v.* **neoðerra, land**); (*the Sowthesyde of*) *New Crosse* 1535 (*v.* **nīwe, cros(s)**); *the Norther Lake* 1591 (*v.* **norðerra, lacu**); *Ockemed* 1547, *Okemeade* 1591 (*v.* **āc, mǣd**); *Oyles* 1591 (probably a surname); *Paphill* 1562, *Paper Hill Furlonge* 1591 (the earlier form may be a mistake for *Pamphill* (*v.* **par.** name *supra*), the later may be a reinterpretation of the mistake); *Pater Noster Crosse* 1591 ('cross where the Lord's Prayer was repeated while beating the bounds'; like *Gosspell Bushe supra*, in the bounds of Kingston Lacy); *Pemphamm'* 1591 (*v.* **hamm**, cf. par. name *supra*); *Peppinges Haye* 1591 (*v.* **(ge)hæg**, cf. Hugh *Pipyn* 1327, *-Pepyn* 1332); *Perihey*

1468 (v. **pirige** 'pear-tree', **(ge)hæg**, cf. *Purley infra*); *le Pykydehey* 1409 (v. **pīcede** 'pointed', **(ge)hæg**); *Pipe Hilles* 1547 (perhaps from **pīpe** 'pipe, conduit', but possibly belonging with *Paphill supra*); *ij claus' voc' ij Pokes* 1547 (v. **poke** 'bag', but perhaps for *Parokes* from **pearroc**); *la Portwey(e)* 1306 (1372) (v. **port-weg**); *Pottmoore* 1591 (v. **pot(t)** 'a pot' or **potte** 'a pit', **mōr**); *Preslye Copes* 1564, *Presleye* 1598 (probably 'priests' wood or clearing', from **prēost** and **lēah**, with **copis**); *Priors Grove* 1545 (16), 1546 (parcel of the priory of Christchurch Twyneham Ha (Hutch³ 3 235), v. **prior, grāf(a)**); (*bosc' de*) *Purley* 1468 (probably from **pirige, pyrige** 'pear-tree' and **lēah**, cf. *Perihey supra*); *Pussox* 1559; *Pynnocks* 1591 (cf. Agnes *Pynnok'* 1332); (*Coppes...called*) *Quarters* 1552, 1564, 1598 (v. **quarter**); *Rakcloose* 1541, *Racke Close* 1564² (v. **rakke**); *Richis* 1547, *Ryches* 1552 (the surname *Rich*); *tenementes called the Rieve Holdes* 1598 (v. **(ge)rēfa, hold**); *la Rydeforlong'* 1306 (1372) (v. **rēad** 'red', **furlang**); *cottage called Ridinges Coate* 1591 (from **ryding** 'a clearing' or the surname *Riding*, and **cot**); *Rollehylle* 1523 (cf. William *Rolle* in the same document, v. **hyll**); *Roomes Barne* 1591 (the surname *Room*); *Rounde Hamm' Furlonge* 1591 (v. **round, hamm**); *Rudgis* e16 (in *South Fd infra*, v. **hrycg**); *Sanelaye* 1598 (or *Saue-*, v. **lēah**, first el. uncertain); *la Schaphous* 1306 (1372) (v. **scēap, hūs**); *Sextons Thornes* 1591 (the surname *Sexton*, v. **þorn**); *Shawes house* 1664; *Sheaffes* 1591 (a common, perhaps to be associated with foll.); *Shelffes-, Shelles Furlonge* 1591 (first el. possibly **scelf** 'a ledge', or a surname); *Shephey apud Kyngeston als. Stubles* 1468 (v. **scēap, (ge)hæg, stubbil**); *Shonehey* 1547, *Shore-, Sharehaie* 1591 (v. **(ge)hæg**; first el(s). uncertain, whether or not all three forms belong together); *le Smalelande* 1547 (v. **smæl, land**); *Smale Water* 1591 (v. **smæl, wæter**); *long-, shorte snake* e16, *Longe-, Shorte Snake Furlonge* 1591 (v. **snaca** 'a snake'); *in campo australi* n.d. (1372), *the Southfyeld'* e16, *Sowthfeld* 1535, *South field* 1591 (v. **sūð, feld**); *Southwode, Nyther-, Ouersouthwode* 1306 (1372) (v. **sūð, wudu, neoðerra, uferra**); *Splatlackes* 1591 (perhaps from **splott** 'small plot' and **lacu** 'stream'); *Stadgrowe* 1535 (second el. probably **grāf(a)** 'grove'); *Stonyham* 1468 (v. **stānig, hamm**); *ye stony leye* e16, *Stony laye* 1535, *-Leey* 1547, *Stonie Leise, Stoney Ley Corner* 1591 (v. **stānig, lēah**); *campis voc' Stupvull vele* 1523 (v. **feld**, first el(s). uncertain); *Sweten-* 1294 *Queens, Swetynham* 1444 *ib* (v. **hamm**, first el. **swēte** 'sweet' or the OE pers.n. *Swēta*, cf. Swettenham Ch 2 283); *Attetoneseynde* 1327, *atte Toneshende* 1332 both (p) (v. **atte, tūn, ende**¹); *the towne Fielde* 1598; *twenty acres* e16; *de la Watere* 1270 (1372) (p) (v. **wæter**); *atte Well'* 1468, *Atte Wolle* c.1500 both (p) (v. **atte, well(a), wyll(a)**); *in campo Occidentali de Kingestone* c.Ed I ('west field'); *Wey(e) Furlong(e)* e16, 1591 (v. **weg**); *Wheate Close* 1591 (v. **hwǣte**); *White hole pytte* 1535 (v. **hwīt, hol**¹, **pytt**); *White-* n.d. (1372), *Whytewell'* 1372 (v. **hwīt, well(a)**); *Whyte Waye lane end* 1535, *Whitteyes lane* 1654 (v. **hwīt, weg, lane, ende**¹); *Wolgrove Furlonge* 1591 (v. **wyll(a), grāf(a)**, cf. *atte Well' supra*); *Worley Closse* 1591; *Wydefoldessherde* 1306 (1372) (v. **wīd, fald, sceard**); *Wyteschere dones* 1551 (cf. *Joh' Paulet miles comes de Wylsthere* (sic)...*ter' et ten't in Kyngeston'* in the same document, v. **dūn**).

Shapwick
Part of this par. was transferred to Witchampton par. *infra* in 1886.

SHAPWICK (ST 937017)
> *Scapeuuic* 1086 DB, *-wyk'* 1280 *Ass, Escapewihc* 1086 Exon
> *Sapewic* c.1170 CartAnt, 1212 Fees, *-wyc* 1242 Ch (p), *-wyk'*
> 1280 *Ass, -wike* 1547 DLMB, *S(c)hapewyk(e)* 1176–89 AD
> VI, 1280 *Ass*, 1291 Tax *et freq* to 1431 FA, *-wik* 1412 ib,
> *Sapwic'* 1212 Fees, *-wikes* 1228 FF, *-wyk(')* 1244 *Ass (lib'*
> *de-)*, 1285 FA, *S(c)hapwyk(e)*, *-wik(e)* 1244 *Ass*, 1267 Ch
> *et passim, Chapwyk* 1253 FF, *-wick* 1591 DLMB, *Sabwyk*
> 1266 Ipm, *S(c)happewyk(e)* 1280 *Ass*, 1317 Pat, 1513 *Pars,*
> *Shaupwyk* 1318 FF, *Shapweke* 1504 Ipm, *-wick* 1577 *AD*
> *Sepewich* 1191–93 P, *-wic* 1195 ib, *-wyk'* 1265 Cl, *Sepwik*
> 1235–6 Fees, *-wyk* 1265 Pat, *Shepwyk(e)* 1238 ib, 1431 FA,
> 1593 *Lane, -wyc, -wic* 1256 FF, *Schepwyk'* 1244 *Ass* (p),
> 1268 *ib, Shepewic* 1256 FF, *-wyk'* 1288 *Ass, Schepike* 1265
> Misc, *Scepwyk(')* 1275 RH
> *Shopewyk'* 1288 *Ass, Shopwick* 1575 Saxton
> *Shapwick(e) Champaigne* 1346, 1587 Hutch³, *Shapwike Cham-*
> *payn* 1469 IpmR
> *Shapwick Plecy* 1407 Hutch³, *Shapewik Plecy* 1417 IpmR,
> *Sheepwick als. Camells lands als. Camells Shapwicke* 1564
> Hutch³

'Sheep farm', from WSax scēap (gen.pl. *-a*) and wīc, identical in origin with Shapwick So (DEPN) and Shopwyke Sx 76. The spellings in *Escape-* and *Sap(e)-, Sep(e)-* show AN influence, *v*. IPN 103, 113. The affixes *Champaigne* and *Plecy* are manorial. The manor of *Shapwick Champaigne* was named from Henry and Ralph *de Champaines* who held a knight's fee here in 1212 Fees, cf. Roger *de Chaunpayne* 1256 FF, Joan-, Roger (*de*) *Chaumpaign(e)* 1332 SR, *mes' voc' Champeynsplase, -place* 1429–30 DLCt (*v*. **place**), and the f.n. Champayne Cl *infra, v*. Hutch³ 3 160–1. The manor of *Shapwick Plecy* was named from John *Plecy* 1389 DLRent, 1407 IpmR, cf. *Playseys Wode* 1509 DLCt (*v*. **wudu**), *v*. Hutch³ 3 165–6; this manor was later called *Camells* (*Shapwicke*) (cf. *mansionem Roberti Cammell, Cammelles Place* 1509 DLCt (*v*. **place**), *Cammellondes* 1548 *ib* (*v*. **land**), *the manor of Shapwick called Cammels* 1569

Hutch³, *mannor farme and scyte of the mannor . . .formerly called Camells* 1591 *DLMB*), from John *Cammell* 1451 Hutch³, 1472 *DLCt*. A third manor in Shapwick was *Vinter's Fee, v. infra.*

BADBURY CLUMP & RINGS (ST 964030), *Vindogladia, Vindocladia* 4 AntIt, *æt Baddan byrig wið Win burnan* e10 ASC (A), 11 ib (D) both s.a. 901, *Baddebir'* 1244 *Ass* (p), *-bury* 1508 *DLCt, -bery* 1551 *ib, Badbury* 1468 *MinAcct* (*bosc'* de-, *parc'* de-), 1518 *HarlRoll* (*molend'* de-, *Warennam cuniculorum* de-), *a castelle now caullid Badbyri, but clerely down . . .now conyes borough in it* 1535–43 Leland, *the warren of Connyes and Copsys of Badburye* 1564 *DLComm, Badburie Castell* 1591 *DLMB*, cf. Badbury Down *infra*. On the identification of *Vindogladia, -cladia* in AntIt with Badbury Rings, an Iron Age hill-fort, *v.* A.L.F. Rivet in *Britannia* 1 61, cf. RCHMDo 5 61. *Vindocladia* (this variant represents the correct form) is a Brit name meaning '(the town with) the white ditches', from **ɥindo-* 'white, bright', and **clad-* 'to dig' or **clādo-* 'that which is dug, a ditch', *v.* K. Jackson in *Britannia* 1 81; this is clearly a reference to the chalk of which the hill-fort is constructed. The name Badbury itself apparently means 'Badda's fortified place', from the OE pers.n. *Badda* and **burh** (dat.sg. *byrig*), again with reference to the hill-fort, *v.* **hring, castel(l)**. It gives its name to Badbury hundred *supra*. This name has several analogies in other counties, including Badbury W 281, Badbury Brk 362, Badby Nth 10 and Baumber L (DEPN); the three first of these, like Badbury Rings, refer to prehistoric hill-forts, a fact which led Ekwall (DEPN) to suggest that *Badda* may have been a legendary hero associated with ancient camps (the idea finds support in the probable derivation of the pers.n. *Badda* from the base of OE *beadu* 'war', *v.* Redin 40, Anderson 130). However, the first el. of Badbury Do, and of some or all of the analogous names, may rather be pre-English in origin. Badbury Do, like Badbury W, has been identified by various historians (the first of whom was E. Guest, *Origines Celticæ*, London 1883, II 189), with the possible site of the battle of *Mons Badonicus*, in which according to Gildas the Britons won a resounding victory over the Saxons about the year 500 (Jackson 199, 202). Phonologically this identification is feasible, *Baddan-* being a possible anglicization, with substitution of OE *d* for Late Brit lenited *d*, = [ð], of a pre-English name. For an important recent discussion in support of the identification of *Mons Badonicus* with Badbury, *v.* K. Jackson, *Journal of Celtic Studies* 2 152–55.

VINTER'S FEE (lost), 1548–1750 Hutch³, *Vyntersfe* 1469 *DLCt*, *Vynterfee* 1548 *ib*, *Vynton* als. *Vynters Fee* 1591 *DLMB*, *Vinter's Fee* als. *Winterfield* 1684 Hutch³, a manor named from the family of Walter *le Vineter* 1256 FF, *v.* **fee** 'estate held on condition of feudal homage', Hutch³ 3 166.

WHITE MILL (ST 958006), *Wytemull'* 1341 *Wim*, *-mylle* 1550 *DLCt, album molendinum, Whitemellie* (sic) (*magne vie de Wymborn' ad-*) n.d. (1372) *ChrP, la Whitemulle* 1389 *DLRent, Whytemulle-* 1404, *Whitemullecroft(e)* 1433 *Marten, molend' blad' voc' Whitemull* 1429 *DLCt, Whit(e)-, Whytemyll(e), -mill(e)* 1504 *ib et passim, Whitte Mill* 1690 *Weld¹* (*the casway to-*), 'the white mill', from **hwīt** and **myln**, with **croft**, **cauce**; it gives name to White Mill Bridge in Sturminster M. par. *supra*, to Mill Lane *infra*, and probably to *Milham* 1469 *DLCt*, *v.* **hamm**.

BISHOP'S FM, *-Fm Ho* 1848 *TA*, cf. *Bishops Down* 1811 OS, 1848 *TA, Bishops Md(w)* 1848 *ib*, *v.* **biscop**; in 1416, the main manor of Shapwick was granted to the archbishop of Canterbury and the bishops of Winchester and Durham, etc, afterwards reverting to the Crown (Hutch³ 3 160). BLANDFORD DOWN (lost), 1811 OS, cf. *Gt & Lt Blandford Way* 1848 *TA*, land by the road to Blandford Forum. BOUNDARY COPSE, near the par. bdy. CRAB FM, probably an allusion to the legend of the 'Shapwick Monster' (a giant crab), *v.* Udal 293, Douch 106 (M.H., and Mr D. Hawkins). THE DROVE, cf. *Drouelane* 1469 *DLCt, le droves* 1551 *ib, The Drong at White Drove, White Drove Cl* 1848 *TA*, *v.* **drāf** 'herd, road on which cattle are driven', **lane, drong**. KING'S FM, *Kings Fm (Down)* 1848 *ib*, cf. *terra-, pratum domini regis* 1448–49 *DLCt, Kinges Leese, -Meade* 1591 *DLMB*; Shapwick was royal demesne in 1086 DB (VCHDo 3 65) and so remained until the 17th cent. (Hutch³ 3 160), *v.* **cyning**, but cf. Roger (*le*) *Kyng'* 1327 *SR*, 1332 SR. MILL LANE, *Millane* 1508 *DLCt, Mille Lane* 1547 *DLMB*, cf. *Mill Lane Cl* 1848 *TA*, leading to White Mill *supra*, *v.* **lane**, cf. *the casway to Whitte Mill* 1690 *Weld¹*, *v.* **cauce**. NEW BARN CTGS & FM.

NEW RD. PARK LANE, leading to Kingston Lacy Park in Pamphill par. *supra*. PICCADILLY LANE, a lane in the village, no doubt jocularly named from the London street. PRIORY FM, cf. *the toft or messuage called the priory* 1583 Hutch[3], *Priory Cl & Down, Priory Burnbake* 1848 *TA, the priory lands* 1869 Hutch[3], all named from the supposed cell of the priory of Sheen Sr formerly here ('site of Priory' marked 6″, but 'clearly no more than a grange' according to VCHDo 2 48), cf. *terris nuper Prioris de Schenne* 1551 *DLCt, v.* priory, burnbake. RAM LANE, 1848 *TA*, cf. *Ramlane Cl* 1848 *ib, v.* ramm. ST BARTHOLOMEW'S CHURCH, *ecclesiam de Shapwick* 1577 *AD*, cf. *cotag' voc' le Churchehouse* 1547 *DLMB*. SHAPWICK DOWN (lost), 1811 OS, *The Down* 1848 *TA*, cf. *Downefurlonge* 1591 *DLMB, v.* dūn. STEWARD'S LANE, *Stewardeslane* 1448, 1509 *DLCt*, from ME stiward 'steward (of a manor)', or from the surname *Steward*. STRAW BARROW, 1811 OS, *Shawbarrow* (sic) 1848 *TA*, possibly to be identified with *Staw Barra* 1591 *DLMB* (in bounds of Kingston Lacy), *v.* beorg, perhaps with strēaw 'straw'. SWAN WAY (COPSE). TARGET WD. VICARAGE, cf. *claus' Rectoris* 1448 *DLCt*, (*Will' West firmare*) *Rectorie* 1507 *ib, Parsones Crofte, Parsons is Furgelonge* 1509 *ib, v.* persone, croft, furlang. WILLS WD, *Willswood Coppice* 1848 *TA*, first el. well(a), WSax will(a) 'spring, stream'; a stream rises here (6″). WITHY BED.

FIELD-NAMES

The undated forms are 1848 *TA* 183. For fields in Shapwick *TA* now in Witchampton, *v.* Witchampton f.ns. *infra*. Spellings dated 1306, 1347 are Ipm, 1332 SR, Hy 6, 1474 *DLRent*, 1468[1] *MinAcct*, 1512–1514 *Pars*, 1515, 1542 Hutch[3], 1535 *Midd*, 1547, 1591 *DLMB*, 1564, 1598 *DLComm*, 1690 *Weld*[1], and the rest *DLCt*.

(a) Badbury Down (*Badbery downe* 1535, *the tenantes Downe at Badbury* 1547, *hills and downs called Badbury* 1598, from Badbury Rings *supra, v.* dūn); Bradbury (for Bad-) Plant. (*v.* prec.); Biddle Grove (cf. *Bittelgore* 1449, *v.* grāf(a), gāra, first el. probably bitula, bitela 'a beetle', cf. *biddle, bittle* 'a beetle', Barnes 49); Birchill, Priory Birchell (perhaps 'birch-tree hill', from birce and hyll; for Priory-, *v.* Priory Fm *supra*); Brick Croft; Bridge Cl; Burbush (cf. *Bur-Furlong* 1515); Chalk Pit (Cl), Green Chalk Pit Fd (cf. *Chalkepit furlonge* 1591, *v.* cealc, pytt); Champayne Cl (*v.* par. name *supra*); Cowleaze; Close at Cross Drove (*v.* cross 'crosswise', cf. The Drove *supra*); Earths Pit Fd; Froglane Cl; Further Fd; Graves Cl; Great Croft; Herring Grove (probably to be identified with *Hydynggrove* 1448, *Hedyngrove* 1449, *Hedyngegrove* 1508 (a coppice at Badbury), *Heddyngs Grove* 1564, *Heddingrove*

1598, 'grove near the headland (of a common field)', from ME **hefding** and **grāf(a))**; Hod Pit; Home Cl; Homery (probably to be associated with *Holemereshende* 1448, which is from **hol**[1] 'a hollow' or **hol**[2] 'deep', **mere**[1] 'a pool', and **ende**[1] 'end, edge'); Hook Hays (*v.* **hōc, (ge)hæg**); Horse Ham (*v.* **hamm**); Hunts Croft; Leachmoor (Cl) (*v.* **mōr** 'marshy ground', with **lece** 'stream, bog' or **lǣce**[2] 'leech'); Longbury Cl & Cmn, Longbury Gate (Cl) (second el. perhaps **burh** (dat. sg. *byrig*) 'fortified place'; these fields are near the site of Priory marked 6″, *v.* Priory Fm *supra*); Marsh (*Sapewykmerhys* 1306, *La Mersh'* 1449, *Schap(pe)wyk(k)e Marsche (yeate)* 1512–1514, *Shapswicks marsh* 1690, cf. *Michael de la Merse* 1280 *Ass, Mersche mede furlonge* Hy 6, *Merssh-* 1468[1], *Marshemede* 1469, *v.* **mersc, geat, mǣd, furlang**); Middle Fd (*Mydle-* 1591); Moor (Lane) Cl (cf. *Morelake* 1449, *le More* 1468[2], *Mowre* 1508, *le Comyn' More* 1509, *v.* **mōr** 'marshy ground', **lacu, comun**); Orchard Plot; Ovens Cl; Port Lane Cl (*venell' voc' Portlane* 1449, 'lane leading to a town', *v.* **port**[2], **lane**); Red Lake Cl (*Ridelake* 1475, 'red stream', *v.* **rēad, lacu**); Ryalls Cl; Scarcrow Cl (*v.* **scarecrow**); Seven Lds; Sheep Bridge, Sheepbridge Mdw (cf. *Sheeplandes* 1591, par. name *supra*, *v.* **scēap, land**); Small Plot; Spear Bed (cf. *Spirefurlong* 1469, *v.* **spīr**, Do dial. *spear* 'a reed'); Town End Cl; The 12 Acres; Waterslade(s) (*v.* **wæter, slæd**); Well Fd; Westbrook Cl (cf. *quandam insulam domini Regis . . . iuxta Brokeacre* 1504, *v.* **brōc, æcer**); West Hedge; White Lane Cl; White Mill Fd, Grd & Mdw (*Whitmyll Field* 1591, from White Mill *supra*); Wimborne Way Cl (cf. *Wymborneway furlonge* 1591, by the road to Wimborne M., *v.* **weg**).

(b) *Atnoke* 1509 (p) ('at the oak-tree', *v.* **atte(n), āc**); *Arundelesmede* 1448 (a surname, with **mǣd**); *Beanehill field* 1591 (*v.* **bēan**); *Blakemore* 1469 (*v.* **blæc, mōr**); *Bordelande* 1468[1] (*v.* **bord-land**); *Broade Close* 1591 (*v.* **brād**); *Buckescrofte* 1509 (the surname *Buck*, *v.* **croft**); *Castelwode* 1468[1] (*v.* **castel(l)**, perhaps with reference to Badbury Rings *supra*, **wudu**); *aqua vocat' la Chemere* 1449 (perhaps from **mere**[1] 'pool' with **ceg** 'stump'); *Clerkescote* 1508 (the surname *Clerk*, *v.* **cot**); *Cropelsherde* 1448 (*v.* **sceard** 'cleft, gap', first el. uncertain); *Estlane* 1469, *le Estrete* 1508 (*v.* **ēast, lane, strǣt**); *2 lytle hammes called Two Eies* 1591 (*v.* **ēg** 'island, land by water', **hamm**); *Everlong Furlonge* 1591 (perhaps from **ēa** 'river' and **furlang**, with later explanatory addition, but cf. PN Brk 308); *xv*[en] *Acres* 1591; *Finalley* (or *Fiu-*) Hy 6; *toft' voc' Forsters* 1474, *Forstershay* 1508 (cf. *Walter le Forester* 1332, *v.* **(ge)hæg**); *Gosemede* 1469 (*v.* **gōs** 'goose', **mǣd**); *Goultknapp furlonge* 1591 (*v.* **cnæpp** 'hillock', first el. uncertain); *ten' cum prat' voc' Halfeplace* 1509 (*v.* **half, place**, cf. *le Whole Place infra*); *Harreys Housse* 1508 (the surname *Harrie(s)*, **hūs**); *Hokydedich* 1515 (*v.* **hōcede** 'curved', **dīc**); *Howingsham* 1515 (*v.* **hamm**, probably with a surname, cf. *ten' nuper Ricardi Haveryng'* 1468[1]); *Hullewode* 1347 (*v.* **hyll, wudu**); *Jurdanestile* 1468[1], *Jorden Style* 1591 (the surname *Jordan*, **stigel** 'stile'); *cotag' cum prat' voc' Kewleys* 1508, *-Cules* 1509, *Keeles* 1591 (a surname); *in thelane* 1332 (p) (*v.* **lane**); *Langmery* 1472, *Langemere* 1509, *a voyed grounde called Lange Mery* 1547 (probably 'long pool', from **lang**[1] and **mere**[1], cf. Homery *supra*); *Litulney* Hy 6, 1469 ('little island', *v.* **lȳtel** (wk.obl. *-an*), **ēg**); *Longe Lynch furlonge* 1591 (*v.* **lang**[1], **hlinc**); *in inferior' campo* 1551 ('lower field'); *Medelane* 1448 (*v.* **mǣd**); *Metescherte Furlong'* Hy 6, *Metesherde* 1431, *Medesherde* 1448, *-furlong* 1469 (probably from **mǣd** 'meadow' and **sceard** 'gap'); *the Mydle Furlonge* 1591 (*v.* **middel**); *Oldehouselane* 1473 (*v.* **ald, hūs**); *Picked Close* 1591 (*v.* **pīcede**); *Place Ilande* 1591 (perhaps from the *Plecy* family, cf. par. name *supra, v.* **ēg-land,** WSax **īeg-land**); *tenement called Porpors* 1591 (a surname); *terre voc' Poundesfald'* 1476 (*v.* **pund-fald** 'pinfold, pound'); *ten'...voc' Potters* 1508 (a surname); *claus' voc' Pynnerds* 1547 (probably a surname); *Rabbettes* 1547, *Rabbattes ham* 1552 (a surname, *v.* **hamm**); *Rudge furlonge* 1591 (*v.* **hrycg**); *Sandell Field* 1591 (perhaps from **sand** and **hyll**); *Shapwick Mead* 1542, *pratum de Shapewyke* 1552, *Shapwikwode* 1468[1] (*v.* **mǣd, wudu**, par. name *supra*); *Skitterlinch furlonge* 1591 (*v.* **hlinc**, first el. possibly **scitere** 'a sewer'); *Smalle* 1469 (*v.* **smæl, lēah**); *le Stevelese* 1509 (*v.* **lǣs**); *Stubbelese* 1449 (*v.* **stubb, lǣs**); *tenement called Symes* 1591 (a surname); *Syrewall* 1515 (*v.* **wall**); *reche voc' la Wade* 1449 (*v.* **rǣc** 'stretch of water', (**ge**)**wæd** 'ford'); *Waterlese* 1448 (*v.* **wæter, lǣs**); *in campo frumental'* 1509 ('wheat field'); *tenement called le Whole Place* 1591 (cf. *Halfeplace supra*).

Tarrant Crawford

TARRANT CRAWFORD (ST 923035)
Tarente 1086 DB (f. 77b), *Tar(r)ent(e)* (?) c.1185 Templar, 1227 FF, 1237 Cl *et passim, Thar(r)ent(e)* 1237 Ch *et freq* to 1403 Pat, *Terent* 1242 Ch, Lib, *T(h)ar(r)enta* 1244 *Ass,* c.1270 *Seymer, litle tarenta, lyteltarente* n.d. (1372) *ChrP, Nuns Tarent* 1377 (1381) Pat, *Tarent Monachorum als. Tarent Abbey* 1582 Hutch[3], *Tarrant* 1598 *Drax Little-, Parua Craweford* 1280, *Parua Craueford'* 1288 *Ass, Parva Craweford* 1291 Tax, 1429 *EgCh, Little-, Lit(t)el Crauford* 1347 Pat *et freq* to 1386 Cl, *Parva Crauford* 1412 FA, -*Craw-, -Croweford* 1428 ib, *Craford* 1575 Saxton, *Lordshipp of Lyttle Craford within Tarrant* 1598 *Drax, Craford parva* 1599 *ib, Crawford Tarrant, Parva or Little* 1795 Boswell, *Preston or Tarrant Crawford* 1869 Hutch[3]

Named from R. Tarrant, *v.* RNs. *infra,* cf. Tarrant H. par. *supra;* *Nuns-, -Monachorum* (for *-arum*, 'of the nuns'), *-Abbey* with reference to the former abbey here, *v.* St Mary & All Saints' Abbey *infra. Little Crawford,* originally comprising a large part of the present par., is so named to distinguish it from *Great Crawford* (*q.v.*) in Spettisbury par. *supra* on the opposite bank of R. Stour, *v.* **lȳtel**. *Preston Crawford* is from Preston Fm (earlier *Tarrant Preston*) which formerly formed a tithing with (Tarrant) Crawford (Hutch[3] 3 118, cf. *Preston cum Craford*

Tithing 1664 HTax), and which is now in Tarrant Rush. par. *infra*.

ST MARY & ALL SAINTS' ABBEY (Remains of) (ST 922034), 'the Blessed Place (*locus benedictus*) upon (the) *Tar(r)ent(e)*' 1237 Ch, Pat, 'the abbey of *T(h)arent(e)*' 1237 Ch *et freq, locus* (*benedictus*) *Regine super T(h)arente, -a* 1260 FF, 1347 Pat, *Locus Richardi Episcopi* 1383 Hutch[3], *Tarent(e) Abbe* 1384 Cl, *-Abbey* 1450 *Weld*[1], 'the Cistercian house of St Mary the Virgin, Tarent...called *Locus Regine* on *Tarent*' 1449 Pat, *Tarente nunnery* 1535–43 Leland, ' *Terenta* of the Nuns' 1535 VCHDo, *v.* par. name *supra*, St Mary's Church, Tarrant Abbey Fm *infra*, VCHDo 2 87–90. *Locus Regine* 'the place of the Queen' alludes to Eleanor, wife of Hy 3, in whose patronage the abbey was placed (VCHDo 2 88), or to Joan, wife of Alexander 2 of Scotland and sister of Hy 3, who was buried here (*loc.cit.*); *Locus Richardi Episcopi* 'the place of bishop Richard' alludes to Richard le Poor, bishop of Chichester, Salisbury and Durham, who rebuilt the abbey c.1230 (*op.cit.* 87).

CROSS (Remains of), cf. 'the cross' 1280 Ch. ELLEN'S COPPICE, perhaps an allusion to Queen Eleanor, *v*. St Mary & All Saints' Abbey *supra*. LT HUNDRED COPPICE. MILL (disused), cf. 'the mill of *Tarent*' 1242 Ch, '(Abbess's) mills of *Tarente*' 1253 FF; there was a mill at Tarrant Crawford in 1086 DB (VCHDo 3 73). ST MARY'S CHURCH, 'the church of All Saints' 1235 VCHDo, 'the church of St Mary (on) *T(h)arent*' 1240, 1280 Ch, *ecclesie sancte marie de litle tarenta* n.d. (1372) *ChrP*, 'church of All Saints, Little Crauford, otherwise called St Margaret's chapel' 1377 (1381) Pat, *v.* St Mary & All Saints' Abbey *supra*. TARRANT ABBEY FM, named from St Mary & All Saints' Abbey *supra*.

FIELD-NAMES

The undated forms are 1809 *EnclA* (DRO Record Bk V p. 320). Spellings dated 1243 are FF, 1280 Ch, 1542 Hutch[3], and 1850 *TA* 219.

(a) Alders Mdw; Estate called Austens; Backsom(e) Mdw; Castle Fd; Cowleaze 1850; the Down (cf. *Donforlang, -forlong* 1280, *v*. **dūn, furlang**); Estate called Fills; 14 Acres 1850; Home Cl; Home or Cox's Fd; Estate called Kings; Little Fd; Mapperton Drove (cf. Mapperton in Almer par. *supra*); Middle Mdw; West Fd (*Westfield* 1542).

(b) Bottes 1280 (v. **butte**); *Brecche* 1280 (v. **bræc**); *Cherleberge* 1280 ('hill of the peasants', v. **ceorl** (gen.pl. -*a*), **beorg**); *Craford Mead* 1542 (v. **mæd**, par. name *supra*); *Gretebergh, Gretedich* 1243 (v. **beorg, dīc**, first el. **grēat** 'great' or **grēot** 'gravel'); *Northfield* 1542; *Rackheis* 1542 (v. **rakke, (ge)hæg**); *Radenhull* 1280 ('red hill', v. **rēad** (wk.obl. -*an*), **hyll**); *Riforlang* 1280 (v. **ryge** 'rye', **furlang**); *Selfurlang* 1280 (v. **s(e)alh** 'willow'); *Seueloze* 1280; *Southfield* 1542.

Wimborne Minster

The pars. of Colehill, Holt and Pamphill all *supra* were formed out of the old par. of Wimborne M. in 1894.

WIMBORNE MINSTER (SZ 009999)
  (æt) *Winburnan* lg ASC (A) s.a. 718, 871, 12 ib (E) s.a. 718, *þone ham æt Win burnan* e10 ib (A), 11 ib (D) s.a. 901, (æt) *Wimburnan* l10 ib (A) s.a. 961, *Winburnan monasterium* 893 (ell) Asser, (on) *Winburnan mynstre* c.1000 Saints, (æt) *Winburnan mynstre* 12 ASC (E) s.a. 871
  Winburne 1086 DB (4×), Exon, *Winborne* 1086 DB, -*borna* Exon, *Winburna* 1154–8 (1340) Ch, -*burn(e)* 1184–5 P, 1224 FF *et freq* with variant spelling *Wyn-* (to 1463 *MinAcct*) and with affix -*Ministr'* (1288 *Ass*), -*mynstre* (from 1315 Pat); *Wyn-, Winbo(u)rn(e)* n.d. (1372) *ChrP et freq* to 1547 *AD* with affix -*Mynstre, -mynstre, -Mynster, -Minstre, Wynbourn Mynster* als. *Wymbourne Mynstre* 1459 Pat, *Wynneborn Mynstre* 1474 *Wim, Winborne Minsterne* 1646 *Bartelot*
  Wimburn(e) c.1165 Osm, 1214 P, 1222 Pat *et passim* with variant spellings *Wym-* (from 1229 Pat), -*born(e)* (from 1268 *Ass*), -*bourn(e)* (from 1280 *ib*) and with affix -*Mistre* (1236 FF), -*Min(i)str(e)* (1236 *ib et passim*), -*Monaster'* (1281 FF), -*Munstre* (1286 *Wim*, 1330 FF, 1333, 1348 *Wim*, 1361 Pat), -*Mynistr'* (1288 *Ass*), -*Menstre* (1297 Cl, Pat, 1341 *Wim*, 1391 Pat), -*Mynstre* (1312 *ib et freq*), -*Mynster* (1452 *ib et freq*), *Wymburnysmynster* 1306 Cl, *Wymborn(e) Burgus* 1385, 1475 *DCMCt*, 1563 *DLCt*, *Great Wimborne* 1533 Hutch[3]
  Wumburn Ministre 1256 Pat, *Womborne* 1386 Cl

'Meadow stream', from **winn**[1], **wynn** and **burna**, originally the name of the river here, now called R. Allen, v. Canford

Bridge, RNs. *infra*, cf. Wimborne St G. par. *infra* which also takes its name from this river. The addition *-Minster* is from **mynster** '(the church of) a monastery', originally with reference to the nunnery which was founded here by Queen Cūðburh at the beginning of the 8th cent. (cf. (*in*) *monasterio quod juxta fluvium qui dicitur Winburna situm est* 705 (12) BCS 114), and which was later converted into a house of secular canons presided over by a dean, *v.* VCHDo 2 107 ff, cf. Dean's Court, The Minster *infra*. In the 9th cent. *Life of St Leoba* by Rudolf of Fulda (ed. Waitz, *Monumenta Germaniae historica Scriptores* xv. 1, pp. 118–31) Wimborne is referred to as *locus quidam antiquo gentis illius vocabulo Winbrunno vocatur, quod Latine interpretatum 'vini fons' dici potest;* for later, and equally fanciful, speculations about the origin of the name, *v.* Hutch³ 3 178–180.

WIMBORNE MINSTER STREETS AND BUILDINGS

ALLEN RD, ALLENVIEW RD, from R. Allen. BASKETTS LANE, cf. *Basketts Mdw* 1847 *TA*, John *Basket* 1475 WimCW, now Lewens Lane *q.v. infra*. BLIND LANE. CATTLE MARKET, *v.* High St. *infra*. CHAPEL LANE, from Congregational Chapel which is *The Meeting House* 1869 Map. CHURCH ST., from The Minster *infra*. COOKS ROW, *la-, le Couk(e)rewe* 1364, 1429 *Wim*, (*la-, le*) *Cokerewe* 1428 *ib et freq* to 1483 *ib, Cokerewe streate* 1564 *Glyn*, (*the*) *Cooke Ro(w)e* 1591 *DLMB*, 'row of shops where cooks sold their wares', from *cōc* and **rǣw**. CUTHBURGA RD, CUTHBURY CL, *Cutborough Close* 1593 Hutch³, cf. *Cudburghpole* 1427 *HarlRoll, Cuthbert-* (sic) 1547 *DLMB, Cutburie Poole* 1591 *ib* (in R. Stour), *Cudborough-* 1554 Hutch³, *Codtburrowe-* 1591 *DLMB, Cudbury Fd* 1847 *TA*, all named from *St Cūðburh*, founder of the AS nunnery, *v.* **pōl**¹ 'a pool', par. name *supra*. DEANS COURT LANE, cf. *via de ecclesia Sancte Cuthburge versus curiam domini Decani Wymbornie* 1349 *Wim, v.* Dean's Court *infra*. EAST BOROUGH, 1774 Hutch¹, *Crooked Borough* 1784 CleggWim, cf. West Borough *infra*, named from 'The Manor of the Borough' which 'contains the north part of the town, and consists of two streets, *East-Borough* and *West-Borough* streets... Though stiled a borough, it was never a corporation' (Hutch¹ 2 76). This 'new town extension', originally part of the manor of Kingston Lacy, was probably laid out in the early 13th cent. (Taylor, DoNHAS **89** 168–9), and the following may belong here: *in novo Burgagio de Wymbornemunst(e)re* 1278, 1321, *forum de la Burgage* 1311, *le Burgage* 1477 all *Wim*, cf. also Richard *de Burgh'* 1332 SR, *v.* **burgage, burh**. The S end of East Borough was earlier *viam (regalem) de la Blakelane* 1311, 1350 *Wim, Blakelane* 1432–1501 *ib, Black Lane* 1869 Map, *v.* **blæc, lane**. EAST ST., cf. *viam...de Byestebrok' versus ecclesiam Sancte Cithburge* (sic) *virginis* 1306 *Wim, v. Sluggeslane*, East Brook, The Minster *infra*. HANHAM RD, from the family of *Hanham*, v. Hutch³ 3 230. HIGH ST., *Highe Streate* 1591 *DLMB*, but called *Markett St.* 1869 Map and part of it formerly also *Cheapside* (n.d., CleggWim 175), cf. *in foro decani Wymbornie* 113 *Wim*, *le lyeu de la market le Dean de Wymborne* 1426 *ib*, *locum mercati* 1427 *HarlRoll*, *Mondayshamell'* 1468 *MinAcct*, *schamellys* 1495, 'the fish shambles' 1499 WimCW, *le yarne markett* 1564 *Glyn*, *the Marckett Place* 1591 *DLMB*, *The Corn Markett* 1869 Map, v. **market, cēap** 'market', **sc(e)amol**; on early markets in Wimborne, including a Monday market, v. Hutch³ 3 180. JULIAN'S RD, named from Julian's Bridge *infra*. KING ST., 1869 Map, *Kings streate* 1591 *DLMB*, cf. *Kings Plot* 1847 *TA*; Wimborne M. was royal demesne from the time of DB, v. VCHDo 3 65. KNOBCROOK, a st.n. in TPlan, v. *infra*. LEGG LANE, *Legg Cl*, *Legg Lane* (*Gdn*) 1847 *TA*, v. **leg** 'a long narrow meadow'. LEIGH RD, cf. *viam...de Wymborne versus Leghe* 1286 *Wim*, v. Leigh in Colehill par. *supra*. LEWENS LANE, from Lewens *infra*; earlier Basketts Lane *supra*. MARKET WAY, named from the modern Cattle Market, cf. High St. *supra* for earlier markets in Wimborne. MILL LANE, named from *The Town Mill* 1869 Map, perhaps identical with *Milstrete* 1483 *Wim*, v. **myln, strǣt**, cf. *molendinum fullonum* 1427 *ib*, *molendini domini aquatici* 1427 *HarlRoll*, *a mille at Winburn town ende* 1535–43 Leland, *molend' aquat' granatic' infra Wymborne Mynster* 1564 *Glyn*, *Mill Md* 1847 *TA*, although some of the above forms may strictly belong under *Walford Mill*, v. Walford Bridge & Fm *infra*; for other early mills in or near Wimborne M., cf. *Bydemulle, Brigg Mills, Bucket(t)'s Mill(s)* all *infra*, *Caynesmilne* and *Moremyll'* in Pamphill par. *supra*. NEW BOROUGH RD, from the ecclesiastical par. of 'New Borough and Leigh' formed in 1876 (Kelly). POOLE RD, cf. *viam de Wymborn' versus Caneford'* 1286 *Wim*, *via regia...versus la Poole* 1427 *ib*, *Poole Lane* 1591 *DLMB*, 1847 *TA* (*-Mdw*), v. Poole par. and Canford M. par. *supra*. PRIORS WALK, probably so called because a former house in this street was thought to be the birthplace of the poet Matthew *Prior* 1664–1721; it was formerly called *Lockeslane* 1356 *Wim*, *Lukes Lane* 1591 *DLMB*, 1869 Map, cf. *close called Lockes* 1591 *DLMB*, from the surname *Lock*. REDCOTTS (RD & LANE), named from *Rodecotyscroft* (*in Westrete iuxta-*) 1411 *Wim*, (*terr' voc'*) *Rodecote(s)* 1472–7 *Weld¹*, 1483 *Wim*, (*an orcharde neare unto*) *Reddcottes* 1591 *DLMB*, from the family of Maud *Rotecod* 1327 *SR*, cf. St Margaret's Almshouses in Pamphill par. *supra*, West St. *infra*, v. **croft**. ST CATHERINE'S, *Seynt Kateryns* 1518 *HarlRoll*, *St Catharine's* als. *Le Hermitage* 1550 Hutch³, 'messuage and garden...called the Hermitage' 1593 *ib*, *Catherines* (*Fd*), *Saint Catherines* (a field) 1847 *TA*; thought by Hutch³ 3 226, 228, 243 to have been the site of a chapel, but in view of the above forms, it was clearly rather (or also) a hermitage, cf. the *Herimite* associated with this place in 1518 *HarlRoll*, and cf. the f.n. Anchor Md *infra*. THE SQUARE, 1869 Hutch³. VICTORIA RD, cf. *vie Regie versus Seint Margarete* 1483 *Wim*, cf. St Margaret's Almshouses in Pamphill par. *supra*. WEST BOROUGH, 1774 Hutch¹, *Straight Borough* 1784 CleggWim, cf. East Borough *supra*; the S end of West Borough was earlier *La Pylrystret* 1390, *la Pyllery-* 1411, *Peilleri-* 1417, *Pillerystret(e)* 1483 all *Wim*, *Pyllorie-, Pillorie Stre(e)te* 1591 *DLMB*, *Pillory St.* 1869 Map, v. **pillory**; another instrument of punishment in Wimborne was *le Cokelynstole* 1527 DCMCt ('the cucking-stool'). WEST ROW. WEST ST., *Weststrete* 1281 *Wim*, (*le*) *Westret(e)* 1353 *ib et freq* to 1591 *DLMB*, v. **west,** strǣt; the E end of West St. was earlier (or alternatively) *Puddle St.* 1869 Map, no doubt to be identified with the street which 'presents a stagnant pool from side to side' (Hutch³ 3 180, quoting 2nd ed.), *v.* **puddel**.

Lost street-names include *le Chauntrey strete* 1411 *Wim* (near *Cimiterium Sancte Cutburge*, cf. The Minster *infra*), *Chaunt(e)ristrete* 1426, 1457 *ib* (cf. 'the chantry of *Wymbourn Mynstre*' 1365 Pat, *ten' in le Chauntery* 1476 *Weld*¹, *Cantre de Wymborne* 1518 *HarlRoll*, 'a toft called the Great Chantry' 1593 Hutch³, *v.* **chantry, strǣt**, cf. Great or Brembre's Chantry in The Minster *infra*); *Clackestret* 1318, 1359, *Clakstret* 1332 *Wim* (perhaps 'street noisy with chatter', from ME *clacke* 'din of speech' (from c.1440 NED), but cf. **clacc** 'hill' and the surname *Clack* evidenced in Do, e.g. John *Clak'* 1332 SR (Charminster)); *Colly Lane* 1560 *DLCt* (probably in Wimborne, perhaps from the surname *Colly(n)*); *Crabbelane* 1351 *HarlRoll* (p), 1385 *DCMCt* (p), 1427 *HarlRoll*, *-land* (sic) 1427 *ib* (p), *Crablane* 1468 *MinAcct* (*v.* **crabbe** 'crab-apple (tree)'); *la Grenestret(e)* 1288, 1373 *Wim*, *le Greynestret* 1350 *ib*, *Grenestrete* 1591 *DLMB* (*v.* **grēne**¹ 'green'); *Kaytildestret'* 1330 *Wim*, *Kayteldstrete* 1341 *ib* (first el. perhaps a surname); *Pudding Lane* 1591 *DLMB* (no doubt analogous with the same name in London, where **pudding** probably meant 'butchers' offal', *v.* Ekwall, Ln 102–3); *Sluggeslane* 1349 *Wim* (the ME surname *Slug(g)*, found in 1332 SR; according to CleggWim 111, this was an earlier name for East St. *supra*); *Stoke-* 1547, *Stocke Lane* 1591 *DLMB* (from **stoc** 'secondary settlement', or **stocc** 'tree-trunk'); *Yarne Closse Streate* 1591 *ib* (cf. *le yarne markett* 1564 *Glyn*, *v.* **gearn** 'yarn', **clos(e)**).

Buildings include *Countess of Exeters Almshouses* 1869 Map (founded by Gertrude Courtenay, Marchioness of Exeter in 1557, *v.* Hutch³ 3 249, and now known as the Courtenay Hospital); *libere scole* 1564 *Glyn*, *libere schole grammaticalis regine Elizabethe* 1639 Hutch³ (founded 1496, now Queen Elizabeth's School, cf. *le Scolehouse infra*); *the towne hospitall of Wimbourne* 1647 SC (cf. Alice *atte Spitele* 1327 *SR*, *iv acr' hospital'* 1427 *HarlRoll*, *v.* **atte, spitel**, cf. *Seynt Mary hous infra*); *The Markett House* 1869 Map (cf. High St. *supra* for early references to markets in Wimborne); *La-, Le Priest(s') Houses* 1639 Hutch³, *The Priest's House* 1869 Map (now a museum, *v.* **prēost**); *Pybakers' house* 1495 WimCW (perhaps in Cooks Row *supra*); *shoppam Sancte Marie* 1429, *domus Sancte Marie* 1444, 1456 all *Wim*, *Seynt-, Saynt-, Seint Mary-, -Mar(i)e hous(e)* 1456 *ib et freq* to 1524 WimCW, 'tenement *late called Saynte Marye howse*' 1552 ib (according to Hutch³ 3 223 'an ancient hospital, or rather workhouse, called St Mary's House, which was once set apart for the relief and employment of the poor and impotent', cf. CleggWim 167); *ecclesiam beati Petri* 1330, 1473 *Wim*, *cimiterio Sancti Petri* 1444 *ib*, *Seynt Peter's chyrchyard* 1530 WimCW, *-church* 1532 ib, *ye new chirche hows otherwise called Saynct Peter's* 1544 ib, *the church(e)howse (which was once St Peter's Church)* 1566, 1573 ib, *St Peters yarde* 1583 ib, *the new towne house als. Church Howse* 1591 *DLMB* (for this church, which once stood near where The Square *supra* now is, *v.* Hutch³ 3 180, 226, 228, CleggWim 168, cf. *le cherch house* 1495 WimCW which perhaps refers to a different building, before the conversion of St Peter's, *v.* **cirice, hūs**); *le Scolehouse* 1564 *Glyn*, *Le Scholehouse* 1639 Hutch³, *The School House* 1869 Map (cf. *libere scole supra*); *the Towne Hall* 1591 *DLMB* (*v.* Hutch³ 3 228, cf. *ecclesiam beati Petri supra*); *le Werke house* 1477 *Wim*, *le Wurkehous* 1479 WimCW, *le Workehous*

1483 *Wim* (*-ad finem occid' Turris ecclesie de Wymborn'*) (cf. *The Work House* 1869 Map, built 1759, *v.* Hutch³ 3 230); 'the *yelde halle'* 1499 WimCW (*v.* **gild-hall**). On buildings in Wimborne, *v.* further CleggWim 162ff.

Inns (spellings dated 1824 are from Pigot) include *the Angell* 1663 Hutch³ (*house called-*, *the signe of-*); *Case is Altered* 1824; *Coach & Horses* 1824; *Crown* 1664 CleggWim, *Crown Hotel* 1824; *the crystoffer* 1542 WimCW (*tenement agaynst the syne of-*); *the George* 1524 WimCW, 1547 *DLMB* (*tenement voc' The Signe of-*) *et freq* to 1824, *ye Jorge* 1548 WimCW; *Green Man* 1824; *Greyhound Inn* 1847 *TA*; *King's Arms* 1824; *King's Head* 1824; *Mail Coach* 1824; *New Bell* 1824; (*the*) *New Inn* 1681 CleggWim, 1824; *Old Bell* 1824; *Red Lion* 1824; *Rising Sun* 1824; *Silent Women* (sic) 1824, -*Woman* 1847 *TA*; *Swan* 1824; *Three Lions* 1824; *White Hart* 1824. On these and other inns in Wimborne, *v.* further CleggWim 169ff.

CANFORD BRIDGE (SZ 017992), 1593 Hutch³, (-*Md*) 1822 *EnclA*, *great Canford bridge* 1591 *DLMB*, named from Canford Magna par. *supra*. It was earlier *Aldewynebrigg' extra Wynburn'* 1268 *Ass*, *Ald(e)winesbrigg(e)*, *Aldwynesbrigg' subter Wymborn'*, *A(y)lwynes-*, *Alwinesbrigg'*, *Alwynesbrugg' subter Wymburn'* 1280 *ib*, QW, *pontem Aldewini* n.d. (1372) *ChrP*, *Alwynsbrygge* c. 1500 *Fry*, *Aleyn bridg(e)* 1535–43 Leland, *Aleynsbrydge* 1543 *Ct*, *Alwins Bridge* 1618 *Map*, *Aldwyn Bridge* 1620 Hutch³, 'Ealdwine's bridge', from the OE pers.n. *Ealdwine* and **brycg**, cf. Nicholas *atte Brigge* 1327 *SR*, William *atte Brygge* 1340 NI, *v.* **atte**. As pointed out by Ekwall RN 4 and Fägersten 88–9, the bridge gave name to R. Allen, earlier called *Wimborne*, *v.* RNs. *infra*. The *Ealdwine* in question is perhaps the *Aldwin* who held TRE an unidentified manor of 1 hide called *Winburne* in 1086 DB (*v.* VCHDo 3 104, Fägersten 88 fn. 1, cf. Eyton 111).

DEAN'S COURT (SZ 010997), 1795 Boswell (-*or Deanery*), *curiam domini Decani Wymbornie* 1349 *Wim*, *the deanry* 1593 Hutch³, *Deanes Court* 1664 HTax, formerly the residence of the dean of the College of Wimborne Minister (*collegium de Wymborne* 1518 *HarlRoll*), cf. *The Deane hath a fair house* 1535–43 Leland, *v.* Hutch³ 3 184, 232, VCHDo 2 107ff, The Minster *infra*; belonging to *The Manor of the Deanry* (1774 Hutch¹ 2 76) were *campus domini Decani Wymbornie* 1349 *Wim*, (*le*) *Denesfelde* 1427 *HarlRoll*, *Deanfelde* 1518 *ib*, *gardinum domini decani* 1518 *ib*, *Deans Gdn* 1847 *TA*, *Dean's Mead* 1593 Hutch³, *Deanes Coppice* e18 *Weld¹*, *v.* **dene**, **court**, **feld**, cf. also High St. *supra*, *Evans* and *The Leaze infra*. The ancient Fish Pond here (6″) may be that referred to as *vivarium regis* 1261 Cl.

EAST BROOK (SU 013001), *By-*, *Biestebro(u)k'* 1286 *Wim et freq* to 1359 *ib*, *By Ystebroke* 1411 *ib*, *Byyestebroke* 1426 *ib*, *Estbroke* 1444 *ib et freq* to 1567 Hutch³ ('the bridge of-'), *Isebroke-*, *Isebek* (sic) *Bridges* 1535–43 Leland, *Eastbrooke* 1591 *DLMB*, *Eastbrook great Bridge, -little Bridge* 1869 Map, '(place) to the east of the brook', from bī, ēastan, brōc (with reference to R. *Wimborne*, now R. Allen).

LEIGH PARK (SZ 024995), *Leye park* 1348 Ipm, (*postes Railes et palicia de*) *Le(i)gh'park'* 1374 *MinAcct*, *Leyghparke* 1463 *ib*, *Lye Parke* 1477 *Wim*, 1583 *SPDom*, *Lyghe parke* 1495 WimCW, *Lytell park of Canford* 1519 *Ct*, *the lyttle parke or Leyth parke* 1587 *DCMDeed*, named from Leigh in Colehill par. *supra*, 'little' in relation to Canford Park in Canford M. par. *supra*, *v.* **park, lȳtel**; on the medieval deer-park here, *v.* Wilson, DoNHAS 98 6–9.

THE MINSTER (SZ 009999), 'the church of *Winburne*' 1189–99 France, *ecclesiam de Wymburneminstr'* 1244 *Ass et freq*, *capelle regis de Winburn'* 1246 Cl *et freq*, *scalarium cymiterii beate cuhtburge virginis* 113 *Wim*, *ecclesia Sancte Cithburge* (sic) *virginis* 1306 *ib*, *ecclesia Sancte Cudburge virginis* 1313 *ib et freq* with variant spellings *-C(h)ut(h)burge-*, 'king's free chapel of St Cuthburga in *Wymb(o)urne Min(i)stre'* 1328 Cl, 1440 Pat *et freq*, *chirch of Saynt Cutborrowgh* 15 *Wim*, *libere capelle regis sive ecclesie collegiate de Wymborn Minster* 1511 Hutch³, *The Collegiate Church* 1869 Map, perhaps on the site of the AS nunnery founded by Queen Cūðburh (*v.* par. name *supra*) and of *ecclesiam de Winburne* 1086 DB (VCHDo 3 70), cf. also the chapel (*ecclesiola*) in Wimborne belonging to the abbey of Horton at the same date (ib 3 81). In the Minster is the Lady Chapel ('the chapel of St Mary' 1495 WimCW, *owre lady chappell* 1506 ib), and the Great or Brembre's Chantry (*magne Cantar'...voc' Brenbrischauntry* 1577 *AD*) founded by dean Thomas *de Brembre* 1351 *HarlRoll*, *v.* **chantry**, VCHDo 2 110, and the lost st.n. *le Chauntrey strete supra*. The Minster gives name to *le Churchestile* 1483 *Wim*, *Cherchstyle* 1495 WimCW ('the house at-', on E side of church, *v.* **stigel**), cf. also *the howse att the chyrche end* 1504 WimCW, *the chyrche yarde* 1506 ib, *church lytten walls* 1590 ib (*v.* **līc-tūn**).

ODENHAM (lost), 1350, 1427 *HarlRoll* (*camp' vocat'*-), *Ode(a)nhamfelde* 1518 *ib*, *Odyham* n.d. AD I (p), to be identified with *Odeham* 1086 DB, a manor held by the Bishop of London and assessed at ½ hide (VCHDo 3 73, 129), thus confirming the supposition made by Eyton 88, 113f that *Odeham* was in the old par. of Wimborne M. The ME forms in *Oden-* show that the first el. is the OE pers.n. *Od(d)a* (gen.sg. *-an*) (cf. Fägersten 87, Kökeritz 124), this *Od(d)a* being no doubt the man called *Ode* in DB (*Odo* the treasurer (*thesaurarius*) in Exon) who held TRE a manor called simply *Winburne* which was also assessed at ½ hide and which never paid geld (VCHDo 3 68, 129), the evidence thus suggesting a division of a one-hide unit at some earlier date. The second el. is **hamm** 'enclosure, river meadow', with **feld**. The location of this place is suggested by *camp' vocat' Odenham iuxta Cudburghpole* 1427 *HarlRoll*; *Cudburghpole* was a pool in R. Stour, cf. Cuthburga Rd, Cuthbury Cl in st.ns. *supra*.

SELAVESTUNE (lost), 1086 DB (VCHDo 3 100), an unidentified manor assessed at 4 hides and 1½ virgates, almost certainly in Badbury hundred (op.cit. 3 129) and, like prec., supposed by Eyton 88, 113f to have been in the old par. of Wimborne M. The second el. is **tūn** 'farm', the first is probably the OE pers.n. *Sǣlāf*, although an OE pers.n. *Sigelāf* would be a possible alternative (on *Se-* for *Sige-* in DB, *v.* Feilitzen 352, 360).

WALFORD BRIDGE (SU 009007) & FM
Walteford 1086 DB, c.1140 (1340) Ch, 1225 FF (p), 1268 *Ass* (p), 1275 RH (p), 1280 *Ass* (p), 1307, 1326 FF, *Ass*, 1350 *Wim* (*Ponte de-*), 1365 Inq aqd, Pat, *-forde* 1412 Cl, *Waltelforth'* (sic) 1280 *Ass* (p), *Waltford* 1323 Pat, *Walte-fford* 1409 *Midd*
Waltesford c. 1140 *AddCh*, 1154–8 (1340) Ch
Welteford l13 *Wim* (p)
Waldeford 1280 QW, *Ass*, 1326 *ib*, *Waldford* 1620 Hutch[3]
Walford(e) 1535 VE, 1547 *DLMB* (*molend' follonicu' apud-*), 1554 Hutch[3] (*East-*), 1560 *DLCt* (*-brydge*), 1591 *DLMB* (*-Bridge, -Mill*) *et passim*, *-Fm* 1869 Hutch[3], *Walleford bridg of 4 archis* 1535–43 Leland, *hundr' de Wallef(f)ord* 1552 *DLCt*, *Waleford Bridge* 1591 *DLMB*, *Whafford Fm* 1861 Hutch[3]
Wallsford als Wayford Bridge 1791 Boswell

Probably 'shaky, unsteady ford, i.e. ford difficult to cross', from w(e)alt and ford, as suggested by Ekwall DEPN. The first el. has been taken to be a pers.n. in the two 12th cent. *Waltesford* forms (unless these are for *Waltefford*), and shows influence from w(e)ald 'woodland' in some forms. The road from Cranborne into Wimborne crosses R. Allen here. For possible earlier references to the mill(s) here (*ii mol' aquatic' vocat' Waltefordmylles* 1508 Cecil, *Waltfford' myll* 1578 Fry, *Walford Mill* 1869 Map), v. Mill Lane *supra*.

ALLENDALE, from R. Allen. BIG LEAZE HOLE, apparently a deep place in R. Stour, named from The Leaze *infra*, v. hol[1], cf. Founder Hole *infra*. EVANS (lost), *Evans's Court* 1593 Hutch[3] (3 232), *Evans (manor)* 1774 Hutch[1] (2 76), from the surname *Evans*, cf. Edith *Evinns* 1591 *DLMB*; it belonged to the *Manor of the Deanry*, v. Dean's Court *supra*. FIMARO, a house-name. FOUNDER HOLE, in R. Stour, cf. Big Leaze Hole *supra*, first el. perhaps to be associated with ModE *founder* 'to sink, etc'. GREEN CLOSE DAIRY, *Green Close (Orchd)* 1847 *TA*, v. Green Close in Colehill par. *supra*. GRIFFIN HOTEL. JULIAN'S BRIDGE, *Juliane bridge* 1535–43 Leland, *Jelian-* 1591 *DLMB*, *Gilian-* 1593 Hutch[3], *Julian-* 1822 *EnclA*, *Julien Bridge* 1869 Hutch[3], cf. *Julian Bridge Fd*, *Julian Island* 1847 *TA*, probably named from (the family of) Walter *Julien* t. John Hutch[3] (3 268), witness in a deed concerning St Margaret's Almshouses in Pamphill par. *supra*, as supposed by Hutch[3] 3 182, cf. *pons de Wymbourn'* 1341 *Wim*, Thomas *atte Brigge* 1327 *SR*, *-atte Brygge* 1333 *Wim*, John *atte Brygge* 1353 *ib*, v. atte, brycg. KNOBCROOK, a quarter of the town near R. Allen (6"), also the name of a short curving lane (TPlan), perhaps from knob 'a knoll' and crōc 'a bend' (either in the river or in the lane), cf. *Crokelandes* 1427 *HarlRoll* which may contain the latter el. with land 'strip in a common field', and v. Knob's Crook in Woodlands par. *infra*. THE LEAZE, *Hr, Lr & Middle Lease* 1847 *TA*, probably to be identified with *le Deneslese* 1427 *HarlRoll*, *Deaneslease* 1518 *ib*, *Deans-Lease* 1550 Hutch[3], 'the dean's pasture', v. lǣs, Dean's Court *supra*. LEIGH FM, cf. *Leigh Cowleaze* 1847 *TA*, from Leigh in Colehill par. *supra*. LEWENS, from a family here in the 17th cent., cf. Robert- 1620 WimCW, Henry *Lewen* 1664 HTax. ROWLANDS, 1561 Hutch[3], 1847 *TA* (-*Plot*), *Reulonde* (probably for *Rou-*) 1350 *HarlRoll*, *Roulond*

1355 *Wim, Littell Rowlandes* 1591 *DLMB*, from rūh (wk.obl.
rūwan) 'rough' and **land** 'cultivated land, strip in a common
field', with lȳtel. ST JOHN'S, an ecclesiastical par., named from
the church of St John the Evangelist. STOURFIELD, by R. Stour.
WESTFIELD, *West Fd 5 & 12 Acres* 1847 *TA*, W of the town.

FIELD-NAMES

The undated forms are 1847 *TA* 246; fields in this *TA* but now in Colehill,
Holt or Pamphill are included under those pars. all *supra*. Spellings dated
c.Ed 1, 1312, 1476, 1553, 1554, Eliz, 1569, 1593, 1639, 1800, and 1869 are
Hutch", 1288 *Ass*, 1327 *SR*, 1332 *SR*, 1347, 1350, 1351, 1427, 1518 *HarlRoll*,
n.d. (1372) *ChrP*, 1400, 1403 Cl, 1413 SoDoNQ (1917), 1468 *MinAcct*, 1474,
e18 *Weld*[1], 1481, 1495, 1505, 1524, 1538, 1548, 1566, 1569[2] WimCW, c.1500
Fry, 1512, 1515 *Pars*, 1541, 1564 *Glyn*, 1547, 1591 *DLMB*, 1552 *DLCt*, 1598
DLComm, 1664 HTax, and the rest *Wim*. Some of the lost f.ns. in (b) may
well have been in the area out of which the new pars. of Colehill, Holt and
Pamphill were formed in 1894.

(*a*) Anchor Md (probably to be associated with *Aumcorite de Wymbourn'*
(*biestebrouk' ex opposito-*) 1359, *Anchoriste* (*toft. . .ex parte boriali-*) 1427,
which are from *anchoret, -ite* (from 1460 NED), *anchorist* (from 1651 ib) 'a
recluse, a hermit', and where the use is apparently elliptical for 'anchorite
cell, i.e. hermitage', cf. St Catherine's (st.n.) and East Brook both *supra*);
Barrow Pool Shallow 1869 (in R. Stour, named from nearby barrow (Hutch[3]
3 179), perhaps that marked 6″ near Big Leaze Hole, cf. John *atte Berghe* 1331,
v. atte, beorg); Bells (cf. f.ns. in Holt par. *supra*); Boxleys and Rashleys (cf.
Thomas *Boxly* 1561 Hutch[3] 3 249, who gave lands for charity); Broad Mdw
(*Brademede* n.d. (1372), *Brade Mede* 15, *v.* brād, mǣd; the forms
Bradmede 1468, c.1500, *Brodemede* 1468, 1547, *Broadmeade* 1591, may belong
here or to a name of identical origin in the manor of Kingston Lacy, *v.*
Pamphill par. *supra*); Budge Mdw; Bullpits (*v.* bula, pytt); Canford Bridge
Fd (from Canford Bridge in Canford M. par. *supra*); Coneygar (*v.* coninger);
Delph Fd & Orchd (cf. *depedelf'* 1468, *v.* dēop, (ge)delf 'pit'); 18 Acres; 4
Acres; Giddy Lake Plot(*v.* gydig); Goods Plot (cf. Roger *Gud* 1327, Richard
le God' 1332); Green Hayes (*Les Greneheyes* 1427, *v.* grēne[1], (ge)hæg);
Lavender Acres (no doubt where lavender grew); Leggs and Bldgs (probably
a surname *Legg*, but cf. Legg Lane *supra*); Little Bridge 1791 Boswell; Little
Md 1800; Mayo's Fd; (Islands near) Paper Mill, Paper Mill Fd; The Parks
(possibly from pearroc 'small enclosure', but cf. Leigh Park *supra*); Press
Mdw (*Prestemede* 1411, 1552, *Presse Meade* 1591, 1598, 'priests' meadow',
from prēost and mǣd, perhaps to be associated with *Preston* 1553 (*West-*),
1554 (*Little-*), *Preston Meade* 1591, 'priests' farm', *v.* tūn); Reynolds Plot
(cf. Walter *Renald'* 1332, John *Reynold* 1417); Rick Yd; Roman T (no doubt
so called from its shape); Rushy 7 Acres; Searls (cf. Richard-, Walter *Cerle*
1332, John *Serle* 1332, 1664); Selry Fd; Stoney Croft; Streets Mdw (cf.
Richard *Streete* 1664); Sunmer Fd; 10 Acres; Toll House; Walfords 5 & 14
Acres (from Walford *supra*).

(b) *lande sometime Ankettells* 1591 (cf. *ten' nuper Willelmi Anketell'* 1468); *Beckyn* 1569 (perhaps (ge)bēacon 'a beacon'); *Bydemylne* 1288 (p), *stangnum* (sic for *stagnum* 'pond') *de Bydemulle* 1321, 1322, *Bydemul(l)more* 1410, 1411, (*gurgitem aque vocat'*) *Bydemyl(le)watere* 1467, 1501, *Bedemyll Water* 1473 (possibly 'mill with a pond', or 'mill in a valley', from byden 'a vessel, a hollow', and myln, with mōr and wæter; however, in view of the absence of *u*-spellings, Professor Löfvenberg thinks the first el. is perhaps rather an OE pers.n. *Bida*, *v*. DEPN s.n. Biddenden K); *Bylcombe* 1474 (*v*. cumb); *La Blak(e)hall(e)* n.d. (1372) (*curia...voc'*-), 1382 (*placeam terre nuper edificat'...voc'*-) ('the black hall', *v*. blæc, h(e)all); *Brigg Mills* 1476, *Brygemyll* 1518 ('mill at the bridge', *v*. brycg, myln); *Bucket(t)'s Mill(s)* Eliz, 1593, 1639 (near Canford Bridge in Canford M. par. *supra*, named from the family of Thomas *Boket* 1481); *Cal(l)ys* 1404, 1505, 1548 (a surname); *Cartereshouwe, unius houwe nuper Carter* 1427 (the surname *Carter* with howe 'enclosure'); *Champaynes* 1427 (cf. 'land of Thomas *Champeyne*' 1413); *la Charnel* 1404 (*v*. charnel 'a mortuary'; on the charnel house in Wimborne, *v*. Hutch³ 3 227); *Clavells Lande* 1591 (the surname *Clavell*); *Le-, La Clefhous* 1305, 1315 (*v*. clif, hūs); 'Clements' house' 1495; *ten'...Ducis (Lancastr')* *vocat'* *Cokro(se)isplace* 1450, 1456 (*v*. place; first el. probably a surname); *Corellys-, Corylliscroft(e)* 1411 (at East Brook *supra*, *v*. croft, perhaps to be associated with *Curlesmylle* in Colehill par. *supra*; first el. probably a surname); (*the*) *Croked Close* 1547, 1591 (*v*. croked); *Crokkerne fyldys* 1512, *-fyldis* 1515 ('place where pots were made', from crocc and ærn, with feld); *la Croiz* 1307 (p), *atte Croys, -Crois* 1316 (p) (cf. *Ric' de Cruce* 1333, *tenement' Ricardi de la Croyz* 1335, *v*. crois 'a cross', atte); *Dedde Poolee* (*a lyte poole...callyd-*) 1512 (*v*. dēad, pōl¹, cf. *Deadpool* Sr 125); 'a cottage called *Dedhouse*' 1495, cf. *la Charnel supra*); *de La Dene* 1244 *Ass* (p), 1307 FF (p) (*v*. denu); *Dillington* 1541; *duyes* 1548 (possibly an inn, cf. Thomas *Dewye* 1566); *pontem orientalem* 1512, *Eastebridge, East Bridge* 1591 (*v*. ēast, brycg); (*campum voc'*) *Eldebury* 1312, 1333, 1411, *Oldebury* 1350, *Eldbury* 1427, *Eldeburyfelde* 1518 ('old fortified place', from (e)ald and burh (dat.sg. *byrig*), with feld); *Etthulle* c.Ed 1 (*v*. hyll); *Finchcombe* 1593 (*v*. finc, cumb); *Freeman-, Free Mann Meade* 1591 (cf. *Fremanshowe (claus' voc'-*) 1468, *v*. frēo-mann, mæd, howe); *Gaueleresshegge, -heighe* 1427 (*v*. hecg, (ge)hæg, cf. Gilbert *Gaueler*' 1332); *le Grynye* 1412, *clausum voc' greny* 1427² (perhaps from grēne¹ 'green' and ēg, ī(e)g 'island'); *les Hammes* 1427 (*v*. hamm); *Hardemanneshouwe* 1427 (cf. *1 houwe nuper Johannis Hardeman* 1427, *v*. howe); *atte Hide* 1327, *-Hyde* 1332, 1341, 1355 all (p) (*v*. atte, hīd, cf. Roger *de la Hyde* 1288); *Holemor* 1353 (*v*. hol², mōr¹); *the How, the Three How Closes* e18 (cf. *clausis...vocat' Howys* 1427, *v*. howe 'enclosure'); *in the hurne* 1363 (p) (*v*. hyrne); *atte Hurst* 1340, 1347 both (p) (*v*. atte, hyrst); 'tenement called *Jolywattes*' 1400, 1403 (a surname or nickname, *Watt* being a pet-form for *Walter*); *Langehe(g)hes* 1347, 1350 (*v*. lang¹, (ge)hæg); 'tenement called *Mapoudre*' 1400, 1403 (*v*. mapuldor 'maple-tree'); *Middle Close* e18; *Moore Closes* e18; *Mustardesplace* 1427 (the surname *Mustard*, *v*. place); *the Parsons acre* e18; *de la Pyle* 1311 (p) (*v*. pīl 'a stake'); *Pittmans Lande* 1591 (cf. Robert *Pytman* 1569²); '*certi putei* of pasture called *Pitts*' 1593 (near Julian's Bridge, *v*. pytt); *Plecyes* 1427 (cf. John *Plecy* who held 6 messuages in 1407 Hutch³

3 233); *Ponde Close* 1547 (*v.* **ponde**); *Scrivener's Mead* 1800; *tenement' voc' Sevyars* 1493 (cf. Thomas *Sevier* 1591); *Seynt Ellyn's Cros* 1524 (*v.* **cros**); *Seynte Sythes felde* 1564, *St. Scythe's Field* 1593 (no doubt dedicated to *St Sytha* (Zita of Lucca)); *grangia...voc' Squyers barn'* 1402 (the surname *Squier*, *Squire*, *v.* **bere-ærn**); *le Sterte* 1427 (*v.* **steort**); *Great Stonehill* e18; *the Stony Close* e18; *Vylescombeshouwe* 1427 (*v.* **howe**; first part of the name probably a surname); *Water Close* e18 (cf. *atte Water(e)* 1327, 1332, 1351 all (p), *v.* **atte, wæter**); *croft'...voc' La Worthe* c.Ed 1 (*v.* **worð**).

CRANBORNE CHASE

bosc' de Craneburn' 1234 Cl, 1393 *MinAcct*, *chaceam de-, foresta de Craneburn'* 1236 Cl, *foresta de Cranebourne* 1280 *Ass*, *chacie...de Craneburn* 1280 QW, 'chace of *Craneburn'* 1281 Pat *et passim*, 'the king's chace of *Cramburne'* 1461 ib, *chacea domine Regine*, *Craneborne Chacea* 1547 *Ct*, *Cranburne Chace* 1618 *Map*, *Cranborne Chase* 1620 Hutch³, named from Cranborne par. *infra*, since the lords of the manor of Cranborne were always lords of the Chase, *v.* **chace**. The bounds of the Chase (both the 'in-bounds' or 'short bounds' which extended into Wiltshire, and the 'out-bounds' or 'large bounds' which extended into both Wiltshire and Hampshire) are described in 1280 *Ass* (203, 204, 205, 783, the last printed in QW, cf. also Hutch³ 3 407) and in 1620 Hutch³ 3 415, and are mapped in 17 *CecilMap* (Legal 231/15) and in 1618 *Map* (printed in A. Pitt Rivers, *King John's House*, 1890), cf. 'the chace and woods called *le Outewod* of *Crambourne'* 1486 Pat, *v.* **ūt(e), wudu**. The nine parks in the Chase included three in Dorset, viz Alderholt Park (in Alderholt par. *infra*), Blagdon Park (in Cranborne par. *infra*), and Gunville Park (in Tarrant G. par. *infra*), cf. 'the new park called *Le Mote park'* 1505 Pat (*v.* **mote** 'a moat, a ditch'), said to be within the bailiwick of *Battyllysbayll* (the surname *Battyll* with **baillie** 'a bailliff's jurisdiction or district') and associated with 'the new tower or lodge called *le Towar in the Heth'* (*v.* **hǣð**). The eight 'walks' in the Chase included those at Bussey Stool (in Tarrant G. par. *infra*), Chetterwood (in M. Crichel par. *supra*), and Cobley (in Pentridge par. *infra*), as well as *West Walk(e)* 17 *CecilMap*, 1618 *Map* (partly in Tarrant G. par., partly in Ashmore par. *infra*) and one in Alderholt par. *infra*, *v.* Hutch³ 3 410–11. The court of the Chase (*curiam de*

Craneburn' 1234 Cl, *curia chacie* 1331 *Cecil*) was formerly held at Cranborne, *v.* the Court Close in Cranborne par. *infra*, Hutch³ 3 411.

XV. CRANBORNE HUNDRED

The main part of this hundred along the Hampshire border contains Cranborne itself but there are three other detached parts. In c.1086 GeldR, the main part of the present hundred was in *Albretesberge* hundred, which included the pars. of Pentridge, Cranborne, Alderholt, Edmondsham and Verwood, as well as Wimborne St G. (now in Wimborne St Giles hundred). At the same date, the pars. of Ashmore, Tarrant G., Farnham and Tarrant Rush. were in *Langeberge* hundred, Shillingstone and Turnworth were in *Hunesberge* hundred (for both these GeldR hundreds, *v.* under Pimperne hundred *supra*), Witchampton was in Badbury hundred, and Hampreston and W Parley were in *Canendone* hundred (*v.* under Badbury hundred *supra*) (Eyton 111ff, Anderson 130–1, VCHDo 3 128ff). Turnworth was in Pimperne hundred in 1316 FA, 1332 SR. Various other pars. and parts of pars. now in other hundreds were formerly in Cranborne hundred, including in 1327 *SR* Chettle par., Tarrant M. par., Bagber in Sturminster N. par., Monkton Up Wimborne in Wimborne St G. par., Petersham in Holt par., and Lower Fifehead or Fifehead St Quintin in Fifehead N. par., and in 1795 Boswell, Belchalwell in Okeford F. par. The whole of Cranborne hundred was appurtenant to the manor of Cranborne and belonged to the Honour of Gloucester, this accounting both for the change in the name of the hundred and for the inclusion in the hundred of other manors belonging to the Honour (Anderson 131).

ALBRETESBERGE HUNDRED (lost), *Albretesberge hundret* c.1086 GeldR, *Hundredum de Alvredesberge* 1212 Fees, 'Ælfrǣd's hill or barrow', from the OE pers.n. *Ælfrǣd* and **beorg**. The site of the hill or barrow is unknown.

CRANBORNE HUNDRED, *Craneburnehdr'* 1168, 1175, 1182, 1196, *Craneburn'hundredum* 1178, *Craneburgehundredum* 1195 all P, *Craneburnehundredum* 1196 ChancR, *Craneburn(e)* 1244, 1268, 1288 all *Ass*, 1265 Misc, 1269 Cl *et freq* to 1324 ib ('honour of-'), 1346 FA, *Croneburne* 1268 *Ass*, *Craneborn(e)* 1268 *ib*, 1297, 1314 Ipm ('-foreign hundred') *et freq* to 1439 Cl, *Cranebourne* 1280 *Ass*, 1542 LP, *Cranburn* 1382 Pat, *Crambo(u)rne* 1428 FA, 1509 BrEll, 1664 HTax. Named from Cranborne par. *infra* which was the *caput* of the hundred and to which it was annexed. In the 1314 form, 'foreign' no doubt renders Lat *forinsecus* denoting the 'out-hundred'.

Alderholt

This par. was formed in 1894 out of the old par. of Cranborne.

ALDERHOLT (SU 115125)
  Alreholt(e) 1285 *Cecil*, 1288 *Ass*, 1314 Ipm *et freq* to 1332 SR,
  Alreolte, Halre(h)olte 1325 *MinAcct, Halreholt* 1328 *Cecil*,
  Al(l)erholt 1398 Pat, 1404 *Cecil*
  Arleholte 1318 *Cecil*
  Altherholt 1369 *MinAcct (bosc' de-)*, 1382 *Cecil, Cran(e)borne*
    Alderholt 1508 *ib*, 1611 Hutch[3], *Alderholt(e)* 1509 BrEll *et*
    passim, -hoult 1614 *Cecil, Aldderholt* e17 *CecilMap*
  Alderwod 1530 *Cecil, -wood* 1535 VE

'Alder wood', from **alor** and **holt** (in two 16th-cent. forms
replaced by **wudu**), cf. Cranborne par. *infra*; there is a f.n.
Aldersholt in 1845 *TA*.

CRENDELL (CMN) (SU 085135), *Crundole (Close, -Droue, -Plott,*
-Ponde) e17 *CecilMap, Crendall* 1620 *Cecil*, 1621 *CH (-plat)*,
1622 *ib (-gate), Crundall* 1622 *ib, Crendle Common* 1811 OS,
Crandall Gate & Little Cmn 1846 *TA*, from **crundel** 'a pit, a
quarry', with **drāf, plot, plat**[2]. In this instance the pit may have
been a clay pit, cf. *Pitts of Potters Clay* e17 *CecilMap*, although
there are also chalk pits nearby; it is noted in 1774 Hutch[1] 2
143 that 'here is found good potter's clay', cf. Old Pottery Kiln
infra, Old Claygrounds in Cranborne par. *infra*.

DAGGONS (FM) (SU 106126), LR DAGGONS, *Daggans* 1553 *Cecil*,
Dagens 1574 Hutch[3], *Daggyns* e17 *CecilMap, Dagons* 1618 *Map*,
Daggens 1621 *CH*, 1774 Hutch[1], *Daghams* 1811 OS, *Little*
Daggons 1845 *TA, Daggans Lodge* 1846 *ib*, named from the
family of Richard *Dagon* 1327 *SR*, 1332 SR.

PERRY COPSE & FM (SU 132139), *atte Purie* 1324 *MinAcct*, 1328
Cecil both (p), *La Purye* 1404 *ib*, *(Ferme de) Perr(e)y(e)* e17
CecilMap, Perry Copse, Md & Moors 1845 *TA*, 'the pear-tree',
v. **pyrige, atte** 'at the'; there is another Perry Copse 3½ miles
W in Cranborne par. *infra*.

VALE ACRE COPSE & FM (SU 087117), *Vellak(e)* 1314 Ipm, 1318
Cecil, 1325, 1369 *MinAcct (bosc' apud-)*, 1382 *Cecil (-brech')*,
Fenlak 1324 *MinAcct, Wellake(brech')* 1382 *Cecil, bosc' domini*
voc' Fellake 1404 *ib, Bosc' de Velacre* 1508 *ib, Vellker* e17

CecilMap, Fell Acre Row 1846 *TA*, probably 'fen stream', from
fenn and **lacu**, as indicated by the 1324 form, with early
assimilation of *-nl-* to *-ll-* and voicing of the initial consonant
in the first el., and more recent reshaping of the name due to
popular etymology; *v.* **brǣc, rāw.** The name refers to a small
tributary of R. Crane.

ALDER COPSE, cf. *Alderbed Copse* 1845 *TA*, par. name *supra*.
ALDERHOLT BRIDGE, cf. *(Inner) Bridge Grd* 1845 *ib.* ALDERHOLT
CMN, 1845 *ib*, cf. *communia de Alderholt* 1618 *CH*. ALDERHOLT
GRAVEL PIT, cf. *Gravel Pit Grd & Pce* 1845 *TA*. ALDERHOLT
HEATH (lost), 1811 OS, *Hethe* 1318 *Cecil, Bruera de Altherholt*
1382 *ib, Bruere comune de Aldderholt* e17 *CecilMap, v.* **hǣð,** cf.
the f.ns. Heath Fd & Pce *infra*. ALDERHOLT MILL (FM), *-Mill*
1811 OS, *-Mill Ho* 1845 *TA.* ALDERHOLT PARK (a house), 1811
OS, *Aldersholt Park Mansion* 1845 *TA*, named from *parc' de
Alreholt(e)* 1285 *Cecil*, 1324 *MinAcct et freq, Alderholt Parke*
1583 *SPDom, -Parcke* 1621 *CH, The Park* 1845 *TA, v.* **park**;
on this medieval park, *v.* Cantor & Wilson 14 47. ANDREW'S
COPSE, 1845 *TA, Andrews, Androwes* e17 *CecilMap, Inner &
Outer Andrews, Lt Andrews* 1845 *TA*, from the pers.n. or
surname *Andrew*. BAILEY'S PLANT., cf. Cranborne f.ns. *infra*.
BARTLEYS ROW & WD, *Barteley* e17 *CecilMap, Bartley (Row),
Bartley's Copse* 1846 *TA*, probably to be identified with
Berk(e)le 1285 *Cecil, Bercley* 1324 *MinAcct, Berkleye* 1325 *ib,
Barkly* 1621 *CH*, 'birch wood', from **beorc** and **lēah**, with **rāw**;
for the development to *Bart-*, cf. Bartley Ha (DEPN) and Wo
348. BATTERLEY DROVE, *Batherligh* 1614 *Cecil, Batterley Drove
(Pce), Batterley (Plot)* 1846 *TA*, probably from **lēah** 'wood,
clearing', *v.* **drāf**; the first part of the name cannot be explained
without earlier spellings. BIRCH HILL. BLACKWATER, *Black-
waters* 1846 *TA*, named from a stream called *Black Water* 1811
OS, now Sleep Brook *infra, v.* **blæc, wæter.** BONFIRE HILL.
BOXBURY ROW, *Boxby (Row)* 1845 *TA, v.* **row.** BROXHILL,
Brooke Hill e17 *CecilMap, v.* **brōc**; possibly to be associated
with *(an) brokhurste* 944–6 (14) BCS 817 (S 513), *v.* **hyrst.**
BULLHILL COPSE & FM, HIGHER BULHILL, *Bull hill* e17 *ib,
Bulhill (Lane)* 1618, 1621 *CH, Bull Hill Farm Ho, Bull Hill Pce*
1845 *TA, v.* **bula, hyll.** CAMELGREEN, cf. *crofta terr' voc'
Cameleshow* 1382 *Cecil*, from the surname *Camel* and **howe**

'enclosure', **grēne**². CHARING CROSS, at a cross roads, no doubt a transferred name from the Ln place, v. **cross**. CHEATER'S LANE, cf. *le yate voc' Chaters yate* 1621 *CH, Chaters Gate Grd* 1845 *TA*, named from the family of William *Chatere* 1530 *Cecil*, v. **geat**. CHUBBS COPSE, 1846 *TA*. COW BRIDGE, a railway bridge. CRANBORNE CMN, 1846 *TA, Cramborne Common* 1583 *SPDom*, v. Cranborne par. *infra*. CRIPPLESTYLE (PLANT.), *Cripplestile (Pce)* 1846 *TA*, no doubt 'stile that could be crept through (by sheep)', from **crypel** and **stigel**, cf. **crypel-geat** and *cripple-gap* (NED). CROSS ROADS FM & PLANT., near Charing Cross *supra*. CURTIS, *Curtis*(') *Md & Plot* 1845 *TA*, named from the family of John *Curtes* 1530 *Cecil*, William *Curtis* 1664 HTax. DAGGONS RD, cf. *viam...a Cramborne...ad Daggens* 1621 *CH*, v. Daggons *supra*. FURTHER & HITHER DAGGONS WD, *copicia apud Daggans* 1553 *Cecil, Daggyns Bushes* e17 *CecilMap*, (*Lr & Upr*) *Daggons Wd* 1846 *TA*, cf. *Daggans Plot* 1846 *ib*, *Daggons Row* 1845 *ib*, v. Daggons *supra*. DROVE END, cf. *Drove (Plot)* 1845 *TA*, v. **drāf, ende**¹; the drove itself is Harbridge Drove (6″), which begins across the county bdy in Harbridge Ha. FELTHAM'S COPSE, *Felthams (Copse)* 1846 *TA*. FOX HILL, *Foxhill* 1846 *ib*. GARETT'S COPSE, *Garretts* c17 *CecilMap*, *Garretts Copse, Inner & Outer Garretts* 1845 *TA*, cf. John *Garrett* 1664 HTax. GOLD OAK, *Goldeoke* e17 *CecilMap, Gould oke* 1618 *Map*, perhaps named from an oak-tree so called from the colour of its foliage, v. **gold, āc**; it is on the county bdy. HART'S COPSE & FM, *Harts Copse, Farm Ho, & Grd* 1845 *TA*, cf. Edmund *Hart* 1664 HTax. HAWKHILL DITCH & MILL, (*molendinum de*) *Hawkhill* e17 *CecilMap, Hockle Mill* 1811 OS, *Hawkhill Mill Ho* 1845 *TA*, cf. *Hawkhill lane* e17 *CecilMap*, *Hawkhill Green, Hawkhill Lane Grd, Hilly Hawkhills* 1845 *TA*, v. **hafoc, hyll**; on hawking in Cranborne Chase, v. Hutch³ 3 414. The form *Hockle* would seem to show confusion of this name with Huckle Copse just over the county bdy in Damerham Ha, v. PNW 401. HIGH WD, 1845 *TA*. HILLBERRY, perhaps 'barrow on a hill', v. **beorg**; it is on the county bdy and gives name to Hilbury Wd (6″) in Fordingbridge par. (Ha). HILL COPSE (1845 *ib*), CTG, & FM (1811 OS), cf. John *de la Hulle* 1288 *Ass*, Stephen *atte Hulle* 1404 *Cecil, Hill* e17 *CecilMap*, (*Gt & Lt*) *Hill Moor(s)* 1845 *TA*, v. **hyll, atte**. HOME FM. JOSHUA'S COPSE, cf. *Joshuas Fd* 1846 *TA*. KING BARROW (a natural mound), 1811

OS, *Kyngbor'ghe* 1404 *Cecil, Kingbarowe* e17 *CecilMap*, cf.
Kingborrowe Heathe 1619 *CH, King Barrow Patch & Pce* 1846
TA, King Barrow Hill 1869 Hutch[3], from **cyning** and **beorg** (in
two forms showing confusion with **burg** 'a burrow'); it is
possibly to be identified with (*on*) *kingberwes* 944–6 (14) BCS
817 (S 513) in the bounds of Damerham Ha, as suggested by
Forsberg 207. LITTLE CMN, *Crandall Little Cmn* 1846 *TA*, v.
Crendell *supra*. LONDONDERRY, *-Plot* 1846 *ib*, no doubt a
transferred name from the Irish place. MINNOWS HOLE, 1846
ib, 'hole where minnows are found', v. **hol**[1]; it is at a ford
(marked 6″) over Sleep Brook near Blackwater *supra*. NORTH
LODGE. PARK BOTTOM RD, cf. *Parke Lane* e17 *CecilMap*, *callem*
('track') *in parco de Alderholt* 1618 *CH*, v. **botm**, Alderholt
Park *supra*. PARK CHAPEL, cf. prec. PARRICK'S COPSE, *Parricks
Copse* 1846 *TA*, cf. *Parricks Arable, Pasture & Pce* 1846 *ib*.
POND CL, 1845 *TA*, OLD POTTERY KILN (at Crendell *supra*),
cf. *Pitts of Potters Clay* e17 *CecilMap*, *Potteries* 1811 OS
(further E near Daggons *supra*), *Pottery and Yard* 1846 *TA*, and
the f.ns. Brick Kiln (Bottom) and Potsherd Green & Pce *infra*.
PUG'S PLANT., cf. ModE *pug* in various senses (NED). THE
ROOKERY, *Rookery* 1845 *ib*. ST JAMES'S CHURCH, cf. Chapel
Close *infra*. SAMMEL'S COPSE & LEG, *Samuels Copse* 1846 *TA*,
v. **leg**. SLEEP BOTTOM & BROOK (*Black Water* 1811 OS),
probably from **slæp** 'a slippery, muddy place', cf. Slepe in
Lytchett Min. par. *supra*, with **botm** and **brōc**, cf. Blackwater
supra. STANFORD POINT, probably the home of Richard *de
Stanford* 1283 *Cecil* mentioned in connection with Edmondsham par. *infra*, 'stony ford', from **stān** and **ford**, with **point**
'promontory'; it is on Sleep Brook *supra* near a ford (marked
6″). STROUDS FIRS, cf. William *Stroud* 1664 HTax. TELEGRAPH
PLANT., named from Telegraph (Remains of) (6″), *Telegraph*
1811 OS, cf. Hutch[3] 3 383. LT THANES COPSE, *Thians* 1846 *TA*,
cf. Thanes Copse in Cranborne par. *infra*. WARREN FM, *Lodge
Fm* 1811 OS, cf. *Cranborne Warren* 1577 Hutch[3], v. **wareine**.
WHITEFIELD BOTTOM, on the county bdy, v. **botm**. WITHY BED,
1846 *TA*, v. **wīðig**. WOLVERCROFT, *Wolver Crofte* 1621 *CH*, on
the county bdy and giving name to Wolvercrate Copse (6″) in
Fordingbridge par. (Ha); *Wolver-* may represent the OE pers.n.
Wulfhere or the like, or **wulf** 'wolf' with some other el., v. **croft**
'small enclosed field'.

FIELD-NAMES

The undated forms are 1845 *TA* 3 or (those marked†) 1846 *ib* 73 (Cranborne).
Spellings dated 1244, 1268, 1280, 1288 are *Ass*, 1324, 1325 *MinAcct*, 1327
SR, 1332 SR, 1574, 1584 Hutch³, e17 *CecilMap*, 1611 Hutch³, 1621, 1622,
1623 *CH*, 1664 HTax, and the rest *Cecil*.

(*a*) †The acre (*v.* **æcer**); Aldersholt (cf. par. name *supra*); Apps Grd;
†Arable Patch & Pce; Arable Plot; †Bank Pce; Barley Croft; †(Big) Barn Cl,
Barn Fd & Pce (cf. Walter *de la Berne* 1280, *Bernlondes* 1404, *v.* **bere-ærn,
land**); Barn Cl, Fd & Grd; Bathers (*Bat(t)hyes* e17, probably a surname);
Baulk (*v.* **balca**); Bean Grd; Beggars (e17, *Baggardesham* 1382, *Baggesham*
1398, *hammum voc' Baggers* 1623, from the ME surname *Baggard*, cf. John
Bagard' 1332 (Fordington), and **hamm**); Big Pasture; Brewers and Breachers
(*Brewers* e17, cf. William *Brewer* 1664 (Edmondsham) and Cranborne f.ns.
infra; *Breacher* is probably also a surname); †Brick Kiln (Bottom) (*Brick kilne*
e17, *Brickall* 1614, from **brick-kiln** (with loss of -*n* in the 1614 form), cf. Old
Pottery Kiln *supra*, Kiln Grd *infra*); Broad Cl (e17); †Broken Rough; †Buck
Mdw (*Buck(e)*, *Buckelane* e17, perhaps from **bucc** 'a buck, a male deer' if
the simplex *Buck(e)* is elliptical for *Buck(e)mead* or the like); (Lr, Middle &
Upr) Burnbake (*v.* **burnbake**); Carrotts Cl; Cart House Grd; Cats Holes,
Catsholes (*v.* **cat(t), hol¹**); Chalk Cl; (Gt & Lt) Chapel Cl, The New Chapel
& Yd (cf. *St Clement's Chapel, Chapel-close* 1574; on the former chapel in
Alderholt dedicated to St Clement, *v.* Hutch³ 3 383, 397); Clapper Gate Orchd
(probably an altered form of **clap-gate** rather than from ME **clapper** 'a rough
bridge' or dial. **clapper** 'fox earth, rabbit burrow'); †Clay Grd(s) (near to
Old Claygrounds in Cranborne par. *infra*); †The Clothiers, Clothiers Md;
Colts Cl; Common Corner, Fd, Grd & Plot(s); †Common En-, Inclosure,
Common Patch; Lr & Middle Compse (possibly **camp¹** 'enclosed piece of
ground', in a pl. form, unless this is an erratic spelling of *copse*); †Copse (Cl);
Copse (Cl & Fd); †Corner Orchd, Patch & Pce; Cow Leaze (Pce);
Cunnerberry (Orchd) (*v.* **cony-burrow** 'rabbit-warren'); †Daisy Md;
(Drove in) Ditch Herons (*Dytchearne Close* 1621, cf. *Hearneditchlane ib, v.*
dīc, hyrne 'angle, corner'); Divers (*Dyuers* e17, a surname); Doctors;
Drinkwater (probably a surname); †Drove (Corner & Pce) (*le Drove* 1621,
v. **drāf**); Gt & Lt East Fd; †Elliots Grd (cf. John *Elliott* 1664); †Enclosure
(from Common); †Falls (probably a surname); The Far Pce; Lr & Upr
Ferney Cl, †Ferney Grd (*v.* **fearnig**); †Fern Hill (*v.* **fearn**); †Fir Plant.;
Fishpond Pce; 5 Acre, (The) 5 Acres, †The 5 Acres, 5 Acre Pce; †French
Grass; Gt & Lt French Grass (*v.* **french grass**); †Furze Cl; Furzy Grd (cf.
Fursey close e17, *v.* **fyrsig**); Lt Gallopers; Lt Garbage, Garbage Md (perhaps
ModE *garbage*); †Garden Tillage (cf. *garden grownd* 1553, *v.* **gardin, tillage**);
Grandmothers Plot; (†) Great Grd; Gt & Lt Green Cl; Hall Hill Grd; †Hart
Hill (Pce & Strip) (*v.* **heorot**); Hayters Plot; †Haywards (cf. Cranborne f.ns.
supra); †Heath Fd & Pce (*la Heth'felde* 1404, cf. *hethy close* 1553, *le Heathe
Gate* 1622, *Alderholt Heath supra, v.* **hǣð, feld**); Hedgerow; †Hibbards Plot;
Hilly, Lt, Peaked & Square Higdens (*Higdons* e17, cf. Cecilia *Hykedon'* 1328,
v. **peked** 'pointed'); †Hill Pce; Lt Hilly Fd; Lr & Upr Hintons Md, Middle
& Outer Hintons (*Hintons* e17, a surname from one of the Do Hintons); Home

Cl, Fd & Grd, Far & Near Home Plot, †Home Cl, Pce & Plot (*Home Close* e17); Hostile Grd; Hotkins; †House Mdw; Hilly Hunts (Leg), Tea Hunts (*Hunts* e17, cf. Henry *Hunt* 1664, *v.* leg; *Tea* perhaps means 'T-shaped'); Inner Md; †Kiln Grd, Lr Kiln Grd (Pce), Top Kiln Grd (Peak), Upr Kiln Grd (Patch) (cf. Brick Kiln *supra*); Kinchertons Md; Kings (cf. Cranborne f.ns. *infra*); †Knap Md & Pce, Knaps (*v.* cnæpp); Knights Grd & Md (cf. Thomas *Knygh* (sic) 1327, -*le Knyghtz* 1332); †Land Pce; Lane (Plot); Latch(es), †Latch (*v.* læc(c) 'stream, bog'); †Leasow (*v.* lǣs); Little Cmn, Copse, Grd & Pasture; Little Firs; †Little Gains (cf. Small Gains *infra*); †Little Grd, Orchd & Pce; Little Hat (*v.* hæt(t) 'hat-shaped hill', cf. *Hatcombe* (p), *Hattecombe* 1324 which may contain the same el. with cumb 'valley'); †Little Knap (*v.* cnæpp); †Lockyers; Long Cl; †Long Grd (cf. *Longe Groundes* e17); Long Gut (Grd) (*v.* gut 'water-channel'); Long Md (*Langemede* 1318, 1324, *Longemede* 1382, *Long Meade* e17, *v.* lang¹, mǣd); †Long Pce; Lucerne (*v.* lucerne (a crop)); Lushs; Majors Copse, Home Cl & Md; (†) The Mead; Meadow; †Mead Plot; Middle Cl (*Midle Close* 1553, *v.* middel); (†) Middle Grd; Middle Md & Pce; The Moors, Mower (cf. William *de La More* 1244, *Attemore* 1268 (p), John *de la More* 1288, *v.* mōr, atte); Mortar Holes; †Mountains; Mowlands (*v.* mow); Muckle Cl (*v.* muckle); New Pce & Plot; North Fd (cf. *in campo borial*' 1318); Old Grd & Plot; The Old Orchd; (†) Orchard; Outlet (*v.* utlete); Pasture Fd; †Pasture Pce & Plot; †Patch (*v.* patche); Peak, †(Gt, Inner & Middle) Peak (*v.* pēac); †Peakes Pce; †Pear Tree Mdw; Pear Tree Pce; (Roughland in) Peat Mower (*v.* pete, mōr); Picked Cl (*Pyked close* e17, *v.* pīcede 'pointed'); †Picked Pce, Nicklens Picket Pce (*v.* prec.); †Hr, Lr & Upr Piece; †Plack (*v.* plack); Plantation; Plot; †(The Far) Pond Cl, Pond Pce; Pools; †Open in Potsherd Green, Potsherd Pce (*v.* potsherd, cf. Old Pottery Kiln *supra*; *Open* must be elliptical for *open ground*); The Pound (*v.* pund); Priory Copse Cl, Priory Grd & Pasture, (Far) Priory Pce (cf. *Pryors Cops*, -*Groue* e17, *Priors Coppice* 1611, land once belonging to Cranborne Priory in Cranborne par. *infra*, *v.* prior, copis, grāf(a)); Rickyard Pce; †Far & Near Road Pce; Roadway; †Rough (Pce); Rough Pce; Row (freq, *v.* row); †The Rows; †Ryegrass Pce; Sandpits; †Lt Saw Pit Grd (*v.* saw-pit); 7 Acres (Cow Leaze), †The 7 Acres (cf. *7 acr crofte* e17); Sheep Croft (*Schapecroft* 1292, 1325, *Shepcroft*' 1324, cf. *le Shephouse ib*, *v.* scēap, croft, hūs, cf. foll.); Gt & Lt Shop Cl (probably sc(e)oppa 'shed'); (Upr) Sims's; †(The) 6 Acres (*Sixe Acres* e17); (†) Small Gains (a derogatory name for unproductive land, cf. Little Gains *supra*); †Spring Pce; †Square Patch & Pce; †Square Pits; Stile Grd (*v.* stigel); †Stone Quarry; Streets Grd (cf. George *Streete* 1664); †Strip; †Tappers; †10 Acres; (The) 10 Acres; 3 Acres; †Three Cornered Patch; †Tillage (Fd & Pce) (*v.* tillage); †Triangles; Turf House Grd; Upper Grd & Pce; †Warwicks; Water Cl; Way Grd; †Well Copse & Plot; (Lr, Middle & Upr) Well Plots (*v.* well(a) 'spring, stream'); Wiggins; Withey Bed (Row), †Withy Plot (*v.* wīðig); †Wood; Lr, Middle & Upr Woodlands; Yew Tree Fd; Yonder Pce.

(b) *le Backeside Ricardi Cooke* 1622 (*v.* backside); *Bourne close, Bourn lake* e17 (cf. *la Borne* 1318, *v.* burna 'spring, stream', lacu 'stream'); *Breache* e17 (*v.* brǣc); *prat*' *voc*' *Buckes* 1621 (the surname *Buck*); *Butt(s) Lane* e17, 1621 (*v.* butte); *Cole close* e17; *molend*' *de feadenore* 1328 (possibly

'Feadenore's mill', cf. William *feadenore ib*; however these forms are perhaps corrupt and may belong under *Padner infra*); *Groue* e17 (*v.* **graf(a)**); *Hopkins* e17 (a surname); *How Coppice* e17 (*v.* **howe**); *Jollye Marchants* e17; (*claus' voc'*) *Jolly Robins* 1614, 1619, *Jolly Robyn* e17 (cf. Chaucer's *Troilus and Criseyde* Book V, l. 1174, Shakespeare's *Hamlet* IV, 5, 181, etc); *Kerleys* 1614 (cf. Henry *Kirley* 1584 (Edmondsham)); *Kickapace* e17; *Lack(e)moore* 1621, 1622 (*v.* **mōr**, first el. probably **lacu** 'stream'); *Long(e)lande* e17 (*v.* **lang**[1], **land**); *Moorye Close* 1621 (*v.* **mōrig**); (*molendinum de*) *Padner* e17, *Padner Mylle* 1620, *terr' voc' Padnors alias Tadnor* 1621 (the *alias* forms suggest that the first el. is **padde** 'toad' alternating with **tadde** 'toad', perhaps with **ōra**[1] 'bank', *v.* **myln**, cf. *feadenore supra*; medial -*n*- is from the gen.sg. -*an* or gen.pl. -*ena*); (*claus' voc'*) *Palmers* e17, 1623 (a surname); *Poole* e17 (*v.* **pōl**[1] 'pool, pond'); *Sandy lane, Sandylaneyate* e17 (*v.* **sandig, lane, geat**).

Ashmore

ASHMORE (ST 913178)
Aisemare 1086 DB, -*mara* Exon
Essemera, -*mere* 1100–35 (1496) Pat, 1107 (1300) Ch, 1194 P, 1230 Cl, 1284 Banco, 1289 Pap, *Essemor(e)* 1247, 1250 Cl, *Esmere* 1268 Ass, *Esshemere* 1284 Banco, *Eshemere* 1399 Cl
Ashesmera 1233 Cl
Assemere 1235 Cl, 1268, 1280, 1288 Ass, 1291 Tax, 1303 FA, *Aysmere* 1242–3 Fees, *Ayssemere* 1268 Ass (p), *Asmere* 1280 ib, *Aysschemere* 1283 Cecil, *Has(s)emer(e)* 1288 Ass, *Aschemer(e)* 1303 FA, 1332 SR, 1536 AD, *Asshemer(e)* 1305 FF *et freq* to 1494 Cecil, *Ashmere* 1314 Ipm, 1619 CH (-als. *Ashmore*), 1661 CollA (-als. *Aysmer*), *Asshemore* 1316 FA, *Asshmer(e)* 1340 NI, 1346 FA, *Aysshmer* 1412, 1431 ib, *Aysemere* als. *Ashemeer* 1579 CollA, *Ashmeere* 1618 CH, 1664 HTax, *Ashmore* 1618 CH, *Aishmere* 1619 ib

'Pool where ash-trees grow', from **æsc** and **mere**[1], cf. Ashey Knap *infra*, with reference to the pond at the centre of this hill-top village (700′), situated on a ridgeway and beside the Badbury Rings-Kingston Deverell Roman road (Margary 46). OE **(ge)mǣre** 'boundary', with reference to the situation of Ashmore on the county bdy with Wiltshire, is a formally possible but perhaps less likely alternative, as is the OE pers.n. *Æsca* for the first el. (DEPN). The second el. has been confused with, and eventually replaced by, **mōr** 'marshy ground'.

GT & LT ALDERWOOD COPPICE, *Great Aldred Coppice*, *close*

called Aldred 1590 *LRMB, Alderhead, Alder wood* (two adjacent coppices) 1618 *Map, Alderwood Coppice, Fd & Pce* 1842 *TA*; there are probably two names here, both containing **alor** 'alder', one with **hēafod** 'end of a ridge', the other with **wudu** 'wood'. ALNER'S COPPICE, 1842 *TA*, cf. *Alners Corner* 1842 *ib*, Stephen *Alner* 1664 HTax. ASHEY KNAPP, *Ashton cops* 1618 *Map, Ashen Nap Coppice* 1842 *TA*, cf. *Ashe Coppice* 1590 *LRMB, v.* **æsc** 'ash-tree', **tūn, æscen** 'growing with ash-trees', **cnæpp** 'hill-top', cf. par. name *supra*. ASHMORE CMN (lost), 1811 OS, *Ashmore greene* 1618 *Map, The Common* 1842 *TA*. ASHMORE DOWN, 1811 OS, *Tennants Downe* 1618 *Map*, cf. *Free Down, Hr & Lr Down, The North Down* 1842 *TA, v.* **dūn**. ASHMORE FDS (lost), 1811 OS, *Ashmere Fieldes* 1618 *Map*. BALL COPPICE, 1842 *TA, Bald Coppice* 1590 *LRMB, Ball cops, Ashmere ball* 1618 *Map, v.* **ball** 'rounded hill', with epenthetic -d in the 16th cent. form, cf. foll. GT & LT BENCH COPPICE, *Nether Binche Coppice* 1590 *LRMB, Double bench* 1618 *Map, Hr, Lr & Middle Bench, Gt Bench Coppice, Ball or Lr Bench Hill* 1842 *TA, v.* **benc** 'shelf, ledge', cf. prec.; the feature described is a prominent squared hill-spur rising to 600′. BOYNE BOTTOM, *v.* **botm**. BROADRIDGE CMN, LR & UPR BROAD-RIDGE COPPICE, *Longe Brodriche Coppice* 1590 *LRMB, Brod-ridge, Longe Broderidge or Longe seege Cork* 1618 *Map, Broadridge Cmn, Coppice, Gate & Wd* 1842 *TA, v.* **brād, hrycg**, Sedge Oak Coppice *infra*. CRABTREE COPPICE, *Crabtree otherwise called Paltable Coppice* 1590 *LRMB, Crabtree, Patable* (two adjacent coppices) 1618 *Map, v.* **crabbetre**; *Pa(l)table* is obscure, unless it is for eModE *palatable* 'agreeable to the palate, pleasant to the taste' (with reference to the crab-apples?) (NED from 1669). DEADMAN'S COPPICE, 1829 *EnclA, Dead mans* 1618 *Map*. HR & LR DOWNEND COPPICE, *Downe end* (a coppice) 1618 *Map*, 'the end of the down', *v.* **dūn, ende**[1]. ELDEREN COPPICE & ROW, *Est-, West Elden Copps* 1590 *LRMB, Est-, West Elden* 1618 *Map, East & West Eldren Coppice* 1842 *TA, v.* **elle(r)n** 'elder-tree', **copis**, with **ēast, west, rāw**, cf. the f.n. Elderland *infra*. GARDINER FOREST (1″), cf. West Wd *infra*. GATEHOUSE ROW, *Gatehouse's Row* 1842 *TA*, cf. *Gatehouse's Plot* 1842 *ib*, William *Gatehouse* 1664 HTax. GORE FM, cf. *Gore Close, Gores Coppices* 1590 *LRMB, Gore close, Gore cops* 1618 *Map, Gore Coppice, Fd & Pleck* 1842 *TA, v.* **gāra** 'triangular plot of ground, point of land', with **plek**; the farm is situated in the pointed NW corner of the par. HATTS BARN & COPSE, *Winsons hatts* (a coppice) 1618 *Map*, *Hats Barn* 1811 OS, *Hatts Barton and Barn*, *Hatts Coppice* 1842 *TA*, probably from **hæt(t)** 'hat-shaped hill', perhaps with reference to the prominent hill which reaches 810′ just W of Hatts Barn; *Winson* is a surname. HOOKLEY COPSE, (*-Cops*) 1618 *Map*, *-Coppice* 1842 *TA*, cf. *Houkle Close* 1590 *LRMB*, *Gt & Lt Hookley*, *Hookley Close* (*Mdw*), *Hookley Row* 1842 *TA*, 'wood or clearing at the bend', from **hōc** and **lēah**, with reference either to the hill-spur here or to the curve in the county bdy; *Howke Grene* 1590 *LRMB*, *Hook's Green* (a coppice) m18 Hutch[3], containing the same first el. with **grēne**[2], may also have been near here. THE HUT. KEEPER'S LODGE. LAMBERT'S COPPICE, *Lamberts* (*Coppice*) 1842 *TA*, cf. William *Lambert* 1664 HTax. MANOR FM (formerly Manor House), *maner place of Aschemer* 1536 *AD*, cf. foll. MANOR HO. GT & LT MORRIS CLOSE, *Moris close* 1618 *Map*, *Gt Morris Cl*, *Morris Cl Coppice*, *Flg & Path*, *Norris Cl Flg* 1842 *TA*, cf. *Mores Coppice* 1590 *LRMB*, *Morris Plant.* 1842 *TA*, from the surname *Mores* or *Morris*. MUDOAK WD, *Maddox* (a coppice) m18 Hutch[3], *Mudoak* 1842 *TA*, but called *Mudwaye* (a coppice) 1618 *Map*: first el. probably **mudde** 'mud' with **weg** 'way' and with **āc** 'oak' or **hōc** 'bend' (it is near Hookley *supra*). NORTH FM. RECTORY, cf. *Rectorie et ecclesie de Aysemere* 1565 *CollA*, *Parsonage Ho*, *Vicarage Ho* 1829 *EnclA*. ST NICHOLAS'S CHURCH, built 1874 replacing an earlier church, cf. *ecclesia de Essemere, -mera* 1100–35 (1496) Pat, 1107 (1300) Ch, *-de Hassemere* 1288 *Ass*. GT & LT SEDGE OAK COPPICE, *Shide Oke Coppice* 1590 *LRMB*, *Shideoke* (possibly *Shidtoke*), *Long Broderidge or Longe seege Cork* (adjacent coppices) 1618 *Map*, *Sedge Oak* 1839 *TA* (Tarrant G.), on the par. bdy, *v.* Broadridge Coppice *supra*. The older forms may represent two names for two different trees, or two names for the same tree, the modern form apparently combining the two: *Shide Oke* may be from **scīd** 'board, plank, beam' and **āc**, although **scite** 'excrement' cannot be ruled out for the first el. in view of the form *seege Cork* which may be from ME *sege* (ModE *siege*) 'privy, excrement' and *cork* 'cork-oak tree', cf. also Bussey Stool Fm 1 mile SE in Tarrant G. par. *infra*. SHEPHERD'S BOTTOM, *Ashmore Bottom* 1811 OS, *v.* **botm**, cf. William *bercarius* 1332 SR (Tarrant G.).

SOUTH'S FM, named from the *South* family which held land in Ashmore in the 18th cent. (Hutch³ 3 370). STONE DOWN COPPICE, *Estonden-, Westonden Coppice* 1590 *LRMB, West Stonden* 1618 *Map, Stone-down Coppice* 1842 *TA*, 'stony valley', from **stān** and **denu** (replaced by *down* from **dūn**), with **ēast, west,** a hill-spur which took its name from the adjacent valley, *v.* foll. STONY BOTTOM, *Stonedeane bottome* 1618 *Map, Stoney Bottom* 1842 *TA, v.* **botm,** the valley which gave name to prec. TURKEY PLANT., *Turkey (Acre)* 1842 *ib.* WAGBUSH COPPICE, 1829 *EnclA, Waites bush* 1618 *Map,* a surname with **busc.** WASHERS PIT (COPPICE), *Washers Pit Coppice* 1842 *ib.* WELL BOTTOM, cf. *Well Cl* 1842 *ib,* perhaps to be associated with John *atte Welle* 1327 *SR,* 1332 SR (Compton A. and Melbury A.), *v.* **well(a), atte.** WEST WD, *West(e)wode* 1280 *Ass,* QW, *West Wood* 1590 *LRMB, West Wd (Drove), South West Wd, North West Wd* 1842 *TA, v.* **west, wudu;** for earlier evidence of woodland in the par., cf. *foresta de Ashesmera* 1233, *-de Assemere* 1235, *-de Essemore* 1247 all Cl, no doubt part of Cranborne Chase.

FIELD-NAMES

The undated forms are 1842 *TA* 9. Spellings dated 1283 are *Cecil,* 1332 SR, 1340 NI, 1590 *LRMB,* 1618 *Map,* 1664 HTax, and m18 Hutch³.

(*a*) Jack Allen's Md; Apsey Coppice (*Apes* (a coppice) 1618, *Appice* (a coppice) m18, perhaps from **æspe** 'aspen-tree'); Ash Acre (cf. par. name *supra*); Bastard Crooked Pce, Bastards 4 Acres; Beals Barn and Barton, Beals Md (*Beales* (a coppice) 1618, cf. Robert *Beale* 1664); Bennety Coppice (*Bennett Coppice* 1590, *Benettie* (a coppice) 1618, *Bennett's* (a coppice) m18, probably from **beonet** 'bent grass', later confused with the surname *Bennett*; in the 1618 and *TA* form, *-ie, -y* may be adjectival, *v.* **-ig³**); Bottom Pce, Hr & Lr Bottoms (*v.* **botm**); Bowling Green; Bratch (2 Acres) (*v.* **bræc** 'land broken up for cultivation'); British School and Gdn; Broad Md; Hr & Lr Burnbake (*v.* **burnbake**); Bush Pce, Lt Bushy Cl (cf. *Busshe Close* 1590, *v.* **busc**); Bussey Stool Coppice (*Burses Stolle Coppice* 1590, *Bursey cops* 1618, *Bursey Stool* (a coppice) m18, named from Bussey Stool in Tarrant G. par. *infra*); Butland (Acre, Flg & Head), Butts (Cl) (*v.* **butte, land, hēafod** 'headland (in a common field)'); Craft Head, Flg & Pce, Croft Flg (*v.* **croft, hēafod**); Coppice; Corner Acre; Cowleaze; Cross Pce (*v.* **cross**); Elderland (Head) (*v.* **elle(r)n,** cf. Elderen Coppice *supra*); (Lt) Field Gate Pce; Middle 5 Acres; Footpath Pce; 40 Acres; Garden Plot; Goose Acre; Great Pce; Green Fd; Green Lane (Flg); Green Md 1829 *EnclA;* Halfpence-, Halfpenny Pce (no doubt an allusion to a rental or charge, cf. PNBrk 543); Lt Hatchet Acre, Hatchet Pce (probably **hæcc-geat** 'a hatch-gate'); Head Acre & Pce (*v.* **hēafod** 'headland (in a common field)'); Higher Fd & Pce; Holmy Nap, Holney Acre & Bottom (*v.* **holegn** 'holly', **cnæpp**; -(*e*)*y* may be adjectival, *v.* -**ig³**); Home Md & Plot; Horder(')s Flg; Kite Corner (*v.* **cȳta**); Knowle (Acre, Pce & Stile) (*v.* **cnoll** 'hill-top, hillock', **stigel**); Lane End (Pce), Lane-end Flg & Head (cf. William *in the lane* 1332, -*de la Lane* 1340, *v.* **lane, ende¹**); Large Pce; Little Acre, Coppice, Half & Plot (*v.* **half**); Long Cl; Long Coombe (Head) (*v.* **cumb**); Long-hedge Drove; Long Lds, Md & Pce; Lower Acre; Marlpit; Middle Acres, Fd & Md; Large Middle Pce; Mullens Md & Row (cf. Lewis *Mullen*, George *Mullens* 1664); (Lr & Upr) New Cl, New Cl Acre & Md; New Orchd; Noad Cl, End, Flg & Plot (probably from a ME *atten ode* '(place) at the beacon', *v.* **ād, atte(n)**); Northovers Md; Orchard; Parish Pound; Picked Acre & Pce (*v.* **pīcede** 'pointed'); Pincushion (Head) (perhaps with reference to the shape of the field); Pit Acre & Pce; Plat Mdw (*v.* **plat²** 'a plot'); Pleck (*v.* **plek** 'a small plot'); Pollard Green Coppice (perhaps the surname *Pollard*); Rapshill Fd (*close called Robsholl* 1590 (spelling uncertain)); Road Flg; Row; Sandpit Flg, Sandpits (*Sandpit(t)* 1618, *v.* **sand, pytt**); Sawpit Coppice (m18, *v.* **saw-pit**); Shaftesbury Way (*v.* Shaftesbury par. *infra*); Sharps 2 Acres; (Lr) Shelves Corner; Short Coombe (*v.* **cumb**); Slades Bush; Slip Roadway; Socketts (Head), Sockett's Cleaver (*Sockett* is probably a surname, *Cleaver* is obscure); Stickway (*Estickway Coppice* 1590, *Stick way* (a coppice) 1618, *Stickway* (a coppice) m18; this coppice is near the par. bdy, *v.* Stickway in Tarrant G. par. *infra*); 10 Acres; 3 Acres; 3 Halves (*v.* **half**); Triangular Cmn; 12 Acres 1829 *EnclA*; Way Acre; Way Flg, Head Littleway Flg; Way Pce & Side (*v.* **weg**); (Lt) West Fd; West Hill; White Acre (*v.* **hwīt**); Yonder Pce.

(*b*) *Borders* (a coppice) 1618 (a surname); *Brode Oke Coppice* 1590 (*v.* **brād, āc, copis**); *Cowe Close* 1590; *Erpittes Coppice* 1590 (first two letters uncertain); *Greene Coppice* 1590; *Hony Feld Close* 1590 (*v.* **hunig** 'honey'); *Peinke Pitt Coppice* 1590 (*v.* **pinc** 'a minnow', **pytt**, cf. Minnows Hole in Alderholt par. *supra*); *viam que dicitur Rygeweye* 1280 *Ass*, *viam que dicitur Rugwyk*(') *que ducit versus Salesbyr*', -*ber*' 1280 *ib*, *QW*, *Ridgwaye, The Ridgwaie* 1618 *Map* (*v.* **hrycg-weg**; along N par. bdy); *Stenefeld* 1590 (from **stǣne** 'stony place', or a reduced form of **stǣnen** 'stony'); *Stony Coppice* 1590 (*v.* **stānig**); *Tollard Grene Coppice* 1590, *greene cops* 1618, *Tollard Green* (a coppice) m18 (from Tollard Green in Tollard Royal par. W 208–9); *attetoneseynd*' 1283, *atte Toneseynde* 1327, -*Toneshende* 1332 all (p) (*v.* **atte, tūn, ende¹**); *messuage called West Living* m18 (*v.* **living**).

Cranborne

The pars. of Alderholt and Verwood were formed out of this par., formerly the largest in the county, in 1894. Part of this par. (Oakley and Monkton Up Wimborne) was transferred to Wimborne St G. in 1886.

CRANBORNE (SU 055133)

Creneburne 1086 DB (3 ×, once (p)), -*borna* Exon, -*bornam* 1100–35 (1496) Pat

Craneburna(m) 1154–89 (1496) Pat, 1163 P (p), -*burn(e)*
1187–1210 ib, 13 *Cecil*, 1205 ChancR, 1226 Cur (p), 1228
Cl *et freq* to 1535–43 Leland, -*born(e)* 13 *Cecil*, 1207 FF,
1229 ib (p) *et freq* to 1553 *Cecil*, -*bourn(e)* 1280 *Ass*, 1283
Cecil et freq to 1447 Pat, *Kraneborn* 1275–83 Ipm
Crannborne 13 (14) *Cecil*, *Cranbourn(e)* 1252 Pat *et passim*
with variant spellings -*burn(e)*, -*born(e)*
Cramburn(e) 1255 *AD et freq* to 1664 HTax with variant
spellings -*born(e)*, -*bourn(e)*; *Cramburn als. Cranborne* 1483
IpmR
Cranebroke als. Cranbourn 1398 IpmR

'Stream frequented by cranes or herons', from **cran** and
burna (in one form replaced by **brōc**), with reference to the
stream here now called R. Crane (a back-formation from the
p.n.). The same name occurs in Brk and Ha. There were two
manors in Cranborne, that of *Cranborne Borough* (1795 Boswell,
Craneborne Burgus 1508 *Cecil*, *borough of Cramborne* 1509 BrEll,
Cramborne Borough 1664 HTax, *The Manor of Borough* 1774
Hutch[1], *v*. Hutch[3] 3 375) and that of *Cranborne Priory* (1795
Boswell, *Craneborne Prioratus* 1553 *Cecil*, *Cramborne Pryory*
1664 HTax, *The Manor of Cranborn-Prior or Manor of the
Priory* 1774 Hutch[1], *v*. Hutch[3] 3 382), the latter so called
because it once belonged to Cranborne Priory *infra*.

STREET-NAMES: CASTLE ST., -*Streete* 1553 *Cecil* (named from the earthworks
at Castle Hill *infra*); GRUGS LANE; HIGH ST.; PENNY'S LANE (cf. Penny's Fm
infra); SALISBURY ST., *Salesburystrete*, *Regiam viam versus Sarum* 1508 *Cecil*
('street leading to Salisbury W'). Lost st.ns. include *belstreete* 1623 *ib* (*v*.
Bellows Cross *infra*); *Cranborne Lane* 1869 Hutch[3]; *Ensham Lane* 1784 ib
('lane to Edmondsham par. *infra*'); *in vico mercati* 1382 *Cecil* (cf. *the Marquet
Howse infra*). Buildings include *Coopers Shop* 1846 *TA*; *the Marquet Howse*
1618 *CH*, *le Marckett Howse* 1619 *ib* (cf. *in foro de Craneborne*, *les shameles*
1382 *Cecil*, *le Butchers Shambles* 1622 *CH*, *in vico mercati supra*, *v*. **market,
sc(e)amol**; on markets and fairs in Cranborne, *v*. Hutch[3] 3 375); *house called
Melledge's* 1869 Hutch[3] (cf. William *Melledge* 1654 ib); *Toll House* 1846 *TA*.
Inns include *Cross Keys*, *Fleur-De-Lis*, *Sheaf of Arrows* all 1846 *TA*, *the
Whitehart* 1631 Hutch[3], cf. *Red Lion Fd* 1846 *TA*.

BELLOWS CROSS (SU 066139), 1846 *TA*, *Bellyes Crosse* 1621
CH, named from *Belleye* 1382 *Cecil*, *Belly(e)* (*Home Close*) e17
CecilMap, *Bellyes* 1621 *CH*, cf. *Belly Lane* 1619 *ib*, *Bellow(s)
Cross Fd & Pce* 1846 *TA*. *Belleye* may be from **belle** 'bell-shaped

hill' and **lēah** 'wood, clearing in a wood'; **bēl**[1] (Angl), **bǣl** (WSax) 'fire, pyre' is a less likely first el. in view of the absence of forms with -*a*- which would probably have arisen from shortening of WSax **bǣl** in the cpd; Cross is probably **cross** 'cross-roads' with reference to the five lane junction here. The form *duos campos vocat' belstreete* 1623 *CH* should perhaps also be associated with this name, if the 'street' is that entering Cranborne from Damerham Ha.

BIDDLESGATE FM (SU 078144), ? *bi talayate* 944–6 (14) BCS 817 (S 513), *butelesheite* 1236 Hutch[3], *Butelesheyte* 1247 (c. 1340) Glast, *Buttelyte* 1268 *Ass* (p), *Butlesgate* 1283 *Cecil* (p), 1325 *MinAcct* (p), 1327 *SR* (p), 1332 *SR* (p), *Butlegate* 1284 *Cecil* (p), *Butel(es)gate* 1285 *ib* (p), *Buttlesgate* 1324 Hutch[3], *But(t)elgate* (*juxta Cran(e)bo(u)rn*) 1332, 1386 FF, *Buttelgate* 1463 Cl, *Buttylgats* 1535 VE, *Byddelgates* 1570 PN W. Probably 'But-(t)el's gate', from an OE pers.n. *But(t)el* (suggested by Ekwall DEPN for Buston Nb) and **geat**; it is on the county bdy where the road from Damerham Ha enters the county. It gives name to Bittlegate Copse (1902 6″) in Damerham (PNW 401). For the late change *u* > *i* before a dental, cf. Didcot Brk 517, PN Gl 4 70. The form *bi talayate*, in the bounds of Damerham Ha, probably belongs here but is corrupt, the first part of the name having been confused with the prep. **bī**.

(WEST) BLAGDON FM, BLAGDON HILL (SU 056180), BLAGDON HILL WD, *Blakedon(e)* 1234 Cl (*chacie de-, foresta de-*), 1235 *ib*, 1240 *ib* (*foresta regis de-, manerio de-*), 1280 *Ass*, 1285 *Cecil et freq* to 1495 Pat (-*park*), *parcus de Blakedon'* 1324, 1325, 1369 all *MinAcct*, 'the (king's) park of *Blakedon* (within the chace of *Cranbourne*)' 1382 Pat *et freq* to 1486 *ib*, *foresta regis de Blakedun* 1251 Cl, *Blakyndon'* 1331 *Cecil*, *Blakedoun'* 1399 Pat ('the park of-'), 1508 *Cecil* (*parcum de-*), *Blakdon* (*park*) 1460 Pat, 1465 Hutch[3], 1499 Pat, *Blacdon* 1482 (1610), 1530 *Cecil*, *Blagdon* 1535 VE, 1553 *Cecil* (*warrena iuxta-*), 1575 Saxton (-*Parke*), e17 *CecilMap* (*Parci de-*), 1869 Hutch[3] (*North-, West-*), *Blakden the kinges great park* 1535–43 Leland, *Blacke-don'* 1547 Ct, *Blagedon als. Cranborne Park* 1577 Hutch[3], *Blagden* (*Parke*) 1583 SPDom, 1621 CH. 'Dark-coloured hill', from **blæc** (wk.obl. *blacan*) and **dūn**; the hill reaches 529′ and lies on the county bdy, *v.* PN W 402 and Bockerly Ditch in

Pentridge par. *infra*. There was a large medieval deer-park here, *v*. **park**, Cantor & Wilson 4 165–170, 9 196, cf. Park Row *infra*.

BOVERIDGE (SU 062147), BOVERIDGE FM & HO ['bɔvərɪdʒ], *Bovehric* 1086 DB, *Bogerugg*', *Bobrugge* (sic) 1154–89 (1496) Pat, *Bowerigg(e)* c.1183 (14) *Cecil*, 1288 *Ass*, *-rugge* 1381 (1408) Pat, 1383 Fine, *-ridge* 1620 *Cecil*, *Bewerugg*' 1245 Cl, *Boverug*, *-rig* 1256 FF, *-rigge* 1285 *Cecil* (p), *-ryg* 1327 *SR*, *-regge* 1390 IpmR, *-rugge* 1504 Pat, *-ridge* 1553 *Cecil*, 1580 Hutch³ (*-als. Borage*) *et passim*, *Bouerigg(e)* 1268, 1280, 1288 *Ass*, 1382 Fine, *-rig*' 1288 *Ass*, *-rugg(e)* 1324 *MinAcct*, 1482 (1610) *Cecil*, *-ryg*' 1332 SR, *-regge* 1390 Cl, *Buuerigg*' 1280 *Ass*, *Bourigh*' 14 *Cecil*, *-rigg* 1382 Fine, *-ridge* 1620 *Cecil*, *Bowrigge* 1535 VE, *-ridge* 1620 *Cecil*, 1811 OS, *Borage* 1621 *CH*, cf. *Boveridge Heath* 1795 Boswell. Probably '(place) above the ridge', from **bufan** and **hrycg**, as suggested by Fägersten 100, cf. Bowood in Netherbury par. *infra*. However some of the forms show early confusion or alternation of the first el. with **boga** 'bow', often used in hill-names to describe the shape of a hill; in fact 'bow-shaped, i.e. curved, ridge' would equally well suit the topography of Boveridge.

BURWOOD (SU 062142), 1811 OS, *Borwod(e)* 1285 *Cecil* (*sub-bosc*' *in-*), 1324, 1325 *MinAcct* (*bosc*' *in-*), *Borewode* 1292, 1318 *Cecil*, *Bourewode* 1314 Ipm, 1508 *Cecil*, *Burwod*' 1369 *MinAcct*, *Burwood coppice* 1573 Hutch³, *Borrowwood*, *Burrow wood* (*close, -feyld*) e17 *CecilMap*, *Burrowood* 1619 *CH*, *Burwoodd* 1621 *ib*, *Burrow Fd & Wd* 1846 *TA*, probably 'wood at or near the fortified place', from **burh** and **wudu**, although it is not apparent to what **burh** referred; this is still a wood. The spellings for the first el. may suggest confusion with ˈbūr¹ 'cottage' (cf. *terr*'...*iuxta la Boure* 1382 *Cecil* which may represent this el.) and **burg** 'burrow'.

CASTLE HILL (LANE & WD) (SU 059127), *Castlehill-, -hyll Close* 1553 *Cecil*, *Castle Hill coppice* 1573 Hutch³, *Castle Hill* (*cops*), *Mons Castrensis* e17 *CecilMap*, *Castle Hill Fd* 1784 Hutch³, *Castle Hill* (*Copse*) 1846 *TA*, cf. *Castell*' 1324 *MinAcct*, 1382 *Cecil*, *ten*' *de Castello* 1325 *MinAcct*, *Castelfeld(e)* 1292 *Cecil*, 1385 Cl, 1393 FF, *-feldes* 1482 (1610) *Cecil*, *Castellond* 1382 *ib*, Fine, *Castle Streete* 1553 *Cecil*, *Castelwode* 1285 *ib*, 1324

MinAcct, 1508 *Cecil*, from **castel(l)**, with reference to the undated motte and bailey here (marked 6″, *v*. RCHM 5 15), *v*. **hyll, copis, feld, land, strǣt** and **wudu**.

CRANBORNE PRIORY (lost), founded c.930 as a Benedictine abbey, later a priory subject to Tewkesbury; the church of St Mary and St Bartholomew in Cranborne, rebuilt 1252, was formerly attached to the priory: *Abbatia Creneburnensis, Ecclesia Sanctae Mariae Creneburnensis, Æcclesiae de Creneburne* 1086 DB, *Sancte Marie et Sancto Petro et Sancto Bartholomeo de Cranb'na* 1102 (14) *Cecil, ecclesiam Sanctæ Mariæ de Craneburna* 1109 Hutch[3], *eccl' Beate Marie de Craneburne* a1327 *Cecil*, 'the church of St Mary, St Peter and St Bartholomew, *Craneburne*' 1381 (1408) Pat, *prioratum de Cranburne* 1530 *Cecil, Craneborne Prioratus* 1553 *ib*. On the history of the priory here, *v*. VCHDo 2 70–1; according to Hutch[3] 3 397, the *Priory House* was pulled down c.1703. The priory buildings formerly stood just S of the church (M.H.). The priory gave name to the manor of *Cranborne Priory* (*v*. par. name *supra*) and to Priory Copse Close and other f.ns. in Alderholt par. *supra*.

CROCKERTON HILL (SU 046167), probably to be associated with *Crokkerneweye* 1325 *MinAcct, Crockherne yate* e17 *CecilMap*, 'way to-, gate at the pottery', from **crocc** and **ærn**, with **weg** and **geat**, cf. *Crockern Stoke* in Haselbury B. par. *supra*; Crockerton may mean 'farm or hill at *Crokkerne*', or 'farm or hill of the potters', *v*. **tūn, dūn, croccere**. For other evidence of pot-making in the old par. of Cranborne, cf. Crendell and Old Pottery Kiln in Alderholt par. *supra*, Potterne Fm in Verwood par. *infra*, and the f.n. Potten Hill *infra*.

HIGH WD (lost, SU 069155), 1811 OS, *Haywod'* c.1250 PN W, *Hai-, Haywod(e)* 1285–1318 *Cecil*, 1324, 1325 *MinAcct, (Casies-, Godderds-, Vowles) Haywood* e17 *CecilMap, (Fowles-, Goddardes) Hey(e)wood(d)* 1623 CH, cf. *Hai-, Haywodebrech(e)* 1285, 1318 *Cecil*, 1324, 1325 *MinAcct, Haywood Hams, Haywood Rediche* e17 *CecilMap*. 'Enclosed wood', from **(ge)hæg** and **wudu**, with **brǣc, hamm**; it is on the county bdy and gives name to Highwood Copse and High Haywood Copse (both 6″) in Damerham Ha (PN W 400). For the surnames of the 17th-cent. tenants, cf. Goddard's Barn and the f.ns. *Casies* and *Vowles infra; Rediche* is obscure, but may be a poor spelling.

(Lt & Lr) HOLWELL FM (SU 066133) ['houlwel], *Holewella* 1194 P, *Hole-, Halewelle* 1328 *Cecil, Holewell(e)* 1332 SR, 1335 Orig, 1383 Fine, 1385 Cl *et freq* to 1620 *CH, Holwelle* 1378 Cl, *Holewyll* 1393 FF, *Craneborne Hol(e)well* 1508 *Cecil, Holwell* 1614 *ib et passim, Hollwell* 1623 *CH, Holliwell* 1774 Hutch[1], Lr *Holwell Fm* 1869 Hutch[3], cf. *Holwell Close, -Moore* e17 *CecilMap*, 'hollow stream, stream in a deep valley', from hol[2] (wk.obl. *holan*) and well(a), cf. Holwell Hrt 12, *v.* Corn Mill and Holwell Mill *infra*.

HORSYTH (lost), *horside* 13 *Cecil* (*iter versus-*), *Horsyth(e)* 1249, 1256, 1331 all FF, 1338 Cl, Ipm, *Horseth* 1256 FF, *Horsith(e)* 1311 Cl, 1327 *SR* (p), 1463 Cl, *Horsiche* (for *-sithe*) 1330 FF, 1369 (1372) *ChrP, Horshide* 1412 FA, *Horsetts* 1535 VE, *Horsych* (for *-syth*) 1774 Hutch[1], 1795 Boswell, 1869 Hutch[3]. Possibly 'dirt pit', from horu and sēaŏ, as suggested by Kökeritz 130; the compound is recorded in OE (BT), and the same derivation is suggested by Smith EPN 2 116 for Horseheath C 108 (interpreted in PN C and DEPN as from hors and hæŏ). However, Professor Löfvenberg suggests that this name is probably a cpd of hors 'horse' and īgoŏ, īgeŏ 'small island', comparing Nythe W 284 and (for the meaning) Horse Eye Sx, Horsey Nf, So (DEPN), *v.* Löfvenberg 114–115. *Horsyth* was probably in the S of the old par. of Cranborne; according to Hutch[3] 3 386 it may have comprehended 'the manors of Eastworth and Westworth', *v.* Eastworth Fm now in Verwood par. *infra*, Westworth Fm in Edmondsham par. *infra*.

HYDE (lost), 1530 *Cecil*, e17 *CecilMap*, 1846 *TA, La Hide* 1318 *Cecil*, cf. *la Hide* 1244 *Ass* (p), *Hidewod* 1553 *Cecil, Middle & Upr Hyde, Hyde Fd, Lr Hyde Mdw, Hyde Shoot* 1846 *TA*, 'the hide of land', *v.* hīd, with wudu, scēot[3] 'steep slope' or scyte '(steep) slope or hill'. The *TA* fields indicate the location of this place in the SE corner of the present par. at about SU 070124.

KNAP BARROW (SU 051150), 1811 OS, *plac' voc' Knappedebergh* 1382 *Cecil, Knapped Barrowe* e17 *CecilMap*, (*Rough Bank in*) *Knapped Barrow* 1846 *TA*, cf. *Cnappedeberghe* 1344 Cl (probably not this place, but a point on the county bdy near here), *v.* beorg 'a hill, a mound'; it is described as a tumulus (6″), but it is in fact a natural feature, the remains of Tertiary capping overlying the chalk. The significance of the first el. is not clear, cf. *Knappydehalle* 1 184; however it is most probably a derivative in **-ede** of **cnæpp** 'top, cop', meaning 'provided with a top', cf. **coppede, pīcede, peked**; it is perhaps less likely to be the pa.part. of the ME vb. *knap(p)* 'to break, snap, etc' (NED *knap*[1] from c.1470), cf. ModE *knapped* 'broken' (of flints) (NED from 1861), Brokenborough W 53 which is from **brocen** 'broken' and **beorg**.

ASHES FM, 1846 *TA*, *Ashes* 1811 OS, the surname *Ash* or from **æsc** 'ash-tree'. BLACK BUSH, BLACKBUSH DOWN, *Blackbushe(s)* e17 *CecilMap*, *Black Bush* 1811 OS, *Blackbush* 1846 *TA*, v. **blæc, busc**; Blackbush Down is named *Black Heath* 1826 Gre. BRATCH COPSE, *Brach Wd* 1811 OS, cf. foll. BREACH COPSE, *Breache(s)* e17 *CecilMap*, *Breach Coppice & Grd* 1846 *TA*, v. **bræc** 'land broken up for cultivation', cf. prec. which contains a form of the same word in which early shortening has taken place. BURWOOD PIT, *Burrowwood Pitt* e17 *CecilMap*, *Burrowed Pit Fd* 1846 *TA*, v. **pytt**, Burwood *supra*; *Burrowed* is a contracted form of *Burrow wood*; there are gravel pits in the vicinity (6″). CHALK PIT, cf. *chalke in le magno Putes* (probably for *Puteo*) *iuxta viam...a Cramborne...ad Daggens* 1621 *CH*, *Royal Chalk Pit Fd* 1846 *TA*, v. Daggons in Alderholt par. *supra*. CHURCH (St Mary and St Bartholomew), v. Cranborne Priory *supra*. CHURCHILL DROVE, 1846 *TA*, *Churckehill Droue* e17 *CecilMap*, cf. *Churchhill* 1623 *CH*, v. **drāf**; not near any known church, so perhaps from PrWelsh or PrCorn **crūg* 'hill' with explanatory OE **hyll** as in (Long) Crichel par. *infra*; the drove extends for a mile over the top of Jordan Hill *infra* to the top of another (now unnamed) hill near Rushmore Fm. OLD CLAYGROUNDS, *Old Clay Grd* 1846 *TA*, cf. Crendell and f.ns. in Alderholt par. *supra*. CORN MILL, *Higher Holwell Mill* 1811 OS, cf. *Upr Mill Grd, Mill Plot & Pond* 1846 *TA*, Holwell Mill *infra*; there were four mills in Cranborne, as well as one at Boveridge, in 1086 DB (VCHDo 3 67, 74), and mills in Cranborne are also mentioned in 1236 FF, 1268 *Ass*, 1280 Ch ('the mill in *Craneburne* which Edmer held'), and 1285 *Cecil* (with repairs to a *flodgat* ' *a floodgate* '), cf. the f.n. Mill Downs *infra*. CRANBORNE FM, 1811 OS, -*Md* 1846 *TA*, *Cranburne farme*

1618 *Map*. CRANBORNE LODGE, 1788 Hutch³. CURRIES, *Curries*
(*Copse & Fir Plant*.), *Upr Carries* (sic) 1846 *TA*, cf. Thomas
Curry 1664 HTax. DEAD MAN, a cross-roads, no doubt where
a corpse was found. EAST HAYS, apparently an alteration of *Cast
Hayes* 1846 *TA*, which may be from ModE *cast* 'what is
thrown, a heap', *v.* (ge)hæg; East Hays lies alongside Chalk Pit
supra. FIR COPSE. GILHAM'S COPSE, *Gillams* e17 *CecilMap*, *Hr
& Lr Gilliams, Gilliams Furzy Pce & Plant*. 1846 *TA*, from the
surname *Gill(i)am*. GODDARD'S BARN, *claus' voc' Goddards* 1621
CH, Godhead 1811 OS, cf. *Mr Goddard* 1664 HTax (Pentridge),
High Wd supra. HARE LANE FM, named from *Hare Lane* e17
CecilMap, cf. *Harehill* e17 *ib*, 1618 *CH*, perhaps from **hara** 'a
hare'. HOLWELL MILL, *Lower Mill* 1811 OS, giving name to
Mill Copse in Edmondsham par. *infra*, cf. Holwell Fm, Corn
Mill *supra*, Mill Lane *infra*. JACK'S HEDGE CORNER, *Jacks Hedge*
1846 *TA*, cf. *Iacks Style* e17 *CecilMap*, Thomas *Jackes* 1332
SR (Pentridge), *v.* hecg, stigel. JORDAN HILL (PLANT.), *Iurden
Hill* e17 *CecilMap*, *Jordan Hill* (*Patch*) 1846 *TA*, *v.* patche, cf.
Jordan Hill I 231. KENNEL POND. LONG COPSE, 1846 *TA*.
MANOR FM, near foll. MANOR HO, 1846 *TA*, *manor of Cranborne
Howse* 1509 BrEll, *Cranborne house* 17 CecilMap, cf. *Manor
Drove & Md* 1846 *TA*; the earlier building here (a fortified
hunting lodge built by King John) is referred to as *castri de
Craneburn'* 1241, *prisona* (*regis*) *de Cran(e)burn'* 1261, 1270 all
Cl, *v.* Hutch³ 3 380–1, RCHMDo 5 5. MEAR'S POND, a pool on
the par. and county bdy, possibly to be identified with (*bi weste*)
widemere 944–6 (14) BCS 817 (S 513) in the bounds of
Damerham Ha, 'wide pool', *v.* wīd, mere¹. MILL LANE,
leading to Corn Mill and Holwell Mill both *supra*. NODDLE
HILL (WD). PARK ROW, cf. *West Park* 1314 Ipm, *Park,
Westpark* 1318 *Cecil*, (*the*) *Park, North Park, Park Fd & Pce*
1846 *TA*, *v.* park, rāw, and cf. the medieval park at Blagdon
supra. PAUL'S COPSE, *Pauls* (*Copse & Wd*) 1846 *ib*. PEAKED
CORNER, *Pyke* (*Corner*) e17 *CecilMap*, *v.* pīc¹ 'point', peked
'pointed', corner; at the N corner of the par. PEAKED PLANT.,
a triangular wood, cf. prec. PENNY'S FM, cf. *Penneys Md* 1846
TA. PERRY COPSE, cf. an identical name in Alderholt par. *supra*.
PETERS FM (lost, SU 050168), 1811 OS. PURBECK LANE, cf. 'the
land which Ralph *Burbik* held' 1280 Ch, John *de Purbke* n.d.
(1372) *ChrP* (Wimborne St G.); perhaps a surname from Isle

of Purbeck 1 1. PYE LANE, *Py Lane* e17 *CecilMap*, from pēo
'insect' or pie² 'magpie'. REVEL'S POND, *Revels Pond* 1846 *TA*,
cf. *Rebles Meade* e17 *CecilMap*, *Rebbles-* 1620, *Revels Bridge*
1622 *CH*; the pond is beside R. Crane, near a foot-bridge
(marked 6″). ROKE HILL, (*pasture in*) *Roke* 1846 *TA*, probably
'(place) at the oak-tree', from ME *atter oke*, *v.* atter, āc, cf.
Roke 1 276; the form *Rake* 1614 *Cecil* may belong here.
ROOKERY WD. ROUND COPSE. RUSHMORE FM, *Rushmore* e17
CecilMap, 1620 *Cecil* (-*nere Crendall*), *Rushmoor* 1846 *TA*, *v.*
risc, rysc, mōr, Crendell in Alderholt par. *supra*. ST ALDHELM'S
CHURCH, cf. an earlier chapel at Boveridge mentioned in 1595
RCHM. SALISBURY HALL, no doubt named from the Earls of
Salisbury, lords of the manor since the early 17th cent.
STANDRIDGE, -*Cl*, -*Fd*, -*Hill* 1846 *TA*, *Sandridge* 1811 OS,
Stanridge 1869 Hutch³, perhaps to be associated with *Stanrigge*
1236 FF, from stān 'stone' and hrycg 'ridge'; stān may allude
to the line of stones (shown 6″) marking the par. bdy here.
STONE HILL GATE & WD (1811 OS), perhaps named from a stone
here (shown 6″) marking the county bdy, cf. Ralph *atte Stone*
1398 *Cecil*, *v.* atte, stān. TARGETT'S FM, *Targetts Farm Ho* 1846
TA, cf. *Targets Home Fd*, *Targetts Long Fd & Md* 1846 *ib*.
TELEGRAPH CTG, on Jordan Hill, 2 miles from Telegraph Plant.
in Alderholt par. *supra*. TENANTRY WD, *Tenantry* 1811 OS, *v.*
tenantry. THANES COPSE, *Thians-* 1846 *TA*, cf. Lt Thanes
Copse in Alderholt par. *supra*. TOBY'S BOTTOM, cf. *Tobys gate*
e17 *CecilMap*, *Tobys Fm* 1811 OS, *v.* geat, botm. THE WELL,
a spot of swampy ground…called the well 1869 Hutch³, *v.*
well(a). WELLSNARE (lost, SU 060166), 1811 OS. WHITE HO
(COPSE). WITHY BED. WOODWARD'S COPSE, *Woodwards-* 1846
TA, cf. *Hilly & Upr Woodwards* 1846 *ib*.

FIELD-NAMES

The undated forms are 1846 *TA* 73. For some fields in Cranborne *TA* now
in Alderholt, *v.* Alderholt f.ns. *supra*. Spellings dated 1234, 1344 are Cl, 1236,
1296, 1599, 1784, 1869 Hutch³, 1280, 1288 *Ass*, 1280² Ch, 1314 Ipm, 1320,
1324, 1325, 1411 *MinAcct*, 1327 *SR*, 1332 SR, 1382² Fine, e17 *CecilMap*,
1618, 1619, 1620, 1621, 1622, 1623 *CH*, 1664 HTax, and the rest *Cecil*.

(a) The Acre; Alderman; Allotment Fd; Aplangs; Ashy Fd; Baileys Fd (cf.
Nicholas *Baille* 1332); Barlows Copse; Barn Cl, Fd & Grd, Barn Mdw or
Moor; Bean Acre; Berry Grd; Biddlecombs Barn and Fold, Biddlecombs

Md; Bird Pit Fd; Blagden-, Blagdon Lane Pce (cf. *in regia via de Blakedon'* *in vill' de Craneburne* 1280, *Blackedoneweye* 1518 PN W 402, *v.* Blagdon *supra*); Bottom Cl (*v.* **botm**); Brewers Bank (*-Bancke* e17, *v.* **bank(e)**, cf. Alderholt f.ns. *supra*); Broad Fd; Brown Adams (e17); Burnbeck (*v.* **burn-bake**); Bushy Gdn; Buttons (cf. Henry *Bodyn* 1382, John *Budden* 1599 (in possession of Holwell Fm *supra, v.* Hutch³ 3 386), Richard *Budden* 1664, cf. Verwood f.ns. *infra*); Charity Fd & Grd (on charitable benefactions in Cranborne, *v.* Hutch³ 3 398); The Close; Coles('s) (*Coles* e17, cf. *Cowles Moore* 1621, *prat' voc' Collis* 1623, the surname *Cole(s)*, or *Coll(s)*, *v.* **mōr**); Collar Maker (no doubt elliptical for 'land belonging to the collar maker'); Comptons (Fd & Ho) (cf. Charles *Compton* 1664); Coneys Acre (cf. Andrew *Cony*, William *Conny* 1664); Copse Cl; the Court Cl 1869 (cf. *curiam de Craneburn* 1234, 'the close of the court of Cranborne' 1296, *curia chacie* 1331, *the Courte barton and backside* 1623, *v.* **court, bere-tūn, backside**, Cranborne Chase *supra*); Cow Grd, Lr & Upr Cow Leaze; Cranborne Gate, (Far & Near) Cranborne Gate Pce; Crossway Pce (*v.* **cross**); Decoy Pond (*v.* **decoy**); 8 Acres (cf. *8 acr peece, eighte acre close* e17); 11 Acres; Far Copse; Farleys Md; Fishers and Goulds (cf. Nicholas *Fisher* (Edmondsham), Richard *Goold*, *-Gould* 1664); 5 Acres; The 4 Acres; Four and a half acres; The 14 Acres (cf. *fourteen acre Peece* e17); Fridays Heron (*Fryday(e)s Herne* e17, 1621, cf. *ten' Joh' Friday* 1328, *Frydayes close* e17, *v.* **hyrne** 'angle, corner'); Gipsies Pit Fd (named from Gipsies' Pit in Edmondsham par. *infra*); Grass Grds; Gravel Pit and Waste (cf. Gravel Pits 6"); Green Cl & Plot; Greens Further & Nearer Water Md (cf. Nicholas *Grene* 1664, *v.* **wæter**); Hannans (perhaps to be associated with the family of James *Hanham* who held the manor of Blagdon *supra* in 1597 Hutch³ 3 383); (Lt) Hardings (cf. George *Harding* 1664); Hayters Fd; Hayward Hill Cl (*Haywardes Hill* 1619), Hr, Lr & Middle Haywards (cf. John *Langehayward* 14, Samuel *Hayward*, Walter *Heyward* 1664); Hedge Row; Holdins, Long Holdens (*Holdene* 1404, *-den* e17, 1622, 'deep valley', from **hol²** and **denu**); Home Cl, Fd & Orchd; Hop Gdn (*v.* **hoppe**); Hopper Cl; Horse Leaze (*Horslease* 1553, *Horseleaze* e17, *v.* **hors, lǣs**); Island Mdw; Kings (*cl' terr' voc' kinges* 1553, *Kings Close* e17, *claus' voc' Kinges* 1621, cf. *unam acram...quam Rogerus le Kyng quondam tenuit* 13, Walter *Kyng'* 1332); New Lidden (*-Litton* e17, *v.* **līc-tūn** 'burial ground'); Little Md; Long Close & Fd; Long Lawrence; Lonnens Fd & Pce; Lower Mdw; Luckhams Md (*-Mead(e)* e17, 1621, a surname, *v.* **mǣd**); Marling Pit(s) Fd (*Marlepytts* 1621, *v.* **marle, marling, pytt**); The Mead, (Lr & Upr) Meadow; Middle Cl; Middle Fd (*Midlefild* 1553, *v.* **middel, feld**); Middle Grd & Md(w); Mile-, Mill Downs (*Mill downs* e17, cf. Corn Mill *supra*); Lr & Upr Moor (cf. Alderholt f.ns. *supra*); The Mount; New Drove (Fd & Pce) (*v.* **drāf**); New Grd; 9 & 19 Acres; Hr & Middle Normans, Leg Normans (*Normans Lande* e17, perhaps from the surname *Norman*, but probably to be associated with *Nonemannes lond* 13, 1382, 'no man's land', *v.* **nān, mann, land, leg**; the three TA fields lie along the par. bdy); Nursery Copse; Oats Grd & Orchd (probably the surname *Oats*); Orchard (cf. *the Orchard* 1620); Paradise (*v.* **paradis**); Picks (*terr' voc' Pykes* 1622, cf. *Pikes-, Pukes Lane* 1619); Pig Oak; Pit Cl (*Pitt-* e17, *v.* **pytt**); Pit Copse & Grd (cf. prec.); Pond Cl; Potten Hill (perhaps 'place where pots are made', from pot(t) and **ærn** or **tūn**); The Pound, Pound Fd (*v*. **pund**); Red Lion Fd (no doubt from the name of an inn); Rickyard; Rough (*v*. **rūh**); Rough Bank & Pasture; Row (freq, *v*. **row**); Rushy Corner, (Far & Near) Rushy Mdw; Rye Grd; Sandy Plot; 7 Acres under Jordan Hill (*v*. *supra*); Shepherds Cl (cf. William *Shepheard* 1664); 6 Acres (*terr' in Sixacres* 1553, *claus' voc' le Six Akers* 1621, *v*. **sex, æcer**); Skinners (*Skynners Feyld* e17, *-Field, -Fyeld* 1621, cf. Michael *le Skynner'* 1332, *v*. **feld**); Smock Acre (*v*. **smoke** 'smoke'); Square Grd; Storeys Md, Inner Storeys White Hill (the surname *Storey, v.* White Hill *infra*); Strip (under Wood) (*v*. **strip**); Strongs (*Stronges* e17, the surname *Strong*); Tappers Half (*v*. **half**, cf. Alderholt f.ns. *supra*); (The) 10 Acres; 30 Acres (*the thirtye Akers* 1621); Three Cornered Fd; 12 Acres (cf. *Twelve acre close* e17); Two Houses; Ubgins; Vales (*Vales (Breache)* e17, a surname, with bræc 'land broken up for cultivation'), Wadleys Drove (Fd) (cf. William *Wadeclay* (sic) 1327, *v*. **drāf**); Warny Cl (perhaps to be associated with *Wernham infra*); Over the Water Md (to be construed as 'meadow over the water', cf. John *del Watere, -de Watre* 1288, *le Water lane* 1619, *v*. **wæter**; the field is encircled by two arms of R. Crane); (Gt & Lt) White Hill (*Whithull'* 1382, *Whitehill, Withill* 1553, *Whyte Hill, Whytehill furlonge* e17, *White Hill Fd* 1784, *v*. **hwīt, hyll**, 'white' in allusion to chalk); Winborne Lane (to Wimborne St G. par. *infra*); Yew Tree Fd (cf. *ad quendam arborem le hiis* 1236 Hutch³ 3 386 (in bounds of Boveridge *supra* and Damerham Ha), which may represent the pl. of **īw** 'yew-tree'; a yew-tree is still marked (6″) on this stretch of the county bdy, near Yewtree Copse in Damerham, *v*. PN W 402); Yonder Cl.

(*b*) *Ables meade* 1553 (the pers.n. or surname *Abel, v*. **mǣd**); *pastur' voc' le backsid* 1553, *the backside* 1621 (*v*. **backside**); *atte Barre* 1324, 1325, 1328, 1332 all (p), *ten' Nich' atte Barre* 1325 (*v*. **barre** 'bar, rod, barrier', **atte**); *Batchelers* e17 (a surname); *atte beche* 1328 (p) (*v*. **bece¹** 'stream, valley', or **bēce²** 'beech-tree', **atte**); *Benshams* e17, *Bensons Lane* 1619 (a surname); *Boochers Close* e17 (a surname); *terr'...iuxta la Boure* 1382 (*v*. **būr¹** 'cottage', cf. Burwood *supra*); *Brodforlang* 13 (*v*. **brād** 'wide', **furlang**); *Brod(e)lond(')* 1382 (*v*. **land**); *brode meade* 1553 (*v*. **mǣd**); *Brodmoore* 1553 (*v*. **mōr**); *ten' voc' Bulls* 1620 (a surname); *Burches* 1619 (*v*. *Suddon infra*); *Bushops* e17 (a surname); *Casies, Casyes* e17 (a surname, cf. *High Wood supra*); *Chalvecroft* 1318 (*v*. **calf** (WSax gen.pl. *cealfa*), **croft**); *Chinnocks Pitt* e17 (a surname, *v*. **pytt**); *Clarkes* e17 (a surname); *Cnoklarde Lane* 1620; *Codebregie, Codemor* 1285, *Coudebrec(c)h(e)* 1318, 1324, *Coudemor* 1318, 1325, *Schoudebrech* 1325, *Coudehouwe* 1328, *Scudhow(e)* e17, 1621 (the first el. of these names would seem to be an OE pers.n. *Cōda* suggested for Cooden Sx 491, cf. also the ME surname *Coude* freq in 1332 SR, with **bræc, mōr** and **howe**; the form in *Scud-* may have arisen through metanalysis of a surname with possessive -*s* and *Cud-*); *Colver(h)eye* 1285, 1318 (*v*. **culfre, (ge)hæg**); *Comon Crofte* e17 (*v*. **comun**); *Cookesgrove* 1382 (the surname *Cook, v*. **grāf(a)**); *de Cruce* 1320, *atte Cruche* 1327, *atte Crouch(e)* 1328, 1332, *at Crosse* 1614 all (p) (*v*. **crux, crūc³**, **cros** 'cross', **atte**); *Cunygere Bottome* e17 (*v*. **coninger, botm**); *Depemore* 1344 (near Cranborne on Do-Ha county bdy, *v*. **dēop, mōr**); *The Droue* 1618 *Map* (*v*. **drove**); *le farme* 1530 (*v*. **ferme**); *Fiftie acre feylde* e17; *Glebeland* 1553 (belonging to Cranborne Priory *supra, v*. **glebe**); *Godesacre, Godesgore* 1382 (the ME surname *Gode, v.* **æcer, gāra**); *Godfryes Drove* e17 (the pers.n. or surname *Godfrey, v.* **drāf**); *la Goreacr(e)* 1324, 1325 (*v.* **gāra, æcer**); *de la Grene* 1288 (p) (*v.* **grēne**[2]); *Hallewode* 1314 (*v.* **hall, wudu**); *Haselley* e17 (*v.* **hæsel, lēah** or **(ge)hæg**; *hemefild* 1553 (*v.* **hǣme, feld**); *Hennings close* e17 (cf. Richard *Hening* 1664); *Hermgroue yate* e17 (*v.* **grāfa, geat,** first el. uncertain); *Hoggen Bottom* e17 (*v.* **hogg** (ME gen.pl. *-en(e)*) 'young sheep', **botm**); *Hoksesplace* 1398 (the surname *Hooks, v.* **place**); *Holweton* 1318 ('farm in a hollow', *v.* **hol**[1], **tūn**); *Hoppehull* 1280[2] (*v.* **hyll**; the first el. may be **hoppa** 'grass-hopper', perhaps used as a pers.n.); *atte Horewode* 1331 (p) (*v.* **wudu, atte**; first el. **hār**[2] 'grey' or **horu** 'dirt'); *le Inclose, (lez) Incloses* 1553 (*v.* **in** 'inner'); *Kenteliscombe* 1236 Hutch[3] 3 386, *Kenelescomb(e)* 1247 (c. 1340) Glast (in bounds of Boveridge *supra* and Damerham Ha, 'Centel's valley', from an OE pers.n. *Centel* (for which *v.* DEPN s.n. Kentisbeare D) and **cumb**); *Les Layes* 1318 (probably a poor spelling for foll.); *le layns* 1285 (*v.* **leyne** 'tract of arable land'); *Le Lodge* e17 (near Crockerton Hill *supra, v.* **logge**); *Longdene close, -yate* e17 (*v.* **lang**[1], **denu, geat**); *camp' de Luuenesburg* 13 ('Lēofwine's fortified place', from the OE pers.n. *Lēofwine* and **burh**); *Lyndhull* 1280[2] (*v.* **lind** 'lime-tree', **hyll**); *Maleckesdene* 1553 (a surname with **denu** 'valley'); *Merghedene* 1344 (near Cranborne on Do-Ha county bdy, 'pleasant valley', *v.* **myrge, denu**); *Middeldone* 1318 (*v.* **middel, dūn**); *Midle Droue* e17 (*v.* **drāf**); *Mournes* e17 (a surname); *atte Nassche* 1331 (p) (*v.* **atte(n), æsc**); *la Newecroft'* 1404 (*v.* **nīwe, croft**); *sepem domini voc' la Neweheigge, -heighe* 1404 (*v.* **hege** 'hedge, fence'); *Newelaund* 1280[2] (p), *la Newelond* 1382, *Newlandes* e17 (*v.* **land**); *le Northdowne yate* 1622 (*v.* **norð, dūn, geat**); *Northholt* 1411 (*v.* **holt**); *Nywedolveneford* 1344 (near Cranborne on Do-Ha county bdy, 'newly dug ford', i.e. probably 'ford that has been recently built up', from **nīwe, gedolfen** pa.part. of *delfan* 'to dig', **ford**); *Owtfild* 1553 (*v.* **ūt** 'outer', **feld**); *Parretts howse, -meadowe* 1614 (the surname *Parrett*); *burgag' voc' Paynettes* 1508 (the surname *Pa(y)nett*); *Pyked feylde* e17 (*v.* **pīcede** 'pointed'); *atte Pyle* 1324, 1332, 1340, *atte Pile* 1325, 1327 all (p) (*v.* **pīl** 'shaft, stake', **atte**); *(claus' pastur' in) le nether eddynge, -(le) overed(d)ynge, -inge* 1553 (probably **ryding** 'clearing', *v.* **neoðerra, uferra**); *Redewode* 1325 (*v.* **rēad, wudu**); *Redhill, -holl* e17 (*v.* **hyll**); *Redpitts* e17 (*v.* **pytt**); *Rewe ground* 1620[2] (*v.* **rǣw**); *Roddokeslane* 1404 (the surname *Ruddock* (from OE *ruddoc* 'robin'), *v.* **lane**); *Ruggeweye* 1325 (*v.* **hrycg-weg**); *Rullecochesclo(o)s* 1382 (a surname with **clos(e)**); *firm' molendini de Scoudmell, -Scoutemull'* 1382, 'watermill called *Scondmulle*' 1382[2] (*v.* **myln** 'mill'; Professor Löfvenberg suggests that the first el. might be *Stond-* reflecting OE **stande** 'pond', a word found in two OE charters relating to Brk, *v.* Forsberg 112 fn. 2, PN Brk 638); *la Schulue* 1325 (*v.* **scielf, scylf** 'ledge'); *Smalemede* 1318, 1324 (*v.* **smæl, mǣd**); *Smalryn* 1344 (near Cranborne on Do-Ha county bdy, 'narrow stream or ditch', *v.* **smæl, ryne**); *Smythes Bushe* e17, 1621 (the surname *Smith(e)* and **busc**); *Somergate* 1344 (near Cranborne on Do-Ha county bdy, *v.* **sumor, geat**); *Southe Feylde* e17, *in campo australi* 1621 (*v.* **sūð**); *Stene* e17 (*v.* **stǣne** 'stony place'); *Stockmead* 1553 (*v.* **stocc, mǣd**); *Stoudlond* 14 (*v.* **stōd, land,** cf. Studland 1 43); *Stretacre* 1344 (*v.* **strǣt, æcer**); *Tailecopice close* 1553 (*v.* **tægl** 'tail of land', **copis**); *Tallowe Bridge* 1618; *Thornyham* 1553 (*v.* **þornig, hamm**); *Thorps* e17 (probably a surname);

Threescore acre feylde e17; (*atte*) *Twychene* 1325 (p) (*v.* twicen(e) 'cross-roads', atte); *Twyne Feylde* e17 (probably from **betwēonan** 'between'); *Vowles* e17 (a surname, cf. *High Wood supra*); *Wakes* e17 (a surname); *Weede crofte* e17 (*v.* **wēod**); *Warners ham* 1553 (probably from the surname *Warner* and **hamm**, but perhaps to be associated with *Wernham* 1288, which may be from **wrǣna**, **wærna** 'stallion' or **wrenna**, **wærna** 'wren', cf. also Warny Cl *supra*); *Westfeld* 1324 (*v.* **west**); *Wildlese* 1553 (*v.* **wilde, lǣs**); *Willeie* 1382 (*v.* **lēah**, first el. perhaps **w(i)ell(a), wyll(a)** 'spring, stream' as in foll.); *le dytche apud Wolbrach* 1622 (*v.* **dīc, wyll(a), brǣc**); *Woodclose* e17; *Wood Crampe* e17 (second el. probably **cramb** 'bend', cf. dial *cramp* 'bend in a ditch or fence' (Ha, *v.* EDD)); *atte Wych'* 1332 (p) (*v.* **wīc** or **wice, atte**); *Zeale Crofte* e17 (*v.* **sealh** (WSax dat.sg. *sēale*) 'willow').

Edmondsham

A small detached part of Gussage All Sts par. was transferred to this par. in 1886. Westworth in this par. was in Bindon liberty (1 107–8).

EDMONDSHAM (SU 061116) ['edmənʃəm, 'enʃəm]
  Amedesham 1086 DB, *Medesham* 1086 ib (2 ×), c.1150 MontC,
  Medessan 1086 Exon, *Emedesham* 1280 *Ass*
  Ædmodesham 1176, 1186 P (p), *Edmodesham* 1196 ChancR
  (p), 1197 *AddCh* (p), P (p), 1205 Cur, 1214 P (p), 1226 FF,
  1236 ib (p), *Emodesham* 1206 P, 1251 Ch, 1253 Cl (p), 1268,
  1288 *Ass*, 1303 FA, *Eumodesham* 1268 *Ass*
  Agemodesham 1177 P (p), *Aumodesham* 1244 *Ass* (p), *Aug-
  modesham* n.d. AD I (p)
  Edmundesham 1195 P (p), 1196 ChancR (p), 1248 Ipm, 1283
  Cecil *et freq* to 1438 Queens, *Emondesham* 1283 *Cecil*, 1370
  Pat, 1393 FF, *Eymondesham* 1316 FA, *Edmondesham* 1332
  Ipm *et freq* to 1563 Hutch³ (*-alias Ensham alias Edynsham*),
  Emundesham 1378 Cl, *Edmonsam* 1536 VE, *Edmondsham*
  1618 *CH*
  Edmondesham Paine c.1346, *Edmundes Champayne*, *Edmondes-
  ham Payne juxta Cranborne* 1469, *Edmundeschampayne*
  (*juxta Cranborn*) 1484, 1554 all Hutch³
  Ensom 1664 Hutch³

'Ēadmōd's or Ēadmund's homestead or enclosure', from an unrecorded OE pers.n. *Ēadmōd*, or the common *Ēadmund*, and **hām** or **hamm**; the forms in *Age-, Au-, Augmodes-* are probably best explained as showing further alternation of the pers.n. with an OE *Ealhmōd*, cf. Amersham Bk 209. The moiety of the manor

formerly known as *Edmondesham Paine* belonged to the family
which gave its name to Stourpaine par. *supra* (Bartholomew
Payn 1316, 1332 Hutch³, Richard- 1332 SR, Edward *Payne* c.
1346, 1388 Hutch³), cf. Pains Moor Copse *infra*; *-Champayne*
is due to metanalysis of *-sham Payne* and association of this
manor with *Shapwick Champaigne* named from the *Champaigne*
family, *v.* Shapwick par. *supra.*

ROMFORD (BRIDGE & MILL), ROMFORD EAST FM (SU 074094),
Runford 1268 *Ass*, *Rungeford* 1308 Banco, *Rongford* 1403 *Midd*,
1407 Hutch³, *Rough-* (for *Rongh-*) 1407 IpmR, *Rougeford* (for
Ronge-) 1417 ib, *Runggeforde* 1489 Ipm, *Rumforthe* 1575
Saxton, *-ford* 1618 *Map*, *Bomford Mill* (sic) 1811 OS, 'ford
marked by a pole', from **hrung** and **ford**, a name similar in
meaning to the common p.n. Stapelford (C, Ch, Ess, etc). The
Cranborne-Ringwood road crosses R. Crane here. The mill here
is probably (on the site of) the water-mill in Westworth *infra*
mentioned in 1546 Hutch³ 3 425, cf. also *molend' de Emodesham*
1268 *Ass*, *Mill and Gdn* 1838 *TA*, and the two mills in two of
the manors of Edmondsham in 1086 DB (VCHDo 3 68, 101).

WESTWORTH FM (SU 077103), *Worth'* 1268 *Ass*, 1318 *Cecil*,
(*communia de*) *Worthe* 1575 Saxton, 1621 *CH*, *Worth W.* 1795
Boswell, *Worth Fm* 1811 OS, *Westworth Common* 1838 *TA*,
West Worth 1869 Hutch³, *v.* **worð** 'enclosure', **west** 'west' to
distinguish this farm from Eastworth Fm in Verwood par. *infra*
½ mile SE, cf. *Horsyth* in Cranborne par. *supra.*

AVENUE LODGE, at the top of the avenue leading to St Giles's
Ho in Wimborne St G. par. *infra.* BARN FD, cf. *Barn Cl* 1838
TA. BOTTOM COPSE, 1838 *ib*, cf. *Bottom Fd* 1838 *ib*, *v.* **botm**
'valley'. BRAMBLES FM, cf. Bramble's Fm in W Parley par.
infra. CHEATER'S COPSE, cf. *Cheaters Fd*, *Cheatersfield* 1838 *ib*,
cf. Cheater's Lane in Alderholt par. *supra.* COCK ROW, *Cock
Row Wd* 1838 *ib*, possibly from **cocc-rodu** 'clearing where
woodcock were netted'. COOK'S MOOR, *venell' ad Cookes Moore*
1620 *CH*, *v.* **mōr**, cf. Thomas *Cocus* 13 *Cecil*, Widow *Cooke*
1664 HTax. CRANBORNE COPSE, *Cram-* 1838 *TA*, near the bdy
with Cranborne par. *supra.* EDMONDSHAM HO. FURZE CMN
COPSE. GIPSIES' PIT, *Gipsies Pit Fd* 1846 *TA* (Cranborne), cf.
Sibyl *atte Putte* 1332 SR, *v.* **pytt** 'a pit', **atte**, cf. Mutton Hole

infra. GOTHAM (CMN, COPSE & FM), *Goathams* 1838 *TA*, probably 'goat enclosures', from **gāt** and **hamm**. GRAINS HILL, *Gt & Lt Grains, Grains Md* 1838 *ib*, probably a surname. GRAVEL PIT (2 ×). IRONMONGERS COPSE, 1838 *ib*. LODGE. LONG COPSE. LOWER FM, cf. Upper Fm *infra*. MARLEY'S ROW, *Marrowe leaze* 1621 *CH, Murrel Leaze* 1841 *TA* (Gussage All Snts), *v*. **lǣs** 'pasture', **rāw**; the first el. may be ModE *marrow* in the figurative sense 'rich food, essence', used to denote good pasture along a small tributary of R. Crane; however if the form *prat' vocat' Morleyrs* 1494 *Cecil* belongs here, the name may have a different origin. MILL COPSE, (*Lane by*) *Mill Copse, Mill Cl* 1838 *TA*, named from Holwell Mill in Cranborne par. *supra*. MUTTON HOLE, like Gipsies' Pit *supra*, a pit on the par. bdy, *v*. **hol**[1]; *Mutton* is probably a surname, cf. Richard *Moton* 1332 SR (Holt). NELLIE'S COPSE, *Nellys Cl & Pce* 1838 *TA*. PAINS MOOR COPSE, *Paynsmore* 1444 *Queens, Paynes Moore* 1621 *CH, Coppice adjoining Payne's Moor, Paynes' Moor Coppice* 1841 *TA* (Gussage All Snts), *v*. **mōr**, par. name *supra*. PINNOCKS MOOR (BRIDGE & CTGS), *Pinnock bridge* 1618 *Map, Pynnocks Bridge greene* 1621 *CH, Pinnick's Moor Bridge* 1791 Boswell, *Pennicks Moor* 1811 OS, *Pinnocks Md* 1838 *TA, Pinnock's Moor* 1869 Hutch[3], *v*. **mōr, brycg, grēne**[2], cf. William *Pynnok'* 1332 SR (Wimborne St G.). PISTLE DOWN (1811 OS) & HILL (1811 ib), at the extreme E corner of the par., possibly from ModE (*e*)*pistle* with reference to a reading from the scriptures during beating the bounds. RECTORY, *The parsonage-house* 1869 Hutch[3]. GT & LT RHYMES COPSE, *Rimes Copse, Lt Rimes (Copse)* 1838 *TA*, on the par. bdy, so perhaps from **rima** 'border', cf. PN Brk 377. THE ROUGHS, *v*. **rūh**. ST NICHOLAS'S CHURCH, 'the church of *Emondesham*' 1370 Pat, 'St Nicholas *Edmondesham*' 1385 Cl, 'the church of St Nicholas' 1396 Hutch[3], called alternatively 'the church of St Michael of *Edmondesham*' 1393 ib, cf. *Church Lands* 1869 ib ('four acres...appropriated for the repair of the church'). There was formerly also a chapel here, referred to as *capella de Edmondesham* 1340 NI, 'the church of St Quintin' 1396 Hutch[3], 'a chapel...called St Quintin's' 1587 ib, cf. 'tenement called St Quintin's' 1684 ib. SANDY'S HILL, cf. Sampson *Sanders* 1664 HTax. SMALLBRIDGE COPSE & FM, *Smallbridge gate* 1621 *CH, Smallbridge Copse, Small*

Bridge Cow Lease & Fd 1838 *TA, v.* smæl 'narrow', brycg; by a tributary of R. Crane. UPPER FM, cf. Lower Fm *supra.*

FIELD-NAMES

The undated forms are 1838 *TA* 79, but forms marked † are 1841 *TA* 94 (Gussage All Snts). Spellings dated 1332 are SR, 1494 *Cecil*, n.d. (16), 1546 Hutch³, 1618 CH, 1664 HTax, and 1916 *TA* alt.app.

(*a*) Anthonys Md; Ashen Style (*v.* æscen); Baines Wet Mdw; (Wood in) Bar Cl (*v.* barre); Barns Md; High & Lr Basketts (cf. Thomas *Baskett* 1664 (Cranborne)); Bason Grd; †Bornett Dry and Water Mds (perhaps from bærnet 'land cleared by burning'); Breach (*v.* bræc); Brick Cl; Lt Brinstead (perhaps from stede 'place, site' with bryne 'burning'); Chitterne Copse & Fd, Gt & Lt Chitterne Md(w) (perhaps analogous with Chitterne W 163); Clap Gate (*v.* clap-gate); Common; Copse Cl & Md; Gt & Lt Covenbury; Cow Leaze; Cuckolds Md (perhaps a reference to cuckolding, cf. Cuckolds Parlor 1 27, but possibly from the family of Henry *Guggell* n.d. (16)); Daffyclose 1916; (Gt & Lt) Down (*v.* dūn); Drove; Dunns Md (cf. Edmund *Dunne* 1664); Dunocks (cf. *Dunockes Lane* 1618, from dunnoc 'hedge-sparrow' or a surname from this); Eunucks Md (from ModE *eunuch,* unless this is an error for *Dunucks-, v.* prec.); Giffords Cl; Goose Copse; Gorr Copse (*v.* gāra); Great Md; Green Cl; Grove Copse, the Grove, (The) Groves, Short Groves (*v.* grāf(a)); Hedge Row; Higher Fd; High Hills, †Gt & Inner Highhills; Home Cl, Cmn, Grd & Md; Hospital Md; Humber Md (perhaps an instance of the pre-English r.n. Humber; the field lies alongside R. Crane); Hungry Grd & Hill (*v.* hungrig, denoting poor land); Lr, Middle & Upr Irish, Irish Copse (from the family of Robert *Irishe* 1562 Hutch³ 3 423); Gt & Lt Ister (perhaps from ēstre 'sheep-fold'); Kimbridge; Lime Kiln Gdn; Little Fd & Mdw; Long Cl, Croft & Mdw; Lynchet Stile Fd (*v.* linchet); Maldry Fd (named from Maldry Wd in Wimborne St G. par. *infra*); (the) Meadow (cf. *pratum voc' Meadhayes* 1618, *v.* mǣd, (ge)hæg); Mertins Plot; Middle Moor Cmn (cf. John *atte More* 1332, *v.* mōr, atte); Newbury Fd, Lt Newburys ('pasture called *Newbury'* 1546, perhaps a manorial name; the fields are at Pinnocks Moor *supra*); Hthr & Yonder Newmans; North Fd; (Wood in) Northover (from ōfer¹ 'bank' or ofer² 'hill'); Dry & Wet Olivers, Lt Olivers; (N) Orchard, Orchard Cl; Outlets (*v.* utlete); Piles and Painters (both surnames; for the first cf. *atte Pyle* in Cranborne f.ns. *supra*); The Park, Gt Park (for a park at Edmondsham in 1228 Ipm, *v.* Cantor & Wilson 1 112); The Peak (*v.* pēac); Peal Pits; Picked Grd (*v.* pīcede 'pointed'); Pit Cl; Pond Cl; Richardsons (cf. Widow *Richardson* 1664); Half of River; Rooks (Copse, Long Grd & Md); Rose Grd; Rushy Pce; Russells Cl (cf. William *Russel* 1332 (Cranborne); Rusty Copse; Gt & Lt Sadlers; Sandy Cl; Sangers Cl (cf. John *Sanger* 1664); School Ho; Sling (*v.* sling); Sonsoms Md (cf. *Mellior Samson* 1664 (Cranborne)); Sprotts Ld; Stanbridge Cmn & Grd (an error for *Stan(d)ridge-,* named from Standridge in Cranborne par. *supra*); Strattons Grd; 10 Acres 1916; Thistle Cl; Turnpike Rd; Water Md(w); Gt & Lt Wood Cl, Wood Cl Coppice; Woods.

(b) *Boudykes lane* 1494 (perhaps 'curved ditch', from **boga** and **dīc**); *the mansyon howse att Huckelake* n.d. (16) (perhaps from an OE pers.n. *Hucca* (for which v. DEPN s.n. Hucknall) and **lacu**).

Farnham

FARNHAM (ST 957151)
> *Fernham* 1086 DB (4 ×), 1201 Cur, FF, 1263 Ipm, 1282 FF *et freq* to 1486 *Eton*, '-by *Hanley*' 1405 Pat, *Ferneham* 1086 DB, Exon, 1281 Cl, c.1333 BM I *et freq* to 1553 *Cecil*, *Fernaam* 1089 (1371) Pat, *Vernham* 1288 *Ass*, *Fernaham* 1338 Pat, *Fernhaump* 1412 FA, *Fern(n)am* 1431 *ib*, 1475 Pat
> *Farnham* 1199 CurR, 1261 FF, 1280 *Ass*, 1285 *Cecil et passim*, -*Deverel* 1283 *Cecil*, '-by *Guss(h)ygge*' 1432 Pat, *Farneham* 1205 RC, 1466 *Weld*[2] *et freq* to 1547 *AD*, *Farnam* 1263 Ipm, 1408 BM I, *Farenham* 1288 *Ass*, *Gounvyle Farnham* 1547 Ct, *Little Farnham* 1829 *EnclA*
> *Farham* 1261 FF, *Ferham* 1288 *Ass*
> *Firnham* 1283 *Cecil*, -*Cary* 1362 Pat, *Fyrnham* 1324 FF
> *Fornham* 1314, 1399 Cl

'Homestead or enclosure where ferns grow', from **fearn** and **hām** or **hamm**, cf. Six. Handley par. *infra*, Gussage St M. par. *supra*. This p.n. occurs in several other counties, e.g. Farnham Ess 550, Fernham Brk 371. The affixes -*Deverel*, -*Cary* and *Gounvyle*- are manorial: Elias (*de*) *Deverel* held a fee here in 1261 FF and 1314 Cl, Thomas *Cary* held the principal manor in 1357 Hutch[3] (3 430), and *Gounvyle*- must be from the family which gave name to the adjacent par. of Tarrant Gunville *infra*.

HALF HIDE COPPICE & DOWN (ST 954167), named from *Alueyde*, *Halueyde* 1288 *Ass*, *halfhide* 1618 *Map*, *Half Hide* c.1840 *TA*, cf. *Halfe Hide end* 1619 *CH*, 'the half hide', from **half** and **hīd**, with **ende**[1], cf. *Halfhide* in Sydling St N. par. *infra*. This is no doubt to be identified with one of the two manors of *Fern(e)ham* assessed at ½ hide in 1086 DB (VCHDo 3 101, 105). Half Hide Down is *Farneham Downe* 1618 *Map*.

OSMOND'S MANOR (lost), 1774 Hutch[1], 'the manor of *Osmondes*' 1475 Pat, *Osmunds* 1485 Hutch[3], *Osmond* 1795 Boswell, clearly manorial, although no one with this name has been noted in connection with Farnham. If the assumption in Hutch[3] 3 431 is correct, that this 'second manor' of Farnham once belonged to the *Lucy* family, then *Dec' Johannis de Lucy in Farnham* 1285 *Cecil* belongs here.

TOLLARD FARNHAM (ST 950160), 1811 OS, *Farnham* 1224 Cur, *Toulard, Fernham* 1282 FF (sic, the comma is editorial), *Tollard Farneham* 1500 Pat. The affix *Tollard-* is manorial, from the family of Brian *de To(u)llard'* 1202, 1224 Cur, *To(u)llard'* being Tollard Royal in Wiltshire (*v.* PN W 208) which par. borders on Farnham. In the indexes to the printed sources the forms *Tollar* 1202 Cur, *Tollard(e)* 1242–3 Fees, 1409 Cl are identified with this place, and *Toller* 1541 *Glyn* probably also belongs here.

HR & LR BEASDEN COPPICE, *copicia voc' Basedeane* 1541 *Glyn, Basens* 1618 *Map,* Hr & Lr *Bearsden* c.1840 *TA, v.* **denu** 'valley', first el. uncertain. BUSSEY STOOL LODGE, c.1840 *TA, Bursey Lodge* 1618 *Map,* from Bussey Stool Fm in Tarrant G. par. *infra.* CHALK PIT, cf. *The Chalk Pit* (arable) c.1840 *TA.* COMMON DROVE. CROSS WAYS, 1842 *TA, Cross Way Fd* 1786 Hutch[3], at a cross-roads, *v.* **cross.** DOWNEND COPPICE, cf. *Easte Downe* 1619 *CH, the Downe* 1703 *Mont, Heath Down, The Down Pce* 1842 *TA, v.* **dūn, ende**[1]. DUNSPIT LANE, cf. Hr & Lr *Dunspitt* 1842 *ib,* probably the surname *Dun, v.* **pytt.** FARNHAM COMMON WD, cf. *Farneham Comon* 1618 *Map, Farnham Common* 1811 OS, *Farnham Lr Common, Tollard-Farnham Common* c.1840 *TA.* FARNHAM FM & WDS. FURZEY WOOLLY COPPICE, *old wilhay* 1618 *Map, Chettle Wilhay, Furzey Wilhay* c.1840 *TA,* probably from **will(a), wyll(a)** 'spring, stream' and **(ge)hæg**, cf. Chettle par. *infra.* GORE COPPICE, c. 1840 *TA, Yonge Johns Cops' alias Goorecops* 1541 *Glyn, Goore cops* 1618 *Map, v.* **gāra.** HAND IN HAND (P.H.). HOOKSWOOD CMN, COPPICE & FM, *Hookes-Wood* 1774 Hutch[1], *Hookswood* 1795 Boswell, *Hooks Wood (Fm)* 1811 OS, *Hooks Coppice* 1829 *EnclA, Hookswood Cmn & Coppice* 1842 *TA,* cf. *Hookes (farme)* 1618 *Map, Hoockes Downe* 1619 *CH, in campo ante Hoke, Hooks gate* 1621 *ib, v.* **hōc** 'hook, angle, bend', perhaps with reference to the valley in which the farm lies, with **wudu, dūn, geat.** LARMER TREE, on par. and county bdy, named from Larmer

Grd in Wiltshire, *v.* PN W 208; the form *lawmoote gate* 1619 *CH* also belongs here. NEW TOWN, 1811 OS, cf. *Newton Furland* c.1840 *TA, New Town Fd* 1842 *ib.* PARK VIEW POINT, cf. *Hr & Lr Park* 1842 *TA*, named from Tollard Park in Tollard Royal par. (PN W 209), cf. also *cl' voc' lez Parkes, copic' voc' Parkecopes* 1541 *Glyn* which may have been named from the same park, *v.* park, copis. RECTORY, *The Parsonage Ho* 1842 *TA*, cf. *Parsonage Fd, The Parsonage Md* 1842 *ib.* ROOKERY COPPICE & FM, *the Rookery, Rookery Copse* c.1840 *TA*, cf. *parua claus' voc' Rowkhey* 1541 *Glyn*, *v.* hrōc 'rook', (ge)hæg. ST LAWRENCE'S CHURCH, cf. 'church of *Farham*' 1261 FF, *Eccl' Sancti Laur' de Farnham* 1280 *Ass*, 'the chapel of *Fernham* by *Hanley*' 1405 Pat, 'church of St Laurence, *Fernnam*' 1475 ib, 'church of All Saints in Farnham' 1485 Hutch[3], *Church Close* 1786 ib, *Church Fd* c.1840 *TA*. SERRAUD'S FM (6", Surrands in Kelly). STONE-WAY COPPICE, *Stonewaie* 1618 *Map*, *v.* stān, weg.

FIELD-NAMES

The undated forms are 1842 *TA* 82, but those marked † are c.1840 *ib* 38/265 (Tollard Royal par. W). Spellings dated 1261 are FF, 1327 *SR*, 1332 SR, 1407 Hutch[3], 1486 *Eton*, 1541 *Glyn*, 1618, 1621 *CH*, 1629 *Ilch*, 1795 Boswell, and 1829 *EnclA*.

(*a*) †Abbey Mdw, Abbey Orchd (no doubt from their former possession by the Abbey of Shaftesbury, *v.* Hutch[3] 3 431); †Apsey Coppice; †Ayle's Ctgs; †Barn Cl; †Barretts' Ho; †Baws' Cl; Bayleys Fd; †Bottom Cl & Pce; Bottom Fd; †Bowers' Ho; †Brach Furland (cf. *iij braches* 1541, *v.* brǣc, furlang); (Further, Hr & Lr) Brofland (*brokefurlonge* 1621, *v.* brōc, furlang); Brooks Coppice 1829; †Brook 6 Acres; †Bugden Gate Mdw; Chettle Down Fd (from Chettle Down in Chettle par. *infra*); †Clapham Pce; †Close; †Combes' Pce (cf. *Combes Close* 1618 *Map*); †Common Cl; †Common Coppice (cf. *Comon Cops* 1618 *Map*); †Corner Pce (cf. *Corner Cops* 1541, *v.* corner); †Corn Fd; †Cridges' Furland (*v.* furlang); †Croft Cl; †Cuckolds' Corner; †Denicks' Grd; †Dericks' Ho; †Dinnis' and Groves' Ho; †Down Cl; Duke of Bolton's 1795 (a manor and farm belonging to the Duke of Bolton, *v.* Hutch[3] 3 431); Dun Cl, Lr Dunclose (possibly from dūne 'down, below'); †East Fd (*Estfeld*' 1541, *v.* ēast); †8 Acres; †Entrance Pce; Farmers Cl; Fern Croft; †Fields' Cl; †Fluels' Gdn; †Gate Furland, -furlong; †Goddards' Ho; †Great Grd; Groves Md & Orchd; †Hackney's Barn & Cl; †Harpers' Ho; †Harts' Plot and Mdw; †Harveys' Ho; †Hatchet Pce (*v.* hæcc-geat); †Headland; †Head Pce; †Henvilles' (Ho); †Higher Furland; †Home Mdw; †Hoopers' Mdw; †Horse Path; †Kearleys' Ho; †Knights' Ho; †Lamberts' Cl; †Lane Cl, †Lane End; †Limekiln; Lodge Walk; Mandling, †(Peaked)

Manland (*Manelond, Moneland* 1621, cf. *Manlondisdene* 1486, *Mounelondes Downe* 1541, 'common land', from (ge)**mǣne** and **land**, with **denu, dūn, peked**; the fields with this name lie along the par. body); Manor Ho; †Middle Furland; Hr & Lr New Grd; †New Ho; †Next the Orchard; The Old Ash Inn; Old Barn and Orchd; Hr & Lr Peak (*v.* **pēac**); †Peaked Furland & Pce; †Pigs' Cl; †Pound Fd & Furland, †The Pound-House; †7 Acres; †Shortland; †South Fd (*Southefeld'*, *-fild* 1541, *Southfield* 1618); †Stonehay (*v.* (ge)**hæg**); †Sweatmans' Ho; Tanners Cl 1829; Tippetts Md (cf. Walter *Terpaud* 1332); †Tomkins' Barn; †Triangle Pce; †Turners' Ho; †20 Acres; †2 Acres; †The Upper Barn and Barton; Westhay (*v.* (ge)**hæg**); Hr & Lr Wimblebarrow (1618, *Wymble Barrow* 1621, *v.* **beorg**; the first el. may be the OE pers.n. *Winebeald*, cf. foll.); †Wimbletons' (Ho); †Wirethorn (probably *wire-thorn* 'yew'); †Wood Plot; †Yew Tree Mdw.

(*b*) *Brode Aker* 1621 (*v.* **brād, æcer**); *Burdens close* 1618 *Map*; *Chiteborne furlonge* 1621 (*v.* **burna, furlang**, first el. uncertain); *Common streate of Farnham* 1629; *la Deane* 1621 (*v.* **denu**); *Esthill'* 1541 (*v.* **ēast, hyll**); *Farneham closes, -fieldes* 1618 *Map*; *claus' voc' Gilbertes* 1541 (the pers.n. *Gilbert*); *tenement' voc' la Gywesplace* 1486 (*v.* **place**, cf. Walter *le Gyw* 1327, Ralph *le Gyn* (for *Gyu*) 1332); *la Hangehedge* 1621 (perhaps for *Lange-, v. le longehedge infra*); *in campo by West le Langefeherth* 1621 (probably 'field to the west of the long projecting piece of ploughed land', from **lang¹** and **forierð, -yrð**); *parua claus' voc' Lielane* 1541 (spelling not certain); *Longecraft* 1541, *Longcroft* 1618 *Map* (*v.* **lang¹, croft**); *Long(e)deane* 1541 (*v.* **denu** 'valley', perhaps to be identified with Langden in Tollard Royal, *v.* PN W 209); *le longehedge* 1621 (*v.* **hecg**); *vij acr' voc' Marchuntes* 1541 (a surname); *Les Moures* 1407 (cf. John *de la More* 1261, *v.* **mōr**); *Myddelfeld'* 1541 (*v.* **middel**); *Nuedecrowe* 1621 (form probably unreliable); *mess' voc' pecutes* 1541 (probably the surname *Picot*); *la Undelewey* 1621 (form perhaps unreliable); *Westdeane* 1621 (*v.* **west, denu**); *Westfeld'* 1541 (*v.* **feld**); *Wodlondes, Woodlond'feld'* 1541 (*v.* **wudu, land, feld**).

Hampreston

Part of this par. (Glynville, Pilford, Middle Hill, Canford Bottom, etc) was transferred to Colehill par. *supra* in 1913. Part of W Parley par. *infra* is now in this par. (1960 1″).

HAMPRESTON (SZ 055988) ['hɑːm'prestn]
　　Hame 1086 DB (4 ×), Exon, *Hama* Exon, *Hamma* 1100–35 (1496) Pat, 1107 (1300) Ch, 1263 Ipm, *Hammes* 1196 ChancR, 1208 FineR, P, 1244 *Ass*, 1275 RH, n.d. (1372) *ChrP*, 1367 (1372) *ib* (*-in Hammespreston'*), *Hames* 1204 Cur, *Hamme* 1204 ib, 1216 ClR, 1258 FF, 1262 Ipm, 1268 *Ass et freq* to 1583 *Glyn*, *Hamnes* 1288 *Ass*, *Hamne* 1428 FA

Hamme Preston(e) 1244 *Ass*, 1283 FF, 1285 *Cecil*, 1291 Tax
et freq with variant *Hammepreston(e)* to 1431 FA, *Ham-
mespreston* 1244 *Ass*, n.d. (1372) *ChrP, Hamepreston* 1299
Pap, *Hamne Preston* 1304 Ipm, *Hamme et Prestone* 1327
SR, *Hampme Preston* 1361 Pat, *Hampreston(e)* n.d. (1372)
ChrP, 1380 Cl *et passim, Hamperston* 1411 Fine, 1664
HTax, *Ham Preston* 1612 *DCMDeed*
Hamme Chamberlayn 1291 Tax, 1321 FF, *-Chamberleyne*
1428 FA
Hammedaumarle 1298 FF, *Hamme Daumarle* 1348, 1349,
1352 *Wim, -Dammarl(e)* 1352, 1399 *ib, -Aumarle* 1381 *ib,
-Aumerle* 1479 IpmR
Preston 1575 Saxton

'The enclosure(s) or river meadow(s)', *v.* **hamm**, cf. Walter-,
William *atte Hamme* 1332 SR, Hamworthy and Hammoon pars.
both *supra*; Hampreston is on R. Stour. The affix *Preston* is
'priest farm', from **prēost** and **tūn**, probably in allusion to lands
here belonging to the College of Wimborne Minster, *v.* Hutch[3]
3 433–4, VCHDo 2 110. The other affixes are manorial. The
largest of the four DB manors of *Hame* was held by *Aiulfus
Camerarius* 'Aiulf the chamberlain', *v.* VCHDo 3 100. (D)*au-
marle* is from the family of Geoffrey *de Albemarle* mentioned
in connection with *Hamme* in 1216 ClR, cf. William *Daumarle*
1333 *HarlCh, v.* Longham *infra.*

Lt CANFORD (FM) (SZ 047997), 1619 *CH, Parva Caneford* 1263
Ass, 1276 Banco, 1321, 1382 FF, *lytel Canefford* 1381 *Wim,
Litelcaneford* 1386 FF, *Lytill-* 1479 IpmR, *Lytle-, Parua Canford* 1583 *Glyn, parva Canneford* 1523 *AddCh*, 'little' to
distinguish it from Canford Magna par. *supra* on the opposite
bank of R. Stour, *v.* **lȳtel**.

FERN DOWN (HILL & NURSERY) (SU 072009), FERNDOWN (1″),
Fyrne 1321 FF, *Ferne* 1358 ib, possibly from OE **fergen** (WSax
fiergen) 'wooded hill', as suggested by Ekwall Studies[2] 140, cf.
Verne Yeates 1 220, Ferne Ho W 188, *v.* **dūn**. The forms *Ferne*
13 *Cecil*, 1244 *Ass* both (p) may also belong here. The hill is
a low one in an otherwise fairly flat area between Uddens Water
and R. Stour. However, as Professor Löfvenberg points out, all
the forms can be derived from OE **fearn** 'fern' (in a collective

sense 'ferny place', cf. PN Brk 290) or a derivative of it, an OE *(ge)fierne 'fern brake', and this explanation is probably to be preferred.

HILLAMSLAND (SZ 071984), *firma voc' Hillamlands* 1553 *Cecil*, *Hullamland(e)* 1562 Hutch³, 1618 *CH*, *Hullomslonde* 1620 *ib*, *Hillham Lands Fm* 1822 *EnclA*, *Halham or Hillham's Lands* 1869 Hutch³, to be identified with *Hull* 1330, 1403 Hutch³ 3 421 ('the manor of -'), *Hyll'*, *Hile* 1583 *Glyn*, *Hull' als. Hullamlande* 1620 *CH*, cf. *Hill Howe* 1583 *ib*, (*An halve on*) *Hill* 1837 *TA*, 'the hill', *v.* **hyll, howe, half**. *Hillam-* is then probably 'enclosure at the hill', or 'enclosure at *Hill'*, *v.* **hamm**, with **land** 'estate'; earlier forms are needed to support a different possibility, that the medial *-am-* represents an earlier **hǣme** 'inhabitants', cf. Speenhamland Brk 259. The farm at Hillamsland is situated just below the hill on which Belle Vue Barrow *infra* stands.

LONGHAM (BRIDGE, FM & HO) (SZ 066986), *Longeham* 1541 *Glyn*, *Longham* 1575 Saxton, *Longham* (*Head'*) 1583 *Glyn*, *Longham Bridge* 1756 (1774) Hutch¹, *Long Ham* 1811 OS, 'long enclosure', or perhaps 'long part of Ham(preston)', *v.* **lang¹, hamm**, with **hēafod** probably in the sense 'promontory, spit of land round which a river flows' with reference to the course of R. Stour here. This place is possibly to be identified with *Hamme* (*D)aumarle* (*v.* par. name *supra*) as suggested in DoNHAS **22** 127, and is probably also *Esthamme* 1280, 1288 *Ass*, *Estehame Preston'* 1288 *ib*, *Yest Hamme* 1321 Drew, *villa de Est Hamme*, *Esthamme* 1333 *HarlCh*, cf. *claus' voc' Eastham* 1621 *CH*, Longham being situated ¾ mile ESE of Hampreston, *v.* **ēast**.

ALL SAINTS' CHURCH, cf. 'the church of *Hampme Preston'* 1361 Pat, 'All Saints church in *Hampreston'* 1465 Hutch³, cf. Church Moor Copse *infra*, Church Coppice Cl, Church Fd 1837 *TA*. AMEYSFORD (RD), *Aimesford Bridge* 1791 Boswell, possibly to be associated with the John and Roger *Arney* (for *Amey* ?) who in 1598 *DLComm* had 'inclosed and shutt upp a lane...at Uddinges...called Ringwood Waye', cf. *Arneys* (for *Ameys* ?) *Cl* 1837 *TA*, *v.* Uddens and the f.n. Old Road in Holt par. *supra*; for the surname *Amey*, *v.* Kinson f.ns. *supra*; the ford was where a road crossed Uddens Water, *v.* **ford**. ANGEL INN. BAROONA, a house name, like several of the names in this list. BARTLETT'S CLIFF. BEAUFOYS (AVE). BEDBOROUGH FM & PLANT. BELLE VUE BARROW & PLANT., *Bell View* 1811 OS, *Bellevue Plant*. 1837 *TA, v.* Hillamsland *supra,* cf. Belle Vue 1 57. BIG COPSE. THE BIRCHES. BLUNT'S FM. THE BOG. BROADMOOR COPPICE. BIG & LT BURLES, BURRELL'S COPSE, *claus' voc' Burdels* 1541 *Glyn,* (*E & W*) *Burl(e)s* 1837 *TA,* from a ME surname *Burdel,* cf. Burleston 1 301. BUTLER'S COPPICE, cf. *Butler's Moor* 1837 *TA.* CANFORD BOTTOM, *v.* **botm**, Lt Canford *supra.* CANON HILL, 1811 OS, possibly the lost *Canendone* which gave name to a GeldR hundred, *v.* Badbury hundred *supra.* CAPTAIN'S ROW. CHURCH MOOR COPSE, 'ham or meadow called *Churchmore*' 1663 Hutch[3], (*Silbys*) *Church Moor* 1837 *TA, v.* **cirice, mor**, cf. Thomas *Selbye* 1664 HTax; not near a church, so perhaps a reference to ownership. CLAYFORD AVE & RD, cf. *le Howe apud Clayford* 1583 *Glyn, Clayford Cl* 1837 *TA, v.* **clæg, ford, howe**. CLIVEDEN. CLONMEEN. CONEYGAR LANE, named from *Coniger, Connyger* 1583 *Glyn, Conegar* 1811 OS, cf. (*le Howe voc'*) *Conyger Howe* 1541, 1583 *Glyn, v.* **coninger** 'rabbit-warren', **howe**, cf. The Warren *infra*. CORLEONE. CROW COPSE, cf. (*how voc'*) *Cro(w)thorne* 1541, 1583 *Glyn, v.* **cräwe, þorn**. DOWDEN'S COPSE. FAULKLAND LODGE. FIR CTG. FOX AND HOUNDS INN. FOX FM. FRYER'S COPSE. GLYNVILLE. GRAVEL PITS. GREAT BARROW, 1811 OS. GREEN WORLDS. HAMPRESTON LANE. HAM-WOODS COPSE. HAWTREE. HAYES LANE, *Haise lane* 1583 *Glyn,* cf. *terr' voc' Hays* 1583 *ib, Hay(e)s Coppice, Hay's-, Hayes Pce* 1837 *TA,* from **hæs** 'brushwood' or a pl. form of **(ge)hæg** 'enclosure'. HEATH FM, cf. (*lez*) *Heath'* 1541 *Glyn, le Hethe* 1583 *ib, Hampreston Heath* 1811 OS, *Heath Cl and Ho, Heath Pce* 1837 *TA, v.* **hæð**. HEATHER EDGE. HIGH MEAD LANE, named from *Imeade* 1541 *Glyn, Ymede, Yemed(d)e* 1583 *ib, Eye Md* 1837 *TA,* analogous with Eye Md in Pamphill par. *supra* also used of meadows by R. Stour. HOLMWOOD (PARK), *v.* **holegn** 'holly'. KING'S ARMS INN. LAUREL CTGS. LAWN FM. LAYMOOR COPSE & LANE, *howe voc' Leymoore* 1541 *Glyn, Laymoor* (*Coppice & Md*), *Laymoor Lane Pce* 1837 *TA, v.* **mōr** 'marshy ground', first el. perhaps **lay** 'a pool'. LEIGH HO, named from Leigh in Colehill par. *supra*. LEWER'S COPSE. LITTLE MOORS FM, *Litle-, Lyttle Moore* 1583 *Glyn, Little-Moores* 1774 Hutch[1],

Little Moors 1811 OS, *-Moor* 1837 *TA*, *v*. **lȳtel, mōr**. MANOR
FM (HO). MANOR HO. MIDDLE HILL (HO & RD). MOOR HO, cf.
atte More 1352, *atte Moure* 1393 *Wim* both (p), (*lez*) *Moores*
1541, 1583 *Glyn*, (*le*) *Moore* 1583 *ib*, (*the*) *Moor* 1837 *TA*, *v*.
mōr, atte, cf. f.ns. *infra*. THE MOUNT, cf. *Mount* 1837 *ib*, *v*.
mont. OLIVERS HO. PARK HOMER, a house name. PILFORD (FM),
terr' voc' Pilforde 1583 *Glyn*, *Pilfords* 1811 OS, *Pilford* 1837
TA, cf. Pilford Copse & Lane in Holt par. *supra, v*. **ford**, first
el. **pīl** 'a stake' (hence 'ford marked by a stake'), or **pyll** 'a
pool in a river, a small stream'; the farm lies beside a small
tributary of Uddens Water. PILGRIMAGE. PINEHULME. POMPEY'S
CORNER. POOR CMN. QUARRY CORNER, gravel pits marked 6″.
RABBIT'S COPSE, cf. *Rabbits Corner* 1837 *TA*. RECTORY, cf. *the
Parsonage house* 1664 HTax. RED BRIDGE. THE ROUGHS, *v*. **rūh**.
ST MARY'S CHURCH. ST MARY'S R.C. CHAPEL. SANDY LANE (2
×). STAPEHILL, *Staphill'* 1583 *Glyn*, *Stapes-Hill* 1774 Hutch[1],
Steep Hill 1811 OS (*-Nunnery*, = Cistercian Priory 6″), *Stape
Hill Cl & Pce* 1837 *TA*, *Stapes Hill or Stape Hill* 1869 Hutch[3],
v. **stēap** 'steep', **hyll**, cf. Stapenhill St (PN Db 662); there is
only a low hill here, so it is possible the name is ironical. STOUR
BANK, by R. Stour. TOM'S COPPICE. THE WARREN. WELL HO.
WHIN CROFT. WHITE BRIDGE. WINKLEY CTG, 1811 OS.
WOLVERTON. WOOLSLOPE COPPICE, named from Woolslope Fm
in W Parley par. *infra*.

FIELD-NAMES

The undated forms are 1837 *TA* 98. Spellings dated 1208 are P, 1283 FF,
1285 *Cecil*, 1288 *Ass*, 1327 *SR*, 1330, 1562 Hutch[3], 1332 SR, 1333 *HarlCh*,
1340 NI, n.d. (1372) *ChrP*, 1541, 1583 *Glyn*, 1664 HTax, 1822 *EnclA*
(Canford M.), and the rest *Wim*.

(a) Acre Pce; Ansteys Ham (probably a surname from Ansty in Hilton par.
infra, v. **hamm**); Barner's two Plots; Benyham 1822 (*Bennehame* 1583, *v*.
hamm, cf. Benham Brk 267); Boathouse Md; Bo(u)lton(')s Coppice, Bolton's
Copse Cl, Bolton's Md; Bolts Lane; Bowling Green; (Hr) Breach, Breach
Md (cf. 'meadow of *la Breche*' 1283, *Bratch Coppice & Md* 1822, *v*. **brǣc**);
Brensons-, Brinsons Cl; Broad Md; Butts Cl (*v*. **butte**); Canford Milestone
(Pce at-) (*v*. Canford M. par. *supra*); Capons How Cowleaze (*v*. **howe**); Castle
(East) Cl (*v*. **castel(l)**, with reference to Duds Bury in W Parley par. *infra*);
Clapper (Lane End) (*v*. **clapper** 'rough bridge', or 'rabbit-burrow'); Cole
(perhaps an elliptical form to be associated with *Coolehowe* 1541, which is
named from John *Coole ib, v*. **howe**); Colly; Common (Cl) Plot; Comptons

Moor; Compty (*Compte Mdw* 1822); Coppice Cl; Corner Cl; Cowleaze thousand Acres (a very small field); Crooked (Coppice) Cl; Cross Cl; Curtis's Cl; Dawns Plot; Coppice near Deweys; Downes Plot; East Cl & Md; East and Home Plots; (Picked) 8 Acres (*v.* **pīcede** 'pointed'); 11 Acres; Elmy Fd; Ensbury-, Hensbury Hill Cl (named from Ensbury in Kinson par. *supra*); Fent Md 1822 (*Vyntemede* 1333, *Fent-, Fint-, Fyntmeade* 1583, *v.* **mǣd**, first el. probably **fyniht** 'fenny, marshy', cf. *Finford* Wa 156); 5 Acres; 5 Ashes Close(s); Fo(r)sters Cl; 4 Acres; Fuzzey Hays (*fursehais* 1541, *Fursey Hayes* 1583, *v.* **fyrs, fyrsig, (ge)hæg**); Georges Stile; Giddy Mead Cl (cf. *Lt Giddy Md* 1822, *v.* **gydig**, or a surname); Gilberts Cl; Glissons Hill Cl (probably to be identified with *Lyssenhill* 1541, *Lycenshill'* 1583, *v.* **hyll**, first el. probably a surname, *v.* Reaney s.n. *Lysons*); Gore (*Gore (Close)* 1583, *v.* **gāra**); E, N & W Grange, Grange Coppice (*claus' voc' Graung'* 1541, *v.* **grange**, perhaps to be associated with lands in Hampreston belonging to Tewkesbury abbey, *v.* Hutch³ 3 434, cf. Monks How *infra*); Ham Fd (*Ham(m)efield, -Fylde* 1583, cf. *campo de Hamme Daumarle* 1348, *unam acram in campo de Hamme* 1352, *v.* **hamm, feld**, par. name *supra*, Preston Fd *infra*); Hardeys Gdn; Hartly Green; Haskels-, Haskolls Hay (*v.* **(ge)hæg**); Hatchet Cl (*v.* **hæcc-geat** 'hatch-gate'); Herne Corner (*paruo campo voc' Hurne, Horne* 1583, *v.* **hyrne** 'angle, corner'); High Street Coppice; Hiscocks Platt (*v.* **plat²**); Hoare Stone ((*claus' apud*) *Horestone* 1583, 'grey (boundary) stone', *v.* **hār, stān**); Home Cl, Corner & Md, Home Plot alias Spencers; Hope Hill Pce; How (Coppice), Long & Short How, N & S How (cf. *le Howe, Howeham, 3 claus' voc' Howes* 1583, *v.* **howe** 'enclosure', **hamm**); Hundred Acres (a small field); Hunger Hill (a name for poor land, *v.* **hungor**); Inner Cl; Kidney Md (perhaps named from its shape); Kingstone-, Kinson Lane Pce (*v.* Kinson par. *supra*); Lane side (cf. William *in le Lane* 1332, *v.* **lane**); Leg, Leg(g) Cl (*v.* **leg**); Little Ham (*v.* **hamm**); Little Moors Corner Coppice (*v.* Little Moors Fm *supra*); Little Platt (*v.* **plat²**); Long Cl; Lower Cl; Lype (*terr' in Lype* 1583, *v.* **hlīep** 'a leaping place'); Marshall(s) (Craft or) Plot (*v.* **croft**, cf. *Mascalshey, Maskalshay* 1541, *Mascolls Acr', -Haye* 1583, from the surname *Mascall*, a form of *Marshall, v.* **æcer, (ge)hæg**); Mead Acre; Meakes How (cf. *Alice-* 1583, John *Meake* 1664, *v.* **howe**); Middle Plot; Mile Stone Fd & Plot (*v.* **mīl-stan**); Near(e) the Mill (cf. *molend' de Hamme*, Richard *de Molyns de Hamme* 1288, Ralph *de molendino* 1333, Walter *At(t)e Mulle* 1333, 1340, *v.* **myln, atte**, par. name *supra*; the 1288 reference makes it clear that the mill in question was near a certain bridge on R. Stour, and the *TA* field is near Longham Bridge *supra*); Monks (alias Abreys) How (*Munuckes Howe* 1583, *v.* **munuc, howe**, cf. Grange *supra*; *Abreys* is perhaps for *Abbeys*); (Hr & Lr) Moor Cl, Moor Coppice Cl, Moor Md (*Mo(o)reme(a)de* 1541, 1583, *v.* **mōr, mǣd**, cf. Moor Ho *supra*); Morris' Ham 1822 (*Morris Hamme* 1583, from the surname *Morris* and **hamm**); Mule's Park (*Mules'-* 1822), Park Cl (cf. *prat' iuxta le Parke pale* 1583, *v.* **park** (probably with reference to Leigh Park in Wimborne M. par. *supra*), **pale**; *Mule* is a surname); New Cl; 9 Acres; North Plot & Wd; Orchard; Peppins How, Reppins (*Pypens Howe* 1541, the surname *Pepin, v.* **howe**); Picks Hays (*v.* **(ge)hæg**); Place Lane Cl (*Plashlane, Plac' Lane* 1583, *v.* **plæsc** 'pool'); Playford Cl ('ford where sports were held', *v.* **plega, ford**, cf. Plyford D 597, Playford Sf (DEPN)); Plot; Preston Fd (Cl) (*Preston' field*, *campis de Hampreston'* 1583, *v.* par. name, Ham Fd *supra*); Rails Lane Coppice; Gt & Lt Rough Grd; 7 Acres; Shortlands (5 Acres) (*Shortlond* 1583, *v.* sc(e)ort, land); Signpost Cl; 6 Acres; Slough Ditch (cf. *terr' in (le) dyche*, *terr' in dyches* 1583, *v.* dīc, slōh); Small Cl & Plot; Spencers Ditch; Square Cl; Stock Md (*Stokmede* 1300, 1444, 1483, *-meade* 1541, *Stockmeade* 1583, *v.* mǣd, first el. probably stocc 'tree-stump' rather than stoc 'secondary settlement'); W Stoney Ld (*v.* stānig); Stopples; Stubb (*prat' apud Stubbes*, *-Stubbsford'* 1583, *v.* ford, first el. stubb 'tree-stump' or the surname *Stubb(s)*); Summer Lane Cl (*Somerlane (grene)* 1541, 1583, 'lane used (only) in summer', *v.* sumor, lane, grēne[2]); Tent Md Cl; 3 Acres; Towers Moor; E & W Tuckers; 12 Acres; Lt 20 Acres; 2 Acres; Wade Lane Cl, Waylane Cl (*pastur' iacen' in Wadelane* 1583, *v.* (ge)wæd 'a ford'); Walls Cl; Water Lane Cl; West Fd; (Hr & Lr) West Grd; West Platt & Plot (*v.* plat[2], plot); Wet Cl; Bess Whites (cf. Thomas- 1583, John *White* 1664); Winchtons How (*v.* howe); Wood Flg; E & W Woods (probably a surname).

(*b*) *Bakers Howe* 1583 (the surname *Baker*, *v.* howe); *Bilberys* 1583 (probably a surname); *Brodeaker* 1541, *Broadacre* 1583 (*v.* brād, æcer); *Brodehowe* 1541 (*v.* brād, howe); *Cleypit* 1583 (*v.* clæg, pytt); *Collyns Place* 1583 (the pers.n. or surname *Collin*, *v.* place); *le Howe voc' the Comon' Howe* 1583 (*v.* howe); *Crode Lane* 1583; *claus' voc' Downhouse* 1583 (perhaps a rationalization of *Downers*, cf. John *le Douner'* 1332, but *-house* may represent a pl. form of howe); *Dyghays* 1583 (probably the surname *Dyg*, a voiced form of *Dick*, *v.* (ge)hæg); *orientali campo* 1583 ('east field'); *Esthowe* 1541 (*v.* ēast, howe); *parua claus' voc' Farthinge How* 1583 (*v.* fēorðung 'fourth part', with reference either to a measure of land or to a rental of a farthing, *v.* howe); *Fernforlong'* 1352, *Fernyforlange* 1399 (*v.* fearn, fearnig, furlang); *atte Forde* 1332 (p) (*v.* atte, ford); *Frithefeld'* 1541, *Frithfeilde* 1583 (*v.* fyrhð 'wood', feld); *Goseaker, Gosham* 1541, *Gooseacre* 1583 (*v.* gōs 'goose', æcer, hamm); *Grenehay* 1541 (*v.* grēne[1], (ge)hæg); *Gurnay crosse* 1541 (*v.* cros(s)); *Gurnay* may be a metathesized form of *Grenehay*; *Hack(s)-howe* 1541 (cf. Stephen *Hak'* 1393, *v.* howe); *Hethy howe* 1583 (*v.* hethy, howe); *Horsehaye* 1583 (*v.* hors, (ge)hæg); *atte Knolle* 1332 (p) (*v.* atte, cnoll); *Lavermeade* 1583 (*v.* lǣfer 'rush, reed, yellow iris', mǣd); *claus' voc' Lonneds* 1541 (spelling not certain); *Lucye-, Lacy Breche* 1583 (*v.* brǣc; probably to be connected with the family of *de Lucy* which held the manor of Hampreston at an early date, cf. Margaret *de Luci* 1208 P, John *de Lucy* 1285, *v.* Hutch[3] 3 433–4); *claus' voc' Lymans* 1541 (the surname *Liman*); *Lyneham* 1583 (*v.* hamm, first el. perhaps līn 'flax'); *atte Ock* 1327, *-Ok'* 1332 both (p), *Okehey* 1541 (*v.* āc 'oak-tree', atte, (ge)hæg); *Pryggesplace* 1381 (the surname *Prigg*, *v.* place); *Rawlettes Moore* 1583 (the surname *Rawlett*, *v.* mōr); *pastur'-, prat' voc' ropes* 1583 ('allotments measured out with a rope', *v.* rāp); *prat' in La Rytha* n.d. (1372) (*v.* rīð 'a stream'); *Sle(e)pe hedge* 1583 (*v.* slǣp 'a slippery, muddy place', hecg); *Smale Mo(o)re* 1583 (*v.* smæl, mōr); *Southmeade* 1541 (*v.* sūð, mǣd); *atte Stone* 1332 (p) (*v.* atte, stān); *Thachehowe* 1541 ('enclosure where thatching materials are got', *v.* þæcce, howe); *Theven'howe* 1541 (*v.* howe; *Theven'-* may be a gen. pl. form in *-en* of þēof 'thief', *v.* -ena, or represent 'the even', from efen 'even, flat'); *Westhowe* 1541 (*v.* west); *Wythy bedde* 1541, *Webedd* 1583 (*v.* wīðig, bedd); *terr' voc' Wolberes* 1583 (probably a surname); *Woodles* 1583 (*v.* **wudu, lǽs**); *Yollande, Yowlond* 1583 (*v.* **eald, land,** cf. Yolland D 465); *Yuymede* n.d. (1372) (*v.* **īfig, mǽd**).

West Parley

Part of this par. is now in Hampreston par. *supra*, and West Moors is now a separate par. (1960 1″).

WEST PARLEY (SZ 090980)
  Perlai 1086 DB, *-lea* 1187 P, *-lee* 1228 FF, 1428 FA, *-le* 1244
    Ass et freq to 1618 *CH* with *West-* from 1331 Cl, *-legh* 1303
    FA *et freq* to 1428 FA, *-ley* 1303 ib, 1494 *Cecil*, 1575
    Saxton, *-lyghe* 1314 Ipm, *Westperele* 1305 FF, *West Per-*
    leygh 1431 FA
  Parlea 1194 P, *-le* 1399 Cl, *-ley* 1558 *PlR et passim* with
    West- from 1618 *CH*, (*West*) *Parly* 1618 *ib*

'Pear wood', from **peru** and **lēah**, cf. Parnham in Beaminster par. *infra*; *West* to distinguish it from East Parley in Hurn par. just over the county bdy in Ha, *v.* **west.**

DUDS BURY (Camp), DUDSBURY (SZ 078982), *Dodesberie* 1086 DB, *-bery* 1280 *Ass*, *-bir'* 1281 Banco, *Dudesbir'* 1235–6 Fees, *-bery* 1280 *Ass*, *Duddesbury* 1312 FF, 1381 *Wim*, 1393 FF, 1479 IpmR, *-burie* 1591 *DLMB*, *Dudisbur'* 1432 *Wim*, *Tudesburye* 1558–79 ChancP, *Dudsbury* 1774 Hutch[1], 1811 OS (-*Camp*), *Dusbury* 1795 Boswell, 'Dudd's fortified place', from the OE pers.n. *Dudd* and **burh** (dat.sg. *byrig*), with reference to the Iron Age hill-fort here which is dissected by the Hampreston-W Parley par. bdy, cf. Castle Rings *infra*.

ST LEONARD'S BRIDGE, CMN, COPPICE & FM (SU 095015), *St Leonards common* 1556 Ipm, *Sct. Leonarde* 1575 Saxton (chapel marked), *St Leonardes* 1618 *Map, pontem voc' S'ct Leonards* 1620 *CH, St Leonard's, a farm on a common of that name* 1869 Hutch[3], all named from the medieval religious house here as shown by C. D. Drew, DoNHAS **64** 34–42, cf. Hutch[3] 3 463, VCHDo 2 105–6 where this house is ascribed to a site in Tarrant Rushton par. *infra*. It is *domus Sancti Leonardi de Russeton'* 1288 *Ass*, 'the house of St Leonard of *Rushton* near *Palmeres-brugg'* 1332 VCHDo 2 106, 'the house of St Leonard, *Risshton* by *Palmeresbrigge'* 1333 Pat, cf. 'the chantry of *Rissheton*

Chapel', 'the chapel of *Ryshton*' 1331 Pat. The settlement here also occurs as *Ryston* 1282 Banco, *Rushton juxta Parley* 1288 *Ass*, *Rushton* 1535 VE, *Rousheton* 1556 Ipm, and is 'rush farm', from **risc, rysc** and **tūn**, cf. 1 147. *Palmeresbrugg, -brigge* is now Palmer's Ford (6″), just on the Ha side of the county bdy in the par. of St Leonards & St Ives (which apparently takes the first part of its name from those here discussed). Drew (*loc.cit.*) may be correct in further suggesting that the settlement of *Rushton*, along with lands to the N, may represent the unidentified DB manor of *Langeford*, this ('the long ford') having perhaps been an earlier name for *Palmeresbrigge*, cf. 1 373 where, following VCHDo 3 74, etc., this form is tentatively assigned to Langford in Stratton. In support of the DB identification, Drew cites a form *Langford* 1568 (said to be in W Parley par.), and to this can be added the form *Langfordes* 1562 Hutch[3] 3 423, cf. also Thomas (*de*) *Lang(e)ford(e)* 1330 ib 3 421, 1332 SR, 1340 NI (mentioned in connection with this par.), *v.* **lang**[1], **ford**.

WEST MOORS (FM) (SU 079030), *La More juxta Westperle* 1310, 1312 Banco, *More juxta Westperle* 1316 ib, *la More* 1364, 1380 Cl, 1557 Hutch[3], *Le Moure* 1412 FA, *le more* 1558 *PlR*, *More* 1562 Hutch[3]; *Moures* 1407 IpmR, *Mores* 1489 Ipm, 1620 *CH*, (*the*) *Moores* 1575 *PlR*, 1619 *CH*, *le Morys* 1618 *ib*, *West Moors* 1591 Hutch[3], 1811 OS, -*Moores* 1620 *CH*, 'the marshy ground(s)', *v.* **mōr**; *West* in relation to East Moors Fm (*Great or East Moors* 1591 Hutch[3]) just over the county bdy in St Leonards & St Ives par. (Ha), *v.* **west**, cf. Little Moors *infra*.

ABEL'S COPPICE. ALDER BED, 1839 TA. ALL SAINTS' CHURCH, cf. *the Church Yd* 1839 *ib*. BARN CLOSE, cf. *Barn Fd & Plot*, *Barnhead* 1839 *ib*. BARNES'S FM. BARTLETT'S PLANT. BRAMBLE'S FM, cf. James *Bramble* 1777 Hutch[3]. CASTLE RINGS, *The-* 1839 *TA*, cf. *Castle Copse & Wd* 1839 *ib*, *Castle* (*East*) *Cl* 1837 *ib* (Hampreston), named from the ramparts of the earthwork at Duds Bury *supra*, *v.* **castel(l), hring**. CHURCH FM, near All Saints' Church *supra*. DOLMAN'S FM. DOWAGER'S COPSE, *Dowges Copse* 1839 *TA*, cf. *Dudge Forde* 1591 *DLMB*, *the lane at Dowgers Forde* 1595 *DLComm*, *Dowdges 5 & 6 Acres* 1839 *TA*, named from the family of Walter *Do(u)ge* 1327 *SR*, 1340 NI, *v.* **copis, ford**. DUDSBURY LANE, 1839 *TA*, cf. *Dudsbury Mdw & Pit* 1839 *ib*, *v.* Duds Bury *supra*. EGYPT, 1839 *TA*,

-*Fd* 1840 *ib* (alt. app.), so called from its remoteness; it is in heathland near the par. bdy. FORD LANE. GOULD'S FM. GULLIVER'S FM & FIRS, -*Plant*. 1839 *TA*, named from Isaac *Gulliver* 1745–1822, *v*. Lilliput in Parkstone par. *supra*. GUNDRYS FM & INCLOSURE. HATCHARD'S COPSE, *Hatche's Coppice* 1839 *TA*, cf. *Hatches Md* 1839 *ib*, from the surnames *Hatch* or *Hatchard*. HORNS INN, 1839 *ib*. INNISFAIL. LAYFIELD (lost), 1774 Hutch[1], 1839 *TA* (*Inner-*, *Lower-*, *Outer-*), 1869 Hutch[3], first el. probably **lǣge** 'fallow'. LITTLE MOORS (lost), 1811 OS, near to West Moors *supra*. MAG'S BARROW, cf. *Maggs* (*Barn*, *Cl & Lane*) 1839 *TA*, the surname *Magg(s)*. NEW BRIDGE (lost), 1811 OS (2 ×). NIGHTINGALE COPSE, *Nightingale's Coppice* 1839 *ib*. OAKLEE. OLD PINES. PARLEY BARROW. PARLEY CMN, 1811 OS, *The* (*Great*) *Cmn*, *West Parley Cmn* 1839 *ib*. W PARLEY HALL. PARLEY WD, cf. (*Gt & Lt*) *Wood* 1839 *ib*. PENNINGTON'S COPSE, *Peniton's-* 1839 *ib*, cf. *Late Penningtons* 1839 *ib*. PERCY'S COPPICE. PINE HILLS. PUNTIS COPSE, *Pontis-* 1839 *ib*, cf. *Gt & Lt Pontis* 1839 *ib*, the surname *Pontis*. RALPH'S BARROW, cf. *Old Ralphs* 1839 *ib*, the pers.n. or surname *Ralph*. RECTORY, cf. *Parsons Plot* 1839 *ib*. REDDINGS COPPICE. REVEL'S CROSSING (railway). ST MARY'S CHURCH. STOCKS FM, cf. *Stocks Bridge* 1791 Boswell. STURT'S FM, *Sturts* 1811 OS, *v*. steort 'tail of land', or a surname. THORNY HAM, *v*. **hamm**. TRICKETT'S CROSS, a cross-roads, *v*. **cross**. WOOD TOWN FM, *Woodtowne* 1620 *CH*, cf. *Wood Town Green*, *Grd & Md* 1839 *TA*, probably a late name, *v*. **wudu, tūn**. WOOLBRIDGE HEATH (lost), 1811 OS, cf. *terre in le Heath voc' le old Forest* 1618 *CH*, named from Woolsbridge in Verwood par. *infra*, *v*. **hǣð, forest**. WOOLSLOPE FM, *Woolslap* 1811 OS, cf. *Woolslap Bridge* 1791 Boswell, possibly from **wyll(a)** 'spring, stream' and an OE **slæp* 'mud, mire, marsh' (*v*. Löfvenberg 189), later influenced by ModE *slope*; the farm is by sloping ground and a small stream rises here to join Uddens Water.

FIELD-NAMES

The undated forms are 1839 *TA* 164. Spellings dated 1327 are *SR*, 1332 SR, 1541, 1583 *Glyn*, 1618, 1620, 1621 *CH*, 1664 HTax, and the rest Hutch[3].

(a) Arable Pce; Back Door Grd; (Lt) Benjamins; Berry Croft; Birchy How (*v*. **howe**); Boar Cl; Bob Grd; Bot Md; Break (*v*. **bræc[1]** 'brake'); Brick Kiln Grd; Bridge Md adjoining River; Broad Cl; Browns Grd; Bushy Grd; Butts and Lt Wood (*v.* **butte**); Calves Cl Plot; Catmoor (Md) (probably to be identified with *Tatmoore* 1620, *v.* **cat(t)** 'wild-cat', **mōr**); Chubbs 16 & 10 Acres; Claypits; Coakers (cf. Alice *Coker* 1664); Cockpit (*v.* **cockpit**); Common Grd (cf. *le com'on Dytche* 1620, *v.* **comun, dīc**); Copse Cl & Grd; Corfe Charity Md (probably to be associated with the acre of land that belonged to the trustees of Lockyer's Charity, Corfe Mullen (M.H.), cf. Corfe M. par. *supra*); Corner Grd; Cowleaze, The hanging Cowleaze (*v.* **hangende**); Cow Pen Grd; Crooked Cl & Md; Dorsetshire Cl (no doubt near the county bdy); (Gt & Lt) Down (*v.* **dūn**); The Drove, Drove Cl or Sams Cl (*v.* **drāf**); Duck Md; 8 Acres (or Hr Reeks, -or Lr Reeks) (cf. Thomas *Reeks* 1775); 11 Acres; (Lt) Emberl(e)ys (cf. John *Emberly* 1664); Ferny Cl; Fir Plant.; (Lr) 5 Acres; The folly (*v.* **folie**); (Lt, Lr & Upr) 4 Acres; Front Fd & Grd; Furze Grd; Furzy Lane & Pce; Gallows Acre (*v.* **galga**); Galton's Bridge 1791 Boswell; Garden Plot; Gillingham Grd; Gore Acre (*v.* **gāra**); Grammers Grd; Great Mdw Ham (*v.* **hamm**); Harbins; Harveys Md; Hedge Row; Highmoor Pasture Fd; Holcroft (*v.* **hol²**, **croft**); Home Cl; How Pce (*v.* **howe**); Howses (a possessive form of the surname *Hows(e)*, or a double pl. of **howe**); Inner Cl; The Island; Jacks Cl; Kellaways; Kings Md (cf. Adam *le Kyng*' 1332, Thomas *Kinge* 1541 (Hampreston)); The Lawn (*v.* **launde**); Little Coppice & Plot; Late Lockyers (cf. John *Lockeir* 1664); Long Grd & Plot; Malthouse Grd; The Marsh; Mead Lane, Hr & Lr Mead (cf. *le meadowe Ditche* 1620, *v.* **mǣd, dīc**); The Middle Pce; Milliards; Moors Md(w) (cf. West Moors *supra*); New Inclosure & Plant.; Newmans 3 Acres; 9 Acres; Nursery Grd; Old Orchd; Paradise Md (*v.* **paradis**); Pardy's Plot; Pasture Fd & Pce; (The) Peake (*v.* **pēac**); Peaked Pce (*v.* **peked** 'pointed'); Lt Pennings (*v.* **penning**); Pheasant Coppice; Plantation; Pollard Grd; Pond or Middle Cl; Potatoe Plot; Pump Md; Roger's Ham (*v.* **hamm**); Rook Hay Md (*v.* **hrōc, (ge)hæg**); Rough Grd; Round Grd; Rushy Pce; Rye Grd (cf. *prat' in-, loco voc' Rye* 1583, probably '(place) at the island or at the dry ground in marsh', *v.* **atter, ī(e)g**); Sage Grd; Scaffold Plot; 7, 6, & 16 Acres; Sour Plot; Square Cl; Stable Cl; Sweet Mdw; 10 & 3 Acres; 3 Acre Wd; 3 Corner Pce; Trims Md (cf. John *Trim* 1664 (Hampreston)); Trokes Cl (cf. Ann *Trock* 1664 (Hampreston), Jonadab *Troke* 1856); Trouble Fd (no doubt a derogatory name for difficult ground); 12, 20, & 2 Acres; The Upper Pce; Usleys, Lt Usley Plot; Way Grd & Md; West Moors Cmn (*v.* West Moors *supra*); West Pce; Wheat or Duck Grd; Withey Bed (*v.* **wīðig**).

(b) *atte Asshe* 1327 (p) (*v.* **atte, æsc**); *Berwood Corner* 1618; *Broome close* 1620 (*v.* **brōm**); *Frezells* 1615 (probably a surname); *little close* 1620 (*v.* **lȳtel**); *Littleforde* 1621 (*v.* **lȳtel, ford**); *Longe close* 1620; *Netherfield* 1620 (*v.* **neoðerra**).

CRANBORNE HUNDRED235

Pentridge

The pars. of East and West Woodyates *infra* were joined to this par. in 1933.

PENTRIDGE (SU 033178)

?*Pentric* 762 (13) Muchelney Cartulary (SoRecSoc 14), *Pentric* 1086 DB, 1100–35 (1496) Pat, 1107 (1300) Ch, *Pentrich(e)* 1100–35 (1496) Pat, 1264 Ipm, 1280 *Ass*, 1283 *Cecil*, 1288 *Ass*, 1303 FA *et freq* to 1428 ib, *Pentric'* 1236 Cl, *Pentrice* 1244 *Ass*, *Pentryz* 1244, 1268 *ib*, *Pentryhc* 1280 *ib*, *Pentrishe* 1291 Tax, *Pentrech* 1316 FA, *Pentrych(e)* 1340 NI, 1398 *Cecil*, 1416 Pat, 1431 FA, *Pentryssh* 1346 ib, *Penterych* 1389 Pat
Pentringtone 944–46 (14) BCS 817, -*yngton'* Glast (both S 513)
Pencriz 1187, 1188, 1194, 1201, 1202 P, 1234 Cl, n.d. (1372) ChrP, *Pencrico* (ablative) 1234 Cl, *Pencrich* 1297 ib, *Pencrych vel Pentrich* 1398 IpmR
Pent(t)rig(') 1288 *Ass*, 1382 *Cecil*, *Peyntreg'* 1288 *Ass*, *Pentryg(g)e* 1494 *Cecil*, 1535 VE, *Penterigge* 1548 *Ct*, *Pentridge* 1618 *CH*
Pontrich 1382 *Cecil*   *Pantridge* 1575 Saxton

A British hill-name, the first el. of which is PrWelsh or PrCorn *penn*[1] 'a hill', with reference to Pentridge Hill *infra*. The second el. may be *tyrch*, an old gen.sg. of Welsh *twrch* 'a boar', as suggested by Ekwall DEPN for this name and the analogous Pentrich Db 490; Professor Jackson agrees that 'the hill of the boar', with second el. *tyrch* (PrWelsh *türk* or PrCorn *tirk*), is perfectly plausible. The 10th cent. form *Pentringtone* probably means 'farm of the men of Pentridge', *v.* -inga-, tūn, Karlström 15. The spellings in -*criz*, -*crich*, etc are due to orthographic confusion of *c* and *t*, cf. Fägersten 103 who wrongly interprets the name on the basis of these forms as containing PrWelsh *crüg* 'a hill, a barrow' as in Penkridge St (DEPN).

BOKERLY DITCH (SU 023200–063168), *Bockedic* 1280 *Ass*, *fossat' voc' Bucke Ditche* 1618 *CH*, *Bockl(e)y Dyke* 1869 Hutch[3], cf. *Inner & Outer Bockerley, Lt Bockerley, Bockerley Cowleaze, Grds & Lane* 1838 *TA*, Grim's Ditch *infra*, *v.* bucc 'a buck, a male deer', dīc, -*l(e)y* perhaps representing lēah 'wood, clearing', cf. Buckley So (EPN 1 56); on the killing of bucks in Cranborne Chase, *v.* Hutch³ 3 414. This late RB ditch, crossing four miles of downland, is earlier referred to in (*ende lang*) *dich* 944–6 (14) BCS 817 (S 513) (in the bounds of Martin Ha), and as *magnum fossatum de Blakedounesdich* 1236 Hutch³, i.e. 'the ditch at *Blakedoun* ('the dark-coloured hill')', *v.* Blagdon in Cranborne par. *supra.*

CHETTLE HEAD COPSE (SU 025210), (*to*) *coteleshed* 944–6 (14) BCS 817 (S 513), (*on*) *cheotoles heafde* 955 (14) ib 917 (S 582), *Chettleslesheved* 1278 QW, *Chetelesheved(e)* 1280–1 ib, *Cheteles-, Chetteslesheued* 1280 *Ass, Chytelheved* 1281, 1289 *ib, chateshead woods* 17 *CecilMap, Chettelhead* 1618 PN W, *Chettlehed, -head Cops* 1618 *Map, Hr & Lr Chittle Head Coppice* 1838 *TA,* cf. (*to*) *cotelesburgh'* 944–6 (14) BCS 817 (S 513), (*to*) *chetoles beorge* 955 (14) ib 917 (S 582), which is identified with the nearby KITT'S GROVE on the county bdy in PN W 204. Tengstrand MN 98 is no doubt correct in taking the first el. of these two names to be an OE **ceotol**, a variant of **cetel, cytel** 'a kettle', used topographically of 'a deep valley surrounded by hills', cf. Chettle par. *infra*; the valley referred to was perhaps that now called Chickengrove Bottom (6″) lying E from Chettle Head Copse in Broad Chalke par. (Wiltshire). Chettle Head Copse is just below a 600′ ridge, *v.* hēafod 'head', either in the sense 'hill, ridge' or 'upper end of a valley'; at Kitt's Grove (1902 6″, called Kitt's Grave in PN W 204), on the site of *cotelesburgh', chetoles beorge*, there is a barrow, *v.* **beorg.**

GRIM'S DITCH, *Grym(m)esdich(e)* 1280 QW, *Ass, Grymes-, Grimesdych'* 1280 *Ass, Grimsditch* 17 *CecilMap, Grymes Ditche* 1618 *Map, Grime ditch or Boccoli ditch* 1774 Hutch¹, from *Grīm,* probably a by-name of Woden, and dīc; this earthwork runs partly parallel to Bokerly Ditch *supra,* crossing the county bdy into Wiltshire, *v.* PN W 16, cf. DEPN 205 for other examples of ditches with this name.

BOKERLY DOWN (*Bockerly-* 1838 *TA*) & FM, cf. Bokerly Ditch *supra, v.* dūn. BOWLING GREEN LANE. COBLEY FM, cf. *Cobley Lodge* 17 *Cecil,* 1618 *Map,* 1811 OS, *Cobly (walke)* 17 *CecilMap,* 1617 *Cecil, Cobley Walke* 1618 *Map, Cobley* 1838 *TA, v.* lēah 'wood, clearing', **log(g)e**, **walk** (this was one of the 'walks' in Cranborne Chase *supra*); the first el. may be an OE pers.n. *Cobba*, or **cobb(e)** 'round lump', cf. Cobb in Lyme R. par. *infra*. EARTHPITS LANE, *vie vocat' Earthpits* 1618 *CH, Earth pit Lane* 1838 *TA*, from eorðe and **pytt**, probably with reference to the earthworks SW of Bokerly Ditch which the lane crosses. KITT'S GROVE, *v*. Chettle Head Copse *supra*. MORGAN'S LANE, cf. William *Morgan* 1548 *Ct*, Six. Handley f.ns. *infra*. PEAKED POST, *v*. **peked** 'pointed', post. PENBURY-KNOLL, *Penbury hill* 1774 Hutch[1], cf. *Knowl Fd* 1838 *TA*; this is the 600' summit of Pentridge Hill, *v*. ***penn**[1] (cf. par. name *supra*), **burh** (with reference to the hill-fort here, marked Camp 6″), **cnoll** 'hill top'. PENTRIDGE DOWN (1811 OS, cf. *The tenants Common Down* 1838 *TA*), FM (cf. *The Farm East Down* 1829 *EnclA*), & HILL (1811 ib, cf. par. name, Penbury-Knoll *supra*). RECTORY, *Parsonage* 1826 Gre, cf. *Parsonage Home & Upr Cl, Parsons Cl* 1838 *TA*. ST RUMBOLD'S CHURCH, cf. *ecclesia de Pentric(h)* 1100–35 (1496) Pat, *ecclesie de Pencriz* 1234 Cl, cf. *Church Croft* 1838 *TA*. SHAFTESBURY ARMS (P.H.), *v*. foll. SHAFTSBURY COPSE (lost), 1811 OS, cf. *Shaftesbury Fd* 1838 *TA*, from the Earls of Shaftesbury, lords of the manor. WHITEY TOP, cf. *Whiteway Fd* 1829 *EnclA, Whiteway* (or *Stoney Lane*) 1838 *TA*, *v*. **hwīt, weg**, cf. Whiteway 1 90. WOODYATES HO, *v*. W Woodyates par. *infra*.

FIELD-NAMES

The undated forms are 1838 *TA* 165. Spellings dated 1332 are SR, n.d. (1372) *ChrP*, 1618 *Map*, 1664 HTax, and 1829 *EnclA*.

(a) Barr Grd (*v*. **barre**); Barretts Fd & Grd (-*Lane* 1829); Bottom Coppice (*Bottome cops* 1618, *v*. **botm**); Brewers Grd; Hr Burnbake (*v*. **burnbake**); Butlers Home Cl, Butler's Ho 1829; Droveway; East pitts (-*Pitt* 1829, *Estpitte* 1242 Ch, *v*. **ēast, pytt**); 8 & 11 Acres; 4 & 14 Acres; Frost Lds; The Further Grd 1829; Gate Grd (cf. Yatt Heron *infra*); Greenfield; Harris's Picked Grd, Harris's 10 Acres & Upper Grd (*v*. **pīcede** 'pointed', cf. John *Harris* 1664 (Cranborne)); Heron Grd (-*Grove* 1829, *v*. **hyrne** 'angle, corner', **grāf(a)**, cf. Yatt Heron *infra*); Higher Grd; Hill Coppice; Home Cl & Grd; Kite Hill (*v*. **cȳta**); Lawn Fd (*v*. **launde**); Little Johns Grd or Whites Hill and Stoney Closes (cf. Alice *Whittes* 1332); Long Cl and Loders Grds (a surname from Loders par. *infra*); Lodge Coppice (*Lodg cops* 1618, named from the lodge at Cobley *supra*); Lower Grd; Lynch Grd (*v*. **hlinc**); Malthouse Plot; Manswood Coppice (*Mangewood* 1618, cf. Manswood in M. Crichel par. *supra*); Merry Md (*v*. **myrge**); Middle Grd; E & W Mill Way Coppice (*Myllway cops* 1618, *v*. **myln, weg**); 9 Acres (or Barrow Fd) (*v*.

beorg); Oaks Cl; Orchard; Parricks Md (cf. *The Parricks* 1829, *v.* **pearroc**); Peak (*v.* **pēac**); Pentridge Street (the main street of the village); Percy's Grd (cf. Richard *Percy* 1664); Picked Coppice & Grd (*Picked cops* 1618, *v.* **pīcede** 'pointed'); Play Cl 1829 (*v.* **plega** 'play, sport', cf. Merry Md *supra*); Pond Grd; The Pound; Race Post (Fd); E & W Rowles, Rowles Coppice (*Rowells* 1618, a surname); 6 Acres; Stoney Closes (*v.* Little Johns Grd *supra*); 10 Acres; Tibbs Fd; Townsend Fd (*v.* **tūn, ende**[1]); Triggalls Cl & Grd (cf. Henry *Trigoll* 1664); Two Closes; Watch Oak Coppice (perhaps 'oak tree from which watch was kept', *v.* **watch**, cf. Watchoak Plant. Brk 32); Weares three Closes (cf. Timothy *Weare* 1664); Weary Hill (cf. the same name, PN Brk 226); Whites Hill (cf. Little Johns Grd *supra*); Woodyates Street (the main street of Woodyates, *v. infra*); Hr & Lr Yatt Heron 1829 (*v.* **geat** 'gate, opening, pass', **hyrne** 'angle, corner', cf. Gate Grd, Heron Grd *supra*); Yonder Grd.

(*b*) *terram...de la borna iuxta Pencriz* n.d. (1372) (*v.* **burna** 'spring, stream', perhaps with reference to the upper course of R. Crane, which rises near Pentridge).

Shillingstone

SHILLINGSTONE (ST 825115) ['ʃilənstn]

Alford (sic) 1086 DB, *Akeford*(') 1199 Cur, 1244 *Ass* (p), 1303 FA, *Acford*(') 1201 P, Hy 3 *AddCh*, 1227 FF, 1263 Ipm *et freq* to 1428 FA, *Acforth'* 1280 *Ass*, *Akford* 1303 FA; *Okford*(') 1283, 1398 *Cecil*, *Ocford'* 1398 *ib*

Acforde Eskelin a 1155, 1298 MontC, *Acforde of Robert Eskylling* c.1155 *ib*, *Acford*(*e*) *Eschellinch* 1189–99 *ib*, -*Eskelling* 1215 ClR *et freq* to 1285 Cl, -*Eschelling* 1236 FF, -*Scillinge* 1268 MontC, -*Skelling*('), -*yng'* 1288 *Ass*, 1297 Pat, -*Schilling'* 1288 *Ass*, -*Eskylling* 1303 BM I, 1330 (15) *AddCh*, -*Skilling*, -*yng*(*e*), -*Skyllyng* 1316 FA *et freq* to 1383 *Cecil*, -*Skillynges* 1328 *HarlCh*, -*Shillyng*, -*shillyng* 1336 Cl *et freq* to 1407 Pat, *Akeford Skelling* 1220 ClR, *Akford' Eschelling* 1242–3 Fees, *Hacfordeskelling'* 1268 *Ass*, *Hakeford Eskellyng* 1268 FF, *Akfordskyllyng'* 1318 *Cecil*, *Hacford Shillyng* 1348 Pat; *Ocford*(') *Sculling'* 1280 *Ass*, -*Skillyng* 1327 SR, -*Skyllyng'* 1332 SR, -*skylling* 1405 (15) *AddCh*, *Hocfordeskelling* 1286 FF, *Okfordskelling* 1302 AD I, *Ok*(*e*)*ford*(*e*) *Skylling*, -*yng*(*e*) 1314 Ipm *et freq* with variant spellings -*Skellyng*, -*Scilling*, -*Skillyng*(*e*) to 1431 FA, *Okford' Eschyllinges* 1320 *AddCh*, *Ok*(*e*)*ford*(*e*) *Shillyng*(*e*) 1355 Pat *et freq* with variant spellings -*Shyllyng*, -*Shilling* to 1558 PlR, *Okeford*(*e*) *Eskylling* 15 *AddCh*,

-Eskyllyng 1507 (1530) *ib, Okesford Esskylling* 1546 *PlR, Ockford Shilling* 1664 HTax

Skillyng Okeford 1407 Pat, *Skyllyng Ocford* 1412 FA, *Shillyngokford(e)* 1418 Cl, *Shillyngesokeford(e)* 1443 ib, 1453 IpmR, *Shillingaukford* 1575 Saxton, *Shilling Okeford* 1795 Boswell

Shillyngeston 1444 IPN, *Shyllyng(e)ston(e)-, Shyllengeston' ys Okeford(')* 1494 Cecil, *Shillingston, vulgarly Ockford-Shilling* 1774 Hutch[1]

'Oak-tree ford' *v.* **āc, ford.** In 1086 DB the manor of *Alford* (for *Acford*) was held by *Schelin* (also called *Eschelinus* in Exon p. 31), and his descendants here were Robert son of *Eskelin* a1155 MontC, Robert *Eskylling*, Robert son of *Scilling* c.1155 ib, John *Eskelingh'* 1199 Cur, *-Eskelling* 1201 P, Hy 3 AddCh, Walter *Eschelling'* Hy 3 *ib*, etc; on the alternation of *Esc-, Sc-* in the pers.n., *v.* ANInfl 55. The affix *-Eskelin, -Eskelling*, etc, later *-Shilling*, served to distinguish this place from the neighbouring pars. of Child Okeford and Okeford Fitzpaine. The modern form Shillingstone is a late formation with **tūn** 'village', *v.* IPN 131.

ALDERS COPPICE (ST 837108), 1838 *TA*, cf. (meadow) *sub Alneto de Alfrikesham* c.1250 AddCh (cf. also Hutch[3] 3 445), *desuper Alnetum* c.1270 *ib, Alres, Alreweye, bovenalre, eynythe Alre* 1330 (15) *ib, Gt & Lt Alders, Alder Ways* 1838 *TA, v.* **alor** 'alder', with **weg** 'way', **bufan** '(the place) above', **beniðan** '(the place) beneath' (the form *eynythe* showing loss of initial *b-*); *Alfrikesham* is 'Ælfrīc's enclosure or river meadow', from the OE pers.n. *Ælfrīc* and **hamm.**

BERE MARSH CTGS, FM & MILL (ST 823124), *molendinum de la Bere* 1268 *Ass, la Bere* c. 1270 *AddCh* (p), *La Bere* 1384 IpmR, *Bere* 1412 FF (*-juxta Okford Fytz Payn*), 1412, 1431 FA *et passim* to 1869 Hutch[3], *Berre marshe* 1546 *PlR, Be(e)re Marshe* 1553, 1597 *ib, -marshe* 1618 *CH, Bere als. Bere Marsh* 1611 Hutch[3], *Beer als. Beer Marsh* 1795 Boswell, probably from **bǣr**[2] '(woodland) pasture', cf. Bere R. 1 273, with **mersc** 'marsh'; the place is by R. Stour. There was a mill at Shillingstone in 1086 DB, *v.* VCHDo 3 102, Mill Race *infra.*

THE CLIFF (ST 844104), *cultura que vocatur Super La Clive* c.1270 *AddCh*, (2 acres) *super la Clive* 1330 (15) *ib*, *Clift (Coppice)* 1838 *TA*, *v*. **clif** (dat.sg. *clife*) 'cliff, bank'; it is beside R. Stour.

BONSLEY CMN, *Bowslye Common* 1583 *SPDom*, *Bonslate* 1774 Hutch[1], 1795 Boswell, *-or Bonsleigh* 1869 Hutch[3], *Bonsley (Down)* 1811 OS, 1838 *TA*; Professor Löfvenberg suggests that the first el. may be the OE pers.n. *Buna*, and that the second is probably **slæget** alternating with **slege** 'sheep pasture'. BURT'S WATER CTGS, cf. John *Burt* 1664 HTax. CHURCH OF HOLY ROOD, cf. 'the church of *Acforde Eskelin*' a1155 MontC, *Ecclesia de Atford* (for *Acford*) *Skellyngg* 1291 Tax, cf. *Church Cl* 1838 *TA*. EASTBROOK FM, (*Long*) *East Brook* 1838 *TA*, *v*. **ēast, brōc**. EASTCOMBE CTG & WD, *East Combe Coppice* 1838 *ib*, cf. *West Coombe* 1838 *ib*, *v*. **cumb**. GAIN'S CROSS (FM), *Gains Cross* 1811 OS, (*Long-*) 1838 *TA*. HILLCOMBE BOTTOM & COPPICE, *Elcombe* 1330 (15) *AddCh*, *Elcomb Wood* 1811 OS, *Hill Coombe Coppice* 1838 *TA*, *v*. **cumb**; the first el. may be the OE pers.n. *Ella*. HODWAY LANE, (*viam que vocatur*) *Hodweye* c.1270 *AddCh*, *Hodwaysende* 1548 *Weld*[1], *Hod Way* (*11 & 7 Acres*) 1838 *TA*, 'the road to *Hod*' *v*. **weg**, Hod Hill in Stourpaine par. *supra*, cf. *Hoddefelde* 1548, *-feeld Close* 1600, *Hoddemore* 1548, 1600 all *Weld*[1], *Hod Moor*, (*Lt*) *Hod Mills* 1838 *TA*, also named from their proximity to this hill, *v*. **feld, mōr**. HOLLOWAY LANE, *v*. **hol**[2], **weg**. KITE HILL COPPICE, *Kitehills* 1838 *TA*, *v*. **cȳta, hyll**. LAMB HOUSE FM, cf. *Lamb Grd* 1838 *ib*. LANDCHARD LANE, *Hansheir Lane* 1618 *CH* (for *Lan-*), cf. *Lanchard* 1838 *TA* (the name of two fields on the par. bdy), *v*. **land-sc(e)aru** 'boundary', perhaps to be associated with *Rivulum qui vocatur Landsore* c.1270 *AddCh* which is from the related and synonymous **land-scoru**. MANOR FM. MARSH BRIDGE, cf. Bere Marsh *supra*. MILL RACE, cf. *Mulham* 1330 (15) *AddCh*, *Mill Ham*, (*Lt*) *Mill Md* 1838 *TA*, all named from Bere Marsh Mill *supra*, *v*. **myln, hamm**. NEW BARN. NEW CROSS GATE, *New Cross* 1838 *ib*, a cross-roads, *v*. **cross**. PUXEY LANE, cf. Puxey in Sturminster N. par. *infra*. SHILLINGSTONE HILL, 1838 *ib*, cf. *versus montem* c. 1270 *AddCh*. SHILLINGSTONE HO. WHITE HILL (lost), 1811 OS, *Gt & Lt White Hills* 1838 *TA*, near to foll. WHITE PIT, 1838 *TA*, cf. *Whitepit Coppice*, *White Pit Grd* 1838 *ib*, *v*. **hwīt, pytt**. WITHY BED, cf. *Wytihoug*' 1330 (15) *AddCh* which may be 'heel

of land growing with willows', from **wīðig** and **hōh**. WOOLAND
(lost), 1774 Hutch[1], 1869 Hutch[3], *Woolland* 1576 ib, *Woollands*
1838 *TA*, probably from **wyll(a)** 'spring, stream' and **land**, but
cf. Woolland par. *infra*.

FIELD-NAMES

The undated forms are 1838 *TA* 188. Spellings dated n.d. (e13), n.d. (l13),
1311 are Hutch[3], 1283, 1398 *Cecil*, 1454 *HarlCh*, 1543, 1546, 1548[2] *PlR*,
1548[1], 1600 *Weld*[1], 1618, 1619 *CH*, 1664 HTax, 1711 *WRO*, 1791 Boswell,
and the rest *AddCh*.

(*a*) Acre and Half; Barcombe; Barley Grove; Beer Fd, Beer Marsh Pound
(from Bere Marsh *supra*); Best Buttery (no doubt a complimentary name for
productive land); Boat Acre (by R. Stour); (Lt) Broad Cl; Brought em away
(a phrase name of uncertain significance); Calves House Grd; Clackel;
Cobourn's Grd; Coles's Grd; Crowsty's Plot; Cuckwell Bridge 1791 (named
from Cookwell Brook, *v*. RNs. *infra*); Culverhay (*v*. **culfre** 'dove', **(ge)hæg**,
cf. Dotflen (Coppice) *infra*); Dogs Cl; Dotflen (Coppice) (perhaps to be
associated with *cultura que vocatur Dufurlang*' c.1270, which may be 'dove
furlong' from **dūfe** and **furlang**, and which may be identical with *cultura que
vocatur desuper Columbar*' c.1270, from MedLat *columbare* 'dove-cot', cf.
Culverhay *supra*; Dublin *infra* may be another form of the same name);
Downtons Orchd (cf. John *Dounton*' 1389); (Hr & Lr) Dry Grd; Hr, Lr &
Middle Dublin (cf. Dotflen (Coppice) *supra*); 8 Acres; Enford Bottom Grd,
Endford End Plant. (from Enford (Bottom) in Durweston par. *supra*); Farr's
Orchd (cf. John *Farr* 1664); 40 & 4 Acres; (Lt) Gandle, Gandle Coppice (*terr*'
voc' *Gandelles* 1548[1], 1600, perhaps a surname); Goodfellows Md (cf. Thomas
Goudfelowe 1389, John *Goodfellow* 1664); Gt Gooselands, Lt Gooselands
(Coppice) (cf. *cultura que vocatur Gosfurlang*' c.1270, *v*. **gōs, furlang**, cf. foll.);
Goswells (possibly from **gōs** and **well(a)**, cf. prec.); Grammers Md; Great
Grd; Ham Down ('down belonging to *Ham*', i.e. Hammoon par. *supra*);
Hanfords Ford (by a ford (marked 6″) across R. Stour to Hanford par. *infra*);
Hazell (*v*. **hæsel**; Gt Headland, Lt Head Lands (cf. *hevedacre* 1330 (15), *v*.
hēafod-land, hēafod, æcer); (Gt & Lt) Hill Nap (*v*. **hyll, cnæpp** 'hill-top');
Hill(')s Foot (*v*. **hyll, fōt**, but cf. *prat*' *voc*' *Helys* 1548[1], 1600); Hilly Grd;
Home Grd & Md; Knit Down; Lankley Acre (*v*. **lēah**; first el. uncertain);
Laws Brook; Leg, Leg's (*v*. **leg**); Little Grd; Hr & Lr Long Md; Meadland;
Milking Barton (*v*. **bere-tūn**); Miss Stichings (*v*. **sticcen**; *Miss* perhaps
represents *Mistress's*); Morey's Orchd; Newless Hedge; Newmans Drove;
New Yate (*v*. **geat**); 9 Acres; Gt & Lt Norbury; Nursery; Orchard; Oxen
Leaze (*v*. **oxa, læs**); Paddock; Parish Pound; Park (cf. *locum qui vocatur le
Parke iuxta Ripam de Stoure* 1330 (15), *v*. **park**; the same park is probably
referred to as *parcum Abbatis de Forth* 1330 (15), lands in Shillingstone having
been granted to the abbey of Forde at least as early as the 13th cent., *v*. Hutch[3]
3 444–5); Parsonage Cl; Pasture and Orchd; Peak (*v*. **pēac**); (Gt) Penhill,
Penhill Coppice & Md (first el. possibly PrWelsh or PrCorn *penn[1] 'head,
end, hill', with explanatory OE **hyll**); Play Cross (*v*. **plega** 'play, sport');

Cow, Horse & Lt Pussell, Pussell Plant. (perhaps 'pease hill' from **peosu** and **hyll**); Gt & Lt Raglands, Raglands Lane (*v.* **ragge**); Randalls; Rush Cl; Bennets & Shepherds Ryals, Parsonage & Sandy Ryals, Ryals Coppice (probably 'rye hill' from **ryge** and **hyll**, cf. Peter *Beneyt* c.1270, *Rylond* 1330 (15), *v.* **land**); Scotch Cl; Scuffles Cowleaze; Shrow Pits (probably from **scrēawa** 'shrew-mouse' with shift of stress as in Shroner Ha (EPN)); 6 Acres; Sleek Beard; Snook's Orchd; Hr Sprouse, Sprouse Cowleaze; Stone's Md; Stoney Stile; Sydenhams; 3 Acres; Tom's Grd; Townsend (*v.* **tūn, ende**[1]); Turnpike Ho and Gdn; 12 Acres; 12 and 5 Acres; Water Slade (*v.* **slæd**); Thomas Whites Grd, Whites Home Grd (cf. William *White* 1664); Williams's Md; Youngs Drove.

(*b*) *terr' nuper Basterds* 1619 (cf. Matthew *le Bastard* 1272); *Berelane* 1398, 1548[2], *Beerelane* 1618 ('lane to *Bere*', *v.* Bere Marsh *supra*); *Bocfurlang'* c.1270 (*v.* **furlang**, probably with **bōc**[1] 'beech-tree'); *Brode acre* 1546 (*v.* **brād**, **æcer**); *ten' voc' Castell* 1543, *le Castell* 1546 (*v.* **castel(l)**, probably with reference to the earthworks near Bere Marsh Fm on which *v.* RCHM 3 241); *Downeslond'* 1548[1], *Downsland'* 1600 (*v.* **land**, first el. **dūn** 'hill' or a surname); *Godlynhay* 1546 (the pers.n. or surname *Godelin*, cf. Godlingston 1 54, and (**ge)hæg**); *Goldacra* c.1270 (*v.* **æcer**, first el. **gold** 'gold' or **golde** 'marigold'); *de la Grave* Hy 3 (p) (*v.* **grāf(a)**); *Guldrunethon'* Hy 3 (the fem. OE pers.n. *Goldrūn* with **tūn** 'farm'); *Hare Acres* 1330 (15) (probably from **hara** 'a hare'); *Hole Mead* n.d. (e13) (*v.* **hol**[2]); *Littlemead* 1711; *Ludefurlang'* c.1270 (*v.* **furlang**, with **hlȳde** 'noisy stream' or the OE pers.n. *Luda*); *attelupȝete* 1283 (p) (*v.* **atte, hlīep-geat** 'a leap-gate'); *Melkwell'*, *Melke-wellemede* 1330 (15) ('(meadow by) the spring or stream with milky coloured water', from **meoluc** and **well(a)**, with **mǣd**, cf. the f.n. Milk Wells in Fifehead N. par. *supra*); *la Metelond* 1330 (15) (cf. an analogous 14th cent. f.n. in Winfrith N. 1 184); *Middeldich'* Hy 3 (*v.* **middel, dīc**); *la More* n.d. (l 13), 1311, *More* 1454, *Moracra* c.1270 (*v.* **mōr, æcer**); *in campo Boreali* c.1270 ('north field'); *Northehay* 1546 (*v.* **norð, (ge)hæg**); *Oteresfen* Hy 3 (*v.* **oter** 'an otter', **fenn**); *Rodforlang* 1330 (15) (*v.* **hrēod** 'reed', **furlang**); (*Rivulum de*) *Sevewelle* c.1270 ('seven springs', *v.* **seofon, well(a)**, cf. Seawell Nth 40); *Sourlond* 1330 (15) (*v.* **sūr** 'sour, damp', **land**); *in campo Australi* c.1270, 1320 ('south field'); *prat' de Stures, -Sturesiside* c.1250, *Ripam de Stoure* 1330 (15) ('land alongside R. Stour, bank of R. Stour', *v.* **sīde**, RNs. *infra*); *Twyth hevheud* 1330 (15) (form uncertain, probably for *Twychhen hend* 'the end of the narrow lane', from **twicen(e)** and **ende**[1]); (2 acres in) *la Worth* 1330 (15) (*v.* **worð** 'enclosure').

Tarrant Gunville

TARRANT GUNVILLE (ST 926127)
> ? *Tarente* 1086 DB (f. 75b), ? *Tarenta* Exon, ? *Terente* 1086 DB (f. 82b), *Tarent(e)* 1180–1 P, 1233 Cl, FF, 1320 *MinAcct*, *Tarrent, Torrent* 1382 Fine
> *Tarente Gundevill* 1233 Ch, 1236 FF *et passim* with variant

spellings *Tar(r)ent(e)-*, *Tar(r)ant(t)-* (from 1316 FA),
Tar(r)aunt- (from 1504 Ipm), *-Gund(e)-*, *-Gond(e)-* (from
1263 Cl), *-Gound(e)-* (from 1316 FA), *-Gun-* (from 1475
Pat), *-Gon-* (1503 Ipm), *-Goun-* (1538 *Rawl*), *-vil(l)(e)*,
-uil(l)(e), *-vyl(l)(e)*, *-uyl(l)(e)*, *-fylde* (1504 Ipm), *-feld(e)*
(1510 AD V, 1541 *Glyn*), *-field* (1619 *CH*); *Tharrente
Gundeuill'* 1244 *Ass*, *Terantgonnevyle* 1407 Pat, *Terra(u)nt
G(o)undevyle* 1492, 1500 ib, *-Gunvile* 1591 *Rawl*, *Torrent
Gounvyle* 1542 *ib*, *-Gounvyll* 1548 *Ct*
Gondevileston 1264 Ipm, *Gundevyleston* 1303 FA, *Go(u)nde-
uyleston'* 1405 *Weld*[1]
Goundeuill' 1395 *Rawl et freq* with variant spellings *Gunde-,
Gonde-, -vyle, -uyle, -vile* to 1494 *Cecil*, *Goundeville maner'*
1466 IpmR, *Gounvyll* 1547 *Ct*, *-vyle, -vyld* 1548 *ib*, *Gunfild*
1553 *Cecil*, *-feld* 1575 *Saxton*, *-field* 1618 *Map*, *Gunvill(e)*
1563 Hutch[3], 1664 HTax, *Gundfield* 1619 *CH*

Named from R. Tarrant which rises near Stubhampton *infra*,
v. Tarrant H. par. *supra*, RNs. *infra*; on the probable identification of the DB forms, *v.* Eyton 131–2, VCHDo 3 69, 100. The
affix *Gunville* is manorial; Robert *de Gundeuill'* held a fee here
in 1180–1 P, cf. Hugh *de Gundevil(l)e* 1211–2 RBE, 1212 Fees,
1233 FF, Tarrant H. par. and Farnham par. *supra*, *v.* **tūn**
'estate'; the 16th and 17th cent. spellings in *-fyld*, *-feld*, etc show
confusion with **feld** 'field'.

HR & LR BARN DOWN (lost), 1829 *EnclA*, *Berendon'* 1244 *Ass*,
Brandon(') 1280 QW, *Ass*, *Braun-, Brendon(e)* 1280 *ib*, *pastur'
voc' La Barndedon'* 1397, *(La) Barndedon(e)* 1397–1408, *Gouitz
Barndedon'* 1397, 1398, *(la) Barn(e)do(u)n(e)* 1398–1407, *Barn-
do(u)n(e) Gouys* 1398, *-Gouytz* 1400–1408, *Barndedon' Gouytz*
1402–1409, *Barendon'* 1402 all *Weld*[1], *Barne Downe* 1541 *Glyn*,
Barren Downe 1618 *Map*, 'burnt hill', from **berned, bærned**
and **dūn**; the affix is manorial, cf. Brian *de Gouyz* mentioned
in connection with *Tarente* and Stubhampton *infra* in 1282 FF.
The documents cited as 1397–1409 *Weld*[1] are court rolls of
Barn(d)edon (Gouytz), which is referred to as a hundred in the
headings of the rolls for 1397 and 1398.

BUSSEY STOOL FM (ST 927148), BUSSEY STOOL PARK & WDS,
BUSSEY'S DOWN, *Burcyes* 1432 Cl, *manerium de Burces* 1558

PlR, *Burses Stolle* (*Coppice*) 1590 *LRMB*, *Burcistoole walk* 17 *CecilMap*, *Bursie house*, -*Downe*, *Burs*(*e*)*y cops*, -*Walke* 1618 *Map*, *Bursey Stool*(*e*) *Walk* 1620, 1869 Hutch[3], *Bursies* 1659 *Salkeld*, *Burseyes* 1674 *ib*, *Bushey Stool Fm*, *Bushy Down* 1811 OS, *Pusseys Down* 1829 *EnclA*, *Bussey Stool Ho*, *Busseys Down* 1839 *TA*, *Busseystool walk* 1869 Hutch[3], named from the family of Roger *Burcy* 1327 *SR*, 1332 SR, John *Busse* 1664 HTax, *v.* **walk** (this was one of the 'walks' of Cranborne Chase *supra*), **dūn**. *Stool* is apparently from **stōl** 'stool, seat; tree-stump, etc'; the precise significance is not clear, but on the possible analogy of the nearby Sedge Oak Coppice in Ashmore par. *supra*, perhaps 'commode, privy' (from 1501 NED). However Dr Gelling points out that **stōl** may have been used of 'a flat-topped hill', the possible sense of this el. in Stoulton Wo.

EASTBURY DAIRY, Ho (ST 933127) & PARK, Richard *apud Estbury* 1391 *Rawl*, *Gunvil-Eastbury* 1511 Hutch[1], *Gounvyle Estbury* 1547 *Ct*, *Gunvile Estbury* 1558 *PlR*, *Estbury* 1569 Hutch[3], *Eastbury* 1619 *CH*, 1774 Hutch[1] (-*or Gunvil-Eastbury*), *East Bury Park* 1811 OS, *Eastbury Ho*, *Plot & Wd*, *Front & Gt Park* 1839 *TA*, no doubt ME **bury** (from dat.sg. *byrig* of OE **burh**) in the sense 'manor house, centre of an estate', 'east' to distinguish it from Westbury Fm *infra*, *v.* **ēast**. For the affix *Gunvil*, cf. par. name *supra*; on the park here, enclosed in the 18th cent. and originally five miles round, *v.* Hutch[1] 2 165.

MAIN DOWN (PLANT.) (ST 932138), (*pastur' montana voc' la*) *Menedon*(*e*) 1397, 1398 *Weld*[1], *Main Down* 1811 OS, -*Plant.* 1839 *TA*, 'common hill or down', from (**ge**)**mǣne** and **dūn**, with reference to its situation near the E par. bdy, cf. foll. and *Monelandes Downe* 1541 *Rawl* which may have the same first el., with **land**.

MANOR COPPICE & HILL (ST 923155), *Manors Hill* (*Coppice*) 1829 *EnclA*, *Hr Manor* (a coppice), *Lr Manors Coppice*, *Manor hill Down* 1839 *TA*, named from *Manewode*(*s*)*hull*(*e*) 1397, 1398 *Weld*[1], *bosc' voc' Manewode* 1423 *Rawl*, *copicia juxta Mamewoodhill'* 1541 *Glyn*, *the Copps upon Manwood* 1590 *LRMB*, *Manwood* (*Downe*) 1618 *Map*, '(hill and down at) the common wood', *v.* (**ge**)**mǣne**, **wudu**, **hyll**, **dūn**, cf. prec.; Manor Coppice is in fact adjacent to Common Coppice *infra*, both of them being on the N par. bdy.

STUBHAMPTON (FM) (ST 917138)
   Stibemetune 1086 DB
   Stubehampton(e) 1233 FF, 1280 *Ass, Stubhamtune* 1262 Ipm,
   Stubhampton(e) 1280 Ch, QW, *Ass,* 1282 FF, 1283 Ipm *et
   passim, Tarente Stubhampton(e)* 1318 *Cecil,* 1397, 1404
   Weld¹, Tarentestubhampton 1324 FF, *Stubamton'* 1388
   Rawl, Stubbehamton 1541 *Glyn, Stubhampton* or *Tarent-
   Stubhampton* 1774 Hutch¹, *-or Stepington* 1795 Boswell
   Stibampton' 1268 *Ass* (p), *Stibhampton(')* 1280 Ch (p), 1288
   Ass, Tarente Stibhampton' 1405 *Weld¹ Stebhampton* 1276
   FF (p)
   Stupehampton 1280 *Ass, Stupham(p)ton'* 1384, 1423 *Rawl,*
   1402 *Weld¹*
   St(h)uham(p)ton' 1405, 1421 *Rawl*
   Stupyngton' 1471 *Rawl, Stipyng-, Stypyngton'* 1534–1580 *ib,*
   1549 *Ct, Stepington* 1575 Saxton

   Probably, as indicated by the DB form in *-eme-*, 'farm of the
Stybbhǽme', i.e. 'farm of the dwellers at a place called *Stybbhām*
('tree-stump village')', or 'farm of the dwellers by the
tree-stump', *v.* **stybb, hām, hǣme** (gen.pl. *hǽma*), **tūn,** cf.
Bockhampton 1 367, Witchampton par. *infra,* Tengstrand MN
97. The affix *Tarente-* is from R. Tarrant which rises here, *v.*
par. name *supra.*

   WESTBURY FM (ST 925129), *Westbury* 1414 *Rawl, Gunavile
Westbury* 1423 *ib, West Bury* 1811 OS, 'west manor house', *v.*
Eastbury *supra.*

   ASHMORE BOTTOM, from Ashmore par. *supra, v.* **botm.** BALL
COPPICE, 1839 *TA, v.* **ball.** BISHOP'S COPPICE, *Bishops Cl &
Coppice* 1839 *ib.* BLOOD-WAY COPPICE, 1869 Hutch³, *una
copicia apud Fludway* 1541 *Glyn, Blindway* (a coppice) 1618
Map, Fludice Coppice & Fd 1839 *TA.* The two earlier names
(perhaps denoting two different ways since several tracks meet
here) mean 'way liable to be flooded', *v.* **flōd, weg,** and 'way
that leads nowhere', *v.* **blind;** *Fludice* no doubt represents a
reduced gen.sg. form *Fludway's.* The modern Blood-way may
be partly the result of confusion with the next name, partly the
result of popular etymology: Hutch³ (3 412) reports that this
place and the adjacent Bloody Shard Gate were by tradition

scenes of battles between keepers of Cranborne Chase and deer-stealers, and an alteration of *Flood-* to *Blood-* may have been further encouraged by a misinterpretation of the neighbouring Gore Coppice in Farnham par. *supra* as containing *gore* 'blood'. BLOODY SHARD GATE, 1869 Hutch[3], *bluds gate* 1618 *Map*, near prec. on the par. bdy, *v.* **sceard** 'gap', **geat**. The early form *bluds* may represent a surname *Blood* rather than the word *blood*, but it has clearly influenced the change *Flood-* > *Blood-* in prec.; *Bloody* no doubt represents a reduced form of *Blood-way*. BOSSLETON COPPICE, *Bokeldeane* 1618 *Map*, *Bossleton* 1839 *TA*, *v.* **denu** 'valley'. BRAMBLE HEW COPPICE, *Bramble Yew* 1829 *EnclA*, *-Hugh* 1839 *TA*. BUILDING GDN COPPICE, cf. *pastura in gardino* 1320 *MinAcct*. COMMON COPPICE, 1839 *TA*, *Comen' Cops* 1541 *Glyn*, *Common Cops* 1618 *Map*, *v.* **comun, copis**, cf. Manor Coppice *supra*. DAIRY LODGE, 1811 OS. HIGH DITCH COPPICE, *Great ditch, Little ditch* (two coppices) 1618 *Map*, *Ditch Coppice, Higher Ditch* (a coppice) 1839 *TA*, *v.* **dīc**, no doubt with reference to the circular earthwork marked 6″. DROVE BARN, cf. *xxxvij acr'*...*bywestedraue* 1320 *MinAcct* ('to the west of the drove'), *the drove hedge* 1591 *Rawl, North of Drove, South of Drove* 1839 *TA*, *v.* **drāf, bī, westan, hecg**. DUNGROVE FM, HILL & ROWS, *Don(e)groue* 1408, 1409 *Weld*[1], *Doune Grove* 1541 *Glyn, Dungroue* 1618 *Map*, *Gt & Lt Dungrove* 1829 *EnclA, Dungrove Barn, Ctg & Fd* 1839 *TA*, 'copse on the hill', *v.* **dūn, grāf(a), rāw**, cf. *Le Dunfurlong* 1356 *Rawl*, which has the same first el. with **furlang**. EARL'S HILL (COPPICE), *Earles hill* 1618 *Map, Earls Hill* 1839 *TA*, cf. *Erleswod(e)* 1402–1421, *Erliswod'* 1403, *Yerles-* 1541, *Erles Coppes* 1542 all *Rawl*, *v.* **eorl, hyll, wudu, copis**; the manor of Tarrant G. was held in turn by the earls of Gloucester and Hertford, of March, and of Cambridge, *v.* Hutch[3] 3 451. FILBERD'S COPPICE, *Filberds-* 1839 *TA, Field beard Coppice* 1829 *EnclA*, perhaps to be associated with John *Phelpot* 1471 *Rawl*, Peter *Fylpott* 1548 *Ct*. FURZEY CLOSE ROW, *Furzey Close* (*Row*) 1839 *TA*, cf. *Fursehedge drove* 1578 *Rawl, Furzhedge* (*hedge*) 1725 *ib*, *Furz(e)y hedge* 1839 *TA*, *v.* **fyrs, fyrsig, hecg, rāw**. GLEBE FM, *Cleave* 1811 OS (sic, possibly an error, but perhaps representing **clif** (dat.sg. *clife*) 'cliff, bank'). GUNVILLE COPPICE (cf. *Coppice* 1829 *EnclA*), DOWN (1784 *SalisT*, cf. *xxxvij acr' bouedoune* 1320 *MinAcct, Dounes* 1406 *Rawl, Down Cl* 1829

EnclA, Down 1839 *TA, v.* **dūn, bufan** 'above', cf. *Smethedon(e) infra*), Ho (*Goundeville maner*' 1466 IpmR), LODGE, & PARK (cf. Harbin's Park *infra*), all named from par. name *supra.* HALIFAX. HANDCOCK'S BOTTOM, *v.* **botm.** HANGING COPPICE, 1839 *TA, -cops* 1618 *Map, v.* **hangende, copis.** HARBIN'S PARK, formerly *parcus...de Tarente Gundeuile* 1280 *Ass, bosc'...voc' la Park' de Goundevile* 1423 *Rawl, bosc' domine voc' la Parke* 1470 *ib, Parke of Gunville* 1563 Hutch³, *Gunfield Parke* 1618 *Map, Gunville Park* 1811 OS, cf. *subbosc'...in parco* 1320 *MinAcct,* 'park of...*Tarente*' 1398 Pat, *Parke yeat coppis* 1535 *Rawl, Park Cops'* 1541 *Glyn, Park Pleck* 1839 *TA, v.* **park, geat, copis plek,** par. name *supra,* cf. Gunville Park *supra.* The present name of the park is from the family of *Harbin* which possessed the manor of Tarrant G. in the 18th cent. (Hutch³ 3 452), cf. 'Here is a small seat and park belonging to the Harbins' (Hutch¹ 2 165). For further references to this park, the best preserved of Dorset's medieval deer parks, *v.* Cantor & Wilson 4 170–2. HARBIN'S PARK FM, from prec., earlier *New Barn* 1811 OS. HERON GROVE COPPICE, *Irmegraue* 1405 *Weld¹, Earn Grove* 1839 *TA, v.* **grāf(a),** first el. perhaps an OE pers.n. *Irma* suggested for Irmingland Nf (DEPN). HOLMES AND PUDDLEWAY COPPICE, HOLMES CMN, *Homes, Pudleway* (coppices) 1618 *Map, Holmes (Hill)* 1829 *EnclA, Holmes and Puddleway, Holmes's hill* 1839 *TA,* from the surname *Home(s),* **puddel** 'puddle, shallow pond', **weg,** cf. Stainer's (Holmes) Coppice *infra.* JOE'S GROVE. KENNEL QUARTER, THE KENNELS, *Kennel (Park)* 1839 *TA, The Eastbury Kennel* 1869 Hutch³, *v.* **kenel, quarter,** Eastbury *supra.* LAMB HOUSE WDS. LILY BANK FIRS, *Lily bank* 1839 *TA,* perhaps to be associated with Geoffrey *le Lilie* 1327 *SR, -Lylie* 1340 NI, *v.* **bank(e).** LIME PIT COPPICE, *Limepit-*1839 *TA.* LONG PLANT. LOOSE PATH COPPICE, *Loose path* 1829 *EnclA,* first el. probably **hlōse** 'pigsty'. MARLBOROUGH FM. MAY LANE, perhaps to be associated with Richard *le May* 1327 *SR.* PERCY'S ROW, 1839 *TA, v.* **rāw;** *Percy's* may be an alteration of *Bursey's* since this is near Bussey Stool Fm *supra.* POND COPPICE, 1839 *ib.* PURLEY WD (lost), 1811 OS, *John Swaines purliew within his Manor of Gunvill* 1563 Hutch³ (3 452), *v.* **purlewe** 'outskirts of a forest'; it was N of Harbin's Park *supra* and adjoined Cranborne Chase. ROWDEN COPPICE, *Manwood or Rowden* 1618 *Map, Rowdens* 1829 *EnclA, -den* 1839

TA, *v.* **rūh, denu,** cf. Manor Coppice *supra.* ST MARY'S CHURCH, cf. *ecclesie de Tarente Gondevyle, -Gundevyle* 1318 *Ct, Church Plot* 1829 *EnclA, -Close* 1839 *TA.* SCHOOL HOUSE QUARTER, *v.* **quarter.** SEDGE OAK COPPICE, *Sedge Oak* 1839 *ib, v.* Gt & Lt Sedge Oak Coppice in Ashmore par. *supra.* SIR JOHN'S COPPICE, 1839 *ib, Surgeons* (a coppice) 1618 Map, *St John's Coppice* 1829 *EnclA,* from the surname *Surgeon.* SOLOMON'S QUARTER, *Solomons-* 1839 *TA, v.* **quarter.** SQUIRE COPPICE, *Squires* (a coppice) 1618 *Map, Esquire or Square* 1829 *EnclA, Squire* 1839 *TA,* from the surname *Squire.* STAINER'S (HOLMES) COPPICE, *Stainers, Stayners* 1618 *Map,* (*Stainers*) *Holmes* 1829 *EnclA, Hr & Lr Stainers* 1839 *TA,* cf. John *Steyner* 1518 Hutch[1], Richard *Stayner*(*s*) 1541 *Glyn,* 1548 *Ct, v.* Holmes and Puddleway Coppice *supra.* STUBHAMPTON BOTTOM (1811 OS) & DOWN (1839 *TA*), from Stubhampton *supra.* TOLLARD GREEN BOTTOM, cf. *Tollardesgore* 1397 *Weld*[1], *Grene* 1541 *Glyn,* near the county bdy and named from Tollard Green in Tollard Royal par. (W 208), *v.* **gāra, grēne**[2]. WINDMILL PLANT., cf. *Windmill Fd & Pce* 1839 *TA,* named from *old windmill* 1618 *Map* (marked just E of Harbin's Park), *v.* **windmill.** WOODHOUSE LANE, cf. *Woodhouse Md* 1829 *TA,* named from *Woodhay* 1618 *Map, v.* **wudu, (ge)hæg.** ZAREBA CLUMP, ModE (from Arabic) *zariba* 'fenced enclosure or camp in the Sudan'.

FIELD-NAMES

The undated forms are 1839 *TA* 220. Spellings dated 1280 are QW, 1283, 1285 *Cecil,* 1288 *Ass,* 1318, 1548, 1549 *Ct,* 1320, 1322 *MinAcct,* 1332 SR, 1340 NI, 1397, 1398, 1401[1], 1402[2], 1404, 1405[2], 1407[2] *Weld*[1], 1432 Cl, 1541[1] *Glyn,* 17 *CecilMap,* 1618 *Map,* 1664 HTax, 1829 *EnclA,* and the rest *Rawl.*

(a) Abbey Cl & Fd (cf. *Abbeis-* 1337, 1414, *Abbey*(*e*)*swode* 1396, 1414, *Ab*(*b*)*ey*(*e*)*s-, Abbei*(*e*)*stenement* 1378 *et freq* to 1402, *Abbeis-* 1391, *Abbaisplace* 1395, *Abbeyes place* 1403, *Abbes copps', Abbey londe* 1534, from the family of John *Abbay* 1332, 1340, *v.* **wudu, tenement, place, copis, land;** the lost name *Abbeyweye infra* is probably unrelated to these names); Ashey Coppice (probably from **æsc** and **(ge)hæg**); Barn Yd & Plant.; Bastards Cl; Belt (*v.* **belt**); Bottom Md 1829, Bottom Orchd or Home Cl (*v.* **botm** 'valley bottom', cf. *Bitome* 1337, *le Butme* 1353, from the related and synonymous **bytme**); Boyce's Plot; Broad Cl; Bugle horn Inn; Calf Hay (*v.* **(ge)hæg**); Calves Cl; Further, Middle & Nether Chalcots (the common p.n. 'cold cottage(s)', from **ceald** and **cot,** cf. *lez Cotes* 1534, or the surname from such a p.n.); Cheese Croft; Cinkum Pits; Corn Grd (cf. *camp' frument' de Stypyngton'* 1548, *the Corn-Fields* 1725, *v.* Stubhampton *supra*); Corner Grd; Crabtree Coppice;

Crowters (cf. Thomas *Crowter* 1664); Culverhay Cl & Coppice 1829, Culverhay (Row) (*v.* **culfre** 'a dove', **(ge)hæg**, cf. Pigeon house Fd *infra*); Dags Cl & Row 1829, Dags (the surname *Dag(g)*); Damsels hays; Dean Fd (*v.* **denu** 'valley'); Dry Cl; Dunwood 1829, Durnwood (first el. perhaps **dierne, dyrne** 'hidden'; however *claus' voc' Thurneord'* 1541[1] may belong here, in which case the first el. is **þyrne** 'thorn-bush' with an uncertain second el.); East Fd (*le East fyld* 1578, *v.* **ēast, feld**); Eweleaze; (Peaked) Fern Down, Fern Down Flg (*v.* **peked, fearn, dūn**); Flippings (cf. William *Flopyn* 1340, Robert *Flippen* 1664); 4 Acres (*Foureakers* 1541[1]); Great Md or Eweleaze; Grove Cl (Row) & Gdn (cf. *Groves* 1618, *v.* **grāf(a)**); Scite of Gumbletons 1829; (Hanham's) Gunville Fd (*Gunfield fields* 1618, *v.* par. name *supra*); Lr Ham Fd, Ham Cl (cf. *terr' voc' le Hamp'hegge* 1534, 1535, *Hamhege* 1535, 1538, *Ham-hedge* 1725, *v.* **hamm, hecg**); Hanging Grd 1829, -Cl (*v.* **hang-ende**); Harry's Gore 1829 (*v.* **gāra**); Hawking Down (perhaps ModE *hawking*, or an altered form of *Hogging-*, *v. infra*); Hide Cl 1829, Hides (*la Hyde* 1401[1], 1404, *v.* **hīd** 'a hide of land'); Higher Fd by Down; Hoggen- 1829, Hogging Down (a gen.pl. form in *-en* (*v.* **-ena**) of **hogg** 'young sheep'); Home Fd; Homers Fd; Kiddles 8 Acres & Md; Lay Fd 1829 (*v.* **lǣge**); (Gt, Lr & Upr) Lines (*le Laynes in campo frument' de Stypyngton'* 1548, *lez leynes* 1578, *Lynes* 1618, *v.* **leyne, lain**, Stubhampton *supra*); Little Coppice & Md; Hr & Lr Lodge Coppice, Lodge Grds & Row; Longbarrow Fd (named from Chettle Long Barrow in Chettle par. *infra*); Long Bottom (*v.* **botm**); Long Md (*Langemed* 1356, *v.* **lang**[1], **mǣd**); Long Walk (*v.* **walk**); Lower Fd; Mead 1829; Middle Fd; Moreys Grove (cf. Thomas *Morey* 1664, *v.* **grāf(a)**); Mount Fd; Mundys (Dags) (cf. John *Munday* 1664, *v.* Dags *supra*); Mustons Cl; Lr & Upr New Cl; New Inclosure 1829; Newlands Fd (*v.* **nīwe** 'newly cultivated', **land**); No Mans Ld (near to Main Down *supra* and par. bdy); North Fd & Plot; The Paddock; Parsons Piddle (probably **piddle** 'small enclosure', *v.* PN Brk 896); Peaked Cl 1829, -Coppice (*v.* **peked** 'pointed'); Pigeon house Fd (near Culverhay *supra*); Pleasure Grd Plant.; Pleck Coppice, Furzy Pleck, Park Pleck (*v.* **plek** 'small plot of ground', *v.* Harbin's Park *supra*); Pond Cl; Pot Craft (*v.* **croft**; the first el. may be a surname, cf. William *Puttes* 1351, (*ten' voc'*) *Pottes Place* 1401[2]); Pot Hook 1829, -Oak (*Potthook'* (a coppice) 1618, perhaps from its shape); Ragged Row (*v.* **ragged, row**); Rick Barton (*v.* **rickebarton**); Rodford 1829, -fords (*v.* **hrēod, ford**, or a surname); Rough Cl (Row); Round (a round plant.); Round about Coppice; Row (freq, *v.* **row**); South Mead Plant.; Stars (-and Robs 1829) (*claus' voc' Steres* 1541[1], the surnames *Ste(e)r* and *Robb*); Stickway (*copicia...voc' Stikwey* 1541[1], this field is at ST 926162 beside the Roman road from Badbury where it climbs to 500′, *v.* **sticol** 'steep', **weg**); Straw house Coppice; Stubhampton Fd 1829 (*-field* 1618, *v.* Stubhampton *supra*); 30 Acres 1829; Middle Thorns (cf. *Taillorsthorne, Wilemannesthorn'* 1337, *v.* **þorn**, with the surnames *Taillor, Wilman*); Three Cornered Plant.; Threshers Cl; Tinkers Cl; Townsends- 1829, Townsend Cl; 20 Acres; Vimiels Cl (*pratum voc' Clariswenyllis* 1405, *-Clarice Wyneles* 1406, *-Clarice Wymeles* 1410, *-Claricewyvulles* (sic) 1414, *-Claricie Wyveles* (sic) 1416, *cot' voc' Wevels* (sic) 1538, cf. Roger *Wynel* 1327 SR, 1351, Walter *Wynel* 1332, some forms of the surname showing scribal confusion of *n* and *u* (*v*)); the same family probably gave name to *Bysouthe-*

wymullepath' 1397, '(land) to the south of Wymull's path', *v.* **bī, sūðan, pæð**, although Professor Löfvenberg points out that this form may mean 'to the south of the path to the windmill', *v.* **windmulle**); Gt & Lt Wears (probably a surname); Gt & Lt Well Coppice; Well Plot 1829; Lr West side Fd (cf. *la West Feld'* 1401², *-felde* 1423, *le West fyld* 1578, *v.* **west, feld**); North part-, South part Yonder Pce.

(b) *Abbeyweye* 1320, *Abwey* 1322, 1337, 1541², *Abney* (sic) 1549, *Abway-Gate*, *Abway hedge* 1725 ('road to the abbey', *v.* **abbeye, weg**, probably with reference to Tarrant abbey in Tarrant C. par. *supra*, cf. Abbey Cl & Fd *supra*); *Alstanesdich* 1337 (from **dīc**, with the OE pers.n. *Æðelstān*, *Ælfstān* or *Ealhstān*); *AspeCops* 1541¹, *Apse* (a coppice) 1618 (*v.* **æspe** 'aspen-tree', **copis**); *le Backesyd'* 1591 (*v.* **backside**); *Beals ground* 1725 (cf. Joseph *Beale ib*); *(copis'* . . . *voc'*) *Bere Knapp(e)* 1535, 1538 (perhaps 'hillock where barley was grown', from **bere** and **cnæpp**); *Bitelegh'* 1322, *Byteleyghe* 1337 (*v.* **lēah**; first el. perhaps **bitula, bitela** 'beetle'); *Blaneford(e)wey* 1351, 1356, *Blanefordesweye* 1410 ('road to Blandford (Forum)', *v.* **weg**); *claus' voc' lez breache* 1541¹ (*v.* **bræc**); *Brokeforlang'* 1391 (*v.* **brōc, furlang**); *Burnegate* 1595 (perhaps analogous with Burngate I 130); *lez Close* 1541¹ (*v.* **clos(e)**); *Cosynesplace* 1407, 1408, *Cosynes-, Cosinesthyng(e)*, *-thing'* 1407-1409, *Cosynes* 1432 (cf. John *Cosyn* 1405, *v.* **place, þing**); *parva claus' iuxta Cruce* 1541¹ ('small close next to the cross'); *prat' voc' Crynes(place)* 1401², 1412 (cf. Walter *Cryne* 1384, *v.* **place**); *Eldeden'* 1405 (*v.* **eald, denu**); (*By weste*) *Eyryscroftyftes* 1397 (form probably corrupt); *Frankham* 1337 *et freq* to 1396, *Frankenham* 1396, 1405², *Frankhampme, Franham* 1401² ('Franca's enclosure', from an OE pers.n. *Franca* and **hamm**); *Fries (hatts)* 1618 (the surname *Frie* with **hætt** 'hat-shaped hill'); *Gronsylles* 1535, *grounshilles* 1539 (probably a surname); *atte Hale* (p) 1384, 1407 (*v.* **atte, healh** 'nook', dat.sg. *heale* (with a short diphthong from the nom. form)); *Hamundesacres* 1391 (the ME surname *Hamund, v.* **æcer**); *Holethorne* 1337 ('hollow thorn', or 'thorn in a hollow', *v.* **hol¹, hol², þorn**); *le Howe* 1423 (*v.* **howe**); *loc' voc' Hullewerk* 1389 (possibly 'earthwork on the hill', from **hyll** and **(ge)weorc**, perhaps with reference to the Iron Age hill-fort (marked 6″) in Bussey Stool Park *supra*, cf. other instances of this name in PN W 320. However Dr Gelling draws my attention to F. Emery, *The Oxfordshire Landscape* (1974), p. 66-7, where *hillwork* is shown to have been a piece of woodland in which a community had cutting rights); *la Inlond(e)* 1397, 1398 (*v.* **inland**); *ten' voc' Ive house* 1544 (reading uncertain); *toft'* . . . *voc' Janewynes* 1421 (cf. Richard *Janewenes* 1351); (*claus' voc'*) *Knoyel(l)es* 1400, 1403 (cf. John *Knoiel* 1351, *-Knoyel* 1384); *Langelond(e)* 1320 *et freq* to 1356 (*v.* **lang¹, land**); *le Launde* 1356, 1396 (*v.* **launde**, perhaps also the first el. of *Landefeld'* 1541¹, *v.* **feld**); *la longeforurde* 1407 (*v.* **lang¹, forierð, -yrð**); *Louches* 1318 (probably a manorial name, cf. Richard *de Louches* 1285 (mentioned under Cranborne hundred), *-de Luches* 1306 Banco (Tarrant Rush.)); *le Mere* 1337, *Merefurlong'* 1353 (*v.* **mere¹** 'pool', **furlang**); *de la Mire, -Myre* 1322 (p) (*v.* **mire**); *de la More* 1288 (p) (*v.* **mōr**); *Musebergh'* 1320, *Mous-, Moseberghe* 1337 ('hill or barrow infested with mice', *v.* **mūs, beorg**); *New-Field* 1725; *Noddeneszete* 1337 (*v.* **geat**; the first part of the name could be a surname, or a p.n. in **denu**); *la Northdon'* 1406, 1408 (*v.* **norð, dūn**); *Northwod(e)* 1403, *Nortwode* 1414 (*v.*

norð, wudu); *le Orcherd'* 1351, *pastur' del Orchard'* 1353, *le Orcherdmed'* 1356 (*v.* **orceard, mæd**); *les Outwodes* 1381, *le Outwode, le Oute wode* 1386 (*v.* **ūt(e), wudu**); *Paltonesplace* 1401², *prat' voc' Paltounes* 1417 (cf. John *Palton* 1403, *v.* **place**); *Paynes Cote* 1534 (the surname *Payne, v.* **cot**); (*ten' voc'*) *Plankettes* 1400, *Blankettes* 1423 (a surname); *Pondfald'* 1337 (*v.* **pund-fald**); (*pastur' de*) *Poushull(e)* (or *Pons-*) 1337, 1351, *Pulshull'* 1353, *Pushel* 1356 (*v.* **hyll**; Professor Löfvenberg suggests that the first el. would seem to be the word *pulse* 'plant yielding pulse' (cultivated in England since the 13th cent.), *v.* NED, EDD, cf. the f.n. Pulse Hill Db 658, Field 175); *Prattestenement* 1423 (the surname *Pratt, v.* **tenement**); *Prest(e)wey* 1322, 1353 (*v.* **prēost, weg**, cf. Priest's Way 1 39); *claus' voc' Rodberdes* 1541¹ (cf. Richard *Rodbard* 1340); *Rugewey* 1390 (*v.* **hrycg-weg**); *Rytheresdene* 1280 QW, *-denn(e)* 1280 ib, *Ass, Rothersdeane* 17, *Rotherdene, Rothers Dene* 1618 (*v.* **hrīðer, hrȳðer** 'an ox, cattle', **denu** 'valley'); (*prat' voc'*) *Sawyer(e)s* 1417, 1421, *Sawerys* 1417, *Saw(y)ers* 1423 (cf. Robert *Sawiar', -Sawyare* 1351); *Scam(m)ellysplace* 1397 (cf. Alice *Scammel* 1332 (Pimperne), *v.* **place**); *Schepe-*1320, *Shapecroft* 1332, 1396 (cf. *la Shephous* 1402, *v.* **scēap** 'sheep', **croft, hūs**); *Schortelond* 1320, 1322 (*v.* **sc(e)ort, land**); *Shafteburys-, Shefteburyswey* 1397 ('road to Shaftesbury', *v.* **weg**); *pastur' de Shoyetdone* 1397 (*v.* **dūn**, first el(s). uncertain); *Sixeakers* 1541¹ (*v.* **sex, æcer**); *Slades-Bottom-hedge* 1725 (*v.* **slæd, botm**); *Smethedon(e)* 1320, 1322, *Smith doune* 1618 (*v.* **smēðe¹** 'smooth, level', **dūn**); *le Strete* 1549 (*v.* **strǣt**, no doubt with reference to the Roman road from Badbury (Margary 46) which crosses the par.); *T(h)omelyn(e)stenement* 1395, 1399, 1400, *Thomlenestenement* 1396, *Thomelyneslond'* 1402 (the surname *T(h)omelyn, v.* **tenement, land**); *claus' voc' Trompers* 1423 (a surname); *Vyncentyswonyenge* 1402² (cf. Richard *Vyncent ib, v.* **wunung** 'dwelling'); *acr' apud Vyni* 1320, (*pastura super*) *Vyny* 1320, 1337, *le Vyny(e), -Vyni* 1351, 1353, 1356, *la Vyny* 1471 (*v.* **vinye** 'a vine', cf. Phoenice Fm Sr 100); *Wof'* 1283 (perhaps for *Wofurlong*, in which case the first el. is identical with foll.); *Wowelond* 1356 (*v.* **wōh** 'crooked', **land**); *prat' voc' Writhell'* 1414, 1415, *-Wrythell'* 1417 (cf. John *W(h)rithel* 1351).

Tarrant Rushton

TARRANT RUSHTON (ST 938060)
? *Tarente* 1086 DB (f. 75b), ? *Tarenta* Exon, *Tarent(e)* 1194 Cur, 1199 FF, 1225, 1226 Cur, ClR, 1227 FF, 1244 *Ass Tarente Petri de Russell'* 1242–3 Fees, *Tar' Russ'* 1264 Ipm, *Tarente Russe(a)us* 1280, 1288 *Ass, -Russeals* 1289 Orig, 1290 Fine, *-Russeale* 1290 Pat, *-Russchnes* 1296 Ipm, *-Russe(a)ux* 1314, 1399 Cl
Rus(s)cheuston(e) 1283 Cecil, 1327 *SR, Russe(a)uston(e)* 1315 Ipm, 1318 Cecil, *Russheston* 1326 Ipm, *Russ(c)heton(e)* 1326 ib, 1332 SR, 1494 Cecil, *Russe Auxton* 1399 Cl, *Ryssheton* 1463 IpmR, *Rushton* 1588, 1611 Cecil, 1811 OS; *Tarent(e)*

Russcheweston 1307 Ipm *et freq* with variant spellings
-*Russea(u)ston*, -*Russeauxton*, -*Ruysscheustone*, -*Russh(es)-
ton*, -*Ru(y)ss(h)enston* (for -*eus*-), -*Rousshton*, -*Rissheton*,
-*Ryssheton* to 1432 Cl, *Tarrante Russeaston* 1316 FA,
Rushton' Tarente 1367 (1372) ChrP, *Tarrant Rushton* 1609
Cecil
Tarente Vileres 1291 Tax, *Tarent(e) Vylers* 1297 Cl, Pat *et freq*
with variant spellings -*Viler(e)s*, -*Villers*, -*vil(i)ers*, -*vylers*,
-*villers* to 1432 Cl, *Terent Vilers* 1428 FA

Named from R. Tarrant, *v.* Tarrant H. par. *supra*, RNs.
infra; on the probable identification of the DB form, *v.* Eyton
131–2, VCHDo 3 69. The affixes are manorial: land in *Tarente*
was held by William *de Vilers* in 1194 Cur and 1199 FF, various
estates in Do, Ha and So belonging to Roger *de Vilers* were
granted by the king to Peter *de Rusceaus* in 1216 ClR, and Roger
de Vilers acknowledged the manor of *Tarente* to be right of Peter
de Russeous in 1227 FF, cf. also Peter *de Russea(u)ls* 1224 ClR,
1238 Ch, -*de Russell'* 1226 ib, -*de Russels* 1227 ib, -*de Ruscheaus*
1244 *Ass.* The later forms of *Rushton* 'the estate of *(de)*
Rusceaus', *v.* **tūn**, have been influenced by the common p.n.
Rushton from **risc, rysc** 'a rush' and **tūn**, cf. 1 147.

PRESTON FM (ST 937050), *Prestetune* 1086 DB, *Prusteton* 1212
Fees, *Presteton(a)* 1268 *Ass*, n.d. (1372) ChrP, *Preston(e)* 1280
Ass, 1285 FA *et passim*, *Preston' Tarente* 1280 *Ass*, *Tar(r)ent(e)*
Preston 1306 Banco, 1318 FF *et freq* to 1774 Hutch[1], *Prestetarente*
n.d. (1372) ChrP, *Tarraunt Preston* 1545 (16) *Bartelot*, *Preston*
parva 1559 DLCt, *Tarrant Presson* 1646 SC, *Tarrant Preston*
1869 Hutch[3], 'priests' farm (on R. Tarrant)', from **prēost**
(gen.pl. *prēosta*) and **tūn**, cf. Tarrant Crawford par. *supra*
(formerly *Preston Crawford* from its having been a tithing in
Badbury hundred with this place, cf. *Preston cum Craford*
Tithing 1664 HTax). In 1086 DB the manor of *Prestetune*
belonged to the bishop of Lisieux, and Edward *clericus* held it
TRE (VCHDo 3 73).

ABBEYCROFT COPPICE & DOWN, *Abbey Croft* 1542 Hutch[3],
Abbeycraft Down 1811 OS, cf. *Tarronte Downe* 1591 DLMB,
v. **abbeye, croft, dūn**, cf. par. name *supra*; it belonged to
Tarrant abbey. BRATCH COPPICE & LANE, cf. *Pitmans Brach*

1609 *Cecil*, from **bræc** 'land broken up for cultivation', with the surname *Pitman*. CHALCOTT'S COPPICE, *Chalcotts* 1621 Hutch[3], -*Coppice* 1829 *EnclA, Chalkitts Coppice* 1842 *TA*, 'cold cottages', from **ceald** and **cot**, or a surname. CRANE HILL PLANT. DEAN HILL (COPPICE), 1838 *TA* (Tarrant K.), cf. *Dean Drove* 1840 *TAMap*, named from Dean Fm in Witchampton par. *infra.* HARRY'S COPPICE, cf. William *Harris* 1664 HTax. HOGSTOCK (COPPICE), *Hogstocke Lane, Hogstoke waie* 1609 *Cecil, Hogstock* 1811 OS, first el. **hogg** 'a hog' or a pers.n. *Hogg*, probably with **stoc** 'outlying farmstead, secondary settlement', cf. Ekwall Studies[2] 41. LEG ROW, *v.* **leg, rāw**. LONG ROW COPPICE, *v.* **rāw**. PRESTON CTGS & PLANT., cf. Preston Fm *supra*. RUSHTON FM (1842 *TA*), HILL (1621 Hutch[3], -*Hills* 1829 *EnclA*), & MILL (*water Myll called...the Wheate mill* 1588 *Cecil, Rushton Mills* 1842 *TA*, cf. *the Myll close* 1609 *Cecil*), *v.* **hyll, myln**, par. name *supra*. ST LEONARD'S HOSPITAL (Site of); as shown by C. D. Drew, DoNHAS **64** 34–42, the medieval house of St Leonard, ascribed to this site by Hutch[3] 3 463, VCHDo 2 105–6, really belongs to a lost *Rushton*, now St Leonard's Fm in W Parley par. *supra.* ST MARY'S CHURCH, cf. *Church Cl* 1842 *TA*. SHEEP PARK COPPICE, *Sheepeparke* (*Field*) 1611 *Cecil, v.* **scēap, park**; there was a medieval deer-park, first mentioned in 1296 Ipm, just N of here, *v.* Cantor & Wilson 8 242. SING CLOSE COPPICE. SMITH'S CTGS, cf. 'land of John the smith' 1280 Ch, Henry *Smith* 1664 HTax.

FIELD-NAMES

The undated forms are 1842 *TA* 218; the form dated 1838 is from Tarrant K. *TA* 222. Spellings dated 1270 (1372) are *ChrP*, 1327 *SR*, 1332 SR, 1609, 1611 *Cecil*, and 1621 Hutch[3].

(a) Calves Cl (cf. *Cheluemede* 1270 (1372), 'meadow used for calves', from **cealf** (gen.pl. *cealfa*) and **mæd**); Common Ld; Coppice Wd; Glebe Ld; Stourton Gore (*v.* **gāra**; *Stourton* may be a surname from Stourton W, St or Wa); Wadhouse Fd 1838.

(b) *Bull meade* 1611 (*v.* **bula, mæd**); *Courtfield* 1611 (*v.* **court**); *Crook(e)field* 1611 (*v.* **crōc** 'a bend'); *in le Hurne* 1327, *in the hurn* 1332 both (p) (*v.* **hyrne** 'angle, corner'); *Little Hill* 1621; *Mory* 1609 (perhaps 'dry ground in marshland', from **mōr** and **īeg**); *Munck(e)s meade* 1611 (*v.* **munuc, mæd**); *Newberry Close, claus' voc' Nuberries* 1611 (probably a surname, *v.* **clos(e)**); *Northfield, -feilde* 1611 (*v.* **norð**); *the pidgeon howse* 1609; *great Pikes, -Pykes* 1611 (the surname *Pike*); *Rushton Drove* 1609 (*v.* **drāf**, par. name *supra*);

Wheden (*howse*) 1609, *tenement' voc' Wheyden* 1611 (perhaps 'whey valley', from **hwǣg** and **denu**, cf. Wheadown D 399).

Turnworth

A detached part of this par. (Thorncombe) was transferred to Blandford St Mary par. *supra* in 1887.

TURNWORTH (ST 822075)
> *Torneworde* 1086 DB, -*worth(e)* 1280 *Ass*, 1285, 1318 *Cecil*, 1325 *MinAcct*, 1327 *SR*, -*word'* 1288 *Ass*
> *Turnewrd(a)*, -*wrd'e* John *AddCh*, -*wrd'i* ? John *ib*, -*wordam* 1204 (1313) Ch, -*wurth(')* 1234 Cl, Pat, 1237 FF, -*wurþe* 1255 *AD*, -*worth(')* l13 *ib*, 1268, 1288 *Ass*, 1291 Tax, 1332 SR *et freq* to 1530 *AddCh*, -*word'* 1288 *Ass*, -*w'rth* 1291 Tax, *Turnet* 1412 FA, *Turnwood* 1575 Saxton, *Turnworth als.*
> *Turnwood* 1795 Boswell
> *Thurneworda* John *AddCh*
> *Thornewr'he* ? John *AddCh*, -*worth(e)* 1280 *Ass* (p), 1316 FA, 1382 *Cecil*
> *Tourneworth* 1428 FA

'Thorn-bush enclosure, enclosure formed by thorn-bushes', from **þyrne** (alternating with the cognate **þorn**) and **worð** (replaced once by **worðig**). On AN *T*- for *Th*-, *v.* ANInfl 39ff, IPN 98, Feilitzen 100ff; the strong AN influence on the name of this place may reflect its early possession by the great Norman family of *de Lincoln, v.* Hutch[3] **3** 466.

BROCKHAM (ST 814071), (6 acres in) *Brocam* John *AddCh, bosco voc'-, pastura in* (*le*) *Brokham* 1507 (1530) *ib, Brokeham* (*Wood*) 1546 Hutch[3], *Brock hams* 1840 *TA*, possibly 'enclosure or meadow by a brook', from **brōc** and **hamm**; there is no brook marked on the maps, but Brockham lies beside the valley called Coombe Bottom in Ibberton par. *infra.* Alternatively, the first el. could be **brocc** 'a badger', cf. Brockham Sr 282.

RINGMOOR (CTG) (ST 810087), *Hringmere* John *AddCh*, 'pool near the circular enclosure', *v.* **hring, mere**, cf. Ringmer Sx 355; **hring** no doubt refers to the oval enclosure among the prehistoric or Romano-British earthworks NW of the village, *v.* RCHMDo **3** 241.

CLAPPER PLANT., *v.* **clapper** 'rough bridge; rabbit burrow or fox's earth'. THE CLIFF, *Cliff* 1840 *TA*, *v.* **clif** 'cliff, bank, escarpment', cf. Elias *de La faleyse* 1255 *AD* (a witness in a charter concerning Turnworth), from OFr *faleise* 'cliff'. THE COMMON, *Turnworth Common* 1811 OS, *Lr & Upr Common* 1840 *TA*. EWERN DOWN PLANT., *(Hr) Ewens Down, Ewens Down Orchd* 1840 *ib*, *v.* **dūn**; *Ewe(r)n-* may represent gen.pl. *eowena* of OE **eowu** 'a ewe', cf. Young Creech 1 194. HOLE PLANT., *Hole* 1840 *ib*, *v.* **hol**[1] 'a hollow'. LINES DEAN BOTTOM, *Lines Down* 1840 *ib*, *v.* **denu, dūn**, cf. Robert *Line* ? John *AddCh* (a witness in a charter concerning Turnworth). MISLE WD (lost), 1811 OS. THE PARK. ST MARY'S CHURCH, cf. *the Church Hatch* 1747 Hutch[3], *v.* **hæc(c)** 'hatchgate'. TURNWORTH CLUMP *(Clump of Firs* 1840 *TA*), DOWN (1811 OS, cf. *Down* 1840 *TA*), FM, HO (1811 OS) & WD, *v.* par. name *supra*.

FIELD-NAMES

The undated forms are 1840 *TA* 233. For fields in the former detached part of this par. (Thorncombe), *v.* Blandford St M. par. *supra*. Spellings dated John, ? John, 1337, 1507 (1530) are *AddCh*, 1255 *AD*, 1327 *SR*, 1332 SR, 1546, 1634 Hutch[3], and 1784 *SalisT*.

(a) Bondsley Drove & Md (named from Bonsley Cmn in Shillingstone par. *supra*); Bowdens Orchd; Carbons Grd; Coombe (*v.* **cumb**); 4 Acres; Gt & Lt Furze Cl; Frys Md & Orchd; Upr Gravelly Way; Great-Orchard; Grove (*v.* **grāf(a)**); Hedgerow; Hevilands (*v.* **hēafod-land**); Hogsleaze (cf. 'hogs lease for fourteen hogs in *Allern*' 1634, *v.* **hogg** 'hog, young sheep', **læs** 'pasture'; *Allern* may reflect an OE dat.pl. form *al(o)rum* of **alor** 'alder'); Home Md; Kitchen Gdn; Lambing Pound; Little Md; Fifth, Second & Third Long Down, Lt Long Down (named from Ibberton Long Down in Ibberton par. *infra*); Lower Md; (Lr) Melyotts; Middle Fd (cf. *the middle Farm Field* 1634); Hr & Middle North Fd; North Md; Parsons Pce; Peate (*v.* **pete**); Stoney Pce; Turnworth Fd 1784; 20 Acres; Wansley; Well Plot (cf. *pond called Wellspring* 1634, *v.* **well(a), spring**); Yonder Fd (cf. *the yonder Farm Field* 1634).

(b) *montis qui dicitur Alwardun'* John (*v.* **dūn** 'hill'; the first el. is possibly the OE pers.n. *Ælf-* or *Æðelweard*); *atte Berne* 1337 (p) (*v.* **atte, bere-ærn**); *Blandford Linch* 1634 (*v.* **hlinc**, Blandford F. par. *supra*); *the East Field* 1634; *Everland* (in *South Field*) 1634; *del Ham* ? John (p) (*v.* **hamm**); *Hengstelega* John, *-legh'* 1332 (p) (*v.* **hengest** 'stallion', **lēah** 'wood, clearing'); *Hildeweie* John (*v.* **hielde** 'slope', **weg**); *hwata-* John, *Watacumba* ? John (*v.* **hwǣte** 'wheat', **cumb** 'valley', cf. Whatcombe in Winterborne W. par. *supra*); *neteldene* John (*v.* **netel(e)** 'nettle', **denu** 'valley'); *bosc' voc'-, pastura in Okedene* 1507 (1530), *Okeden* (*Wood*) 1546 (*v.* **āc** 'oak-tree', **denu**); *(atte*

Putte 1327, 1332 both (p) (*v.* **atte, pytt** 'pit'); *Shakham Coppice* 1546; *the common South Field* 1634; *Stokeleweie* John ('way to *Stokele*', *v.* **weg**; *Stokele* is from **lēah** 'wood, clearing', with either **stoc** 'outlying farm' or **stocc** 'stump'); *de La Strode* 1255 (p) (*v.* **strōd**); *close called Thickets* 1634 (*v.* **ρiccett**).

Verwood

This par. was formed in 1894 out of the old par. of Cranborne.

VERWOOD (SU 088090) ['vəːwud, 'vəːrud], *Beubo(y)s* 1288 *Ass*, *Fairwod(e)* 1329 FF, 1374 *MinAcct*, 1404 *Cecil*, 1416 Hutch[3] (*le-*), 1436 FF, *-wood* 1618 *CH*, 1846 *TA*, *Fair(e)woude* 1378 Hutch[3], *Fayr(e)wod(e)* 1404 *Cecil*, 1422 *Midd*, 1436 FF, 1477 Hutch[3], *-wood(d)*, *-wodd* 1619 *CH*, *Fairewode* 1412 FA, 1416 IpmR (*Le-*), 1508 *Cecil*, *-wood* 1553 *ib*, *Feyyrwud'* 1530 *ib*, *Wer-Wood* 1575 Saxton, *Ferwood* 1614 *Cecil*, *Fayerwoodd* 1620 *CH*, *Wayrewood* 1621 *ib*, *Verwood* 1774 Hutch[1], 'beautiful wood', from **fæger** and **wudu**. The 13th cent. Fr forms (from OFr **be(a)u, bois**) bear out the suggestion in Hutch[3] 3 421 fn. b, that this place gave its name to the family of *de Beauboys* (latinized as *de Bello Bosco*), which had lands here and in Edmondsham par. *supra* in the 14th cent., cf. Richard *de Bello Bosco* 13 *Cecil*, John *de Bello Bosco* 1329 FF, Maud-, John *de Beauboys* 1332 SR, William *de Bello Bosco* 1378 Hutch[3].

STREET-NAME: BURNBECK RD, cf. *Burnbake* 1846 *TA*, *v.* **burnbake**.

EBBLAKE (BRIDGE) (SU 108078), *Abbelake, Abbeslak(e)* 1280 *Ass*, *Albel(l)ak(e)* (for *Abbe-*), *Aweslake* (for *Abbes-*) ·1280 *ib*, QW, *Albelake* (for *Abbe-*) 1618 *Map*, *Alblake* (for *Abb-*) 1620 Hutch[3], probably 'Abba's stream', from the OE pers.n. *Abba* and **lacu**, with reference to Ebblake Stream which forms the county bdy here. As Professor Löfvenberg points out, the early forms in *Abbes-* are probably due to an OE side-form *Æbbi* (cf. Ekwall *Studies*[1] 2 ff). The modern form of the name has perhaps been influenced by ModE *ebb*.

LEFTISFORD (lost), *Levetesford* 1086 DB, *Luuedesford* 1170, 1171 P (p), *Leftesford(e)* 1244 *Ass*, 1288 *ib* (p), 1325 *MinAcct*, *Lefte(s)ford, Le Efteford* 1280 *Ass*, *Esteford* (for *Efte-*) 1280 QW, *Leftusforde* 1285 *Cecil*, *Le Steford* 1309 Drew, *Lestesford(e)* (for *Leftes-*) 1318 *Cecil*, 1416 IpmR (*-juxta le Fairewode*), *Lestisford* (for *Leftis-*) 1329 FF, *Listisford* (for *Liftis-*) 1378 Hutch³, *Leftisford* 1436 FF, *Letteford* (sic) 1582 Hutch³, *Lestford* (for *Left-*) 1620 ib, 'Lēofgēat's ford', from the OE pers.n. *Lēofgēat* and **ford**; the ford was no doubt across R. Crane, perhaps that marked (6″) near Potterne Fm *infra*, or that called *Verwood Ford* 1811 OS at Bridge Ctgs in Horton par. *supra*.

POTTERNE FM (SU 095075), *villat' de Poterne* 1280 *Ass*, *Potern(e)* 1283 *Cecil*, 1303 Hutch³, 1332 SR all (p), *Wynter(ne)burne* (sic) *Poterne* 1288 *Ass*, *Poternne* 1340 NI (p), *Wymbo(u)rne Pot(t)erne* 1384 IpmR, 1430 ib, Cl, *Poterneswimborn* 1396 IpmR, *Winborne Pottern* 1397, 1428 Hutch³, *Pottern anciently Winborn-Pottern* 1774 Hutch¹, *Wimborne Pottern* 1795 Boswell, 1869 Hutch³, *Potters Fm* 1811 OS, 'building where pots are made, a pottery', *v.* **pott, ærn**, cf. Potterne W 244. The affix *Wimborne-* is from the association of this manor with Monkton Up Wimborne in Wimborne St G. par. *infra* (5 miles NW): according to Hutch³ 3 387, Verwood (which contains Potterne) was a tithing in Monkton Up Wimborne hundred *infra*, and Boswell places Potterne and Verwood in the tithing of Monkton Up Wimborne itself (all three places then having been in the par. of Cranborne); earlier evidence of this association is that a Walter *de Poternne* is mentioned under Wimborne St G. in 1340 NI, and that land in *Winborne Pottern*, along with land in Wimborne St G., was held by a family called *Bryt* in 1397, 1428 Hutch³ 3 601, cf. All Hallows Fm in Wimborne St G. par. *infra*. For the confusion of *Wynburne* with *Wynterburne* in the 1288 form, cf. the form from 1242–3 Fees for Wimborne St G. par. *infra*.

ALL SAINTS' CHURCH. BAILEY'S PLANT. (cf. Cranborne f.ns. *supra*). BAKER'S FM, cf. John *le Bakere* 1283 *Cecil*, Richard *le Baker'* 1332 SR. BLACK HILL, *Blackhill* 1618 *CH*, *v.* **blæc, hyll**. BLACK MOOR, cf. *Peat Moors* 1811 OS, *v.* **mōr**. BOVERIDGE HEATH, *Verwood Heath* 1811 ib, named from Boveridge in Cranborne par. *supra*. BUGDEN'S COPSE, *Bugden(s) Copse, Bugdens Drove Plot* 1846 *TA*, perhaps to be associated with *Bucke mead…alias Ferwood* 1614 *Cecil*, from **bucc** and **mæd**, *v.* par. name *supra*, but cf. Bugden in Six. Handley par. *infra*. BURROWS COPSE, FM & LANE. CHURCH (St Michael and All Angels). CHURCH HILL, cf. *Far Church Plot, Near Church Pce* 1846 *TA*, named from prec. CLAYLAKE (COPSE), cf. *Clay Lake Corner &*

Plot 1846 *ib*, 'clay stream', from **clǣg** and **lacu**, with reference to a small tributary of R. Crane. CRAB ORCHD, *Crab Orchd Cl & Copse* 1846 *ib*, *v*. **crabbe** 'crab-apple'. DEWLANDS CMN, HILL & WDS, *v*. **dēaw, land**. EASTWORTH FM, *Estwurt'* 1530 *Cecil*, *Worth als. Eastworth* 1545 Hutch[3], cf. Westworth in Edmondsham par., *Horsyth* in Cranborne par. both *supra*, *v*. **ēast**. FOSTER'S WD, *Fosters* (*Copse*) 1846 *TA*, cf. Richard *Forestarius* 13 *Cecil*, Thomas *le Forester* 1332 (Cranborne). HALFWAY HILL (lost), 1811 OS, by the road 'half way' between Cranborne par. *supra* and Ringwood Ha. HAYWARD'S FM, cf. *Horethornesacre alias Haywardesacre* 1508 *Cecil*, *v*. **æcer**; *Horethorn* and *Hayward* are probably both surnames, cf. Isabel *Attehorethorne* 1284 *ib* ('at the grey thorn-tree', *v*. **atte, hār**[2], **þorn**), Cranborne and Alderholt f.ns. *supra*. HEATHY HOW, (-*Md*) 1846 *TA*, *v*. **howe**. LADIES' COPSE. LR COMMON, *Woolbridge Cmn* 1811 OS, cf. *The South Cmn* 1846 *TA*, *v*. Woolsbridge *infra*. MANOR HO. MARGARDS LANE. MIDDLE COPSE. MOUNT ARARAT, a remote hill on Boveridge Heath, named from the mountain on which Noah's ark is said to have rested. NEW TOWN. NOON HILL. OWRE CMN (lost, at SU 092082), 1811 OS, from **ōra**[1] 'bank', perhaps to be associated with *Beuerore* 1288 *Ass* (p), *Beverehoare* 1582 Hutch[3], which is from the same word with **beofor** 'a beaver'; the reference is probably to the bank of R. Crane. POTTERNE HILL & WD, cf. *Pottern Cl, Ham & Md* 1846 *ib*, named from Potterne *supra*, *v*. **hamm**. RUSHMOOR POND, probably analogous with Rushmore in Cranborne par. *supra*. ST MICHAEL'S CTG, cf. Church *supra*. SANDY LANE, cf. (Old) Sand Pit (6″). STEPHEN'S CASTLE (Tumulus), *v*. **castel(l)**. THREE LEGGED CROSS, 1811 OS, -*Crosse* 1591 *DLMB*, perhaps a term for a T-junction, *v*. **cross**, but *Three Legged* may be an allusion to the gallows, nicknamed *Three legged mare* (NED from 1685). Cf. 'The name is. . .from a tripod surmounted by a wooden cross that was a direction beacon. . .to persons crossing the heaths' (TGuide). VERWOOD CMN, 1811 OS, cf. *The North Cmn* 1846 *TA*. VERWOOD FM. VERWOOD MANOR FM, *Verwood Fm* 1811 OS. WILD CHURCH BOTTOM, 1869 Hutch[3], cf. Church Hill *supra*, *v*. **wilde, botm**. WITHY BED, 1846 *TA*. WOOLS BRIDGE (*Woolles bridge* 1618 *Map*, *Wool Bridge* 1811 OS), where the Horton-Ringwood road crosses Moors River, giving name to WOOLSBRIDGE (FM)

(*Woolbridge Fm* 1811 ib), *v.* **brycg**; *Wool-* is probably from **wyll(a)** 'stream' with reference to the river, cf. Woolbridge 1 148.

FIELD-NAMES

The undated forms are 1846 *TA* 81. Spellings dated 1244, 1280[1] are *Ass*, 1280[2] QW, 1332 SR, 1530 *Cecil*, 17 *CecilMap*, 1620, 1869 Hutch[3], and 1664 HTax.

(*a*) Arable Fd, Patch & Plot; Furzy & Lt Bait, Bait Md & Orchd (Professor Löfvenberg suggests that this is probably dial. *bait* 'food (for men and horses)' (EDD), used here in the sense 'pasture'; the fields are in marshy ground between two streams); Barley Grd; Barn Cl; The Boot (so named from its shape); (Lt) Bottom Grd; Brickells; Bulleters; Bungeys Plot; Buttons (Copse, Ctg, Ham, Md, Orchd & Plot) (cf. William *Buddyn* 1530, *v.* Cranborne f.ns. *supra*); Calves Cl; Carters Cl (cf. Richard *Carter* 1664); Chalk Cl; Chapel Hays Copse & Fd (*v.* **(ge)hæg**); Common Grd; (Pce under) Copse; (Lr) Cow Leaze; Dobbins (Copse) (cf. William *Dobyn* 1332 (Cranborne)); Drove, Near Drove Plot; Gt Dukes and Coppice, Lt Dukes Copse & Plot, Long Dukes; The 8 Acres; End Pce; Far Brow Pce (*v.* **brū**); Far Pce; The 5 Acres; Gallows (near the cross-roads at Potterne Hill, *v.* **g(e)alga**); Garden Patch; Gastons (*v.* **gærs-tūn**); Dry & Wet Goldimoor; Granaly Grd; Grays Md (cf. Thomas *Gray* 1664 (Cranborne)); Great Md & Plot; Lr & Upr Hand; Hanging Grd (*v.* **hangende**); Pce by Haskills (cf. William *Haskoll* 1664); Heath pce; Hilly Grd; Home Fd, Grd & Plot; Horners; Hurdles Hill Ctg and Gdn; Kiln Grd; Lay Moor (Plot) (cf. Laymoor in Hampreston par. *supra*); Little Acre; Long Grd Copse; Long How (*v.* **howe**); Long Md & Patch; Meadow; Middle Grd, Pce & Plot; Mill Md; New Grd; Plot new Leaze; Orchard; Outlet (*v.* **utlete** 'a channel'); Pasture Fd, Pce & Plot; (Near) Patch; Middle Plot; Picked Moor & Pce (*v.* **pīcede** 'pointed'); Plot; Pond Cl; Popes Md; Red Gate Grd; Rick Yd; (Gt, Inside & Outside) Rough Pce; Round Cl & How; Sandy Balls (*v.* **ball**, PN W 422, EPN 1 18–19); 7 Acres; Sheivers; Shop plot; The 6 Acres; Snow Hill (*v.* **snāw**); Square Grd & Pce; Thornes Grd (cf. Euphrony *Thorne* 1664 (Cranborne)); Toads Cove (Cmn, Copse & Md); Tuppiers Md; The 12 Acres; 2 Acres; Way Grd; West Fd & Md; Whites (Mdw) (cf. Roger *Whit'*, Robert *le White* 1332 (Cranborne)); Wickets Copse, Grd & Md; the Wurstone 1869 (described in Hutch[3] 3 388 as 'a large block of sandstone standing on the heath, not far from the Ringwood Road', and probably to be identified with *le Horeston'*, (*la*) *Horestone* 1280[1], 1280[2], *Horesham* (sic) 17, *the Horestone* 1620, a point in the bounds of Cranborne Chase, 'the grey (boundary) stone', *v.* **hār**[2], **stān**).

(*b*) *de la Clyue* 1244 (p) (*v.* **clif**); *de la Cnolle* 1244 (p) (*v.* **cnoll**); *de* (*la*) *Dene* 1244 (p) (*v.* **denu**); (*La*) *Horewich'*, *Le Horewichie* (sic), *le-*, *la Horewych'* 1280[1], *la Horewyeche*, *le Hordewych'* (sic) 1280[2], *Horewith* 17, 1620 ('the grey wych-elm', *v.* **hār**[2], **wice**, cf. Horwich La (DEPN); this was a point in the bounds of Cranborne Chase); *de la Penne* 1244 (p) (*v.* **penn**[2] 'a pen, a fold').

Witchampton

A detached part of Shapwick par. *supra* was transferred to this par. in 1886.

WITCHAMPTON (ST 988065) [witʃˈæmtən], *Wichemetune* (2 ×) 1086 DB, *Wichamatuna* Exon, *Wichamton*(') 1216 ClR, 1280, 1288 *Ass*, *Wich*(*h*)*ampton*(*e*) 1242–3 Fees, 1280 *Ass*, 1318 *Cecil et freq* to 1412 FA, *Wycham*(*p*)*ton*(*e*) 1263 Ipm, 1268 *Ass* (p), 1280 *ib*, QW, 1281 FF *et freq* to 1456 Pat, *-toun* 1349 Ipm, *Wichehampton* 1271 Pat (p), 1280 *Ass*, *Wychehampton*(') 1278 Pat *et freq* to 1494 *Cecil*, *Whichampton*' 1280 *Ass*, *Wycampton*' 1370 *Ilch*, *Wykehampton* 1375 IpmR, *Wich-*, *Wych Hampton* 1633 Hutch[3]. Probably, as indicated by the DB forms in *-heme-*, 'farm of the *Wīchǣme*', i.e. 'farm of the dwellers at a place called *Wīchām*', or 'farm of the dwellers at the *wīc*', *v*. **wīc**, **wīc-hām**, **hǣme** (gen.pl. *hǣma*), **tūn**, cf. Tengstrand MN 97. In fact 'farm of the dwellers at a place called *Wīchām*', with **wīc-hām** in the sense 'village associated with a Romano-British settlement or *vicus*', would seem to be the more likely meaning in view of the site of Witchampton, as pointed out by M. Gelling, *MedArch* 11 104: there are extensive Roman remains here including a villa at Hemsworth (cf. Wall's Ctgs *infra*), the Roman road from Badbury Rings to Old Sarum (Margary 4c) crosses the par., and the junction of Roman roads at Badbury Rings is only 2½ miles SW. There is no evidence to support the supposition (made by Ekwall DEPN, Smith EPN 1 216) that Witchampton was owned by the inhabitants of Wimborne Minster, and the suggested meaning 'farm of the dwellers at the *wīc* (i.e. Wimborne Minster)' is therefore extremely unlikely.

DEAN FM (ST 969064), 1811 OS, *La Dene* 1243 FF, 1256 *ib* (p), 1409 Inq aqd, *Dene* 1412 FA, *graungia*...*voc*' *Deane House* 1547 *DLMB*, *Deane* 1591 *ib*, *Dean* 1795 Boswell, 'the valley', *v*. **denu**, cf. Deans Leaze Ctgs & Fm *infra*.

E & W HEMSWORTH (ST 969057, 966055) ['hemzud]
    Hemedesw(*o*)*rde* 1086 DB, *-wurth* 1243 FF, *Emmedeswurtha* 1180 P (p), *Hemmesdeswurda* 1194 *ib*, *Hemmedeswrda* 1195 *ib*, *Emedeswurth* 1238 Ch, *Hemdesworth* 1278 Pat *Hemeleswurth* 1224 ClR, *-worth*(') 1288 *Ass*, 1290 FF (*West-*),

1302 Ch, 1303 FA, 1304 Ch (*Est-*), 1312 Cl, 1320 Pat, 1340
NI (*West-*), 1346 FA, 1392 Pat (*Wes-*), 1399 Cl, *Emeleswurth*
1224 ClR, *-worth* 1291 Tax, 1303, 1346, 1428 FA,
Hemlesworth' 1280 *Ass*, *Hemelisworth*(') 1337 FF, 1387
(e15) *MiltRoll*, *West Hemelsworth* 1412, *Hemmelesworth*
1428 FA
Hendesworth 1235–6 Fees, *Hyndesworth*' 1288 *Ass*
Hamelesw(o)rth 1257 FF, 1303 Ch (*West-*)
Emmeswurth 1278 Pat, *Hemmesworth* 1428, 1431 FA (*West-*),
Hemsworth 1553 *Cecil*, 1774 Hutch[1] (*-East or Lower-*, *West-*
or Higher-), 1838 *TA* (*-Fm*)
Henlesworth' 1280 *Ass*
Hemblesworth Giffard 1348 FF
Hanlesworth 1361 Cl
Elmesworth 1412 FA
Hammesworth(') 1428 FA, 1494 *Cecil*

Probably 'Hem(m)ede's enclosure', from **worð** and an OE
pers.n. *Hem(m)ede*, a derivative of *Hemma* found also in Hemps-
hill Nt 150, *v.* ēast, west. During the 13th cent. the forms for
the first el. show alternation with, and eventual replacement by,
the recorded OE pers.n. *Hemele*. Ekwall, DEPN s.n. Hemsworth, suggests that the two Hemsworths may once have had
different names, *Hemedesworth* and *Hemelesworth*, but this seems
unlikely. *Giffard-* is clearly a manorial affix; *Gif(f)ard* occurs in
Do as the byname of two DB landholders (VCHDo 3 97) and
as a surname in 1332 SR and other 13th and 14th cent. sources,
though not in connection with this place, cf. however Henry
Giffard' 1332 SR taxed under Kingston Lacy in Pamphill par.
(adjacent to Witchampton), *v.* the f.n. Giffards in Holt par.
supra.

ABBEY BLDGS & HO, cf. 'Near it [the church] is a very large old
barn, supposed by the inhabitants to have been a chapel, and
called by them *The Abbey Barn*' (1774 Hutch[1] 2 174), *v.* RCHM
5 106. BIRCH COPPICE. BUSHY PARK, cf. *Wich Hampton Park*
1633 Hutch[3], Parkham Rows *infra*, *v.* **park**; for a park at
Witchampton in 1294 Banco, *v.* Cantor & Wilson 1 112.
CHURCH (St Mary, St Cuthberga & All Saints), cf. *ecclesie de*
Wycampton' 1370 *Ilch*, 'the church of All Saints' 1383 Hutch[3],
'parish church of *Wychampton*' 1456 Pat. THE COTTAGE.

CRICHEL LANE, leading to M. Crichel par. *supra*. CUCKOO POUND, cf. 1 38 for an identical name. CUTLER'S COPPICE, -*Copse* 1811 OS, -*Cl & Coppice* 1848 *TA* (Shapwick), cf. John *Cutler* 1664 HTax (Shapwick). DARK LANE. THE DARK WALK. DEANS LEAZE CTGS & FM, *Deane's Leaze* 1633 Hutch[3], *Deans Lease* 1811 OS, *Hr Dean Leaze*, (*Lr*) *Deans Leaze* 1829 *EnclA*, probably 'pasture belonging to Dean', *v.* læs, *Dean Fm supra*, although *Dean* is possibly a surname, note the coincidence that the manor of Witchampton was sold to a family called *Dean* in 1692 (Hutch[3] 3 477). DOWNLEY CTG & COPPICE, probably 'hill clearing' from dūn and lēah. FERN HILL. HAGGATES CTGS, *Haggetts* (*Coppice, Ctg & Orchd*) 1829 *EnclA*, the surname *Haggett*. HEMSWORTH DOWN (lost), 1591 *DLMB*, 1811 OS, *v.* Hemsworth *supra*. HILDA CTGS. HUSSY'S COPPICE. IVY HO. LITTLE COPPICE. MALT HO, 1811 OS. NEW TOWN, the site of a new village built in the late 18th cent. to rehouse the displaced inhabitants of More Crichel (Taylor 161). PARKHAM ROWS, cf. Bushy Park *supra*, *v.* hamm, rāw. POUND HILL, *v.* pund. RECTORY, cf. *the Parsonage* 1664 HTax. ROWBARROW LANE, 'rough hill or barrow', *v.* rūh, beorg, cf. 1 4. SHEEPHOUSE (DROVE & ROW), cf. *Drove* 1848 *TA* (Shapwick), *v.* drāf, rāw. STEP HO. WALL'S CTGS, cf. *Walls* 1848 *TA* (Shapwick); near the site of the Roman villa at Hemsworth *supra*, *v.* wall, cf. Walls Coppice 1 342. WHITE FM. WITCHAMPTON CMN (lost), 1811 OS. WITCHAMPTON MILL, *Mill* 1811 OS, cf. the mills at both of the manors of Witchampton in 1086 DB (VCHDo 3 68, 86). WOODSIDE CTGS, cf. *boscus de Wychampton'* 1288 *Ass*. ZANNIES COPPICE & CTGS, *Sannys* 1811 OS, a surname.

FIELD-NAMES

There are no f.ns. in 1838 *TA* 260 (Witchampton). The undated forms are 1848 *TA* 183 (Shapwick). Spellings dated 1332 are SR, 1340 NI, 1387 (e15) *MiltRoll*, 1473 DLCt, 1663, 1869 Hutch[3], 1829 *EnclA*.

(a) Calves Plot Orchd; Cookroad (Cl) (*v.* cocc-rodu 'wood clearing where woodcocks are netted'); Coppice 1829; 18 Acres; the Ewe Leaze 1869; 5, 40, 4 and 14 Acres; Hedge Row; Hounds Castle 1829; New Grd; Park Coppice & Fd (near Dean Fm *supra*, *v.* park); Peaked Grd 1829 (*v.* peked 'pointed'); Pit Fd; Plick (*le Plek'* 1473, *v.* plek 'small plot of ground'); (Lt) Pond Cl, Pond Fd; Row (freq, *v.* rāw); The Walk.

(b) *in laa* (sic) *Hurne* (p) 1387 (e15) (*v.* hyrne 'angle, corner'); *Sley Yates*

1633 (v. slege 'sheep pasture', geat 'gate'); atte Watere (p) 1332, 1340 (v. atte, wæter).

East Woodyates

This small par., originally a tithing in Cranborne hundred, is included in Pentridge par. *supra* by Boswell and Hutch[3], although marked as a separate par. on 6" (1902 ed.); it was finally joined to Pentridge par. in 1933 along with West Woodyates par. *infra, q.v.* for early forms and etymology of the name.

XVI. WIMBORNE ST GILES HUNDRED

This is not an old hundred: Wimborne St G. and W Woodyates were in the GeldR hundred of *Albretesberge* (v. Cranborne hundred *supra*), *Philipston* was in Knowlton hundred in c.1086 GeldR (and is still included in that hundred in 1795 Boswell), and Wimborne St G. was in Knowlton hundred in 1332 SR (v. Hutch[3] 3 578, Eyton 111 f, Anderson 131). Monkton Up Wimborne was in Cranborne hundred in 1332 SR and in Monkton Up Wimborne hundred in 1664 HTax and 1795 Boswell, and All Hallows was in Cranborne hundred in 1664 HTax and 1795 Boswell.

Hd of Upwymbourne Seynt Gylis 1542 LP, *Wimborne St Giles hd* 1570 Anderson, *Hundred and Parish of St Giles Vpwimborne* 1664 HTax, named from Wimborne St G. *infra*.

Wimborne St Giles

Monkton Up Wimborne and Oakley were transferred to this par. from Cranborne par. in 1886, and at the same date Sutton, formerly a detached part of Gussage St M. par., was also transferred to this par.

WIMBORNE ST GILES (SU 032120)
  Winburne 1086 DB (2 ×, ff. 84, 85)
  Up Wimburn, Up Wymburne 1154–89 (1496) Pat, *Vpwymborne* c.1183 (14) Cecil, *Upwym-, -wimburn(e)* 1213 ClR, 1231 Pat, 1232 Cl *et freq* with variant spellings *Hup-* 1263–70 Ipm, 1281 Queens, n.d. (1372) ChrP, *Uppe-* 15 Queens, 1455 Cl, *-born(e)* (from 1268 Ass), *-bourn(e)* (from 1327 Cl); *Upwinburn(e)* 1180 P, 1199 Cur, 1207 PatR, 1212 Fees *et freq* to 1262 Cl, *Opwinburne, Upwinborne* 1212 Fees, *Up Vinborne* 1263–70 Ipm, *Upwynborne* 1359 Cl, *-burn(e)* 1442 Pat, 1530 Cecil

Uppingburn' 1187–1194 P, 1230 Cl

Winterborn' (sic, for *Winborn'*) *Malemains* 1242–3 Fees, *Vpwynburn' Malemeins* 1280 *Ass, Opwymborn' Malemeyns* 1288 *ib, Vpwymburne Malemayns* 1296 FF, *Upwymbo(u)rn(e)-, -burn Malemeyns* 1301 Ipm, 1303, 1346, 1431 all FA, *Up Wymborn Malemayns* 1303 ib, *Uppe Wynbourne Malmayns* 1428 ib

Vpwymburn' Sancti Egidi(j) 1268 *Ass, parochia Sancti Egidij de Upwymbourn* 1340 NI, *Wymbourn St Giles* 1394 Pat, *Upwymbourn(e) St Giles* 1399 Cl, 1494 Pat, *Up Wymborn St Giles* 1494 Ipm, *St Giles Upwymbourne* 16 *Midd, S. Giles Winburne* 1535–43 Leland, *St Giles's* 1811 OS

Upwymburn Pleycy 1347 Cl, *Upwymbo(u)rne Plecy* 1374 Pat, 1403 *Midd*, 1489 Ipm, *St Giles Upwymborn Plecy* 1375 Cl, *Wymborn' Plecy* 1398 *Cecil*

Like Wimborne M. par. *supra*, named from the river here (formerly the *Wimborne*, now called R. Allen, *v.* RNs. *infra*); *Up* means 'higher up (the river)', *v.* **upp**, cf. All Hallows *infra*, Upwey 1 245. The affixes *Malemayns* and *Plecy* are manorial: Nicholas *Malemains, -meins* was here in 1227 FF, 1230 Cl, and the manor belonged to Robert *de Plassetis, -de Plecys* in 1259 FF, 1275 RH, cf. Maud *de Plecy* 1332 SR, Peter- 1403 *Midd*, John *Plecy* 1489 Ipm, *v.* Hutch[3] 3 578 ff. *St Giles* is from the dedication of the church, *v.* St Giles's Church *infra*.

ALL HALLOWS FM (SU 023127)

Opewinburne 1086 DB, *Obpe Winborna* Exon

Wymborn Karentham 1291 Tax, *-Carentham* 1340 NI, *Upwimborn Karntham* 1408 IpmR, *Wymbourne Karentham* 1428 FA

'*Vpwymburne* All Saints' 1294 FF *et freq* with variant spellings *Up-, -wyn-, -bo(u)rn(e)-* to 1346 Pat, *Vpwymbourn' Omnium Sanctorum* 1297 CoramR (p), *Wynborn Sanctorum* 1394 *Midd*, 'the manor of *Wymborne Allhallows* otherwise *Upwymborne* called *Brytys place*' 1430 Cl, *Alhalowes Wimborn* 1575 Saxton, *Upwimborne Omnium Sanctorum* 1618 CH, *Wymborne All Saincts* 1620 ib, *Alhallou* 1621 ib, *Athollous* (for *Al-*) 1664 HTax, *Upp Wimborne All Saynts* 1677 *Salkeld, Winborn-All-Saints or All-Hallows* 1774 Hutch[1] *v.* par. name *supra.* The affix *Karentham* is manorial, from the family of Alice- 1242 Ch, Richard *de Karenthem* n.d. (1372) *ChrP,* William *de Carent(h)am* 1243 FF, 1276 Banco, Henry *de Carenteym* 1251 FF. *All Hallows* is from the dedication of the former church here (site marked 6″), once the mother church (*v.* St Giles's Church *infra,* Hutch[3] 3 602), cf. 'the church of *Vpwymburn*' 1249 FF, *ecclesiam de Vpwymborn*' 1268 *Ass, capell' de Wynborn Sanctorum* 1394 *Midd.* The manor here known as *Brytys place* in 1430 (also *Brittes Place* 1556 Hutch[3]) takes its name from the family of Ralph *le Bret* 1249 FF, n.d. (1372) *ChrP,* Thomas-, William *le Bret* 1294 FF, John *Bryt* 1385 Hutch[3], 1430 IpmR, *v.* **place,** Hutch[3] 3 601.

FERNE (lost), 1244 *Ass* (p), 1280 *ib* (p), 1296 FF (p), 1358 Hutch[3] (*-juxta Upwinborne*), 1401, 1403 *Midd,* 1431 Fine, 1434 Pat, 1441 Cl, *via regia usque Fernwod*' 1401 *Midd,* possibly from **fergen, fiergen** 'wooded hill', but more probably from **fearn** 'fern' in a collective sense 'ferny place', cf. Fern Down in Hampreston par. *supra.*

FRENCH'S FM (SU 027125), *Frensshes* 1394 *Midd,* 1412 FA, (*la*) *Frenssh(e), le Frenche* 1394 *Midd, Freinsshes* 1422 Cl, Pat, *Frenches* 1774 Hutch[1], cf. *Frenches* (*Lt*) *Mead* 1838 *TA,* a manorial name, cf. France Fm in Stourpaine par. *supra;* Richard *le Franc*' held a hide of land in *Upwinborne* in 1212 Fees (p. 92), cf. also *acra Ricardi le fraunceis, Ricardus-, Willelmus franciscus* n.d. (1372) *ChrP,* Robert *Franceys* 1301 Hutch[3], William *le Fraunceys, -le Frenche* 1310 FF (held land in ' *Upwymburne* All Saints'), Nicholas *le Frensche* 1327 *SR, -le Freynssh*' 1332 SR (taxed in Monkton Up Wimborne, *v. infra*), Thomas *Frenshe* 1435 *Midd* (held land in *Baggeridge* in the adjacent par. of Woodlands).

MONKTON UP WIMBORNE (SU 016136), SOUTH MONKTON FM (SU 022133), *Winburne* 1086 DB (f. 77b), *Wynburne* 1236 FF; *Vpwimburn*' *Abbatis* 1268 *Ass, Vpwynburne-, Vpwymborne Abbatis* 1288 *ib, Wymburne Abbatis* 1316 FA, *Wymborn(e) Abbatis* 1327 SR, 1332 SR, 1430 Cl, *Wymborne Abbotts* 1621 CH; *Wymborne Monkton* 1504 Ipm, *Munkton* 1575 Saxton, *Mounckton Up Wimborne* 1617 Cecil, 1664 HTax, *Mouncton* 1621 CH, *Upwinborn-Monkton* 1774 Hutch[1], *Munckton Up*

Wimborne 1795 Boswell, *v.* par. name *supra.* The affixes *Abbatis* and *Monkton* allude to its possession by the priory of Cranborne (in 1086 DB, *v.* VCHDo 3 74) and later by the abbey of Tewkesbury (as in 1236 FF, *v.* Hutch³ 3 388), *v.* **munuc, tūn,** cf. Tarrant Monkton par. *infra.* It gave name to the hundred of Monkton Up Wimborne *infra.* There was once a chapel here dedicated to St Andrew, alluded to as 'the chapel of *Upwinborne*' 1550 Hutch³ 3 389.

OAKLEY DOWN & FM (SU 010183)
>   *on litlen ac lee estward of aclee,* (*to*) *anclee* (sic) *estward* 956 (14) *ShaftR* (S 630), (*æt*) *áclee on westsæxum* c.970 Durham Ritual (Surtees Society 140)
>   *Ockeleghe* (*camp' de-*) 1280 *Ass, boscum de Ocleye* 1288 *ib, Ocle* 1332 SR (p), *Oakley Wood* 1524 Hutch³, *Okeleywod* 1542 Dugd, *Okeley* 1618 *Map*
>   *Workly Down* 1811 OS

'Oak wood', from **āc** and **lēah,** with **lȳtel, wudu**; in 1524, oaks in this wood were not to be felled without leave of the lord (Hutch³ 3 388). Ekwall DEPN may be correct in identifying *Aclaeh* 805 (9) BCS 321 (S 161), *æt Aeclea* 844 BCS 445 (S 1439), the name of a place where synods were held, with this Oakley, but the form (*to*) *acclei* 944–6 (14) BCS 817 (S 513) in the bounds of Damerham and Marten Ha, identified with this place by Fägersten 97, can hardly belong here. For the form *Workly* with prosthetic *w-, v.* Phonol.

PHILIPSTON (lost, about SU 027108)
>   *Winburne* 1086 DB (f. 79)
>   *Philipeston'* 1206 Cur, *Filippes-, Phylepeston'* 1244 *Ass, Philippes-* 1351 Cl, *Phileppes-* 1510 *MP, Phillipston* 1535 VE
>   *Felipston'* 1235–6 Fees, *Phelip(p)eston(e)* 1236, 1244 FF, 1285 FA *et freq* to 1346 FA, *Felipeston* 1239 Cl, 1327 Pat, *Phelypeston'* 1288 *Ass, Phelipston* 1331 Ch, Pat, 1336 Ch, 1428 FA
>   *Phelpeston* 1318 FF, 1346 Ipm *et freq* to 1469 *Midd, Phelpston* 1348 Pat, *Phelipston* 1380 Cl, *Phelpyston* 1431 FA
>   *Phepeston* 1394 *Midd*   *Phipiston* 1455 Cl
>   *Philpston* 1465 Pat   *Phillips(t)on* 1795 Boswell

'Philip's manor', a post-Conquest name in **tūn** like Forston 1 340, *v.* IPN 131; possibly named from the *Philip de Winburne* mentioned in 1166 RBE (239) in connection with the abbey of Wilton, which held this manor in 1086 DB and 1235–6 Fees. The pers.n. occurs frequently in ME as *Phelip* beside *Philip*, and the contracted forms *Phelp*, *Philp* occur as surnames, *v.* Reaney s.n. *Philip*. For the identification of the DB form *Winburne*, *v.* Eyton 119–20, VCHDo 3 83. The site of this lost manor, on the E bank of R. Allen (formerly the *Wimborne*) S of St Giles Ho, is located by Taylor, DoNHAS 88 210–211. There is reference to a mill here in 1086 DB (VCHDo 3 83), to a church in 1510 *MP*, and there was also a medieval deer-park, *v.* Park Copse *infra*.

SUTTON FM & HILL (SU 064098), SUTTON HOLMS, *Suddon(')* 1226 FF, 1244 *Ass*, 1288 *ib* (p), 1393 Hutch³, 1489 Ipm, 1548 *Ct*, 1619 *CH* (*-alias Sutton*), 'the wood of *Suthdun*' 1241 DoNHAS (88 211), *Sudden* 1407, 1601 Hutch³, *Suddons* 1562 ib, *Sutton Holms* 1811 OS, *Sutton*, (*Hr*) *Suttons* 1842 *TA* (Gussage St M.), 'south hill', from **sūð** and **dūn**, 'south' perhaps in relation to Edmondsham par. *supra*. *Holms* is the pl. of Do dial. *holm* '*holly*', *v.* **holegn**, cf. Gore Holmes 1 125.

BARN (lost, at SU 033165), 1811 OS. BIRCHES COPSE, *Burches* 1619 *CH*, *Birch's Coppice* 1842 *TA* (Gussage St M.), from **birce** 'birch-tree', or a surname. BONE ACRE COPSE, *-Coppice* 1838 *TA*, *Park Cops* 1811 OS, perhaps **bān** 'bone', from bones having been discovered here. BOTTLEBUSH CLUMP, CTGS, DOWN (*Bottle Bush Down* 1811 OS), LANE & PLANT., perhaps an allusion to the distinctive shape of a conspicuous bush. BOWL-DISH POND, a round pond, perhaps thought to resemble a bowl (cf. **bolla**) or a dish. However, as Professor Löfvenberg points out, Bowldish may mean 'bull pasture' from **bula** and **edisc**. BOYS WD, 1838 *TA*, perhaps to be associated with *terram Rob'* *de Bosco in Felipeston* 1239 Cl, John *Boys* 1333 Hutch³, John *atte Wode* 1403 *Midd*, *v.* *Philipston supra*, **atte**, **wudu** 'wood'; the surname (*de*) *Boys* is from OFr **bois** 'wood'. BROOK HO, by R. Allen, *v.* **brōc**. BULL BRIDGE, *pontem de Belbrug'* 1403 *Midd*, *Bill* [bridge] 1791 Boswell, *Bellbridge Md* 1838 *TA*, *v.* **brycg** 'bridge' (over R. Allen); the first el. is probably **belle** 'bell', perhaps in the sense 'bell-shaped, i.e. humpbacked', cf.

Bell Bridge O 261 (no early forms). CASHBROOK CTGS, -*Md* 1838 *TA*, 'brook where water-cress grows', from **cærse** and **brōc**; there are still water-cress beds here (marked 6″) by R. Allen. (OLD) CHALK PIT, cf. *Chalk pit by Park Gate, Chalkpit Fd, Chalk Grd* 1838 *TA*. COACH RD. COLD HARBOUR, called *Philipston Fm* 1839 *TAMap, v.* **cald, here-beorg** 'shelter, lodging', *Philipston supra*; it is by the Cranborne-Wimborne M. road where it is joined by an old road through St Giles's Park. CORN MILL, cf. Robert *atte Mulle* 1332 SR, *unam acram apud Mulepad* n.d. (1372) *ChrP, Sr. H. Asheleys Mylle* 16 *Midd, Mill Lane Grd* 1838 *TA, v.* **atte, myln, pæð** 'path'; there was a mill at one of the manors of *Winburne* in 1086 DB (*v.* par. name *supra*, VCHDo 3 113), and there is mention of a mill at *Vpwymburn*' in 1268 *Ass* and at *Upwymbourn All Saints* (*v.* All Hallows Fm *supra*) in 1321 FF. CRANBORNE LODGE, near the road to Cranborne par. *supra*, cf. *Cranbo(u)rne Lane Grd* 1838 *TA*. CREECH HILL (FM & WD), *Screech Hill* 1811 OS, *E Critchill, Critchill Fd* 1838 *TA*, probably from PrWelsh or PrCorn ***crūg** 'mound, hill' with explanatory OE **hyll** 'hill', in which case it is analogous with Long Crichel par. *infra* (4 miles SW); the hill is 300′ high and stands where the par. boundaries of Cranborne, Edmondsham and Wimborne St G. meet. DEER PARK FM & PONDS, *Deer Park including Ponds* 1838 *TA*, apparently identical with *St Gile's Park* 1765 Tayl and probably a medieval deer-park, *v.* Cantor & Wilson 8 246. THE DRIVE PLANT. (3 ×), *v.* **drive**. FARRINGDON CLUMP & COPSE, -*Fd & Grove* 1838 *TA*, 'fern-covered hill', *v.* **fearn, dūn**, cf. Farrington in Iwerne C. par. *infra*, Faringdon Brk 365. FURZE BRACH LANE, cf. *Furze Brake, Furze Break Coppice* 1842 *TA* (Gussage St M.), *v.* **fyrs, bræc**[1] 'brake, thicket' (though the 6″ map form suggests rather **bræc** 'land broken up for cultivation'). GLEBE CTGS, on Parsonage Lane *infra*. GRAVEL PITS PLANT. HOBBYS COPSE, 1838 *TA*, perhaps to be associated with *Hobeleswell* 1227 FF, ME *Hobel* being a diminutive of the ME pers.n. *Hob(b)*, a pet-form of *Robert, v.* **well(a)**. HOME FM. THE INCLOSURE. KING'S WD, 1838 *TA, Kinges, Kynges* 1280 *Ass*, QW, *King(e)s* 1618 *Map*, 1620 Hutch[3], perhaps alluding to royal possession, *v.* **cyning**, but cf. Robert *Kyng*' 1332 SR. LODGE COPSE, from Keeper's Lodge (6″), cf. *Wood by the Keepers Ho* 1838 *TA*. LOWER FM, on low land by R. Crane. MAINSAIL

HAUL, called MANOR HO 1". MALDRY WD, 1838 *TA*, cf. *Maldry Fd & Wd* 1838 *ib* (Edmondsham). MANOR FM. MONKTON DROVE, *v.* **drāf**, Monkton Up Wimborne *supra*. NINE YEWS. NINNEY-COX WD. NORTH BARN. PARK COPSE, -*Cops* 1811 OS, -*Coppice* 1838 *TA*; this probably marks the site of the medieval deer-park at *Philipston supra*, cf. *parcis de Philippeston et Wodlond* 1394 *Midd, parci de Phelpeston*' 1429 *ib*, *v.* Woodlands par. *infra*, Cantor & Wilson 8 244. PARSONAGE LANE, leading to Rectory (6"), cf. *Parsonage (West) Cl, Parsonage Little Grd* 1838 *TA*. PERT COPSE, -*Coppice* 1838 *TA*, 'the *rifletum* ['osier-bed'] of *Pert*' 1227 FF, probably to be compared with Peart So (*le Perte* c.1250), Pertwood W 176, Solport Cu 107, all of which may be from PrWelsh or PrCorn *****perth** 'a hedge, a bush, a brake'. PINETUM. REMEDY GATE, cf. the oak here on which is a brass tablet inscribed: 'Beneath this oak King Edward VI touched for the King's Evil'. RINGWOOD LANE, named from Ringwood Ha. GT & LT ROUGH COPSE. ROUND HO, *Summer Ho* 1811 OS, a gazebo. THE ROW, a strip of woodland, *v.* **rāw**. RYE HILL, 1838 *TA*, *v.* **ryge**. ST GILES'S CHURCH, cf. *Capella Sancti Egidii* 1291 Tax, 'the church of St Giles, *Upwymbourne Plecy*' 1374 Pat, *v.* par. name, All Hallows Fm *supra*, Hutch[3] 3 602–3. ST GILES'S HO & PARK (1811 OS), cf. *S. Giles Winburne, wher Mr. Asscheley hath his maner place and park* 1535–43 Leland, *The Park, Park Gate, (The) Horse Park, Horse Park Grd(s)* 1838 *TA*. SIX ACRE COPSE, *Six Acres Coppice* 1838 *TA*. SQUIRREL'S CORNER. SUTTON CMN (1811 OS, *Sudden-* 1838 *TA, Suttons Cmn* 1842 *ib* (Gussage St M.)) & COPSE (*Suttons Coppice* 1842 *ib*), from Sutton *supra*. THE WARREN. WARWICK'S LANE. WATER LAKE (BOTTOM), *v.* **lacu, botm**. WIMBORNE LODGE, by the road to Wimborne M. par. *supra*. WOODLANDS GATE, where the road from Wimborne St G. enters Woodlands par. *infra*. cf. *Ground adjoining Woodlands* 1838 *TA*. WOR BARROW, 1811 OS, a tumulus by the par. bdy (with Six. Handley par. *infra*) and on the highest part of Oakley Down; the references to *a place callyd Werebarewe, watch and ward duty at Warbarrow* 1546 *Surv* (SC 12/7.11 p. 17) possibly belong here, and the name is probably analogous with Worbarrow 1 103, *v.* **weard** 'watch', **beorg** 'barrow', cf. the lost f.n. *la Weyte infra*, and cf. *Wyreberge* in Canford M. par. *supra*.

FIELD-NAMES

Most of the undated forms are 1838 *TA* 247, but those marked † are 1842 *ib* 95 (Gussage St Michael), comprising the old detached manor of Sutton. Spellings dated 13, 1404, 1530 are *Cecil*, 1227, 1253, 1296 FF, 1268, 1288 *Ass*, 1327 *SR*, 1332 SR, 1334 (1372), n.d. (1372) *ChrP*, 1340 NI, 15, 1444 *Queens*, 1403 *Midd*, 1421, 1591 Hutch³, 1430 Cl, 1620 *CH*, 1664 HTax, and 1791 Boswell.

(*a*) Further and Hither Acres; Allhallows Fm Down, Allhallows Fd (*v.* All Hallows Fm *supra*); Answorth Six Acre; †Arable Plot; Baileys Hill (the surname *Bayli, Bayly* occurs in connection with *Vpwymburn'* in 1268); †Barley Grd; Barrow Fd (*v.* **beorg**); †Beames's Grd; †Bean Grd; Blakes Fd; (†) Bottom Fd; The Breach (*La Breche* 15, *v.* **bræc** 'land broken up for cultivation'); Bull Md; Bungys Cl; Burnbake Grd (*v.* **burnbake**); †Butter Md (*v.* **butere**); Carpenters Cl (cf. Robert *Carpentar'* 1327, *-Carpenter* 1332); Clarkes Cl (cf. Henry *le Clerk* 1340 (Woodyates)); Cobbs 15 Acres, Cobbs Grd; Cole(s)'s 11, 15, 5, 4 & 10 Acres, Coles's Md, Plot & South Grd; The Common Grd; Comptons Fd, †Hr & Lr Comptons Lake; The Coneygar and Orchd (*v.* **coninger**); Coppice; Cow Drove & Pasture, Lr Cowleaze; Deadman Fd (cf. Dead Man in Cranborne par. *supra*); Down (Pce) (*v.* **dūn**); †Droveway, the Drove; Dry Md; Dunsmoor Wd; The East and West Pieces; (The) 8 Acres, †The 8 Acres; (The) Farm Down; The 5, 4 & 14 Acres; Frenches Bridge 1791 (from French's Fm *supra*); Old French Grass Grd (*v.* **french grass**); Frost Fd; Seven Goods Heath (perhaps elliptical for '7 Acres on-', cf. Thomas *Good* 1591); Goulds Cl & Moor; Granary Fd; Griffins Pdk; Hayters Cl (cf. Widow *Haytor* 1664); Lt Heath, Heath Grds (cf. *la Hethfeld* 1403, *v.* **hǣð, feld**); Hedge Row; South Heron (probably **hyrne** 'angle, corner'); †Higher Mdw; Home Cl, Fd & Grd (all freq), †Home Grd, Md & Plot; Picked Horse Leaze (*v.* **pīcede** 'pointed'); Hospital Fd; The Lawn; †The Leg (*v.* **leg**); Ley Cl (*v.* **lǣge** 'fallow'); Long Bridge 1791; Long Cmn, Grd & Md; †Long Mdw; †Lower Grd & Md; Martins and Sansums Moor (cf. Thomas *Sansome* 1664, Richard *de la More* 1280 *Ass*, Walter *atte More* 1327, *v.* **atte, mōr**); (The) Meadow, †The Meadow; Merry Fd (*v.* **myrge**); New Cl & Fd; North Fd (cf. *campo de North'* n.d. (1372), *v.* **norð**); North Md; Orchard, The (Old) Orchard, †Orchard Fd & Plot; †Parker's Md; †Parsons; Pasture; The Peak (*v.* **pēac**); Philipstone Lr & Upr Fd (*v. Philipston supra*); †Picked Grd (*v.* **pīcede** 'pointed'); Plantation Play Cl (*v.* **plega**); Plot of Meadow, The Plot; Pond Cl (Mead); Potters Cl; The Road Fd; †Rough Pce; Rumford Cmn (from Romford in Edmondsham par. *supra*); Lr & Upr 7 Acres; Sheppards (Down) Cl, 18 Acres & Moor (cf. John *Shepheard* 1664); †6 Acres; The 6 Acres; (The) 10, 30, 3 & 20 Acres, †The 10 & 3 Acres; Thorney Down (*Thorney Downe Hedge* 1620, *v.* **þornig, dūn**); Upper Cl; Waddocks Coppice & Md, Upr Waddocks (probably a surname from Waddock 1291); †Walnut Cl; (Gt) Water Md(w); †Well Cl; Whatcomb Warren (perhaps analogous with Whatcombe in Winterborne W. par. *supra*); (The) Withy Bed; Wood; Yewtree Fd.

(*b*) *atte Assch'* 1332 (p) (*v.* **atte, æsc**); *pastura de Bardesberghe* 15 (*v.* **beorg** 'hill, tumulus', first el. possibly the OE pers.n. *Beornrǣd*); *Bochelaueshull*

1227 (v. **hyll**, first el. probably a pers.n., though the form is not certain); *Brokfirlong* 1311 Banco (v. **brōc, furlang**); *La Brodelande* 1227 (v. **brād, land**); *Cheldelond'* 15 (v. **land**, first el. **ceald** 'cold, exposed' or **celde, cielde** 'a spring'); *Eldelond'* 15 (v. **eald, land**); *campo qui dicitur Erneborge* n.d. (1372) (v. **earn** 'eagle', **beorg** 'hill, tumulus'); *locus qui vocat' Forthdon'* 1288 ('(ground) in front of the hill', or 'projecting hill', v. **forð, dūn**); *de la Gore* 1268 (p), *atte Gore* 1332 (p) (v. **atte, gāra**); *hauedacram* n.d. (1372) (v. **hēafod, æcer**); *Hupmede* n.d. (1372) (v. **upp(e)** 'higher up', **mǣd**); *Hymondesmede* n.d. (1372) (probably an error for *Symondes-*, v. *infra*); *la landshore* n.d (1372) (v. **land-scoru** 'boundary'); *lefdie crofta* n.d (1372) (probably 'enclosure dedicated to Our Lady', v. **hlǣfdige, croft**); *Oclefurlong* 1328 Banco (v. **furlang**, Oakley *supra*); *Rygweye* 15 (v. **hrycg, weg**, perhaps with reference to the Badbury Rings–Old Sarum Roman road (Margary 4c) where it crosses the par. on Bottlebush Down); *Sabeleye* 15 (perhaps to be compared with Sapley Hu 208, which is 'fir wood' from **sæppe** and **lēah**); *Seventditches* 1613 Hutch³ (with reference to earthworks, v. **dīc**); *Symondsmede* 1421 (the pers.n. or surname *Simon(d)*, v. **mǣd**, cf. *Hymondesmede supra*); *terre...vocat' lez Sperkes* 1404 (in spite of the def.art., probably to be connected with the family of John *Spark* 1340 (Edmondsham), Joan *Sparke* 1530, William *Sparkes* 1664); *Stodenhull* 1227 (perhaps 'hill at *Stoden*' ('valley where horses were kept'), v. **stōd, denu, hyll**); *La Suelghesheude* 1227 (v. **(ge)swelg** 'abyss, whirlpool', **hēafod** 'head, upper end, source'); *La Surelonde* n.d. (1372) (v. **sūr** 'sour', **land**); *tokkedemor* n.d. (1372) (perhaps for *cokkede-*, with the meaning 'marshy ground with heaps or mounds on it', from **cocc¹, -ede, mōr**); *Tounyshend* 1444 (p) (v. **tūn, ende¹**); *le Westhide in Upwymborne* n.d. (1372), *Westhide pres de Upwymborne* 1334 (1372), *le west Hyde* 1421 (probably to be associated with Roger- 1280 *Ass*, Hugh *de la Hyde* 1296, Ralph *atte Hyde* 1332, cf. also *the wood of Hyde* 1421, v. **hīd** 'a hide of land', **west, atte**); 'pasture...called *la Weyte*' 1253, *the Wayt* 1430 (ME *waite* 'a watch, a look-out place', cf. Wor Barrow *supra*); *campum de Wimborne* 13; *ten' voc' Wynes* 1438 Queens, *ii cotag'...vocat' wyne howse* 1444 (probably the surname *Wyne*, with **hūs**).

West Woodyates

This small par., along with East Woodyates (in Cranborne hundred *supra*), was joined to Pentridge par. in 1933. Early forms that may strictly belong under East Woodyates are included here.

WOODYATES (SU 028194), EAST & WEST WOODYATES ['wudiəts, 'udiəts]

in publico loco qui dicitur at Wdegeate 859 ?for 870 (15) *ShaftR* (S 334), *in þare stowe þat is inemned at wudegate* ?870 (15) *ib* (S 342), (*to*) *wideyate* 944–6 (14) BCS 817 (S 513), ?*Widamgate* 959–975 Finberg (S 1772), *besuðan wudigan gæte* c.970 Durham Ritual (Surtees Society 140)

Odiete 1086 DB

Widiate 1199 FF

Wudiete 1199, 1213 ib both (p), *Wdiate* 1201 Cur (p), *Wodiat(e)* 1208 ib (p), 1213 ib, *Wud(e)iat(e)* 1213 ib (p) *et freq* to 1233 Cl, *Wodiet'* 1244 *Ass*, *Wodeyate* 1244, 1288 *ib* both (p) *et freq* to 1428 FA, *-hyate* 1244 *Ass* (p), *-yet(e)* 1268 *ib*, 1428 FA, *Wodyete* 1288 *Ass* (p), *-yate* 1409 Cl, *Wdehette*, *Wudehate* n.d. (1372) *ChrP*

Wudegat(e) 1199 Cur (p), 1244 *Ass*, *-geith'* n.d. (1372) *ChrP*, *Wodegat(e)* 1199 Cur (p), 1242 Ch *et freq* to 1325 Pat, *Wdegete* n.d. (1372) *ChrP*

Wudigat' 1244 *Ass* (p)

Wudesate 1251 FF, *Wodezete* 1291 Tax, *-zate* 1340 NI (p)

Wodeyats 1535 VE, *Woodyates* 1618 *Map*, *East-Woodyates*, *West-Woodyates* 1774 Hutch[1]

'(At) the gate or gap in the wood', from **wudu, widu** and **geat**, the first el. apparently alternating with **wudig** 'wooded' in the form from Durham Ritual and perhaps in *Wudigat'* 1244. There is mention of a wood here in 1251 FF. The gate or gap may have been at Bokerly Junction, where Bokerly Ditch, a late RB earthwork built across the Badbury Rings-Old Sarum Roman road, was later breached by the road from Blandford F. to Salisbury. Ekwall DEPN makes an alternative suggestion for the first el., the OE pers.n. *Widia, Wudga, Wudia* found in Withington Gl 1 186, but the topographical terms seem more likely in this name. The late appearance of *-s* in Woodyates is noteworthy; it would seem to have originally represented a pl. form, 'the (two) places called *Woodyate*'.

BOKERLY JUNCTION (1"), named from Bokerly Ditch in Pentridge par. *supra, v.* also par. name *supra*. CHAPEL (Remains of), cf. 'the church of St Nicholas of *Wodegate*' 1242 Ch. DENBOSE WD, *Denbows Coppice* 1829 *EnclA*, cf. *Great Denwalls* (sic) 1618 *Map*, from the family of Philip (*de*) *Denebaud*, *-de Denebald'* 1233 Cl, *-Denebaud* 1234 ib, 1244 *Ass*, William *Denebaud* 1316 FA, 1317 FF, John *Denebaude* 1390 Ipm, cf. Denbow Fm D 588. HILL COPSE, *-Coppice* 1829 *EnclA*, *hill cops* 1618 *Map*, *v.* **hyll**. HORSE LEYS PIT, cf. *Horse Cl & Leaze* 1829 *ib*, *v.* **læs** 'pasture'. THE MOUNT, 1829 *EnclA*, *v.* **mont**. PILL ASH, *Pill Ash Coppice* 1829 *ib*, first el. perhaps **pīl** 'shaft' or **pyll** 'small

stream'. WOODYATES INN (lost), 1774 Hutch[1], 1811 OS. WEST
WOODYATES MANOR.

FIELD-NAMES

The undated forms are 1829 *EnclA* (DRO 21). Spellings dated 1242 are Ch,
n.d. (1372) *ChrP*, 1618 *Map*, 1838 *TA* 165 (Pentridge), and 1839 *TAMap*
(Pentridge).

(*a*) Barley Md; Bear Coppice & Plot (*La Bere* 1242, from **bǣr**[2] '(woodland)
pasture' or **bearu** 'wood, grove'); Bottom Bushes & Coppice (*v.* **botm**);
Broad Fd; Hr & Lr Canon hill; Cook Pond; Coppice Row; Hr Cow Leaze;
Cunnegar (*v.* **coninger** 'rabbit-warren'); Gt, Lesser, Lr & Middle Down,
The Down; Goar (*v.* **gāra**); Hr & Lr Grove (cf. *Estgroue* 1618, *v.* **ēast**,
grāf(a)); Hanover Corner; Home Coppice (*Home cops* 1618); The Lawn,
Lawn Coppice (*Lawne cops* 1618, *v.* **launde**); Leg (*v.* **leg**); The Mead; New
Cl; Gt & Lt Piddle (probably **piddle** 'small enclosure'); Row (*n.* **row**); Saxon
pit Fd; Scotch Croft; Smugglers Rd 1839; Stone Croft; Tunicks Coppice;
Well Fd; Hr & Lr Wick Fd (*Witch Fd* 1838, *v.* **wīc** 'dwelling, farm');
Woodyates Gt & Lesser Fd.

(*b*) *Carrants* (*hill*) 1618 (a surname); *Hoopers* 1618 (a surname); *Inokes* 1618
(*v.* **inhoke**); *Langfordes closs* 1618 (probably a surname, *v.* **clos(e)**); *lega, la
leiga, la leige* n.d. (1372) (*v.* **lēah** 'wood, clearing'); *Puweysend* 1242 (*v.*
ende[1]); *Stomed* 1242 (probably 'stony meadow', from **stān**, **mǣd**).

XVII. KNOWLTON HUNDRED

In c.1086 GeldR this hundred also contained M. Crichel (now in Badbury
hundred) and *Philipston* in Wimborne St G. (still included in this hundred
in 1795 Boswell), *v.* VCHDo 3 138–9, cf. Eyton 119f, Anderson 132.
Wimborne St G. was in this hundred in 1332 SR (*v.* Wimborne St G. hundred
supra). The hundred was appurtenant to the manor of Knowlton (*v. infra*).

Chenoltune hundret c.1086 GeldR, *Cnolton' hdr'* 1168 P, (*Hundredum de*) *Cnolton(e)* 1212 Fees, 1244 *Ass*, 1246 Ch *et freq* to
1346 FA, *Cnoutone* 1244 *Ass*, *Knolton(')* 1244 *ib*, 1258 FF *et freq*
to 1564 *Glyn*, *Cnowelton'* 1280 *Ass*, *Knowlton* 1664 HTax,
named from the royal manor of Knowlton in Woodlands par.
infra, the *caput* of the hundred.

Long Crichel

LONG CRICHEL (ST 977103)

(*to*) *chircelford* 935 (15) *ShaftR* (S 429)

Circel 1086 DB (f. 80b), ?*Chirce* 1086 ib (ff. 75, 83), Exon

Kerichel, Kerechel 1202 FF, *Longa Kerechel* 1285 FA

Crechel 1204 FF, *Langecrechel Roberti de Luscy et Briani Tollard* 1208 P, *Crechill Govitz, Longe Crechill* 1541 *Glyn*

Kerchel 1208 FineR, 1233 Cl, 1244 *Ass* (p), 1251 FF, (*Longa-*) 1258 ib, 1280 *Ass* (*Lang-*), *Langeker(c)hil, -kerhul, Kerhill'* (sic) 1288 *ib, Kerchehull* 1297 Pat

Kercle 1208 P

Longcherchel 1219 FF

Curchel 1244 *Ass* (p), 1280 *ib* (*Lan-, Longe-*), *Lang-, Longe Kurchel* 1280 *ib, Lange-, Longekurchel*(') 1288 *ib, Kurchul* 1288 *ib,* 1333 *HarlCh* (*Longe-*), *Lange Curchille* 1324 Ipm, *Langekurchill* 1348 ib, *Curchell juxta Gussych St Michael* 1410 Hutch[3], *Kurchell Govytz, -Govitz* 1422, 1469 *Midd, Longekurchell* 1441 Cl, *Kurchell Lucy* 1469 *Midd, Long-curchell* 1575 Saxton

Churethel (for *-chel*) 1262 Ipm, *Churchell, Churchill* 1411 IpmR

Langecruchel 1268 *Ass* (p), *Cruchell Longa* 1366 IpmR, *Long Cruchel* 1366 Pat

Langecrichel 1268 *Ass,* 1297 Pat, *Langge-, Longecrichil* 1268 *Ass, Lancrichull* 1428 FA, *Lang(e) Crychell* 1494 *Cecil, Crichell als. Long Crechehill* 1534 Hutch[3], *Longe Crichell' als. Crechill' Govis* 1547 *AD, Longe Crychell* 1564 *Marten, Crichel-Gouis, Crichel-Lucy* 1774 Hutch[1]

Kirchel, Langekyrchil, -kyrchyl 1288 *Ass, Longa Kyrchyl* 1291 Tax, *Kirchil* 1298 Pat *et freq* with variant spellings *Kyrchil(l), Kirchill(e), Kyrchel(l), Kirchell, Kyrchyll* and with additions *Lang(e)-* (to 1431 FA) and *Long(e)-* (from 1416 Pat) to 1500 Pat, *Kirchull* 1346 Fine, *Longekyrhull* (sic) 1381 Pat, *Kyrchhylle* 1378 Cl, *Lange Kyrchull* 1412 FA, *Longa Kyrchile* 1428 ib, *Langkyrchill Govice, Langkirchell Govice* 1564 *Glyn*

Kirkechil 1288 *Ass, Kyrkechil(l)* 1288 *ib* (p)

Langechirchil 1303 FA, *Lanchirchull* 1388 IpmR

Langecriechill 1316 FA, *Long Creechill* 1618 *Map*

Crouchull' 1332 SR (p)

From PrWelsh or PrCorn *crūg 'mound, hill, barrow', with explanatory OE **hyll** 'hill', thus identical in origin with Church Hill So (DEPN), Creech Hill in Wimborne St G. par. *supra*, etc, cf. Ekwall Studies[1] 33ff. The hill referred to is Crichel Down (347′) *infra*. *Long* distinguishes this place from More Crichel par. *supra* and *Little Crichel* in More Crichel, 'on account of its greater length' (Hutch[3] 3 482), v. **lang**[1]. The other affixes are manorial: *Crichel Lucy* (1869 Hutch[3], 'the eastern half of the vill') was named from the family of Robert *de Lucy* 1202 Hutch[3], Robert *de Luscy*, Margaret *de Luci* 1208 P; *Crichel Govis* (1869 Hutch[3], 'the westerly part of the parish') was named from the family of Roger *de Gouiz* 1233 Cl, Brian *de Gouiz* 1258 FF, John *Gouytz* 1375 Cl. The form *to chircelford* 'to the ford of Crichel', occurs in the AS bounds of Tarrant Hinton, and describes the point where the Salisbury–Blandford F. road (earlier 'Week Street', v. Week Street Down in Gussage St M. par. *supra*) crosses the small stream which flows through the Crichels to join R. Allen, v. **ford**. On the identification of the DB forms, some of which may strictly belong under More Crichel, v. VCHDo 3 65, 92, 100, DBGazetteer 119; some of the other early forms without affix may also strictly belong under More Crichel or *Little Crichel*.

BAYTON'S COPPICE, named from the *Bainton* or *Baynton* family which held the manor of *Crichel Lucy* from 1411 to 1543, v. *Hutch*[3] 3 486, par. name *supra*. CHETTERWOOD LODGE, 1795 Boswell, *Chettered-Lodge* 1774 Hutch[1], named from the ancient wood of Chetterwood, included under More Crichel par. *supra*. COUTMAN'S CROFT, cf. *Croft* 1268 *Ass* (p), *The Croft* 1842 *TA*, v. **croft**; *Coutman* is perhaps an altered form of the surname *Cook(e)man* found in this par., cf. John-, Mathew *Cook(e)man* 1664 HTax. CRICHEL DOWN, *le Downe* 1564 *Glyn*, *Common Down* 1842 *TA*, v. **dūn**, par. name *supra*. HIGHER FM, cf. Lower Fm *infra*. HORSE DOWN, 1842 *ib*, *Long Critchell Horse Down* 1811 OS. LOWER FM, 1842 *TA*, cf. *Lower Bridge* 1791 Boswell, Higher Fm *supra* and foll. MIDDLE FM. NURSERY. PARSON'S CLOSE, 1842 *ib*. PRINCE'S COPPICE, 1842 *ib* (Gussage St M.), cf. Thomas *Prynce* 1547 *Ct* (Gussage St M.); this coppice is next to Queen's Coppice in More Crichel par. *supra*. ST MARY'S CHURCH, cf. 'the church of *Kirchil*' 1375 Pat, *ecclesie de Longkirchill* 1452 *Marten*, 'church of St Mary the Virgin,

Longkirchill' 1475 Pat, *Church Mdw* 1842 *TA*. SHORT COPPICE. STRAWBERRY COPPICE. THICKTHORN DOWN, FM & WD, *Thickthorn Bridge* 1791 Boswell, *Thick Thorn* 1811 OS, *Thickthorn Enclosure* 1842 *TA*, *v.* þicce² 'thick, dense', þorn, cf. Thickthorn W 272, Bk 33, and the lost f.n. *Senethorn infra*. VEINY CHEESE POND, so called from its resemblance to blue *vinny cheese*, from Do dial. *vinny* 'mouldy' (Barnes 115, EDD), with later rationalization.

FIELD-NAMES

The undated forms are 1842 *TA* 74. Spellings dated 1202, 1258 are FF, 1332 SR, 1541, 1564 *Glyn*, 1791 Boswell, and 1829 *EnclA* (DRO 21).

(*a*) Allotment Fd; Down Cl 1829; East Fd 1829; 15 Acres 1829; French Grass Fd (from the crop); Glebe Cl & Down, Glebe Ho and Pdk; Gough land cl 1829; Higher Fd 1829; Holly Fd; Home Cl; Homes Mdw 1829; Honeygrove; Little Fd; Long Mdw 1829; Middle Fd 1829; The Moor; North East Fd; Northeast Pasture 1829; North Fd 1829; Old Enclosure; Paddock; Gt South West Fd; South West Mdw & Pasture; Square Cl; 10 Acres 1829; Tenants Down; Turnpike Bridge 1791; Upper Mdw; Great West Fd.

(*b*) *Brocforlang* 1202 (*v.* brōc, furlang); 'two acres beyond the *Court of Gades*' 1202 (?perhaps the name of an inn); *lez drove* 1541, *boscum voc' le Drove* 1564 (*v.* drāf); *Hamme* 1258 (*v.* hamm); *Landshori* 1202 (*v.* land-scoru 'boundary'); *in thelane* (p) 1332 (*v.* lane); *parok voc' Mannefels* 1541 (a form of the surname *Mandeville, v.* Reaney *s.n.*); *Myllers place* 1564 (the surname *Miller, v.* place); *Senethorn* 1202 (probably for *Seuethorn*, 'seven thorn-trees', from seofon and þorn, cf. Seven Ash D 50, Sevenoaks K, etc); *Withwye Cops* 1541 (*v.* wīðig 'willow', copis); *Wood cloose* 1541 (*v.* wudu).

Gussage All Saints

Mannington, formerly a detached part of this par., was added to Wimborne Minster in 1886, and became part of Holt par. in 1894.

GUSSAGE ALL SAINTS (ST 998108 ['gʌsidӡ, 'gisidӡ]
    (*æt*) *Gyssic* 966–975 (e12) ASWills
    Gessic 1086 DB, *Gessich(e)* 1183 P, 1205, 1215 ClR, 1236 FF (*-Gentil*), 1240 Ch, 1242–3 Fees (*-Omnium Sanctorum*), 1244 Cl, 1282 Pat (p), 14 *Queens*, n.d. (1372) *ChrP*, *Gessing(')* 1195 P, 1231 Cl, *Gessiz* 13 *Queens*, 1212 Fees, *Gessi* 1210, 1211 P, *Gessigh(')* 1245 Cl (*-Omnium Sanctorum*), 14 *Queens*, *Gessege* 1429 Pat
    Gersic 1091–1104, 1107–22, 1135–37, 1152–58 (all p1305) MontC, *Gersich(e)* 1100–18 (p1305) ib, 1100–22 (1270) Ch,

1107–22, 1155 (-*Omnium Sanctorum*), 1189–99 (all p1305) MontC, ?1192 *Queens*, 1221 Cur, 1227 ClR, 1230 FF, 1232, 1233 Cl, *Gersiz* 1183–88, 1194–95 P, 1196 ChancR, 13 *Queens*, *Gersihc* ?1192, 1198 (15) *ib*, *Gersingg'* 1222 ClR, *Gersis* 1230 P, *Gersy* 1232 Cl

Gissig(') ?Hy I *Queens*, 1281 *Salis* (-*Regis*), *Gissich*(*e*) 1217 ClR, 1226–8 Fees, 1244 *Ass* (p), 1268 *ib*, 1275 Banco, 1277 *Queens*, 1280 Ch ('-All Saints'), 1288 FF, *Ass*, 1318 *Queens*, 1346 FA, 15 *Queens*, 1412 FA, *Gissic* 1219 Fees, *Gyssyk'* 1244 *Ass* (p), '*Gissik* All Saints' 1258 Ch, *Gyssich*(*e*) 1273 Banco ('-All Saints'), 1288 *Ass*, 1294 *Queens* (-*Regis*), 1406 Pat, *Gissinge-*, *Gisich' Gentil* 1280 *Ass*, *Gyssych*(') 1281 *Queens* (-*Omnium Sanctorum*), 1300 Pap, 15 *Queens*, *Gissegge* 1475 Pat, *Gyssege* 1476 IpmR

Garsic 1207 ClR

Gussiz Regis e13 *Queens*, *Gussich*(*e*) 13 *ib* (-*regis*), 1211 ClR, 1244 FF, 1245 Ch ('-All Saints'), 1253 Ipm, 1276 FF ('-All Saints'), 1285 FA (-*Regis*) *et freq* to 1445 Pat ('-All Saints') with affixes '-All Saints' (1332 Cl, Ipm, 1374 Pat) and -*Regis* (1428 FA), *Gutsich'* 1233 Cl, *Gusich*(') 1254 Cl (p), 1268 *Ass*, *Gusik'* 1254 Cl (p), *Gussuch* 1291 Tax (-*Regis*), 1324 Pat, *Gusshich* 1347 Cl, 1389 ib ('-All Saints'), *Gussych*(*e*) 1351 *Weld*[1], 1360 Ipm, n.d. (1372) *ChrP*, 1384 Cl (-*Allhallows*), 1402 FA (-*Omnium Sanctorum*), *Gussynch* 1407 Pat, *Gussehich All Saints* 1425 AD III, *Gusshigge Omnium Sanctorum* 1432 BM I, *Gusshyche Sanctorum* 1438 *Queens*, *All Hallow Gussege* 1466 IpmR, *Gussege All Saints* 1500 Pat, *Gussage* Hy 8 *Queens*, 1535 VE (-*Omnium Sanctorum*), 1618 *Map* (*All Saints-*), 1664 HTax (-*All Snts'*), *Alhollowne Guusshedge* Eliz Kelly, *Gussage All Saints* (*Lower*) 1795 Boswell

Cussigh' 1237 Cl, *Cussith* (for *Cussich*) 1291 Tax, *Cussich* 15 *Queens*

Kissich Gentil 1242 Ch

Girsech' 1239 Cl

Gostyche 1402 FA

Gwyssych 1419 *DLRent*

For other spellings of the name Gussage, *v*. Gussage St Michael par. *supra* and Gussage St Andrew in Six. Handley par.

infra (note especially *Gissic, Gersicg* 871–877 (15) *ShaftR* (S 357 (1 and 2)); early forms of the name without affix, where precise identification is uncertain, have been included here. Ekwall (DEPN, RN 187) is no doubt right in taking the name to be from an OE **gyse* 'a gush of water' (corresponding to OHG *gusi* 'water suddenly breaking forth') and sīc 'a water-course, a small stream', with reference to the stream which rises at Gussage St Andrew and which flows through Gussage St Michael and this par. to join R. Allen. The Devon stream-names Gessage and Gissage Lake are probably analogous, *v.* PN D 6, cf. also Gisburn YW 6 164 which may contain a related word OE **gysel* 'gushing'. The *e*-spellings for the first el. (*Gessic*, etc) are probably due to AN influence, *v.* Feilitzen 56. The *-r-* spelling in *Gers-* (frequent between the end of the 11th cent. and the middle of the 13th cent., and found also in the form *Gersicg* 871–877 (15) noted above), *Gars-* (once) and *Girs-* (once), is possibly inorganic, cf. Ekwall DEPN who notes that the spelling with *rs* is 'probably erroneous, but it seems to have had a certain vogue'; the frequent occurrence of *-r-* with *-e-*, as against its rarity with *-i-* and its non-occurrence with *-u-*, might suggest further AN influence, cf. Feilitzen 84. However, Professor Löfvenberg notes: 'The *r*-spellings are easily accounted for if we postulate an OE side-form **gyre* 'gushing' formed in the same way as the masc. abstract nouns *cyre, dryre, hryre, lyre*. Such a form is actually suggested by Ekwall in *Meijerbergs Arkiv* 3 (1941) 38–39. It is not mentioned, however, in DEPN. There must also have been an OE fem. noun **gyre* 'dirt, mud', on which *v.* Löfvenberg 85'.

The affix *Gentil* is manorial: Robert *le Gentil* was chief lord of the fee of *Gessich Gentil* in 1236 FF, cf. Robert *le Gentil* (of *Gessich*) 1242 Ch, John *le Gentil* (*de Gessich*) 1244 Cl, FF. The affix *Regis* may belong to a different manor: the manor of *Gissich*' was the King's escheat in 1227 Fees (p. 378). *All Saints* (*Omnium Sanctorum, All Hallows*, etc) is from the dedication of the church, *v. infra*. The late affix *Lower* (first noted 1774 Hutch[1]) is from its position relative to Gussage St Michael (*Middle*) and Gussage St Andrew (*Upper*).

BIDCOMBE MILL (SU 014094), *Byncomb* (sic, perhaps for *Byttcomb*) *mill* 1631 Hutch[3], *Bidecomb Mill* 1811 OS, cf. *Bidcomb*

Cowleaze, Fd & Md 1841 *TA*, possibly to be associated with John *de Bitcombe* 1327 *SR*, *-de Bitecomb*' 1332 SR (Petersham in Holt), Robert *Bitcombe* 1435 *Midd* (Woodlands), in which case the name may mean 'Bit(t)a's valley', from an OE pers.n. *Bit(t)a* (suggested by DEPN for Bidborough K) and **cumb**. There was a mill at the manor of *Gessic* in 1086 DB (VCHDo 3 86), and other references to mills probably in this par. (some of them perhaps belonging here) include *molend*' *de Gusich* 1268 *Ass*, Roger *atte mille* 14 *Queens*, Maud *atte Mulle* 1318 *ib*, Cristina *atte Mulle* 1332 SR, Robert *atte Mulle* 1332 Cl, *Terresmull*' 1444 *Queens*, *Cheryottes* (*myll*) 16 *Midd*, v. **myln**, **atte**; *Terre-* is probably a form of the surname *Terry*, and *Cheryott* is also a surname.

BOWERSWAIN FM (SU 009099) & HOLLOW ['bouswein, 'bousən]

> *Baresfeld(e)* 1091–1104, 1100–18 (both p1305) MontC,
> 1100–22 (1270) Ch, 1135–37 (p1305) MontC, *Baresfelt*,
> *Boresfeu[d]* c.1155 (p1305) ib
> *Boresfe'rne* (sic) e13 *Queens*, *Boresfen* 1288 *Ass*, 1332 SR (p),
> n.d. (1372) *ChrP*, 1406, 1438 *Queens*, *Boressen* (probably
> for *Boresfen*) 1316 FA, 1469 *Midd*, *Boreswain* 1546 Hutch[3],
> *Bareswayne* 1590 Drew, *Bowerswayne* 1795 Boswell
> *Boreston* n.d. (1372) *ChrP*, *Boreson* 1575 Saxton, 1774
> Hutch[1], 1869 Hutch[3], *Barston Moor* 1841 *TA*

The first el. of this name is probably an OE pers.n. *Bār*, as suggested by Ekwall DEPN for Barsham Nf, Sf, Husbands Bosworth Lei, rather than OE **bār**[2] 'a boar (wild or domestic)', though both are formally possible; the pers.n. occurs once in DB (spelt *Bar*), once as a byname (*Æilmar Bar* 1087–98), and may well be a nickname from the animal name (*v.* Ekwall DEPN *s.n.* Barsham, Tengvik 359, Smith EPN *s.v.* **bār**[2], cf. Feilitzen 192). The earliest forms (*Baresfeld, -felt*) represent 'Bār's open country', *v.* **feld**. However, from the 13th cent. the el. **fenn** 'fen, marsh, marshland' is apparently substituted for **feld**; the farm, situated by the *Gussage* stream near its confluence with R. Allen, is low-lying. It is from these forms (*Boresfen*, etc) that the present name Bowerswain, with some influence from popular etymology, is derived. A third naming tradition may be evidenced in the forms *Boreston, Boreson, Barston*, in which the second el. is apparently **tūn** 'farm'. However this is not certain, since *Boreston* may be an error for *Boresfen*; *Boreson* may be a form of *Boresfen*, *-wain* with weakly stressed final syllable (cf. also the alternative local pronunciation cited); and *Barston* may be a rationalization of this on the analogy of *-ston* > *-son* in other names, e.g. Kinson par. *supra*, Herrison 1 340, Bhompston 1 367, etc. The change from *feld* to *fen* is probably not simply 'a curious corruption' as suggested by Fägersten 92 (presumably he had in mind scribal confusion whereby *feld* > *feud* > *fend* > *fen*, this in turn influencing pronunciation); it is more likely that *Baresfeld* and *Boresfen* were from the beginning distinct though related names for adjacent parts of the same manorial unit, or that there was genuine substitution of one el. for another in the name of the unit itself at the end of the 12th cent.; and if **tūn** is also to be reckoned with, a further partial substitution of **tūn** for **fenn** may have taken place during the 14th cent. The f.n. *Bower Ditch* 1841 *TA* also belongs here; it is *Borysdych* 1330 FF (p), 'Bār's ditch', *v.* **dīc**.

BROCKINGTON FM (SU 019107)
> *Brochemtune* 1086 DB
> *Brochamton* 1204 FineR, 1225 FF, 1268 *Ass* (p), *Brochampton*(') 1225 Pat, 1262 FF, 1280 *Ass* (p) *et freq* to 1367 *Queens*, *Brokham*(*p*)*ton*(') 1268 *Ass* (p), 1288 *ib* (p) *et freq* to 1432 Fine, '*-by Gussych Allhallows*' 1384 Cl, *-juxta Gussyche Omnium Sanctorum* 1402 FA, *Brockamton*' 1288 *Ass* (p), *Brokehampton* 1444 *Queens*, 1469 *Midd*, *Brockehampton* 1564 *Marten*
> *Brechamton* (probably for *Broc-*) 1244 *Ass* (p)
> *Broghampton*(*e*) 1294, 1295 *Queens*
> *Brokinton* 1575 Saxton, *Brockington* 1620 *CH*, 1774 Hutch[1], *-or Brockhampton* 1869 Hutch[3]

Probably, as indicated by the DB form in *-hem-*, 'farm of the *Brōchǣme*' ('dwellers by the brook'), *v.* **brōc, hǣme** (gen.pl. *hǣma*), **tūn**, cf. Witchampton par. *supra*; on the possible presence of, or influence from, OE **hām-tūn** in the forms, *v.* Tengstrand MN 97. For the DB identification, *v.* Eyton 111–2, Fägersten 93, DBGazetteer 117; VCHDo 3 87 identifies the DB form with Brockhampton in Buckland N. par. *infra*, a name which may be identical in origin with Brockington, cf. also Brockhampton Gl 1 178. The farm lies beside R. Allen.

HARLEY DOWN (SU 006133), HARLEY GAP, LANE & WD, BURTT'S HARLEY, *Hardelyedun'* 1281, *Hardeleydune* 1281, 1349, *Harendeledone* (sic) 1294 all *Queens, Harley Bushes, Down & Wd* 1841 *TA*, '(hill or down at) the hard clearing', from **heard** (probably with reference to hard soil), lēah, dūn, cf. Hardley Ha (DEPN), Wt 37. *Burtt* is a surname, cf. Henry *Birt* 1664 HTax.

LOVERLEY FM (SU 005089) ['lʌvəli]
> *Loverlay* 1091–1104, 1100–1118, 1107–1122 (all p1305)
> MontC, *-lai* c.1155 (p1305) ib, *-lee* l13 Salis (p), 1288 *Ass*
> (p), *-le* 1303 FA (p), 1383 IpmR, *Louerle* 1285 Banco, *-lay*
> 1288 *Ass* (p), *-leygh* 1341 FF, *-legh* 1590 Drew, *-leigh* 1774
> Hutch[1]
> *Luverlay* 1100–22 (1270) Ch, 1135–7 (p1305) MontC, *Lun-*
> *erlea* (for *Luuer-*) 1285 FA (p)
> *Lowerleygh* 1341 FF, *-leigh* 1795 Boswell
> *Leverley* 1462 IpmR, *-legh* 1546 Hutch[3]

Probably 'Lēofwaru's wood or clearing', from the OE fem. pers.n. *Lēofwaru* (Searle 333, Feilitzen 316) and lēah, as suggested by Fägersten 93. Professor Löfvenberg comments that the constant early spellings with *u* and *o* are noteworthy, and draws attention to the complete absence of similar spellings for Leverton Brk 304, which clearly contains this pers.n.

WYKE FM (SU 013137), *Wike* 1596 Hutch[3], *Wike-Farm, Week-Farm* 1774 Hutch[1], *Wyke* 1795 Boswell, *Wick Fm* 1811 OS, probably to be associated with Robert *de Wyk'* 13 *Queens*, Walter *de Wyke* 1276 FF, John *de Wyke* 1332 SR all mentioned in connection with this par., v. wīc 'dwelling, (dairy) farm', cf. Week Street Down in Gussage St M. par. *supra*.

ALL SAINTS' CHURCH, cf. 'the church of All Saints, *Gersic(he)*' 1091–1104, c.1155 (both p1305) MontC, *ecclesie de Gissig* ?Hy 1 *Queens, ecclesiam de Gissig' Regis* 1281 Salis, 'church of *Gussich'* 1297 Pat, v. par. name *supra*. AMEN CORNER, 1869 Hutch[3] ('where tradition states a chapel anciently stood'). ASS HILL. BROCKINGTON BEECHES, DOWN (1841 *TA*) & LANE, cf. Brockington Bridges 1791 Boswell, *Brockington Moor* 1841 *TA*, from Brockington Fm *supra*. CAUSEWAY BRIDGE, where a lane crosses the *Gussage* stream at Bowerswain Fm *supra*, v. **cauce**.

CUSTARD HILL, possibly from **cot-stōw** 'collection of cottages', cf. PN Brk 860. DANCING DROVE. THE DRIVE PLANT. HORSE PIT, *Hurst Pit late Barns* 1841 *TA*, *v.* **hyrst** 'copse, wooded hill'; for the surname *Barn(es)*, *v.* f.ns. *infra*. JAMES CROSS LANE, *James' Croft* 1841 *ib*, from **croft** 'small enclosure' with the surname *James*. LOVERLEY LANE, *v.* Loverley *supra*. MANOR FM & HO. MEAD LANE, cf. *Mead Flg* 1841 *TA*, *v.* **mǣd**, Ton Bridge *infra*. THE MOOR, cf. *Moor* 1841 *ib*, *v.* **mōr**. NEW BARN. RECTORY, cf. *Parsonage Fd & Md* 1841 *ib*. RICHMOND CTG, cf. *Richmonds' Moor* 1841 *TA*, Ralph *Richmond* 1664 HTax. TENANTRY DOWN, cf. *The Tenants Down* 1838 *TA* (Wimborne St G.), *v.* **tenantry**. TON BRIDGE, *Tunbridge* 1791 Boswell, probably 'bridge belonging to the village', *v.* **tūn**, cf. *Tonmede* 1294 Queens, *Tun mede* n.d. (1372) ChrP, *Tun Md* 1841 *TA*, from the same first el. with **mǣd** 'meadow', and cf. John *atte Tounesende* 1318 Queens, Richard *atte Toneshende* 1332 SR, 'at the end of the village', *v.* **ende**[1]. WELL HO. WHITEWAY HILL, where a lane climbs the chalk down, cf. Whiteway 1 90, 103. WYKE DOWN, 1841 *TA*, from Wyke Fm *supra*.

FIELD-NAMES

The undated forms are 1841 *TA* 94. For fields in this *TA* belonging to former detached parts of this par., *v.* f.ns. in Holt par. and Edmondsham par. both *supra*. Spellings dated 1091–1104, c.1155 (both p1305) are MontC, 1100–22 (1270) Ch, 1268 *Ass*, l13 *Salis*, 1332 SR, n.d. (1372) ChrP, 16 *Midd*, 1564 *Glyn*, 1596 Hutch[3], 1664 HTax, 1791 Boswell, and the rest Queens.

(*a*) Arundel's Cl; Awes Md (perhaps to be associated with *Aluesmede* 1406, *Aleysmede* 1438, *Allesmed lake* 16, the first el. of which is probably a surname, cf. Reaney *s.n. Alway, Alley*, *v.* **mǣd**, **lacu**); Late Barbers' Orchd (cf. *John Barbers house* 1664); (Late) Barnes' Grd & Md, Barn's Dry Grd, Barn's Fd & Moor (the surname *Barn(es)*)*;* Batlands (*v.* **batte**); Beacon Hill (and Barn) (*v.* **(ge)bēacon**); Black Gate Fd; Bone Mill and Shed; (Lr) Bottom Fd (*v.* **botm**); Bowerswayne Bridge 1791 (from Bowerswain *supra*); Bramble Hill (*Brembelhull'* 1281, 1349, 1367, cf. *Brembelsaʒ(h)e* 1295, *v.* **brēmel**, **brembel** 'bramble, blackberry bush', **hyll**, **sc(e)aga** 'small wood, copse', cf. Bramshaw Ha (DEPN)); Hr & Lr Brick Fd; Burnbake (*v.* **burnbake**); Caseleys Ham Md (*v.* **hamm**); Coachway Fd; Coped Bush Fd (*v.* **(ge)coppod** 'pollarded'); Cranborne Fd & Md (perhaps named from Cranborne par. *supra*); Dean Fd (*v.* **denu** 'valley'); Doves Grd; East Md; (Lr) 18 Acres; Enter Common (from *intercommon* 'the practice of sharing in the use of the same common', cf. *in comuna...ville de Gessich'* n.d. (1372)); Fore Down (*v.* **fore**); 40 Acres; Late Framptons' (Md), Framptons' Moor (cf. Walter *Frampton* 1664); Furzy Cl;

Gallops' Grd; Goddards' Grd, Late Goddards' Md; Green Cl; Gussage Fd
(v. par. name *supra*); Harts' Cl, Fd & Living (cf. Anthony *Harte* 1564,
Edmund *Hart* 1664); Higher Fd; Home Cl & Fd; Honey Grd & Md (v.
hunig); Hulbarrow (v. **beorg** 'hill, mound, tumulus'; the first el. may be **ūle**
'owl' or **hulu** 'hovel, shed', cf. Oldberrow Wo 267, Holberrow ib 327);
Humpheyes Closes and Gdn (probably for *Humphreyes*, from the pers.n.
Humphrey); late Ingrams (cf. Elizabeth *Ingram* 1664); Late Kelly's Moor (cf.
Stephen *Kelly* 1664); Kite Hill (v. **cȳta**); Little Down and Chalk Pit; Long
Fd & Md(w); Inner Longway; Loverly Cowleaze, Grd, Higher Fd, & Row
(from Loverley *supra*, v. **rāw**); May Croft; Mower Bridge 1791; New Fd;
Newmans Fd (cf. *Newman's Lane Bridge* 1791); 19 Acres; Oak Tree Fd; One
Sheard (*Wenchierd, la Wemherde* (probably for *Wencherde*) n.d. (1372), 'gap
fit for a wagon', v. **wægn, sceard**, cf. Hr Sheard *infra*); Lr & Upr Park Fd,
Horse Park (v. **park**); Large Peaked Fd (v. **peked** 'pointed'); Pit Cl; Pitman's
Living & Moor (cf. Walter *Pytman* 1564); (Second & Third) Plantation Fd;
Play Cl (v. **plega**); Poors' Altmt; The Pound; Late Princes' Fd; Late Prouts
(cf. Gussage St M. f.ns. *supra*); Punters(') Cl; (Gt) Red Lane (*la Redelane*
l13, v. **rēad, lane**); Rogers Dry Grd; Rubbing Bush; Hr Sheard (v. **sceard**
'a gap', cf. One Sheard *supra*); South Down Moors (*Sothdone* 1295,
Southdon' 1367, *-downe* 1438, *Suthdown* 1444, *South Downe* (*Comon*) c.1618
DROSurv, v. **sūð, dūn** 'hill, down'); South Fd (*in australi campo* n.d. (1372),
cf. Sovell Down in Gussage St M. par. *supra*); Sparkes' Plot (cf. Robert
Sparke(s) 1664); Square Cl; Stag's Moor & Plot, Stays' Plot (sic); Sweetmans'
Grd; Late Talbots; Three Cornered Grd; Tinkers' Drove (v. **tynkere**); Tops'
Grd (perhaps to be associated with *ten' nuper...Brountoppes* 1438, where
Brountopp is a ME surname); Tulby's Moor; 20 Acres; Wall Fd (v. **w(e)all**);
Water Mdws; Well Bottom Cl (v. **well(a)** 'spring, stream', **botm** 'valley');
West Bridge 1791; West Md (*Westmede* n.d. (1372), v. **west, mǣd**); West Plick
(v. **plek** 'small plot'); Wheelers Moor; Withy Bed; Wortheys'-, Worthies Md
(perhaps to be associated with Godfrey *de la Worthe* 1268, Henry *atte Worth'e*
1332, v. **worð, worðig** 'enclosure', **atte**); Wyke Burn Bake (v. **burnbake**,
Wyke Fm *supra*); Yew Tree Pce; Late Youngs' (Fd) (cf. *John Youngs house*
1664).

(b) *Estbath', Westbath* 1367 (v. **bæð** 'bathing place, pool'); *Bighendebrok'*
1318 (p) ('beyond the brook', v. **begeondan, brōc**); *les butacres* Hy 8 (v. **butte**
æcer); *terr' voc'...Danyelles* Hy 8, *Daniels* 1596 (the surname *Daniel*); *Dottes*
1367 (a surname, cf. Robert *Dotes* 1332 (Tarrant L.)); *Fiveacres hedge* Hy 8
(v. **fīf, æcer, hecg**); *la Forde* 1277 (p) (v. **ford**); *herneshulle* e13, *Erneshull'* 1318
(v. **hyll**; first el. probably **earn** 'eagle'); *holeueye* e13, *Ollewey* (*furlang*) 1367
('hollow way', v. **hol², weg, furlang**); *terris...vocatis howys* 1444 (v. **howe**);
Hunecroft 1091–1104 *et freq* to c.1155, 1100–22 (1270), *Hunescroft* c.1155
('Huna's enclosure', from the OE pers.n. *Hūna* (in one form alternating with
the strong form *Hūn*) and **croft**); *Middel-, le myddelacre* Hy 8 (v. **middel**,
æcer); *Nonham* 1444 (v. **hamm**, first el. perhaps **nunne** 'a nun'); *Northfild*
Hy 8 (v. **norð, feld**); *de la pentiz* 13 (p), n.d. (1372) (p) (v. **pentis** 'a penthouse,
an annex'); *Redmore* 1294, *Radmore* 1438 (v. **rēad** 'red', **mōr**); *la Rydelond*
1367 (v. **(ge)ryd(d)** 'cleared', **land**); *Sc(h)ochleham* c.1618 *DROSurv* (v.
hamm; the first el. may be **scucca** 'evil spirit', *-le-* perhaps representing **hyll**

or lēah); *ten' nuper Trenchefeldes* 1438 (the surname *Trenchefoyl*, cf. Woodlands f.ns. *infra*); *Wexihamme* 1294 (*v.* **hamm**; the first el. would seem to be an early form of ModE *waxy* (NED from 1552), no doubt with reference to soft ground, from **weax, -ig³**).

Woodlands

This was formerly a manor and chapelry in Horton par. (Hutch³ 3 151).

WOODLANDS (SU 051090) ['wudlændz, 'udlənz], *Wodelande* 1244 *Ass* (p), 1345 FF (*La*-), *-launde* 1244 *Ass* (p), 1268 *ib* (*la*-), *-lond*(*e*) 1268, 1288 *ib*, 1303 FA (*La*-) et passim to 1495 *Midd*, *Woodland*(*e*) 1321 Inq aqd *et freq* to 1664 HTax, *Wodlond* 1394 *Midd*, *Wudlond* 1486 Ipm, *Wodelond or Wedelond* 1499 ib, *Woodlands* 1774 Hutch¹, 'wood land', i.e. perhaps 'wooded estate or tract of land', or 'land cleared for cultivation near or within a wood', *v.* **wudu, land**, cf. DEPN for other examples of this common name. The late appearance of the final *-s* (presumably a pl. form) is to be noted.

BAGGERIDGE (lost, about SU 030090)
   Bag(*g*)*herug'*, *Bageregge, -rug*(*h*)' 1250 Fees (p), *Bagerughe* 1250 *ib*, *Bargarich'* (sic) 1251–2 ib (p), *Baggerigg*(*e*) 1268 *Ass* (p), 1274–86 Ipm (p), 1275 RH (p), 1280 *Ass*, 1285 FA (p), *-riche* 1268 *Ass* (p), *-rig* 1275 RH (p), *Bagerig* 1274 Ipm (p), *-rigge* 1274–86 ib, *Baggeridge or Baggeridge-Street* 1774 Hutch¹, *Baggridge* 1795 Boswell
   Bagrichstrete 1251–2 Fees, *Baggerigsted'* (sic) 1260 Cl, *Baggeriggestrete* 1268 *Ass*, 1275 RH, 1285 FA, *Bagerichesstrete*, *Baggerugestrete* 1274 Ipm, *Bagerigestrete* 1288 *Ass*, *Bagrigstret* 1325 Inq aqd, *Baggeruggestrete* 1353 Fine *et freq* to 1446 ib, *Bageryngestrete* 1429, 1435 *Midd*, *Baggeringe Strete* 1551 *ib*

The first el. of both this and the following name is probably an OE **bagga** 'bag', either as a topographical word 'bag-like hill' or as the name of some animal, possibly 'badger', although the OE pers.n. *Bacga* is also formally possible, *v.* the discussion in EPN 1 17, DEPN *s.n.* Bagley. The second el. of *Baggeridge* is **hrycg** 'ridge', referring to the narrow 230'-high ridge S of Knowle Hill; cf. Badgemore O 65, Baggridge So

(DEPN). The alternative form *Baggeridge Street* probably means 'hamlet at *Baggeridge*', with ME **strete** in the sense 'hamlet, straggling village'. The spellings in *-sted*' (1260) and *-rynge-*, *-ringe-* (15th and 16th cent.) are probably errors. In 1774 Hutch¹ 2 60, it is stated that *Baggeridge* (*Street*) 'seems formerly to have been a hamlet. Its situation and name is now scarcely known'; on the location of the site of this settlement near Bagman's Copse (foll.), *v.* C. C. Taylor, DoNHAS **88** 209–210.

BAGMAN'S COPSE (SU 032091) & LANE, BAGMAN'S FM (1″, called SMITHY 6″), *Bagerham* (probably for *Bagenham*) 1237, 1242 Ch, *Baggeham* (a wood) 1305 Ipm, *bosco domini apud Bagenham* 1435 Midd, *copse called Baggnam, Baggenamcopse* 1551 *ib, Gt & Lt Bagenham Coppice, Bagenham Grd* 1840 *TA*. This name has the same first el. as *Baggeridge* (prec.), medial *-n-* no doubt reflecting an OE gen.sg. form in *-an*. The second el. is probably **hamm** 'enclosure'. For the late change *Bagnam > Bagman*, cf. dial. *vemon* for *venom* and the forms for the f.n. Newnham's 1 127.

CHARLTON DAIRY FM (SU 025107), *Cherleton juxta Wymburn* 1266 FF, *Charleton* 1432 BM I, 1450 Fine, 1620 *CH*, 1774 Hutch¹, *Charlton* 1795 Boswell, 'farm of the peasants', *v.* **ceorl** (gen.pl. *ceorla*), **tūn**, cf. Charlton M. par. *supra*; *Wymburn* is Wimborne St G. par. *supra*.

KNOWLE HILL (SU 033097), *Cnolle* 1212 Fees, 1268 *Ass*, 1298 FF, *Knol* 1242 Ch, *Knolle* 1244 *Ass* (p), 1268, 1280 *ib et freq* to 1469 *Midd, Cnoll* 1346 FA, *Knoll* 1388 Fine, *Knoll-Hill farm* 1650 Hutch¹, *Knoll Hill* 1811 OS, *Knowlhill* (*Fd*) 1840 *TA*, from **cnoll** 'hill top, hillock', with the later addition of **hyll**, cf. Church Knowle 1 87. Knowle Hill rises to just over 250′, and gives name to Knowlton (foll.) ½ mile W.

KNOWLTON (SU 024100)
  Chenoltune, -tone 1086 DB, *-tona* Exon
  Cnoltun n.d. (12) *SherC, Cnolton*(') 1212 Fees, 1236 Cl, 1244
    Ass et freq to 1340 NI, *Knolton*(') 1242 Ch, 1243 Fees, 1244
    Ass et freq to 1863 Hutch³, *Knollton* 1618 *Map*
  Cnouton(') 1205 P, 1237 Ch, 1239 Cl, 1244 *Ass, Cnowton*
    1237 Ch
  Gnolton 1214 ClR

Chinouton' 1217 ClR
Cnelton 1244 *Ass*
Chnoldon', *Cheltun'* (sic) 1250 Fees
Knowlton or Knowlhill 1795 Boswell

'Farm by the hillock', from **cnoll** (*v.* prec.) and **tūn** (once replaced by or confused with **dūn** 'hill'). The DB spellings, and the 13th cent. spellings in *Cnou-*, *Gnol-*, *Chinou-*, show AN influence, cf. Church Knowle 1 87, *v.* ANInfl 49, 137, 146. This place gave name to the hundred, *v. supra*.

MATTERLEY CTGS (SU 021092), *on mapoldor lea middeweardne*, *of mapoldor lea* 1033 (12) *SherC* (S 969), *on mapeldurelea midewarde* n.d. (12) *ib* (f. 24v), *claus' voc' Materlie* 1551 *Midd*, *Matterly* 1774 Hutch[1], 1840 *TA* (*-Cow Leaze*, *-9 & 10 Acres*), 'maple-tree wood or clearing', *v.* **mapuldor, lēah**, cf. Mapperley Db 583. The earliest forms occur in the Anglo-Saxon bounds of Horton par. *supra*.

ASH PIT, *-Fd* 1840 *TA*, *v.* **æsc**. BOLEHAYS COPSE, (*-Coppice*) 1840 *ib*, *claus'. . .voc' Bolleheyes* 1429 *Midd*, 'bull enclosure(s)', *v.* **bula, (ge)hæg**, cf. Bowleaze 1 234. BURGESS'S FM, cf. *Burgess Md* 1840 *TA*, probably to be associated with *byrches* (*copse. . .lyinge in Whitmore under-*) 1551 *Midd*, *v.* **birce** 'birch-tree', Whitmore *infra*, cf. Birches Copse in Wimborne St G. par. *supra*. CHALK PIT, *Chalk Pit* (*Cl & Fd*) 1840 *TA*, cf. *puteu' chalceti voc' a chalkepitte* 1551 *Midd*, *v.* **cealc, pytt**. CHAPEL, *capella de Woodlande* 1551 *ib*, *The Chapel* 1840 *TA*. CHURCH OF THE ASCENSION. DAVID'S CROSS, where several lanes meet, *v.* **cross**. FROME (lost), 1774 Hutch[1] ('a place now swallowed up in Woodlands'), 1863 Hutch[3]; this is probably a transferred or manorial name, from the family called (*de*) *Frome* which held the manor of Woodlands in the 14th and early 15th centuries, cf. William *Frome* of Woodlands e14, Reginald *de Frome* 1333, Edward *Frome* of *Frome* (who purchased 3 messuages in *Frome* and Woodlands) 1400, John *Frome* 1405 all Hutch[3] 3 151. The *Frome* from which the family took its name was probably one of the Do Fromes, e.g. Frome Billet 1 243, Frome St Q. par. or Frome V. par. both *infra*. HAYTHORN COPSE, from Haythorn in Horton par. *supra*. IVORY HILL COPSE, (*-Coppice*) 1840 *TA*, *claus' voc' Everyehill* 1551 *Midd*, cf. *Ivery lake* 16 *ib*; the first el. is a surname, cf. John *Iverey* 1358, *terr' nuper Rogeri Yverey* 1435 *ib*, *v.* **hyll, lacu** 'stream'. IVY CTG. KNOB'S CROOK, probably an allusion to the sharply curved ridge at Peat's Hill *infra*, from **knob** 'a knoll' and **crōc** 'a bend', cf. Knobcrook in Wimborne M. par. *supra*. KNOWLTON CHURCH (ruins), cf. *capell' de Cnoltun* n.d. (12) *SherC* (f. 35r), *Knowlton Church* (*Fd*), *Church Fd* 1840 *TA*. LUMBER LANE. MARTIN'S LIVING, cf. *Martins Md* 1840 *ib*, Joan *Marten* 1664 HTax (L. Crichel). MONMOUTH'S ASH, cf. *Monmouths Fd* 1840 *TA*, *Monmouth('s) Cl* 1869 Hutch[3], named from the Duke of Monmouth who was captured hiding in an ash-tree here (no longer standing) after the battle of Sedgemoor (1685), *v.* Hutch[3] 3 156. NEW BARN. OLD DOWN CTGS, cf. *Old down fd*, *The Down* 1840 *TA*, *v.* **dūn**; *old* probably means 'long used', *v.* **(e)ald**. PARK HO, in Woodlands Park *infra*. PARSONAGE. PEAT'S HILL, *Peats Hill* 1840 *TA*, *v.* Horton par. f.ns. *supra*. PIT COPSE, earlier *King Lane Coppice* (*v.* f.ns. *infra*), cf. *Pit Fd*, *Pit(s)* 1840 *ib*, *v.* **pytt**. POUND, cf. *pounde called the greate pounde, pounde called Rodways pounde* 1551 *Midd*, *v.* **pund**; *Rodway* is a surname, cf. *Roddeways copse*, John *Rodwaye* 1551 *ib*, *v.* **copis**. ROUND HO. SHEEPCROFT ROW, *la Shepcroft* 1394, *Shepecrofte* 1551 both *Midd*, *Sheep Croft* (*Coppice & Row*) 1840 *TA*, 'enclosure for sheep', from **scēap** and **croft**, with **rāw** 'strip of woodland'. STEPPING STONES, where a footpath crosses a small stream. WEDGE HILL, 1840 *TA*, perhaps 'wedge-shaped hill', from ModE **wedge** (OE *wecg*), but cf. *weggeleawe* in Horton par. *supra*. WELL HO. WHITMORE, 1551 *Midd*, *Hr & Lr Whitemore Bridges* 1791 Boswell, *v.* **hwīt, mōr**, cf. Burgess's Fm *supra*. WOODLANDS COPSE (*Park Coppice* 1840 *TA*), CMN (1811 OS), & (DAIRY) FM. WOODLANDS PARK, *parcis de Philippeston et Wodlond* 1394 *Midd*, *Wo(o)dlande Parke* 1551 *ib*, *Wood Lande Parke* 1583 *SPDom*, *the Park* 1587 *Midd*, *Woodland Park* 1840 *TA*, cf. *Parkemede*, *claus'...voc' Kerpinges Parke* 1551 *Midd*, *v.* **park, mǣd**, cf. *Philipston* in Wimborne St G. par. *supra*; *Kerping* is no doubt a surname. On this medieval deer-park, *v.* Cantor & Wilson 9 201. YEWTREE PIT.

FIELD-NAMES

The undated forms are 1840 *TA* 113. Spellings dated 1237, 1242 are Ch, 1280, 1288 *Ass*, 1318 FF, 1320 Ipm, 1332 SR, 1340 NI, 16² *Antiquity* (Vol. 35, No. 139, p. 231, note 44), 1541 *Glyn*, 1562, 1620¹ Hutch³, 17 *CecilMap*, 1620² *CH*, 1664 HTax, and the rest *Midd*.

(a) Alder Moor Md (*claus' voc' Aldermore* 1551, *v.* **alor, mōr**); Barrow Fd (*v.* **beorg**); Bean Grd; Hr & Middle Berrill, Lr Berrell; Bottom Fd; Bowden; Brick Coppice & Place (cf. *domus voc' le bricke howse, claus'...voc' bryckepitte* 1551, *v.* **brick, hūs, pytt**, cf. Brickplace Copse in Horton par. *supra, puteu' voc' a cleypitte* 1551); Brockington Fd & Md (from Brockington in Gussage All Snts par. *supra*); Bushy Grd; Butts Md (*v.* **butte**); Calves Plot (cf. *Calves lease* 1551, *v.* **calf, lǣs** 'pasture'); Lr & Upr Charlton Fd (from Charlton *supra*); Chilkill Coppice, Lt Chilkill (*Chilkehill, Chilkill* 1551, possibly 'hill at the chalky place', from WSax **cielce** (with influence from **cealc** 'chalk') and **hyll**, cf. Chalk Pit *supra* which is nearby); Common Md; Coombes Lawn (*v.* **launde**; *Coomb* is probably a surname); Court Fd & Md (*v.* **court**); (Further) Cow Leaze; Droveway; Gardens; Goods Fd & Md (cf. Thomas *Good* 1562 (acquired manor of Knowlton)); Harts Grd (cf. William *Hert* 1340, Roger *Hart* 1664, Hart's Bridge in Horton par. *supra*); Hedge Row; Hill Fd & Grd (cf. *la Hill* 1394, *v.* **hyll**); Home Cl; Hop Gdn; Horse Leaze ((*le*) *Horselese* 1394, 1429, *Horselease* 1551, *v.* **hors, lǣs** 'pasture'); Horse Md; How (Croft) (*claus' voc' Howcrofte* 1551, *v.* **howe, croft**); Gt & Lt James's(s) (cf. widow *James* 1664 (Horton)); King Lane Coppice (*venelle voc' Kyngeslane* 1469, *claus' voc' Kingeslayne* 1551, cf. *Kyngestret(e)* 1394, 1398, 1422, *v.* **lane, strǣt** (perhaps in the ME sense 'hamlet', cf. *Baggeridge supra*); the first el. is probably **cyning** 'king' in allusion to royal possession, since one of the two DB manors of Knowlton belonged to the King, *v.* VCHDo 3 65, cf. the f.n. *Kingescrofte* in Horton par. *supra*; the coppice (now called Pit Copse) lies alongside the lane running E into Woodlands village); Kitchen Cl; Knackers Hole (cf. 1 41); Knowlton Md (*prat' de Knolton* 1358, *Knoltonesmede* 1394, *Knoltonmede* 1398, -*Me(a)de* 1551, *v.* **mǣd**, Knowlton *supra*, cf. also *Knollton arable feild, Knollton streame* 16¹); Lane (Grd); The Lawn (*v.* **launde**, cf. Coombes Lawn *supra*); Little hill (probably from **hyll**, but possibly to be associated with *claus' voc' Litlehile* 1551, where -*hile* may be·from **healh** (WSax dat.sg. *hēale*) 'nook of land' or **hygel** 'hillock', cf. 1 120, *v.* **lȳtel**); Little Md; Lodge Cl; Long Cl; Lonnens Grd (cf. John *de London* 1318 (Horton)); Lower Md; Madmans Pce; The Meadow; Middle Fd; Mill Md (cf. *le Milleham* 1435, named from *molendinum de Knolton* 1398, *Knollton Mylle* 16, *v.* **myln, hamm**, Knowlton *supra*; there was a mill at Knowlton in 1086 DB, *v.* VCHDo 3 86, cf. also (*le*) *Muledych*', -*dich*' 1280, *Milldith* (for -*dich*) 1618 *Map*, *Mulditch* 1620 Hutch³, mentioned in the 'outbounds' of Cranborne Chase, which may belong here, *v.* **dīc**); North Fd (*in campo boriali* 1358, *Northfilde* 1551, *v.* **norð, feld**); The Orchard, New & Old Orchard (cf. *pomaria* 1551); Oxleaze; The Pasture; Pond Cl; Ramshorn (probably in allusion to its shape, cf. 1 24); Redmans Grd (cf. Redman's Hill in Horton par. *supra*); Ridings Coppice; Rooky Md; Sandells (Coppice) (*claus' voc' Sandehilles, Sandhilles copse* 1551, *v.* **sand, hyll, copis**; however it is possible that *Sandehill, Sandell* in these names is a surname, cf. Katherine *Sandell'* 1541 (L. Crichel)); Shags Fd (cf. *Shags Heath* in Horton par. *supra*); 16 Acres; Sows Md (cf. Horton par. f.ns. *supra*); Taylors Md (cf. Adam *le Taillur* 1332 (L. Crichel)); Wallnut Walk; Gt Water Mdw; Wet Md; Wet Moor (probably an aphetic form of *Swotemour* 1358, *prat' de Swetemor(e)* 1394, 1398, 'sweet marshland', *v.* swēte, mōr); Wimborne Shear (cf. dial. *shear* 'crop (of grass)' (Barnes 98); the field lies ½ mile from the par. bdy with Wimborne St G.); With(e)y (Bed) (*v.* wīðig); Woodlands Heath.

(b) *Alesford* 1435 (possibly *Alefford, v.* ford, first el. uncertain); *Artoureslond* 1435 (the ME surname *Artour* (*v.* Reaney *s.n. Arthur*), land); *Bailliesmede* 1398, *Baylyesclose* 1429 (from mǣd and baillie 'a bailiff' or the surname, cf. Thomas *Bayllyf* 1394); *Bodyslond* 1435 (the surname *Body, v.* land); *Brodefilde* 1551 (*v.* brād, feld); *le Brodemede* 1435 (*v.* mǣd); *Brokkehulle* 1429, *-hille* 1435 (cf. John *Brokke* 1429, *v.* hyll); *Chamberlein Breche* 1394 (the surname *Chamberlein, v.* brǣc); *Comingere closes* 1551 (*v.* coninger); *in campo frument'* 1495 ('the corn field'); *claus' voc' Dowges* 1551 (a surname); *Est(e)wod(e)* 1280, *Estwode* 1358, 1429, *-lande* 1551, *Estwood* 1618 *Map*, 1620[1], *Eastwood* 17 (*v.* ēast, wudu; this wood is mentioned in the 'outbounds' of Cranborne Chase *supra*); *claus'...voc' Fosters* 1551 (the surname *Foster*); *Foxbergh'* 1280 (*v.* fox, beorg); *Fries close* 1551 (cf. *toft'...nuper Nicholi Frie* 1435); *Fryerne* c.1618 *DROSurv*; *Ham* 1237 ('meadow called-'), 1242 (*v.* hamm); *Haytereslond* 1435 (*v.* land, cf. Wimborne St G. f.ns. *supra*); *Herodesacre* 1320 (the surname *Herod, v.* æcer); *(la) Holcroft* 1394 (*v.* hol[2], croft); *Hollaneyate* (*portam voc'*-) 1495 (*v.* hol[2], lane, geat); *prat' de La Lake* 1358 (*v.* lacu 'stream'); *Laudeclose* 1551 (first el. probably a surname); *(ad) longam hay(h)am* 1280, *la Langehey* 1394 (*v.* lang[1], (ge)hæg); *la longlond* 1394, *la Langelond* 1398 (*v.* land); *Lowcasmore* 1394 (the surname *Lucas, v.* mōr); *le Louseslappe* 1435 (apparently from lūs 'louse' and slæp 'mud, mire, marsh', *v.* Löfvenberg 189); *Mecherlesbreh* 1237, *Micheleberg* 1242 (shown by the documentary context to refer to the same place, so that one or other of the forms may be corrupt; the final el. of the earlier form would seem to be brǣc 'land broken up', whereas the later form would seem to represent 'large hill or barrow', from micel and beorg); *atte Mere* 1332 (p) (*v.* atte, mere[1] 'pool'); *le Mershe* 1551 (*v.* mersc); *La Moure, Middelmour* 1358, *-mor* 1398 (*v.* middel, mōr); *Nic(h)olesclos(e)* 1398, 1429, *Nicholeslondes* 1435 (the surname *Nichol, v.* clos(e), land); *East Nordon* 1620[2] ('north hill', *v.* norð, dūn); *La Northfrith* 1358, *-ffryth* 1394 (*v.* fyrhð 'wood'); *le Oteberne* 1435 ('barn for oats', *v.* āte, bere-ærn); *atte Ouene* 1332 (p) (*v.* atte, ofen 'an oven, a furnace'); *(le) Rowemere* 1358, 1398, *le Roughmere* 1394, *le Rowmere* 1429, 1435, *Rowemore* 1551 ('the rough pool', *v.* rūh (wk. obl. rūwan), mere[1]); *Shirmedesdal* 1237 (perhaps '(valley at) the bright meadow', from scīr[2], mǣd, dæl[1]; according to the documentary context, *Surredesburg* 1242 would seem to refer to the same place, *-burg* perhaps representing burh 'fortified place'); *Southfilde* 1551 (cf. *in camp' austral'* 1495, *v.* sūð, feld); *Stockley* 1620[2] (*v.* stocc 'stump', lēah, cf. 1 277); *copicii apud Stonyhull* 1429, *Stonye copse* 1551 (*v.* stānig, hyll, copis); *Trenchefoilleshide* 1398 (cf. Peter *Trenchefoyl* 1288, *v.* hīd); *Venellys* 16[2] (a barrow at Knowlton, probably from the surname *Vennel*); *Waggefryth Copse* 1551 (*v.* fyrhð 'wood'; the first el. may be an OE *wagge 'quaking bog, marsh', on which *v.* Löfvenberg 218); *tenement voc' Wayres* 1551 (a surname); *claus'...voc' Wilkeshire* 1551 (the surname *Wiltshire*); *Wixiesmede* 1358 (the surname *Wicks, Wix, v.* mǣd); *atte Wode* 1332 (p) (*v.* atte, wudu); *Wolvesham, ten' le Wolf* 1358, *Wolfeslond* 1435 (the surname (*le*) *Wolf, v.* hamm, land).

XVIII. MONKTON UP WIMBORNE HUNDRED

This small hundred consists of the pars. of Chettle and Tarrant M., together with Blagdon and Boveridge in Cranborne par. and Monkton Up Wimborne in Wimborne St G. par. (formerly also in Cranborne par.). Chettle and Tarrant M. were in the GeldR hundred of *Langeberge* (*v.* Pimperne hundred *supra*, Eyton 131–2, Anderson 132, VCHDo 3 138), and were in Cranborne hundred in 1327 *SR*. All the vills in the hundred belonged to the abbeys of Cranborne and Tewkesbury, *v. Cranborne Priory* in Cranborne par. *supra*.

Hundredum de Upwymburn' -Upwimburne, -Upwynburn' 1244 *Ass, Upwymborn* 1275 RH, 1285 FA, *Up Wymborn(e)* 1346, 1431 FA, *Hundred of Munckton Vp Wimborne* 1664 HTax. Named from Monkton Up Wimborne in Wimborne St G. par. *supra*, the *caput* of the hundred.

Chettle

CHETTLE (ST 952133)
  Ceotel 1086 DB, 1107 (1300) Ch, *Cheotel* 1369 (1372) *ChrP*
  Chetel 1100–35 (1496) Pat, 1154–89 (1496) ib, c.1183 (14)
    Cecil, 1234 Cl (*bosco de-*), 1237 ib (*foresta regis de-*), 1280,
    1288 *Ass*, 1291 Tax, 1294 Pat, 1320 Pat *et freq* to 1428 FA,
    Chettel 1233 Lib, *Chettell(')* 1235 Cl, 1547 *Ct*, 1553 *Cecil*,
    Chetell(e) 1388 Fine, 1390 Cl, *Chettle* 1575 Saxton
  Chetil 1288 *Ass, Chettille* 1390 Cl, *Chetyll* 1530 *Cecil*
  Chetul 1327 *SR*, 1332 SR, *Chettul'* n.d. (1372) *ChrP*
  Chittel n.d. (1372) *ChrP*

Probably, as suggested by Tengstrand MN 97, from an OE ceotol, a variant of cetel, cytel 'a kettle', here in the topographical sense of 'a deep valley surrounded by hills', with reference to the situation of the village, cf. Chettle Head Copse in Pentridge par. *supra*.

LITTLE WOOD (ST 943133), *littlen wde* 935 (15) *ShaftR* (S 429), *Little Wood* (*Down*) 1839 *TA*, 'little wood', *v.* **lȳtel, wudu**. The early form occurs in the AS bounds of Tarrant H. par. *supra*. For other references to woodland in this par., *v.* foll. and the lost *Hida infra*.

CHETTLE CHASE COPPICE, *Chettle cops* 1618 *Map*, cf. *bosco de Chetel* 1234, *foreste de Chettell'* 1235, *foresta regis de Chetel* 1237 all Cl, *chacea...de Blakedone et Chetel* 1288 *Ass*, Little Wood *supra*; both Blagdon (in Cranborne par. *supra*) and Chettle were within Cranborne Chase *supra*. CHETTLE CMN (*Common* 1618 *Map*), DOWN (1839 *TA*, *-downe* 1618 *Map*), FM (cf. *Farm House, Hr Chettle Fm* 1839 *TA*) & HO. CHETTLE LONG BARROW, cf. *Gt Barrow Fd, Long Barrow Fd* 1839 *ib*, *v.* **beorg** (tumulus marked 6"). GREENCLOSE FM. (LT) HATTS COPPICE, *Chettle hatts* 1618 *Map*, *Hats Coppice, Fd & Thickett* 1839 *TA*, *v.* **hæt(t)** 'hat-shaped hill', **piccett**. THE LODGE. LONG BARROW (1"), *Hinton Down Long Barrow* 1839 *ib*, cf. Tarrant Hinton Down in Tarrant Hinton par. *supra*. NEW BARN. NEW COPPICE. THE PARK. ST MARY'S CHURCH, cf. *Church Yd* 1839 *ib*.

FIELD-NAMES

The undated forms are 1839 *TA* 56. Spellings dated 1332 are SR, n.d. (1372) *ChrP*, 1572 Hutch³, 1664 HTax, and 1829 *EnclA*.

(*a*) Bottom Fd (*v.* **botm**); (Yonder) Brawflings (perhaps 'broad furlongs', from **brād** and **furlang**); (Lr) Burnbake (*v.* **burnbake**); Burts Cl (cf. William *Burt* 1664); Butlers Md; Calves Cl; Crabtree Fd; (Hr & Further) Drove Fd; Farm Mdw; Lr Farm Yd & Orchd; 5 & 4 Acres; Furze Cl; (Yonder) Gidlings; Glebe Fd; Hr & Lr Hill Coppice; Hodges; Home Down; Gt & Lt Home Fd; Home Mdw; Kitchen Gdn; Little Down Fd; Lofters Cmn, Coppice & Ctg (*Losters* (sic, a coppice) 1618 *Map*); (Gt & Middle) Longlands; Long Md; Manlands (*v.* **(ge)mǣne** 'common'); Mead(ow); Middle Fd; The Nursery 1829; Paddock or Rookery; Plantation of Ash; Rabits Farm Ho & Mdw (cf. John *Robet'* 1332); Roll Way (*Rowlewaie* (a coppice) 1618 *Map*); Spiers Plot; Willow Hay (*Chettle wilhais* 1618 *Map*, near to Furzey Woolly Coppice in Farnham par. *supra q.v.*).

(*b*) the cunygere 1572 (*v.* **coninger**); ¼ *bosci de Hida in Chittel* n.d (1372) (*v.* **hīd** 'a hide of land'; the DB manor of *Ceotel* was assessed at one hide, *v.* VCHDo 3 100, cf. *Chetel cum hida Aiulfi* 1100–35 (1496) Pat).

Tarrant Monkton

Part of this par. was transferred to Pimperne par. *supra* in 1933.

TARRANT MONKTON (ST 944088)
   Tarente 1086 DB (f. 77b), *Tarenta* 1107 (1300) Ch
   Tarenta Monachorum 1154–89 (1496) Pat, c.1183 (14) *Cecil,*
      Tarent(e) Monachorum 1291 Tax *et freq* to 1428 FA,
      Terrunt(e)- Hy 8 Hutch[3], *Tarrent*- 1530 *Cecil, Tarraunte*
      Monachorum 1556 Dugd
   Tarent(e) Moneketon(e) 1280, 1288 *Ass,* 1327 *SR,* 1335, 1340
      Pat, 1366 (1372) *ChrP,* -*Monketon(')* 1288 *Ass,* 1332 SR,
      1340 NI, 1380 Cl, 1400, 1402 Pat, -*Monkton* 1332 ib,
      -*Munketon* 1367 ib
   Monks' Tarente 1384 Pat
   Munketon 1575 Saxton, *Munckton Tarrant* 1795 Boswell

Named from R. Tarrant, *v.* Tarrant H. par. *supra*, RNs. *infra*;
for the DB identification, *v.* VCHDo **3** 74. Monkton means
'farm of the monks', from **munuc** (gen.pl. *munuca*) and **tūn**,
cf. the alternative Lat affix -*Monachorum* 'of the monks', with
reference to the possession of this manor by the priory of
Cranborne (1086 DB) and by the abbey of Tewkesbury (1154–89
(1496) Pat), *v.* Hutch[3] **3** 572, cf. Monkton Up Wimborne in
Wimborne St G. par. *supra*. There was a mill here in 1086 DB,
v. VCHDo *loc.cit.*

LUTON FM (ST 942072)
   Tarente Loueton', Louente Tarente (sic) 1280 *Ass, Tarente*
      Loueton 1323 FF, *Tarant Loveton* 1435 ib, *Tarrant Love-*
      towne 1619 *CH*
   Loueton(') 1280, 1288 *Ass* both (p), 1317 Banco, 1323, 1376,
      1408 FF all (p), 1432 Cl, *Loveton(')* 1283 *Cecil,* 1412 FA,
      1494 *Cecil, Lovetowne* 1618 *CH*
   Luueton' 1288 *Ass* (p)
   Loffeton 1478 IpmR, *Luffeton* 1486 Ipm
   Lovington alias Luton 1542 Hutch[3]
   Luton 1869 Hutch[3]

The farm stands on R. Tarrant, *v.* par. name *supra*. Luton
probably means 'Lufa's farm', from the OE pers.n. *Lufa* and
tūn.

ALL SAINTS' CHURCH, cf. 'church of *Tarente Munketon*' 1367
Pat. ASH PLANT. BLACKLAND PLANT., *Blackland* 1839 *TA*, *v.*
blæc, land. BLANDFORD RACE COURSE (disused), *Blandford Race
Ground* 1811 OS, *v.* Race Down in Tarrant L. par. *supra.*
COMMON DROVE, cf. *West Drove Fd* 1839 *TA*, *v.* **drāf.** CUCKOO
CLUMP. EAST FM, E of the village. FIELD BARN. HIGH ST. HORSE
COPPICE, *Monkton horse Coppice* 1839 *ib*, *v.* par. name *supra.*
LITTLE DOWN, 1839 *ib*, *v.* **dūn.** LUTON DOWN (1839 *ib*) & DROVE
(cf. *Droveway* 1839 *ib*), from Luton Fm *supra.* MONKTON
COMMON HIGHER & LOWER, *Monkton Comn.* 1811 OS, *v.* par.
name *supra.* MONKTON DOWN, 1811 ib, *v.* **dūn.** OLD BUTTS, *v.*
butt[2] 'an archery butt'. PIPPIN LODGE, probably from the
surname *Pippin*, cf. *Lodge Plot* 1839 *TA.* POND BOTTOM
(PLANT.), *v.* **ponde, botm.** RACE DOWN PLANT., *v.* Race Down
in Tarrant L. par. *supra.* REDLAND PLANT., *Redland* 1839 *ib*, *v.*
rēad, land. THE SANCTUARY. TARRANT MONKTON FM, cf.
Monkton Farm Down, Hr Farm Down 1839 *TA.* TURNER'S
LANE, cf. John *Turner* 1664 HTax and the f.n. *Longland infra.*
VICARAGE, cf. *Parsonage Mdw, Vicarage Mdw* 1839 *TA.* WEEK-
LEY COPPICE & LANE, *Weekly Coppice* 1839 *ib*, probably from
lēah 'wood, clearing in a wood', first el. perhaps **wīc** 'dairy
farm'.

FIELD-NAMES

The undated forms are 1839 *TA* 223. Spellings dated 1327 are *SR*, 1332 SR,
1664 HTax, 1699 Hutch[3], and 1791 Boswell.

(*a*) Barn Cl; Bolton Cl; Bottom Fd (*v.* **botm**); Broad Cl; Buckston; (New)
Burnbake (*v.* **burnbake**); Calves hay (*v.* **(ge)hæg**); Carters Fd (cf. widow
Carter 1664); Chalk Pits; Collarmaker's Md; Coneygarth (Coppice) (*v.*
coninger 'rabbit-warren'); Cozens's; Crate (*v.* **croft**); Cross Lds (*v.* **cross**);
Cutler's Grd (and Homers) (cf. Stephen *Cutler* (Chettle), Thomas *Honer*
1664); First, Second, Third & Lr East Fd; 5 & 4 Acres; Fox brake (*v.* **bræc**[1]
'a thicket'); Gaston (*v.* **gærs-tūn** 'a paddock'); Great Farm Bridge 1791;
Haymoor Ld (*v.* **hēg, mōr**); Hayward's Cl (cf. *Hayward Corner Bridge* 1791,
Robert *Hayward* 1664); Higher Bridge 1791; Higher Fd & Md; Hill(')s Mdw
& Orchd (cf. John *le Hulle* (Chettle) 1332); Holmar's Bridge 1791; Home Cl,
Fd & Grd; Hunger hill (a derogatory name, *v.* **hungor**); King's Md (cf.
Geoffrey *le Kyng*' 1327, 1332); Lambert(')s Grd & Mdw (cf. William *Lambert*
1664); Little Bridge 1791; Long Fd; Turner's & West's Longland (*v.* **lang**[1],
land, cf. Turner's Lane *supra*); Luton Cowleaze (from Luton Fm *supra*);
Meadlanes; Middle Fd; Muston's Orchd and Barn (cf. Margaret *Muston*
1699); New & Old Orchd; Paul's Cl (cf. Christopher-, John *Paull* 1664);

Peaked Cl & Grd (*v.* **peked** 'pointed'); Pick(')s; Poor Ld; Scotland (*v.* **scot** 'tax, payment'); Shop Cl (*v.* **sc(e)oppa** 'shed'); 6 Acres; Sow path; Square Fd; Stainer's Grd & Orchd; 10 & 3 Acres; Three Gates Fd; Tuffins Md (cf. Thomas *Tuffen* 1664); Two Stiles (*v.* **stigel**); Undercliff ('(ground) beneath the bank', with reference to The Cliff in Tarrant Raw. par. *supra*); Water Md (Cowleaze) (cf. Henry *atte Watere* 1327, 1332, *v.* **atte, wæter**); Well Fd & Plot (*v.* **well(a)**); Hr Woodway; Yard Grd & Mdw.

LIST OF DORSET PARISHES

Parishes followed by 1 or 2 and page number are dealt with in Part I or Part II respectively; the rest will appear in subsequent Parts. Abbreviated forms of affixes, if used in the text, are given in brackets.